HOW TO PREPARE FOR THE GRADUATE MANAGEMENT ADMISSION TEST

GMAT

SEVENTH EDITION

BY

EUGENE D. JAFFE, M.B.A., Ph.D.
Associate Professor and Director of the Management Training Center, Bar-Ilan University, Israel
Formerly Professor of Marketing, Graduate School of Business, St. John's University

STEPHEN HILBERT, Ph.D.
Associate Professor of Mathematics, Ithaca College

BARRON'S

Barron's Educational Series, Inc.
New York • London • Toronto • Sydney

All inquiries should be addressed to:

Barron's Educational Series, Inc.
250 Wireless Boulevard
Hauppauge, New York 11788

International Standard Book No. 0-8120-3882-7

Library of Congress Cataloging-in-Publication Data

Jaffe, Eugene D.
    How to prepare for the graduate management admission test GMAT /
by Eugene D. Jaffe, Stephen Hilbert. — 7th ed.
    p.   cm.
    ISBN 0-8120-3882-7
    1. Graduate Management Admission Test.   2. Management —
Examinations, questions, etc.   3. Business — Examinations,
questions, etc.   I. Hilbert, Stephen.   II. Title.
HD30.413.J33 1987
650'.076 — dc 19   87-18619

PRINTED IN THE UNITED STATES OF AMERICA

78   100   98765432

For Liora, Iris and Nurit
and for Susan

Contents

Preface

Barron's How to Prepare for the Graduate Management Admission Test (GMAT) is designed to assist students planning to take the official Graduate Management Admission Test administered by the Educational Testing Service of Princeton, New Jersey. Since the results of the GMAT are used by many graduate schools of business as a means for measuring the qualifications of their applicants, it is important that the prospective student do as well as he possibly can on this exam. His admission to business school may well depend on it.

A study guide, although not able to guarantee a perfect score, can provide a good deal of assistance in test preparation by enabling the student to become familiar with the material he will encounter on the exam and supplying him with ample opportunity for practice and review. With this in mind, we have developed a study guide that goes further than the simple simulation of the official GMAT in its effort to offer a sound basis of test preparation. Besides containing six practice tests with questions (and answers) similar to those the student will encounter on the actual exam, it offers invaluable advice on *how* to prepare for the exam, ranging from a general discussion of the purpose and various formats of the GMAT to a step-by-step program of subject analysis and review designed to help the student discover his weak points and take measures to correct them.

Review sections for each subject area appearing on the exam have been especially developed to meet the specific needs of students who may feel a deficiency in any of these areas. Each review provides both an explanation of the material and exercises for practical work. The six practice exams included in the guide have self-scoring tables to help the student evaluate his results and check his progress. All answers to the test questions are fully explained to ensure complete understanding.

The authors would also like to extend their appreciation to Mrs. Susan Hilbert and Ms. Dawn Murcer for their excellent job in typing the manuscript, to Professor Shirley Hockett for several helpful discussions, and to Professor Justin Longenecker for his generous advice.

How to Use This Guide

The step-by-step study program appearing below outlines the recommended study plan you should follow when preparing for the GMAT. By making use of this procedure, you will be able to take full advantage of the material presented in this guide.

1. Familiarize yourself with the purpose and general format of the GMAT (Chapter One).

2. Study the analysis of each type of question on the exam (Chapter Two).

3. Take the GMAT Diagnostic Test (Chapter Three) and use the Self-scoring Table at the end of the test to evaluate your results.

4. Study the review sections (Chapter Four), spending more time on areas where you scored poorly on the Diagnostic Test.

5. Take the five sample GMAT tests (Chapter Five) and evaluate your results after completing each one.

6. Review again any areas you discover you are still weak in after you have evaluated your test results.

Acknowledgments

The authors gratefully acknowledge the kindness of all organizations concerned with granting us permission to reprint passages, charts, and graphs. The copyright holders and publishers of quoted passages are listed on this and the following pages.

Sources and permissions for charts and graphs appear on the appropriate pages throughout the book through the courtesy of the following organizations: the New York Times Company; U.S. Department of Labor; Dow Jones & Company, Inc.; U.S. Department of Health, Education, and Welfare; United Nations Economics Bulletin for Europe; Social Security Bulletin, Statistical Abstract of the U.S., U.S. Department of Commerce, Bureau of Economic Analysis; Federal Reserve Bank of New York; European Economic Community; U.S. Department of Commerce, Bureau of the Census; New York State Department of Labor; Federal Power Commission; U.S. Treasury Department; U.S. Bureau of Labor Statistics; Institute of Life Insurance; and the Statistical Abstract of Latin America.

Page 7, Sample Passage: Reprinted with permission of the author, Virgil Thomson.

Page 10, Sample Passage: Maynard and Davis, *Sales Management,* © 1957, reprinted by permission of John Wiley & Sons, Inc., New York.

Page 23, Passage 1: Reprinted from *The Bible on Broadway* by Arthur T. Buch © Arthur T. Buch 1968, Hamden, CT., Archon Books, with the permission of The Shoe String Press, Inc.

Page 28, Passage 3: Petra Karin Kelly, "Cancer A European Conquest?" *European Community,* April–May, 1976, pp. 23–24. Reprinted from *Europe* Magazine.

Page 36, Passage 2: Reprinted with permission from Boyd, Clewett, and Westfall, *Cases in Marketing Strategy* (Homewood, Ill.: Richard D. Irwin, Inc., 1957), pp. 97–100, © 1957.

Pages 44-48, Section V, 25 Questions (with Explained Answers): Murray Rockowitz et al., *Barron's How to Prepare for the New High School Equivalency Examination (GED),* © 1979 Barron's Educational Series, Inc., Woodbury, N.Y.

Page 51, Passage 2: Reprinted with permission from Boyd, Clewett, and Westfall, *Cases in Marketing Strategy* (Homewood, Ill.: Richard D. Irwin, Inc., 1957), pp. 77–80, © 1957.

Page 55, Passage 1: Kenneth R. Seeskin, "Never Speculate, Never Explain: The State of Contemporary Philosophy." Reprinted from *The American Scholar,* Volume 49, No. 1, Winter 1979–80. Copyright © 1979 by the United Chapters of Phi Beta Kappa. By permission of the publishers.

Page 57, Passage 2: By Michael Useem, Professor of Sociology, Boston University, "Government Patronage of Science and Art in America," from *The Production of Culture,* Richard A. Peterson, ed., © 1976 Sage Publications, Inc. Reprinted by permission of the author and the publisher.

Portions of the "Reading Comprehension Review": Eugene J. Farley, *Barron's How to Prepare for the High School Equivalency Examination Reading Interpretation Test,* © 1970 Barron's Educational Series, Inc., Woodbury, N.Y.

Page 85, Example 2: "Skye, Lonely Scottish Isle," *Newark Sunday News,* June 9, 1968, C 16, Sec. 2.

Page 86, Example 4: David Gunter, "Kibbutz Life Growing Easier," *Newark News,* May 6, 1968, p. 5.

Page 91, Example 2: Reprinted with permission from "Understanding Foreign Policy," by Saul K. Padover, *Public Affairs Pamphlet #280.* Copyright, Public Affairs Committee, Inc.

Page 95, Exercise B: Marina Gazzo and Catherine Browne, "Venice Rising," *European Community,* November–December, 1975, pp. 15–16.

Page 235, Passage 1: From *Our Dynamic World: A Survey in Modern Geography* by A. Joseph Wraight. © 1966 by the author. Reproduced by permission of the publisher, Chilton Book Company, Radnor, Pennsylvania.

Page 239, Passage 3: From W.D. Howells, "The Man of Letters as a Man of Business," in *Literature and Life.* Copyright 1911 by Harper & Brothers. Reprinted with permission of William White Howells.

Page 248, Passage 2: Reprinted with permission from Boyd, Clewett, and Westfall, *Cases in Marketing Strategy* (Homewood, Ill.: Richard D. Irwin, Inc., 1957), pp. 55–58, © 1957.

Pages 255–258, Section V, 25 Questions (with Explained Answers): Samuel C. Brownstein and Mitchel Weiner, *Barron's How to Prepare for College Entrance Examinations (SAT),* © 1980 Barron's Educational Series, Inc., Woodbury, N.Y.

Page 261, Passage 2: Reprinted with permission from Boyd, Clewett, and Westfall, *Cases in Marketing Strategy* (Homewood, Ill.: Richard D. Irwin, Inc., 1957), pp. 124–128, © 1957.

Pages 265–269, Section VII, 5 Questions (with Explained Answers): Murray Rockowitz et al., *Barron's How to Prepare for the New High School Equivalency Examination (GED),* © 1979 Barron's Educational Series, Inc., Woodbury, N.Y.

Page 291, Passage 1: *Improving Executive Development in the Federal Government,* copyright 1964 by the Committee for Economic Development.

Page 293, Passage 2: G. R. Crone, *Background to Geography,* 1964, by permission of Pitman Publishing Ltd., London.

Page 295, Passage 3: Jean Hollander, "Cops and Writers." Reprinted from *The American Scholar,* Volume 49, No. 2, Spring 1980. Copyright 1980 by the United Chapters of Phi Beta Kappa. By permission of the publishers.

Page 298, Passage 1: "Open Admissions Assessed: The Example of The City University of New York, 1970–1975" by Irwin Polishook, Professor of History, Lehman College, CUNY. "Open Admissions Assessed" originally appeared in *Midstream* (April, 1976), © 1976, The Theodor Herzl Foundation.

Page 300, Passage 2: Robert D. Hershey, Jr., "A Perilous Time for World Trade," *New York Times*, August 1, 1982. © 1982 by The New York Times Company. Reprinted by permission.

Page 311, Passage 2: Reprinted with permission from Cateora and Hess, *International Marketing*, Third Edition (Homewood, Ill.: Richard D. Irwin, Inc., 1975), pp. 721–727, © 1975. The Cost-of-Living Indexes is reprinted by permission from *Sales and Marketing Management* magazine. Copyright 1974.

Page 324, Passage 1: Reprinted with permission from Cruickshank and Davis, *Cases in Management* (Homewood, Ill.: Richard D. Irwin, Inc., 1954), © 1954.

Page 326, Passage 2: Reprinted with permission from Cateora and Hess, *International Marketing*, Third Edition (Homewood, Ill.: Richard D. Irwin, Inc., 1975), pp. 727–732, © 1975.

Pages 331–335, Section VIII, 21 Questions (with Explained Answers): Samuel C. Brownstein and Mitchel Weiner, *Barron's How to Prepare for College Entrance Examinations* (*SAT*), © 1980 Barron's Educational Series, Inc., Woodbury, N.Y.

Pages 331–335, Section VIII, 3 Questions (with Explained Answers): Murray Rockowitz et al., *Barron's How to Prepare for the New High School Equivalency Examination* (*GED*), © 1979 Barron's Educational Series, Inc., Woodbury, N.Y.

Page 355, Passage 1: *The Hebrew Impact on Western Civilization*, edited by Dagobert Runes. The Philosophical Library.

Page 357, Passage 2: *Budgeting for National Objectives*, copyright 1966 by the Committee on Economic Development.

Page 359, Passage 3: From *The American Guide*, edited by Henry G. Alsberg. Copyright © 1949, by permission of Hastings House, Publishers.

Page 364, Passage 1: From *Basic Problems in Marketing Management* by Edwin C. Greif. © 1967 by Wadsworth Publishing Company, Inc., Belmont, California 94002. Reprinted by permission of the publisher.

Page 367, Passage 2: Daniels, Ogran, and Radebaugh, *International Business* (Reading, Mass.: Addison-Wesley Publishing Company, 1982 ©), pp. 528–532. The following have given permission for the use of data in this article: 1. © 1977 by The New York Times Company. Reprinted by permission. 2. Reprinted by permission of *The Wall Street Journal*, © Dow Jones & Company, Inc. (1978 and 1979). All Rights Reserved. 3. Reprinted with permission from the April 14, 1980 issue of *Advertising Age*. Copyright 1980 by Crain Communications, Inc. 4. Reprinted by permission of *Barron's*, © Dow Jones & Company, Inc. (1980). All Rights Reserved. 5. Reprinted by permission from *Sales & Marketing Management* magazine. Copyright 1979. 6. Reprinted with permission of *Beverage World* magazine. 7. Reprinted by permission of *Business Week*. 8. Reprinted by permission of *Fortune*.

Pages 375–378, Section V, 17 Questions (with Explained Answers): Murray Rockowitz et al., *Barron's How to Prepare for the New High School Equivalency Examination* (*GED*), © 1979 Barron's Educational Series, Inc., Woodbury, N.Y.

Page 409, Passage 1: *Trade Policy Toward Low-Income Countries*, copyright 1967 by the Committee for Economic Development.

Page 411, Passage 2: James Hitchcock, "Postmortem on a Rebirth: The Catholic Intellectual Renaissance." Reprinted from *The American Scholar*, Spring 1980. Copyright 1980 by the United Chapters of Phi Beta Kappa. By permission of the publishers.

Page 420, Passage 1: Reprinted with permission from Cruickshank and Davis, *Cases in Management* (Homewood, Ill.: Richard D. Irwin, Inc., 1954), © 1954.

Page 423, Passage 2: Reprinted by permission of The World Publishing Company from *Basic Marketing* by Robert S. Raymond. Copyright © 1967 by Robert S. Raymond.

Pages 429–433, Section V, 14 Questions (with Explained Answers): Sharon Green and Mitchel Weiner, *Barron's How to Prepare for the Test of Standard Written English*, © 1982, Barron's Educational Series, Inc., Woodbury, N.Y.

Pages 429–433, Section V, 6 Questions (with Explained Answers): Samuel C. Brownstein and Mitchel Weiner, *Barron's How to Prepare for the College Entrance Examinations* (*SAT*), © 1980, Barron's Educational Series, Inc., Woodbury, N.Y.

Page 433, Passage 1: Reprinted by special permission from the July 1977 issue of *International Management*. Copyright © 1977 McGraw-Hill International Publications Company Limited. All rights reserved.

Page 467, Passage 2: From *The Social Bond*, by Robert A. Nisbet. Copyright © 1970 by Alfred A. Knopf, Inc. Reprinted by permission of the publisher.

Page 475, Passage 1: Reprinted by special permission from the May 1978 issue of *International Management*. Copyright © 1978 McGraw-Hill International Publications Company Limited. All rights reserved.

Pages 485–489, Section V, 9 Questions (with Explained Answers; Sharon Green and Mitchel Weiner, *Barron's How to Prepare for the Test of Standard Written English*, © 1982, Barron's Educational Series, Inc., Woodbury, N.Y.

Pages 485–489, Section V, 3 Questions (with Explained Answers): Samuel C. Brownstein and Mitchel Weiner, *Barron's How to Prepare for the College Entrance Examinations* (*SAT*), © 1980, Barron's Educational Series, Inc., Woodbury, N.Y.

Page 490, Passage 1: Maynard and Davis, *Sales Management*, © 1957, reprinted by permission of John Wiley & Sons, Inc., New York.

ONE
AN INTRODUCTION TO THE GMAT

The most productive approach to undertaking the actual study and review necessary for any examination is first to determine the answers to some basic questions: What? Where? When? and How? In this case, what is the purpose of the Graduate Management Admission Test (GMAT)? What does it measure? Where and when is the exam given? And most important, how can you prepare to demonstrate aptitude and ability to study business at the graduate level?

The following discussion centers on the purpose behind the Graduate Management Admission Test and presents a study program to follow in preparing for this exam, including a special section to acquaint you with the general format and procedure used on the GMAT.

The Purpose of the GMAT

The purpose of the GMAT is to measure your ability to think systematically and to employ the reading and analytical skills that you have acquired throughout your years of schooling. The types of questions that are used to test these abilities are discussed in the next chapter. It should be noted that the test does not aim to measure your knowledge of specific business or academic subjects. No specific business experience is necessary, nor will any specific academic subject area be covered. You are assumed to have knowledge of basic algebra, geometry, and arithmetic.

In effect, the GMAT provides business school admission officers with an objective measure of academic abilities to supplement subjective criteria used in the selection process, such as interviews, grades, and references. Suppose you are an average student in a college with high grading standards. Your overall grade average may be lower than that of a student from a college with lower grading standards. The GMAT allows you and the other student to be tested under similar conditions using the same grading standard. In this way, a more accurate picture of your all-around ability can be established.

Where to Apply

Information about the exact dates of the exam, fees, testing locations, and a test registration form can be found in the "GMAT Bulletin of Information" for candidates published by ETS. You can obtain a copy by writing:

Graduate Management Admission Test
Educational Testing Service
CN 6103
Princeton, New Jersey 08541-6103

The GMAT is generally given in October, January, March, and June. Since the majority of business schools send out their acceptances in the spring, it is wise to take the exam as early as possible to ensure that the schools you are applying to receive your scores in time.

The Test Format

In recent years, the GMAT has contained questions of the following types: Reading Comprehension, Problem Solving, Analysis of Situations, Data Sufficiency, Writing Ability (2 types: Usage and Sentence Correction), Verbal Ability, and Reading Recall. The most recent tests, however, have contained the following types: Reading Comprehension, Problem Solving, Analysis of Situations, Data Sufficiency, and Writing Ability (only Sentence Correction). Questions on Critical Reasoning may also be included.

Recent GMAT examinations have contained eight sections, with each section allotted thirty minutes. Some possible test formats are:

Form A

SECTION	TYPE OF QUESTION	NUMBER OF QUESTIONS	TIME (MIN.)
I	Reading Comprehension	25	30
II	Reading Comprehension	25	30
III	Problem Solving	20	30
IV	Analysis of Situations*	35	30
V	Data Sufficiency	25	30
VI	Analysis of Situations	35	30
VII	Writing Ability	25	30
VIII	Problem Solving	20	30
Total		210	240

*NOTE: Recent Analysis of Situations sections have included two passages, with a total of 35 questions (usually 18 and 17 questions each).

Form B

SECTION	TYPE OF QUESTION	NUMBER OF QUESTIONS	TIME (MIN.)
I	Reading Comprehension	25	30
II	Analysis of Situations	35	30
III	Problem Solving	20	30
IV	Analysis of Situations	35	30
V	Data Sufficiency	25	30
VI	Writing Ability	25	30
VII	Writing Ability	25	30
VIII	Problem Solving	20	30
Total		210	240

Additional forms are possible wherein sections may be repeated—e.g., Problem Solving or Analysis of Situations may appear three times in one test. However, the content of question types has not changed. Usually only six of the eight sections are counted in your score. The other two sections either contain experimental questions or are used to calibrate different versions of the GMAT. However, you will not know which sections are going to count, so you must do your best on every section.

Each section of the GMAT must be completed within the specified time limit. If you finish the section before the allotted time has elapsed, you must spend the remaining time working on that section *only*. You may *not* work on other sections of the test at all.

Specific directions telling you exactly how to answer the questions appear at the beginning of each section of the exam. Keep in mind that although the directions for answering the sample questions in this guide are designed to simulate as closely as possible those on the actual test, the format of the test you take may vary. Therefore, it is important that you read the directions on the actual test very carefully before attempting to answer the questions. You also should be certain of the exact time limit you are allowed.

GMAT Test-Taking Techniques

First, you must be prepared. Make sure you bring several sharpened number two pencils, a good eraser, and a watch (the test center may not have a visible clock).

Use your pencil and blacken your answer choices completely. Be sure erasures are done cleanly. If you skip a question, make sure you skip that answer space in your answer sheet.

Read the directions carefully. Make sure you answer the questions which are asked. Consider *all* choices. Remember you must pick the *best* choice, not just a good choice. For many questions, it is helpful to read the answers before trying to answer the question.

Budget your time. Calculate the time you may spend on each question, so that you will have time to look at each question. You want to answer as many questions correctly as you can, so try to work quickly but accurately. Check your watch a few times while you are working on each section to make sure you are working sufficiently fast. Be sure not to linger on a question you can't answer, or spend time worrying about questions you can't answer. You should not expect to answer every question correctly. If you have no idea what the answer to a question is, leave the space blank on your sheet and move on. Since one quarter of your wrong answers is subtracted from your total of correct answers to get your raw score, it is better to leave an answer blank if you cannot eliminate any of the choices. However, if you can eliminate even one answer it is to your advantage to guess one of the remaining answers.

You will not be allowed to use rulers, slide rules, or calculators on the exam. If you usually use a calculator to do arithmetic, practice doing arithmetic without it.

The GMAT exam takes over four hours, and you will have only one fifteen-minute break. To ready yourself for this physical strain, do each practice exam entirely in one sitting. Try to be well rested and eat a good meal before the exam. Remember: a question answered correctly on the last section of the exam counts just as much as a question answered correctly on the first section. If you are tired by the end of the exam, you may not do as well as you could on the later sections.

Your Scores and What They Mean

You will receive three scores on the GMAT exam: a total score, a verbal score, and a quantitative score. The total score ranges from 200 to 800; the verbal and quantitative scores range from 0 to 60. You will also be given a percentile ranking for each of the three scores. The percentile ranking gives you the percentage of the test scores in the last three years lower than yours. Thus, a percentile ranking of 75 would mean that 75% of the test scores in the last three years were below your score.

All of the scores you receive are *scaled scores*. Since there are many different versions of the exam, the use of scaled scores allows test results based on different versions of the exam to be compared. The same *raw score* (total number of correct answers minus one fourth of the number of wrong answers) will be converted into a higher scaled score if you took a more difficult version of the exam. If you take several versions of the exam, your scaled scores should cluster about your "true" scaled score. Thus, your scaled score in some sense represents a range of possibilities. A score of 510 means that your "true" score is probably between 480 and 540.

In general, no particular score can be called good or bad, and no passing or failing grade has been established. Scores above 700 or below 250 are unusual. In recent years, about two thirds of all scores have fallen between 350 and 570, with the average between 460 and 470. In the verbal and quantitative scores, grades above 46 or below 10 are unusual. About two thirds of these scores fall between 22 and 38, with the average about 30.

Your score on the GMAT is only one of several factors examined by admissions officers. Your undergraduate record, for example, is at least as important as your GMAT score. Thus, a low score does not mean that no school will accept you, nor does a high GMAT score guarantee acceptance at the school of your choice. However, since your score is one important factor, you should try to do as well as you can on the exam. Using this book should help you to maximize your score.

How to Prepare for the GMAT

You should now be aware of the purpose of the GMAT and have a general idea of the format of the test. With this basic information, you are in a position to begin your study and review. The rest of this guide represents a study plan which will enable you to prepare for the GMAT. If used properly, it will help you diagnose your weak areas and take steps to remedy them.

Begin your preparation by becoming as familiar as possible with the various types of questions that appear on the exam. The analysis of typical GMAT questions in the next chapter is designed for this purpose. When you feel you understand this material completely, take the Diagnostic Test that follows and evaluate your results on the self-scoring table provided at the end of the test. (An explanation of how to use these tables appears below.) A low score in any area indicates that you should spend more time reviewing that particular material. Study the review section for that area until you feel you have mastered it and then take one of the sample GMATs at the back of the book. Continue this pattern of study until you are completely satisfied with your performance. For best results, try to simulate exam conditions as closely as possible when taking sample tests: no unscheduled breaks or interruptions, strict adherence to time limits, and no use of outside aids.

The Self-scoring Tables

The self-scoring tables for each sample test in this guide can be used as a means of evaluating your weaknesses in particular subject areas and should help you plan your study program most effectively.

After completing a sample test, first determine the number of *correct* answers you had for each section. Next, subtract *one-fourth* the number of *wrong* answers for each part from the number of correct answers. This is done to eliminate the benefits of wild guessing. Do *not* subtract for any answers left blank. For example, suppose that in Section I you answered 15 out of 25 questions correctly, with 6 incorrect responses and 4 blanks. Subtract ¼ of 6 (1½) from 15 to obtain a final score of 13½. Record this score in the appropriate score box in the Self-scoring Table as shown below.

Self-scoring Table

SECTION	SCORE	RATING
1	13½	FAIR
2		
3		
4		
5		
6		
7		
8		

Then compare this score with those contained in the Self-scoring Scale. Insert your rating, either POOR, FAIR, GOOD, or EXCELLENT, in the appropriate box in the Self-scoring Table.

Self-scoring Scale—RATING

SECTION	POOR	FAIR	GOOD	EXCELLENT
1	0–12+	13–17+	18–21+	22–25
2	0–9+	10–13+	14–17+	18–20
3	0–17+	18–24+	25–31+	32–35
4	0–12+	13–17+	18–21+	22–25
5	0–12+	13–17+	18–21+	22–25
6	0–17+	18–24+	25–31+	32–35
7	0–12+	13–17+	18–21+	22–25
8	0–9+	10–13+	14–17+	18–20

In the table, numbers such as 12+ mean numbers larger than 12 but less than 13. For example, if your raw score on Section 6 of the exam was 24½, then this translates to FAIR on the self-scoring table.

A rating of FAIR or POOR in any area indicates that you need to spend more time reviewing that material.

Scaled Scores

The rules below will give you a method for converting your raw score on a practice exam into a scaled score. This is not the same procedure that the GMAT uses, but it should give you some idea of what your scaled score would be on the exam. Note that your raw score on an exam is the number of correct answers minus one fourth of the incorrect answers, with no deduction for answers left blank.

Use the following rule to convert your raw score into a scaled score.

Call N the number of questions in the test. Then the rule is:

$$\text{SCALED SCORE} = 3.5 \times (\text{RAW SCORE}) + (800 - 3.45N)$$

If the rule gives a scaled score greater than 800, then the scaled score is 800.
If the rule gives a scaled score less than 200, then the scaled score is 200.

EXAMPLE: You have a raw score of 142.5 on a test with 200 questions.

(A) Use the rule SCALED SCORE = $3.5 \times$ (RAW SCORE) + (800 − 3.45N).
(B) Since N = 200, (800 − 3.45N) = 800 − 690 = 110.
(C) So the scaled score is 3.5 (142.5) + 110 = 498.75 + 110 = 609.

If your scaled scores are low on the first practice exams you take, don't get discouraged. Your scaled score should improve on the later practice exams after you have used the various reviews to strengthen your weaknesses. The tests were made hard. That way you can discover your weaknesses and try to correct them. Easy practice tests are not good practice for a difficult exam. Remember that, on the GMAT itself, you shouldn't expect to be able to answer every single question. Don't worry about that. To maximize your score, you want to answer as many questions as you can correctly in the given amount of time.

After You Take the Exam

You will usually receive your scores about four weeks after the exam.

You may take the GMAT as many times as you wish. However, if you repeat the test, your scores from that test and the two most recent previous test results will be sent to all institutions you designate as score recipients. Many schools average your scores if you take the test more than once. So unless there is a reason to expect a substantial improvement in your score, it usually is *not* worthwhile to retake the exam.

Currently, you can receive a copy of your answer sheet, a booklet containing all questions that were counted in scoring your exam, an answer key, and the scale used to translate your raw scores into scaled scores. You should obtain this information if you are considering retaking the exam. You can see if there was any particular section which hurt your score and concentrate on those questions as you study.

You can also cancel your scores if you act *before* receiving them. If you wish to cancel your scores, you must indicate this on your answer sheet, notify the supervisor before you leave the test center, or notify ETS by mail within 7 days of the test administration. If you cancel your scores, the fact that you took the test will be reported to all the places you designated as score recipients. Thus, it is generally not advantageous to cancel your scores unless there is reason to believe that you have done substantially worse on the test than you would if you took the test again; for example, if you became ill while taking the exam. Once a score is cancelled from your record it cannot be put back on your record or reported at a later date.

As a general rule, it is better to retake the exam after looking over your previous results (questions, answers, and so on) than it is to cancel your scores. You can do well on the exam without finishing every section of the exam. In addition, each version of the exam contains questions or sections which are experimental and are not counted towards your score, so your score may be better than you expect. Thus, you usually are better off waiting to see your score before deciding whether or not to retake the exam.

TWO
AN ANALYSIS OF TYPICAL GMAT QUESTIONS

A logical first step in preparing for the GMAT is to become as familiar as possible with the types of questions that usually appear on this exam. The following analysis of typical GMAT questions explains the purpose behind each type and the best method for answering it. Samples of the questions with a discussion of their answers are also presented. More detailed discussions and reviews for each type of question are presented elsewhere in this book.

Reading Comprehension

The Reading Comprehension section tests your ability to analyze written information and includes passages from the humanities, the social sciences, and the physical and biological sciences. The typical Reading Comprehension section consists of three or four passages with a total of 25 questions which must be completed in 30 minutes. You will be allowed to turn back to the passages when answering the questions. However, many of the questions may be based on what is *implied* in the passages, rather than on what is explicitly stated. Your ability to draw inferences from the material is critical to successfully completing this section. You are to select the best answer from five alternatives.

The following passage will give you an idea of the format of the Reading Comprehension section. Read the passage through and then answer the questions, making sure to leave yourself enough time to complete them all.

Sample Passage and Questions

TIME: 10 minutes

Political theories have, in fact, very little more to do with musical creation than electronic theories have. Both merely determine methods of distribution. The exploitation of these methods is subject to political regulation, is quite rigidly regulated in many countries. The revolutionary parties, both in Russia and else-
(5) where, have tried to turn composers on to supposedly revolutionary subject-matter. The net result for either art or revolution has not been very important. Neither has official fascist music accomplished much either for music or for Italy or Germany.

Political party-influence on music is just censorship anyway. Performances can
(10) be forbidden and composers disciplined for what they write, but the creative stimulus comes from elsewhere. Nothing really "inspires" an author but money or food or love.

That persons or parties subventioning musical uses should wish to retain veto power over the works used is not at all surprising. That our political masters (or (15) our representatives) should exercise a certain negative authority, a censorship, over the exploitation of works whose content they consider dangerous to public welfare is also in no way novel or surprising. But that such political executives should think to turn the musical profession into a college of political theorists or a bunch of hired propagandists is naïve of them. Our musical civilization is older (20) than any political party. We can deal on terms of intellectual equality with acoustical engineers, with architects, with poets, painters, and historians, even with the Roman clergy if necessary. We cannot be expected to take very seriously the inspirational dictates of persons or of groups who think they can pay us to get emotional about ideas. They can pay us to get emotional all right. Anybody can. (25) Nothing is so emotion-producing as money. But emotions are factual; they are not generated by ideas. On the contrary, ideas are generated by emotions; and emotions, in turn, are visceral states produced directly by facts like money and food and sexual intercourse. To have any inspirational quality there must be present facts or immediate anticipations, not pie-in-the-sky.

(30)   Now pie-in-the-sky has its virtues as a political ideal, I presume. Certainly most men want to work for an eventual common good. I simply want to make it quite clear that ideals about the common good (not to speak of mere political necessity) are not very stimulating subject-matter for music. They don't produce visceral movements the way facts do. It is notorious that musical descriptions of hell, (35) which is something we can all imagine, are more varied and vigorous than the placid banalities that even the best composers have used to describe heaven; and that all composers do better on really present matters than on either: matters like love and hatred and hunting and war and dancing around and around.

The moral of all this is that the vetoing of objective subject-matter is as far as (40) political stimulation or censorship can go in advance. Style is personal and emotional, not political at all. And form or design, which is impersonal, is not subject to any political differences of opinion.

1. Ⓐ Ⓑ Ⓒ Ⓓ Ⓔ   **1.** The author is making a statement defending

      I. intellectual freedom
     II. the apolitical stance of most musicians
    III. emotional honesty

    (A) I only
    (B) II only
    (C) I and II only

    (D) I and III only
    (E) I, II, and III

2. Ⓐ Ⓑ Ⓒ Ⓓ Ⓔ   **2.** The tone of the author in the passage is

    (A) exacting
    (B) pessimistic
    (C) critical
    (D) optimistic
    (E) fatalistic

3. Ⓐ Ⓑ Ⓒ Ⓓ Ⓔ   **3.** The author's reaction to political influence on music is one of

    (A) surprise
    (B) disbelief
    (C) resignation
    (D) deference
    (E) rancor

4. According to the author, political attempts to control the subject-matter of music   4. Ⓐ Ⓑ Ⓒ Ⓓ Ⓔ

    (A) will be resisted by artists wherever they are made
    (B) may succeed in censoring but not in inspiring musical works
    (C) will succeed only if the eventual goal is the common good
    (D) are less effective than the indirect use of social and economic pressure
    (E) have profoundly influenced the course of modern musical history

5. The author refers to "musical descriptions of hell" (line 34) to make the point that   5. Ⓐ Ⓑ Ⓒ Ⓓ Ⓔ

    (A) musical inspiration depends on the degree to which the composer's imagination is stimulated by his subject
    (B) composers are better at evoking negative emotions and ideas than positive ones
    (C) music is basically unsuited to a role in support of political tyranny
    (D) religious doctrines have inspired numerous musical compositions
    (E) political ideals are a basic motivating force for most contemporary composers

6. The author implies that political doctrines usually fail to generate artistic creativity   6. Ⓐ Ⓑ Ⓒ Ⓓ Ⓔ
because they are too

    (A) naïve
    (B) abstract
    (C) rigidly controlled
    (D) concrete
    (E) ambiguous

Answers:

  1. **(D)**   2. **(C)**   3. **(C)**   4. **(B)**   5. **(A)**   6. **(B)**

Analysis:

1. **(D)** The author is arguing that musicians will not conform to any control over their creativity. Thus, they want to be intellectually free and emotionally honest. It does not mean that they could not be active in politics (apolitical).

2. **(C)** The author is critical of attempts to censor the arts, especially music.

3. **(C)** The author does not find censorship surprising (line 13), nor does he take it seriously (line 21). He is resigned to attempts at censorship, although he does not believe it can inspire creativity.

4. **(B)** See paragraph 2.

5. **(A)** See lines 34–35.

6. **(B)** See paragraph 4, in which the author states that "ideals" do not inspire music as "facts" do; and also see lines 11–12 and 28–29.

Writing Ability

In spite of its name, the Writing Ability part of the exam tests not writing ability but rather your understanding of the basic rules of English grammar and usage. To succeed in this section, you need a command of sentence structure including tense and mood, subject and verb agreement, proper case, parallel structure, and other basics. No attempt is made to test for punctuation, spelling, or capitalization.

The Writing Ability section is comprised of *Sentence Correction* questions. You will be given a sentence in which all or part of the sentence is underlined. You will then be asked to choose the best phrasing of the underlined part from five alternatives. (A) will always be the original phrasing.

Sample Question

Ⓐ Ⓑ Ⓒ Ⓓ Ⓔ   Since the advent of cable television, at the beginning of <u>this decade, the video industry took</u> a giant stride forward in this country.

(A) this decade, the video industry took
(B) this decade, the video industry had taken
(C) this decade, the video industry has taken
(D) this decade saw the video industry taking
(E) the decade that let the video industry take

Answer:

(C)

Analysis:

The phrase "Since the advent . . ." demands a verb in the present perfect form; thus, "*has taken*," not "*took*," is correct. Choice (E) changes the meaning of the original sentence.

Analysis of Situations

The objective of the Analysis of Situations section is to test your ability to analyze business situations and draw conclusions about them. In this section, you are asked to read a passage discussing various aspects of a business situation leading to the need for a decision. After you complete the passage, you are given questions to answer containing a number of factors relating to the passage, each of which you must evaluate as being a *Major Objective*, a *Major Factor*, a *Minor Factor*, a *Major Assumption*, or an *Unimportant Issue* in the decision-making process. You are permitted to refer to the passage while answering the questions.

It is helpful to underline main points as you read. However, when reading the Analysis of Situations passages, you should concentrate on defining decision-making factors that fit into the categories for evaluation in the Data Evaluation questions.

The sample passage that follows is considerably shorter than a typical Analysis of Situations passage on the exam. Read the passage, underlining what you feel to be

1. Major Objectives
2. Major Factors
3. Minor Factors
4. Major Assumptions
5. Unimportant Issues

After you have finished, answer the questions that follow. Allow yourself 12 minutes to complete the entire exercise. You may consult the passage for assistance.

Sample Passage and Questions

TIME—12 minutes

Early in 1953, the soft drink world began to watch an interesting experiment: the introduction of soft drinks in cans. Grocery outlets up to that time had enjoyed about one-half of all sales, but it was felt that if the new package was successful, local bottling plants might give way to great central plants, possibly operated by companies with established names in the grocery fields, with shipments being made in carload lots. Local bottlers faced a great decision. If the change were to prove permanent, they should perhaps hasten to add can-filling machines lest they lose their market. Coca-Cola, Canada Dry, White Rock, and many other bottlers experimented with the new plan. An eastern chain put out privately branded cans.

A basic limitation was the cost factor of about three cents per can, whereas bottle cost was but a fraction of a cent, since a bottle averaged about twenty-four round trips. It was known, however, that at that time about one third of all beer sales were made in cans and, furthermore, that other beverages had paved the way for consumer acceptance of a canned product. Beer prices were normally from three to four times those of soft drinks.

Many leaders in the industry felt that it might well be that consumer advertising emphasizing the convenience of using a nonreturnable package might offset both habit and the extra cost to the consumer. One of the principal bottling companies undertook a large-scale market research project to find useful guides to future action.

DIRECTIONS: The questions that follow relate to the preceding passage. Evaluate, in terms of the passage, each of the items given. Then select your answer from one of the following classifications, and blacken the corresponding space on the answer sheet.

(A) A MAJOR OBJECTIVE in making the decision: one of the goals sought by the decision maker

(B) A MAJOR FACTOR in making the decision: an aspect of the problem, specifically mentioned in the passage, that fundamentally affects and/or determines the decision

(C) A MINOR FACTOR in making the decision: a less important element bearing on or affecting a Major Factor, rather than a Major Objective directly

(D) A MAJOR ASSUMPTION in making the decision: a projection or supposition arrived at by the decision maker before considering the factors and alternatives

(E) AN UNIMPORTANT ISSUE in making the decision: an item lacking significant impact on, or relationship to, the decision

1. Introduction of soft drinks in cans   1. Ⓐ Ⓑ Ⓒ Ⓓ Ⓔ

2. Results of the market research project   2. Ⓐ Ⓑ Ⓒ Ⓓ Ⓔ

3. Cost of soft drinks in cans   3. Ⓐ Ⓑ Ⓒ Ⓓ Ⓔ

4. Inappropriateness of cans for more than a single use prior to scrapping   4. Ⓐ Ⓑ Ⓒ Ⓓ Ⓔ

5. Size of the beer market as compared to that for soft drinks   5. Ⓐ Ⓑ Ⓒ Ⓓ Ⓔ

6. Power of consumer advertising to eliminate resistance to canned soft drinks   6. Ⓐ Ⓑ Ⓒ Ⓓ Ⓔ

The sample passage with suggested underlining appears below.

Early in 1953, the soft drink world began to watch an interesting experiment, the introduction of soft drinks in cans. Grocery outlets up to that time had enjoyed about one-half of all sales, but it was felt that if the new package was successful, local bottling plants might give way to great central plants, possibly operated by companies with established names in the grocery fields, with shipments being made in carload lots. Local bottlers faced a great decision. If the change were to prove permanent, they should perhaps hasten to add can-filling machines lest they lose their market. Coca Cola, Canada Dry, White Rock, and many other bottlers experimented with the new plan. An eastern chain put out privately branded cans.

A basic limitation was a cost factor of about three cents per can, whereas bottle cost was but a fraction of a cent, since a bottle averaged about twenty-four round trips. It was, however, known that at that time about one-third of all beer sales were made in cans, and furthermore, that other beverages had paved the way for consumer acceptance of a canned product. Beer prices normally were from three to four times those of soft drinks.

Many leaders in the industry felt that it might well be that consumer advertising emphasizing the convenience of using a nonreturnable package might offset both habit and the extra cost to the consumer. One of the principal bottling companies undertook a rather large-scale market research project to find useful guides to future action.

Answers:

1. (A) 2. (B) 3. (B) 4. (C) 5. (E) 6. (D)

Analysis:

1. **(A)** The introduction of soft drinks in cans is certainly the *Major Objective* here, since it is the ultimate goal toward which the executives were working.

2. **(B)** The market research project would gather information allowing management to make a decision; without such information, presumably, no decision could be reached. Therefore, the results of the project are a *Major Factor* influencing the decision.

3. **(B)** The cost of canned soft drinks is a *Major Factor* in making the decision because it is crucial to consumer acceptance. If the soft drinks are priced too high, consumers may not be willing to purchase them.

4. **(C)** Because cans may only be used once, their cost per use is higher than that of bottles. Since this factor has a peripheral effect on a major factor—namely, overall costs—it constitutes a *Minor Factor*.

5. **(E)** The size of the beer market is of minimal importance in the decision as to whether soft drinks in cans will prove a success. Therefore, the only possible answer to this question is (E), *Unimportant Issue*.

6. **(D)** The executives alluded to in the passage merely *suspect* that advertising will be capable of effecting the desired attitude change. No facts are given to support this belief. Thus, this item is a *Major Assumption*.

Critical Reasoning

Critical reasoning questions consist of a short statement followed by a question or assumption about the statement. Each question or assumption contains five possible answers, only one of which is correct.

The objective of this type of question is to test your ability to evaluate an assumption, inference, or argument that is presented in a short statement. Your task, therefore, is to evaluate each of the five answer choices and select the one that is the best alternative.

There are a number of different question types:

1. Inferences or assumptions. You will be given a statement, position argument, or fact. You will then be asked to choose the best alternative that either summarizes the statement or may be inferred from the statement. This type of question may be worded, "From which of the following can the statement above be properly inferred?"

2. Flaws. In this type of question you are asked to choose the best alternative answer that either represents a flaw in the statement position, or, if true, would weaken the argument or conclusion. Example question: "Which of the following, if true, would weaken the answer above?"

3. Statements of fact. You will be instructed to find the best answer that agrees or summarizes the statement. Question example: "If the information above is accurate, which of the following must be true?"

Strategy for Critical Reasoning Questions

1. If the statement given presents an argument,

   "In studying the effects of inflation on wages, some economists conclude that. . . ."

   make sure you identify and understand the writer's thesis and conclusions before you examine the answer alternatives.

2. If a statistical trend is given in the passage,

   "In 1950 there were 50 deaths per 100,000 population; in 1960, 40 deaths and in 1970, 30 deaths. This trend seems to be continuing."

   you will be asked to choose the alternative answer that best summarizes the trend or to identify from a list of factors the one that does *not* explain the trend. In most cases, the relationship between the trend and the factors can be determined from common sense.

3. Do not let your personal opinion affect your answer. Accept each statement, argument, or trend as a fact and proceed accordingly.

4. Do not worry about unfamiliar subjects. Technical terms will be defined for you.

5. Read actively, marking the facts you feel are important.

Sample Questions

1. From a letter to the editor:

   "Many people are murdered by killers whose homicidal tendencies are triggered by an official execution. There was a murder rate increase of at least 66% of executions since 1977 . . . If each of the 1,788 death row prisoners were to be executed, up to 7,152 additional murders would be one of the results."

   Which of the following, if true, would weaken the above argument?

   (A) The rate of murders to executions is 1 to 1.66
   (B) There is no relation between executions and murders.
   (C) Executions result from the higher incidence of violent crime.
   (D) The death penalty will be abolished.
   (E) Not all death row prisoners will be executed.

   Analysis: **(B)** The author's assumption is that there *is* a relation between executions and homicides. As executions increase, so will homicides—at a given rate. Of course, if (D) occurred, presumably the homicide rate, according to the author's argument, will decline. However, (B) is the strongest argument—if true—against the author's premise.

2. When Herodotus wrote his history of the ancient world, he mixed the lives of the famous with those of the everyday. He wanted not only to record the events that shaped his world but also to give his readers a taste of life in past times and faraway places.

   Which of the following statements best summarizes the above?

   (A) Herodotus performed the tasks of both historian and journalist.
   (B) Historians alone cannot reconstruct times and social circles.
   (C) Herodotus relied upon gossip and hearsay to compile his essays.
   (D) Herodotus' history was based on scanty evidence.
   (E) Herodotus preferred writing about the elite, rather than the lower classes.

   Analysis: (A) Herodotus wrote about all classes of people, recording not only momentous events but also the mundane. Therefore, he could be classified both as an historian and a journalist.

3. Four years ago the government introduced the Youth Training Program to guarantee teenagers leaving school an alternative to the dole. Today, over 150,000 16- and 17-year-olds are still signing on for unemployment benefits.

Each of the following, if true, could account for the above outcome EXCEPT:

(A) The program provides uninteresting work.
(B) It is difficult to find work for all the program's graduates.
(C) The number of 16- and 17-year-old youths has increased over the past four years.
(D) Unemployment benefits are known while future salaries are not.
(E) Youths are unaware of the program's benefits.

Analysis: **(C)** While the number of 16- and 17-year-olds has increased, it does not explain why *unemployed* high school graduates do not opt for the training program. All other answer alternatives do.

Problem Solving

The Problem Solving section of the GMAT is designed to test your ability to work with numbers. There are a variety of questions in this section dealing with the basic principles of arithmetic, algebra, and geometry. These questions may take the form of word problems or require straight calculation. In addition, questions involving the interpretation of tables and graphs may be included.

The typical Problem Solving section that has appeared on recent tests consists of 20 questions that must be answered within a time limit of 30 minutes. These questions range from very easy to quite challenging and are not always arranged in order of difficulty. Make sure you budget your time so that you can try each question.

Strategy for Problem Solving Questions

In order to maximize your score on this section, you must answer all the questions you can. *Don't waste time* on a question you can't figure out in a minute or two. You will score better if you answer 2 or 3 easy questions in the time it would take to answer one difficult one. Since the last questions may be easier for you than the first questions, try to *budget your time* so that you will have a chance to try each question.

Don't waste time on *unnecessary calculations*. If you can answer the question by *estimating* or doing a rough calculation, the time you save can be used to answer other questions. Keep this in mind especially when considering problems that involve tables and graphs. In many cases you can make estimates which will simplify your calculations and still be accurate enough to answer the question. Using estimates is a skill that can turn a good score into an excellent one.

For line and bar graphs, use your pencil as a ruler. It is more accurate than simply "eyeballing" columns which are not adjacent.

You should understand that random guessing will not help your score on these sections, since a percentage of your wrong answers is subtracted from your correct answers. If you can eliminate at least one of the answers for a particular question, it will probably help your score to guess an answer for that question.

Solve the sample questions below, allowing yourself 12 minutes to complete all of them. As you work, try to make use of the above strategy. Any figure that appears with a problem is drawn as accurately as possible to provide information that may help in answering the question. All numbers used are real numbers.

Sample Questions

TIME—12 minutes

1. A train travels from Albany to Syracuse, a distance of 120 miles, at the average rate of 50 miles per hour. The train then travels back to Albany from Syracuse. The total traveling time of the train is 5 hours and 24 minutes. What was the average rate of speed of the train on the return trip to Albany?

   1. Ⓐ Ⓑ Ⓒ Ⓓ Ⓔ

   (A) 60 mph
   (B) 48 mph
   (C) 40 mph
   (D) 50 mph
   (E) 35 mph

2. A parking lot charges a flat rate of X dollars for any amount of time up to two hours, and ⅙X for each hour or fraction of an hour after the first two hours. How much does it cost to park for 5 hours and 15 minutes?

   2. Ⓐ Ⓑ Ⓒ Ⓓ Ⓔ

   (A) 3X
   (B) 2X
   (C) 1⅔X
   (D) 1½X
   (E) 1⅙X

Use the following table for questions 3–5.

Number of Students by Major in State University		
	1950	1970
Division of Business	990	2,504
Division of Sciences	350	790
Division of Humanities	1,210	4,056
Division of Engineering	820	1,600
Division of Agriculture	630	1,050
TOTAL	4,000	10,000

3. From 1950 to 1970, the change in the percentage of university students enrolled in Engineering was

   3. Ⓐ Ⓑ Ⓒ Ⓓ Ⓔ

   (A) roughly no change
   (B) an increase of more than 4%
   (C) an increase of more than 1% but less than 4%
   (D) a decrease of more than 4%
   (E) a decrease of more than 1% but less than 4%

4. The number of students enrolled in Business in 1970 divided by the number of Business students in 1950 is

   4. Ⓐ Ⓑ Ⓒ Ⓓ Ⓔ

   (A) almost 3
   (B) about 2.5
   (C) roughly 2
   (D) about 1
   (E) about 40%

5. By 1970 how many of the divisions had an enrollment greater than 200% of the enrollment of that division in 1950?

   5. Ⓐ Ⓑ Ⓒ Ⓓ Ⓔ

   (A) 0
   (B) 1
   (C) 2
   (D) 3
   (E) 4

6. Ⓐ Ⓑ Ⓒ Ⓓ Ⓔ 6. Which of the following sets of values for w, x, y, and z respectively are possible if *ABCD* is a parallelogram?

I. 50, 130, 50, 130
II. 60, 110, 70, 120
III. 60, 150, 50, 150

(A) I only
(B) II only
(C) I and II only
(D) I and III only
(E) I, II, and III

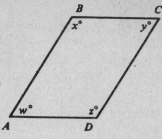

7. Ⓐ Ⓑ Ⓒ Ⓓ Ⓔ 7. John weighs twice as much as Marcia. Marcia's weight is 60% of Bob's weight. Dave weighs 50% of Lee's weight. Lee weighs 190% of John's weight. Which of these 5 persons weighs the least?

(A) Bob
(B) Dave
(C) John
(D) Lee
(E) Marcia

Answers:

1. **(C)**   4. **(B)**   7. **(E)**
2. **(C)**   5. **(D)**
3. **(D)**   6. **(A)**

Analysis:

1. **(C)** The train took 120/50 = 2⅖ hours to travel from Albany to Syracuse. Since the total traveling time of the train was 5⅖ hours, it must have taken the train 3 hours for the trip from Syracuse to Albany. Since the distance traveled is 120 miles, the average rate of speed on the return trip to Albany was (1/3)(120) mph = 40 mph.

2. **(C)** It costs X for the first 2 hours. If you park 5 hours and 15 minutes there are 3 hours and 15 minutes left after the first 2 hours. Since this time is charged at the rate of $X/6$ for each hour or fraction thereof, it costs $4(X/6)$ for the last 3 hours and 15 minutes. Thus the total $X + ⅔X = 1⅔X$.

3. **(D)** Since 820/4,000 = .205, the percentage of university students enrolled in Engineering in 1950 was 20.5%; since 1,600/10,000 = .16, the percentage in 1970 was 16%. Thus the percentage of university students enrolled in Engineering was 4.5% less in 1970 than it was in 1950.

4. **(B)** In 1950 there were 990 Business students and in 1970 there were 2,504. Since (2.5)(1,000) = 2,500, the correct answer is thus (B), about 2.5. Note that this is an easy way to save yourself time. Instead of dividing 990 into 2,504 to find the exact answer, simply use numbers close to the original numbers to get an estimate. In many cases this gives enough information to answer the question and saves valuable time.

5. **(D)** If a division in 1970 has more than 200% of the number of students it had in 1950 that means that the number of students more than doubled between 1950 and 1970. Therefore simply double each entry in the 1950 column and if this is less than the corresponding entry in the 1970 column, that division has more than 200% of the number of students it had in 1950. Since (2)(990) = 1980, which is less than 2,504, the number of Business students more than doubled. Since (2)(1,210) = 2,420, which is less than 4,056, Humanities more than doubled, and because (2)(350) = 700, which is less than 790, Sciences more than doubled. Engineering did not double in size because (2)(820) = 1,640, which is larger than 1,600. Also since (2)(630) = 1,260, which is larger than 1,050, the number of Agricultural students in 1970 was less than 200% of the number of Agricultural students in 1950. Therefore three of the divisions (Business, Humanities, and Sciences) more than doubled between 1950 and 1970.

6. **(A)** The sum of the angles of a parallelogram (which is 4-sided) must be $(4 - 2)180°$ $= 360°$. Since the sum of the values in III is 410, III cannot be correct. The sum of the numbers in II is 360, but in a parallelogram opposite angles must be equal so x must equal z and y must equal w. Since 60 is unequal to 70, II cannot be correct. The sum of the values in I is 360 and opposite angles will be equal, so I is correct.

7. **(E)** John weighs twice as much as Marcia, so John cannot weigh the least. Marcia's weight is less than Bob's weight, so Bob's weight is not the least. Dave's weight is ½ of Lee's weight, so Lee can't weigh the least. The only possible answers are Marcia or Dave. Let J, M B, D, and L stand for the weights of John, Marcia, Bob, Dave, and Lee respectively. Then $D = .5L = .5(1.9)J$. So $D = .95J$. Since $J = 2M$, we know $M = .5J$. Therefore Marcia weighs the least.

Data Sufficiency

This section of the GMAT is designed to test your reasoning ability. Like the Problem Solving section, it requires a basic knowledge of the principles of arithmetic, algebra, and geometry. Each Data Sufficiency question consists of a mathematical problem and two statements containing information relating to it. You must decide whether the problem can be solved by using information from: (A) the first statement alone, but not the second statement alone; (B) the second statement alone, but not the first statement alone; (C) both statements together, but neither alone; or (D) either of the statements alone. Choose (E) if the problem cannot be solved, even by using both statements together. A typical section will consist of 25 questions to be answered in 30 minutes. As in the Problem Solving section, time is of the utmost importance. Approaching Data Sufficiency problems properly will help you use this time wisely.

Always keep in mind the fact that you are never asked to supply an answer for the problem; you need only determine if there is sufficient data available to find the answer. Therefore, *don't waste time figuring out the exact answer*. Once you know whether or not it is possible to find the answer with the given information you are through. If you spend too much time doing unnecessary work on one question you may not be able to finish the entire section.

Strategy for Data Sufficiency Questions

A systematic analysis can improve your score on Data Sufficiency sections. By answering three questions, you will always arrive at the correct choice. In addition, if you can answer any one of the three questions, you can eliminate at least one of the possible choices so that you can make an intelligent guess.

The three questions are:
   I. Is the first statement alone sufficient to solve the problem?
   II. Is the second statement alone sufficient to solve the problem?
   III. Are both statements together sufficient to solve the problem?

As a general rule try to answer the questions in the order I, II, III, since in many cases you will not have to answer all three to get the correct choice.

Here is how to use the three questions:

If the answer to I is YES, then the only possible choices are (A) or (D). Now, if the answer to II is YES, the choice must be (D), and if the answer to II is NO, the choice must be (A).

If the answer to I is NO then the only possible choices are (B), (C), or (E). Now, if the answer to II is YES, then the choice must be (B), and if the answer to II is NO, the only possible choices are (C) or (E).

So, finally, if the answer to III is YES, the choice is (C), and if the answer to III is NO, the choice is (E).

A good way to see this is to use a decision tree.

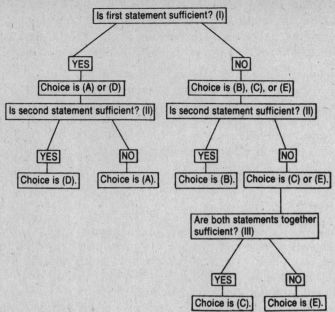

To use the tree simply start at the top and by answering YES or NO move down the tree until you arrive at the correct choice. For example, if the answer to I is YES and the answer to II is NO, then the correct choice is (A). (Notice that in this case you don't need to answer III to find the correct choice.)

The decision tree can also help you make intelligent guesses. If you can only answer one of the three questions, then you can eliminate the choices that follow from the wrong answer to the question.

EXAMPLE 1: You know the answer to I is YES. You can eliminate choices (B), (C), and (E).

EXAMPLE 2: You know the answer to II is NO. You can eliminate choices (D) and (B) since they follow from YES for II.

EXAMPLE 3: You know the answer to III is YES. You can eliminate choice (E) since it follows from NO for III.

EXAMPLE 4: You know the answer to I is NO and the answer to III is YES. You can eliminate (E) since it follows from NO to III. You also can eliminate (A) and (D) since they follow from YES to I.

Since you get one raw score point for each correct choice and lose only one quarter of a point for an incorrect choice, you should guess whenever you can answer one of the three questions.

Read the following directions carefully and then try the sample Data Sufficiency questions below. Allow yourself 8 minutes total time. All numbers used are real numbers. A

Sample Questions

TIME—8 minutes

DIRECTIONS: Each of the following problems has a question and two statements which are labeled (1) and (2). Use the data given in (1) and (2) together with other available information (such as the number of hours in a day, the definition of *clockwise*, mathematical facts, etc.) to decide whether the statements are *sufficient* to answer the question. Then choose

   (A) if you can get the answer from (1) alone but not from (2) alone;

   (B) if you can get the answer from (2) alone but not from (1) alone;

   (C) if you can get the answer from (1) and (2) together, although neither statement by itself suffices;

   (D) if statement (1) alone suffices *and* statement (2) alone suffices;

(E) if you cannot get the answer from statements (1) and (2) together, but need even more data.

All numbers used are real numbers. A figure given for a problem is intended to provide information consistent with that in the question, but not necessarily consistent with the additional information contained in the statements.

1. A rectangular field is 40 yards long. Find the area of the field.

1. Ⓐ Ⓑ Ⓒ Ⓓ Ⓔ

   (1) A fence around the entire boundary of the field is 140 yards long.
   (2) The field is more than 20 yards wide.

2. Is X a number greater than zero?

2. Ⓐ Ⓑ Ⓒ Ⓓ Ⓔ

   (1) $X^2 - 1 = 0$
   (2) $X^3 + 1 = 0$

3. An industrial plant produces bottles. In 1961 the number of bottles produced by the plant was twice the number produced in 1960. How many bottles were produced altogether in the years 1960, 1961, and 1962?

3. Ⓐ Ⓑ Ⓒ Ⓓ Ⓔ

   (1) In 1962 the number of bottles produced was 3 times the number produced in 1960.
   (2) In 1963 the number of bottles produced was one half the total produced in the years 1960, 1961, and 1962.

4. A man 6 feet tall is standing near a light on the top of a pole. What is the length of the shadow cast by the man?

4. Ⓐ Ⓑ Ⓒ Ⓓ Ⓔ

   (1) The pole is 18 feet high.
   (2) The man is 12 feet from the pole.

5. Find the length of RS if z is 90° and $PS = 6$.

5. Ⓐ Ⓑ Ⓒ Ⓓ Ⓔ

   (1) $PR = 6$
   (2) $x = 45°$

6. Working at a constant rate and by himself, it takes worker U 3 hours to fill up a ditch with sand. How long would it take for worker V to fill up the same ditch working by himself?

6. Ⓐ Ⓑ Ⓒ Ⓓ Ⓔ

   (1) Working together but at the same time U and V can fill in the ditch in 1 hour 52½ minutes.
   (2) In any length of time worker V fills in only 60% as much as worker U does in the same time.

7. Did John go to the beach yesterday?

7. Ⓐ Ⓑ Ⓒ Ⓓ Ⓔ

   (1) If John goes to the beach, he will be sunburned the next day.
   (2) John is sunburned today.

Answers:

1. **(A)**	4. **(C)**	7. **(E)**
2. **(B)**	5. **(D)**	
3. **(E)**	6. **(D)**	

Analysis:

   1. **(A)** The area of a rectangle is the length multiplied by the width. Since you know the length is 40 yards, you must find out the width in order to solve the problem. Since statement (2) simply says the width is greater than 20 yards you cannot find out the exact width using (2). So (2) alone is not sufficient. Statement (1) says the length of a fence around the entire boundary of the field is 140 yards. The length of this fence is the perimeter of the rectangle, the sum of twice the length and twice the width. If

we replace the length by 40 in $P = 2L + 2W$ we have $140 = 2(40) + 2W$ and solving for W yields $2W = 60$, or $W = 30$ yards. Hence the area is $(40)(30) = 1200$ square yards. Thus (1) alone is sufficient but (2) alone is not.

2. **(B)** Statement (1) means $X^2 = 1$, but there are two possible solutions to this equation, $X = 1$, $X = -1$. Thus using (1) alone you can not deduce whether X is positive or negative. Statement (2) means $X^3 = -1$ but there is only one possible (real) solution to this, $X = -1$. Thus X is not greater than zero which answers the question. And (2) alone is sufficient.

3. **(E)** T, the total produced in the three years, is the sum of $P_0 + P_1 + P_2$, where P_0 is the number produced in 1960, P_1 the number produced in 1961, and P_2 the number produced in 1962. You are given that $P_1 = 2P_0$. Thus $T = P_0 + P_1 + P_2 = P_0 + 2P_0 + P_2 = 3P_0 + P_2$. So we must find out P_0 and P_2 to answer the question. Statement (1) says $P_2 = 3P_0$; thus by using (1) if we can find the value of P_0 we can find T. But (1) gives us no further information about P_0. Statement (2) says T equals the number produced in 1963, but it does not say what this number is. Since there are no relations given between production in 1963 and production in the individual years 1960, 1961, or 1962 you cannot use (2) to find out what P_0 is. Thus (1) and (2) together are not sufficient.

4. **(C)** Sometimes it may help to draw a picture. By proportions or by similar triangles the height of the pole, h, is to 6 feet as the length of shadow, s, + the distance to the pole, x, is to s. So $h/6 = (s + x)/s$. Thus $hs = 6s + 6x$ by cross-multiplication. Solving for s gives $hs - 6s = 6x$, or $s(h - 6) = 6x$, or, finally we have $s = 6x/(h - 6)$.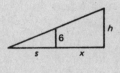
Statement (1) says $h = 18$; thus $s = 6x/12 = x/2$, but using (1) alone we cannot deduce the value x. Thus (1) alone is not sufficient. Statement (2) says x equals 12; thus, using (1) and (2) together we deduce $s = 6$, but using (2) alone all we can deduce is that $s = 72/(h - 6)$, which cannot be solved for s unless we know h. Thus using (1) and (2) together we can deduce the answer but (1) alone is not sufficient nor is (2) alone.

5. **(D)** Since z is a right angle, $(RS)^2 = (PS)^2 + (PR)^2$, so $(RS)^2 = (6)^2 + (PR)^2$, and RS will be the positive square root of $36 + (PR)^2$. Thus if you can find the length of PR the problem is solved. Statement (1) says $PR = 6$, thus $(RS)^2 = 36 + 36$, so $RS = 6\sqrt{2}$. Thus (1) alone is sufficient. Statement (2) says $x = 45°$ but since the sum of the angles in a triangle is 180° and z is 90° then $y = 45°$. So x and y are equal angles and that means the sides opposite x and opposite y must be equal or $PS = PR$. Thus $PR = 6$ and $RS = 6\sqrt{2}$ so (2) alone is also sufficient.

6. **(D)** (1) says U and V together can fill in the ditch in $1\frac{7}{8}$ hours. Since U can fill in the ditch in 3 hours, in 1 hour he can fill in one-third of the ditch. Hence, in $1\frac{7}{8}$ hours U would fill in $(1/3)(15/8) = \frac{5}{8}$ of the ditch. So V fills in $\frac{3}{8}$ of the ditch in $1\frac{7}{8}$ hours. Thus V would take $(8/3)(15/8) = 5$ hours to fill in the ditch working by himself. Therefore statement (1) alone is sufficient. According to statement (2) since U fills the ditch in 3 hours, V will fill $\frac{3}{5}$ of the ditch in 3 hours. Thus V will take 5 hours to fill in the ditch working by himself.

7. **(E)** Obviously, neither statement alone is sufficient. John *could* have gotten sunburned at the beach, but he might have gotten sunburned somewhere else. Therefore (1) and (2) together are not sufficient. This problem tests your grasp of an elementary rule of logic rather than your mathematical knowledge.

Answer Sheet—Diagnostic Test

Section I
Reading Comprehension

1. Ⓐ Ⓑ Ⓒ Ⓓ Ⓔ
2. Ⓐ Ⓑ Ⓒ Ⓓ Ⓔ
3. Ⓐ Ⓑ Ⓒ Ⓓ Ⓔ
4. Ⓐ Ⓑ Ⓒ Ⓓ Ⓔ
5. Ⓐ Ⓑ Ⓒ Ⓓ Ⓔ
6. Ⓐ Ⓑ Ⓒ Ⓓ Ⓔ
7. Ⓐ Ⓑ Ⓒ Ⓓ Ⓔ
8. Ⓐ Ⓑ Ⓒ Ⓓ Ⓔ
9. Ⓐ Ⓑ Ⓒ Ⓓ Ⓔ
10. Ⓐ Ⓑ Ⓒ Ⓓ Ⓔ
11. Ⓐ Ⓑ Ⓒ Ⓓ Ⓔ
12. Ⓐ Ⓑ Ⓒ Ⓓ Ⓔ
13. Ⓐ Ⓑ Ⓒ Ⓓ Ⓔ
14. Ⓐ Ⓑ Ⓒ Ⓓ Ⓔ
15. Ⓐ Ⓑ Ⓒ Ⓓ Ⓔ
16. Ⓐ Ⓑ Ⓒ Ⓓ Ⓔ
17. Ⓐ Ⓑ Ⓒ Ⓓ Ⓔ
18. Ⓐ Ⓑ Ⓒ Ⓓ Ⓔ
19. Ⓐ Ⓑ Ⓒ Ⓓ Ⓔ
20. Ⓐ Ⓑ Ⓒ Ⓓ Ⓔ
21. Ⓐ Ⓑ Ⓒ Ⓓ Ⓔ
22. Ⓐ Ⓑ Ⓒ Ⓓ Ⓔ
23. Ⓐ Ⓑ Ⓒ Ⓓ Ⓔ
24. Ⓐ Ⓑ Ⓒ Ⓓ Ⓔ
25. Ⓐ Ⓑ Ⓒ Ⓓ Ⓔ

Section II
Problem Solving

1. Ⓐ Ⓑ Ⓒ Ⓓ Ⓔ
2. Ⓐ Ⓑ Ⓒ Ⓓ Ⓔ
3. Ⓐ Ⓑ Ⓒ Ⓓ Ⓔ
4. Ⓐ Ⓑ Ⓒ Ⓓ Ⓔ
5. Ⓐ Ⓑ Ⓒ Ⓓ Ⓔ
6. Ⓐ Ⓑ Ⓒ Ⓓ Ⓔ
7. Ⓐ Ⓑ Ⓒ Ⓓ Ⓔ
8. Ⓐ Ⓑ Ⓒ Ⓓ Ⓔ
9. Ⓐ Ⓑ Ⓒ Ⓓ Ⓔ
10. Ⓐ Ⓑ Ⓒ Ⓓ Ⓔ
11. Ⓐ Ⓑ Ⓒ Ⓓ Ⓔ
12. Ⓐ Ⓑ Ⓒ Ⓓ Ⓔ
13. Ⓐ Ⓑ Ⓒ Ⓓ Ⓔ
14. Ⓐ Ⓑ Ⓒ Ⓓ Ⓔ
15. Ⓐ Ⓑ Ⓒ Ⓓ Ⓔ
16. Ⓐ Ⓑ Ⓒ Ⓓ Ⓔ
17. Ⓐ Ⓑ Ⓒ Ⓓ Ⓔ
18. Ⓐ Ⓑ Ⓒ Ⓓ Ⓔ
19. Ⓐ Ⓑ Ⓒ Ⓓ Ⓔ
20. Ⓐ Ⓑ Ⓒ Ⓓ Ⓔ

Section III
Analysis of Situations

1. Ⓐ Ⓑ Ⓒ Ⓓ Ⓔ
2. Ⓐ Ⓑ Ⓒ Ⓓ Ⓔ
3. Ⓐ Ⓑ Ⓒ Ⓓ Ⓔ
4. Ⓐ Ⓑ Ⓒ Ⓓ Ⓔ
5. Ⓐ Ⓑ Ⓒ Ⓓ Ⓔ
6. Ⓐ Ⓑ Ⓒ Ⓓ Ⓔ
7. Ⓐ Ⓑ Ⓒ Ⓓ Ⓔ
8. Ⓐ Ⓑ Ⓒ Ⓓ Ⓔ
9. Ⓐ Ⓑ Ⓒ Ⓓ Ⓔ
10. Ⓐ Ⓑ Ⓒ Ⓓ Ⓔ
11. Ⓐ Ⓑ Ⓒ Ⓓ Ⓔ
12. Ⓐ Ⓑ Ⓒ Ⓓ Ⓔ
13. Ⓐ Ⓑ Ⓒ Ⓓ Ⓔ
14. Ⓐ Ⓑ Ⓒ Ⓓ Ⓔ
15. Ⓐ Ⓑ Ⓒ Ⓓ Ⓔ
16. Ⓐ Ⓑ Ⓒ Ⓓ Ⓔ
17. Ⓐ Ⓑ Ⓒ Ⓓ Ⓔ
18. Ⓐ Ⓑ Ⓒ Ⓓ Ⓔ
19. Ⓐ Ⓑ Ⓒ Ⓓ Ⓔ
20. Ⓐ Ⓑ Ⓒ Ⓓ Ⓔ
21. Ⓐ Ⓑ Ⓒ Ⓓ Ⓔ
22. Ⓐ Ⓑ Ⓒ Ⓓ Ⓔ
23. Ⓐ Ⓑ Ⓒ Ⓓ Ⓔ
24. Ⓐ Ⓑ Ⓒ Ⓓ Ⓔ
25. Ⓐ Ⓑ Ⓒ Ⓓ Ⓔ
26. Ⓐ Ⓑ Ⓒ Ⓓ Ⓔ
27. Ⓐ Ⓑ Ⓒ Ⓓ Ⓔ
28. Ⓐ Ⓑ Ⓒ Ⓓ Ⓔ
29. Ⓐ Ⓑ Ⓒ Ⓓ Ⓔ
30. Ⓐ Ⓑ Ⓒ Ⓓ Ⓔ
31. Ⓐ Ⓑ Ⓒ Ⓓ Ⓔ
32. Ⓐ Ⓑ Ⓒ Ⓓ Ⓔ
33. Ⓐ Ⓑ Ⓒ Ⓓ Ⓔ
34. Ⓐ Ⓑ Ⓒ Ⓓ Ⓔ
35. Ⓐ Ⓑ Ⓒ Ⓓ Ⓔ

Section IV
Data Sufficiency

1. Ⓐ Ⓑ Ⓒ Ⓓ Ⓔ
2. Ⓐ Ⓑ Ⓒ Ⓓ Ⓔ
3. Ⓐ Ⓑ Ⓒ Ⓓ Ⓔ
4. Ⓐ Ⓑ Ⓒ Ⓓ Ⓔ
5. Ⓐ Ⓑ Ⓒ Ⓓ Ⓔ
6. Ⓐ Ⓑ Ⓒ Ⓓ Ⓔ
7. Ⓐ Ⓑ Ⓒ Ⓓ Ⓔ
8. Ⓐ Ⓑ Ⓒ Ⓓ Ⓔ
9. Ⓐ Ⓑ Ⓒ Ⓓ Ⓔ
10. Ⓐ Ⓑ Ⓒ Ⓓ Ⓔ
11. Ⓐ Ⓑ Ⓒ Ⓓ Ⓔ
12. Ⓐ Ⓑ Ⓒ Ⓓ Ⓔ
13. Ⓐ Ⓑ Ⓒ Ⓓ Ⓔ
14. Ⓐ Ⓑ Ⓒ Ⓓ Ⓔ
15. Ⓐ Ⓑ Ⓒ Ⓓ Ⓔ
16. Ⓐ Ⓑ Ⓒ Ⓓ Ⓔ
17. Ⓐ Ⓑ Ⓒ Ⓓ Ⓔ
18. Ⓐ Ⓑ Ⓒ Ⓓ Ⓔ
19. Ⓐ Ⓑ Ⓒ Ⓓ Ⓔ
20. Ⓐ Ⓑ Ⓒ Ⓓ Ⓔ
21. Ⓐ Ⓑ Ⓒ Ⓓ Ⓔ
22. Ⓐ Ⓑ Ⓒ Ⓓ Ⓔ
23. Ⓐ Ⓑ Ⓒ Ⓓ Ⓔ
24. Ⓐ Ⓑ Ⓒ Ⓓ Ⓔ
25. Ⓐ Ⓑ Ⓒ Ⓓ Ⓔ

Section V
Writing Ability

1. Ⓐ Ⓑ Ⓒ Ⓓ Ⓔ
2. Ⓐ Ⓑ Ⓒ Ⓓ Ⓔ
3. Ⓐ Ⓑ Ⓒ Ⓓ Ⓔ
4. Ⓐ Ⓑ Ⓒ Ⓓ Ⓔ
5. Ⓐ Ⓑ Ⓒ Ⓓ Ⓔ
6. Ⓐ Ⓑ Ⓒ Ⓓ Ⓔ
7. Ⓐ Ⓑ Ⓒ Ⓓ Ⓔ
8. Ⓐ Ⓑ Ⓒ Ⓓ Ⓔ
9. Ⓐ Ⓑ Ⓒ Ⓓ Ⓔ
10. Ⓐ Ⓑ Ⓒ Ⓓ Ⓔ
11. Ⓐ Ⓑ Ⓒ Ⓓ Ⓔ
12. Ⓐ Ⓑ Ⓒ Ⓓ Ⓔ
13. Ⓐ Ⓑ Ⓒ Ⓓ Ⓔ
14. Ⓐ Ⓑ Ⓒ Ⓓ Ⓔ
15. Ⓐ Ⓑ Ⓒ Ⓓ Ⓔ
16. Ⓐ Ⓑ Ⓒ Ⓓ Ⓔ
17. Ⓐ Ⓑ Ⓒ Ⓓ Ⓔ
18. Ⓐ Ⓑ Ⓒ Ⓓ Ⓔ
19. Ⓐ Ⓑ Ⓒ Ⓓ Ⓔ
20. Ⓐ Ⓑ Ⓒ Ⓓ Ⓔ
21. Ⓐ Ⓑ Ⓒ Ⓓ Ⓔ
22. Ⓐ Ⓑ Ⓒ Ⓓ Ⓔ
23. Ⓐ Ⓑ Ⓒ Ⓓ Ⓔ
24. Ⓐ Ⓑ Ⓒ Ⓓ Ⓔ
25. Ⓐ Ⓑ Ⓒ Ⓓ Ⓔ

Section VI
Analysis of Situations

1. Ⓐ Ⓑ Ⓒ Ⓓ Ⓔ
2. Ⓐ Ⓑ Ⓒ Ⓓ Ⓔ
3. Ⓐ Ⓑ Ⓒ Ⓓ Ⓔ
4. Ⓐ Ⓑ Ⓒ Ⓓ Ⓔ
5. Ⓐ Ⓑ Ⓒ Ⓓ Ⓔ
6. Ⓐ Ⓑ Ⓒ Ⓓ Ⓔ
7. Ⓐ Ⓑ Ⓒ Ⓓ Ⓔ
8. Ⓐ Ⓑ Ⓒ Ⓓ Ⓔ
9. Ⓐ Ⓑ Ⓒ Ⓓ Ⓔ
10. Ⓐ Ⓑ Ⓒ Ⓓ Ⓔ
11. Ⓐ Ⓑ Ⓒ Ⓓ Ⓔ
12. Ⓐ Ⓑ Ⓒ Ⓓ Ⓔ
13. Ⓐ Ⓑ Ⓒ Ⓓ Ⓔ
14. Ⓐ Ⓑ Ⓒ Ⓓ Ⓔ
15. Ⓐ Ⓑ Ⓒ Ⓓ Ⓔ
16. Ⓐ Ⓑ Ⓒ Ⓓ Ⓔ
17. Ⓐ Ⓑ Ⓒ Ⓓ Ⓔ
18. Ⓐ Ⓑ Ⓒ Ⓓ Ⓔ
19. Ⓐ Ⓑ Ⓒ Ⓓ Ⓔ
20. Ⓐ Ⓑ Ⓒ Ⓓ Ⓔ
21. Ⓐ Ⓑ Ⓒ Ⓓ Ⓔ
22. Ⓐ Ⓑ Ⓒ Ⓓ Ⓔ
23. Ⓐ Ⓑ Ⓒ Ⓓ Ⓔ
24. Ⓐ Ⓑ Ⓒ Ⓓ Ⓔ
25. Ⓐ Ⓑ Ⓒ Ⓓ Ⓔ
26. Ⓐ Ⓑ Ⓒ Ⓓ Ⓔ
27. Ⓐ Ⓑ Ⓒ Ⓓ Ⓔ
28. Ⓐ Ⓑ Ⓒ Ⓓ Ⓔ
29. Ⓐ Ⓑ Ⓒ Ⓓ Ⓔ
30. Ⓐ Ⓑ Ⓒ Ⓓ Ⓔ
31. Ⓐ Ⓑ Ⓒ Ⓓ Ⓔ
32. Ⓐ Ⓑ Ⓒ Ⓓ Ⓔ
33. Ⓐ Ⓑ Ⓒ Ⓓ Ⓔ
34. Ⓐ Ⓑ Ⓒ Ⓓ Ⓔ
35. Ⓐ Ⓑ Ⓒ Ⓓ Ⓔ

Section VII
Reading Comprehension

1. Ⓐ Ⓑ Ⓒ Ⓓ Ⓔ
2. Ⓐ Ⓑ Ⓒ Ⓓ Ⓔ
3. Ⓐ Ⓑ Ⓒ Ⓓ Ⓔ
4. Ⓐ Ⓑ Ⓒ Ⓓ Ⓔ
5. Ⓐ Ⓑ Ⓒ Ⓓ Ⓔ
6. Ⓐ Ⓑ Ⓒ Ⓓ Ⓔ
7. Ⓐ Ⓑ Ⓒ Ⓓ Ⓔ
8. Ⓐ Ⓑ Ⓒ Ⓓ Ⓔ
9. Ⓐ Ⓑ Ⓒ Ⓓ Ⓔ
10. Ⓐ Ⓑ Ⓒ Ⓓ Ⓔ
11. Ⓐ Ⓑ Ⓒ Ⓓ Ⓔ
12. Ⓐ Ⓑ Ⓒ Ⓓ Ⓔ
13. Ⓐ Ⓑ Ⓒ Ⓓ Ⓔ
14. Ⓐ Ⓑ Ⓒ Ⓓ Ⓔ
15. Ⓐ Ⓑ Ⓒ Ⓓ Ⓔ
16. Ⓐ Ⓑ Ⓒ Ⓓ Ⓔ
17. Ⓐ Ⓑ Ⓒ Ⓓ Ⓔ
18. Ⓐ Ⓑ Ⓒ Ⓓ Ⓔ
19. Ⓐ Ⓑ Ⓒ Ⓓ Ⓔ
20. Ⓐ Ⓑ Ⓒ Ⓓ Ⓔ
21. Ⓐ Ⓑ Ⓒ Ⓓ Ⓔ
22. Ⓐ Ⓑ Ⓒ Ⓓ Ⓔ
23. Ⓐ Ⓑ Ⓒ Ⓓ Ⓔ
24. Ⓐ Ⓑ Ⓒ Ⓓ Ⓔ
25. Ⓐ Ⓑ Ⓒ Ⓓ Ⓔ

Section VIII
Problem Solving

1. Ⓐ Ⓑ Ⓒ Ⓓ Ⓔ
2. Ⓐ Ⓑ Ⓒ Ⓓ Ⓔ
3. Ⓐ Ⓑ Ⓒ Ⓓ Ⓔ
4. Ⓐ Ⓑ Ⓒ Ⓓ Ⓔ
5. Ⓐ Ⓑ Ⓒ Ⓓ Ⓔ
6. Ⓐ Ⓑ Ⓒ Ⓓ Ⓔ
7. Ⓐ Ⓑ Ⓒ Ⓓ Ⓔ
8. Ⓐ Ⓑ Ⓒ Ⓓ Ⓔ
9. Ⓐ Ⓑ Ⓒ Ⓓ Ⓔ
10. Ⓐ Ⓑ Ⓒ Ⓓ Ⓔ
11. Ⓐ Ⓑ Ⓒ Ⓓ Ⓔ
12. Ⓐ Ⓑ Ⓒ Ⓓ Ⓔ
13. Ⓐ Ⓑ Ⓒ Ⓓ Ⓔ
14. Ⓐ Ⓑ Ⓒ Ⓓ Ⓔ
15. Ⓐ Ⓑ Ⓒ Ⓓ Ⓔ
16. Ⓐ Ⓑ Ⓒ Ⓓ Ⓔ
17. Ⓐ Ⓑ Ⓒ Ⓓ Ⓔ
18. Ⓐ Ⓑ Ⓒ Ⓓ Ⓔ
19. Ⓐ Ⓑ Ⓒ Ⓓ Ⓔ
20. Ⓐ Ⓑ Ⓒ Ⓓ Ⓔ

THREE
GMAT DIAGNOSTIC TEST

Now that you have become familiar with the various types of questions appearing on the GMAT and have had a chance to sample each type, you probably have an idea of what to expect from an actual exam. The next step, then, is to take a sample test to see how you do.

The Diagnostic Test that follows has been designed to resemble the format of recent GMATs. When taking it, try to simulate actual test conditions as closely as possible. For example, time yourself as you work on each section so that you don't go over the allotted time limit for that section. After you have completed the test, check your answers and use the self-scoring chart to evaluate the results. Use these results to determine which review sections you should spend the most time studying before you attempt the 5 sample GMATs at the end of the book. To assist you in your review, all answers to mathematics questions are keyed so that you can easily refer to the section in the Mathematics Review that discusses the material tested by a particular question.

Diagnostic Test

Section I   Reading Comprehension

TIME: 30 minutes

DIRECTIONS: This part contains three reading passages. You are to read each one carefully. When answering the questions, you *will* be able to refer to the passages. The questions are based on what is *stated* or *implied* in each passage. You have thirty minutes to complete this section.

Passage 1:

Morally and culturally, American society, as reflected in our TV programs, our theatrical fare, our literature and art appears to have hit bottom.

Gen. David Sarnoff felt prompted to issue a statement in defense of the TV industry. He pointed out that there was much good in its programs that was being
(5) overlooked while its occasional derelictions were being overly stressed. It struck me that what he was saying about TV applied to other aspects of American culture as well, particularly to the theatrical productions.

Without necessarily resting on his conviction that the good outweighed the bad in American cultural activity, I saw further implications in Gen. Sarnoff's decla-

(10) ration. Audiences needed to be sensitized more and more to the positive qualities of the entertainment and cultural media. In addition, through such increased public sensitivity, producers would be encouraged to provide ever more of the fine, and less of the sordid.

Here is where questions arise. If the exemplary aspects of TV are not being (15) recognized, what is the reason for such a lack of appreciation? Similarly, and further, if the theatre, including in this term the legitimate stage, on and off Broadway as well as the moving pictures, has large measures of goodness, truth and beauty which are unappreciated, how are we to change this situation?

All in all, what should be done to encourage and condone the good, and to (20) discourage and condemn the unsavory in the American cultural pattern?

These are serious and pressing questions—serious for the survival of the American Way of Life, and pressing for immediate and adequate answers. Indeed the simple truth is that the face that America shows the world affects seriously the future of democracy all over the globe.

(25) Since the theatre in its broadest sense is a large aspect of American culture—its expression as well as its creation—I saw the urgent importance of bringing the worthwhile elements in the American Theatre to the fore. Especially was this importance impressed on me when I realized how much Hollywood was involved in exporting American life to the world, and how much Broadway with all its (30) theatres meant to the modern drama.

Then the thought of the Bible came to me in this connection. Was not the Bible the basis of Western civilization as far as morals are concerned? Why not use the Bible as guide and touchstone, as direction and goal in the matter of the cultural achievements of Western society? Thus was born "The Bible on Broadway."

(35) The birth of the idea accomplished, rearing it brought the usual difficulties of raising a child—albeit in this case a "brain" one. There was first the fact that the Bible, although the world's best seller, is not the world's best read book. Second was the current impression that "message-plays" must necessarily be dull and unpopular. . . .

(40) Still, I was drawn to the project of a series of lectures on the Bible and the contemporary theatre. What if the Bible is not well known? Teach it! Plays with a message dull? All plays by reason of their being works of art have been created by their authors' selection and ordering of experience. As such, plays are proponents of ideas—and certainly they are not meant to be uninteresting. . . .

(45) That there are spiritual, even religious ideas, in the contemporary theatre should be no cause for wonderment. It is well known that the drama had its origin in religion. The Greeks, the Romans, as well as the early Hebrews, all had forms of the drama which among the first two developed into our classical plays.

In the Middle Ages, it was the Church in the Western World that produced the (50) morality and mystery plays. With such a long history it is not surprising to find an affinity between the Bible and the Theatre.

1. The author is primarily concerned with

   (A) the declining pattern of morality in America
   (B) promoting American theatre
   (C) the role of the Bible in the contemporary theatre
   (D) comparing the theatre with other art forms
   (E) preserving the "American Way of Life"

2. With which of the following statements regarding the theatre would the author most likely agree?

   (A) The theatre does not reflect American culture.
   (B) Critics of American cultural life are biased.
   (C) While the entertainment media can be criticized, they contain much wholesome material.
   (D) The advertising media are largely to blame for criticisms leveled at the theatre.
   (E) The Bible should be used as our primary source of entertainment ideas.

3. Which of the following statements best reflects the author's own ideas?

   (A) American art forms have degenerated to a new low.
   (B) The good outweighs the bad in American cultural activity.
   (C) American culture has positive content, but it is not appreciated by the public.
   (D) Only the Biblical content of American theatre has positive meaning.
   (E) American theatre is currently dull and unpopular.

4. The author implies that he will deal with which of the following questions?

   I. What is the reason for the lack of appreciation of the theatre?
   II. To what extent have Bible themes been used in or influenced American theatrical productions?
   III. What should be done to encourage the good in American culture?

   (A) I only
   (B) II only
   (C) I and II only
   (D) I and III only
   (E) I, II, and III

5. It can be inferred from the passage that the author's background might be in any of the following occupations *except*

   (A) theatrical producer
   (B) thespian
   (C) humorist
   (D) writer
   (E) critic

6. The author implies that, if the public is made aware of the positive qualities of American entertainment, it will

   I. demand more high-quality entertainment
   II. demand less low-quality entertainment
   III. attend the theatre more often

   (A) I only
   (B) II only
   (C) I and II only
   (D) I and III only
   (E) I, II, and III

7. When the author uses the expression "the Bible as guide and touchstone" in line 33, he probably means to refer to

   (A) the interrelationship of the Bible and the "American Way of Life"
   (B) an academic approach to researching the theatre and religion
   (C) the relationship of Biblical concepts to basic ideas and values contained in theatrical productions
   (D) the use of the Bible as a guide to everyday life
   (E) the Bible as a source of inspiration for all

8. According to the author, which of the following media have low cultural and moral values?

   I. Movies
  II. TV
 III. Literature

  (A) I only
  (B) II only
  (C) I and II only
  (D) II and III only
  (E) I, II, and III

9. The author believes that high American moral and cultural values are important because they determine

  (A) what is produced in Hollywood
  (B) the future of world democracy
  (C) whether the Bible will be studied
  (D) the basis for Western civilization
  (E) educational trends in the school system

Passage 2:

It is easy to accept Freud as an applied scientist, and, indeed he is widely regarded as the twentieth century's master clinician. However, in viewing Marx as an applied social scientist the stance needed is that of a Machiavellian operationalism. The objective is neither to bury nor to praise him. The assumption is
(5) simply that he is better understood for being understood as an applied sociologist. This is in part the clear implication of Marx's *Theses on Feurbach*, which culminate in the resounding 11th thesis: "The philosophers have only interpreted the world in different ways; the point, however, is to change it." This would seem to be the tacit creed of applied scientists everywhere.

(10) Marx was no Faustian, concerned solely with understanding society, but a Promethean who sought to understand it well enough to influence and to change it. He was centrally concerned with the social problems of a lay group, the proletariat, and there can be little doubt that his work is motivated by an effort to reduce their suffering, as he saw it. His diagnosis was that their increasing misery and alienation
(15) engendered endemic class struggle; his prognosis claimed that this would culminate in revolution; his therapeutic prescription was class consciousness and active struggle.

Here, as in assessing Durkheim or Freud, the issue is not whether this analysis is empirically correct or scientifically adequate. Furthermore, whether or not this
(20) formulation seems to eviscerate Marx's revolutionary core, as critics on the left may charge, or whether the formulation provides Marx with a new veneer of academic respectability, as critics on the right may allege, is entirely irrelevant from the present standpoint. Insofar as Marx's or any other social scientist's work conforms to a generalized model of applied social science, insofar as it is profes-
(25) sionally oriented to the values and social problems of laymen in his society, he may be treated as an applied social scientist.

Despite Durkheim's intellectualistic proclivities and rationalistic pathos, he was too much the product of European turbulence to turn his back on the travail of his culture. "Why strive for knowledge of reality, if this knowledge cannot aid us

(30) in life," he asked. "Social science," he said, "can provide us with rules of action for the future." Durkheim, like Marx, conceived of science as an agency of social action, and like him was professionally oriented to the values and problems of laymen in his society. Unless one sees that Durkheim was in some part an applied social scientist, it is impossible to understand why he concludes his monumental
(35) study of *Suicide* with a chapter on "Practical Consequences," and why, in the *Division of Labor*, he proposes a specific remedy for anomie.

Durkheim is today widely regarded as a model of theoretic and methodologic sophistication, and is thus usually seen only in his capacity as a pure social scientist. Surely this is an incomplete view of the man who regarded the *practical* effec-
(40) tiveness of a science as its principal justification. To be more fully understood, Durkheim also needs to be seen as an applied sociologist. His interest in religious beliefs and organization, in crime and penology, in educational methods and organization, in suicide and anomie, are not casually chosen problem areas. Nor did he select them only because they provided occasions for the development of his
(45) theoretical orientation. These areas were in his time, as they are today, problems of indigenous interest to applied sociologists in Western society, precisely because of their practical significance.

10. Which of the following best describes the author's conception of an applied social scientist?

(A) A professional who listens to people's problems
(B) A professional who seeks social action and change
(C) A student of society
(D) A proponent of class struggle
(E) A philosopher who interprets the world in a unique way

11. According to the author, which of the following did Marx and Durkheim have in common?

(A) A belief in the importance of class struggle
(B) A desire to create a system of social organization
(C) An interest in penology
(D) Regard for the practical applications of science
(E) A sense of the political organization of society

12. It may be inferred from the passage that the applied social scientist might be interested in all of the following subjects *except*

(A) the theory of mechanics
(B) how to make workers more efficient
(C) rehabilitation of juvenile delinquents
(D) reduction of social tensions
(E) industrial safety

13. According to the passage, applied social science can be distinguished from pure social science by its

(A) practical significance
(B) universal application
(C) cultural pluralism
(D) objectivity
(E) emphasis on the problems of the poor

14. Which of the following best summarizes the author's main point?

(A) Marx and Durkheim were similar in their ideas.
(B) Freud, Marx, and Durkheim were all social scientists.
(C) Philosophers, among others, who are regarded as theoreticians can also be regarded as empiricists.
(D) Marx and Durkheim were applied social scientists because they were concerned with the solution of social problems.
(E) Pure and applied sciences have fundamentally similar objects.

15. All of the following are mentioned as topics of interest to Durkheim *except*

(A) suicide
(B) psychiatry
(C) crime
(D) education
(E) religion

16. What action did Marx prescribe for the proletariat?

  I. Class consciousness
 II. Passive resistance
III. Alienation

(A) I only
(B) II only
(C) I and II only
(D) II and III only
(E) I, II, and III

17. Marx sought to
  I. understand society
 II. change the educational system
III. apply science to philosophy

(A) I only
(B) II only
(C) I and III only
(D) II and III only
(E) I, II, and III

Passage 3:

In Aachen, Germany, and environs, many children have been found to have an unusually high lead content in their blood and hair. The amount of lead in the children tested has risen above the amount found in workers in heavy-metal industries. The general public is no longer surprised that the lead has been traced
(5)   to Stolberg near Aachen: Stolberg is surrounded by brass foundries and slag heaps which supply building materials to construct schoolyards and sports halls.

This is but one example. . . .

When Dr. John W. Gofman, professor of medical physics at the University of California and a leading nuclear critic, speaks of "ecocide" in his adversary view
(10) of nuclear technology, he means the following: A large nuclear plant like that in Kalkar, the Netherlands, would produce about 200 pounds of plutonium each year. One pound, released into the atmosphere, could cause 9 billion cases of lung cancer. This waste product must be stored for 500,000 years before it is of no further danger to man. In the anticipated reactor economy, it is estimated that

(15) there will be 10,000 tons of this material in western Europe, of which one table-spoonful of plutonium-239 represents the official maximum permissible body burden for 200,000 people. Rather than being biodegradable, plutonium destroys biological properties.

In 1972 the U.S. Occupational Safety and Health Administration ruled that the
(20) asbestos level in the work place should be lowered to 2 fibers per cubic centimeter of air, but the effective date of the ruling has been delayed until now. The International Federation of Chemical and General Workers' Unions report that the 2-fiber standard was based primarily on one study of 290 men at a British asbestos factory. But when the workers at the British factory had been reexamined by
(25) another physician, 40–70 percent had x-ray evidence of lung abnormalities. According to present medical information at the factory in question, out of a total of 29 deaths thus far, seven were caused by lung cancer and three by mesothelioma, a cancer of the lining of the chest-abdomen. An average European or American worker comes into contact with six million fibers a day. And when this man returns
(30) home at night, samples of this fireproof product are on his clothes, in his hair, in his lunchpail. "We are now, in fact, finding cancer deaths within the family of the asbestos worker," states Dr. Irving Selikoff, of the Mount Sinai Medical School in New York.

It is now also clear that vinyl chloride, a gas from which the most widely used
(35) plastics are made, causes a fatal cancer of the blood-vessel cells of the liver. However, the history of the research on vinyl chloride is, in some ways, more disturbing than the "Watergate cover-up." "There has been evidence of potentially serious disease among polyvinyl chloride workers for 25 years that has been incompletely appreciated and inadequately approached by medical scientists and by
(40) regulatory authorities," summed up Dr. Selikoff in the *New Scientist*. At least 17 workers have been killed by vinyl chloride because research over the past 25 years was not followed up. And for over 10 years, workers have been exposed to concentrations of vinyl chloride 10 times the "safe limit" imposed by Dow Chemical Company. In the United Kingdom, a threshold limit value was set after the dis-
(45) covery of the causal link with osteolysis, but the limit was still higher than that set by Dow Chemical. The Germans set a new maximum level in 1970, but also higher than that set by Dow. No other section of U.S. or European industry has followed Dow's lead.

18. Which of the following titles best describes the contents of the passage?

(A) *The Problems of Nuclear Physics*
(B) *Advanced Technology and Cancer*
(C) *Occupational Diseases*
(D) *Cancer in Germany*
(E) *The Ecology of Cancer*

19. The author provides information that would answer which of the following questions?

(A) What sort of legislation is needed to prevent cancer?
(B) Should nuclear plants be built?
(C) What are some causes of lung cancer?
(D) What are the pros and cons of nuclear energy?
(E) Which country has the lowest incidence of occupational disease?

20. According to the author, all the following are causes of cancer *except*

(A) plutonium
(B) asbestos
(C) vinyl chloride
(D) osteolysis
(E) lead

21. The style of the passage is mainly

    (A) argumentative
    (B) emotional
    (C) factual
    (D) clinical
    (E) vitriolic

22. It can be inferred from the passage that the author believes that

    (A) industrialization must be halted to prevent further spread of cancer-producing agents
    (B) only voluntary, industry-wide application of antipollution devices can halt cancer
    (C) workers are partly to blame for the spread of disease because of poor work habits
    (D) more research is needed into the causes of cancer before further progress can be made
    (E) tougher legislation is needed to set lower limits of worker exposure to harmful chemicals and fibers

23. Some workers have been killed by harmful pollutants because

    (A) they failed to take the required precautions and safety measures
    (B) not enough research has been undertaken to find solutions to the pollution problem
    (C) available research was not followed up
    (D) production cannot be halted
    (E) factory owners have failed to provide safety equipment

24. It is mentioned in the passage that the asbestos level

    (A) should be lowered
    (B) causes heart problems
    (C) is linked with osteolysis
    (D) is similar to the level of vinyl chloride
    (E) is not linked with any known disease

25. The passage is based on evidence of pollutants in the following countries *except*

    (A) United Kingdom
    (B) United States
    (C) Sweden
    (D) Germany
    (E) Netherlands

If there is still time remaining, you may review the questions in this section only.
You may not turn to any other section of the test.

Section II   Problem Solving

TIME: 30 minutes

DIRECTIONS: Solve each of the following problems; then indicate the correct answer on the answer sheet. [On the actual test you will be permitted to use any space available on the examination paper for scratch work.]

NOTE: A figure that appears with a problem is drawn as accurately as possible so as to provide information that may help in answering the question. Numbers in this test are real numbers.

1. If the length of a rectangle is increased by 20% and the width is decreased by 20%, then the area

   (A) decreases by 20%
   (B) decreases by 4%
   (C) stays the same
   (D) increases by 10%
   (E) increases by 20%

2. If it is 250 miles from New York to Boston and 120 miles from New York to Hartford, what percentage of the distance from New York to Boston is the distance from New York to Hartford?

   (A) 12   (D) 48
   (B) 24   (E) 52
   (C) 36

3. The lead in a mechanical pencil is 5 inches long. After pieces ⅛ of an inch long, 1¾ inches long, and 1 1/12 inches long are broken off, how long is the lead left in the pencil?

   (A) 2 in.   (D) 2¼ in.
   (B) 2 1/24 in.   (E) 2½ in.
   (C) 2 1/12 in.

4. It costs $1.00 each to make the first thousand copies of a record and it costs x dollars to make each subsequent copy. How many dollars will it cost to make 4800 copies of a record?

   (A) 1,000   (D) $1,000x + 3,800$
   (B) 4,800   (E) $1,000 + 3,800x$
   (C) $4,800x$

5. If a worker makes 4 boxes of labels in 1⅔ hours, how many boxes of labels can he make in 50 minutes?

   (A) 2   (D) 2⅚
   (B) 2⅓   (E) 3
   (C) 2⅔

6. If $x + y = 3$ and $y/x = 2$, then y is equal to

   (A) 0   (D) 3/2
   (B) ½   (E) 2
   (C) 1

7. A store buys paper towels for $9.00 a carton, each carton containing 20 rolls. The store sells a roll of paper towels for 50¢. About what percent of the cost is the selling price of a roll of paper towels?

(A) 11
(B) 89
(C) 100
(D) 111
(E) 119

8. A history book weighs 2.4 pounds. 12 copies of the history book and 8 copies of an English book together weigh 42.8 pounds. How much will one copy of the English book weigh?

(A) 1 pound
(B) 1.4 pounds
(C) 1.75 pounds
(D) 2.88 pounds
(E) 14 pounds

9. A car goes 15 miles on a gallon of gas when it is driven at 50 miles per hour. When the car is driven at 60 miles per hour it only goes 80% as far. How far will it travel on a gallon of gas at 60 miles per hour?

(A) 12 miles
(B) 13.5 miles
(C) 16.5 miles
(D) 18.75 miles
(E) 20 miles

10. If $x + y = z$ and x and y are positive, then which of the following statements can be inferred?

    I. $x < y$
   II. $x < z$
  III. $x < 2z$

(A) I only
(B) II only
(C) I and II only
(D) II and III only
(E) I, II, and III

11. If it costs x cents to produce a single sheet of paper for the first 800 sheets and if every subsequent sheet costs $x/15$ cents, how much will it cost to produce 5,000 sheets of paper?

(A) 800x¢
(B) 1,080x¢
(C) 1,400x¢
(D) 2,430x¢
(E) 3,500x¢

12. If in 1967, 1968, and 1969 a worker received 10% more in salary each year than he did the previous year, how much more did he receive in 1969 than in 1967?

(A) 10%
(B) 12%
(C) 19%
(D) 20%
(E) 21%

13. If factory A turns out a cars an hour and factory B turns out b cars every 2 hours, how many cars will both factories turn out in 8 hours?

(A) $a + b$
(B) $8a$
(C) $8b$
(D) $8a + 4b$
(E) $8a + 8b$

14. If John makes a box every 5 minutes and Tim takes 7 minutes to make a box, what will be the ratio of the number of boxes produced by John to the number of boxes produced by Tim if they work 5 hours and 50 minutes?

(A) 5 to 6   (D) 7 to 5
(B) 5 to 7   (E) 2 to 1
(C) 6 to 5

15. If a store sells 3¼ crates of lettuce on Monday, 2⅙ on Tuesday, 4½ on Wednesday, and 1⅔ on Thursday, how many crates has the store sold altogether?

(A) 10   (D) 11¾
(B) 11½   (E) 12⅓
(C) 11⁷/₁₂

16. If $x + y > 4$ and $x < 3$, then $y > 1$ is true

(A) always   (D) only if $x = 0$
(B) only if $x < 0$ (E) never
(C) only if $x > 0$

17. If 50 apprentices can finish a job in 4 hours and 30 journeymen can finish the same job in 4½ hours, how much of the job should be completed by 10 apprentices and 15 journeymen in one hour?

(A) ⅑   (D) ⅕
(B) ²⁹/₁₈₀   (E) ³⁹/₁₂₁
(C) ²⁶/₁₄₃

18. If 40% of all women are voters and 52% of the population are women, what percent of the population are women voters?

(A) 18.1   (D) 40
(B) 20.8   (E) 52
(C) 26.4

19. If a bus can travel 15 miles on a gallon of gas, how many gallons of gas will it use to travel 200 miles?

(A) 10   (D) 15
(B) 12½   (E) 20⅓
(C) 13⅓

20. A tank contains 10 gallons of water. If a pump takes $15 - \dfrac{x}{10}$ minutes to pump one gallon of water out of the tank, how many minutes will it take for the pump to empty the tank?

(A) x (D) $150 - x$
(B) $15 - 10x$ (E) $15 - x$
(C) $150 - 10x$

If there is still time remaining, you may review the questions in this section only.
You may not turn to any other section of the test.

Section III Analysis of Situations

TIME: 30 minutes

DIRECTIONS: Read the following passages. After you have completed each one, you will be asked to answer questions that involve determining the importance of specific factors included in the passage. When answering questions, you may consult the passage.

Passage 1:

The B & S Manufacturing Co. for many years had held a dominant but stationary position in the industry which produces small gasoline engines for powering lawn mowers, chain saws, go-carts, compressors, pumps, and the like. Sales in 1970 were approximately $20,000,000. At a 1970 meeting, the board of directors approved a proposal by the corporate marketing manager to introduce a line of outboard motors. This proposal came as the result of a previous commitment by the board to develop a new product for a market related to those presently served.

The general plan involved the marketing of low horsepower motors for utility work and for fishing rather than the high horsepower units required for cruising, water skiing, and so on. A market study by a prominent outdoor magazine revealed that there were approximately 7.5 million active fishermen in 1970. About 15% of these actually owned outboard motors. Fishermen were located throughout the country, but there were major concentrations around inland waterways. Most of the fishermen who owned motors were located in these areas of concentration. A second market which seemed potentially good was the 2,500 fishing resort owners who rented boats and motors by the day or week. The marketing manager at B & S stressed that the company intended to get into the *user* market—not to supply motors for other outboard motor manufacturers, the situation which dominated the rest of the company's business. No consideration, therefore, was given to the possibility of developing O.E.M. customers.

B & S hoped it could establish a strong foothold in its target market by selling 50,000 units in 1971 and 1972. No fewer than 100,000 units should be sold each year thereafter. The general plan called for the development of a franchised distributor and retailer channel of distribution; an aggressive sales and advertising program; and a two-year marketing budget of $5,000,000. The average price of the motors was to be around $200.

The product strategy involved the development of three basic motors—a 2.2 hp unit, a 4.4 hp unit, and a 9.9 hp unit. These motors were all functionally designed to provide maximum convenience and service. Light in weight, relatively compact, and easy to install on almost any type or size of boat, the motors featured a built-in gasoline tank, a rewinding starter device, and a flexible (and adjustable) lower unit to permit operation in almost any depth of water. The motors were given the name of "Big Scout." Each had a very rugged appearance, designed to suggest durability, service, and reliability.

The product was tested under many kinds of conditions and received tremendous approval from fishermen who were asked to use it. However, the research and development expense and the actual cost of manufacturing ran considerably over the original estimates. The tentative introductory price was raised by about one-third.

The marketing manager did not foresee any great difficulty in obtaining distribution, in view of the great response to the initial product tests. He therefore assigned the task of designing the channel strategy to an assistant marketing manager. He told this assistant to prepare a detailed channel plan, studying the detailed marketing research reports if he needed additional information.

The distribution plan worked out by the assistant marketing manager involved the appointment of exclusive distributors and dealers in each of the major areas of concentration of fishermen. These dealers were to be marine and sporting goods retailers not presently handling a competitive line of fishing motors. As an incentive, the dealers would be offered a 40% discount, in contrast to the 33.3% usually expected by these kinds of retailers. A program of dealer training, especially in product service, was included in the channel strategy. It was anticipated that these same dealers would sell to the other market segment—the fishing resort owners.

Shortly after the assistant marketing manager submitted his report, one of the other people on the B & S marketing staff visited a regional trade show attended by marine and sporting goods dealers. He visited with more than a score of these dealers and left the show with the view that the distribution problem was going to be quite serious. He felt that there would be relatively few marine and sporting goods dealers who either could or would take on the new line. A very limited number of new boat dealers who could not get a Mercury, Johnson, or Evinrude franchise were likely to be interested, and some sporting goods shops which had not previously handled motors would probably be interested in at least discussing the possibility of taking on the "Big Scout" motors. But, in all, he judged that fewer than one-third of the major markets could be covered.

The marketing manager, leaning heavily on this report, decided that alternative channel directions would have to be pursued. The idea of exclusive distribution was abandoned. Instead, a wide range of retail outlets was proposed, including hardware stores, department stores, lawn and garden shops, and so on. The principal decision was that the sales estimate of 50,000 units for 1971 would have to be cut in half unless some other way of reaching users could be worked out. To offset this threatened cutback, the marketing manager proposed that Sears, Roebuck & Co. be approached. From informal conversations he had had with Sears personnel at an earlier date, he believed that Sears would be willing to take on the B & S motors, provided modest design modifications were incorporated and the Sears brand name were used.

In view of these overall changes in the plan, the original ideas on promotion had to be reconsidered. An advertising agency was appointed and assigned the task of developing a promotion strategy.

DIRECTIONS: The questions that follow relate to the preceding passage. Evaluate, in terms of the passage, each of the items given. Then select your answer from one of the following classifications, and blacken the corresponding space on the answer sheet.

(A) A MAJOR OBJECTIVE in making the decision: one of the goals sought by the decision maker

(B) A MAJOR FACTOR in making the decision: an aspect of the problem, specifically mentioned in the passage, that fundamentally affects and/or determines the decision

(C) A MINOR FACTOR in making the decision: a less important element bearing on or affecting a Major Factor, rather than a Major Objective directly

(D) A MAJOR ASSUMPTION in making the decision: a projection or supposition arrived at by the decision maker before considering the factors and alternatives

(E) AN UNIMPORTANT ISSUE in making the decision: an item lacking significant impact on, or relationship to, the decision

1. 1970 company sales of $20,000,000

2. Likelihood that fishing resort owners would constitute a potential market

3. Marketing of a new product in order to increase market share

4. Penetration of the final user market

5. Suitability of "Big Scout" motors for any type of boat

6. Wide market coverage for the motors

7. Number of active fishermen in the U.S.

8. Percentage of fishermen currently owning outboard motors

9. Possibility of selling to O.E.M. customers

10. Desirability of the Sears brand name

11. Product service training for dealers

12. Possibility of maximizing sales through franchised distribution

13. Plausibility of achieving annual sales of 100,000 units

14. An aggressive sales and advertising program

15. B & S's stationary market position

16. Sales by marine retailers to fishing resorts

17. Availability of Mercury, Johnson, and Evinrude franchises

18. Boat rentals by day or week

Passage 2:

The Pebble Company manufactured and sold nationally a line of folding wooden doors which were used in the place of swinging or conventional wooden doors in homes and in office buildings, stores, and other commercial buildings. While sales had increased substantially in the years following World War II, the company's president believed his firm was getting only a small part of its potential in the fast-growing home market—both new home construction and remodeling of older homes. He proposed establishing, on a trial basis, a specialty sales staff that would supplement the selling efforts of the existing distributor organization.

Founded in 1927, the company originally specialized in wooden shutters, storm doors and windows, and garage doors. In 1938 the company developed its present folding wooden doors, which were sold under the name Savi Space. Though wooden, these doors were similar in principle and use to fabric folding doors. They were made of boards 2 or 3 inches wide, fitted together vertically with a hinging device on each board to permit the door to fold accordion style. Although slightly more expensive than the fabric folding doors, they were longer lasting, more soundproof, and more "permanent" in appearance, and they could be painted to match the color scheme of the room in which they were installed. The doors were available in seven-ply birch veneer (1 inch thick) or ponderosa pine (1⅙ inches thick). The birch door had a hollow core, while those made of pine came in a louvred style. All parts were prefabricated, and the doors were sanded ready for finishing. Installation was not difficult but required some knowledge of carpentry. While some doors were installed by the homeowner or other buyer, the majority of buyers (about 60 percent) preferred to have the installation work done for them. The doors came in a variety of sizes, and over 75 per cent of all sales were of standard sizes. The remainder consisted of special or custom orders.

The value of such doors was that they saved the space wasted by a swinging or conventional door. While the biggest sale of these doors was for closets, a large number were sold for kitchens and playrooms. The doors also were used as room dividers; for example, one large bedroom could be made into two smaller ones by installing a folding door across the middle of the room. The company estimated that about 65 per cent of its sales of these doors went to the homeowner market, while the remainder went to the commercial market, including offices, funeral homes, hotels, restaurants, schools, and retail stores. Of the 65 per cent sold for homes, more than three-quarters were used in residences already constructed.

The Pebble Company first sold the doors (in 1938) through manufacturers' agents to lumberyards, but sales through these channels were disappointing. The company was in the process of changing its distribution channels policy when the U.S. entered World War II. From 1941 to 1945 Pebble devoted itself exclusively to war work, and it was not until the summer of 1946 that the company began producing folding doors again. At this time a dealer-distributor organization was set up. Distributors were expected to stock, promote, and install the doors; dealers were expected only to have a catalogue and a display door on hand so that customers could place orders. Some dealers did make installations, but most contracted them out when the customer wanted the service. Distributors were located in the large cities of the metropolitan areas of the country, while the dealers were limited to smaller cities and towns. Both distributors and dealers bought direct from the company.

Distributors typically handled related building specialty products and sold to builders of both homes and commercial buildings as well as to homeowners. It was not uncommon, however, for a distributor to sell only Savi Space. For example, the Cincinnati distributor supported a five-man sales organization on Savi Space sales entirely. By 1955 the company had 145 installing distributors in 141 trading areas and more than 400 dealer outlets in smaller cities and towns. Distributors received a discount of 50 per cent off list, while dealers received a 40 per cent discount. The company did not attempt to enforce its suggested list prices, and distributors and dealers were free to set their own installation charges. The average retail sale, including installation, was $165. The company strongly urged distributors to call on architects, since it was thought they could influence the use of such doors by specifying them in customers' plans. It was believed, however, that only a few distributors made such calls.

The company spent about $225,000 a year for advertising in several consumer magazines. Advertisements stressed the advantages of folding doors and urged readers to contact a local distributor or dealer. Inquiry coupons were included in these ads, and any coupons that were received by the company were forwarded to the appropriate distributor or dealer. Less than 10 per cent of distributors' sales, however, resulted from the coupon inquiries. Distributors also obtained leads from their own advertising through newspapers, television, radio, and direct mail. Some subscribed to the Dodge reports[1] to get building leads. A few distributors rented space at local home shows to get prospect names.

Company sales in 1955 were between $8 million and $9 million, which represented a 10 per cent increase over 1954. Since the president felt that the company had a much greater sales potential than this, he suggested that the company experiment with the use of a specialty sales staff. The principal purpose of such a staff would be to serve as a model for distributors. The president felt that, if the company was successful with this type of selling operation, the distributors in the larger metropolitan areas could be persuaded to set up their own specialty staffs. The president did not anticipate the company's continuing the staff beyond the experimental period.

As envisioned by the president, the experimental staff would merely supplement the selling effort of existing distributors and would in no way be a substitute for them. The specialty salesmen would be expected to make cold canvass calls—that is, attempt to locate prospects by random telephone calls or door-to-door selling—in contrast to distributors, who typically did no selling of this type. The president suggested Chicago, Memphis, and Dallas as areas in which to initiate the test. He suggested these cities

[1] The F. W. Dodge Corporation publishes reports on current and planned new construction and major remodeling of both residential and industrial buildings. The reports include the location, estimated cost, and state of completion of each job.

because he felt that people located in different parts of the country might respond differently. A test of three to four months in each area was proposed, with the company supervising and paying for the test work. Special crews for direct home contact would be recruited and trained, as would telephone crews. Specialty salesmen would be paid all expenses and guaranteed a salary of $75 per week. The company would not expect its distributors to contribute financially to this program, although their installation crews would be used. All sales made in a distributor's territory during the test period would be credited to the distributor; thus, he would get his usual margin on the sale.

If the tests were successful, distributors would be strongly urged to establish such staffs, with the details of the company's experiment used as a model. For example, distributors would be told how to select and train the door-to-door salesmen and telephone callers; they would be told what sales appeals had been most successful, and how sales objections had been met. In short, the company's experiment would provide a guide for distributors to follow in considerable detail.

DIRECTIONS: The questions that follow relate to the preceding passage. Evaluate, in terms of the passage, each of the items given. Then select your answer from one of the following classifications, and blacken the corresponding space on the answer sheet.

(A) A MAJOR OBJECTIVE in making the decision: one of the goals sought by the decision maker

(B) A MAJOR FACTOR in making the decision: an aspect of the problem, specifically mentioned in the passage, that fundamentally affects and/or determines the decision

(C) A MINOR FACTOR in making the decision: a less important element bearing on or affecting a Major Factor, rather than a Major Objective directly

(D) A MAJOR ASSUMPTION in making the decision: a projection or supposition arrived at by the decision maker before considering the factors and alternatives

(E) AN UNIMPORTANT ISSUE in making the decision: an item lacking significant impact on, or relationship to, the decision

19. Channel of distribution policy

20. Likelihood of distributors implementing the specialty staff concept

21. Location of test cities

22. Possibility of greater sales potential

23. Pebble's founding in 1927

24. Determining successful sales appeals

25. Pebble's small share of the home market

26. Level of advertising budget

27. Serving as a model for distributors

28. The variety of sizes of folding doors

29. Specialty sales force to make canvass calls

30. Few distributors making calls on architects

31. Some distributors selling only Savi Space

32. Sales made through manufacturers' agents

33. Locating prospects by random telephoning

34. Installation of Savi Space doors by contractors

35. Increasing sales to the home market

If there is still time remaining, you may review the questions in this section only.
You may not turn to any other section of the test.

Section IV   Data Sufficiency

TIME: 30 minutes

DIRECTIONS: Each of the following problems has a question and two statements which are labeled (1) and (2). Use the data given in (1) and (2) together with other available information (such as the number of hours in a day, the definition of *clockwise*, mathematical facts, etc.) to decide whether the statements are *sufficient* to answer the question. Then fill in space

(A) if you can get the answer from (1) alone but not from (2) alone;

(B) if you can get the answer from (2) alone but not from (1) alone;

(C) if you can get the answer from (1) and (2) together, although neither statement by itself suffices;

(D) if statement (1) alone suffices *and* statement (2) alone suffices;

(E) if you cannot get the answer from statements (1) and (2) together, but need even more data.

All numbers used in this section are real numbers. A figure given for a problem is intended to provide information consistent with that in the question, but not necessarily with the additional information contained in the statements.

1. A piece of wood 5 feet long is cut into three smaller pieces. How long is the longest of the three pieces?

   (1) One piece is 2 feet 7 inches long.
   (2) One piece is 7 inches longer than another piece and the remaining piece is 5 inches long.

2. *AC* is a diameter of the circle. *ACD* is a straight line. What is the value of x?

   (1) $AB = BC$
   (2) $x = 2y$

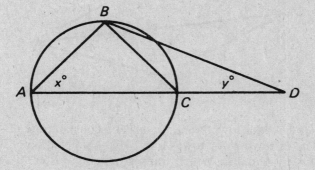

3. What is the value of y?

   (1) $x + 2y = 6$
   (2) $y^2 - 2y + 1 = 0$

4. Two pipes, *A* and *B*, empty into a reservoir. Pipe *A* can fill the reservoir in 30 minutes by itself. How long will it take for pipe *A* and pipe *B* together to fill up the reservoir?

   (1) By itself, pipe *B* can fill the reservoir in 20 minutes.
   (2) Pipe *B* has a larger cross-sectional area than pipe *A*.

5. *AB* is perpendicular to *CO*. Is *A* or *B* closer to *C*?

   (1) *OA* is less than *OB*.
   (2) *ACBD* is not a parallelogram.

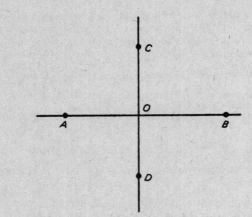

6. Is *xy* greater than 1? *x* and *y* are both positive.

   (1) *x* is less than 1.
   (2) *y* is greater than 1.

7. Does *x* = *y*?

   (1) *z* = *u*
   (2) *ABCD* is a parallelogram.

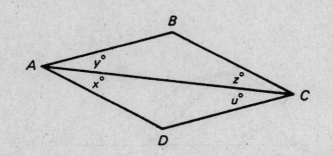

8. Train *T* leaves town *A* for town *B* and travels at a constant rate of speed. At the same time, train *S* leaves town *B* for town *A* and also travels at a constant rate of speed. Town *C* is between *A* and *B*. Which train is traveling faster? Towns *A*, *C*, *B* lie on a straight line.

   (1) Train *S* arrives at town *C* before train *T*.
   (2) *C* is closer to *A* than to *B*.

9. Does $x = y$?

    (1) BD is perpendicular to AC.
    (2) AB is equal to BC.

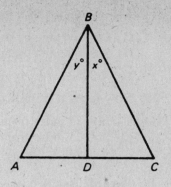

10. What is the value of $x + y$?

    (1) $x - y = 4$
    (2) $3x + 3y = 4$

11. Did the *XYZ* Corporation have higher sales in 1968 or in 1969?

    (1) In 1968 the sales were twice the average (arithmetic mean) of the sales in 1968, 1969, and 1970.
    (2) In 1970, the sales were three times those in 1969.

12. *AB* and *CD* are both chords of the circle with center *O*. Which is longer, *AB* or *CD*?

    (1) Arc *AEB* is smaller than arc *CFD*.
    (2) The area of the circular segment *CAEBD* is smaller than the area of circular segment *ACFDB*.

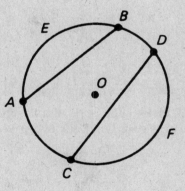

13. Is *ABDC* a square?

    (1) *BC* is perpendicular to *AD*.
    (2) *BE* = *EC*.

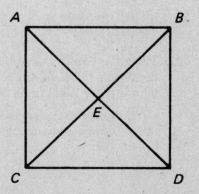

14. k is an integer. Is k divisible by 12?

    (1) k is divisible by 4.
    (2) k is divisible by 3.

15. How far is it from A to B?

    (1) It is 15 miles from A to C.
    (2) It is 25 miles from C to B.

16. Was Melissa Brown's novel published?

    (1) If Melissa Brown's novel was published she would receive at least $1,000 in royalties during 1978.
    (2) Melissa Brown's income for 1978 was over $1,000.

17. Is x an even integer? Assume n and p are integers.

    (1) $x = (n + p)^2$
    (2) $x = 2n + 10p$

18. Did the price of lumber rise by more than 10% last year?

    (1) Lumber exports increased by 20%
    (2) The amount of timber cut decreased by 10%.

19. Find the value of z if $x = 3$.

    (1) $z = (x + 3)^4$
    (2) $z = 2x + y$

20. What was the price of a dozen eggs during the 15th week of the year 1977?

    (1) During the first week of 1977 the price of a dozen eggs was 75¢.
    (2) The price of a dozen eggs rose 1¢ a week every week during the first four months of 1977.

21. Is DE parallel to BC? $DB = AD$.

    (1) $AE = EC$
    (2) $DB = EC$

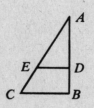

22. There are two drains in the bottom of a water tank. If drain 1 is opened and drain 2 is closed a full tank will be empty in 15 minutes. How long will it take to empty a full tank if drain 1 and drain 2 are both opened?

    (1) If drain 1 is closed and drain 2 is opened it takes 20 minutes to empty a full tank.
    (2) In 3 minutes as much water flows through drain 1 as flows through drain 2 in 4 minutes.

23. Is $x > y$?

    (1) $\dfrac{x}{y} = \dfrac{5}{4}$

    (2) $x^2 > y^2$

24. Does every bird fly?

    (1) Tigers do not fly.

    (2) Ostriches do not fly.

25. Find $x + 2y$.

    (1) $x - y = 12$

    (2) $3x - 3y = 36$

If there is still time remaining, you may review the questions in this section only.
You may not turn to any other section of the test.

Section V   Writing Ability

TIME: 30 minutes

DIRECTIONS: This test consists of a number of sentences, in each of which some part or the whole is underlined. Each sentence is followed by five alternative versions of the underlined portion. Select the alternative you consider both most correct and most effective according to the requirements of standard written English. Answer A is the same as the original version; if you think the original version is best, select answer A.

In considering the answer choices, be attentive to matters of grammar, diction, and syntax, as well as clarity, precision, and fluency. Do not select an answer which alters the meaning of the original sentence.

1. The principal reason for our failure was quite apparent to those whom we had brought into the venture.

   (A) to those whom we had brought
   (B) to them whom we had brought
   (C) to the ones whom we had brought
   (D) to those who we had brought
   (E) to those who we had brung

2. Although he was the most friendly of all present and different from the others, he hadn't hardly any friends except me.

   (A) different from the others, he hadn't hardly any friends except me
   (B) different than the others, he had hardly any friends except me
   (C) different from the others, he had hardly any friends except me
   (D) different than the others, he hadn't hardly any friends except I
   (E) different from the others, he hardly had any friends except I

3. It was us who had left before he arrived.

   (A) us who had left before he arrived
   (B) we who had left before he arrived
   (C) we who had went before he arrived
   (D) us who had went before he arrived
   (E) we who had left before the time he had arrived

4. He is the sort of person who I feel would be capable of making these kind of statements.

   (A) sort of person who I feel would be capable of making these kind of
   (B) sort of a person who I feel would be capable of making these kind of
   (C) sort of person who I feel would be capable of making these kinds of
   (D) sort of person whom I feel would be capable of making these kinds of
   (E) sort of person whom I feel would be capable of making this kind of

5. Due to the continual rain, a smaller number of spectators witnessed the game than had been expected.

   (A) Due to the continual rain, a smaller number
   (B) Due to the continuous rain, a smaller number
   (C) Due to the continual rain, a lesser number
   (D) Because of the rain that kept falling now and then, a smaller number
   (E) Because of the continual rain, a smaller number

6. Beside me, there were many persons who were altogether aggravated by his manners.

    (A) Beside me, there were many persons who were altogether aggravated
    (B) Beside me, there were many persons who were all together aggravated
    (C) Besides me, there were many persons who were altogether aggravated
    (D) Besides me, there were many persons who were altogether irritated
    (E) Beside me, there were many persons who were all together irritated

7. The owner, who was a kind man, spoke to the boy and he was very rude.

    (A) , who was a kind man, spoke to the boy and he
    (B) was a kind man and he spoke to the boy and he
    (C) spoke to the boy kindly and the boy
    (D) , a kind man, spoke to the boy who
    (E) who was a kind man spoke to the boy and he

8. Because we cooperated together, we divided up the work on the report which had been assigned.

    (A) together, we divided up the work on the report which had been assigned
    (B) together, we divided the work on the report which had been assigned
    (C) , we divided up the work on the report which was assigned
    (D) , we divided the work on the assigned report
    (E) we divided up the work on the assigned report

9. The senator rose up to say that, in his opinion, he thought the bill should be referred back to committee.

    (A) rose up to say that, in his opinion, he thought the bill should be referred back
    (B) rose up to say that he thought the bill should be referred back
    (C) rose up to say that he thought the bill should be referred
    (D) rose up to say that, in his opinion, the bill should be referred
    (E) rose to say that he thought the bill should be referred

10. I don't know as I concur with your decision to try and run for office.

    (A) as I concur with your decision to try and
    (B) that I concur in your decision to try to
    (C) as I concur in your decision to try and
    (D) that I concur with your decision to try to
    (E) as I concur with your decision to try to

11. Jones, the president of the union and who is also a member of the community group, will be in charge of the negotiations.

    (A) and who is also a member of the community group
    (B) since he is a member of the community group
    (C) a member of the community group
    (D) also being a member of the community group
    (E) , in addition, who is a member of the community group

12. The instructor told the student to hold the club lightly, keeping his eye on the ball and drawing the club back quickly, but too much force should not be used on the downward stroke.

   (A) to hold the club lightly, keeping his eye on the ball and drawing the club back quickly, but too much force should not be used
   (B) to hold the club lightly, keep his eye on the ball, and drawing the club back quickly, and too much force should not be used
   (C) to hold the club lightly, keep his eye on the ball, draw the club back quickly, and not use too much force
   (D) to hold the club lightly, keep his eye on the ball, draw the club back quickly and too much force should not be used
   (E) he should hold the club lightly, keeping his eye on the ball, drawing the club back quickly, and not using too much force

13. The horse, ridden by the experienced jockey with the broken leg, had to be destroyed.

   (A) horse, ridden by the experienced jockey with the broken leg, had
   (B) horse ridden by the experienced jockey with the broken leg had
   (C) horse with the broken leg ridden by the experienced, jockey had
   (D) horse with the broken leg ridden by the experienced jockey, had
   (E) horse with the broken leg, ridden by the experienced jockey, had

14. Our guest let us know that he would be arriving next week in his last letter.

   (A) that he would be arriving next week in his last letter
   (B) that he was arriving next week in his last letter
   (C) that he will arrive next week in his last letter
   (D) in his last letter that he would be arriving next week
   (E) in his last letter that he was arriving next week

15. Whoever objects to me going to the convention ought to state his position promptly.

   (A) Whoever objects to me
   (B) Whomever objects to me
   (C) Whomever objects to my
   (D) Whoever objects to my
   (E) Whoever has an objection to me

16. There is only five minutes left for us players to recover the initiative we lost because of the delay in the game.

   (A) There is only five minutes left for us players
   (B) There are only five minutes left for us players
   (C) There is only five minutes left for we players
   (D) There are only five minutes left for we players
   (E) There is only five minutes left for all of us players

17. The reason that the number of accidents this year is greater than that of last year is because Americans are uninterested in safety techniques.

   (A) is greater than that of last year is because
   (B) is greater than last year is because
   (C) is greater than last year is that
   (D) is greater than that of last year is that
   (E) is greater than the number of accidents last year is because

18. I was asked <u>not only to contribute to the cause by giving money, but also by participating</u> in its activities.

    (A) I was asked not only to contribute to the cause by giving money, but also by participating

    (B) Not only was I asked to contribute to the cause by giving money, but also by participating

    (C) Not only was I asked to contribute to the cause by giving money, but also to participate

    (D) I was asked not only to contribute to the cause by giving money, but also to participate

    (E) I was asked not only by giving money to contribute to the cause, but also to participate

19. Julio found the new job <u>more preferable to the one he had left so he decided to continue on</u> for a while.

    (A) more preferable to the one he had left so he decided to continue on

    (B) preferable to the one he had left so he decided to continue on

    (C) more preferable to the one he had left so he decided to continue

    (D) preferable to the one he had left so he decided to continue

    (E) more preferable than the one he had left so he decided to continue

20. <u>Since we are living</u> in New York for five years, we are reluctant to move to another city.

    (A) Since we are living

    (B) Being that we are living

    (C) Being that we have been

    (D) Since we have been living

    (E) Since we were living

21. <u>As a child, my parents took me to Chicago to visit my grandfather.</u>

    (A) As a child, my parents took me to Chicago to visit my grandfather.

    (B) My parents took me to Chicago to visit my grandfather as a child.

    (C) My parents took me, as a child, to Chicago to visit my grandfather.

    (D) A child, my parents took me to Chicago to visit my grandfather.

    (E) When I was a child, my parents took me to Chicago to visit my grandfather.

22. His wife <u>awoke him because he forgot to set his alarm before he went</u> to bed.

    (A) awoke him because he forgot to set his alarm before he went to bed

    (B) awoke him because he forgot to set his alarm before he had gone

    (C) had awakened him because he forgot to set his alarm before he went

    (D) had awakened him because he forgot to set his alarm before he had gone

    (E) awoke him because he had forgotten to set his alarm before he went

23. He said that, if <u>he were elected president and that if funds were available, that</u> he would create a national theater.

    (A) he were elected president and that if funds were available, that

    (B) elected president, and funds were available, that

    (C) he were elected president and funds were available, that

    (D) he were elected president and funds were available,

    (E) elected president, and funds were available,

24. Having managed the team for years, he understood the players.

    (A) Having managed the team for years, he understood the players.
    (B) After managing the team for years, the players were understood by him.
    (C) Having managed the team for years, the players were understood by him.
    (D) For years having managed the team, its players were understood by him.
    (E) Because he had managed the team for years, its players were understood by him.

25. "Ours is better than yours" was the disinterested consensus of those gathered to consider the problem.

    (A) "Ours is better than yours" was the disinterested consensus
    (B) "Our's is better than your's" was the disinterested consensus
    (C) "Ours is better than yours" was the disinterested consensus of opinion
    (D) "Ours is better than yours" was the uninterested consensus
    (E) "Ours is better than yours" was the uninterested consensus of opinion

If there is still time remaining, you may review the questions in this section only.
You may not turn to any other section of the test.

Section VI   Analysis of Situations

TIME: 30 minutes

DIRECTIONS: Read the following passages. After you have completed each one, you will be asked to answer questions that involve determining the importance of specific factors included in the passage. When answering questions, you may consult the passage.

Passage 1:

Brooks and Company was a food manufacturer established in 1850. Until 1977, its major product lines had consisted of tomato specialties, such as catsup, pickles, and barbecue sauces. Its consumer products business accounted for 40% of sales; the balance consisted of institutional sales to restaurants, hospitals, and the armed forces. The company had advertised to the institutional market but never to final (household) consumers.

In 1977, the company introduced a new line of Italian specialty products aimed at the final consumer market. The line was composed of a number of prepared pasta dishes, such as spaghetti, lasagne, and ravioli. Each package contained all of the necessary ingredients (except meat) including seasoned tomato sauce, cheese, and noodles.

The idea for the line of Italian pasta products had been conceived by Joe Brooks, son of the company president. Joe's enthusiasm for the product idea was quickly picked up by other executives. The president had married an Italian woman after World War I and their only child, Joe, had been born in Naples. Because they lacked a Neapolitan background, William Johnson, production manager, and Carl Voght, treasurer, approved of the idea on less emotional grounds. Johnson saw in the Italian line certain production possibilities that fitted in well with the company's existing facilities. Mr. Voght had long argued for some type of expansion which would enable the company to solve a number of financial problems associated with its inability to attract outside capital.

Many planning meetings were held throughout the summer. These meetings were attended by both the Brookses, Johnson, and Voght. Charles Welch, an administrative assistant to the president, was instructed to sit in on the sessions after he returned from vacation on August 1. He acted as informal secretary for the group. The original thinking of the committee was that the product line should be introduced at the beginning of the fall food merchandising season, which started about October 1. This deadline, however, subsequently proved to be unrealistic. Production of the first items in the line did not get underway until September 30 and packaging difficulties prohibited introducing the product before mid-December.

In July the problems involved in the product introduction were not foremost in the planners' thoughts. Many hours were spent discussing the name of the product line. Finally, the name *Velsuvio* was adopted as a compromise, but without enthusiasm from Joe Brooks, who believed that a name such as *Valencia* better described the gourmet image that he thought the line should express. With the exception of the name, the younger Brooks directed most of the decisions related to the marketing program. From the beginning, he argued that there were already plenty of "middle class" spaghetti products on the grocers' shelves. What was needed, he believed, was a prestige—even a "gourmet"—line. The popularity of higher-priced Italian restaurants in many cities convinced young Brooks of the opportunity to market a prestige line of Italian food specialties.

Early in the planning it was decided not to limit distribution to those regional markets (West Coast and Southwest) in which Brooks had previously established its reputation. National distribution would be undertaken from the beginning. It was planned that the *Velsuvio* line would be marketed in all major food chains except those handling only private or controlled brands. Sales to chain headquarters would be made by food brokers handling gourmet products rather than by brokers used to the handling of high-volume canned goods.

For the first time in its experience, Brooks planned to undertake an extensive consumer advertising program. A small Los Angeles advertising agency with slight experience in handling food products was appointed. However, by the time the agency had been selected and oriented to the marketing program, the time remaining before the scheduled introduction did not allow for the preparation of magazine advertisements or filmed television commercials. In order to break into the consumer market at the time of the scheduled product introduction on October 1, a consumer advertising program using newspapers, live television commercials, and radio was prepared. Except for the product introduction period, however, relatively little thought was given during the summer planning sessions to the total amount of money required to support the new product with consumer advertising.

A number of circumstances combined to prevent the introduction of the product in October as originally planned. No one had assumed personal responsibility for package design, and production was held up three weeks while the company waited for supplies of packaging materials. Brooks was forced to move very rapidly to obtain a package, and he was the first to admit that the result was neither very well designed functionally nor attractive from a promotional point of view. Time was short, however, and there was no choice but to use this package or abandon the project for the present season and possibly altogether, depending on competitive conditions.

A hastily put together advertising campaign was introduced in November. However, advertising costs had been greatly underestimated, so that the intensity of the campaign was much lower than Brooks had anticipated, even with the limited budget. As a result, most of the budget was allocated to newspapers and radio. Moreover, problems with the scripting of the TV commercials delayed broadcasting until the beginning of December. Newspaper advertisements and radio commercials did commence, however, as planned.

The new product was finally launched in mid-December. However, by February, two major competitors began marketing similar products. Shortly thereafter, a market research survey was sponsored by Brooks to determine whether the Velsuvio name made a favorable impression on housewives. The results of the survey were negative. Only twenty-two percent of the housewives interviewed could recall the Velsuvio name and of those, only twelve percent had tried the products. Consumer evaluation of the product line was far from encouraging. Of those who had tried the product for the first time, only four percent stated that they would buy it again.

Another indication that worried Brooks's management was that few major food chains showed interest in the line. By mid-year, Brooks's product sales were so poor that management established a special committee to determine without delay what immediate steps might be taken to reverse the poor sales record of Velsuvio.

DIRECTIONS: The questions that follow relate to the preceding passage. Evaluate, in terms of the passage, each of the items given. Then select your answer from one of the following classifications, and blacken the corresponding space on the answer sheet.

(A) A MAJOR OBJECTIVE in making the decision: one of the goals sought by the decision maker

(B) A MAJOR FACTOR in making the decision: an aspect of the problem, specifically mentioned in the passage, that fundamentally affects and/or determines the decision

(C) A MINOR FACTOR in making the decision: a less important element bearing on or affecting a Major Factor, rather than a Major Objective directly

(D) A MAJOR ASSUMPTION in making the decision: a projection or supposition arrived at by the decision maker before considering the factors and alternatives

(E) AN UNIMPORTANT ISSUE in making the decision: an item lacking significant impact on, or relationship to, the decision

1. Possibility of using existing production facilities in manufacturing *Velsuvio* products

2. Likelihood of achieving wide consumer acceptance of the *Velsuvio* line

3. Company growth and expansion

4. Age of Brooks and Company

5. The popularity of high-priced Italian restaurants in the U.S.

6. Depth of Brooks's expertise in the sale of consumer products

7. Market survey results

8. Size of the advertising agency hired to promote the *Velsuvio* line

9. National distribution of the *Velsuvio* line

10. Brooks's inability to attract outside capital

11. Appointment of Welch as informal secretary

12. Difficulties with new package design

13. Need for a "gourmet" Italian food line

14. Market entry of competitors

15. Obtaining packaging materials

16. Introducing the new product on October 1

17. Interest of major food chains in *Velsuvio*

18. Scripting of TV commercials

Passage 2:

The Elmstown Manufacturing Company was organized in 1911 to manufacture brass harness hardware. In the late 1930's the market for harness hardware declined substantially, and the company turned to the production of other items, such as hand garden tools and concrete-block makers. Following World War II, the company entered the field of garden tractors and attachments. Production of garden tractors rose from 1,000 units in 1948 to more than 17,000 units in 1952. During this period over 90 percent of the company's output was taken by a large mail-order firm which sold these machines under their private brand. The Elmstown line was the higher of the two price lines carried by the mail-order house. The president of the Elmstown Company felt that the company's place in the market was that of a quality producer who received somewhat higher than the average price.

Prior to World War II the garden tractor and implement market had been restricted to truck gardeners and other commercial growers. Annual industry sales in the five years prior to 1941 had averaged only about 10,000 units. As a result of the increase in farm mechanization, the expansion of suburban living, and the impetus which high food costs gave to home gardening, sales of garden tractors had increased rapidly after 1945 and reached a peak in 1953 of 211,798 tractor units with a value in excess of $29 million. In

1951 several significant trends appeared in the garden tractor market. Sales to farmers dropped, due in part to declining farm income, while sales to suburban dwellers increased. Thus, the bulk of garden tractor sales was shifted from a commercial to a homeowner market. By 1953 Mr. James Burns, president of Elmstown, estimated that 80 percent of the industry's annual sales were to homeowners.

There was also a shift in demand toward tractors of greater power. The proportion of tractors in the two-to-six-horsepower range increased from 28 percent in 1948 to 62 percent in 1952. Motor tillers amounted to 15.6 percent of industry shipments in 1951 and nearly 18 percent in 1952. In this year attachment sales amounted to slightly less than 30 percent of total domestic sales of garden tractors and attachments.[1] Mail-order firms accounted for nearly one-third of all sales, and five manufacturers accounted for the bulk of the remainder.

In 1953 company research showed that the growing suburban market was the primary market for the sale of garden tractors and attachments. Within the suburbs the homeowners with one-half to three or more acres represented the best potential. These were persons who were looking for ways to care for their lawns and gardens more efficiently and in the winter to remove snow from their sidewalks and driveways.

By late 1953 the Elms-Trac line consisted of ten models of powered units, ranging in retail price from $92.50 for a walking rotary power-driven lawn mower to $500 for a riding garden tractor. There were three models of rotary mowers, one of which was a riding mower, three rotary tillers, two walking tractors, and two riding tractors. The company also manufactured 44 attachments, such as lawn rollers, cultivators, and seeders, which could be used in combination with the basic power units.

Besides Elmstown there were 21 other companies selling a general line to the suburban market. These firms accounted for about 75 percent of industry sales. The remaining 25 percent was taken by companies who specialized in only one or two machines or who operated locally. Of the 22 general-line companies only six were considered to have a broad line. Elmstown was one of these.

The relationship between Elmstown and its mail-order house had always been a cordial and satisfactory one. For reasons of general policy, the company decided in 1949 to establish a brand line of its own to be sold nationally through independent dealers. A sales manager and a staff of six salesmen were hired. Sales were made direct to such independent dealers as farm implement stores, hardware stores, lawn and garden shops, large service stations, chain units such as Firestone and Western Auto, and some rural bottled-gas distributors. Manufacturers' representatives and jobbers were not used because the company thought that the problems of servicing, demonstrating, and covering the heterogeneous types of outlets could be handled more effectively by direct factory representatives. Also, the company thought it could do the job for less than the markup which jobbers and manufacturers' representatives received.

The sales manager believed that getting a dealer required a good job of education by company salesmen. Since many retailers had both limited space and capital, they had to be convinced of the merit of equipment and its salability. Salesmen were equipped with station wagons and demonstration units and attachments. They were given freedom to select and franchise dealers. By signing a franchise agreement, the dealer obtained an exclusive right to sell the product in the market area in which he was located. The dealer, in turn, agreed to maintain and display a representative stock of tractors and attachments, to promote sales actively, and to provide service facilities. The regular discount was 25 percent off list price plus 5 percent for cash. Quantity discounts were also offered.

---

[1] Department of Commerce, *Facts for Industry: Tractors* (Washington, D.C.: U.S. Government Printing Office, 1951 and 1952).

The company offered a spring dating plan whereby the dealer could order machinery between September and January 1 in any one year for delivery the following March and not pay until May 1. A credit plan was also offered whereby retail sales could be financed on 10 percent down with 24 months to pay. Dealers handled the application paper work, but payments were made direct to a bank.

The company's consumer advertising program consisted of placing annually one or two full-page ads in a magazine such as *House and Garden* and then using them as merchandising point-of-purchase display pieces for dealers. Some of the company's competitors did considerably more consumer advertising, including the use of magazines, radio, and television. Elmstown placed its primary emphasis on cooperative, direct mail, and trade publication advertising. The company also had exhibits at the hardware shows in New York in October and in Chicago in November. The company's cooperative plan was set up so that Elmstown paid half the cost of any dealer newspaper ads and radio and TV time costs up to 2½ percent of the dealer's Elmstown purchases. This program was available to a dealer only after he had made purchases in excess of $1,000. The company supplied free to its dealers a variety of direct mail literature.

In November, 1953, a total of 375 dealers had been acquired. About 100 dealers who had previously been on the list had been canceled for inactivity. The company's main strength was in the Middle West, but salesmen were working in the Mid-Atlantic and New England states. In 1953 tractor and attachment sales of Elms-Trac were slightly in excess of $100,000. This represented less than 5 percent of the company's total sales. Sales expenses for this line during 1953 exceeded sales.

In reviewing this showing, Mr. Burns stated that, while he had hoped for greater sales of the company's own line, the company had recognized from the beginning that it would take time and money to establish its line. He did feel, however, that an appraisal of selling methods was needed.

Mr. Burns felt that there were four alternatives open to the company as to the best way to sell to dealers. First, the company could use only their own salesmen. Second, the company could use manufacturers' agents. Third, distributors could be used. Fourth, some combination of the first three possibilities could be tried. If the company decided to continue with its policy of using only its own salesmen, then additional men should be hired immediately if sales were to be increased substantially in the near future. Mr. Burns thought that a total of at least 12 men would be needed to obtain and service the desired 600 dealers covering the nation.

If the company decided to use manufacturers' agents exclusively, Mr. Burns felt that more than 12 would be needed since they would be selling other goods besides the Elms-Trac line. The typical industry arrangement was to pay the agents a 7½ percent commission and to bring them together once a year in August or September at the home plant to show them the next year's models. The company would need two or three salesmen to work with and "control" these agents. The company expected that it would not have too much difficulty in locating agents, but realized that good ones were hard to locate and hold. There was no uniformity in the ways in which agents operated. There was considerable variation between them as to geographical area covered, types of dealers contacted, and lines carried.

The third alternative—distributors or wholesalers—presented yet a different situation. Typically such middlemen had handled both manual and power lawn mowers, but had little experience in the sale of other powered garden equipment. Mr. Burns expected, however, that hardware wholesalers would be receptive to the company's complete line, although he was not sure under what conditions. He thought they would probably require at least a 20 percent margin and that many would expect the company to ship direct to the larger retailers. However, the larger hardware wholesalers were experienced merchandisers and had an established clientele of dealers.

DIRECTIONS: The questions that follow relate to the preceding passage. Evaluate, in terms of the passage, each of the items given. Then select your answer from one of the following classifications, and blacken the corresponding space on the answer sheet.

(A) A MAJOR OBJECTIVE in making the decision: one of the goals sought by the decision maker

(B) A MAJOR FACTOR in making the decision: an aspect of the problem, specifically mentioned in the passage, that fundamentally affects and/or determines the decision

(C) A MINOR FACTOR in making the decision: a less important element bearing on or affecting a Major Factor, rather than a Major Objective directly

(D) A MAJOR ASSUMPTION in making the decision: a projection or supposition arrived at by the decision maker before considering the factors and alternatives

(E) AN UNIMPORTANT ISSUE in making the decision: an item lacking significant impact on, or relaltionship to, the decision

19. Growing suburban market

20. Analysis of Elmstown's selling methods

21. Cooperative advertising program

22. Sales expenses exceeding sales

23. Possibility of acquiring new dealers

24. Selecting a distribution channel

25. Receptivity of hardware wholesalers to the Elmstown product line

26. Advertising by Elmstown's competitors

27. Obtaining 600 dealers nationwide

28. Servicing problems of the Elms-Trac line

29. Expansion of suburban living

30. Offering a 20 percent margin to wholesalers

31. Operating methods of agents

32. Three models of rotary motors

33. Competitors' advertising programs

34. Locating good manufacturers's agents

35. Advertising in *House and Garden*

If there is still time remaining, you may review the questions in this section only.
You may not turn to any other section of the test.

Section VII   Reading Comprehension

TIME: 30 minutes

DIRECTIONS: This part contains three reading passages. You are to read each one carefully. When answering the questions, you *will* be able to refer to the passages. The questions are based on what is *stated* or *implied* in each passage. You have thirty minutes to complete this section.

Passage 1:

Although the number of journals has never been greater and the flyers announcing new conferences, colloquia, and societies never as ambitious, it is no secret that something is wrong with philosophy in the English-speaking world. The advances made by Russell, Whitehead, Wittgenstein, and Husserl are now studied
(5) by historians, and the boldness which characterized their age, roughly from 1900 to 1950, has given way to a spirit of caution, qualification, and retreat. This is not to say that talented people no longer study philosophy, nor that worthwhile contributions have ceased. Promising work is being done, but too often it is overwhelmed by pettifogging or left to die in obscurity.

(10)   Those unaware of what is happening in philosophy today may be surprised to learn that few academic philosophers address the sort of problems one studied in college: death, the existence of God, the cardinal virtues, the external world, or the prospects for happiness. Instead, if one walks into a classroom or lecture hall, one is likely to find brief discussions dealing with an odd assortment of issues
(15) about such things as time machines, adverbs, pains, possible worlds, sexual perversion. Even the language has changed. In many cases, English prose has been replaced by codes, symbols, and dialects incomprehensible to those outside the profession and not much better known to some of those inside.

It is not altogether surprising that philosophy has fallen on hard times. Through-
(20) out much of this century, people believed that philosophical questions were the result of logical or linguistic confusions. The task of philosophy was to eliminate them and thereby do away with itself. . . .

The problem is that philosophy is unique among academic disciplines in that the philosopher is forever plagued by the question of what his discipline is about. . . .
(25) A beginning student is usually told that philosophy does not deal with facts but with the analysis of concepts. But this characterization is inadequate because it seems to suggest that the distinction between the factual and the conceptual is absolute and that concepts can be analyzed entirely on their own. The philosopher, in other words, need not bother with what is, has been, or is likely to be the case.

(30)   What emerges is a conception of philosophy that retains its purity by making a radical distinction between itself and virtually every other form of knowledge. C. D. Broad once described philosophy at Cambridge as "almost completely out of touch with general history, with political theory and sociology, and with jurisprudence." Few eyebrows would have been raised if he had thrown in a dozen
(35) other departments and perhaps three or four additional disciplines as well. As for how it is possible to do, say, ethics in such an environment, Broad and his cohorts had a ready answer: the moral philosopher must be distinguished from the moralist. The latter takes a stand on important ethical questions and can be refuted should his evidence prove insufficient. For him to be ignorant of history, political theory,
(40) and jurisprudence is to run the risk of being wrong. The moral philosopher, however, only reflects on the language employed by the moralist. Since the philosopher is not in the business of recommending or criticizing courses of action, he can comfortably ignore the lessons the moralist has to learn.

This conception of philosophy prevailed in the English-speaking world for about
(45) forty years until it fell into disrepute during the turmoil of the sixties. Then sticky
questions began to be asked: To whom was such analysis addressed and for what
purpose? If the moral philosopher had studied the great ethical systems of the
past, why should he not bring his knowledge to bear on the controversial issues
of the present? Recently a number of articles have sprung up in the philosophical
(50) journals dealing with abortion, homosexuality, recombinant DNA research, intelligence testing, and other issues once thought to be beyond the scope of philosophical inquiry. Their presence raises the obvious question: What unique subject
or set of problems distinguishes philosophical inquiry from everything else?

One difficulty is that while other disciplines investigate a specific range of phe-
(55) nomena, philosophy, particularly in the hodgepodge conception of it, investigates
all of existence. Worse, while the natural sciences seem to get better as they get
older, philosophy does not. Without a body of accepted beliefs to build on, philosophers can make interesting points, but not step-by-step progress. A researcher
in physics does not have to make a new beginning each time he walks into his lab;
(60) he can assume that there is a consensus on a large number of issues and thus can
direct his efforts to a few highly restricted problems. Since philosophy prides itself

1. Which of the following titles best exemplifies the passage?

   (A) *Declines and Falls*
   (B) *Nationalism and Philosophy*
   (C) *Contemporary American Literature*
   (D) *The State of Contemporary Philosophy*
   (E) *The Study of Philosophy*

2. According to the passage, philosophers are concerned today with the subject of

   (A) political theory
   (B) philosophical inquiry
   (C) outdated works
   (D) abstract versions of social theory
   (E) public affairs

3. The author states that the philosopher is constantly

   (A) out of touch with general history
   (B) defining his discipline
   (C) determining objectives
   (D) investigating specific phenomena
   (E) providing radical alternatives

4. The moral philosopher does not have to

   (A) be in touch with general history
   (B) recommend a course of action
   (C) account to his colleagues
   (D) study linguistics
   (E) be in touch with reality

5. Many philosophers feel that the study of philosophy should become more

   (A) technical
   (B) popular
   (C) cautious
   (D) moralistic
   (E) dialectic

6. Which of the following subjects *is not* generally studied by academic philosophers?

   (A) Time machines
   (B) Possible worlds
   (C) External worlds
   (D) Linguistics
   (E) Moral issues

7. Recently, the field of philosophy has included

 I. intelligence testing
 II. language training
III. pure research

(A) I only
(B) II only
(C) I and II only
(D) II and III only
(E) I, II, and III

8. Which of the following statements best exemplifies the author's feelings?

(A) Philosophy is in moral decay.
(B) Talented people no longer study philosophy.
(C) Historians have replaced philosophers.
(D) Few academic philosophers are left.
(E) Philosophers are too cautious.

9. A criticism of philosophy is its lack of

(A) models and constructs
(B) concepts
(C) scientific logic
(D) purity
(E) thematic perception

Passage 2:

One of the most rapidly expanding sectors in American life since World War II has been the government. Local, state, and national government expenditures for goods and services rose from 13% of the gross national product in 1950 to 23% in 1970, reflecting a sixfold absolute increase in government spending. The expansion
(5) was not limited to traditional domains, such as defense and welfare. New target areas of government spending include the physical sciences, social sciences, and the arts. Federal outlays for research in the physical sciences rose from $0.6 billion in fiscal 1956 to $2.9 billion in 1963 and $3.8 billion in 1973. Federal support of social science research, which stood at $30 million in 1956, reached $412 million
(10) in 1973 (National Science Foundation, 1970: 243; 1974a: 149). Expenditures by the National Endowment for the Arts (1973: 111–112) evidenced a similar trend: initially appropriated $3 million during its first year of operation in 1966, the National Endowment's budget reached $15 million in 1971 and $61 million by 1974.

The institutions engaged in artistic or scientific activity are centrally concerned
(15) with the maintenance and extension of cultural systems (Parsons, 1961; Peterson, 1976). The growth of government patronage for these areas suggests that the facilitation and production of culture has become a major state activity in the United States. The objectives underlying this state intervention are not well understood. The central purpose of this paper is to evaluate the relative strengths of
(20) several alternative explanations for the government's involvement in the production of culture. A second purpose is to suggest the likely impact of government patronage on the physical sciences, social sciences, and arts in America.

Four distinct models for explaining the state's growing interest in the production of culture can be identified. One model emphasizes the value of patronage for the

(25) maintenance of the cultural institutions in question. A second model stresses the utility of the investment for capital accumulation. A third model points toward the value of supporting science and art for the administration of government programs. The fourth model identifies the ideological potential of science and art as a primary reason for government patronage.

(30) *Science and art for their own sake.* The first model of government patronage is predicated on the structural-functionalist assumption that the government is a relatively neutral instrument for the articulation and pursuit of collective goals in a society with relatively autonomous subsystems (Parsons, 1969). Pure science and art are vital societal subsystems, and the government moves to protect and

(35) develop these areas to ensure the continued production of culture for the benefit of all members of society. Thus, the government intervenes directly as the final patron of public goods that would otherwise be unavailable. Increasingly, the paradigms (Kuhn, 1970: 175) in science and art dictate expenditures that increasingly outstrip the resources of the institutions themselves. Equipment, staff, and

(40) data-processing costs of physical science research far exceed the commercial potential of most scientific projects; the cost of conducting systematic and reliable social scientific investigations can no longer be met through product marketing or private foundations; what is more, artistic organizations are increasingly incapable of underwriting all production costs through income and contributions. Under

(45) these conditions, government patronage is introduced to ensure the flow of cultural goods to society.

Two important corollaries follow from this formulation, which make it empirically testable. First, the timing of government intervention should primarily be related to economic crises faced by the arts and science themselves, not to crises

(50) in the political system, economy, or elsewhere. Second, government intervention should generally take the form of protecting the paradigm of the arts and sciences. Specifically, federal funding should be allocated to the most creative artists and organizations, as defined by the relevant artistic community. Similarly, funding should be preferentially bestowed on scientists whose research is making the

(55) greatest contribution to the advance of the scientific discipline, regardless of its relevance for outside problems or crises.*

10. According to the passage, the growth in federal support was greatest for

   (A) goods and services
   (B) social science research
   (C) defense and welfare
   (D) endowment for the arts
   (E) physical sciences

11. The major objective of the passage is to

   (A) increase appreciation for the arts
   (B) provide an ideological basis for artistic funding
   (C) explain why government supports cultural activities
   (D) argue for more government support of the arts and sciences
   (E) demonstrate cultural activities in the United States

---

* Reprinted from Michael Useem, "Government Patronage of Science and Art in America," pp. 123–142 in Richard A. Peterson, ed., *The Production of Culture*, © Sage Publications, Inc.

12. Which of the models discussed in the passage represents the statement: "Funding should be provided to the best artists and scientists"?

(A) Science and art for their own sake
(B) Science and art for business application
(C) Science and art for government programs
(D) Science and art for ideological control
(E) All models for government investment

13. A corollary of the science and art for government programs is

(A) funding should be provided by government only as a last resort
(B) funding will be geared to projects of value to the government
(C) funding is to be provided only to nongovernmental employees
(D) funding by the government is self-defeating
(E) funding by the government is inflationary

14. A conclusion reached by the author of the passage is that

(A) the arts and sciences have been funded by the government for different reasons
(B) government is a neutral observer of the arts and sciences
(C) government intervention in the arts and sciences is declining
(D) the arts and sciences are not dependent on government funding
(E) politics and science go together

15. Government intervention in the arts and sciences should coincide with

(A) government's ability to pay
(B) fluctuations in the business cycle
(C) political needs
(D) economic needs of the arts and sciences community
(E) the number of needy scientists

16. The idea that government should support the arts and sciences only when the market does not provide enough funds belongs to which school?

(A) "Their own sake"
(B) "Business application"
(C) "Government programs"
(D) "Ideological control"
(E) All of the above

17. The idea that cultural goods can no longer be provided solely by the market system is given by

(A) the author of the passage
(B) the first model of government patronage
(C) the second model of government patronage
(D) the third model of government patronage
(E) the fourth model of government patronage

Passage 3:

Unemployment is an important index of economic slack and lost output, but it is much more than that. For the unemployed person, it is often a damaging affront to human dignity and sometimes a catastrophic blow to family life. Nor is this cost distributed in proportion to ability to bear it. It falls most heavily on the young, the semiskilled and unskilled, the black person, the older worker, and the underemployed person in a low income rural area who is denied the option of securing more rewarding urban employment. . . .

The concentrated incidence of unemployment among specific groups in the population means far greater costs to society than can be measured simply in hours of involuntary idleness or dollars of income lost. The extra costs include disruption of the careers of young people, increased juvenile delinquency, and perpetuation of conditions which breed racial discrimination in employment and otherwise deny equality of opportunity.

There is another and more subtle cost. The social and economic strains of prolonged underutilization create strong pressures for cost-increasing solutions. . . . On the side of labor, prolonged high unemployment leads to "share-the-work" pressures for shorter hours, intensifies resistance to technological change and to rationalization of work rules, and, in general, increases incentives for restrictive and inefficient measures to protect existing jobs. On the side of business, the weakness of markets leads to attempts to raise prices to cover high average overhead costs and to pressures for protection against foreign and domestic competition. On the side of agriculture, higher prices are necessary to achieve income objectives when urban and industrial demand for foods and fibers is depressed and lack of opportunities for jobs and higher incomes in industry keep people on the farm. In all these cases, the problems are real and the claims understandable. But the solutions suggested raise costs and promote inefficiency. By no means the least of the advantages of full utilization will be a diminution of these pressures. They will be weaker, and they can be more firmly resisted in good conscience, when markets are generally strong and job opportunities are plentiful.

The demand for labor is derived from the demand for the goods and services which labor participates in producing. Thus, unemployment will be reduced to 4 percent of the labor force only when the demand for the myriad of goods and services—automobiles, clothing, food, haircuts, electric generators, highways, and so on—is sufficiently great in total to require the productive efforts of 96 percent of the civilian labor force.

Although many goods are initially produced as materials or components to meet demands related to the further production of other goods, all goods (and services) are ultimately destined to satisfy demands that can, for convenience, be classified into four categories: consumer demand, business demand for new plants and machinery and for additions to inventories, net export demand of foreign buyers, and demand of government units, Federal, state, and local. Thus gross national product (GNP), our total output, is the sum of four major components of expenditure; personal consumption expenditures, gross private domestic investment, net exports, and government purchases of goods and services.

The primary line of attack on the problem of unemployment must be through measures which will expand one or more of these components of demand. Once a satisfactory level of employment has been achieved in a growing economy, economic stability requires the maintenance of a continuing balance between growing productive capacity and growing demand. Action to expand demand is called for not only when demand actually declines and recession appears but even when the rate of growth of demand falls short of the rate of growth of capacity.

18. According to the passage, unemployment is an index of

    (A) overutilization of capacity
    (B) economic slack and lost output
    (C) diminished resources
    (D) the employment rate
    (E) undercapacity

19. While unemployment is damaging to many, it falls most heavily upon all except the

(A) black
(B) semiskilled
(C) unskilled
(D) underemployed
(E) white middle class

20. The cost to society of unemployment can be measured by all except

(A) lost incomes
(B) idleness
(C) juvenile delinquency
(D) disruption of careers
(E) the death rate

21. Serious unemployment leads labor groups to demand

(A) more jobs by having everyone work shorter hours
(B) higher wages to those employed
(C) "no fire" policies
(D) cost-cutting solutions
(E) higher social security payments

22. According to the passage, a typical business reaction to a recession is to press for

(A) higher unemployment insurance
(B) protection against imports
(C) government action
(D) restrictive business practices
(E) restraint against union activity

23. The demand for labor is

(A) a derived demand
(B) declining
(C) about 4 percent of the total work force
(D) underutilized
(E) dependent upon technology

24. Gross national product (GNP) is a measure of

(A) personal consumption
(B) net exports
(C) domestic investment
(D) government purchases of goods and services
(E) our total output

25. According to the passage, a satisfactory level of unemployment is

(A) 85 percent of the civilian work force
(B) 90 percent of the civilian work force
(C) 4 percent unemployment
(D) 2 percent unemployment
(E) no unemployment

If there is still time remaining, you may review the questions in this section only.
You may not turn to any other section of the test.

Section VIII   Problem Solving

TIME: 30 minutes

DIRECTIONS: Solve each of the following problems; then indicate the correct answer on your answer sheet. [On the actual exam you will be permitted to use any space available on the examination paper for scratch work.]

NOTE: A figure that appears with a problem is drawn as accurately as possible unless the words "Figure not drawn to scale" appear next to the figure. Numbers in this test are real numbers.

1. .03 times .05 is

   (A) 15%
   (B) 1.5%
   (C) .15%

   (D) .015%
   (E) .0015%

2. Which of the following are possible values for the angles of a parallelogram?

     I. 90°, 90°, 90°, 90°
    II. 40°, 70°, 50°, 140°
   III. 50°, 130°, 50°, 130°

   (A) I only
   (B) II only
   (C) I and III only
   (D) II and III only
   (E) I, II, and III

3. For every novel in the school library there are two science books; for each science book there are seven economics books. Express the ratio of economics books to science books to novels in the school library as a triple ratio.

   (A) 7:2:1
   (B) 7:1:2
   (C) 14:7:2

   (D) 14:2:1
   (E) 14:2:7

4. A store has a parking lot which contains 70 parking spaces. Each row in the parking lot contains the same number of parking spaces. The store has bought additional property in order to build an addition to the store. When the addition is built, 2 parking spaces will be lost from each row; however, 4 more rows will be added to the parking lot. After the addition is built, the parking lot will still have 70 parking spaces, and each row will contain the same number of parking spaces as every other row. How many rows were in the parking lot before the addition was built?

   (A) 5
   (B) 6
   (C) 7

   (D) 10
   (E) 14

5. Which of the following numbers is the closest to 0 (zero)?

   (A) $(1 - .9)^2$
   (B) $1 - (.9)^2$
   (C) $\dfrac{1}{1 - .9}$

   (D) $(.09)$
   (E) $(.09)^2$

6. If the shaded area is one half the area of triangle *ABC* and angle *ABC* is a right angle, then the length of line segment *AD* is

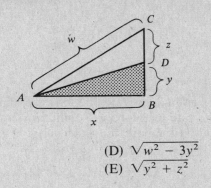

(A) ½*w*

(B) ½(*w* + *x*)

(C) $\sqrt{2x^2 + z^2}$

(D) $\sqrt{w^2 - 3y^2}$

(E) $\sqrt{y^2 + z^2}$

7. There are 50 employees in the office of ABC company. Of these, 22 have taken an accounting course, 15 have taken a course in finance, and 14 have taken a marketing course. Nine of the employees have taken exactly two of the courses, and one employee has taken all three of the courses. How many of the 50 employees have taken none of the courses?

(A) 0

(B) 9

(C) 10

(D) 11

(E) 26

8. If $x + y = 4$ and $x - y = 3$, then $x + 2y$ is

(A) ½

(B) 3.5

(C) 4

(D) 4½

(E) 7½

9. How much interest will $2,000 earn at an annual rate of 8% in one year if the interest is compounded every 6 months?

(A) $160.00

(B) $163.20

(C) $249.73

(D) $332.80

(E) $2,163.20

10. If *BC* is parallel to *AD* and *CE* is perpendicular to *AD*, then the area of *ABCD* is

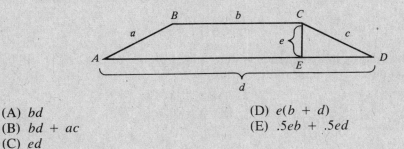

(A) *bd*

(B) *bd* + *ac*

(C) *ed*

(D) *e*(*b* + *d*)

(E) .5*eb* + .5*ed*

11. A company makes a profit of 6% on its first $1,000 of sales each day, and 5% on all sales in excess of $1,000 for that day. How many dollars in profit will the company make in a day when sales are $6,000?

(A) $250

(B) $300

(C) $310

(D) $320

(E) $360

12. If 15 men working independently and at the same rate can manufacture 27 baskets in an hour, how many baskets would 45 men working independently and at the same rate manufacture in 40 minutes?

(A) 27
(B) 35
(C) 40
(D) 54
(E) 81

13. A conveyer belt moves grain at the rate of 2 tons in 5 minutes and a second conveyer belt moves grain at the rate of 3 tons in 7 minutes. How many minutes will it take to move 20 tons of grain using both conveyer belts?

(A) 12
(B) 16 4/7
(C) 18 3/26
(D) 21
(E) 24 4/29

14. A field is rectangular and its width is ⅓ as long as its length. What is the area of the field if the length of the field is 120 yards?

(A) 480 square yards
(B) 2,400 square yards
(C) 4,800 square yards
(D) 5,000 square yards
(E) 7,200 square yards

15. If the price of steak is currently $1.00 a pound, and the price triples every 6 months, how long will it be until the price of steak is $81.00 a pound?

(A) 1 year
(B) 2 years
(C) 2½ years
(D) 13 years
(E) 13½ years

16. If $\dfrac{x}{y} = \dfrac{2}{3}$, then $\dfrac{y^2}{x^2}$ is

(A) $\dfrac{4}{9}$

(B) $\dfrac{2}{3}$

(C) $\dfrac{3}{2}$

(D) $\dfrac{9}{4}$

(E) $\dfrac{5}{2}$

17. The entry following a_n in a sequence is determined by the rule $(a_n - 1)^2$. If 1 is an entry in the sequence, the next three entries are

(A) 0, −1, 2
(B) 0, −1, 1
(C) 0, 1, 2
(D) 2, 3, 4
(E) 0, 1, 0

18. An employer pays 3 workers X, Y, and Z a total of $610 a week. X is paid 125% of the amount Y is paid and 80% of the amount Z is paid. How much does X make a week?

(A) $150
(B) $175
(C) $180
(D) $195
(E) $200

19. What is the maximum number of points of intersection of two circles which have unequal radii?

(A) none

(B) 1

(C) 2

(D) 3

(E) infinite

20. If the area of a rectangle is equal to the area of a square, then the perimeter of the rectangle must be

(A) ½ the perimeter of the square

(B) equal to the perimeter of the square

(C) equal to twice the perimeter of the square

(D) equal to the square root of the perimeter of the square

(E) none of the above

If there is still time remaining, you may review the questions in this section only.
You may not turn to any other section of the test.

Answers

Section I   Reading Comprehension

1. (C)	8. (E)	15. (B)	22. (E)
2. (C)	9. (B)	16. (A)	23. (C)
3. (C)	10. (B)	17. (A)	24. (A)
4. (B)	11. (D)	18. (B)	25. (C)
5. (C)	12. (A)	19. (C)	
6. (C)	13. (A)	20. (D)	
7. (C)	14. (D)	21. (C)	

Section II   Problem Solving

(Numbers in parentheses indicate the section in the Mathematics Review where material concerning the question is discussed.)

1. (B) (I-4)	6. (E) (II-2)	11. (B) (II-3)	16. (A) (II-7)
2. (D) (I-4)	7. (D) (I-4)	12. (E) (I-4)	17. (B) (II-3)
3. (B) (I-2)	8. (C) (II-3)	13. (D) (II-1)	18. (B) (I-4)
4. (E) (II-3)	9. (A) (II-3)	14. (D) (II-5)	19. (C) (I-2)
5. (A) (II-5)	10. (D) (II-7)	15. (C) (I-2)	20. (D) (II-3)

Section III   Analysis of Situations

1. (E)	11. (C)	21. (B)	31. (E)
2. (D)	12. (D)	22. (D)	32. (E)
3. (A)	13. (D)	23. (E)	33. (C)
4. (A)	14. (B)	24. (C)	34. (E)
5. (C)	15. (E)	25. (D)	35. (A)
6. (B)	16. (D)	26. (E)	
7. (B)	17. (B)	27. (A)	
8. (B)	18. (E)	28. (E)	
9. (E)	19. (A)	29. (B)	
10. (B)	20. (D)	30. (C)	

Section IV   Data Sufficiency

1. (D)	8. (C)	15. (E)	22. (D)
2. (A)	9. (C)	16. (E)	23. (E)
3. (B)	10. (B)	17. (B)	24. (B)
4. (A)	11. (A)	18. (E)	25. (E)
5. (A)	12. (D)	19. (A)	
6. (E)	13. (E)	20. (C)	
7. (C)	14. (C)	21. (A)	

Section V   Writing Ability

1. (A)	8. (D)	15. (D)	22. (E)
2. (C)	9. (E)	16. (B)	23. (D)
3. (B)	10. (B)	17. (D)	24. (A)
4. (C)	11. (C)	18. (D)	25. (A)
5. (E)	12. (C)	19. (D)	
6. (D)	13. (E)	20. (D)	
7. (D)	14. (D)	21. (E)	

Section VI   Analysis of Situations

1. (B)	11. (E)	21. (E)	31. (C)
2. (D)	12. (B)	22. (B)	32. (E)
3. (A)	13. (D)	23. (D)	33. (E)
4. (E)	14. (B)	24. (A)	34. (B)
5. (B)	15. (C)	25. (D)	35. (E)
6. (D)	16. (A)	26. (E)	
7. (B)	17. (B)	27. (A)	
8. (E)	18. (C)	28. (B)	
9. (A)	19. (B)	29. (B)	
10. (B)	20. (A)	30. (D)	

Section VII   Reading Comprehension

1. (D)	8. (E)	15. (D)	22. (B)
2. (B)	9. (A)	16. (A)	23. (A)
3. (B)	10. (D)	17. (B)	24. (E)
4. (B)	11. (C)	18. (B)	25. (C)
5. (A)	12. (A)	19. (E)	
6. (C)	13. (B)	20. (E)	
7. (A)	14. (A)	21. (A)	

Section VIII   Problem Solving

(Numbers in parentheses indicate the section in the Mathematics Review where material concerning the question is discussed.)

1. (C) (I-3, I-4)	6. (D) (III-4, III-7)	11. (C) (I-4)	16. (D) (I-2, I-8)
2. (C) (III-3, III-5)	7. (C) (II-4)	12. (D) (II-5)	17. (E) (II-6, II-1)
3. (D) (II-5.3)	8. (D) (II-2)	13. (E) (II-3)	18. (E) (II-3)
4. (D) (I-1)	9. (B) (I-4)	14. (C) (III-7)	19. (C) (III-6)
5. (E) (II-7, I-3)	10. (E) (III-7)	15. (B) (II-6, I-8)	20. (E) (III-7)

Analysis

Section I   Reading Comprehension

1. **(C)** While the author is concerned with the moral and cultural aspects of American society (lines 1, 21–25), his major concern is to show how the Bible has been used as a guide for some theatrical productions. See especially lines 31–34, and 45ff.

2. **(C)** This central theme of the author's concern is contained in lines 3–12.

3. **(C)** Statements (A) and (B) were not originally voiced by the author, but rather by Gen. Sarnoff. See lines 1–2, 8–9. Statements (D) and (E) are taken out of context. See lines 32–39. Statement (C) reflects the author's own ideas. See lines 14–19.

4. **(B)** Question I is found in lines 14–18, question III in lines 19–20. However, the author does not present evidence that he intends to answer them. Only answers to question II are implied throughout.

5. **(C)** The author does not state his background or profession, but it might be any of the choices except (C), since there are no traces of humor in this passage.

6. **(C)** Both these ideas are implied in lines 10–13.

7. **(C)** Examined in context, (C) is the most probable answer. See lines 32–34.

8. **(E)** The answer includes all three items. Movies are included in the answer because they are considered part of "theatrical fare." See lines 1, 2, 16 and 17 of the passage.

9. **(B)** The author believes that the "face that America shows the world"—i.e., its moral and cultural values—"affects seriously the future of democracy all over the globe." See lines 21–24.

10. **(B)** Lines 7–8 quote Marx as saying that philosophers only want to interpret the world, when what should be done is to change it. Change, the author states on line 9, is the "creed of applied scientists everywhere."

11. **(D)** Durkheim also valued the application of science rather than theoretical constructs alone. See lines 39–41.

12. **(A)** Items (B) through (E) deal with *applied* problems, which are the main concern of the social scientist, according to the passage.

13. **(A)** See lines 39–41.

14. **(D)** This point is stressed in lines 5, 12, 18ff., 31–34, 39, and 45ff.

15. **(B)** All but choice (B) are mentioned in the last paragraph.

16. **(A)** Marx prescribed (lines 16 and 17) class consciousness and active struggle. This rules out alternative II. Alternative III was thought to be a causal factor.

17. **(A)** Marx sought to understand *and* change society (lines 10 and 11).

18. **(B)** The passage deals with the harmful effects of certain production processes on workers and others.

19. **(C)** This answer is clear from lines 19–33 of the passage.

20. **(D)** Osteolysis is not mentioned as a cause. (A) can be found in lines 10–13; (B) in lines 19ff.; (C) in lines 34–35; and (E) in lines 2ff.

21. **(C)** The author does not argue for remedial action in the passage, but merely presents the facts concerning cancer-producing occupational hazards.

22. **(E)** This is implied in lines 37ff. Existing legislated-maximum levels of vinyl chloride exposure are higher than that set by Dow Chemical and apparently higher than a medically permissible safe limit.

23. **(C)** The passage relates that at least 17 workers were killed because of the failure by authorities to follow up on available research. See lines 40–42.

24. **(A)** According to the U.S. Occupational Safety and Health Administration, the asbestos level should be lowered. See lines 19–20.

25. **(C)** The United Kingdom is mentioned in line 44, the United States in line 19, Germany in the first paragraph, and the Netherlands in line 11. Sweden is not mentioned.

Section II   Problem Solving

1. **(B)** Let L be the original length and W the original width. The new length is 120% of L which is $(1.2)L$; the new width is 80% of W which is $(.8)W$. The area of a rectangle is length times width, so the original area is LW and the new area is $(1.2)(L)(.8)W$ or $(.96)LW$. Since the new area is 96% of the original area, the area has decreased by 4%.

2. **(D)** The distance from New York to Hartford divided by the distance from New York to Boston is $\frac{120}{250}$ or .48, and $.48 = 48\%$.

3. **(B)** The amount broken off is $\frac{1}{8} + 1\frac{3}{4} + 1\frac{1}{12}$ inches. Since $\frac{1}{8} + 1\frac{3}{4} + 1\frac{1}{12} = \frac{3}{24} + \frac{42}{24} + \frac{26}{24} = \frac{71}{24}$ and the lead was 5 inches long to begin with, the amount left $= 5 - \frac{71}{24} = \frac{120}{24} - \frac{71}{24} = \frac{49}{24} = 2\frac{1}{24}$ inches.

4. **(E)** The first 1,000 copies cost $1 each; so altogether they will cost $1,000. The remaining 3,800 copies $(4,800 - 1,000)$ cost x dollars each; so their cost is $3,800x$. Therefore, the total cost of all 4,800 copies is $1,000 + 3,800x$.

5. **(A)** Since $1\frac{2}{3}$ hours is 100 minutes, 50 minutes is $\frac{1}{2}$ of $1\frac{2}{3}$ hours. Therefore, he should make half as much in 50 minutes as he does in $1\frac{2}{3}$ hours. Since he made 4 boxes in $1\frac{2}{3}$ hours, he makes 2 boxes in 50 minutes.

6. **(E)** Since $\frac{y}{x} = 2$, $y = 2x$. Therefore, $x + y = x + 2x = 3x$ which equals 3. So $3x = 3$, which means $x = 1$. Thus, $y = 2$ because $y = 2x$.

7. **(D)** Since there are 20 rolls in a carton and a carton costs $9, each roll costs $\frac{1}{20}$ of $9 which is 45¢. The roll sells for 50¢, so the selling price divided by the cost is $\frac{50}{45} = \frac{10}{9}$, which is about 111%. (Or divide the total income by the total cost: $\frac{20 \times .50}{9} = \frac{10}{9} = 111\%$.)

8. **(C)** 12 copies of the history book weigh $(12)(2.4)$ or 28.8 pounds. Since the total weight of the books is 42.8 pounds, the weight of the English books is $42.8 - 28.8$ or 14 pounds. Therefore, each English book weighs $\frac{14}{8}$ or 1.75 pounds.

9. **(A)** Let x be the number of miles the car travels on a gallon of gas when driven at 60 miles an hour. Then 80% of 15 is x; so $\frac{4}{5} \cdot 15 = x$ and $x = 12$.

10. **(D)**
    STATEMENT I cannot be inferred since if $x = 2$ and $y = 1$, then x and y are positive but x is not less than y.

    STATEMENT II is true since $x + y = z$ and y is positive so $x < z$.

    STATEMENT III is true. z is positive since it is the sum of two positive numbers and so $z < 2z$. Since we know $x < z$ and $z < 2z$, then $x < 2z$.

    Therefore, only STATEMENTS II and III can be inferred.

11. **(B)** The first 800 sheets cost $800x$ ¢. The remaining 4,200 sheets cost $\frac{x}{15}$ ¢ apiece which comes to $(4,200)\left(\frac{x}{15}\right)$¢ or $280x$ ¢. Therefore, the total cost of the 5,000 sheets of paper is $800x$ ¢ $+ 280x$ ¢, which is $1,080x$ ¢.

12. **(E)** Let S denote the worker's salary in 1967. In 1968 he received 110% of S which is $(1.1)S$, and in 1969 he received 110% of $(1.1)S$ which is $(1.1)(1.1)S$ or $1.21\ S$. Therefore, he received 21% more in 1969 than he did in 1967.

13. **(D)** Factory A turns out $8a$ cars in 8 hours. Since factory B turns out b cars in 2 hours, it turns out $4b$ cars in 8 hours. Therefore, the total is $8a + 4b$.

14. **(D)** In 35 minutes John makes 7 boxes and Tim makes 5. The required ratio, 7 to 5, is constant no matter how long they work.

15. **(C)** The total number of crates sold is $3\frac{1}{4} + 2\frac{1}{6} + 4\frac{1}{2} + 1\frac{2}{3}$ which is equal to $\frac{39}{12} + \frac{26}{12} + \frac{54}{12} + \frac{20}{12} = \frac{139}{12} = 11\frac{7}{12}$. A shorter method would be to add the integral parts of each of the numbers $3 + 2 + 4 + 1 = 10$. Next add the fractional parts $\frac{1}{4} + \frac{1}{6} + \frac{1}{2} + \frac{2}{3}$. Using 12 as a common denominator, you get $\frac{(3 + 2 + 6 + 8)}{12}$ which is $\frac{19}{12} = 1\frac{7}{12}$. Therefore, the answer is $10 + 1\frac{7}{12} = 11\frac{7}{12}$.

16. **(A)** If $x + y$ exceeds 4 and x is less than 3, it is clear that y must exceed 1.

17. **(B)** Since 10 is $\frac{1}{5}$ of 50, the 10 apprentices should do $\frac{1}{5}$ as much work as 50 apprentices. 50 apprentices did the job in 4 hours, so in 1 hour 50 apprentices will do $\frac{1}{4}$ of the job. Therefore, 10 apprentices should do $\frac{1}{5}$ of $\frac{1}{4} = \frac{1}{20}$ of the job in an hour.

Since 15 is $\frac{1}{2}$ of 30, 15 journeymen will do half as much work as 30 journeymen. The 30 journeymen finished the job in $4\frac{1}{2}$ hours, so in

1 hour they will do $\frac{2}{9}$ of the job. Therefore, 15 journeymen will do $\frac{1}{2}$ of $\frac{2}{9} = \frac{1}{9}$ of the job in an hour. So both groups will do $\frac{1}{20} + \frac{1}{9} = \frac{9}{180} + \frac{20}{180} = \frac{29}{180}$ of the job in an hour.

18. **(B)** 40% of the 52% of the population who are women are voters. So $(.40)\ (.52) = .2080 = 20.8\%$ of the population are women voters.

19. **(C)** The amount of gas needed for a bus to travel 200 miles if the bus travels 15 miles on a gallon is $\frac{200}{15}$ or $13\frac{1}{3}$ gallons.

20. **(D)** The time required to pump 10 gallons of water out of the tank is $(10)\left(15 - \frac{x}{10}\right)$ which equals $150 - x$ minutes.

Section III — Analysis of Situations

1. **(E)** The present sales level was not an important issue in the development of corporate strategy. What was important, however, was the fact that the company's *market share* was "stationary," which is an indicator of a lack of growth.

2. **(D)** Fishing resort owners were listed as a potential market in paragraph 2. However, the market research study did not mention any evidence that these resort owners were likely to purchase the proposed product.

3. **(A)** The commitment of the board of directors to the development of a new product to be sold to different (but related) markets was related to the stationary market position of the firm. Introduction of a new product to increase market share was a major objective of B & S.

4. **(A)** Sales to the 7.5 million fishermen—potential users of the product—was a major objective.

5. **(C)** The versatility of the motor was secondary to the consideration of whether fishermen had a *need* for a new low horsepower motor.

6. **(B)** In order to penetrate the diverse market ("located throughout the country"), B & S had to secure wide market coverage.

7. **(B)** The large potential market was a major consideration in the decision to develop the product.

8. **(B)** The fact that only 15% of active fishermen owned an outboard motor was a major consideration in the decision to develop the product.

9. **(E)** Selling to O.E.M. customers was not considered as a possibility by B & S.

10. **(B)** When it was realized that few independent dealers would take on the "Big Scout" line on a franchised basis, it was decided to abandon exclusive distribution (and the "Big Scout" name) and sell through the Sears Roebuck network.

11. **(E)** Provision of dealer training was an insignificant consideration in the decision to market the product.

12. **(D)** The assumption that many dealers would be willing to sell the product was not verified by the facts in the case.

13. **(D)** The sales forecast (in paragraph 3) was not supported by any cited evidence.

14. **(B)** An aggressive sales and advertising program was an important element in the general plan for marketing the new product (paragraph 3).

15. **(E)** There is nothing in the passage that even remotely relates B & S's market position to the decision to market a new product. It is stated in the passage that the decision to develop the motor line was the result of a previous commitment by the board to develop a new product. Therefore, market position is an *Unimportant Issue*.

16. **(D)** The assistant marketing manager "anticipated" that marine retailers would also sell to fishing resort owners. This belief was a *Major Assumption*.

17. **(B)** The availability of well-known motors such as Mercury, Johnson, and Evinrude to most marine and sporting goods dealers was a *Major*

Factor in B & S's marketing manager's decision to find alternative channels of distribution.

18. **(E)** While the fishing resort market was considered as a potential segment, the timing of boat rentals was an *Unimportant Issue*.

19. **(A)** Pebble's president is trying to implement two major goals: to increase sales and their share of market. To do this, he has a number of tools; one is advertising, and another is strengthening the sales effort of his distributors/dealers. A major objective of the latter is to implement a channel of distribution policy, whereby distributors will be convinced to adopt the specialty sales staff concept.

20. **(D)** Pebble's president assumed that if the tests were successful, distributors would adopt their own specialty staff. Note the key word "likelihood."

21. **(B)** The location of the sales experiment is a major factor because the choice of representative cities can determine the success or failure of the experiment. If, indeed, people may respond differently to the experiment according to where they are located, then choice of the cities to be included in the experiment is crucial.

22. **(D)** Pebble's president felt that the company had a much greater sales potential than was being realized. The key word is "possibility." This is an opinion of the decision maker not buttressed by facts in the passage.

23. **(E)** The year of the company's founding does not influence in any way the selection of an alternative course of action.

24. **(C)** The decision to implement the experiment was to determine whether specialty sales staffs would increase sales. The determination of the sales appeals was only one factor associated with the overall experiment.

25. **(D)** Pebble's president *believed* his company was getting only a small part of its sales potential in the home market. See the first paragraph.

26. **(E)** The amount spent on advertising did not influence the decision to launch the sales experiment.

27. **(A)** The major purpose of the specialty sales staff experiment was to serve as a model for distributors. See paragraph 7.

28. **(E)** The number of sizes has no bearing on a decision to be made or consideration of an alternative course of action.

29. **(B)** The way the specialty sales staff will operate in the field may likely determine the success or failure of the experiment. This consideration is a major factor.

30. **(C)** While the fact that few distributors made calls on architects is explicitly mentioned in the passage, it is not directly linked to the consideration of a specialty sales staff. However, it can be implied that the failure to make these calls, in spite of the fact that the company "strongly urged" the calls to be made, was one of the minor factors that led to the decision to go ahead with the experiment.

31. **(E)** The fact that some distributors sold only Savi Space was not a consideration of any alternative course of action.

32. **(E)** Before World War II, sales were made through manufacturers' agents, but this channel proved ineffective and was later discontinued. Therefore, this fact is an *Unimportant Issue* in the present decision consideration.

33. **(C)** Specialty salesmen were to canvass prospects (a *Major Factor*) by a number of methods (*Minor Factors*) including random telephoning.

34. **(E)** The majority of buyers had someone else install the doors for them, but this fact was not a consideration in any alternative course of action. Therefore, it is an *Unimportant Issue*.

35. **(A)** A *Major Objective* of Pebble's president was increasing sales to the home market.

Section IV   Data Sufficiency

1. **(D)** STATEMENT (1) alone is sufficient. 2 feet 7 inches is more than half of 5 feet, so the piece which is 2 feet 7 inches long must be longer than the other two pieces put together.

STATEMENT (2) alone is sufficient. Since one piece is 5 inches long, the sum of the lengths of the remaining two pieces is 4 feet, 7 inches. Since one piece is 7 inches longer than the other, $L + (L + 7 \text{ in.}) = 4 \text{ ft. } 7 \text{ in.}$, where L is the length of the smaller of the two remaining pieces. Solving the equation yields $L + 7$ in. as the length of the longest piece.

2. **(A)** Since AC is a diameter, angle ABC is inscribed in a semicircle and is therefore a right angle.

STATEMENT (1) alone is sufficient since it implies the two other angles in the triangle must be equal. Since the sum of the angles of a triangle is 180°, we can deduce that $x = 45$.

STATEMENT (2) alone is not sufficient. There is no information about the angle ABD; so STATEMENT (2) cannot be used to find the angles of triangle ABD.

3. **(B)** STATEMENT (2) alone is sufficient, $y^2 - 2y + 1$ equals $(y - 1)^2$, and the only solution of $(y - 1)^2 = 0$ is $y = 1$.

STATEMENT (1) alone is not sufficient. $x + 2y = 6$ implies $y = 3 - \dfrac{x}{2}$, but there are no data given about the value of x.

4. **(A)** STATEMENT (1) alone is sufficient. Pipe A fills up $\dfrac{1}{30}$ of the reservoir per minute. STATEMENT (1) says pipe B fills up $\dfrac{1}{20}$ of the reservoir per minute, so A and B together fill up $\dfrac{1}{20} + \dfrac{1}{30}$ or $\dfrac{5}{60}$ or $\dfrac{1}{12}$ of the reservoir. Therefore, together pipe A and pipe B will take 12 minutes to fill the reservoir.

STATEMENT (2) alone is not sufficient. There is no information about how long it takes pipe B to fill the reservoir.

5. **(A)** STATEMENT (1) alone is sufficient. Draw the lines AC and BC; then AOC and BOC are right triangles, since AB is perpendicular to CO. By the Pythagorean theorem, $(AC)^2 = (AO)^2 + (CO)^2$ and $(BC)^2 = (OB)^2 + (CO)^2$; so if AO is less than OB, then AC is less than BC.

STATEMENT (2) alone is not sufficient. There is no restriction on where the point D is.

6. **(E)** STATEMENTS (1) and (2) together are not sufficient. If $x = \frac{1}{2}$ and $y = 3$, then xy is greater than 1, but if $x = \frac{1}{2}$ and $y = \frac{3}{2}$, then xy is less than 1.

7. **(C)** STATEMENT (1) alone is not sufficient. By choosing B and D differently we can have either $x = y$ or $x \neq y$ and still have $z = u$.

STATEMENT (2) alone is not sufficient. It implies that $x = z$ and $y = u$, but gives no information to compare x and y. STATEMENTS (1) and (2) together, however, yield $x = y$.

8. **(C)** STATEMENT (1) alone is not sufficient. If town C were closer to B, even if S were going slower than T, S could arrive at C first. But if you also use STATEMENT (2), then train S must be traveling faster than train T, since it is further than B to C than it is from A to C.

So STATEMENTS (1) and (2) together are sufficient.

STATEMENT (2) alone is insufficient since it gives no information about the trains.

9. **(C)** STATEMENT (2) alone is not sufficient, since D can be any point if we assume only STATEMENT (2).

STATEMENT (1) alone is not sufficient. Depending on the position of point C, x and y can be equal or unequal. For example, in both of the following triangles BD is perpendicular to AC.

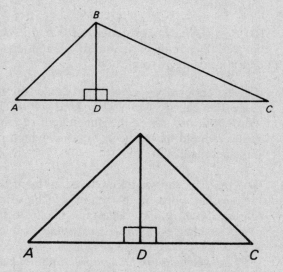

If STATEMENTS (1) and (2) are both true, then $x = y$. The triangles ABD and BDC are both right triangles with two pairs of corresponding sides equal; the triangles are therefore congruent and $x = y$.

10. **(B)** STATEMENT (2) alone is sufficient, since $3x + 3y$ is $3(x + y)$. (Therefore, if $3x + 3y = 4$, then $x + y = \frac{4}{3}$.)

STATEMENT (1) alone is not sufficient, since you need another equation besides $x - y = 4$ to find the values of x and y.

11. **(A)** STATEMENT (1) alone is sufficient. We know that the total of sales for 1968, 1969, and 1970 is three times the average and that sales in 1968 were twice the average. Then the total of sales in 1969 and 1970 was equal to the average. Therefore, sales were less in 1969 than in 1968.

STATEMENT (2) alone is insufficient, since it does not relate sales in 1969 to sales in 1968.

12. **(D)** Since the length of the arc of the circle is proportional to the length of the chord connecting the endpoints, STATEMENT (1) alone is sufficient.

STATEMENT (2) alone is sufficient, since the areas of the circular segments are proportional to the squares of the lengths of the chord.

13. **(E)** STATEMENTS (1) and (2) together are not sufficient, since the points A and D can be moved and STATEMENTS (1) and (2) still be satisfied.

14. **(C)** STATEMENT (1) alone is not sufficient, since 24 and 16 are both divisible by 4 but only 24 is divisible by 12.

STATEMENT (2) alone is not sufficient, since 24 and 15 are divisible by 3 but 15 is not divisible by 12.

STATEMENT (1) implies that $k = 4m$ for some integer m. If you assume STATEMENT (2), then since k is divisible by 3, either 4 or m is divisible by 3. Since 4 is not divisible by 3, m must be. Therefore, $m = 3j$, where j is some integer and $k = 4 \times 3j$ or $12j$. So k is divisible by 12. Therefore, STATEMENTS (1) and (2) together are sufficient.

15. **(E)** STATEMENTS (1) and (2) together are not sufficient, because there is no information about the location of C relative to the locations of A and B.

16. **(E)** Obviously a single statement is not sufficient. However, since Ms. Brown could have other sources of income, even both statements together are not sufficient. If you answered (C) you are making the additional assumption that Ms. Brown's only source of income was royalties from the novel.

17. **(B)** An even integer is an integer divisible by 2. Since $2n + 10p$ is 2 times $(n + 5p)$ using (2) lets you deduce that x is even. (1) by itself is not sufficient. If n were 2 and p were 3, $(n + p)^2$ would be 25 which is not even, but by choosing n to be 2 and p to be 4, $(n + p)^2$ is 36 which is even.

18. **(E)** Both statements give facts that *might* explain why the price of lumber rose. However, even using both statements you can't deduce what happened to the price of lumber.

19. **(A)** Since you know $x = 3$, statement (1) alone is sufficient. However, since no information is given about the value of y, statement (2) is insufficient.

20. **(C)** You need (1) to know what the price was at the beginning of 1977. Using (2) you could then compute the price during the fifteenth week. Either statement alone is insufficient. You should not actually compute the price since it would only waste time.

21. **(A)** (1) alone is sufficient since the line connecting the midpoints of 2 sides of a triangle is parallel to the third side. (2) alone is insufficient. In an isosceles triangle statement (2) would imply that ED is parallel to BC, but in a non-isosceles triangle, (2) would imply that ED and BC are not parallel.

22. **(D)** (1) alone is sufficient. For example, with both drains open, $\frac{1}{15} + \frac{1}{20}$ of the tank would be emptied each minute. You should not waste any time solving the problem. Remember, you only have to decide whether there is enough information to let you answer the question.

 (2) alone is also sufficient. You can deduce (1) from (2) and from the fact that drain 1 alone takes 15 minutes to empty the tank, and we just saw that (1) alone is sufficient.

23. **(E)** If you answered incorrectly you probably assumed that x and y were positive. If $x = 5$ and $y = 4$, then (1) and (2) are both true and $x > y$. However, if $x = -5$ and $y = -4$, (1) and (2) are both true but $x < y$.

24. **(B)** (2) alone is sufficient since ostriches are birds. (1) alone is not sufficient since tigers are not birds.

25. **(E)** Since the equation in (2) has exactly the same solutions as the equation in (1), $3(x - y) = 3x - 3y$ and $3(12) = 36$, you can't determine x and y even by using both (1) and (2). If $x = 12$ and $y = 0$, then (1) and (2) are true and $x + 2y = 12$, but if $x = 6$ and $y = -6$, (1) and (2) are again true but $x + 2y = -6$.

Section V   Writing Ability

1. **(A)** No error.

2. **(C)** This corrects the double negative (*hadn't hardly*). *Different from* is the correct idiom. *Me* is the correct form of the pronoun after the preposition *except*.

3. **(B)** *We* is correct; a predicate pronoun is in the nominative case. *Had went* is an incorrect verb form (either *went* or *had gone*). (E) is not only wordy but the tense sequence is wrong (the *leaving* occurred before the *arriving*).

4. **(C)** An adjective should agree in number with the noun it modifies (*these kinds*). Although in choice (E) *this kind* is also correct, *whom* is not, since *who* is needed as the subject of *would be*. *The sort of a* is not correct idiom.

5. **(E)** *Because of* is used in an adverbial modifier. Although (D) does use *because of*, it is a wordier sentence. (C) is incorrect also because *lesser* is used to refer only to noncountable nouns.

6. **(D)** *Besides* means *in addition to*. *Irritated* is correct. A person is irritated; a situation or condition is aggravated.

7. **(D)** The appositive, *a kind man*, can easily replace the clause *who was a kind man*. The words *and he*, where the antecedent of *he* is vague, should be replaced by *who*, which refers specifically to *boy*.

8. **(D)** *Together* and *up* are included in the meaning of other words in the sentence. The adjective *assigned* is preferable stylistically to the adjective clause *which was assigned*.

9. **(E)** The words *up*, *in his opinion*, and *back* are unnecessary.

10. **(B)** *As* is an incorrect vulgarism after the verb *know*. One concurs *in* a decision. The infinitive *try* should be followed by *to go*.

11. **(C)** Nouns in apposition must be parallel to one another: "Jones, the *president . . .* and a *member . . ."*

12. **(C)** Four infinitives are in parallel form and much clearer than the mixture of an infinitive (*to hold*), two verbals (*keeping* and *drawing*), and a clause (*too much force should not be used*).

13. **(E)** *With the broken leg* is a misplaced modifier. Commas are needed to set off the nonrestrictive clause *ridden by the experienced jockey.*

14. **(D)** The misplaced modifier, *in his last letter*, gives the mistaken impression that the guest would be arriving *in* the letter. The phrase should be near *know*, which it modifies. In choice (E) the tense is incorrect.

15. **(D)** The possessive form of *me* (*my*) is used before a verb form ending in *ing* and used as a noun (*going*). *Whoever* is correct as the subject.

16. **(B)** The correct answer is *There are*, since the use of *is* or *are* depends on the noun that follows the verb (in this case, *minutes*). *Us*, the correct form of the pronoun, is the object of the preposition *for*.

17. **(D)** Don't use the expression *the reason is because*; both *reason* and *because* have similar meanings. Choice (C) is incorrect because it compares *number of accidents* with *last year*.

18. **(D)** The correlatives *not only . . . but also* require parallel structure in the words that follow them. If the infinitive *to contribute* follows *not only*, then an infinitive, *to participate*, must follow the correlative *but also*. In choice (C), *not only* is incorrectly separated from *to contribute*.

19. **(D)** The words *more* and *on* are unnecessary.

20. **(D)** The present perfect tense is required for action begun in the past and continuing into the present. *Being that* is an incorrect idiom.

21. **(E)** This corrects the modifier *as a child*, which is incorrectly referring to *my parents*.

22. **(E)** *Had forgotten* is used to show that the forgetting preceded the going to bed.

23. **(D)** Two *that's* can be dispensed with, as well as one *if*.

24. **(A)** No error. The use of the passive voice in choice (C) is less preferable.

25. **(A)** No error. *Consensus of opinion* is repetitious—choices (C) and (E). No apostrophe is used with the possessive form of the pronouns *ours* and *yours*. *Uninterested* refers to someone lacking interest or concern; *disinterested* refers to someone who has nothing to gain personally from a particular activity but who may still be very much interested or concerned in the matter.

Section VI   Analysis of Situations

1. **(B)** A major consideration of the production manager in endorsing the new product was that it "fit in well" with existing production facilities. See paragraph 3.

2. **(D)** The company's decision to market the new product line was based on the assumption that it would be purchased by consumers. However, nowhere in the passage was there mention of any consumer research to buttress this assumption.

3. **(A)** A *Major Objective* of the new product launching was to generate sales needed to expand the company and enable it to solve some of its financial problems. See paragraph 3.

4. **(E)** The age of the company was an unimportant issue in the passage.

5. **(B)** This fact convinced the president's son of the need for a gourmet line of Italian food products. See paragraph 5.

6. **(D)** The company's experience in the sale of consumer products was limited to the West Coast and the Southwest.

7. **(B)** The survey results indicated a lack of consumer enthusiasm for the product line, which prompted management to appoint the committee to determine the future of the new line.

8. **(E)** The size of the advertising company was not related to any decision alternative.

9. **(A)** National distribution was a *Major Objective* of the company early in the planning stage. See paragraph 6.

10. **(B)** Brooks's inability to attract outside capital was a *Major Factor* which influenced Voght's decision to press for expansion of the company.

11. **(E)** Welch's appointment was inconsequential to the decisions made by management.

12. **(B)** Packaging difficulties resulted in the postponement of the product introduction until mid-December. The failure to design the package in time was a *Major Factor* in management's decision to delay the product's market entry.

13. **(D)** Joe Brooks *believed* that there was an untapped market for a prestige line of Italian food specialties. According to the facts presented in the passage, he based his assumption on the popularity of higher-priced Italian restaurants in many cities. That the same people who patronized these restaurants would want to prepare such food themselves at home was not demonstrated by the facts.

14. **(B)** The fact that competitors had commenced selling similar products was a *Major Factor* influencing management's decision to establish the special committee with the task of determining the fate of the new product line.

15. **(C)** Obtaining packaging materials was a *Minor Factor* that affected the ability to package the new product (a *Major Factor*).

16. **(A)** Brook's management wanted to introduce the new product on October 1 to coincide with the fall merchandising season. The timing, therefore, was a *Major Objective*.

17. **(B)** The little interest shown by major food chains in *Velsuvio* was a *Major Factor* in the decision to establish the special committee.

18. **(C)** Scripting problems were among the constraints that led to the delay in broadcasting commercials. Because the commercials were major considerations, scripting was a *Minor Factor* that affected them.

19. **(B)** Two major decisions were taken by Elmstown management. One was the determination of product policy and strategy—what products to make. The second was the selection of the best way to reach the consumers of their products. The growing suburban market was a major consideration in both decisions.

20. **(A)** Poor sales of the Elms-Trac line and high selling expenses led management to review the company's selling methods. The analysis is an outcome sought by management.

21. **(E)** The company's cooperative advertising program is briefly mentioned in the passage, but it played no role in any decision alternative.

22. **(B)** That sales expenses exceeded sales (in 1953) prompted Mr. Burns to review his company's selling methods.

23. **(D)** The Elmstown's sales manager "believed" that "getting a dealer required a good job of education by company salesmen." The key word in the question is "possibility."

24. **(A)** The determination of what channels of distribution the company should employ is a major objective or outcome desired by management.

25. **(D)** The extent to which hardware wholesalers might take on the Elmstown line was considered by Mr. Burns. He "expected" that such wholesalers "would be receptive," but "was not sure under what conditions."

26. **(E)** The advertising by Elmstown's competition was not considered by a decision maker.

27. **(A)** Note the key word in the passage: "desired" (paragraph 13). Obtaining 600 dealers nationwide was an outcome sought by Mr. Burns.

28. **(B)** Three major factors influenced the choice of sales representatives: servicing, demonstrating and covering retail outlets.

29. **(B)** The expansion of suburban living and the potential it brought for the use of home-garden tractors were a *Major Factor* in the decision to expand Elmstown's selling efforts.

30. **(D)** Mr. Burns "thought" that hardware wholesalers would require at least a 20 percent margin. This was a *Major Assumption* or supposition on the part of a decision maker.

31. **(C)** Use of agents was one of several alternative courses of action considered by Elmstown management. However, the extent to which the operating methods of agents was a consideration in the decision was not emphasized, so it is a *Minor Factor*.

32. **(E)** The number of models was not a consideration or factor in any alternative course of action.

33. **(E)** Although Elmstown's competitors did considerably more advertising, this fact was not considered nor did it affect any alternative course of action.

34. **(B)** Locating *good* agents was a *Major Factor* in the consideration to use manufacturers' agents, one of the decision alternatives.

35. **(E)** Advertising in a particular medium like *House and Gardens* was an *Unimportant Issue* because it was not a consideration in any alternative course of action.

Section VII   Reading Comprehension

1. **(D)** Alternatives (A) and (E) are too general. The passage does not deal with nationalism (B) nor American literature (C). The passage considers the present state or condition of philosophy.

2. **(B)** While philosophers may be concerned with subjects such as (A) and (E), the passage poses a philosophical inquiry in paragraph 6.

3. **(B)** In lines 23–24, the author states that "the philosopher is forever plagued by the question of what his discipline is about," i.e., defining his discipline.

4. **(B)** The difference between a moral philosopher and a moralist is that the latter must present solutions, or courses of action. The moral philosopher, on the other hand, only considers moral questions without taking a position on them. See paragraph 5.

5. **(A)** The author states in the second paragraph that the study of philosophy has, in many cases, embraced the use of codes, symbols, and dialects instead of prose. In short, studies have become more technical (hence the use of symbols).

6. **(C)** Few academic philosophers study the subject of the external world. See paragraph 2.

7. **(A)** Of the three alternatives, only I (intelligence testing) is mentioned. See the last paragraph.

8. **(E)** An examination of the alternatives can be made by reading paragraph 1. Alternatives (A) and (B) are ruled out. (C) is not true; or, rather, some of the subjects studied by philosophers are now studied by historians. (D) is not mentioned anywhere in the passage.

9. **(A)** The author claims that philosophy does not have "a body of accepted beliefs to build on" (last paragraph)—i.e., frameworks, or models and constructs.

10. **(D)** Federal expenditure on goods and services increased sixfold (from 1950 to 1970): for social science research, federal support increased 13 times; for defense and welfare no figures were given; for endowment for the arts expenditures increased 20 times (between 1966 and 1974); and for the physical sciences the increase was 6 times. (See paragraph 1.)

11. **(C)** The author's objective is to provide "alternative explanations for the government's involvement in the production of culture" (paragraph 2).

12. **(A)** See lines 52–56: ". . . federal funding should be allocated to the most creative artists. . . ."

13. **(B)** Alternative (A) belongs to the first model; alternatives (C) through (E) are not given in the passage.

14. **(A)** The author is trying to show empirically how the government funds the arts and sciences, but for different reasons, i.e., as a consumer, as an influencer, and as a subsidizer.

15. **(D)** See the second sentence of the last paragraph.

16. **(A)** The idea expressed in the question is suggested by the "science and art for their own sake" model, in the sentence: ". . . the government intervenes directly as the final patron of public goods that would otherwise be unavailable," i.e., not purchased or supported by nongovernmental or market forces.

17. **(B)** The idea expressed in the question can be found in the section "Science and art for their own sake," especially in the first paragraph of the section.

18. **(B)** See paragraph 1, line 1: "Unemployment is an important index of economic slack and lost output. . . ."

19. **(E)** See paragraph 1: "It falls most heavily on the young, the semiskilled [B] and unskilled [C], the black person [A], the older worker, and the underemployed person [D]."

20. **(E)** See paragraph 2: In the first line are included the costs of involuntary idleness (B) and income lost (A), followed by (C) and (D) in the next sentence.

21. **(A)** See paragraph 3: "On the side of labor, prolonged high unemployment leads to 'share-the-work' pressures for shorter hours . . ."; i.e., if workers are employed fewer hours, there will be "more jobs."

22. **(B)** In paragraph 3: "On the side of business, the weakness of markets [i.e., a recession] leads to . . . pressures for protection against foreign . . . competition"—i.e., protection against imports. (A) was not mentioned, (C) is too vague, and (D) was implied by "protection against . . . domestic competition" but is also vague.

23. **(A)** See paragraph 4: "The demand for labor is derived from the demand for the goods and services which labor participates in producing."

24. **(E)** See paragraph 5: GNP is a measure of the total goods and services produced, "our total output." It consists of the components in (A), (B), (C), and (D).

25. **(C)** Mention was made in paragraph 4 of reducing unemployment to a level of 4 percent (employment of 96 percent of the civilian work force), and it can be inferred that this figure constitutes a "satisfactory level" of unemployment.

Section VIII   Problem Solving

1. **(C)** Remember that the decimal point of the product of two decimals is placed so that the number of decimal places in the product is equal to the total of the number of decimal places in all of the numbers multiplied. Since .03 and .05 each have 2 decimal places, their product must have 4 (2 + 2) decimal places. Because 3 times 5 is 15, you need to add 2 zeros to get the correct number of decimal places, so the product of .03 and .05 is .0015. To change a decimal to a percentage you multiply by 100 (just move the decimal point 2 places to the right), so .0015 is .15%.

2. **(C)** Since a parallelogram is a 4-sided polygon, the sum of the angles of a parallelogram must be $(4 - 2)180° = 360°$. (A diagonal divides a parallelogram into 2 triangles and the sum of each triangle's angles is 180°.) Since the sum of the angles in II is not 360°, II is not possible. But I and III both consist of angles whose sum is 360°.

3. **(D)** If you know two ratios A:B and B:C, you can combine them into a triple ratio if B is the same number and represents the same quantity in both ratios. We know that the ratio of economics books to science books is 7:1 and that the ratio of novels to science books is 1:2. However, we can't combine this into the triple ratio 7:1:2 since 1 in the first ratio represents science books and 1 in the second ratio represents novels. We need science books as the middle term in the triple ratio, so express the second ratio as: the ratio of science books to novels is 2:1. Now, the ratio of economics books to science books is 7:1 and the ratio of science books to novels is 2:1. Since a ratio is unchanged if both sides are multiplied by the same positive number, we can also express the ratio of economics books to science books as 14:2. Finally, we can combine these into the triple ratio 14:2:1 of economics books to science books to novels.

4. **(D)** Call s the number of spaces in each row and r the number of rows in the parking lot before the addition is built. The parking lot had 70 parking spaces, so $sr = 70$. Since after the addition is built there are 4 more rows, 2 less spaces in each row, and a total of 70 spaces, we know that $(s - 2)(r + 4) = 70$. You could solve these two equations by algebra, but there

is a faster method. Since the number of rows and the number of spaces must be positive integers, you are looking for a way to write 70 as the product of two factors s and r with the additional property that $s - 2$ and $r + 4$ also have 70 as their product. Writing 70 as a product of primes, we get $70 = 2 \times 35 = 2 \times 5 \times 7$. Therefore, the only possibilities for s and r are listed here:

s	r	s	r
1	70	10	7
2	35	14	5
5	14	35	2
7	10	70	1

Now just check whether any pair of solutions (s, r) has the property that $s - 2$ and $r + 4$ is a solution. For example, if $s = 5$ and $r = 14$, then $s - 2 = 3$ and $r + 4 = 18$, which are not solutions. But if $s = 7$ and $r = 10$, then $s - 2 = 5$ and $r + 4 = 14$, which is also a solution. It is easy to see this is the only solution that works. So before the addition was built, there were 10 rows each with 7 spaces.

5. **(E)** Since all the expressions give positive results, we need to find the smallest number. (C) can be easily eliminated because the numerator is larger than the denominator, so the result is larger than 1. Since (A) and (E) are squares, simply compare the quantities being squared. (A) $= (.1)^2$ and (E) $= (.09)^2$, so (E) is smaller than (A).

Numbers between 0 and 1 become smaller when squared, so (E), which is $(.09)^2$, is smaller than (D), which is .09. Since (B) is .19, it is larger than (E) also. Therefore (E) is the smallest number and is the closest to 0.

6. **(D)** Since angle ABC is a right angle, we know the length of AD squared is equal to the sum of y^2 and x^2. However, none of the answers given is $\sqrt{x^2 + y^2}$. The area of triangle ABC is $\frac{1}{2}x(y + z)$, and the area of triangle ABD, which is $\frac{1}{2}xy$, must be one half of $\frac{1}{2}x(y + z)$. So $\frac{1}{4}xy + \frac{1}{4}xz = \frac{1}{2}xy$, which can be solved to give $y = z$. Since angle ABC is a right angle, $w^2 = (y + z)^2 + x^2 = (2y)^2 + x^2$. So $w^2 = 4y^2 + x^2$. Since we want $x^2 + y^2$, we subtract $3y^2$ from each side to get $w^2 - 3y^2 = y^2 + x^2$. Therefore, the length of AD squared is $w^2 - 3y^2$.

7. **(C)** A picture helps.

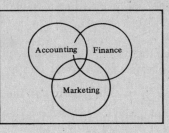

We want to know how many people are not in any of the sets.

The easy way to do this is find the number in at least one of the sets and subtract this number from 50. To find the number of employees in at least one set, *do not count the same employee more than once*. If you add 22, 15, and 14, any employee who took exactly two of the courses will be counted twice and employees who took all three courses will be counted three times. So the number who took at least one course = the number in Accounting + the number in Finance + the number in Marketing − number who took exactly two courses − 2 times the number who took all three courses = $22 + 15 + 14 - 9 - (2 \text{ times } 1) = 51 - 9 - 2 = 40$. Since 40 of the employees took at least one course, $50 - 40 = 10$ took none of the courses.

8. **(D)** Add $x + y = 4$ to $x - y = 3$ to obtain $2x = 7$. Therefore, $x = 3\frac{1}{2}$. Since $x + y = 4$, y must be $4 - 3\frac{1}{2} = \frac{1}{2}$. So $x + 2y = 3\frac{1}{2} + 2(\frac{1}{2}) = 4\frac{1}{2}$.

9. **(B)** The interest is compounded every 6 months. At the end of the first 6 months the interest earned is $\$2,000(.08)(1/2) = \$80$. (Don't forget to change 6 months into 1/2 year since 8% is the annual—yearly—rate.) Since the interest is compounded, \$2,080 is the amount earning interest for the final 6 months of the year. So the interest earned during the final 6 months of the year is $\$2,080(.08)(1/2) = \$83.20$. Therefore, the total interest earned is $\$80 + \$83.20 = \$163.20$.

10. **(E)** Since BC is parallel to AD, the figure $ABCD$ is a trapezoid. The area of a trapezoid is the average of the parallel sides times an altitude. Since CE is perpendicular to AD, e is an altitude. So the area is $e(1/2)(b + d) = (1/2) eb + (1/2)ed$. Since $1/2 = .5$, (E) is the correct answer.

11. **(C)** The profit is 6% of $1,000 plus 5% of $6,000 − $1,000 which is $(.06)($1,000) + (.05)($5,000)$. Therefore, the profit equals $60 + $250, which is $310.

12. **(D)** Since the number of baskets manufactured in an hour is proportional to the number of workers, $\frac{15}{45} = \frac{27}{x}$, where x is the number of baskets manufactured by 45 men in an hour. Therefore, x is 81. Since 40 minutes is $\frac{2}{3}$ of an hour, 45 men will make $\frac{2}{3}$ of 81 or 54 baskets in 40 minutes.

13. **(E)** The first belt lifts $\frac{2}{5}$ of a ton per minute and the second belt lifts $\frac{3}{7}$ of a ton per minute, so both belts together will lift $\frac{2}{5} + \frac{3}{7} = \frac{29}{35}$ of a ton per minute. Therefore, using both belts it will take $\frac{20}{29/35} = \frac{35}{29} \times 20 = \frac{700}{29}$ or $24\frac{4}{29}$ minutes to lift 20 tons.

14. **(C)** Since the width is ⅓ of the length and the length is 120 yards, the width of the field is 40 yards. The area of a rectangle is length times width, so the area of the field is 120 yards time 40 yards, which is 4,800 square yards.

15. **(B)** The price will be $3.00 a pound 6 months from now and $9.00 a pound a year from now. The price is a geometric progression of the form 3^j where j is the number of 6-month periods which have passed. Since $3^4 = 81$, after 4 six-month periods, the price will be $81.00 a pound. Therefore, the answer is two years, since 24 months is 2 years.

16. **(D)** Since $\frac{x}{y} = \frac{2}{3}, \frac{y}{x}$, which is the reciprocal of $\frac{x}{y}$, must be equal to $\frac{3}{2}$. Also, $\frac{y^2}{x^2}$ is equal to $\left(\frac{y}{x}\right)^2$, so $\frac{y^2}{x^2}$ is equal to $\frac{9}{4}$.

17. **(E)** Starting with $a_n = 1$ the rule $(a_n − 1)^2 = (1 − 1)^2 = 0^2 = 0$ so the next entry is 0. Using 0 as a_n gives $(0 − 1)^2 = (−1)^2 = 1$ so the second entry is 1. Since using 1 as a_n gives 0 as the next entry, the entries after 1 should be 0, 1, 0.

18. **(E)** X is paid 125%, or $\frac{5}{4}$ of Y's salary, so Y makes $\frac{4}{5}$ of what X makes. X makes 80% or $\frac{4}{5}$ of Z's salary, so Z makes $\frac{5}{4}$ of what X makes. Thus, the total salary of X, Y, and Z is the total of X's salary, $\frac{4}{5}$ of X's salary and $\frac{5}{4}$ X's salary. Therefore, the total is $\frac{61}{20}$ of X's salary. Since the total of the salaries is $610, X makes $\frac{20}{61}$ of $610, or $200.

19. **(C)** Since the radii are unequal, the circles cannot be identical, thus (E) is incorrect. If two circles intersect in 3 points they must be identical, so (D) is also incorrect. Two different circles can intersect in 2 points without being identical, so (C) is the correct answer.

20. **(E)** Let L be the length and W be the width of the rectangle, and let S be the length of a side of the square. It is given that $LW = S^2$. A relation must be found between $2L + 2W$ and $4S$. It is possible to construct squares and rectangles so that (A), (B), (C), or (D) is false, so (E) is correct. For example, if the rectangle is a square, then the two figures are identical and (A), (C) and (D) are false. If the rectangle is not equal to a square, then the perimeter of the rectangle is larger than the perimeter of the square, so (B) is also false.

Evaluating Your Score

Tabulate your score for each section of the Diagnostic Test according to the directions on pages 4–5 and record the results in the Self-scoring Table below. Then find your rating for each score on the Self-scoring Scale and record it in the appropriate blank.

Self-scoring Table

SECTION	SCORE	RATING
1		
2		
3		
4		
5		
6		
7		
8		

Self-scoring Scale

RATING

SECTION	POOR	FAIR	GOOD	EXCELLENT
1	0–12+	13–17+	18–21+	22–25
2	0–9+	10–13+	14–17+	18–20
3	0–17+	18–24+	25–31+	32–35
4	0–12+	13–17+	18–21+	22–25
5	0–12+	13–17+	18–21+	22–25
6	0–17+	18–24+	25–31+	32–35
7	0–12+	13–17+	18–21+	22–25
8	0–9+	10–13+	14–17+	18–20

The following Review sections cover material for each type of question on the GMAT. Spend more time studying those sections for which you had a rating of FAIR or POOR on the Diagnostic test.

To obtain an approximation of your actual GMAT score, see page 5.

FOUR
REVIEW AND PRACTICE
FOR THE GMAT

Having taken the Diagnostic Test and evaluated your results, you now have an indication of what your strong and weak points are. Your next step is to begin a more intensive review of test material, concentrating particularly on those areas in which you rated FAIR or POOR, but also covering material you did well on so that you will be certain you fully understand all of the topics.

Study the following sections carefully and do all the practice exercises provided. The *Reading Comprehension Review* will assist you in preparing for Reading Comprehension, Analysis of Situations, and Critical Reasoning questions. Problem Solving and Data Sufficiency are covered in the *Mathematics Review,* which is keyed to the answers for sample tests for easy reference. The Writing Ability section reviews those errors in grammar and usage that appear most frequently on the GMAT.

READING COMPREHENSION REVIEW

A large proportion of the GMAT is designed to test your ability to comprehend material contained in reading passages. The Reading Comprehension sections *do* allow you to turn back to the passages when answering the questions. However, many of the questions may be based on what is *implied* in the passages, rather than on what is explicitly stated. Your ability to draw inferences from the material is critical to successfully completing this section. The objective of the Analysis of Situations sections is to test your ability to analyze business situations and draw conclusions about them. The objective of the Critical Reasoning questions is to test your ability to evaluate an assumption, inference, or argument.

In each case, success depends on the extent of your reading comprehension skills. The following discussion is designed to help you formulate an approach to reading passages that will enable you to better understand the material you will be asked to read on the GMAT. Practice exercises at the end of this review will give you an opportunity to try out this approach.

Basic Reading Skills

A primary skill necessary for good reading comprehension and recall is the understanding of the meanings of individual words. Knowledge of a wide and diversified vocabulary enables you to detect subtle differences in sentence meaning that may hold the key to the meaning of an entire paragraph or passage. For this reason, it is important that you familiarize yourself with as many words as possible.

A second reading skill to be developed is the ability to discover the central theme of a passage. By making yourself aware of what the entire passage is about, you are in a position to relate what you read to this central theme, logically picking out the main points and significant details as you go along. Although the manner in which the central theme is stated may vary from passage to passage, it can usually be found in the title (if one is presented), in the "topic sentence" of a paragraph in shorter passages, or, in longer passages, by reading several paragraphs.

A third essential skill is the capacity to organize mentally how the passage is put together and determine how each part is related to the whole. This is the skill you will have to use to the greatest degree on the GMAT, where you must pick out significant and insignificant factors, remember main details, and relate information you have read to the central theme.

In general, a mastery of these three basic skills will provide you with a solid basis for better reading comprehension wherein you will be able to read carefully to draw a conclusion from the material, decide the meanings of words and ideas presented and how they in turn affect the meaning of the passage, and recognize opinions and views that are expressed.

Applying Basic Reading Skills

The only way to become adept at the three basic reading skills outlined above is to practice using the techniques involved as much as possible. Studying the meanings of new words you encounter in all your reading material will soon help you establish a working knowledge of many words. In the same manner, making an effort to locate topic sentences, general themes, and specific details in material you read will enable you to improve your skills in these areas. The following drills will help. After you have read through them and answered the questions satisfactorily, you can try the longer practice exercises at the end.

Finding the Topic Sentence

The term "topic sentence" is used to describe the sentence that gives the key to an entire paragraph. Usually the topic sentence is found in the beginning of a paragraph. However, there is no absolute rule. A writer may build his paragraph to a conclusion, putting the key sentence at the end. Here is an example in which the topic sentence is located at the beginning:

EXAMPLE 1:

The world faces a serious problem of overpopulation. Right now many people starve from lack of adequate food. Efforts are being made to increase the rate of food production, but the number of people to be fed increases at a faster rate.

The idea is stated directly in the opening sentence. You know that the passage will be about "a serious problem of overpopulation." Like a heading or caption, the topic sentence sets the stage or gets your mind ready for what follows in that paragraph.

Before you try to locate the topic sentence in a paragraph you must remember that this technique depends upon reading and judgment. Read the whole passage first. Then try to decide which sentence comes closest to expressing the main point of the paragraph. Do not worry about the position of the topic sentence in the paragraph; look for the most important statement. Find the idea to which all the other sentences relate.

Try to identify the topic sentence in this passage:

EXAMPLE 2:

During the later years of the American Revolution, the Articles of Confederation government was formed. This government suffered severely from a lack of power. Each state distrusted the others and gave little authority to the central or federal government. The Articles of Confederation produced a government which could not raise money from taxes, prevent Indian raids, or force the British out of the United States.

What is the topic sentence? Certainly the paragraph is about the Articles of Confederation. However, is the key idea in the first sentence or in the second sentence? In this instance, the *second* sentence does a better job of giving you the key to this paragraph— the lack of centralized power that characterized the Articles of Confederation. The sentences that complete the paragraph relate more to the idea of "lack of power" than to the time when the government was formed. Don't assume that the topic sentence is always the first sentence of a paragraph. Try this:

EXAMPLE 3:

There is a strong relation between limited education and low income. Statistics show that unemployment rates are highest among those adults who attended school the fewest years. Most jobs in a modern industrial society require technical or advanced training. The best pay goes with jobs that demand thinking and decisions based on knowledge. A few people manage to overcome their limited education by personality or a "lucky break." However, studies of lifetime earnings show that the average high school graduate earns more than the average high school dropout, who in turns earns more than the average adult who has not finished eighth grade.

Here, the first sentence contains the main idea of the whole paragraph. One more example should be helpful:

EXAMPLE 4:

They had fewer men available as soldiers. Less than one third of the railroads and only a small proportion of the nation's industrial production was theirs. For most of the war their coastline was blockaded by Northern ships. It is a tribute to Southern leadership and the courage of the people that they were not defeated for four years.

In this case you will note that the passage builds up to its main point. The topic sentence is the last one. Practice picking out the topic sentences in other material you read until it becomes an easy task.

Finding the General Theme

A more advanced skill is the ability to read several paragraphs and relate them to one general theme or main idea. The procedure involves careful reading of the entire passage and deciding which idea is the central or main one. You can tell you have the right idea when it is most frequent or most important, or when every sentence relates to it. As you read the next passage, note the *underlined* parts.

EXAMPLE 1:

True democracy means direct rule by the people. A good example can be found in a modern town meeting in many small New England towns. All citizens aged twenty-one or over may vote. They not only vote for officials, but they also get together to vote on local laws (or ordinances). The small size of the town and the limited number of voters make this possible.

In the cities, voters cast ballots for officials who get together to make the laws. Because the voters do not make the laws directly, this system is called indirect democracy or representative government. There is no problem of distance to travel, but it is difficult to run a meeting with hundreds of thousands of citizens.

Representation of voters and a direct voice in making laws are more of a problem in state or national governments. <u>The numbers of citizens and the distances to travel make representative government the most practical way</u> to make laws.

Think about the passage in general and the underlined parts in particular. Several examples discuss voting for officials and making laws. In the first paragraph both of these are done by the voters. The second paragraph describes representative government in which voters elect officials who make laws. The last paragraph emphasizes the problem of size and numbers and says that representative government is more practical. In the following question, put all these ideas together.

The main theme of this passage is that   Ⓐ Ⓑ Ⓒ Ⓓ Ⓔ

(A) the United States is not democratic
(B) citizens cannot vote for lawmakers
(C) representative government does not make laws
(D) every citizen makes laws directly
(E) increasing populations lead to less direct democracy

The answer is choice (E). Choices (B), (C), and (D) can be eliminated because they are not true of the passage. Choice (A) may have made you hesitate a little. The passage makes comments about *less direct* democracy, but it never says that representative government is *not democratic*.

The next 3 passages offer further practice in finding the main theme. Answer the question following each example and check the analysis to make sure you understand.

EXAMPLE 2:

Skye, 13 miles off the northwest coast of Scotland, is the largest and most famous of the Hebrides. Yet fame has neither marred its natural beauty nor brought affectation to its inhabitants. The scene and the people are almost as they were generations ago.

The first sight that impresses the visitor to Skye is its stark beauty. This is not beauty of the usual sort, for the island is not a lush green "paradise." It is, on the other hand, almost devoid of shrubbery. Mountains, moorlands, sky, and sea combine to create an overpowering landscape. Endless stretches of rocky hills dominate the horizon. Miles of treeless plains meet the eye. Yet this scene has a beauty all its own.

And then cutting into the stark landscape are the fantastic airborne peaks of the Cuillins, rising into the clear skies above. The Cuillins are the most beloved mountains in Scotland and are frequently climbed. Their rugged, naked grandeur, frost-sculptured ridges and acute peaks even attracted Sir Edmund Hillary.

The main idea of this passage is   Ⓐ Ⓑ Ⓒ Ⓓ Ⓔ

(A) the sky over Skye
(B) the lack of trees on Skye
(C) the natural beauty of Skye
(D) the lack of affectation on Skye
(E) the Cuillins in the skies of Skye

All of the answers have some truth to them. The problem is to find the *best* answer. Four of the choices are mentioned in the passage only by a small comment. But choice (C) is discussed throughout every part of the passage. The clue to the correct answer was how often the same theme was covered.

EXAMPLE 3:

Trade exists for many reasons. No doubt it started from a desire to have something different. Men also realized that different men could make different products. Trade encouraged specialization, which led to improvement in quality.

Trade started from person to person, but grew to involve different towns and different lands. Some found work in transporting the goods or selling them. Merchants grew rich as the demand for products increased. Craftsmen were able to sell more products at home and abroad. People in general had a greater variety of things to choose.

The knowledge of new products led to an interest in the lands which produced them. More daring persons went to see other lands. Others stayed at home, but asked many questions of the travellers. As people learned about the products and the conditions in other countries, they compared them with their own. This often led to a desire for better conditions or a hope for a better life. Trade was mainly an economic force, but it also had other effects.

Ⓐ Ⓑ Ⓒ Ⓓ Ⓔ The general theme of the passage is how

(A) trade makes everyone rich
(B) trade divides the world
(C) products are made
(D) trade changes people's lives
(E) people find new jobs

This is not easy, as you may feel that all the choices are good. Most of them were mentioned in some part of the passage. However, you must select the *best* choice. If you had trouble, let us analyze the passage.

Paragraph one emphasizes a "desire" for "something different" and "improvement." The second paragraph mentions "found work," "merchants grew rich," "craftsmen . . . sell more," and "greater variety of things to choose." The third paragraph covers "interest in the lands," "compared them with their own," "desire for better conditions," and "better life." All these are evidence of the same general theme of how trade brings changes in the lives of people. Choice (D) is the best answer.

Choice (A) is tempting because of the comment on merchants getting rich. However, this idea is not found all through the passage. Choice (B) may catch the careless thinker. Trade does not divide the world, even though the passage talks about dividing jobs. Choice (C) is weak. Some comment is made about making products, but not in all parts of the passage. Choice (E) is weak for the same reason as choice (C).

EXAMPLE 4:

The enormous problems of turning swamps and desert into fields and orchards, together with the ideal of share-and-share-alike, gave birth to the kibbutz.

In those days, the kibbutz member had to plow the fields with a rifle slung over his shoulder.

Today security is still a factor in the kibbutz. Shelters are furrowed into the ground along every walk among the shade trees, near the children's house, where all the young children of the kibbutz live, and near the communal dining room.

But the swamps have been conquered, and the desert is gradually becoming green. And while kibbutz members once faced deprivation and a monotonous diet, today they reap the harvest of hard work and success.

One such kibbutz is Dorot, at the gateway to the Negev desert and typical of the average size Israeli communal settlement.

Life on the kibbutz has become more complex through growth and prosperity. While once the land barely yielded enough for a living, Dorot, like many other kibbutzim, now exports some of its crops. It also has become industrialized, another trend among these settlements. Dorot has a factory which exports faucets to a dozen countries, including the United States.

The main theme of this article is

Ⓐ Ⓑ Ⓒ Ⓓ Ⓔ

(A) the manufacture of faucets is a sign of growth and prosperity in the kibbutz
(B) with the solving of agricultural problems the kibbutz has become a more complex society
(C) since security is a problem for the kibbutz, it has become industrialized
(D) Dorot is the prosperous gateway to the Negev desert
(E) kibbutzim are good places to live, although they are located in swamps and deserts

Choice (A) receives brief mention at the end of the passage. It is an idea in the passage, but certainly not the general idea of the passage. Choice (D) is the same kind of answer as choice (A)—it is too specific a fact. Choice (E) is unrelated to the passage. We now have choices (B) and (C) as possible answers. Choice (C) seems reasonable until you analyze it. Did the need for security *cause* the industrialization? Or are there better examples of how life has become more complex now that agricultural problems have been solved? The evidence leans more to choice (B).

In summary, in order to find the general theme:

1. Read at your normal speed.
2. Locate the topic sentence in each paragraph.
3. Note ideas that are frequent or emphasized.
4. Find the idea to which most of the passage is related.

Finding Logical Relationships

In order to fully understand the meaning of a passage, you must first look for the general theme and then relate the ideas and opinions found in the passage to this general theme. In this way, you can determine not only what is important but also how the ideas interrelate to form the whole. From this understanding, you will be better able to answer questions that refer to the passage.

As you read the following passages, look for general theme and supporting facts, words or phrases that signal emphasis or shift in thought, and the relation of one idea to another.

EXAMPLE 1:

The candidate who wants to be elected pays close attention to statements and actions that will make the voters see him favorably. In ancient Rome candidates wore pure white togas (the Latin word *candidatus* means "clothed in white") to indicate that they were pure, clean, and above any "dirty work." However, it is interesting to note that such a toga was not worn after election.

In more modern history, candidates have allied themselves with political parties. Once a voter knows and favors the views of a certain political party, he may vote for anyone with that party's label. Nevertheless, divisions of opinion develop, so that today there is a wide range of candidate views in any major party.

1. Ⓐ Ⓑ Ⓒ Ⓓ Ⓔ   **1.** The best conclusion to be drawn from the first paragraph is that after an election

    (A) all candidates are dishonest
    (B) candidates are less concerned with symbols of integrity
    (C) candidates do not change their ideas
    (D) officials are always honest
    (E) policies always change

You noted the ideas about a candidate in Rome. You saw the word "however" signal a shift in ideas or thinking. Now the third step rests with your judgment. You cannot jump to a conclusion; you must see which conclusion is reasonable or fair. Choices (A), (D), and (E) should make you wary. They say "all" or "always" which means without exception. The last sentence is not that strong or positive. Choices (B) and (C) must be considered. There is nothing in the paragraph that supports the fact that candidates do not change their ideas. This forces you into choice (B) as the only statement logically related to what the paragraph said.

2. Ⓐ Ⓑ Ⓒ Ⓓ Ⓔ   **2.** A fair statement is that most candidates from the same political party today are likely to

    (A) have the same views
    (B) be different in every view
    (C) agree on almost all points
    (D) agree on some points and disagree on others
    (E) agree only by accident

Here again, the burden rests on your judgment after following ideas and word clues. The paragraph makes the point that there is a wide range of views. That eliminates choice (A). Choice (B) is not logical because the candidates would not likely be in the same party if they disagree on every view. The remaining choices are different degrees of agreement. Choice (E) is weak because candidates are too interested to arrive at agreement only by accident. The wide range mentioned seems to oppose choice (C) and favor choice (D) as a little more likely. You may say that choice (C) sounds pretty good. Again we stress that *you are picking the very best choice,* not just a good choice. This is what we mean by reflecting carefully on all possibilities and selecting the best available choice.

EXAMPLE 2:

In 1812 Napoleon had to withdraw his forces from Russia. The armies had invaded successfully and reached the city of Moscow. There was no question of French army disloyalty or unwillingness to fight. As winter came, the Russian army moved out of the way, leaving a wasted land and burned buildings. Other conquered European nations seized upon Napoleon's problems in Russia as their chance to rearm and to break loose from French control.

Ⓐ Ⓑ Ⓒ Ⓓ Ⓔ   According to the passage, the main reason for Napoleon's withdrawal from Russia was the

    (A) disloyalty of the French troops
    (B) Russian winter
    (C) burned buildings
    (D) planned revolts in other countries
    (E) Russian army

In this passage, only choice (A) is totally incorrect. Choice (E) is very weak because the Russian army was not able to stop the invasion. The choices narrow to which is the best of (B), (C), and (D). It seems that all three answers are supported by the passage. There needs to be some thought and judgment by you. Which of these could be overcome easily and which could be the strongest reason for Napoleon leaving Russia? The burned buildings could be overcome by the troops making other shelters. The Russian winter was severe and the army did not want to face it. However, marching out of Russia in the winter was also a great problem. Napoleon probably would have stayed in Moscow except for a more serious problem—the loss of the control he had established over most of Europe. Thus, answer (D) is best.

EXAMPLE 3:

By 1915 events of World War I were already involving the United States and threatening its neutrality. The sinking of the British liner *Lusitania* in that year by a German submarine caused great resentment among Americans. Over a hundred United States citizens were killed in the incident. President Wilson had frequently deplored the use of submarines by Germany against the United States. Since the United States was neutral, it was not liable to acts of war by another nation.

However, Wilson resolved to represent the strong feeling in the country (notably in the Midwest) and in the Democratic Party that United States neutrality should be maintained. He felt that the United States should have "peace with honor," if possible.

There were also people, mostly in the East, that wanted to wage a preventive war against Germany. Such men as Theodore Roosevelt bitterly attacked Wilson as one who talked a great deal but did nothing.

By 1917 Germany again used unrestricted submarine warfare and Wilson broke off relations with Germany. In February British agents uncovered the Zimmerman Telegram. This was an attempt by the German ambassador to Mexico to involve that nation in a war against the United States. And in March several American merchant ships were sunk by German submarines. His patience at an end, Wilson at last took the position of a growing majority of Americans and asked Congress to declare war on Germany. Thus, the United States entered World War I.

1. This passage tries to explain that   1. Ⓐ Ⓑ Ⓒ Ⓓ Ⓔ

   (A) Wilson wanted the United States to go to war against Germany
   (B) Wilson tried to avoid war with Germany
   (C) Germany wanted the United States to enter the war
   (D) other nations were pressuring the United States to enter the war
   (E) Mexico was our main enemy

2. We can conclude from the passage that most citizens of the United States in 1917   2. Ⓐ Ⓑ Ⓒ Ⓓ Ⓔ
   were

   (A) totally opposed to war with Germany
   (B) in favor of war before Wilson was
   (C) willing to accept war after Wilson persuaded them
   (D) neutral
   (E) trying to avoid war

3. Ⓐ Ⓑ Ⓒ Ⓓ Ⓔ **3.** The last event in the series of happenings that led to a declaration of war against Germany was

   (A) the Zimmerman Telegram
   (B) attacks on U.S. merchant ships
   (C) Wilson's war message to Congress
   (D) a change in public opinion
   (E) the sinking of the *Lusitania*

In question 1, the key is to note Wilson's actions discussed in paragraph two. Near the end of the passage there is a phrase about "his patience at an end." This describes a man who was trying to avoid a conflict, as in answer choice (B).

Question 2 rests on two ideas. There was a change in the feeling of the American people about war. The other idea is that Wilson responded after he felt that they had changed. The phrase "took the position of a growing majority of Americans" tells us that Wilson followed the change in opinion, as in answer choice (B).

In question 3, you need to check the sequence of events. The declaration of war followed the president's request.

Making Inferences

An inference is not stated. It is assumed by the reader from something said by the writer. An inference is the likely or probable conclusion rather than the direct, logical one. It usually involves an opinion or viewpoint that the writer wants the reader to follow or assume. In another kind of inference, the reader figures out the author's opinion even though it is not stated. The clues are generally found in the manner in which facts are presented and in the choice of words and phrases. Opinion is revealed by the one-sided nature of a passage in which no opposing facts are given. It is shown further by "loaded" words that reveal the author's feelings.

It is well worth noting that opinionated writing is often more interesting than straight factual accounts. Some writers are very colorful, forceful, or amusing in presenting their views. You should understand that there is nothing wrong with reading opinion. You should read varied opinions, but know that they are opinions. Then make up your own mind.

Not every writer will insert his opinion obviously. However, you can get clues from how often the same idea is said (frequency), whether arguments are balanced on both sides (fairness), and the choice of wording (emotional or loaded words). Look for the clues in this next passage.

EXAMPLE 1:

Slowly but surely the great passenger trains of the United States have been fading from the rails. Short-run commuter trains still rattle in and out of the cities. Between major cities you can still find a train, but the schedules are becoming less frequent. The Twentieth Century Limited, The Broadway Limited, and other luxury trains that sang along the rails at 60 to 80 miles an hour are no longer running. Passengers on other long runs complain of poor service, old equipment, and costs in time and money. The long distance traveller today accepts the noise of jets, the congestion at airports, and the traffic between airport and city. A more elegant and graceful way is becoming only a memory.

1. Ⓐ Ⓑ Ⓒ Ⓓ Ⓔ **1.** With respect to the reduction of long-run passenger trains, this writer expresses

   (A) regret
   (B) pleasure
   (C) grief

   (D) elation
   (E) anger

Before you choose the answer, you must deduce what the writer's feeling is. He does not actually state his feeling, but clues are available so that you may infer what it is. Choices (B) and (D) are impossible, because he gives no word that shows he is pleased by the change. Choice (C) is too strong, as is choice (E). Choice (A) is the most reasonable inference to make. He is sorry to see the change. He is expressing regret.

2. The author seems to feel that air travel is   2. Ⓐ Ⓑ Ⓒ Ⓓ Ⓔ

  (A) costly (D) elegant
  (B) slow (E) uncomfortable
  (C) streamlined

Here we must be careful because he says very little about air travel. However, his one sentence about it presents three negative or annoying points. The choice now becomes fairly clear. Answer (E) is correct.

EXAMPLE 2:

When the United States was founded at the end of the eighteenth century, it was a small and weak country, made up mostly of poor farmers. Foreign policy, reflecting this domestic condition, stressed "no entangling alliances." The State Department then had a staff of less than half a dozen persons, whose total salary was $6,600 (of which $3,500 went to the Secretary of State), and a diplomatic service budget (July, 1790) of $40,000. Militarily, too, the country was insignificant. The first United States army, soon after the American Revolution, was made up of one captain (John Doughty) and 80 men. Clearly, the United States did not consider itself a real power and was not taken seriously by the rest of the world.

It was not until immense changes took place *inside* the United States that the country began to play an important role in foreign affairs. By the beginning of the twentieth century, the United States had ceased to be a predominantly agricultural nation and had become an industrial one. Its population had grown to more than 30 times its original number. George Washington was president of 3,000,000 Americans; Theodore Roosevelt, of 100,000,000.

1. A country today cannot expect to play an important part in world affairs unless it   1. Ⓐ Ⓑ Ⓒ Ⓓ Ⓔ

   I. has wealth
  II. has a large population
 III. is strong internally

  (A) I only
  (B) III only
  (C) I and II only
  (D) II and III only
  (E) I, II, and III

This is a slightly different style of question. You must look at each of the answer choices in I, II, and III. As you consider the passage and what it suggests, you note that each of the answer choices in I, II, and III make good sense. Therefore, answer choice (E) is the best answer because it includes all of the correct statements. Again, this is not designed to trick you. The purpose of such a question is to be sure that you have read all the choices.

2. Ⓐ Ⓑ Ⓒ Ⓓ Ⓔ **2.** The writer seems to think that a major factor in making the United States a world power was

    (A) industrialization
    (B) the passing of time
    (C) a change in government policies
    (D) the presidency of Theodore Roosevelt
    (E) the avoidance of entangling alliances

The passage does not answer the question directly. You must infer what is meant by the author. However, there is a clue in the author's comment that changes inside a country make a big difference in its foreign policy. The big internal changes noted are the growth of America's population and industrial power. By correctly interpreting the passage, you will be led to choice (A) for this question.

In Example 3 you will find three short statements by three different writers. The questions will require that you make inferences about each writer and then make comparisons of one against the other two.

EXAMPLE 3:

Writer I

No nation should tolerate the slacker who will not defend his country in time of war. The so-called conscientious objector is a coward who accepts the benefits of his country but will not accept the responsibility. By shirking his fair share, he forces another person to assume an unfair burden.

Writer II

A democratic nation should have room for freedom of conscience. Religious training and belief may make a man conscientiously opposed to participation in war. The conscientious objector should be permitted to give labor service or some form of non-combat military duty. His beliefs should be respected.

Writer III

The rights of the conscientious objector should be decided by each individual. No government should dictate to any person or require him to endanger his life if the person, in conscience, objects. There need be no religious basis. It is enough for a free individual to think as he pleases and to reject laws or rules to which he conscientiously objects.

1. Ⓐ Ⓑ Ⓒ Ⓓ Ⓔ **1.** A balanced opinion on this subject is presented by

    (A) Writer I
    (B) Writer II
    (C) Writer III
    (D) all of the writers
    (E) none of the writers

2. Ⓐ Ⓑ Ⓒ Ⓓ Ⓔ **2.** We can conclude that the writer most likely to support a person who refuses any military service is

    (A) Writer I
    (B) Writer II
    (C) Writer III
    (D) all of the writers
    (E) none of the writers

3. An authoritarian person is most likely to agree with

    (A) Writer I
    (B) Writer II
    (C) Writer III
    (D) all of the writers
    (E) none of the writers

Look for clues in the language or choice of words that are loaded with feeling such as "slacker," "so-called," and "shirking" by Writer I and "dictate," "endanger," and "as he pleases" by Writer III. Compare them with the language used by Writer II. Then see if you can connect what these writers say with views you have heard or read. We are not asking you to accept any of these opinions. You are using your skill in reading what the writers think and adding it to your own knowledge. Then you make logical inferences. The correct answers are 1 (B), 2 (C), and 3 (A).

Now that you have spent time reviewing the three basic skills you should master for better reading comprehension ability, try the two practice exercises that follow. Answers to these exercises appear after Exercise B. You should also try to spend time using this reading approach as you read other material not related to the GMAT.

Practice Exercises

The following two reading passages are similar to the Reading Comprehension passages found on the GMAT. You should read each one and then answer the questions that follow according to the directions. Remember that in Reading Comprehension sections you are permitted to refer to the passage while answering the questions.

EXERCISE A

TIME: 9 minutes

DIRECTIONS: This part contains a reading passage. You are to read it carefully. When answering the questions, you *will* be able to refer to the passages. The questions are based on what is *stated* or *implied* in the passage. You have nine minutes to complete this part.

      Above all, colonialism was hated for its explicit assumption that the civilizations of colonized peoples were inferior. Using slogans like *The White Man's Burden* and *La Mission Civilicatrice,* Europeans asserted their moral obligation to impose their way of life on those endowed with inferior cultures. This orientation was

(5)   particularly blatant among the French. In the colonies, business was conducted in French. Schools used that language and employed curricula designed for children in France. One scholar suggests that Muslim children probably learned no more about the Maghreb than they did about Australia. In the Metropole, intellectuals discoursed on the weakness of Arabo-Islamic culture. A noted historian accused

(10)   Islam of being hostile to science. An academician wrote that Arabic—the holy language of religion, art and the Muslim sciences—is "more of an encumbrance than an aid to the mind. It is absolutely devoid of precision." There was of course an element of truth in the criticisms. After all, Arab reformists had been engaging in self-criticism for decades. Also, at least some Frenchmen honestly believed

(15)   they were helping the colonized. A Resident General in Tunisia, for example, told an assemblage of Muslims with sincerity, "We shall distribute to you all that we have of learning; we shall make you a party to everything that makes for the strength of our intelligence." But none of this could change or justify the cultural racism in colonial ideologies. To the French, North Africans were only partly

(20)   civilized and could be saved only by becoming Frenchmen. The reaction of the colonized was of course to defend his identity and to label colonial policy, in the words of Algerian writer Malek Hadad, "cultural asphyxia." Throughout North

(25)

Africa, nationalists made the defense of Arabo-Islamic civilization a major objective, a value in whose name they demanded independence. Yet the crisis of identity, provoked by colonial experiences, has not been readily assured and lingers into the post-colonial period. A French scholar describes the devasting impact of colonialism by likening it to "the role played for us (in Europe) by the doctrine of original sin." Frantz Fanon, especially in his *Studies in a Dying Colonialism,* well expresses the North African perspective.

(30)

(35)

Factors producing militant and romantic cultural nationalism are anchored in time. Memories of colonialism are already beginning to fade and, when the Maghreb has had a few decades in which to grow, dislocations associated with social change can also be expected to be fewer. Whether this means that the cultural nationalism characteristic of the Maghreb today will disappear in the future cannot be known. But a preoccupation with identity and culture and an affirmation of Arabism and Islam have characterized the Maghreb since independence and these still remain today important elements in North African life.

(40)

(45)

(50)

A second great preoccupation in independent North Africa is the promotion of a modernist social revolution. The countries of the Maghreb do not pursue development in the same way and there have been variations in policies within each country. But all three spend heavily on development. In Tunisia, for example, the government devotes 20–25% of its annual budget to education, and literacy has climbed from 15% in 1956 to about 50% today. A problem, however, is that such advances are not always compatible with objectives flowing from North African nationalism. In Morocco, for instance, when the government decided to give children an "Arab" education, it was forced to limit enrollments because, among other things, most Moroccans had been educated in French and the country consequently had few teachers qualified to teach in Arabic. Two years later, with literacy rates declining, this part of the Arabization program was postponed. The director of Arabization declared, "We are not fanatics; we want to enter the modern world."

1. Ⓐ Ⓑ Ⓒ Ⓓ Ⓔ **1.** Which of the following titles best describes the content of the passage?

(A) *Education in the Levant*
(B) *Nationalism in North Africa*
(C) *Civilization in the Middle East*
(D) *Muslim Science*
(E) *Culture and Language*

2. Ⓐ Ⓑ Ⓒ Ⓓ Ⓔ **2.** Which of the following is *not* used by the author in the presentation of his arguments?

(A) Colonialism demoralized the local inhabitants.
(B) Colonialism produced an identity crisis.
(C) Cultural nationalism will soon disappear.
(D) Decolonization does not always run smoothly.
(E) Colonialists assumed that local cultures were inferior.

3. Ⓐ Ⓑ Ⓒ Ⓓ Ⓔ **3.** The author's attitude toward colonialism is best described as one of

(A) sympathy
(B) bewilderment
(C) support
(D) hostility
(E) ambivalence

4. Which of the following does the author mention as evidence of cultural colonialism? 4. Ⓐ Ⓑ Ⓒ Ⓓ Ⓔ

    (A) Native children in North Africa learned little about local culture.
    (B) Science was not taught in the Arabic language.
    (C) Colonial policy was determined in France.
    (D) Colonialists spent little on development.
    (E) Native teachers were not employed in public schools.

5. The author provides information that would answer which of the following questions? 5. Ⓐ Ⓑ Ⓒ Ⓓ Ⓔ

    (A) What was the difference between French and German attitudes toward their colonies?
    (B) Why did Europeans impose their way of life on their colonies?
    (C) Why was colonialism bad?
    (D) Why was colonialism disliked?
    (E) When did colonialism end in North Africa?

EXERCISE B

TIME: **9 minutes**

DIRECTIONS: This part contains a reading passage. You are to read it carefully. When answering the questions, you *will* be able to refer to the passages. The questions are based on what is *stated* or *implied* in the passage. You have nine minutes to complete this part.

      Man and nature were the culprits as Venice sank hopelessly—or so it seemed—into the 177 canals on which the city is built. While nature's work took ages, man's work was much quicker and more brutal. But now man is using his ingenuity to save what he had almost destroyed. The sinking has been arrested and Venice
(5) should start rising again, like an oceanic phoenix from the canals.

      The saving of Venice is the problem of the Italian Government, of course, but Venice is also a concern for Europe. And it happened that in the second half of 1975 Italy was in the chair of the European Council of Ministers. But the EC as such has no program for the salvation of Venice. "The Community is not a cultural
(10) community," explained one Commission official. "There are some areas where it just does not have competence, the preservation of historical landmarks being one of them." So the efforts to save Venice have taken on a worldwide, rather than a Community-wide dimension.

      Industrialization of the Porto Marghera area brought economic benefits to Ven-
(15) ice, but it also raped the city as growing air and water pollution began to take their toll on the priceless works of art and architecture. The danger of the imminent disappearance of Venice's cultural heritage was first brought to public attention in November 1966 when tides rose over six feet to flood Venice's canals and squares. Since then, various national and international organizations have sought
(20) ways and means to halt the destruction of the "queen of the Adriatic," though no one program has proved wholly satisfactory.

      The US "Save Venice" group and the British "Venice in Peril" committee were formed to raise money for the restoration of priceless works of art and monuments. In 1967 the United Nations Educational, Scientific and Cultural Organization
(25) (UNESCO) took on the task of helping to save Venice by setting up a joint international advisory committee with the Italian Government. Such distant lands as Pakistan, no stranger to aid programs itself, joined in the effort, giving UNESCO a gift of 10,000 postage stamps for "Venice in Peril." Even a group of famous cartoonists felt moved to draw attention to the fact that "Venice must be saved"
(30) and organized an exhibit in 1973, with the Council of Europe in Strasbourg, France, and this year a ballet festival drew people and funds to Venice.

Though Venice, the city of bridge-linked islands, was built in the fifth century, the land on which it was built has been sinking "naturally" for a billion years. Movements of the earth's crust have caused the very slow and gradual descent (35) of the Po Valley. And nature's forces aren't easily countered. Each year, Venice has been sinking about one millimeter into the lagoon which holds this Adriatic jewel. To add to Venice's peril, the slow melting of the polar cap causes the level of the sea to rise another millimeter. If nothing is done to reverse nature's work, Venice is doomed to be another Atlantis, lost for ever beneath the murky sea.

(40) Man's part in the sink-Venice movement has been for reasons mainly economic. For the last 400 years, the population of Venice has been drifting toward the mainland to escape the isolation and inconvenience of living on a series of islets. Between 1951 and 1971, Venice lost 63,000 inhabitants. To curtail this migration, new, artificial land areas, on the Dutch model, were added to the old Venice. (45) Venice's original builders had not been far-sighted enough and set the ground level at only a few inches above what they expected to be the maximum tides. The combination of reclaimed land and Porto Marghera industrialization have "squeezed" the lagoon until its waters have no place to go but . . . up.

As Porto Marghera grows as an industrial port, and more and deeper channels (50) are added for larger ships, currents become faster and dikes make the ravaging tides even more violent. The "acqua alta" has always been a problem for Venice, but with increased industrialization, flooding has become more frequent, sometimes occurring 50 times a year. Added to the violent "scirocco" that blows up to 60 miles an hour, Venice is rendered all the more vulnerable.

(55) Yet Venice is not crumbling. Despite the visible decay caused by repeated floods and despite pollution that peels the stucco off the palazzi and eats away at their bottom-most steps, the structures are solid. The Rialto Bridge still stands safely on its ancient foundations supported by 6000 piles.

And something has been done to stop the damage done by water. Indeed, one (60) simple measure has proved to work miracles. The ban on pumping from the thousands of artesian wells in and around the city—an easy source of water, but also a folly that caused a further descent of 5 millimeters a year—has been so effective that Venice should rise an inch in the next twenty years.

1. Ⓐ Ⓑ Ⓒ Ⓓ Ⓔ **1.** According to the passage, between 1951 and 1971, Venice lost approximately how many residents annually?

(A) 475
(B) 3,150
(C) 6,300
(D) 15,500
(E) 63,000

2. Ⓐ Ⓑ Ⓒ Ⓓ Ⓔ **2.** The author's point of view is that Venice

(A) cannot be saved from destruction
(B) is in danger of imminent disappearance
(C) is doomed to become another "Atlantis"
(D) can be saved, but much work is necessary
(E) must become a member of the EC

3. Ⓐ Ⓑ Ⓒ Ⓓ Ⓔ **3.** Which of the following conditions has *not* contributed to Venice's peril?

(A) Movement of the earth's crust
(B) Natural causes
(C) Melting of the polar cap
(D) Industrialization
(E) Shipping on the canals

4. According to the passage, which of the following figures indicates the approximate year when Venice first began sinking?

4. Ⓐ Ⓑ Ⓒ Ⓓ Ⓔ

(A) 400 B.C.
(B) A.D. 1400
(C) A.D. 1966
(D) A.D. 1970
(E) None of the above

5. The author feels that Venice is an example of

5. Ⓐ Ⓑ Ⓒ Ⓓ Ⓔ

(A) a doomed city like Atlantis
(B) uncontrolled conditions
(C) a combination of natural and human destruction
(D) international neglect
(E) benign concern by international agencies

Answers and Analysis

EXERCISE A

1. **(B)** Clearly, the main subject of the passage is nationalism. This is given in the statement on line 1, "Above all, colonialism was hated . . ." and in lines 22ff. and 30ff.

2. **(C)** Choice (E) is given in lines 1–2, (D) in lines 43–45, (B) in lines 24–25, and (A) is implied throughout; while the opposite of (C) is found in lines 34–36.

3. **(D)** See, for instance, the reference to "cultural racism" in lines 18–19, as well as the general tone of paragraph 1.

4. **(A)** This is mentioned in lines 6–8. The fact that children were taught very little about their own culture and history was due to cultural colonialism.

5. **(D)** This theme begins on line 1 and continues throughout much of the passage.

EXERCISE B

1. **(B)** See line 43.

2. **(D)** Venice can be saved, but much work is necessary. See lines 3–5.

3. Answer (A) appears in line 34, (B) in 33, (C) in 37, and (D) in lines 49–53. Choice (E) is not mentioned.

4. **(E)** In lines 32–33 it is stated that the land on which Venice is situated has been sinking for a billion years.

5. **(C)** The theme is given in the first line and repeated in lines 33, 37, 40, 46, 47, and 53.

ANALYSIS OF SITUATIONS REVIEW

The Analysis of Situations section of the GMAT is comprised of Data Evaluation questions. Each passage will present some business problem requiring decision making by one or more of the characters.

You will be asked to evaluate each item given and classify it as either

(A) A MAJOR OBJECTIVE in making the decision: one of the goals sought by the decision maker

(B) A MAJOR FACTOR in making the decision: an aspect of the problem, specifically mentioned in the passage, that fundamentally affects and/or determines the decision

(C) A MINOR FACTOR in making the decision: a less important element bearing on or affecting a Major Factor, rather than a Major Objective directly

(D) A MAJOR ASSUMPTION in making the decision: a projection or supposition arrived at by the decision maker before considering the factors and alternatives

(E) An UNIMPORTANT ISSUE in making the decision: an item lacking significant impact on, or relationship to, the decision

Strategy for the Analysis of Situations Section

---
1. BEFORE READING THE PASSAGE, READ THE QUESTIONS PERTAINING TO IT.

By reading the questions first, CAREFULLY, you familiarize yourself with the type of problem being presented and the factors you will have to take into consideration in choosing your answers.

---
2. USE ONLY INFORMATION MENTIONED IN THE PASSAGE.

Even if the subject of a passage is one about which you have personal knowledge, use only information specifically mentioned in the passage. Inferences and assumptions should be based on the perceptions of the characters in the passage.

---
3. LEARN BY HEART THE FIVE CLASSIFICATIONS USED IN DATA EVAL-UATION QUESTIONS.

Once you have decided that a certain item is a Major or Minor Factor, you should not have to waste time leafing back and forth to find out if you want to mark (A), (B), or (C) on your answer sheet.

The Classifications

(A) Major Objectives

A situation or condition resulting from the decision to be made will be a Major Objective. A Major Objective will often be introduced by expressions of desire: "He wants . . . ," "He would like . . . ," "It is important to him. . . ." The desired result may be one of business condition or of happiness or prestige for a firm or individual.

To illustrate a Major Objective, read the following passage:

Dave Robinson wants to replace his company's present cement mixer with a new model. Dave has been chief building engineer for five years. Dave's calculations show that the newer model can save the company up to $10,000 in operating costs. He is considering ordering one of three models. The three models are all immediately available but vary in cost.

In Analysis of Situations cases, a major decision considered is almost invariably a Major Objective. In the passage quoted, the major decision is whether to buy a new cement mixer. Another clue to locating the Major Objective is the expression of desire: "Dave Robinson *wants* to replace his company's present cement mixer with a new model."

(B) Major Factor

In the decision-making process, the strengths and weaknesses of various alternatives must be weighed and considered. As a result of these considerations the decision maker will choose one alternative over another. The points used to contrast and compare one alternative to another are Major Factors. The final decision will be based on the results of these considerations.

Let us continue with the passage.

Dave is considering three models: A two-ton fully automatic mixer, a two-ton semi-automatic mixer, and a one-ton fully automatic mixer. Dave's decision will depend on some calculations he has made. He will consider total costs, including the purchase price, amortization, and operating costs of each mixer. Dave will compare these costs with the contribution the mixers can make to company earnings. Dave knows the importance of his decision; a wrong choice can result in an operating loss for his company.

In addition to the cost side, Dave considers the quality of the mixers. After examining the technical literature supplied by the mixer manufacturer and talking with users of the equipment, Dave cataloged each mixer's operating characteristics. In particular, he needs a mixer which will have the least maintenance problems, including downtime. Dave is confident that he will be able to reach a correct decision based on his calculations.

Major factors include the key elements that impinge on the decision to be made. Once alternative choices of action have been identified, the pros and cons, or strengths and weaknesses, of each alternative will be weighed.

To reiterate what we explained above, the Major Objective is to acquire a new mixer. The alternative courses of action are (in addition to a "No go" decision—after all, Dave may decide not to buy any of the proposed models) the choice of one of three different models. The Major Factors, therefore, are the strengths and weaknesses of each model as considered by Dave. Specifically, they are *total costs* and the *quality* of the mixers. Both are criteria by which the pros and cons of each mixer can be assessed.

(C) Minor Factor

Minor factors play a less direct part in the decision-making process. They are usually related to or are part of the considerations comprising Major Factors. A Minor Factor may also pertain to only one or some of the alternatives. A Major Factor will involve consideration of all the elements of an alternative course of action.

Referring to our definition of Minor Factors, we can see that a number of secondary factors or items are related to each Major Factor. For example, we are told that the *total cost* of the mixers is comprised of the *purchase price, amortization,* and *operating costs*. A Data Evaluation question mentioning one of the parts of the total cost—say, purchase price—should be labeled a Minor Factor. The price of the mixers is only a sub-element of a Major Factor, total cost. Dave Robinson would not consider only the purchase price of the mixers—or any of the other elements of total cost alone—in making his decision.

Moreover, we read in the passage that total cost is but one of two major considerations in the decision process. The other is *quality*. Quality is defined as the operating characteristics of the mixers. Operating characteristics consist of the incidence of maintenance problems. A Data Evaluation question mentioning the consideration of downtime would be a Minor Factor.

To sum up, Minor Factors are subsets of Major Factors. Minor Factors represent facts that are considered for less than all alternative courses of action or are partial facts considered for less than all alternative courses of action.

(D) Major Assumption

Major Assumptions are feelings, beliefs, or opinions accepted by the decision maker without supporting information. They will mirror expectations of future events and the personal feelings and opinions of the decision maker.

Considering our passage again, note that a Major Assumption is expressed as Dave Robinson's belief or opinion "that he will be able to reach a correct decision based on his calculations." Here, the key word is "confident," which designates an assumption on the part of the decision maker. Dave is assuming that he will be able to choose an alternative course of action based on his calculations. Note that no information is given in the passage about the accuracy of these calculations. Apart from the statement (in paragraph 1) that the newer model can save up to $10,000 in operating costs, nothing more is said about the calculations.

In many cases, Major Assumptions may be based on implications made by the decision maker. Major Assumptions may be identified by such key words as "probability," "likelihood," "estimate," "reliability," and "availability."

(E) Unimportant Issue

Unimportant Issues are those items not significantly influencing the choice of an alternative. Or, by elimination, if an item is not a Major Objective, a Major or Minor Factor, or a Major Assumption, it is an Unimportant Issue.

An example of an Unimportant Issue is that Dave has been chief building engineer for five years. His occupation and length of seniority have no importance in the selection of an alternative course of action and are not Major Objectives, Major or Minor Factors, nor Major Assumptions.

The following decision tree will help you visualize the relationships between the question classifications. To use the tree, simply start at the top and by answering YES or NO move downwards until you arrive at the correct choice. The first YES is the correct answer.

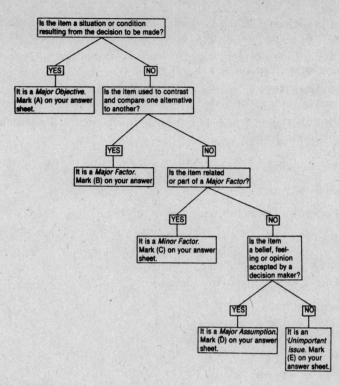

Practice Exercise

This part is designed to give you some practice in reading and answering an Analysis of Situations test. On the actual test you will have 30 minutes to read two passages and answer 35 questions. Because the passage that follows is a shortened version of an actual test, spend no more than 5 minutes reading the passage and answering the questions.

Ed Freed was considering opening a tennis club. Ed was thirty-five years old and had played amateur tennis for over twenty years; the idea of a tennis club would satisfy a long-held dream of making a business out of a favorite pastime. Ed was a traveling salesman for an exporting firm. Because he did not want to give up his present job, he wanted his wife to manage the club. He believed he could convince her to do so because of the extra annual income the club would provide. If his wife would not agree, Ed planned to hire a business manager. Ed spent his spare time looking for a suitable site for the club. He found a piece of real estate on the outskirts of town which was easily accessible by car. The property was large enough to build a club having four indoor courts, showers, restrooms, and a snack bar. There was room for a 30-car outdoor parking lot. Ed had calculated that he needed to operate three courts at a rate of at least 60 percent capacity to break even. The property was particularly attractive because the fourth court would make the operation profitable. Ed estimated that it would take six months to make the club operational. The time necessary to build the club was crucial because Ed could only obtain bank financing for part of the project. Ed had to provide the balance from his savings. If the club was not completed on time, Ed would not be able to repay the bank finance charges. After considering all the facts, Ed decided to make his bid for the property only one day before his option expired.

DIRECTIONS: The questions that follow relate to the preceding passage. Evaluate, in terms of the passage, each of the items given. Then select your answer from one of the following classifications, and indicate your choice in the space provided.

(A) A MAJOR OBJECTIVE in making the decision: one of the goals sought by the decision maker

(B) A MAJOR FACTOR in making the decision: an aspect of the problem, specifically mentioned in the passage, that fundamentally affects and/or determines the decision

(C) A MINOR FACTOR in making the decision: a less important element bearing on or affecting a Major Factor, rather than a Major Objective directly

(D) A MAJOR ASSUMPTION in making the decision: a projection or supposition arrived at by the decision maker before considering the factors and alternatives

(E) AN UNIMPORTANT ISSUE in making the decision: an item lacking significant impact on, or relationship to, the decision

1. Ⓐ Ⓑ Ⓒ Ⓓ Ⓔ   **1.** Location of the property

2. Ⓐ Ⓑ Ⓒ Ⓓ Ⓔ   **2.** Increasing annual income

3. Ⓐ Ⓑ Ⓒ Ⓓ Ⓔ   **3.** Likelihood of operating the club within six months

4. Ⓐ Ⓑ Ⓒ Ⓓ Ⓔ   **4.** Ed's age (thirty-five)

5. Ⓐ Ⓑ Ⓒ Ⓓ Ⓔ   **5.** Size of the property

6. Ⓐ Ⓑ Ⓒ Ⓓ Ⓔ   **6.** Likelihood of Ed's wife's managing the club

7. Ⓐ Ⓑ Ⓒ Ⓓ Ⓔ   **7.** Room for a snack bar

8. Ⓐ Ⓑ Ⓒ Ⓓ Ⓔ   **8.** Time necessary to build the club

9. Ⓐ Ⓑ Ⓒ Ⓓ Ⓔ   **9.** Option for purchasing the property

10. Ⓐ Ⓑ Ⓒ Ⓓ Ⓔ   **10.** Ed's experience as a tennis player

Answers and Analysis

1. **(B)** Major Factor. *Note the first word, "location."* The location of the property is important because it is linked to the potential profitability of the club. Location is not a Major Objective; it is not a goal desired by the decision maker. The goal is the establishment of a tennis club. However, location is one of the Major Factors considered by Ed in his decision to build a club.

2. **(A)** Major Objective. A major goal of Ed was to convert his pastime to an income-producing business. Moreover, he wanted his wife to manage the club because he did not plan to leave his present employment as a traveling salesman. Ed's desire to have his wife manage the club is another major goal.

3. **(D)** Major Assumption. *Note the key word in the question, "likelihood."* The key word in the *passage* is "estimated." "Estimated" mirrors a belief on Ed's part that the club could be opened within six months.

4. **(E)** Unimportant Issue. Ed's age has no bearing on a desired goal, nor is it a factor in the consideration of an alternative course of action.

5. **(B)** Major Factor. Like location, size of the property is a major consideration in the selection of a particular site for the club. Size is linked to profitability. The property had to be large enough to accommodate at least three tennis courts.

6. **(D)** Major Assumption. *Note the key word, "likelihood."* Although employing Ed's wife as club manager is a major goal sought, it is stated in the passage that Ed "believed he could convince her" to take the job. There is no information given to support Ed's belief that his wife will accept the position. Therefore, whether she will accept remains an assumption.

7. **(C)** Minor Factor. Room for a snack bar is secondary to the Major Factor of size.

8. **(B)** Major Factor. *Note the first word, "time."* Time is a major consideration in the decision process. It is stated in the passage that if the club is not completed on time, Ed would not be able to repay his bank loan.

9. **(E)** Unimportant Issue. There is nothing in the passage to suggest that the existence of an option deadline played an important role in the decision process. No relationship was shown between the option and the decision to bid for the property.

10. **(E)** Unimportant Issue. There is no explicit link between Ed's *experience* as a tennis player and the business venture. A better link is his *desire* (goal) to combine a pastime with a business.

WRITING ABILITY REVIEW

As mentioned earlier, the Writing Ability part of the exam tests not writing ability but rather your understanding of the basic rules of English grammar and usage. This section is comprised of Sentence Correction questions.

You will be given a sentence in which all or part of the sentence is underlined. You will then be asked to choose the best phrasing of the underlined part from five alternatives. (A) will always be the original phrasing.

EXAMPLE:

Not having heard clearly, <u>the speaker was asked to repeat his statement</u>.

(A) the speaker was asked to repeat his statement
(B) she asked the speaker to repeat again his statement
(C) the speaker was asked to repeat his statement again
(D) she asked the speaker to repeat his statement
(E) she then asked the speaker again to repeat his statement

Answer:

(D) is the best choice.

Review of Errors Commonly Found in the Writing Ability Section

Since you need only *recognize* errors in grammar and usage for this part of the exam, this section of the book will review those errors most commonly presented in the GMAT and teach you *what to look for*. We will not review the *basic* rules of grammar, such as the formation and use of the different tenses and the passive voice, the subjective and objective cases of pronouns, the position of adjectives and adverbs, and the like. We assume that a candidate for the GMAT is familiar with basic grammar, and we will concentrate on error recognition based on that knowledge.

Verb Errors

1. Errors in Verb Tense

Check if the correct verb *tense* has been used in the sentence.

INCORRECT: When I came home, the children still didn't finish dinner.
CORRECT: When I came home, the children still <u>hadn't finished</u> dinner.

INCORRECT: As we ate dinner, the phone rang.
CORRECT: As we <u>were eating</u> dinner, the phone rang.

In REPORTED SPEECH, check that the rule of *sequence of tenses* has been observed.

INCORRECT:	She promised she will come.
CORRECT:	She promised she would come.

INCORRECT:	She said she doesn't know his phone number.
CORRECT:	She said she didn't know his phone number.

INCORRECT:	She claimed she has never been there.
CORRECT:	She claimed she had never been there.

2. Errors in Tense Formation

Check if the tense has been formed correctly. *Know* the past participle of irregular verbs!

INCORRECT:	He throwed it out the window.
CORRECT:	He threw it out the window.

INCORRECT:	Having just drank some water, I wasn't thirsty.
CORRECT:	Having just drunk some water, I wasn't thirsty.

3. Errors in Subject-Verb Agreement

Check if the subject of the verb is singular or plural. Does the verb agree in number?

Multiple subjects will be connected by the word AND:

Ted, John, and I are going.

If a singular subject is separated by a comma from an accompanying phrase, *it remains singular*:

The bride, together with the groom and her parents, is receiving at the door.

INCORRECT:	There is many reasons why I can't help you.
CORRECT:	There are many reasons why I can't help you.

INCORRECT:	Sir Lloyd, accompanied by his wife, were at the party.
CORRECT:	Sir Lloyd, accompanied by his wife, was at the party.

INCORRECT:	His mastery of several languages and the social graces make him a sought-after dinner guest.
CORRECT:	His mastery of several languages and the social graces makes him a sought-after dinner guest.

4. Errors in Conditional Sentences

In conditional sentences, the word *if* will NEVER be followed by the words *will* or *would*.

Here are the correct conditional forms:

FUTURE:	If I have time, I will do it tomorrow.
PRESENT:	If I had time, I would do it now.
PAST:	If I had had time, I would have done it yesterday.

Sentences using the words *when, as soon as, the moment*, etc., are formed like future conditionals:

I will tell him if I see him.
I will tell him when I see him.

The verb *to be* will ALWAYS appear as *were* in the present conditional:

If I <u>were</u> you, I wouldn't do that.
She wouldn't say so if she <u>weren't</u> sure.

NOTE: Not all sentences containing *if* are conditionals. When *if* appears in the meaning of *whether*, it may take the future:

I don't know <u>if</u> he <u>will be</u> there. (I don't know <u>whether</u> he will be there.)

INCORRECT: If I would have known, I wouldn't have gone.
CORRECT: If I <u>had known</u>, I wouldn't have gone.

INCORRECT: You wouldn't be so tired if you weren't going to bed so late.
CORRECT: You wouldn't be so tired if you <u>didn't go</u> to bed so late.

INCORRECT: Call me the moment you will get home.
CORRECT: Call me the moment you <u>get</u> home.

INCORRECT: We could go to the beach if it wasn't so hot.
CORRECT: We could go to the beach if it <u>weren't</u> so hot.

5. Errors in Expressions of Desire

Unfulfilled desires are expressed by the form "_____ had hoped that _____ would (or *could*, or *might*) do _____."

I <u>had hoped</u> that I <u>would pass</u> the exam.

Expressions with *wish* are formed as follows:

PRESENT: I wish I <u>knew</u> him.
FUTURE: I wish you <u>could</u> (<u>would</u>) <u>come</u>.
PAST: I wish he <u>had come</u>. (or <u>could have come</u>, <u>would have come</u>, <u>might have come</u>)

NOTE: As in conditionals, the verb *to be* will ALWAYS appear as *were* in the present: I wish she <u>were</u> here.

INCORRECT: *I wish I heard that story about him before I met him.
CORRECT: I wish I <u>had heard</u> (or <u>could have heard</u> or <u>would have heard</u>) that story about him before I met him.

INCORRECT: She wishes you will be on time.
CORRECT: She wishes you <u>could</u> (or <u>would</u>) be on time.

6. Errors in Verbs Followed by VERB WORDS

The following list consists of words and expressions that are followed by a VERB WORD (the infinitive without the *to*):

ask	prefer	requirement
demand	recommend	suggest
desire	recommendation	suggestion
insist	require	urge

It is essential/imperative/important/necessary that . . .

INCORRECT: She ignored the doctor's recommendation that she stops smoking.
CORRECT: She ignored the doctor's recommendation that she <u>stop</u> smoking.

INCORRECT: It is essential that you are on time.
CORRECT: It is essential that you <u>be</u> on time.

INCORRECT: He suggested that we should meet at the train.
CORRECT: He suggested that we <u>meet</u> at the train.

7. Errors in Negative Imperatives

Note the two forms for negative imperatives:

a. Please <u>don't do</u> that.
b. Would you please <u>not do</u> that.

INCORRECT: Would you please don't smoke here.
CORRECT: Please <u>don't smoke</u> here.
OR

Would you please <u>not smoke</u> here.

8. Errors in Affirmative and Negative Agreement of Verbs

Note the two correct forms for *affirmative* agreement:

a. <u>I am</u> an American and <u>so is she</u>.
b. <u>I am</u> an American and <u>she is too</u>.

a. <u>Mary likes</u> Bach and <u>so does John</u>.
b. <u>Mary likes</u> Bach and <u>John does too</u>.

a. <u>My father will be</u> there and <u>so will my mother</u>.
b. <u>My father will be</u> there and <u>my mother will too</u>.

INCORRECT: I have seen the film and she also has.
CORRECT: <u>I have seen</u> the film and <u>so has she</u>.
OR

<u>I have seen</u> the film and <u>she has too</u>.

Note the two correct forms for *negative* agreement:

a. I'm not American and <u>he isn't either</u>.
b. I'm not American and <u>neither is he</u>.

a. Mary doesn't like Bach and <u>John doesn't either</u>.
b. Mary doesn't like Bach and <u>neither does John</u>.

a. My father won't be there and <u>my mother won't either</u>.
b. My father won't be there and <u>neither will my mother</u>.

INCORRECT: I haven't seen the film and she hasn't neither.
CORRECT: I haven't seen the film and <u>she hasn't either</u>.
OR

I haven't seen the film and <u>neither has she</u>.

9. Errors of Infinitives or Gerunds in the Complement of Verbs

Some verbs may be followed by either an infinitive or a gerund:

I love <u>swimming</u> at night.
I love <u>to swim</u> at night.

Other verbs, however, may require either one *or* the other for idiomatic reasons. Following is a list of the more commonly used verbs in this category:

Verbs requiring an INFINITIVE:

agree	fail	intend	promise
decide	hope	learn	refuse
expect	want	plan	

Verbs requiring a GERUND:

admit	deny	quit
appreciate	enjoy	regret
avoid	finish	risk
consider	practice	stop

Phrases requiring a GERUND:

approve of	do not mind	keep on
be better off	forget about	look forward to
can't help	insist on	think about
count on	get through	think of

INCORRECT: I intend learning French next semester.
CORRECT: I intend to learn French next semester.

INCORRECT: I have stopped to smoke.
CORRECT: I have stopped smoking.

INCORRECT: We are looking forward to see you.
CORRECT: We are looking forward to seeing you.

10. Errors in Verbs Requiring HOW in the Complement

The verbs KNOW, TEACH, LEARN, and SHOW require the word *HOW* before an infinitive in the complement.

INCORRECT: She knows to drive.
CORRECT: She knows how to drive.

INCORRECT: I will teach you to sew.
CORRECT: I will teach you how to sew.

11. Errors in Tag Endings

Check for *three* things in tag endings:

a. Does the ending use the *same person* as the sentence verb?
b. Does the ending use the *same tense* as the sentence verb?
c. If the sentence verb is positive, is the ending negative; if the sentence verb is negative, is the ending positive?

It's nice here, isn't it?
It isn't nice here, is it?

She speaks French, doesn't she?
She doesn't speak French, does she?

They'll be here tomorrow, won't they?
They won't be here tomorrow, will they?

EXCEPTIONS:

I'm right, aren't I?
We ought to go, shouldn't we?
Let's see, shall we?

NOTE: If there is a contraction in the sentence verb, make sure you know what the contraction stands for:

INCORRECT: She's been there before, isn't she?
CORRECT: She's been there before, hasn't she?

INCORRECT: You'd rather go yourself, hadn't you?
CORRECT: You'd rather go yourself, wouldn't you?

12. Errors in Idiomatic Verb Expressions

Following are a few commonly used idiomatic verb expressions. Notice whether they are followed by a verb word, a participle, an infinitive, or a gerund. Memorize a sample of each to check yourself when choosing an answer:

a. *must have (done)*—meaning "it is a logical conclusion"

They're late. They must have missed the bus.
There's no answer. They must have gone out.

b. *had better* (do)—meaning "it is advisable"

It's getting cold. You had better take your coat.
He still has fever. He had better not go out yet.

c. *used to (do)*—meaning "was in the habit of doing in the past"

I used to smoke a pack of cigarettes a day, but I stopped.
When I worked on a farm, I used to get up at 4:30 in the morning.

d. *to be used to*—meaning "to be accustomed to"

to get used to
to become used to ⎫—meaning "to become accustomed to"

The noise doesn't bother me; I'm used to studying with the radio on.
In America you'll get used to hearing only English all day long.

e. *make* someone *do*—meaning "force someone to do"
have someone *do*—meaning "cause someone to do"
let someone *do*—meaning "allow someone to do"

My mother made me take my little sister with me to the movies.
The teacher had us write an essay instead of taking an exam.
The usher didn't let us come in until the intermission.

f. *would rather*—meaning "would prefer"

I would rather speak to her myself.
I would rather not speak to her myself.

But if the preference is for someone *other than the subject* to do the action, use the PAST:

I would rather you spoke to her.
I would rather you didn't speak to her.

Pronoun Errors

1. Errors in Pronoun Subject-Object

Check if a pronoun is the SUBJECT or the OBJECT of a verb or preposition.

INCORRECT: All of us—Fred, Jane, Alice, and me—were late.
CORRECT: All of us—Fred, Jane, Alice, and I—were late.

INCORRECT: How could she blame you and he for the accident?
CORRECT: How could she blame you and him for the accident?

2. Errors with WHO and WHOM

When in doubt about the correctness of WHO/WHOM, try substituting the subject/object of a simpler pronoun to clarify the meaning:

I don't know who/whom Sarah meant.

Try substituting *he/him*; then rearrange the clause in its proper order:

he/him Sarah meant / Sarah meant him

Now it is clear that the pronoun is the *object* of the verb *meant*, so *whom* is called for.

CORRECT: I don't know whom Sarah meant.

ANOTHER EXAMPLE:

There was a discussion as to who/whom was better suited.

Try substituting *she/her*:

she was better suited / her was better suited

Here the pronoun is the *subject* of the verb *suited*:

CORRECT: There was a discussion as to who was better suited.

3. Errors of Pronoun Subject-Verb Agreement

Check if the pronoun and its verb agree in number. Remember that the following are *singular*:

anyone	either	neither	what
anything	everyone	no one	whatever
each	everything	nothing	whoever

These are *plural*:

both	many	several	others
few			

INCORRECT: John is absent, but a few of the class is here.
CORRECT: John is absent, but a few of the class are here.

| INCORRECT: | Everyone on the project have to come to the meeting. |
| CORRECT: | Everyone on the project has to come to the meeting. |

| INCORRECT: | Either of those dresses are suitable for the party. |
| CORRECT: | Either of those dresses is suitable for the party. |

| INCORRECT: | Neither of them are experts on the subject. |
| CORRECT: | Neither of them is an expert on the subject. |

NOTE: The forms "either . . . or" and "neither . . . nor" are singular and take a singular verb. For reasons of diction, however, if the noun immediately preceding the verb is plural, use a plural verb. An English speaker finds it difficult to pronounce a singular verb after a plural subject, as in ". . . they is coming," even though "they" is preceded by "Neither he nor . . ."

Either his parents or he is bringing it.
Either he or his parents are bringing it.

Neither his parents nor he was there.
Neither he nor his parents were there.

4. Errors of Possessive Pronoun Agreement

Check if possessive pronouns agree in *person* and *number*.

| INCORRECT: | If anyone calls, take their name. |
| CORRECT: | If anyone calls, take his name. |

| INCORRECT: | Those of us who care should write to their congressman. |
| CORRECT: | Those of us who care should write to our congressman. |

| INCORRECT: | Some of you will have to come in their own cars. |
| CORRECT: | Some of you will have to come in your own cars. |

5. Errors in Pronouns after the Verb TO BE

TO BE is an intransitive verb and will always be followed by a subject pronoun.

| INCORRECT: | It must have been her at the door. |
| CORRECT: | It must have been she at the door. |

| INCORRECT: | I wish I were him! |
| CORRECT: | I wish I were he! |

| INCORRECT: | He didn't know that it was me who did it. |
| CORRECT: | He didn't know that it was I who did it. |

6. Errors in Position of Relative Pronouns

A relative pronoun refers to the word preceding it. If the meaning is unclear, the pronoun is in the wrong position.

| INCORRECT: | He could park right in front of the door, which was very convenient. |

Since it was not the door which was convenient, the "which" is illogical in this position. In order to correct the sentence, it is necessary to rewrite it completely:

| CORRECT: | His being allowed to park right in front of the door was very convenient. |

INCORRECT: The traffic was very heavy, which made me late.
CORRECT: I was late because of the heavy traffic.
OR
The heavy traffic made me late.

7. Errors in Parallelism of Impersonal Pronouns

In forms using impersonal pronouns, use *either* "one . . . one's/his or her" *or* "you . . . your."

INCORRECT: One should take your duties seriously.
CORRECT: One should take one's/ his or her duties seriously.
OR
You should take your duties seriously.

INCORRECT: One should have their blood pressure checked regularly.
CORRECT: One should have one's/ his or her blood pressure checked regularly.
OR
You should have your blood pressure checked regularly.

Adjective and Adverb Errors

1. Errors in the Use of Adjectives and Adverbs

Check if a word modifier is an ADJECTIVE or an ADVERB. Make sure the correct form has been used.

An ADJECTIVE describes a noun and answers the question, *What kind*?

She is a good cook. (What kind of cook?)

An ADVERB describes either a verb or an adjective and answers the question, *How*?

She cooks well. (She cooks how?)
This exercise is relatively easy. (How easy?)

Most adverbs are formed by adding *-ly* to the adjective.

EXCEPTIONS:	
Adjective	*Adverb*
early	early
fast	fast
good	well
hard	hard (*hardly* means *almost not*)
late	late (*lately* means *recently*)

INCORRECT: I sure wish I were rich!
CORRECT: I surely wish I were rich!

INCORRECT: The young man writes bad.
CORRECT: The young man writes badly.

INCORRECT: He's a real good teacher.
CORRECT: He's a really good teacher.

2. Errors of Adjectives with Verbs of Sense

The following verbs of sense are intransitive and are described by ADJECTIVES:

be	look	smell	taste
feel	seem	sound	

INCORRECT: She looked very well.
CORRECT: She looked very good.

NOTE: "He is well" is also correct in the meaning of "He is healthy" or in describing a person's well-being.

INCORRECT: The food tastes deliciously.
CORRECT: The food tastes delicious.

NOTE: When the above verbs are used as transitive verbs, modify with an adverb, as usual: She tasted the soup quickly.

3. Errors in Comparatives

a. Similar comparison

ADJECTIVE: She is as pretty as her sister.
ADVERB: He works as hard as his father.

b. Comparative (of two things)

ADJECTIVE: She is prettier than her sister.
She is more beautiful than her sister.
She is less successful than her sister.

ADVERB: He works harder than his father.
He reads more quickly than I.
He drives less carelessly than he used to

NOTE 1: A pronoun following *than* in a comparison will be the *subject pronoun*:

You are prettier than she (is).
You drive better than he (does).

NOTE 2: In using comparisons, adjectives of one syllable, or of two syllables ending in -y, add -er: smart, smarter; pretty, prettier. Other words of more than one syllable use *more*: interesting, more interesting. Adverbs of one syllable add -er; longer adverbs use *more*: fast, faster; quickly, more quickly.

NOTE 3: The word *different* is followed by *from*:

You are different from me.

c. Superlative (comparison of more than two things)

ADJECTIVE: She is the prettiest girl in her class.
He is the most successful of his brothers.
This one is the least interesting of the three.

ADVERB: He plays the best of all.
He speaks the most interestingly.
He spoke to them the least patronizingly.

EXCEPTIONAL FORMS:

good	better	best
bad	worse	worst
much/many	more	most
little	less	least

INCORRECT: This exercise is harder then the last one.
CORRECT: This exercise is harder than the last one.

INCORRECT: He works faster than her.
CORRECT: He works faster than she.

INCORRECT: She is the more responsible person of the three.
CORRECT: She is the most responsible person of the three.

INCORRECT: She was much different than I expected.
CORRECT: She was much different from what I expected.

INCORRECT: This year I'll have littler free time.
CORRECT: This year I'll have less free time.

4. Errors in Parallel Comparisons

In parallel comparisons, check if the correct form has been used.

INCORRECT: The more you practice, you will get better.
CORRECT: The more you practice, the better you will get.

INCORRECT: The earlier we leave, we will get there earlier.
CORRECT: The earlier we leave, the earlier we will get there.

INCORRECT: The busier you become, lesser time you have for reading.
CORRECT: The busier you become, the less time you have for reading.

5. Errors of Illogical Comparatives

Check comparisons to make sure they *make sense*.

INCORRECT: Texas is bigger than any state in the United States.
CORRECT: Texas is bigger than any other state in the United States. (If Texas were bigger than *any state*, it would be bigger than itself!)

INCORRECT: That is the most important of any other reason.
CORRECT: That is the most important reason.

INCORRECT: Of the two books, this one is best.
CORRECT: Of the two books, this one is better.

6. Errors of Identical Comparisons

Something can be *the same as* OR *like* something else. Do not mix up the two forms.

INCORRECT: Your dress is the same like mine.
CORRECT: Your dress is like mine.

OR

Your dress is the same as mine.

7. Errors in Idioms Using Comparative Structures

Some idiomatic terms are formed like comparatives, although they are not true comparisons:

as high as	as much as	as few as
as little as	as many as	

INCORRECT: You may have to spend so much as two hours waiting.
CORRECT: You may have to spend as much as two hours waiting.

INCORRECT: It cost twice more than I thought it would.
CORRECT: It cost twice as much as I thought it would.

8. Errors in Noun-Adjectives

When a NOUN is used as an ADJECTIVE, treat it as an adjective. Do not pluralize or add 's.

INCORRECT: You're talking like a two-years-old child!
CORRECT: You're talking like a two-year-old child!

9. Errors in Ordinal and Cardinal Numbers

Ordinal numbers (first, second, third, etc.) are preceded by *the*. Cardinal numbers (one, two, three, etc.) are not.

We missed the first act.
We missed Act One.

NOTE: Ordinarily, either form is correct. There are two exceptions:

a. In *dates* use only *ordinal* numbers:
   May first (*not* May one)
   the first of May

b. In terms dealing with *travel*, use only *cardinal* numbers, as "Gate Three" may not actually be the third gate. It is Gate Number Three.

INCORRECT: We leave from the second pier.
CORRECT: We leave from Pier Two.

INCORRECT: His birthday is on February twenty-two.
CORRECT: His birthday is on February twenty-second.

10. Errors in Modifying Countable and Noncountable Nouns

If a noun can be preceded by a number, it is a countable noun and will be modified by these words:

a few	many, more	some
few, fewer	number of	

If it cannot be preceded by a number, it is noncountable and will be modified by these words:

amount of	little, less	some
a little	much, more	

INCORRECT: I was surprised by the large amount of people who came.
CORRECT: I was surprised by the large number of people who came.

INCORRECT: You need only a little eggs in this recipe.
CORRECT: You need only a few eggs in this recipe.

Errors in Usage

1. Errors in Connectors

There are several ways of connecting ideas. Do not mix the different forms:

and	also	not only . . . but also
too	as well as	both . . . and

INCORRECT: She speaks not only Spanish but French as well.
CORRECT: She speaks Spanish and French.
              She speaks Spanish. She also speaks French.
              She speaks Spanish and French too.
              She speaks not only Spanish but also French.
              She speaks both Spanish and French.
              She speaks Spanish as well as French.

2. Errors in Question Word Connectors

When a question word such as *when* or *what* is used as a connector, the clause that follows is *not* a question. Do not use the interrogative form.

INCORRECT: Do you know when does the movie start?
CORRECT: Do you know when the movie starts?

INCORRECT: I don't know what is his name.
CORRECT: I don't know what his name is.

INCORRECT: Did he tell you why hasn't he come yet?
CORRECT: Did he tell you why he hasn't come yet?

3. Errors in Purpose Connectors

The word *so* by itself means *therefore.*

It was too hot to study, so we went to the beach.

So that means *in order to* or *in order that.*

INCORRECT: We took a cab so we would be on time.
CORRECT: We took a cab so that we would be on time.

4. Errors with BECAUSE

It is incorrect to say: *The reason is because* . . . Use: *The reason is that* . . .

INCORRECT: The reason he was rejected was because he was too young.
CORRECT: The reason he was rejected was that he was too young.
                        OR
              He was rejected because of his young age.
                        OR
              He was rejected because he was too young.

5. Errors of Dangling Modifiers

An introductory verbal modifier should be directly followed by the noun or pronoun which it modifies. Such a modifier will start with a gerund or participial phrase and be followed by a comma. Look for the modified noun or pronoun *immediately* after the comma.

INCORRECT: Seeing that the hour was late, it was decided to postpone the committee vote.

CORRECT: Seeing that the hour was late, the committee decided to postpone the vote.

INCORRECT: Unaccustomed to getting up early, it was difficult for him to get to work on time.

CORRECT: Unaccustomed to getting up early, he found it difficult to get to work on time.

INCORRECT: Wanting to get feedback, a questionnaire was handed out to the audience.

CORRECT: Since the speaker wanted to get feedback, he handed out a questionnaire to the audience.

6. Errors in Parallel Construction

In sentences containing a series of two or more items, check if the same form has been used for all the items in the series. Do *not* mix infinitives with gerunds, adjectives with participial phrases, or verbs with nouns.

INCORRECT: The film was interesting, exciting, and it was made well.

CORRECT: The film was interesting, exciting, and well made.

INCORRECT: The purpose of the meeting is to introduce new members and raising money.

CORRECT: The purpose of the meeting is to introduce new members and to raise money.

> OR

The purpose of the meeting is introducing new members and raising money.

INCORRECT: He died unloved, unknown, and without any money.

CORRECT: He died unloved, unknown, and penniless.

INCORRECT: He was popular because of his sense of humor, his intelligence, and he could get along with people.

CORRECT: He was popular because of his sense of humor, his intelligence, and his ability to get along with people.

> OR

He was popular because he had a sense of humor, was intelligent, and could get along with people.

7. Errors of Unnecessary Modifiers

In general, the more simply an idea is stated, the better it is. An adverb or adjective can often eliminate extraneous words.

INCORRECT: He drove in a careful way.

CORRECT: He drove carefully.

INCORRECT: The problem was difficult and delicate in nature.

CORRECT: It was a difficult, delicate problem.

Beware of words with the same meaning in the same sentence.

INCORRECT: The new innovations were startling.

CORRECT: The innovations were startling.

INCORRECT: Would you please repeat again what you said?
CORRECT: Would you please repeat what you said?

INCORRECT: He left more richer than when he came.
CORRECT: He left richer than when he came.

Beware of general wordiness.

INCORRECT: That depends on the state of the general condition of the situation.
CORRECT: That depends on the situation.

8. Errors of Commonly Confused Words

Following are some of the more commonly misused words in English:

a. **to lie** lied lied lying to tell an untruth
   to lie lay lain lying to recline
   to lay laid laid laying to put down (*Idiomatic* usage: LAY THE TABLE, put dishes, etc., on the table; CHICKENS LAY EGGS; LAY A BET, make a bet)

b. **to rise** rose risen rising to go up; to get up
   to arise arose arisen arising to wake up; to get up (*Idiomatic* usage: A PROBLEM HAS ARISEN, a problem has come up)
   to raise raised raised raising to lift; bring up (*Idiomatic* usage: TO RAISE CHILDREN, to bring up children; TO RAISE VEGETABLES, to grow vegetables; TO RAISE MONEY, to collect funds for a cause)

c. **to set** set set setting to put down (*Idiomatic* usage: SET A DATE, arrange a date; SET THE TABLE, put dishes, etc., on the table; THE SUN SET, the sun went down for the night; TO SET THE CLOCK, to adjust the timing mechanism of a clock)
   to sit sat sat sitting to be in or get into a sitting position

d. **to let** let let letting to allow; to rent
   to leave left left leaving to go away

e. **formerly**—previously
   formally—in a formal way

f. **to affect**—to influence (verb)
   effect—result (noun)

INCORRECT: He was laying in bed all day yesterday.
CORRECT: He was lying in bed all day yesterday.

INCORRECT: It had laid in the closet for a week before we found it.
CORRECT: It had lain in the closet for a week before we found it.

INCORRECT: The price of gas has raised three times last year.
CORRECT: The price of gas <u>rose</u> three times last year.
OR
The price of gas <u>was raised</u> three times last year.

INCORRECT: He raised slowly from his chair.
CORRECT: He <u>arose</u> slowly from his chair.

INCORRECT: We just set around the house all day.
CORRECT: We just <u>sat</u> around the house all day.

INCORRECT: His mother wouldn't leave him go with us.
CORRECT: His mother wouldn't <u>let</u> him go with us.

INCORRECT: All the men were dressed formerly.
CORRECT: All the men were dressed <u>formally</u>.

INCORRECT: My words had no affect on him.
CORRECT: My words had no <u>effect</u> on him.

9. Errors of Misused Words and Prepositional Idioms

a. in spite of; despite

The two expressions are synonymous; use *either* one *or* the other.

INCORRECT: They came despite of the rain.
CORRECT: They came <u>in spite of</u> the rain.
OR
They came <u>despite</u> the rain.

b. scarcely; barely; hardly

All three words mean *almost not at all*; do NOT use a negative with them.

INCORRECT: I hardly never see him.
CORRECT: I <u>hardly ever</u> see him.

INCORRECT: He has scarcely no money.
CORRECT: He has <u>scarcely any</u> money.

c. Note and memorize the prepositions in these common idioms:

approve/disapprove <u>of</u>	be bored <u>with</u>
be ashamed <u>of</u>	agree/disagree <u>with</u>
capable/incapable <u>of</u>	compare <u>to</u> (point out similarities
be conscious <u>of</u>	between things of a different order)
be afraid <u>of</u>	compare <u>with</u> (point out differences between
independent <u>of</u>	things of the same order)
in the habit <u>of</u>	be equal <u>to</u>
be interested <u>in</u>	next <u>to</u>
except <u>for</u>	related <u>to</u>
dependent <u>on</u>	similar <u>to</u>

d. Confusion of words that *sound alike*:

1. **adapt**—to change, to adjust
   adept—skilled
2. **advice**—counsel (n.)
   advise—to give advice (v.)

3. **affect**—to influence (v.)
   effect—result (n.)
4. **afflicted**—stricken
   inflicted—caused or imposed something negative
5. **affront**—to insult
   confront—to face
6. **alteration**—a change
   altercation—argument
7. **allude**—to refer to indirectly
   elude—to evade
8. **allusion**—a reference to
   illusion—unreal image
   delusion—false belief
9. **apprise**—to let know
   appraise—to estimate the value of
10. **beside**—near
    besides—in addition
11. **capital**—money; punishable by death; large form of letter
    Capitol—the U.S. house of legislature
12. **caret**—a mark used in proofreading
    carat—unit of gem weight
    carrot—an orange vegetable
13. **censor**—one who screens objectionable material
    censure—condemnation
14. **cite**—to quote
    sight—vision
    site—location
15. **coherent**—intelligible
    inherent—a naturally included quality
16. **collaborate**—to work together
    corroborate—to confirm
17. **command**—to order
    commend—to praise
18. **compile**—to collect
    comply—to consent
19. **complement**—to make complete
    compliment—to praise
20. **continual**—happening often
    continuous—happening uninterruptedly
21. **conscientious**—diligent
    conscious—aware; awake
22. **credible**—believable
    creditable—worthy of credit or praise
    credulous—believing anything
23. **depredation**—a robbing
    deprecation—disapproval
24. **detain**—to keep or hold up
    retain—to keep in possession; to remember
25. **detracted**—taken away from
    distracted—diverted
26. **devise**—to create
    revise—to change; to improve
27. **devolve**—to deliver from one possessor to another
    evolve—to develop
28. **discouraging**—seeming to be with no chance of success
    disparaging—belittling

29. **disinterested**—having nothing personal to gain; impartial
    uninterested—having no interest in
30. **elegant**—graceful; refined; with good taste
    eloquent—persuasive; fluent (speech or writing)
31. **elicit**—to draw out
    illicit—unlawful
32. **emigrant**—one who leaves a country to settle in another
    immigrant—one who comes to a new country to settle
33. **eminent**—famous; prominent
    imminent—impending
    immanent—universal
34. **epaulet**—a shoulder decoration (usually on a uniform)
    epithet—a descriptive word or phrase
35. **epic**—a long poem dealing with heroic deeds
    epoch—a period of time marked by noteworthy people or events
36. **flouting**—scorning
    flaunting—showing off provocatively
37. **foreword**—introduction to a book
    forward—toward the front
38. **gorilla**—an ape
    guerrilla—a soldier of the underground
39. **horde**—a crowd
    hoard—to store up a supply
40. **human**—belonging to the race of man
    humane—kind
41. **immoral**—without a sense of morality
    immortal—able to live forever
42. **imply**—to hint
    infer—to conclude from a known fact
43. **in**—within
    inn—a pub or hostel
44. **incandescent**—glowing
    clandestine—secret
45. **incite**—to urge to action
    insight—quality of perceptiveness
46. **incorporate**—to include; to merge
    incarcerate—to imprison
47. **incredible**—unbelievable
    incredulous—doubting
48. **ingenious**—clever
    ingenuous—frank
49. **irrelevant**—having no bearing on a matter
    irreverent—lacking respect
50. **loath**—reluctant
    loathe—to hate
51. **luxuriant**—growing thickly; highly ornamented
    luxurious—rich; having an aura of wealth
52. **perpetuate**—to cause to continue
    perpetrate—to do (something evil)
53. **persecute**—to afflict constantly in order to injure
    prosecute—to institute legal proceedings against
54. **personal**—private
    personnel—employees
55. **perspective**—appearance as determined by distance and position
    prospective—likely

56. **precede**—to come before
    proceed—to continue
57. **prescribe**—to order; to advise (as medicine)
    proscribe—to outlaw
58. **principal**—the amount of a debt; the head of a school
    principle—a fundamental law
59. **profuse**—excessive
    profess—to declare
60. **prophecy**—prediction (n.)
    prophesy—to predict (v.)
61. **relay**—to convey; a race between teams
    relate—to tell; to connect
62. **repel**—to reject
    repeal—to cancel
63. **respectful**—showing regard for
    respective—particular
64. **rightly**—with good reason
    rightfully—having a lawful claim
    righteously—acting in a virtuous way
65. **ruminating**—meditating
    fulminating—shouting
    culminating—ending
66. **sensual**—of the body
    sensuous—appealing to the senses
67. **staple**—basic commodity; a pin holding papers together
    stable—firm; a shed for horses
68. **stationary**—immobile
    stationery—writing materials
69. **supplement**—to add to something
    supplant—to forcefully replace
70. **temerity**—boldness
    timidity—shyness
71. **their**—belonging to them
    there—in that place
    they're—they are
72. **troop**—a group of people
    troupe—a company of singers, dancers, or actors
73. **weigh**—to measure the weight of
    way—road
    whey—a part of milk that is separated from the curds in cheese making
74. **weather**—atmospheric conditions
    whether—if
75. **wholesome**—healthful
    fulsome—disgusting because of excessiveness

Strategy for Sentence Correction Questions

A. Sentence Correction

The first step in the Writing Ability part of the exam is to read the sentence carefully in order to spot an error of grammar or usage. Once you have found an error, eliminate choice (A) and ALL OTHER ALTERNATIVES CONTAINING THAT ERROR. Concentrate on the remaining alternatives to choose your answer. Do not select an alternative that has changed the *meaning* of the original sentence.

EXAMPLE 1:

1. Ⓐ Ⓑ Ⓒ Ⓓ Ⓔ   If I knew him better, I would have insisted that he change the hour of the lecture.

(A) I would have insisted that he change
(B) I would have insisted that he changed
(C) I would insist that he change
(D) I would insist for him to change
(E) I would have insisted him to change

Since we must assume the unmarked part of the sentence to be correct, this is a PRESENT CONDITIONAL sentence; therefore, the second verb in the sentence should read *I would insist*. Glancing through the alternatives, you can eliminate (A), (B), and (E). You are left with (C) and (D). Remember that the word *insist* takes a *verb word* after it. (C) is the only correct answer.

If you do not find any grammatical error in the underlined part, read the alternatives to see if one of them does not use a clearer or more concise style to express the same thing. Do not choose an alternative that changes the meaning of the original sentence.

EXAMPLE 2:

2. Ⓐ Ⓑ Ⓒ Ⓓ Ⓔ   The couple, who had been married recently, booked their honeymoon passage through an agent who lived near them.

(A) The couple, who had been married recently, booked their honeymoon passage through an agent who lived near them.
(B) The couple, who had been recently married, booked their honeymoon passage through an agent who lived not far from them.
(C) The newlyweds booked their honeymoon passage through a local agent.
(D) The newlyweds booked their passage through an agent that lived not far from them.
(E) The couple lived not far from the agent who through him they booked their passage.

Although (A), the original, has no real errors, (C) expresses the same thing more concisely, without distorting the original meaning of the sentence.

Remember: If you find no errors, and if you find that none of the alternatives improve the original, choose (A).

Practice Exercise

DIRECTIONS: This exercise consists of a number of sentences, in each of which some part or the whole is underlined. Each sentence is followed by five alternative versions of the underlined portion. Select the alternative you consider both most correct and most effective according to the requirements of standard written English. Answer (A) is the same as the original version; if you think the original version is best, select answer (A).

In considering the answer choices, be attentive to matters of grammar, diction, and syntax, as well as clarity, precision, and fluency. Do not select an answer which alters the meaning of the original sentence.

1. Ⓐ Ⓑ Ⓒ Ⓓ Ⓔ   **1.** A good doctor inquires not only about his patients' physical health, but about their mental health too.

(A) but about their mental health too
(B) but their mental health also
(C) but also he inquires about their mental health
(D) but also about their mental health
(E) but too about their mental health

2. <u>Knowing that the area was prone to earthquakes</u>, all the buildings were reinforced   2. Ⓐ Ⓑ Ⓒ Ⓓ Ⓔ
with additional steel and concrete.

   (A) Knowing that the area was prone to earthquakes,
   (B) Having known that the area was prone to earthquakes,
   (C) Since the area was known to be prone to earthquakes,
   (D) Since they knew that the area was prone to earthquakes,
   (E) Being prone to earthquakes,

3. John would never have taken the job <u>if he had known</u> what great demands it would   3. Ⓐ Ⓑ Ⓒ Ⓓ Ⓔ
make on his time.

   (A) if he had known
   (B) if he knew
   (C) if he had been knowing
   (D) if he knows
   (E) if he was knowing

4. Anyone wishing to enroll in the program should <u>send in their applications</u> before the   4. Ⓐ Ⓑ Ⓒ Ⓓ Ⓔ
fifteenth of the month.

   (A) send in their applications
   (B) send their applications in
   (C) send in their application
   (D) send their application in
   (E) send in his application

5. Start the actual writing only after having thoroughly researched your subject, organ-   5. Ⓐ Ⓑ Ⓒ Ⓓ Ⓔ
ized your notes, and <u>you have planned an outline</u>.

   (A) you have planned an outline
   (B) planned an outline
   (C) you having planned an outline
   (D) an outline has been planned
   (E) an outline was planned

Answers and Analysis

  1. **(D)** The connective *not only* MUST be accompanied by *but also*. Eliminate (A), (B),
and (E). (C) repeats *he inquires* unnecessarily. (D) is correct.

  2. **(C)** *All the buildings* couldn't have known that the area was prone to earthquakes.
Since the unmarked part of the sentence must be assumed to be correct, eliminate
all alternatives beginning with a dangling modifier: (A), (B), and (E). In (D) the word
they is unclear. Where there is no definite subject, the passive is preferable. (C) is
correct.

  3. **(A)** This is a past conditional sentence. (A) is correct.

  4. **(E)** *Anyone* is singular. At one glance eliminate every choice but (E).

  5. **(B)** Here is a series of three verbs: having *researched, organized,* and *planned.* (B)
is correct.

MATHEMATICS REVIEW FOR THE PROBLEM SOLVING AND DATA SUFFICIENCY SECTIONS

The Problem Solving and Data Sufficiency areas of the GMAT require a working knowledge of mathematical principles, including an understanding of the fundamentals of algebra, geometry, and arithmetic, and the ability to interpret graphs. The following review covers these areas thoroughly and if used properly, will prove helpful in preparing for the mathematical parts of the GMAT.

Read through the review carefully. You will notice that each topic is keyed for easy reference. Use the key number next to each answer given in the Sample Tests to refer to those sections in the review that cover material you may have missed and therefore will need to spend more time on.

I. Arithmetic

I-1. Whole Numbers

1-1

The numbers 0,1,2,3, . . . are called whole numbers or *integers*. So 75 is an integer but 4⅓ is not an integer.

1-2

If the integer k divides m evenly, then we say m *is divisible by k* or *is a factor of m*. For example, 12 is divisible by 4, but 12 is not divisible by 5. 1,2,3,4,6,12 are all factors of 12.

If k is a factor of m, then there is another integer n such that $m = k \times n$; in this case, m is called a *multiple of k*.

Since $12 = 4 \times 3$, 12 is a multiple of 4 and also 12 is a multiple of 3. 5,10,15, and 20 are all multiples of 5 but 15 and 5 are not multiples of 10.

Any integer is a multiple of each of its factors.

1-3

Any whole number is divisible by itself and by 1. If p is a whole number greater than 1, which has *only p* and 1 as factors, then p is called a *prime number*. 2,3,5,7,11,13,17,19 and 23 are all primes. 14 is not a prime since it is divisible by 2 and by 7.

A whole number which is divisible by 2 is called an *even* number; if a whole number is not even, then it is an *odd* number. 2,4,6,8,10 are even numbers, and 1,3,5,7 and 9 are odd numbers.

A collection of numbers is *consecutive* if each number is the successor of the number which precedes it. For example, 7,8,9 and 10 are consecutive, but 7,8,10,13 are not. 4,6,8,10 are consecutive even numbers. 7,11,13,17 are consecutive primes. 7,13,19,23 are not consecutive primes since 11 is a prime between 7 and 13.

1–4

> Any whole number can be written as a product of factors which are prime numbers.

To write a number as a *product of prime factors:*

(A) Divide the number by 2 if possible; continue to divide by 2 until the factor you get is not divisible by 2.

(B) Divide the result from (A) by 3 if possible; continue to divide by 3 until the factor you get is not divisible by 3.

(C) Divide the result from (B) by 5 if possible; continue to divide by 5 until the factor you get is not divisible by 5.

(D) Continue the procedure with 7,11, and so on, until all the factors are primes.

EXAMPLE 1:   Express 24 as a product of prime factors.

(A) $24 = 2 \times 12$, $12 = 2 \times 6$, $6 = 2 \times 3$ so $24 = 2 \times 2 \times 2 \times 3$. Since each factor (2 and 3) is prime, $24 = 2 \times 2 \times 2 \times 3$.

EXAMPLE 2:   Express 252 as a product of primes.

(A) $252 = 2 \times 126$, $126 = 2 \times 63$ and 63 is not divisible by 2, so $252 = 2 \times 2 \times 63$.

(B) $63 = 3 \times 21$, $21 = 3 \times 7$ and 7 is not divisible by 3. Since 7 is a prime, then $252 = 2 \times 2 \times 3 \times 3 \times 7$ and all the factors are primes.

EXAMPLE 3:   A class of 45 students will sit in rows with the same number of students in each row. Each row must contain at least 2 students and there must be at least 2 rows. A row is parallel to the front of the room. How many different arrangements are possible?

Since $45 = $ (the number of rows)(the number of students per row), the question can be answered by finding how many different ways to write 45 as a product of two positive integers each of which is larger than 1. (The integers must be larger than 1 since there must be at least 2 rows and at least 2 students per row.) So write 45 as a product of primes $45 = 3 \times 15 = 3 \times 3 \times 5$. Therefore 3×15, 5×9, 9×5, and 15×3 are the only possibilities. So the correct answer is 4. The fact that a row is parallel to the front of the room means that 3×15 and 15×3 are different arrangements.

1–5

A number m is a *common multiple* of two others numbers k and j if it is a multiple of each of them. For example, 12 is a common multiple of 4 and 6, since $3 \times 4 = 12$ and $2 \times 6 = 12$. 15 is not a common multiple of 3 and 6, because 15 is not a multiple of 6.

A number k is a *common factor* of two other numbers m and n if k is a factor of m and k is a factor of n.

The *least common multiple* (L.C.M.) of two numbers is the smallest number which is a common multiple of both numbers. To find the least common multiple of two numbers k and j:

(A) Write k as a product of primes and j as a product of primes.
(B) If there are any common factors *delete* them in *one* of the products.
(C) Multiply the remaining factors; the result is the least common multiple.

EXAMPLE 1:   Find the L.C.M. of 12 and 11.

(A) $12 = 2 \times 2 \times 3, 11 = 11 \times 1$.
(B) There are no common factors.
(C) The L.C.M. is $12 \times 11 = 132$.

EXAMPLE 2:   Find the L.C.M. of 27 and 63.

(A) $27 = 3 \times 3 \times 3, 63 = 3 \times 3 \times 7$.
(B) $3 \times 3 = 9$ is a common factor so delete it once.
(C) The L.C.M. is $3 \times 3 \times 3 \times 7 = 189$.

You can find the L.C.M. of a collection of numbers in the same way except that if in step (B) the common factors are factors of more than two of the numbers, then delete the common factor in *all but one* of the products.

EXAMPLE 3:   Find the L.C.M. of 27, 63 and 72.

(A) $27 = 3 \times 3 \times 3, 63 = 3 \times 3 \times 7, 72 = 2 \times 2 \times 2 \times 3 \times 3$.
(B) Delete 3×3 from two of the products.
(C) The L.C.M. is $3 \times 7 \times 2 \times 2 \times 2 \times 3 \times 3 = 21 \times 72 = 1,512$.

I–2.   Fractions

2–1

A FRACTION is a number which represents a ratio or division of two whole numbers (integers). A fraction is written in the form $\frac{a}{b}$. The number on the top, a, is called the numerator; the number on the bottom, b, is called the denominator. The denominator tells how many equal parts there are (for example, parts of a pie); the numerator tells how many of these equal parts are taken. For example, $\frac{5}{8}$ is a fraction whose numerator is 5 and whose denominator is 8; it represents taking 5 of 8 equal parts, or dividing 8 into 5.

A fraction cannot have 0 as a denominator since division by 0 is not defined.

A fraction with 1 as the denominator is the same as the whole number which is its numerator. For example, $\frac{12}{1}$ is 12, $\frac{0}{1}$ is 0.

If the numerator and denominator of a fraction are identical, the fraction represents 1. For example, $\frac{3}{3} = \frac{9}{9} = \frac{13}{13} = 1$. Any whole number, k, is represented by a fraction with a numerator equal to k times the denominator. For example, $\frac{18}{6} = 3$, and $\frac{30}{5} = 6$.

2-2

Mixed Numbers. A mixed number consists of a whole number and a fraction. For example, $7\frac{1}{4}$ is a mixed number; it means $7 + \frac{1}{4}$ and $\frac{1}{4}$ is called the fractional part of the mixed number $7\frac{1}{4}$. Any mixed number can be changed into a fraction:

(A) Multiply the whole number by the denominator of the fractional part.
(B) Add the numerator of the fraction to the result of step A.
(C) Use the result of step B as the numerator and use the denominator of the fractional part of the mixed number as the denominator. This fraction is equal to the mixed number.

EXAMPLE 1: Write $7\frac{1}{4}$ as a fraction.

(A) $4 \cdot 7 = 28$
(B) $28 + 1 = 29$
(C)   so $7\frac{1}{4} = \frac{29}{4}$.

A fraction whose numerator is larger than its denominator can be changed into a mixed number.

(A) Divide the denominator into the numerator; the result is the whole number of the mixed number.
(B) Put the remainder from step A over the denominator; this is the fractional part of the mixed number.

EXAMPLE 2: Change $\frac{35}{8}$ into a mixed number.

(A) Divide 8 into 35; the result is 4 with a remainder of 3.

(B) $\frac{3}{8}$ is the fractional part of the mixed number.

(C) So $\frac{35}{8} = 4\frac{3}{8}$.

We can regard any whole number as a mixed number with 0 as the fractional part. For example, $\frac{18}{6} = 3$.

In calculations with mixed numbers, change the mixed numbers into fractions.

2-3

Multiplying Fractions. To multiply two fractions, multiply their numerators and divide this result by the product of their denominators.

> In word problems, *of* usually indicates multiplication.

EXAMPLE: John saves $\frac{1}{3}$ of $240. How much does he save?

$$\frac{1}{3} \cdot \frac{240}{1} = \frac{240}{3} = \$80,\text{ the amount John saves.}$$

2-4

Dividing Fractions. One fraction is a *reciprocal* of another if their product is 1. So $\frac{1}{2}$ and 2 are reciprocals. To find the reciprocal of a fraction, simply interchange the numerator and denominator (turn the fraction upside down). This is called *inverting* the fraction. So when you invert $\frac{15}{17}$ you get $\frac{17}{15}$. When a fraction is inverted the inverted fraction and the original fraction are reciprocals. Thus $\frac{15}{17} \cdot \frac{17}{15} = \frac{255}{255} = \frac{1}{1} = 1$.

To divide one fraction (the dividend) by another fraction (the divisor), invert the divisor and multiply.

EXAMPLE 1: $\frac{5}{6} \div \frac{3}{4} = \frac{5}{6} \cdot \frac{4}{3} = \frac{20}{18}$

EXAMPLE 2: A worker makes a basket every $\frac{2}{3}$ hour. If the worker works for $7\frac{1}{2}$ hours, how many baskets will he make?

We want to divide $\frac{2}{3}$ into $7\frac{1}{2}$, and $7\frac{1}{2} = \frac{15}{2}$, so we want to divide $\frac{15}{2}$ by $\frac{2}{3}$.

Thus $\frac{15}{2} \div \frac{2}{3} = \frac{15}{2} \cdot \frac{3}{2} = \frac{45}{4} = 11\frac{1}{4}$ baskets.

2-5

Dividing and Multiplying by the Same Number. Since multiplication or division by 1 does not change the value of a number, you can multiply or divide any fraction by 1 and the fraction will remain the same. Remember that $\frac{a}{a} = 1$ for any nonzero number a. Therefore, if you multiply or divide any fraction by $\frac{a}{a}$, the result is the same as if you multiplied the numerator and denominator by a or divided the numerator and denominator by a.

If you multiply the numerator and denominator of a fraction by the same nonzero number the fraction remains the same.

If you divide the numerator and denominator of any fraction by the same nonzero number, the fraction remains the same.

Consider the fraction $\frac{3}{4}$. If we multiply 3 by 10 and 4 by 10, then $\frac{30}{40}$ must equal $\frac{3}{4}$.

When we multiply fractions, if any of the numerators and denominators have a common factor (see Section I–1–2 for factors) we can divide each of them by the common factor and the fraction remains the same. This process is called *cancelling* and can be a great time-saver.

EXAMPLE: Multiply $\frac{4}{9} \cdot \frac{75}{8}$.

Since 4 is a common factor of 4 and 8, divide 4 and 8 by 4, getting $\frac{4}{9} \cdot \frac{75}{8} =$ $\frac{1}{9} \cdot \frac{75}{2}$. Since 3 is a common factor of 9 and 75, divide 9 and 75 by 3 to get $\frac{1}{9} \cdot \frac{75}{2} = \frac{1}{3} \cdot \frac{25}{2}$. So $\frac{4}{9} \cdot \frac{75}{8} = \frac{1}{3} \cdot \frac{25}{2} = \frac{25}{6}$.

2–6

Equivalent Fractions.   Two fractions are equivalent or equal if they represent the same ratio or number. In the last section, you saw that if you multiply or divide the numerator and denominator of a fraction by the same nonzero number the result is equivalent to the original fraction. For example, $\frac{7}{8} = \frac{70}{80}$ since 70 = 10 × 7 and 80 = 10 × 8.

In the test there will only be five choices, so your answer to a problem may not be the same as any of the given choices. You may have to express a fraction as an equivalent fraction.

To find a fraction with a known denominator equal to a given fraction:

(A) divide the denominator of the given fraction into the known denominator;
(B) multiply the result of (A) by the numerator of the given fraction; this is the numerator of the required equivalent fraction.

EXAMPLE: Find a fraction with a denominator of 30 which is equal to $\frac{2}{5}$:

(A) 5 into 30 is 6;
(B) 6 · 2 = 12 so $\frac{12}{30} = \frac{2}{5}$.

2–7

Reducing a Fraction to Lowest Terms.   A fraction has been reduced to lowest terms when the numerator and denominator have no common factors.

For example, $\frac{3}{4}$ is reduced to lowest terms, but $\frac{3}{6}$ is not because 3 is a common factor of 3 and 6.

> To reduce a fraction to lowest terms, cancel all the common factors of the numerator and denominator. (Cancelling common factors will not change the value of the fraction.)

For example, $\frac{100}{150} = \frac{10 \cdot 10}{10 \cdot 15} = \frac{10}{15} = \frac{5 \cdot 2}{5 \cdot 3} = \frac{2}{3}$. Since 2 and 3 have no common factors, $\frac{2}{3}$ is $\frac{100}{150}$ reduced to lowest terms. A fraction is equivalent to the fraction reduced to lowest terms.

If you write the numerator and denominator as products of primes, it is easy to cancel all the common factors.

$$\frac{63}{81} = \frac{3 \cdot 3 \cdot 7}{3 \cdot 3 \cdot 3 \cdot 3} = \frac{7}{9}$$

2-8

Adding Fractions. If the fractions have the same denominator, then the denominator is called a *common denominator*. Add the numerators, and use this sum as the new numerator with the common denominator as the denominator of the sum.

EXAMPLE 1: $\quad \frac{5}{12} + \frac{3}{12} = \frac{5 + 3}{12} = \frac{8}{12} = \frac{2}{3}$

EXAMPLE 2: Jim uses 7 eggs to make breakfast and 8 eggs for supper. How many dozen eggs has he used? 7 eggs are $\frac{7}{12}$ of a dozen and 8 eggs are $\frac{8}{12}$ of a dozen. He used $\frac{7}{12} + \frac{8}{12} = \frac{7 + 8}{12} = \frac{15}{12} = \frac{5}{4} = 1\frac{1}{4}$ dozen eggs.

If the fractions don't have the same denominator, you must first find a common denominator. Multiply all the denominators together; the result is a common denominator.

EXAMPLE: To add $\frac{1}{2} + \frac{2}{3} + \frac{7}{4}$, $2 \cdot 3 \cdot 4 = 24$ is a common denominator.

There are many common denominators; the smallest one is called the *least common denominator*. For the previous example, 12 is the least common denominator.

Once you have found a common denominator, express each fraction as an equivalent fraction with the common denominator, and add as you did for the case when the fractions had the same denominator.

EXAMPLE: $\frac{1}{2} + \frac{2}{3} + \frac{7}{4} = ?$

(A) 24 is a common denominator.

(B) $\frac{1}{2} = \frac{12}{24}, \frac{2}{3} = \frac{16}{24}, \frac{7}{4} = \frac{42}{24}$.

(C) $\frac{1}{2} + \frac{2}{3} + \frac{7}{4} = \frac{12}{24} + \frac{16}{24} + \frac{42}{24} = \frac{12 + 16 + 42}{24} = \frac{70}{24} = \frac{35}{12}$.

2–9

Subtracting Fractions. When the fractions have the same denominator, subtract the numerators and place the result over the denominator.

EXAMPLE: $\frac{3}{5} - \frac{2}{5} = \frac{3 - 2}{5} = \frac{1}{5}$

When the fractions have different denominators:

(A) Find a common denominator.
(B) Express the fractions as equivalent fractions with the same denominator.
(C) Subtract.

EXAMPLE: $\frac{3}{5} - \frac{2}{7} = ?$

(A) A common denominator is $5 \cdot 7 = 35$.

(B) $\frac{3}{5} = \frac{21}{35}, \frac{2}{7} = \frac{10}{35}$.

(C) $\frac{3}{5} - \frac{2}{7} = \frac{21}{35} - \frac{10}{35} = \frac{21 - 10}{35} = \frac{11}{35}$.

2–10

Complex Fractions. A fraction whose numerator and denominator are themselves fractions is called a *complex fraction*. For example $\frac{2/3}{4/5}$ is a complex fraction. A complex fraction can always be simplified by dividing the fraction.

EXAMPLE 1: $\frac{2}{3} \div \frac{4}{5} = \frac{\overset{1}{2}}{3} \cdot \frac{5}{\underset{2}{4}} = \frac{1}{3} \cdot \frac{5}{2} = \frac{5}{6}$

EXAMPLE 2: It takes $2\frac{1}{2}$ hours to get from Buffalo to Cleveland traveling at a constant rate of speed. What part of the distance is traveled in $\frac{3}{4}$ of an hour?

$\frac{3/4}{2\text{-}1/2} = \frac{3/4}{5/2} = \frac{3}{4} \cdot \frac{2}{5} = \frac{3}{2} \cdot \frac{1}{5} = \frac{3}{10}$ of the distance.

I–3. Decimals

3–1

A collection of digits (the digits are 0,1,2, . . . 9) after a period (called the decimal point) is called a *decimal fraction*. For example, .503, .5602, .32, and .4 are all decimal fractions.

Every decimal fraction represents a fraction. To find the fraction that a decimal fraction represents:

(A) Take the fraction whose denominator is 10 and whose numerator is the first digit to the right of the decimal point.

(B) Take the fraction whose denominator is 100 and whose numerator is the second digit to the right of the decimal point.

(C) Take the fraction whose denominator is 1,000 and whose numerator is the third digit to the right of the decimal point.

(D) Continue the procedure until you have used each digit to the right of the decimal point. The denominator in each step is 10 times the denominator in the previous step.

(E) The *sum* of the fractions you have obtained in (A), (B), (C), and (D) is the fraction that the decimal fraction represents.

EXAMPLE 1:   Find the fraction .503 represents.

(A) $\dfrac{5}{10}$

(B) $\dfrac{0}{100}$

(C) $\dfrac{3}{1,000}$

(D) All the digits have already been used.

(E) So $.503 = \dfrac{5}{10} + \dfrac{0}{100} + \dfrac{3}{1,000} = \dfrac{500}{1,000} + \dfrac{0}{1,000} + \dfrac{3}{1,000} = \dfrac{503}{1,000}.$

EXAMPLE 2:   What fraction does .78934 represent?

(A) $\dfrac{7}{10}$

(B) $\dfrac{8}{100}$

(C) $\dfrac{9}{1,000}$

(D) $\dfrac{3}{10,000}, \dfrac{4}{100,000}$

(E) So $.78934 = \dfrac{7}{10} + \dfrac{8}{100} + \dfrac{9}{1,000} + \dfrac{3}{10,000} + \dfrac{4}{100,000} = \dfrac{78,934}{100,000}.$

Notice that the denominator of the last fraction you obtain in step (D) is a common denominator for all the previous denominators. Since each denominator is 10 times the previous one, the denominator of the final fraction of part (D) will be the product of r copies of 10 multiplied together (called 10^r) where r is the number of digits which appear in the decimal fraction. Therefore, a decimal fraction represents a fraction whose denominator is 10^r where r is the number of digits in the decimal fraction and whose numerator is the number represented by the digits of the decimal fraction.

EXAMPLE 3: What fraction does .5702 represent?

There are 4 digits in .5702. Therefore, the denominator is $10 \times 10 \times 10 \times 10$ = 10,000, and the numerator is 5,702. Therefore, $.5702 = \dfrac{5,702}{10,000}$.

You can add any number of zeros to the right of a decimal fraction without changing its value.

EXAMPLE: $.3 = \dfrac{3}{10} = \dfrac{30}{100} = .30 = .30000 = \dfrac{30,000}{100,000} = .300000000 \ldots$

3–2

We call the first position to the right of the decimal point the tenths place, since the digit in that position tells you how many tenths you should take. (It is the numerator of a fraction whose denominator is 10.) In the same way, we call the second position to the right the hundredths place, the third position to the right the thousandths, and so on. This is similar to the way whole numbers are expressed, since 568 means $5 \times 100 + 6 \times 10 + 8 \times 1$. The various digits represent different numbers depending on their position: the first place to the left of the decimal point represents units, the second place to the left represents tens, and so on.

The following diagram may be helpful:

```
T  H  T  U     T  H  T
H  U  E  N     E  U  H
O  N  N  I     N  N  O
U  D  S  T  ·  T  D  U
S  R     S     H  R  S
A  E           S  E  A
N  D              D  N
D  S              T  D
S                 H  T
                  S  H
                     S
```

Thus, 5,342.061 means 5 thousands + 3 hundreds + 4 tens + 2 + 0 tenths + 6 hundredths + 1 thousandth.

3–3

A DECIMAL is a whole number plus a decimal fraction; the decimal point separates the whole number from the decimal fraction. For example, 4,307.206 is a decimal which represents 4,307 added to the decimal fraction .206. A decimal fraction is a decimal with zero as the whole number.

3–4

A fraction whose denominator is a multiple of 10 is equivalent to a decimal. The denominator tells you the last place that is filled to the right of the decimal point. Place the decimal point in the numerator so that the last place to the right of the decimal point corresponds to the denominator. If the numerator does not have enough digits, add the appropriate number of zeros *before* the numerator.

EXAMPLE 1: Find the decimal equivalent of $\dfrac{5,732}{100}$.

Since the denominator is 100, you need two places to the right of the decimal point so $\dfrac{5,732}{100}$ = 57.32.

EXAMPLE 2: What is the decimal equivalent of $\dfrac{57}{10,000}$?

The denominator is 10,000, so you need 4 decimal places. Since 57 only has two places, we add two zeros in front of 57; thus, $\dfrac{57}{10,000}$ = .0057.

Do not make the error of adding the zeros to the right instead of to the left of 57; .5700 means $\dfrac{5,700}{10,000}$ not $\dfrac{57}{10,000}$.

3–5

Adding Decimals. Decimals are much easier to add than fractions. To add a collection of decimals:

(A) Write the decimals in a column with the decimal points vertically aligned.
(B) Add enough zeros to the right of the decimal point so that every number has an entry in each column to the right of the decimal point.
(C) Add the numbers in the same way as whole numbers.
(D) Place a decimal point in the sum so that it is directly beneath the decimal points in the decimals added.

EXAMPLE 1: How much is 5 + 3.43 + 16.021 + 3.1?

(A)
```
    5
    3.43
   16.021
 +  3.1
```

(B)
```
    5.000
    3.430
   16.021
 +  3.100
```

(C)
```
    5.000
    3.430
   16.021
 +  3.100
```
(D)
```
   27.551
```
The answer is 27.551.

EXAMPLE 2: If John has $.50, $3.25, and $6.05, how much does he have altogether?

```
  $ .50
    3.25
 +  6.05
   $9.80
```
So John has $9.80.

3–6

Subtracting Decimals. To subtract one decimal from another:

(A) Put the decimals in a column so that the decimal points are vertically aligned.
(B) Add zeros so that every decimal has an entry in each column to the right of the decimal point.
(C) Subtract the numbers as you would whole numbers.
(D) Place the decimal point in the result so that it is directly beneath the decimal points of the numbers you subtracted.

EXAMPLE 1:   Solve 5.053 − 2.09.

(A)   5.053   (B)   5.053
     − 2.09   − 2.090

(C)   5.053
     − 2.090
(D)   2.963   The answer is 2.963.

EXAMPLE 2:   If Joe has $12 and he loses $8.40, how much money does he have left?

Since $12.00 − $8.40 = $3.60, he has $3.60 left.

3–7

Multiplying Decimals. Decimals are multiplied like whole numbers. *The decimal point of the product is placed so that the number of decimal places in the product is equal to the total of the number of decimal places in all of the numbers multiplied.*

EXAMPLE 1:   What is (5.02)(.6)?

(502)(6) = 3012. There were 2 decimal places in 5.02 and 1 decimal place in .6, so the product must have 2 + 1 = 3 decimal places. Therefore, (5.02)(.6) = 3.012.

EXAMPLE 2:   If eggs cost $.06 each, how much should a dozen eggs cost?

Since (12)(.06) = .72, a dozen eggs should cost $.72.

Computing Tip. To multiply a decimal by 10, just move the decimal point to the right one place; to multiply by 100, move the decimal point two places to the right and so on.

EXAMPLE: 9,983.456 × 100 = 998,345.6

3–8

Dividing Decimals. To divide one decimal (the dividend) by another decimal (the divisor):

(A) Move the decimal point in the divisor to the right until there is no decimal fraction in the divisor (this is the same as multiplying the divisor by a multiple of 10).

(B) Move the decimal point in the dividend the same number of places to the right as you moved the decimal point in step (A).

(C) Divide the result of (B) by the result of (A) as if they were whole numbers.

(D) The number of decimal places in the result (quotient) should be equal to the number of decimal places in the result of step (B).

(E) You may obtain as many decimal places as you wish in the quotient by adding zeros to the right in the dividend and then repeating step (C). For each zero you add to the dividend, you need one more decimal place in the quotient.

EXAMPLE 1:   Divide .05 into 25.155.

(A) Move the decimal point two places to the right in .05; the result is 5.

(B) Move the decimal point two places to the right in 25.155; the result is 2515.5.

(C) Divide 5 into 25155; the result is 5031.

(D) Since there was one decimal place in the result of (B), the answer is 503.1.

(E) There is no need to continue the division.

The work for this example might look like this:

$$\underset{.05\,)\overline{25.15\,5}}{\overset{503.1}{}}$$

You can always check division by multiplying.

$$(503.1)(.05) = 25.155 \text{ so we were correct.}$$

If you write division as a fraction, example 1 would be expressed as $\dfrac{25.155}{.05}$.

You can multiply both the numerator and denominator by 100 without changing the value of the fraction, so

$$\frac{25.155}{.05} = \frac{25.155 \times 100}{.05 \times 100} = \frac{2515.5}{5.}.$$

So steps (A) and (B) always change the division of a decimal by a decimal into the division of a decimal by a whole number.

To divide a decimal by a whole number, divide them as if they were whole numbers. Then place the decimal point in the quotient so that the quotient has as many decimal places as the dividend.

EXAMPLE 2:   (100.11)/.8 = ?

(A) Move the decimal point one place to the right in .8; the result is 8.

(B) Move the decimal point one place to the right in 100.11; the result is 1001.1.

(C) Divide 8 into 10011; the result is 1,251, with a remainder of 3. Since the division is not exact, we use step (D).

(D) Add 3 zeros to the right of 1001.1 and repeat (C). So we divide 8 into 10011000; the result is 1251375.

(E) The result must have four decimal places (1 from step (B) and 3 from step (D)), so the answer is 125.1375.

The work for this example might look like this:

$$\underset{.8\,)\overline{100.1\,1000}}{\overset{125.1375}{}}$$

CHECK: (.8)(125.1375) = 100.11000 = 100.11 so this is correct.

EXAMPLE 3: If oranges cost 6¢ each, how many oranges can you buy for $2.52?

6¢ = $.06, so the number of oranges is

$$\frac{2.52}{.06} = \frac{252}{6} = 42.$$

Computing Tip. To divide a decimal by 10, move the decimal point *to the left* one place; to divide by 100, move the decimal point two places to the left, and so on.

EXAMPLE: Divide 5,637.6471 by 1,000.

The answer is 5.6376471, since to divide by 1,000 you move the decimal point 3 places to the left.

3–9

Converting a Fraction into a Decimal. To convert a fraction into a decimal, divide the denominator into the numerator. For example, $\frac{3}{4} = \frac{3.00}{4} = .75$. Some fractions give an infinite decimal when you divide the denominator into the numerator, for example, $\frac{1}{3} = .333 \ldots$ where the three dots mean you keep on getting 3 with each step of division. $.333 \ldots$ is an *infinite decimal*.

If a fraction has an infinite decimal, use the fraction in any computation.

EXAMPLE 1: What is $\frac{2}{9}$ of $3,690.90?

Since the decimal for $\frac{2}{9}$ is $.2222 \ldots$ use the fraction $\frac{2}{9}$. $\frac{2}{9} \times \$3,690.90 = 2 \times \$410.10 = \$820.20$.

You should know the following decimal equivalents of fractions:

$\frac{1}{100} = .01$	$\frac{1}{10} = .1$	$\frac{2}{5} = .4$
$\frac{1}{50} = .02$	$\frac{1}{9} = .111 \ldots$	$\frac{1}{2} = .5$
$\frac{1}{40} = .025$	$\frac{1}{8} = .125$	$\frac{5}{8} = .625$
$\frac{1}{25} = .04$	$\frac{1}{6} = .1666 \ldots$	$\frac{2}{3} = .666 \ldots$
$\frac{1}{20} = .05$	$\frac{1}{5} = .2$	$\frac{3}{4} = .75$
$\frac{1}{16} = .0625$	$\frac{1}{4} = .25$	$\frac{7}{8} = .875$
$\frac{1}{15} = .0666 \ldots$	$\frac{1}{3} = .333 \ldots$	$\frac{3}{2} = 1.5$
$\frac{1}{12} = .0833 \ldots$	$\frac{3}{8} = .375$	

Any decimal with $\ldots$ is an infinite decimal.

I–4. Percentage

4–1

PERCENTAGE is another method of expressing fractions or parts of an object. Percentages are expressed in terms of hundredths, so 100% means 100 hundredths or 1, and 50% would be 50 hundredths or ½.

A decimal is converted to a percentage by multiplying the decimal by 100. Since multiplying a decimal by 100 is accomplished by moving the decimal point two places to the right, *you convert a decimal into a percentage by moving the decimal point two places to the right.* For example, .134 = 13.4%.

If you wish to convert a percentage into a decimal, you divide the percentage by 100. There is a shortcut for this also. To divide by 100 you move the decimal point two places to the left.

Therefore, *to convert a percentage into a decimal, move the decimal point two places to the left.* For example, 24% = .24.

A fraction is converted into a percentage by changing the fraction to a decimal and then changing the decimal to a percentage. A percentage is changed into a fraction by first converting the percentage into a decimal and then changing the decimal to a fraction. *You should know the following fractional equivalents of percentages:*

$1\% = \dfrac{1}{100}$	$25\% = \dfrac{1}{4}$	$80\% = \dfrac{4}{5}$
$2\% = \dfrac{1}{50}$	$33\dfrac{1}{3}\% = \dfrac{1}{3}$	$83\dfrac{1}{3}\% = \dfrac{5}{6}$
$4\% = \dfrac{1}{25}$	$37\dfrac{1}{2}\% = \dfrac{3}{8}$	$87\dfrac{1}{2}\% = \dfrac{7}{8}$
$5\% = \dfrac{1}{20}$	$40\% = \dfrac{2}{5}$	$100\% = 1$
$8\dfrac{1}{3}\% = \dfrac{1}{12}$	$50\% = \dfrac{1}{2}$	$120\% = \dfrac{6}{5}$
$10\% = \dfrac{1}{10}$	$60\% = \dfrac{3}{5}$	$125\% = \dfrac{5}{4}$
$12\dfrac{1}{2}\% = \dfrac{1}{8}$	$62\dfrac{1}{2}\% = \dfrac{5}{8}$	$133\dfrac{1}{3}\% = \dfrac{4}{3}$
$16\dfrac{2}{3}\% = \dfrac{1}{6}$	$66\dfrac{2}{3}\% = \dfrac{2}{3}$	$150\% = \dfrac{3}{2}$
$20\% = \dfrac{1}{5}$	$75\% = \dfrac{3}{4}$	

Note, for example, that $133\dfrac{1}{3}\% = 1.33\dfrac{1}{3} = 1\dfrac{1}{3} = \dfrac{4}{3}$.

When you compute with percentages, it is usually easier to change the percentages to decimals or fractions.

EXAMPLE 1: A company has 6,435 bars of soap. If the company sells 20% of its bars of soap, how many bars of soap did it sell?

Change 20% into .2. Thus, the company sold $(.2)(6,435) = 1287.0 = 1,287$ bars of soap. An alternative method would be to convert 20% to $\frac{1}{5}$. Then, $\frac{1}{5} \times 6,435 = 1,287$.

EXAMPLE 2: In a class of 60 students, 18 students received a grade of B. What percentage of the class received a grade of B?

$\frac{18}{60}$ of the class received a grade of B. $\frac{18}{60} = \frac{3}{10} = .3$ and $.3 = 30\%$, so 30% of the class received a grade of B.

EXAMPLE 3: If the population of Dryden was 10,000 in 1960 and the population of Dryden increased by 15% between 1960 and 1970, what was the population of Dryden in 1970?

The population increased by 15% between 1960 and 1970, so the increase was $(.15)(10,000)$ which is 1,500. The population in 1970 was $10,000 + 1,500 = 11,500$.

A quicker method: The population increased 15%, so the population in 1970 is 115% of the population in 1960. Therefore, the population in 1970 is 115% of 10,000 which is $(1.15)(10,000) = 11,500$.

4–2

Interest and Discount. Two of the most common uses of percentages are in interest and discount problems.

The rate of interest is usually given as a percentage. The basic formula for interest problems is:

$$\boxed{\text{INTEREST} = \text{AMOUNT} \times \text{TIME} \times \text{RATE}}$$

You can assume the rate of interest is the annual rate of interest unless the problem states otherwise; so you should express the time in years.

EXAMPLE 1: How much interest will $10,000 earn in 9 months at an annual rate of 6%?

9 months is $\frac{3}{4}$ of a year and $6\% = \frac{3}{50}$, so using the formula, the interest is $10,000 $\times \frac{3}{4} \times \frac{3}{50} = \$50 \times 9 = \$450$.

EXAMPLE 2: What annual rate of interest was paid if $5,000 earned $300 in interest in 2 years?

Since the interest was earned in 2 years, $150 is the interest earned in one year. $\frac{150}{5,000} = .03 = 3\%$, so the annual rate of interest was 3%.

This type of interest is called *simple interest*.

There is another method of computing interest called *compound interest*. In computing compound interest, the interest is periodically added to the amount (or principal) which is earning interest.

EXAMPLE 3: What will $1,000 be worth after three years if it earns interest at the rate of 5% compounded annually?

Compounded annually means that the interest earned during one year is added to the amount (or principal) at the end of each year. The interest on $1,000 at 5% for one year is $(1,000)(.05) = $50. So you must compute the interest on $1,050 (not $1,000) for the second year. The interest is $(1,050)(.05) = $52.50. Therefore, during the third year interest will be computed for $1,102.50. During the third year the interest is $(1,102.50)(.05) = $55.125 = $55.13. Therefore, after 3 years the original $1,000 will be worth $1,157.63.

If you calculated simple interest on $1,000 at 5% for three years, the answer would be $(1,000)(.05)(3) = $150. Therefore, using simple interest, $1,000 is worth $1,150 after 3 years. Notice that this is not the same as the money was worth using compound interest.

You can assume that interest means simple interest unless a problem states otherwise.

The basic formula for discount problems is:

$$\boxed{\text{DISCOUNT} = \text{COST} \times \text{RATE OF DISCOUNT}}$$

EXAMPLE 1: What is the discount if a car which cost $3,000 is discounted 7%?

The discount is $3,000 × .07 = $210 since 7% = .07.

If we know the cost of an item and its discounted price, we can find the rate of discount by using the formula

$$\text{rate of discount} = \frac{\text{cost} - \text{price}}{\text{cost}}.$$

EXAMPLE 2: What was the rate of discount if a boat which cost $5,000 was sold for $4,800?

Using this formula, we find that the rate of discount equals

$$\frac{5,000 - 4,800}{5,000} = \frac{200}{5,000} = \frac{1}{25} = .04 = 4\%.$$

After an item has been discounted once, it may be discounted again. This procedure is called *successive* discounting.

EXAMPLE 3: A bicycle originally cost $100 and was discounted 10%. After three months it was sold after being discounted 15%. How much was the bicycle sold for?

After the 10% discount the bicycle was selling for $100(.90) = $90. An item which costs $90 and is discounted 15% will sell for $90(.85) = $76.50, so the bicycle was sold for $76.50.

Notice that if you added the two discounts of 10% and 15% and treated the successive discounts as a single discount of 25%, your answer would be that the bicycle sold for $75, which is incorrect. Successive discounts are *not* identical to a single discount of the sum of the discounts. The previous example shows that successive discounts of 10% and 15% are not identical to a single discount of 25%.

I–5. Rounding Off Numbers

5–1

Many times an approximate answer can be found more quickly and may be more useful than the exact answer. For example, if a company had sales of $998,875.63 during a year, it is easier to remember that the sales were about $1 million.

Rounding off a number to a decimal place means finding the multiple of the representative of that decimal place which is closest to the original number. Thus, rounding off a number to the nearest hundred means finding the multiple of 100 which is closest to the original number. Rounding off to the nearest tenth means finding the multiple of $\frac{1}{10}$ which is closest to the original number. After a number has been rounded off to a particular decimal place, all the digits to the right of that particular decimal place will be zero.

EXAMPLE 1:   Round off 9,403,420.71 to the nearest hundred.

You must find the multiple of one hundred which is closest to 9,403,420.71. The answer is 9,403,400.

To round off a number to the *r*th decimal place:

(A) Look at the digit in the place to the right of the *r*th place;
(B) *If the digit is 0,1,2,3, or 4, change all the digits in places to the right of the rth place to 0 to round off the number.*
(C) *If the digit is 5,6,7,8, or 9, add 1 to the digit in the rth place and change all the digits in places to the right of the rth place to 0 to round off the number.*

For example, the multiple of 100 which is closest to 5,342.1 is 5,300. Most problems dealing with money are rounded off if the answer contains a fractional part of a cent. This is common business practice.

EXAMPLE 2:   If 16 cookies cost $1.00, how much should three cookies cost?

Three cookies should cost $\frac{3}{16}$ of $1.00. Since $\frac{3}{16} \times 1 = .1875$, the cost would be $.1875. In practice, you would round it up to $.19 or 19¢.

Rounding off numbers can help you get quick, approximate answers. Since many questions require only rough answers, you can save time on the test by rounding off numbers.

EXAMPLE 3:   If 5,301 of the 499,863 workers employed at the XYZ factory don't show up for work on Monday, about what percentage of the workers don't show up?

(A) 1   (B) 2   (C) 3   (D) 4   (E) 5

You can quickly see that the answer is (A) by rounding off both numbers to the nearest thousand before you divide, because $\dfrac{5,000}{500,000} = \dfrac{1}{100} = .01 = 1\%$. The exact answer is $\dfrac{5,301}{499,863} = .010604$, but it would take much longer to get an exact answer.

EXAMPLE 4: Round off 43.79 to the nearest tenth.

The place to the right of tenths is hundredths, so look in the hundredths place. Since 9 is bigger than 5, add 1 to the tenths place. Therefore, 43.79 is 43.8 rounded off to the nearest tenth.

If the digit in the *r*th place is 9 and you need to add 1 to the digit to round off the number to the *r*th decimal place, put a zero in the *r*th place and add 1 to the digit in the position to the left of the *r*th place. For example, 298 rounded off to the nearest 10 is 300; 99,752 to the nearest thousand is 100,000.

I–6. Signed Numbers

6–1

A number preceded by either a plus or a minus sign is called a SIGNED NUMBER. For example, $+5$, -6, -4.2, and $+\frac{3}{4}$ are all signed numbers. If no sign is given with a number, a plus sign is assumed; thus, 5 is interpreted as $+5$.

Signed numbers can often be used to distinguish different concepts. For example, a profit of \$10 can be denoted by $+\$10$ and a loss of \$10 by $-\$10$. A temperature of 20 degrees below zero can be denoted $-20°$.

6–2

Signed numbers are also called DIRECTED NUMBERS. You can think of numbers arranged on a line, called a number line, in the following manner:

Take a line which extends indefinitely in both directions, pick a point on the line and call it 0, pick another point on the line to the right of 0 and call it 1. The point to the right of 1 which is exactly as far from 1 as 1 is from 0 is called 2, the point to the right of 2 just as far from 2 as 1 is from 0 is called 3, and so on. The point halfway between 0 and 1 is called ½, the point halfway between ½ and 1 is called ¾. In this way, you can identify any whole number or any fraction with a point on the line.

All the numbers which correspond to points to the right of 0 are called *positive numbers*. The sign of a positive number is $+$.

If you go to the left of zero the same distance as you did from 0 to 1, the point is called -1; in the same way as before, you can find -2, -3, $-\dfrac{1}{2}$, $-\dfrac{3}{2}$ and so on.

All the numbers which correspond to points to the left of zero are called *negative numbers*. Negative numbers are signed numbers whose sign is −. For example, −3, −5.15, −.003 are all negative numbers.

> *0 is neither positive nor negative; any nonzero number is positive or negative but not both.* So −0 = 0.

6–3

Absolute Value. The absolute value of a signed number is the distance of the number from 0. The absolute value of any nonzero number is *positive*. For example, the absolute value of 2 is 2; the absolute value of −2 is 2. The absolute value of a number a is denoted by $|a|$, so $|-2| = 2$. The absolute value of any number can be found by dropping its sign, $|-12| = 12$, $|4| = 4$. *Thus $|-a| = |a|$ for any number a.* The only number whose absolute value is zero is zero.

6–4

Adding Signed Numbers.

Case I. Adding numbers with the *same sign:*

   (A) The sign of the sum is the same as the sign of the numbers being added.
   (B) Add the absolute values.
   (C) Put the sign from step (A) in front of the number you obtained in step (B).

EXAMPLE 1: What is $-2 + (-3.1) + (-.02)$?

   (A) The sign of the sum will be −.
   (B) $|-2| = 2$, $|-3.1| = 3.1$, $|-.02| = .02$, and $2 + 3.1 + .02 = 5.12$.
   (C) The answer is -5.12.

Case II. Adding *two* numbers with *different signs:*

   (A) The sign of the sum is the sign of the number which is largest in absolute value.
   (B) Subtract the absolute value of the number with the smaller absolute value from the absolute value of the number with the larger absolute value.
   (C) The answer is the number you obtained in step (B) preceded by the sign from part (A).

EXAMPLE 2: How much is $-5.1 + 3$?

   (A) The absolute value of −5.1 is 5.1 and the absolute value of 3 is 3, so the sign of the sum will be −.
   (B) 5.1 is larger than 3, and $5.1 - 3 = 2.1$.
   (C) The sum is -2.1.

Case III. Adding *more than two* numbers with *different signs:*

   (A) Add all the positive numbers; the result is positive (this is Case I).
   (B) Add all the negative numbers; the result is negative (this is Case I).
   (C) Add the result of step (A) to the result of step (B), by using Case II.

EXAMPLE 3: Find the value of $5 + 52 + (-3) + 7 + (-5.1)$.

   (A) $5 + 52 + 7 = 64$.
   (B) $-3 + (-5.1) = -8.1$.
   (C) $64 + (-8.1) = 55.9$, so the answer is 55.9.

EXAMPLE 4: If a store made a profit of $23.50 on Monday, lost $2.05 on Tuesday, lost $5.03 on Wednesday, made a profit of $30.10 on Thursday, and made a profit of $41.25 on Friday, what was its total profit (or loss) for the week? Use + for profit and − for loss.

The total is 23.50 + (−2.05) + (−5.03) + 30.10 + 41.25 which is 94.85 + (−7.08) = 87.77. So the store made a profit of $87.77.

6-5
Subtracting Signed Numbers. When subtracting signed numbers:

(A) Change the sign of the number you are subtracting (the subtrahend).
(B) <u>Add</u> the result of step (A) to the number being subtracted from (the minuend) using the rules of the preceding section.

EXAMPLE 1: Subtract 4.1 from 6.5.

(A) 4.1 becomes −4.1.
(B) 6.5 + (−4.1) = 2.4.

EXAMPLE 2: What is 7.8 − (−10.1)?

(A) −10.1 becomes 10.1.
(B) 7.8 + 10.1 = 17.9.

So we subtract a negative number by adding a positive number with the same absolute value, and we subtract a positive number by adding a negative number of the same absolute value.

6-6
Multiplying Signed Numbers.

Case I. Multiplying two numbers:

(A) Multiply the absolute values of the numbers.
(B) If both numbers have the same sign, the result of step (A) is the answer— i.e. the product is positive. If the numbers have different signs, then the answer is the result of step (A) with a minus sign.

EXAMPLE 1: (−5)(−12) = ?

(A) 5 × 12 = 60
(B) Both signs are the same, so the answer is 60.

EXAMPLE 2: (4)(−3) = ?

(A) 4 × 3 = 12
(B) The signs are different, so the answer is −12. You can remember the sign of the product in the following way:

$$(-)(-) = +$$
$$(+)(+) = +$$
$$(-)(+) = -$$
$$(+)(-) = -$$

Case II. Multiplying more than two numbers:

(A) Multiply the first two factors using Case I.
(B) Multiply the result of (A) by the third factor.
(C) Multiply the result of (B) by the fourth factor.
(D) Continue until you have used each factor.

EXAMPLE 3: $(-5)(4)(2)(-\frac{1}{2})(\frac{3}{4}) = ?$

(A) $(-5)(4) = -20$
(B) $(-20)(2) = -40$
(C) $(-40)(-\frac{1}{2}) = 20$
(D) $(20)(\frac{3}{4}) = 15$, so the answer is 15.

> *The sign of the product is $+$ if there are no negative factors or an even number of negative factors. The sign of the product is $-$ if there are an odd number of negative factors.*

6–7

Dividing Signed Numbers. Divide the absolute values of the numbers; the sign of the quotient is determined by the same rules as you used to determine the sign of a product. Thus,

$$+ \div + = +$$
$$- \div - = +$$
$$+ \div - = -$$
$$- \div + = -$$

EXAMPLE 1: Divide 53.2 by -4.

53.2 divided by 4 is 13.3. Since one of the numbers is positive and the other negative, the answer is -13.3.

EXAMPLE 2: 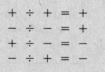 $\dfrac{-5}{-2} = \dfrac{5}{2}$

I–7. Averages and Medians

7–1

Mean. The *average* or *arithmetic mean* of a collection of N numbers is the result of dividing the sum of all the numbers in the collection by N.

EXAMPLE 1: The scores of 9 students on a test were 72, 78, 81, 64, 85, 92, 95, 60, and 55. What was the average score of the students?

Since there are 9 students, the average is the total of all the scores divided by 9.

So the average is $\frac{1}{9}$ of $(72 + 78 + 81 + 64 + 85 + 92 + 95 + 60 + 55)$, which is $\frac{1}{9}$ of 682 or $75\frac{7}{9}$.

EXAMPLE 2: The temperature at noon in Coldtown, U.S.A. was 5° on Monday, 10° on Tuesday, 2° below zero on Wednesday, 5° below zero on Thursday, 0° on Friday, 4° on Saturday, and 1° below zero on Sunday. What was the average temperature at noon for the week?

Use negative numbers for the temperatures below zero. The average temperature is the average of 5, 10, −2, −5, 0, 4, and −1, which is $\frac{5 + 10 + (−2) + (−5) + 0 + 4 + (−1)}{7} = \frac{11}{7} = 1\frac{4}{7}$. Therefore, the average temperature at noon for the week is $1\frac{4}{7}°$.

EXAMPLE 3: If the average annual income of 10 workers is $15,665 and two of the workers each made $20,000 for the year, what is the average annual income of the remaining 8 workers?

The total income of all 10 workers is 10 times the average income which is $156,650. The two workers made a total of $40,000, so the total income of the remaining 8 workers was $156,650 − $40,000 = $116,650. Therefore, the average annual income of the 8 remaining workers is $\frac{\$116,650}{8} = \$14,581.25$.

7–2

The Median. The number which is in the middle if the numbers in a collection of numbers are arranged in order is called the *median*. In example 1 above, the median score was 78, and in example 2, the median temperature for the week was 0. Notice that the medians were different from the averages. In example 3, we don't have enough data to find the median although we know the average.

In general, the median and the average of a collection of numbers are different.

If the number of objects in the collection is even, the median is the average of the two numbers in the middle of the array. For example, the median of 64, 66, 72, 75, 76, and 77 is the average of 72 and 75, which is 73.5.

I–8. Powers, Exponents, and Roots

8–1

If b is any number and n is a whole number greater than 0, b^n means the product of n factors each of which is equal to b. Thus,

$$b^n = b \times b \times b \times \cdots \times b \text{ where there are } n \text{ copies of } b.$$

If $n = 1$, there is only one copy of b so $b^1 = b$. Here are some examples:

$$2^5 = 2 \times 2 \times 2 \times 2 \times 2 = 32, (−4)^3 = (−4) \times (−4) \times (−4) = −64,$$
$$\frac{3^2}{4} = \frac{3 \times 3}{4} = \frac{9}{4},$$

$$1^n = 1 \text{ for any } n, 0^n = 0 \text{ for any } n.$$

b^n is read as "b raised to the nth power." b^2 is read "b squared." b^2 is always greater than 0 (positive) if b is not zero, since the product of two negative numbers is positive. b^3 is read "b cubed." b^3 can be negative or positive.

You should know the following squares and cubes:

$$
\begin{array}{ll}
1^2 = 1 & 8^2 = 64 \\
2^2 = 4 & 9^2 = 81 \\
3^2 = 9 & 10^2 = 100 \\
4^2 = 16 & 11^2 = 121 \\
5^2 = 25 & 12^2 = 144 \\
6^2 = 36 & 13^2 = 169 \\
7^2 = 49 & 14^2 = 196 \\
 & 15^2 = 225 \\
 & \\
1^3 = 1 & 3^3 = 27 \\
2^3 = 8 & 4^3 = 64 \\
 & 5^3 = 125
\end{array}
$$

If you raise a fraction, $\dfrac{p}{q}$, to a power, then $\left(\dfrac{p}{q}\right)^n = \dfrac{p^n}{q^n}$. For example,

$$\left(\frac{5}{4}\right)^3 = \frac{5^3}{4^3} = \frac{125}{64}.$$

EXAMPLE: If the value of an investment triples each year, what percent of its value today will the investment be worth in 4 years?

The value increases by a factor of 3 each year. Since the time is 4 years, there will be four factors of 3. So the investment will be worth $3 \times 3 \times 3 \times 3 = 3^4$ as much as it is today. $3^4 = 81$, so the investment will be worth 8,100% of its value today in four years.

8–2

Exponents. In the expression b^n, b is called the base and n is called the *exponent*. In the expression 2^5, 2 is the base and 5 is the exponent. The exponent tells how many factors there are.

> The *two basic formulas for problems involving exponents* are:
> (A) $b^n \times b^m = b^{n+m}$
> (B) $a^n \times b^n = (a \cdot b)^n$
>
> (A) and (B) are called *laws of exponents*.

EXAMPLE 1: What is 6^3?

Since $6 = 3 \times 2$, $6^3 = 3^3 \times 2^3 = 27 \times 8 = 216$.
or
$$6^3 = 6 \times 6 \times 6 = 216.$$

EXAMPLE 2: Find the value of $2^3 \times 2^2$.

Using (A), $2^3 \times 2^2 = 2^{2+3} = 2^5$ which is 32. You can check this, since $2^3 = 8$ and $2^2 = 4$; $2^3 \times 2^2 = 8 \times 4 = 32$.

8–3

Negative Exponents. $b^0 = 1$ *for any nonzero number b.* By one of the laws of exponents (A) above, $b^n \times b^0$ should be $b^{n+0} = b^n$. If we still want (A) to be true, then b^0 must be 1. (NOTE: 0^0 is not defined.)

Using the law of exponents once more, you can define b^{-n} where n is a positive number. If (A) holds, $b^{-n} \times b^n = b^{-n+n} = b^0 = 1$, so $b^{-n} = \dfrac{1}{b^n}$. *Multiplying by b^{-n} is the same as dividing by b^n.*

EXAMPLE 1: $2^{-3} = \dfrac{1}{2^3} = \dfrac{1}{8}$

$2^0 = 1$

EXAMPLE 2: $\left(\dfrac{1}{2}\right)^{-1} = \dfrac{1}{1/2} = 2$

EXAMPLE 3:   Find the value of $\dfrac{6^4}{3^3}$.

$$\frac{6^4}{3^3} = \frac{(3 \cdot 2)^4}{3^3} = \frac{3^4 \cdot 2^4}{3^3} = 3^4 \times 2^4 \times 3^{-3} = 3^4 \times 3^{-3} \times 2^4 = 3^1 \times 2^4 = 48.$$

8–4

Roots. If you raise a number d to the nth power and the result is b, then d is called the nth root of b, which is usually written $\sqrt[n]{b} = d$. Since $2^5 = 32$, then $\sqrt[5]{32} = 2$. The second root is called the square root and is written $\sqrt{}$; the third root is called the cube root. If you read the columns of the table in Section I–8–1 from right to left, you have a table of square roots and cube roots. For example, $\sqrt{225} = 15$; $\sqrt{81} = 9$; $\sqrt[3]{64} = 4$.

There are two possibilities for the square root of a positive number; the positive one is called the square root. Thus we say $\sqrt{9} = 3$ although $(-3) \times (-3) = 9$.

Since the square of any nonzero number is positive, *the square root of a negative number is not defined as a real number.* Thus $\sqrt{-2}$ is not a real number. There are cube roots of negative numbers. $\sqrt[3]{-8} = -2$, because $(-2) \times (-2) \times (-2) = -8$.

You can also write roots as exponents; for example,

$$\sqrt[n]{b} = b^{1/n}; \text{ so } \sqrt{b} = b^{1/2}, \sqrt[3]{b} = b^{1/3}.$$

Since you can write roots as exponents, formula (B) under Section I–8–2 is especially useful.

$a^{1/n} \times b^{1/n} = (a \cdot b)^{1/n}$ or $\sqrt[n]{a \times b} = \sqrt[n]{a} \times \sqrt[n]{b}$. This formula is the basic formula for simplifying square roots, cube roots and so on. *On the test you must state your answer in a form that matches one of the choices given.*

EXAMPLE 1: $\sqrt{54} = ?$

Since $54 = 9 \times 6$, $\sqrt{54} = \sqrt{9 \times 6} = \sqrt{9} \times \sqrt{6}$. Since $\sqrt{9} = 3$, $\sqrt{54} = 3\sqrt{6}$.

You cannot simplify by adding square roots unless you are taking square roots of the same number. For example,

$$\sqrt{3} + 2\sqrt{3} - 4\sqrt{3} = -\sqrt{3}, \text{ but } \sqrt{3} + \sqrt{2} \text{ is not equal to } \sqrt{5}.$$

EXAMPLE 2: Simplify $6\sqrt{12} + 2\sqrt{75} - 3\sqrt{98}$.

Since $12 = 4 \times 3$, $\sqrt{12} = \sqrt{4 \times 3} = \sqrt{4} \times \sqrt{3} = 2\sqrt{3}$;
$75 = 25 \times 3$, so $\sqrt{75} = \sqrt{25} \times \sqrt{3} = 5\sqrt{3}$;
and $98 = 49 \times 2$, so $\sqrt{98} = \sqrt{49} \times \sqrt{2} = 7\sqrt{2}$.
Therefore, $6\sqrt{12} + 2\sqrt{75} - 3\sqrt{98} = 6 \times 2\sqrt{3} + 2 \times 5\sqrt{3} - 3 \times 7\sqrt{2} =$
$12\sqrt{3} + 10\sqrt{3} - 21\sqrt{2} = 22\sqrt{3} - 21\sqrt{2}$.

EXAMPLE 3: Simplify $27^{1/3} \times 8^{1/3}$.

$27^{1/3} = \sqrt[3]{27} = 3$ and $8^{1/3} = 2$, so $27^{1/3} \times 8^{1/3} = 3 \times 2 = 6$. Notice that 6
is $\sqrt[3]{216}$ and $27^{1/3} \times 8^{1/3} = (27 \times 8)^{1/3} = 216^{1/3}$.

II. Algebra

II–1. Algebraic Expressions

1–1

Often it is necessary to deal with quantities which have a numerical value which is unknown. For example, we may know that Tom's salary is twice as much as Joe's salary. If we let the value of Tom's salary be called T and the value of Joe's salary be J, then T and J are numbers which are unknown. However, we do know that the value of T must be twice the value of J, or $T = 2J$.

T and $2J$ are examples of algebraic expressions. An algebraic expression may involve letters in addition to numbers and symbols; however, *in an algebraic expression a letter always stands for a number*. Therefore, you can multiply, divide, add, subtract and perform other mathematical operations on a letter. Thus, x^2 would mean x times x. Some examples of algebraic expressions are: $2x + y$, $y^3 + 9y$, $z^3 - 5ab$, $c + d + 4$, $5x + 2y(6x - 4y + z)$. When letters or numbers are written together without any sign or symbol between them, multiplication is assumed. Thus $6xy$ means 6 times x times y. $6xy$ is called a term; terms are separated by + or − signs. The expression $5z + 2 + 4x^2$ has three terms, $5z$, 2, and $4x^2$. Terms are often called monomials (mono = one). If an expression has more than one term, it is called a *polynomial* (poly = many). The letters in an algebraic expression are called *variables* or *unknowns*. When a variable is multiplied by a number, the number is called the *coefficient* of the variable. So in the expression $5x^2 + 2yz$, the coefficient of x^2 is 5, and the coefficient of yz is 2.

1–2

Simplifying Algebraic Expressions. *Since there are only five choices of an answer given for the test questions, you must be able to recognize algebraic expressions which are equal*. It will also save time when you are working problems if you can change a complicated expression into a simpler one.

Case I. Simplifying expressions which don't contain parentheses:

(A) Perform any multiplications or divisions before performing additions or subtractions. Thus, the expression $6x + y \div x$ means add $6x$ to the quotient of y divided by x. Another way of writing the expression would be $6x + \dfrac{y}{x}$. This is not the same as $\dfrac{6x + y}{x}$.

(B) The order in which you multiply numbers and letters in a term does not matter. So $6xy$ is the same as $6yx$.

(C) The order in which you add terms does not matter; for instance, $6x + 2y - x = 6x - x + 2y$.

(D) If there are roots or powers in any terms, you may be able to simplify the term by using the laws of exponents. For example, $5xy \cdot 3x^2y = 15x^3y^2$.

(E) Combine like terms. *Like terms* (or similar terms) are terms which have exactly the same letters raised to the same powers. So x, $-2x$, $\frac{1}{3}x$ are like terms. For example, $6x - 2x + x + y$ is equal to $5x + y$. In combining like terms, you simply add or subtract the coefficients of the like terms, and the result is the coefficient of that term in the simplified expression. In the example given, the coefficients of x were $+6$, -2, and $+1$; since $6 - 2 + 1 = 5$ the coefficient of x in the simplified expression is 5.

(F) Algebraic expressions which involve divisions or factors can be simplified by using the techniques for handling fractions and the laws of exponents. Remember dividing by b^n is the same as multiplying by b^{-n}.

EXAMPLE 1: $3x^2 - 4\sqrt{x} + \sqrt{4x} + xy + 7x^2 = ?$

(D) $\sqrt{4x} = \sqrt{4}\sqrt{x} = 2\sqrt{x}$.

(E) $3x^2 + 7x^2 = 10x^2$, $-4\sqrt{x} + 2\sqrt{x} = -2\sqrt{x}$.

The original expression equals $3x^2 + 7x^2 - 4\sqrt{x} + 2\sqrt{x} + xy$. Therefore, the simplified expression is $10x^2 - 2\sqrt{x} + xy$.

EXAMPLE 2:   Simplify $\dfrac{21x^4y^2}{3x^6y}$.

(F) $\dfrac{21}{3} x^4y^2x^{-6}y^{-1}$.

(B) $7x^4x^{-6}y^2y^{-1}$.

(D) $7x^{-2}y$, so the simplified term is $\dfrac{7y}{x^2}$.

EXAMPLE 3:   Write $\dfrac{2x}{y} - \dfrac{4}{x}$ as a single fraction.

(F) A common denominator is xy so $\dfrac{2x}{y} = \dfrac{2x \cdot x}{y \cdot x} = \dfrac{2x^2}{xy}$, and $\dfrac{4}{x} = \dfrac{4y}{xy}$.

$$\text{Therefore, } \dfrac{2x}{y} - \dfrac{4}{x} = \dfrac{2x^2}{xy} - \dfrac{4y}{xy} = \dfrac{2x^2 - 4y}{xy}$$

Case II. Simplifying expressions which have parentheses:

The first rule is to perform the operations inside parentheses first. So $(6x + y) \div x$ means divide the sum of $6x$ and y by x. Notice that $(6x + y) \div x$ is different from $6x + y \div x$.

The main rule for getting rid of parentheses is the distributive law, which is expressed as $a(b + c) = ab + ac$. In other words, if any monomial is followed by an expression contained in a parenthesis, then *each* term of the expression is multiplied by the monomial. Once we have gotten rid of the parentheses, we proceed as we did in Case I.

EXAMPLE 4: $2x(6x - 4y + 2) = (2x)(6x) + (2x)(-4y) + (2x)(2) = 12x^2 - 8xy + 4x.$

If an expression has more than one set of parentheses, get rid of the *inner parentheses first* and then *work out* through the rest of the parentheses.

EXAMPLE 5: $2x - (x + 6(x - 3y) + 4y) = ?$

To remove the inner parentheses we multiply $6(x - 3y)$ getting $6x - 18y$. Now we have $2x - (x + 6x - 18y + 4y)$ which equals $2x - (7x - 14y)$. Distribute the minus sign (multiply by -1), getting $2x - 7x - (-14y) = -5x + 14y$. Sometimes brackets are used instead of parentheses.

EXAMPLE 6: Simplify $-3x\left[\dfrac{1}{2}(3x - 2y) - 2(x(3 + y) + 4y)\right]$

$$= -3x\left[\dfrac{1}{2}(3x - 2y) - 2(3x + xy + 4y)\right]$$

$$= -3x\left[\dfrac{3}{2}x - y - 6x - 2xy - 8y\right]$$

$$= -3x\left[-\dfrac{9}{2}x - 2xy - 9y\right]$$

$$= \dfrac{27}{2}x^2 + 6x^2y + 27xy.$$

1–3

Adding and Subtracting Algebraic Expressions. Since algebraic expressions are numbers, they can be added and subtracted.

The only algebraic terms which can be combined are like terms.

EXAMPLE 1: $(3x + 4y - xy^2) + (3x + 2x(x - y)) = ?$

The expression $= (3x + 4y - xy^2) + (3x + 2x^2 - 2xy)$, removing the inner parentheses;
$= 6x + 4y + 2x^2 - xy^2 - 2xy$, combining like terms.

EXAMPLE 2: $(2a + 3a^2 - 4) - 2(4a^2 - 2(a + 4)) = ?$

It equals $(2a + 3a^2 - 4) - 2(4a^2 - 2a - 8)$, removing inner parentheses;
$= 2a + 3a^2 - 4 - 8a^2 + 4a + 16$, removing outer parentheses;
$= -5a^2 + 6a + 12$, combining like terms.

1–4

Multiplying Algebraic Expressions. When you multiply two expressions, you multiply *each term of the first by each term of the second.*

EXAMPLE 1: $(b - 4)(b + a) = b(b + a) - 4(b + a) = ?$
$$= b^2 + ab - 4b - 4a.$$

EXAMPLE 2: $(2h - 4)(h + 2h^2 + h^3) = ?$

$$= 2h(h + 2h^2 + h^3) - 4(h + 2h^2 + h^3)$$
$$= 2h^2 + 4h^3 + 2h^4 - 4h - 8h^2 - 4h^3$$
$$= -4h - 6h^2 + 2h^4, \text{ which is the product.}$$

If you need to multiply more than two expressions, multiply the first two expressions, then multiply the result by the third expression, and so on until you have used each factor. Since algebraic expressions can be multiplied, they can be squared, cubed, or raised to other powers.

EXAMPLE 3: $(x - 2y)^3 = (x - 2y)(x - 2y)(x - 2y)$.

Since $(x - 2y)(x - 2y)$ $= x^2 - 2yx - 2yx + 4y^2$
$= x^2 - 4xy + 4y^2$,

$(x - 2y)^3 = (x^2 - 4xy + 4y^2)(x - 2y)$
$= x(x^2 - 4xy + 4y^2) - 2y(x^2 - 4xy + 4y^2)$
$= x^3 - 4x^2y + 4xy^2 - 2x^2y + 8xy^2 - 8y^3$
$= x^3 - 6x^2y + 12xy^2 - 8y^3$.

The order in which you multiply algebraic expressions does not matter. Thus $(2a + b)(x^2 + 2x) = (x^2 + 2x)(2a + b)$.

1–5

Factoring Algebraic Expressions. If an algebraic expression is the product of other algebraic expressions, then the expressions are called factors of the original expression. For instance, we claim that $(2h - 4)$ and $(h + 2h^2 + h^3)$ are factors of $-4h - 6h^2 + 2h^4$. We can always check to see if we have the correct factors by multiplying; so by example 2 above we see that our claim is correct. We need to be able to factor algebraic expressions in order to solve quadratic equations. It also can be helpful in dividing algebraic expressions.

First remove any monomial factor which appears in every term of the expression. Some examples:

$$3x + 3y = 3(x + y): 3 \text{ is a monomial factor.}$$
$$15a^2b + 10ab = 5ab(3a + 2): 5ab \text{ is a monomial factor.}$$

$$\frac{1}{2}hy - 3h^3 + 4hy = h\left(\frac{1}{2}y - 3h^2 + 4y\right),$$

$$= h\left(\frac{9}{2}y - 3h^2\right): h \text{ is a monomial factor.}$$

You may also need to factor expressions which contain squares or higher powers into factors which only contain linear terms. (Linear terms are term in which variables are raised only to the first power.) The first rule to remember is that since $(a + b)(a - b) = a^2 + ba - ba - b^2 = a^2 - b^2$, the difference of two squares can always be factored.

EXAMPLE 1:   Factor $(9m^2 - 16)$.

$9m^2 = (3m)^2$ and $16 = 4^2$, so the factors are $(3m - 4)(3m + 4)$.

Since $(3m - 4)(3m + 4) = 9m^2 - 16$, these factors are correct.

EXAMPLE 2: Factor $x^4y^4 - 4x^2$.

$x^4y^4 = (x^2y^2)^2$ and $4x^2 = (2x)^2$, so the factors are $x^2y^2 + 2x$ and $x^2y^2 - 2x$.

You also may need to factor expressions which contain squared terms and linear terms, such as $x^2 + 4x + 3$. The factors will be of the form $(x + a)$ and $(x + b)$. Since $(x + a)(x + b) = x^2 + (a + b)x + ab$, you must look for a pair of numbers a and b such that $a \cdot b$ is the numerical term in the expression and $a + b$ is the coefficient of the linear term (the term with exponent 1).

EXAMPLE 3: Factor $x^2 + 4x + 3$.

You want numbers whose product is 3 and whose sum is 4. Look at the possible factors of three and check whether they add up to 4. Since $3 = 3 \times 1$ and $3 + 1$ is 4, the factors are $(x + 3)$ and $(x + 1)$. Remember to check by multiplying.

EXAMPLE 4: Factor $y^2 + y - 6$.

Since -6 is negative, the two numbers a and b must be of opposite sign. Possible pairs of factors for -6 are -6 and $+1$, 6 and -1, 3 and -2, and -3 and 2. Since $-2 + 3 = 1$, the factors are $(y + 3)$ and $(y - 2)$. So $(y + 3)(y - 2) = y^2 + y - 6$.

EXAMPLE 5: Factor $a^3 + 4a^2 + 4a$.

Factor out a, so $a^3 + 4a^2 + 4a = a(a^2 + 4a + 4)$. Consider $a^2 + 4a + 4$; since $2 + 2 = 4$ and $2 \times 2 = 4$, the factors are $(a + 2)$ and $(a + 2)$. Therefore, $a^3 + 4a^2 + 4a = a(a + 2)^2$.

If the term with the highest exponent has a coefficient unequal to 1, divide the entire expression by that coefficient. For example, to factor $3a^3 + 12a^2 + 12a$, factor out a 3 from each term, and the result is $a^3 + 4a^2 + 4a$ which is $a(a + 2)^2$. Thus, $3a^3 + 12a^2 + 12a = 3a(a + 2)^2$.

There are some expressions which cannot be factored, for example, $x^2 + 4x + 6$. In general, if you can't factor something by using the methods given above, don't waste a lot of time on the question. Sometimes you may be able to check the answers given to find out what the correct factors are.

1–6

Division of Algebraic Expressions. The main things to remember in division are:

(1) When you divide a sum, you can get the same result by dividing each term and adding quotients. For example, $\dfrac{9x + 4xy + y^2}{x} = \dfrac{9x}{x} + \dfrac{4xy}{x} + \dfrac{y^2}{x}$
$= 9 + 4y + \dfrac{y^2}{x}$.

(2) You can cancel common factors, so the results on factoring will be helpful. For example, $\dfrac{x^2 - 2x}{x - 2} = \dfrac{x(x - 2)}{x - 2} = x$.

EXAMPLE 1: $\dfrac{2x + 2y + x^2 - y^2}{x + y} = ?$

$$\frac{2x + 2y + x^2 - y^2}{x + y} = \frac{2x + 2y}{x + y} + \frac{x^2 - y^2}{x + y}$$

$$= \frac{2(x + y)}{x + y} + \frac{(x - y)(x + y)}{x + y}$$

$$= 2 + x - y$$

You can also divide one algebraic expression by another using long division.

EXAMPLE 2: $(15x^2 + 2x - 4) \div 3x - 1$.

$$
\begin{array}{r}
5x + 2 \\
3x - 1 \overline{)15x^2 + 2x - 4} \\
\underline{15x^2 - 5x} \\
7x - 4 \\
\underline{6x - 2} \\
x - 2
\end{array}
$$

So the answer is $5x + 2$ with a remainder of $x - 2$.
You can check by multiplying,

$(5x + 2)(3x - 1) = 15x^2 + 6x - 5x - 2$

$= 15x^2 + x - 2$; now add the remainder $x - 2$

and the result is $15x^2 + x - 2 + x - 2 = 15x^2 + 2x - 4$.

Division problems where you need to use (1) and (2) are more likely than problems involving long division.

II–2. Equations

2–1

AN EQUATION is a statement that says two algebraic expressions are equal.
$x + 2 = 3$, $4 + 2 = 6$, $3x^2 + 2x - 6 = 0$, $x^2 + y^2 = z^2$, $\dfrac{y}{x} = 2 + z$, and
$A = LW$ are all examples of equations. We will refer to the algebraic expressions on each side of the equals sign as the left side and the right side of the equation. Thus, in the equation $2x + 4 = 6y + x$, $2x + 4$ is the left side and $6y + x$ is the right side.

2–2

If we assign specific numbers to each variable or unknown in an algebraic expression, then the algebraic expression will be equal to a number. This is called *evaluating* the expression. For example, if you evaluate $2x + 4y^2 + 3$ for $x = -1$ and $y = 2$, the expression is equal to $2(-1) + 4 \cdot 2^2 + 3 = -2 + 4 \cdot 4 + 3 = 17$.

If we evaluate each side of an equation and the number obtained is the same for each side of the equation, then the specific values assigned to the unknowns are called a *solution of the equation*. Another way of saying this is that the choices for the unknowns satisfy the equation.

EXAMPLE 1: Consider the equation $2x + 3 = 9$.

If $x = 3$, then the left side of the equation becomes $2 \cdot 3 + 3 = 6 + 3 = 9$, so both sides equals 9, and $x = 3$ is a solution of $2x + 3 = 9$. If $x = 4$, then the left side is $2 \cdot 4 + 3 = 11$. Since 11 is not equal to 9, $x = 4$ is *not* a solution of $2x + 3 = 9$.

EXAMPLE 2: Consider the equation $x^2 + y^2 = 5x$.

If $x = 1$ and $y = 2$, then the left side is $1^2 + 2^2$ which equals $1 + 4 = 5$. The right side is $5 \cdot 1 = 5$; since both sides are equal to 5, $x = 1$ and $y = 2$ is a solution.

If $x = 5$ and $y = 0$, then the left side is $5^2 + 0^2 = 25$ and the right side is $5 \cdot 5 = 25$, so $x = 5$ and $y = 0$ is also a solution.

If $x = 1$ and $y = 1$, then the left side is $1^2 + 1^2 = 2$ and the right side is $5 \cdot 1 = 5$. Therefore, since $2 \neq 5$, $x = 1$ and $y = 1$ is not a solution.

There are some equations that *do not have any solutions that are real numbers*. Since the square of any real number is positive or zero, the equation $x^2 = -4$ does not have any solutions that are real numbers.

2–3

Equivalence. One equation is *equivalent* to another equation, if they have exactly the same solutions. The basic idea in solving equations is to transform a given equation into an equivalent equation whose solutions are obvious.

The two main tools for solving equations are:

(A) If you add or subtract the same algebraic expression to or from *each side* of an equation, the resulting equation is equivalent to the original equation.

(B) If you multiply or divide both sides of an equation by the same *nonzero* algebraic expression, the resulting equation is equivalent to the original equation.

The most common type of equation is the linear equation with only one unknown. $6z = 4z - 3$, $3 + a = 2a - 4$, $3b + 2b = b - 4b$, are all examples of linear equations with only one unknown.

Using (A) and (B), you can solve a linear equation in one unknown in the following way:

(1) Group all the terms which involve the unknown on one side of the equation and all the terms which are purely numerical on the other side of the equation. This is called *isolating the unknown*.
(2) Combine the terms on each side.
(3) Divide each side by the coefficient of the unknown.

EXAMPLE 1: Solve $6x + 2 = 3$ for x.

(1) Using (A) subtract 2 from each side of the equation. Then $6x + 2 - 2 = 3 - 2$ or $6x = 3 - 2$.
(2) $6x = 1$.
(3) Divide each side by 6. Therefore, $x = \dfrac{1}{6}$.

You should always check your answer in the original equation.

CHECK: Since $6 \left(\dfrac{1}{6}\right) + 2 = 1 + 2 = 3$, $x = \dfrac{1}{6}$ is the solution.

EXAMPLE 2:   Solve $3x + 15 = 3 - 4x$ for x.

(1) Add $4x$ to each side and subtract 15 from each side; $3x + 15 - 15 + 4x = 3 - 15 - 4x + 4x$.

(2) $7x = -12$.

(3) Divide each side by 7, so $x = \dfrac{-12}{7}$ is the solution.

CHECK: $3\left(\dfrac{-12}{7}\right) + 15 = \dfrac{-36}{7} + 15 = \dfrac{69}{7}$ and $3 - 4\left(\dfrac{-12}{7}\right) = 3 + \dfrac{48}{7} = \dfrac{69}{7}$.

If you do the same thing to each side of an equation, the result is still an equation but it may not be equivalent to the original equation. Be especially careful if you square each side of an equation. For example, $x = -4$ is an equation; square both sides and you get $x^2 = 16$ which has both $x = 4$ and $x = -4$ as solutions. *Always check your answer in the original equation.*

If the equation you want to solve involves square roots, get rid of the square roots by squaring each side of the equation. Remember to check your answer since squaring each side does not always give an equivalent equation.

EXAMPLE 3:   Solve $\sqrt{4x + 3} = 5$.

Square both sides: $(\sqrt{4x + 3})^2 = 4x + 3$ and $5^2 = 25$, so the new equation is $4x + 3 = 25$. Subtract 3 from each side to get $4x = 22$ and now divide each side by 4. The solution is $x = \dfrac{22}{4} = 5.5$. Since $4(5.5) + 3 = 25$ and $\sqrt{25} = 5$, $x = 5.5$ is a solution to the equation $\sqrt{4x + 3} = 5$.

If an equation involves fractions, multiply through by a common denominator and then solve. Check your answer to make sure you did not multiply or divide by zero.

EXAMPLE 4:   Solve $\dfrac{3}{a} = 9$ for a.

Multiply each side by a: the result is $3 = 9a$. Divide each side by 9, and you obtain $\dfrac{3}{9} = a$ or $a = \dfrac{1}{3}$. Since $\dfrac{3}{\frac{1}{3}} = 3 \cdot 3 = 9$, $a = \dfrac{1}{3}$ is a solution.

2-4

Solving Two Equations in Two Unknowns.   You may be asked to solve two equations in two unknowns. Use one equation to solve for one unknown in terms of the other; now change the second equation into an equation in only one unknown which can be solved by the methods of the preceding section.

EXAMPLE 1:   Solve for x and y: $\begin{cases} \dfrac{x}{y} = 3 \\ 2x + 4y = 20. \end{cases}$

The first equation gives $x = 3y$. Using $x = 3y$, the second equation is $2(3y) + 4y = 6y + 4y$ or $10y = 20$, so $y = \dfrac{20}{10} = 2$. Since $x = 3y$, $x = 6$.

CHECK: $\frac{6}{2} = 3$, and $2 \cdot 6 + 4 \cdot 2 = 20$, so $x = 6$ and $y = 2$ is a solution.

EXAMPLE 2: If $2x + y = 5$ and $x + y = 4$, find x and y.

Since $x + y = 4$, $y = 4 - x$, so $2x + y = 2x + 4 - x = x + 4 = 5$ and $x = 1$. If $x = 1$, then $y = 4 - 1 = 3$. So $x = 1$ and $y = 3$ is the solution.

CHECK: $2 \cdot 1 + 3 = 5$ and $1 + 3 = 4$.

Sometimes we can solve two equations by adding them or by subtracting one from the other. If we subtract $x + y = 4$ from $2x + y = 5$ in example 2, we have $x = 1$. However, the previous method will work in cases when the addition method does not work.

2–5

Solving Quadratic Equations. If the terms of an equation contain squares of the unknown as well as linear terms, the equation is called *quadratic*. Some examples of quadratic equations are $x^2 + 4x = 3$, $2z^2 - 1 = 3z^2 - 2z$, and $a + 6 = a^2 + 6$.

To solve a quadratic equation:

(A) Group all the terms on one side of the equation so that the other side is *zero*.
(B) Combine the terms on the nonzero side.
(C) Factor the expression into linear expressions.
(D) Set the linear factors equal to zero and solve.

The method depends on the fact that if a product of expressions is zero then at least one of the expressions must be zero.

EXAMPLE 1: Solve $x^2 + 4x = -3$.

(A) $x^2 + 4x + 3 = 0$
(C) $x^2 + 4x + 3 = (x + 3)(x + 1) = 0$
(D) So $x + 3 = 0$ or $x + 1 = 0$. Therefore, the solutions are $x = -3$ and $x = -1$.

CHECK: $(-3)^2 + 4(-3) = 9 - 12 = -3$
$(-1)^2 + 4(-1) = 1 - 4 = -3$, so $x = -3$ and $x = -1$
are solutions.

A quadratic equation will usually have 2 different solutions, but it is possible for a quadratic to have only one solution or even no real solution.

EXAMPLE 2: If $2z^2 - 1 = 3z^2 - 2z$, what is z?

(A) $0 = 3z^2 - 2z^2 - 2z + 1$
(B) $z^2 - 2z + 1 = 0$
(C) $z^2 - 2z + 1 = (z - 1)^2 = 0$
(D) $z - 1 = 0$ or $z = 1$

CHECK: $2 \cdot 1^2 - 1 = 2 - 1 = 1$ and $3 \cdot 1^2 - 2 \cdot 1 = 3 - 2 = 1$,
so $z = 1$ is a solution.

Equations which may not look like quadratics may be changed into quadratics.

EXAMPLE 3:   Find a if $a - 3 = \dfrac{10}{a}$.

Multiply each side of the equation by a to obtain $a^2 - 3a = 10$, which is quadratic.

(A) $a^2 - 3a - 10 = 0$
(C) $a^2 - 3a - 10 = (a - 5)(a + 2)$
(D) So $a - 5 = 0$ or $a + 2 = 0$

Therefore, $a = 5$ and $a = -2$ are the solutions.

CHECK: $5 - 3 = 2 = \dfrac{10}{5}$ so $a = 5$ is a solution.

$-2 - 3 = -5 = \dfrac{10}{-2}$ so $a = -2$ is a solution.

You can also solve quadratic equations by using the *quadratic formula*. The quadratic formula states that the solutions of the quadratic equation

$$ax^2 + bx + c = 0 \text{ are } x = \frac{1}{2a}[-b + \sqrt{b^2 - 4ac}]$$

$$and \ x = \frac{1}{2a}[-b - \sqrt{b^2 - 4ac}].$$

This is usually written $x = \dfrac{1}{2a}[-b \pm \sqrt{b^2 - 4ac}]$. Use of the quadratic formula would replace steps (C) and (D).

EXAMPLE 4:   Find x if $x^2 + 5x = 12 - x^2$.

(A) $x^2 + 5x + x^2 - 12 = 0$
(B) $2x^2 + 5x - 12 = 0$

So $a = 2$, $b = 5$ and $c = -12$. Therefore, using the quadratic formula, the solutions are $x = \frac{1}{4}[-5 \pm \sqrt{25 - 4 \cdot 2 \cdot (-12)}] = \frac{1}{4}[-5 \pm \sqrt{25 + 96}] = \frac{1}{4}[-5 \pm \sqrt{121}]$. So we have $x = \frac{1}{4}[-5 \pm 11]$. The solutions are $x = \frac{3}{2}$ and $x = -4$.

CHECK: $\left(\dfrac{3}{2}\right)^2 + 5 \cdot \dfrac{3}{2} = \dfrac{9}{4} + \dfrac{15}{2} = \dfrac{39}{4} = 12 - \dfrac{9}{4} = 12 - \left(\dfrac{3}{2}\right)^2$

$(-4)^2 + 5(-4) = 16 - 20 = -4 = 12 - 16 = 12 - (-4)^2$

NOTE: If $b^2 - 4ac$ is negative, then the quadratic equation $ax^2 + bx + c = 0$ has no real solutions because negative numbers do not have real square roots.

The quadratic formula will always give you the solutions to a quadratic equation. If you can factor the equation, factoring will usually give you the solution in less time. Remember, you want to answer as many questions as you can in the time given. So factor if you can. If you don't see the factor immediately, then use the formula.

II–3. Word Problems

3–1

The general method for solving word problems is to translate them into algebraic problems. The quantities you are seeking are the unknowns, which are usually represented by letters. The information you are given in the problem is then turned into equations. Words such as "is," "was," "are," and "were" mean equals, and words like "of" and "as much as" mean multiplication.

EXAMPLE 1: A coat was sold for $75. The coat was sold for 150% of the cost of the coat. How much did the coat cost?

You want to find the cost of the coat. Let C be the cost of the coat. You know that the coat was sold for $75 and that $75 was 150% of the cost. So $75 = 150% of C or $75 = 1.5C$. Solving for C you get $C = \dfrac{75}{1.5} = 50$, so the coat cost $50.

CHECK: $(1.5)\$50 = \$75$.

EXAMPLE 2: Tom's salary is 125% of Joe's salary; Mary's salary is 80% of Joe's salary. The total of all three salaries is $61,000. What is Mary's salary?

Let M = Mary's salary, J = Joe's salary and T = Tom's salary. The first sentence says $T = 125\%$ of J or $T = \dfrac{5}{4}J$, and $M = 80\%$ of J or $M = \dfrac{4}{5}J$. The second sentence says that $T + M + J = \$61,000$. Using the information from the first sentence, $T + M + J = \dfrac{5}{4}J + \dfrac{4}{5}J + J = \dfrac{25}{20}J + \dfrac{16}{20}J + J = \dfrac{61}{20}J$. So $\dfrac{61}{20}J = 61,000$; solving for J you have $J = \dfrac{20}{61} \times 61,000 = 20,000$. Therefore, $T = \dfrac{5}{4} \times \$20,000 = \$25,000$ and $M = \dfrac{4}{5} \times \$20,000 = \$16,000$.

CHECK: $\$25,000 + \$16,000 + \$20,000 = \$61,000$.

So Mary's salary is $16,000.

EXAMPLE 3: Steve weighs 25 pounds more than Jim. The combined weight of Jim and Steve is 325 pounds. How much does Jim weigh?

Let S = Steve's weight in pounds and J = Jim's weight in pounds. The first sentence says $S = J + 25$, and the second sentence becomes $S + J = 325$. Since $S = J + 25$, $S + J = 325$ becomes $(J + 25) + J = 2J + 25 = 325$. So $2J = 300$ and $J = 150$. Therefore, Jim weighs 150 pounds.

CHECK: If Jim weighs 150 pounds, then Steve weighs 175 pounds and $150 + 175 = 325$.

EXAMPLE 4: A carpenter is designing a closet. The floor will be in the shape of a rectangle whose length is 2 feet more than its width. How long should the closet be if the carpenter wants the area of the floor to be 15 square feet?

The area of a rectangle is length times width, usually written $A = LW$, where A is the area, L is the length, and W is the width. We know $A = 15$ and $L = 2 + W$. Therefore, $LW = (2 + W)W = W^2 + 2W$; this must equal 15. So we need to solve $W^2 + 2W = 15$ or $W^2 + 2W - 15 = 0$. Since $W^2 + 2W - 15$ factors into $(W + 5)(W - 3)$, the only possible solutions are $W = -5$ and $W = 3$. Since W represents a width, -5 cannot be the answer; therefore the width is 3 feet. The length is the width plus two feet, so the length is 5 feet. Since $5 \times 3 = 15$, the answer checks.

3–2

Distance Problems. A common type of word problem is a distance or velocity problem. The basic formula

$$\boxed{\text{DISTANCE TRAVELED} = \text{RATE} \times \text{TIME}}$$

The formula is abbreviated $d = rt$.

EXAMPLE 1: A train travels at an average speed of 50 miles per hour for $2\frac{1}{2}$ hours and then travels at a speed of 70 miles per hour for $1\frac{1}{2}$ hours. How far did the train travel in the entire 4 hours?

The train traveled for $2\frac{1}{2}$ hours at an average speed of 50 miles per hour, so it traveled $50 \times \frac{5}{2} = 125$ miles in the first $2\frac{1}{2}$ hours. Traveling at a speed of 70 miles per hour for $1\frac{1}{2}$ hours, the distance traveled will be equal to $r \times t$ where $r = 70$ m.p.h. and $t = 1\frac{1}{2}$, so the distance is $70 \times \frac{3}{2} = 105$ miles. Therefore, the total distance traveled is $125 + 105 = 230$ miles.

EXAMPLE 2: The distance from Cleveland to Buffalo is 200 miles. A train takes $3\frac{1}{2}$ hours to go from Buffalo to Cleveland and $4\frac{1}{2}$ hours to go back from Cleveland to Buffalo. What was the average speed of the train for the round trip from Buffalo to Cleveland and back?

The train took $3\frac{1}{2} + 4\frac{1}{2} = 8$ hours for the trip. The distance of a round trip is $2(200) = 400$ miles. Since $d = rt$ then 400 miles $= r \times 8$ hours. Solve for r and you have $r = \dfrac{400 \text{ miles}}{8 \text{ hours}} = 50$ miles per hour. Therefore the average speed is 50 miles per hour.

The speed in the formula is the average speed. If you know that there are different speeds for different lengths of time, then you must use the formula more than once, as we did in example 1.

3–3

Work Problems.   In this type of problem you can always assume all workers in the same category work at the same rate. The main idea is: If it takes k workers 1 hour to do a job then *each worker does $\frac{1}{k}$ of the job in an hour* or he works at the rate of $\frac{1}{k}$ of the job per hour. If it takes m workers h hours to finish a job then each worker does $\frac{1}{m}$ of the job in h hours so he does $\frac{1}{h}$ of $\frac{1}{m}$ in an hour. Therefore, each worker *works at the rate of $\frac{1}{mh}$ of the job per hour.*

EXAMPLE 1:   If 5 men take an hour to dig a ditch, how long should it take 12 men to dig a ditch of the same type?

Since 5 workers took an hour, each worker does $\frac{1}{5}$ of the job in an hour. So 12 workers will work at the rate of $\frac{12}{5}$ of the job per hour. Thus if T is the time it takes for 12 workers to do the job, $\frac{12}{5} \times T = 1$ job and $T = \frac{5}{12} \times 1$, so

$$T = \frac{5}{12} \text{ hours or 25 minutes.}$$

EXAMPLE 2:   Worker A takes 8 hours to do a job. Worker B takes 10 hours to do the same job. How long should it take worker A and worker B working together, but independently, to do the same job?

Worker A works at a rate of $\frac{1}{8}$ of the job per hour, since he takes 8 hours to finish the job. Worker B finished the job in 10 hours, so he works at a rate of $\frac{1}{10}$ of the job per hour. Therefore, if they work together they should complete $\frac{1}{8} + \frac{1}{10} = \frac{18}{80} = \frac{9}{40}$, so they work at a rate of $\frac{9}{40}$ of the job per hour together. So if T is the time it takes them to finish the job, $\frac{9}{40}$ of the job per hour $\times\ T$ hours must equal 1 job. Therefore,

$$\frac{9}{40} \times T = 1 \text{ and } T = \frac{40}{9} = 4\frac{4}{9} \text{ hours.}$$

EXAMPLE 3:   There are two taps, tap 1 and tap 2, in a keg. If both taps are opened, the keg is drained in 20 minutes. If tap 1 is closed and tap 2 is open, the keg will be drained in 30 minutes. If tap 2 is closed and tap 1 is open, how long will it take to drain the keg?

Tap 1 and tap 2 together take 20 minutes to drain the keg, so together they drain the keg at a rate of $\frac{1}{20}$ of the keg per minute. Tap 2 takes 30 minutes to drain the keg by itself, so it drains the keg at the rate of $\frac{1}{30}$ of the keg per minute. Let

r be the rate at which tap 1 will drain the keg by itself. Then $\left(r + \dfrac{1}{30}\right)$ of the keg per minute is the rate at which both taps together will drain the keg, so $r + \dfrac{1}{30} = \dfrac{1}{20}$. Therefore, $r = \dfrac{1}{20} - \dfrac{1}{30} = \dfrac{1}{60}$, and tap 1 drains the keg at the rate of $\dfrac{1}{60}$ of the keg per minute, so it will take 60 minutes or 1 hour for tap 1 to drain the keg if tap 2 is closed.

II–4. Counting Problems

4–1

An example of one type of counting problem is: 50 students signed up for both English and Math. 90 students signed up for either English or Math. If 25 students are taking English but not taking Math, how many students are taking Math but not taking English?

In these problems, "either . . . or . . ." means you can take both, so the people taking both are counted among the people taking either Math or English.

You must avoid counting the same people twice in these problems. The formula is:

> the number taking English or Math = the number taking English + the number taking Math − the number taking both.

You have to subtract the number taking both subjects since they are counted once with those taking English and counted again with those taking Math.

A person taking English is either taking Math or not taking Math, so there are 50 + 25 = 75 people taking English, 50 taking English and Math and 25 taking English but not taking Math. Since 75 are taking English, 90 = 75 + number taking Math − 50; so there are 90 − 25 = 65 people taking Math. 50 of the people taking Math are taking English so 65 − 50 or 15 are taking Math but not English.

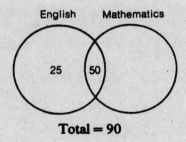

English   Mathematics

25   50

Total = 90

The figure shows what is given. Since 90 students signed up for English or Mathematics, 15 must be taking Mathematics but not English

EXAMPLE 1:   In a survey, 60% of those surveyed owned a car and 80% of those surveyed owned a TV. If 55% owned both a car and a TV, what percent of those surveyed owned a car or a TV or both?

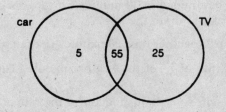

car   TV

5   55   25

The basic formula is:

people who own a car or a TV = people who own a car
+ people who own a TV − people who own both a car and a TV.

So the people who own a car or a TV = 60% + 80% − 55% = 85%. Therefore, 85% of the people surveyed own either a car or a TV.

If we just add 60% and 80% the result is 140% which is impossible. This is because the 55% who own both are counted twice.

This type of problem can involve three or more groups. The basic principle remains to avoid counting the same person more than once.

EXAMPLE 2: 70 students are enrolled in Math, English, or German. 40 students are in Math, 35 are in English, and 30 are in German. 15 students are enrolled in all three of the courses. How many of the students are enrolled in exactly two of the courses: Math, English, and German?

If we add 40, 35, and 30, the people enrolled in exactly two of the courses will be counted twice and the people in all three courses will be counted three times. So if we let N stand for the number enrolled in exactly two courses, then we have the equation $70 = 40 + 35 + 30 − N − 2(15) = 75 − N$. Therefore, N is $75 − 70 = 5$. So there are 5 students enrolled in exactly two of the three courses.

4–2

> If an event can happen in m different ways, and each of the m ways is followed by a second event which can occur in k different ways, then the first event can be followed by the second event in $m \cdot k$ different ways. This is called the *fundamental principle of counting*.

EXAMPLE 1: If there are 3 different roads from Syracuse to Binghamton and 4 different roads from Binghamton to Scranton, how many different routes are there from Syracuse to Scranton which go through Binghamton?

There are 3 different ways to go from Syracuse to Binghamton. Once you are in Binghamton, there are 4 different ways to get to Scranton. So using the fundamental principle of counting, there are $3 \times 4 = 12$ different ways to get from Syracuse to Scranton going through Binghamton.

EXAMPLE 2: A club has 20 members. They are electing a president and a vice-president. How many different outcomes of the election are possible? (Assume the president and vice-president must be different members of the club.)

There are 20 members, so there are 20 choices for president. Once a president is chosen, there are 19 members left who can be vice-president. So there are $20 \cdot 19 = 380$ different possible outcomes of the election.

II–5. Ratio and Proportion

5–1

Ratio. A ratio is a comparison of two numbers by division. The ratio of a to b is written as $a:b = \dfrac{a}{b} = a \div b$. We can handle ratios as fractions, since a ratio is a fraction. In the ratio $a:b$, a and b are called the *terms* of the ratio.

Since a:b *is a fraction,* b *can never be zero.* The fraction $\frac{a}{b}$ is usually different from the fraction $\frac{b}{a}$ (for example, $\frac{3}{2}$ is not the same as $\frac{2}{3}$) so *the order of the terms in a ratio is important.*

EXAMPLE 1: If an orange costs 20¢ and an apple costs 12¢, what is the ratio of the cost of an orange to the cost of an apple?

The ratio is $\frac{20¢}{12¢} = \frac{5}{3}$ or 5:3. Notice that the ratio of the cost of an apple to the cost of an orange is $\frac{12¢}{20¢} = \frac{3}{5}$ or 3:5. So the order of the terms is important.

A ratio is a number, so if you want to find the ratio of two quantities they must be expressed in the same units.

EXAMPLE 2: What is the ratio of 8 inches to 6 feet?

Change 6 feet into inches. Since there are 12 inches in a foot, 6 feet = 6 × 12 inches = 72 inches. So the ratio is $\frac{8 \text{ inches}}{72 \text{ inches}} = \frac{1}{9}$ or 1:9. If you regard ratios as fractions, the units must cancel out. In example 2, if you did not change units the ratio would be $\frac{8 \text{ inches}}{6 \text{ feet}} = \frac{4}{3}$ inches/feet, which is not a number.

If two numbers measure different quantities, their quotient is usually called a rate. For example, $\frac{50 \text{ miles}}{2 \text{ hours}}$, which equals 25 miles per hour, is a rate of speed.

5-2

Proportion. A proportion is a statement that two ratios are equal. For example, $\frac{3}{12} = \frac{1}{4}$ is a proportion; it could also be expressed as 3:12 = 1:4 or 3:12 :: 1:4.

In the proportion $a:b = c:d$, the terms on the outside (*a* and *d*) are called the *extremes,* and the terms on the inside (*b* and *c*) are called the *means.* Since $a:b$ and $c:d$ are ratios, *b* and *d* are both different from zero, so $bd \neq 0$. Multiply each side of $\frac{a}{b} = \frac{c}{d}$ by bd; you get $(bd)\left(\frac{a}{b}\right) = ad$ and $(bd)\left(\frac{c}{d}\right) = bc$. Since $bd \neq 0$, the proportion $\frac{a}{b} = \frac{c}{d}$ is equivalent to the equation $ad = bc$. This is usually expressed in the following way:

In a proportion the product of the extremes is equal to the product of the means.

EXAMPLE 1: Find *x* if $\frac{4}{5} = \frac{10}{x}$.

In the proportion $\frac{4}{5} = \frac{10}{x}$, 4 and *x* are the extremes and 5 and 10 are the means, so $4x = 5 \cdot 10 = 50$.

Solve for *x* and we get $x = \frac{50}{4} = 12.5$

Finding the products ad and bc is also called *cross multiplying the proportion:* $\dfrac{a}{b}\diagdown\diagup\dfrac{c}{d}$. So cross multiplying a proportion gives two equal numbers. The proportion $\dfrac{a}{b} = \dfrac{c}{d}$ is read "*a* is to *b* as *c* is to *d*."

EXAMPLE 2: Two numbers are in the ratio $5:4$ and their difference is 10. What is the larger number?

Let m and n be the two numbers. Then $\dfrac{m}{n} = \dfrac{5}{4}$ and $m - n = 10$. Cross multiply the proportion and you get $5n = 4m$ or $n = \dfrac{4}{5}m$. So $m - n = m - \dfrac{4}{5}m = \dfrac{1}{5}m = 10$ and $m = 50$, which means $n = \dfrac{4}{5} \cdot 50 = 40$. Therefore, the larger number is 50.

CHECK: $\dfrac{50}{40} = \dfrac{5}{4}$ and $50 - 40 = 10$.

Two variables, a and b, are *directly proportional* if they satisfy a relationship of the form $a = kb$, where k is a number. The distance a car travels in two hours and its average speed for the two hours are directly proportional, since $d = 2s$ where d is the distance and s is the average speed expressed in miles per hour. Here $k = 2$. Sometimes the word *directly* is omitted, so a and b are proportional means $a = kb$.

EXAMPLE 3: If m is proportional to n and $m = 5$ when $n = 4$, what is the value of m when $n = 18$?

There are two different ways to work the problem.

I. Since m and n are directly proportional, $m = kn$; and $m = 5$ when $n = 4$, so $5 = k \cdot 4$ which means $k = \dfrac{5}{4}$. Therefore, $m = \dfrac{5}{4}n$. So when $n = 18$, $m = \dfrac{5}{4} \cdot 18 = \dfrac{90}{4} = 22.5$.

II. Since m and n are directly proportional, $m = kn$. If n' is some value of n, then the value of m corresponding to n' we will call m', and $m' = kn'$. So $\dfrac{m}{n} = k$ and $\dfrac{m'}{n'} = k$; therefore, $\dfrac{m}{n} = \dfrac{m'}{n'}$ is a proportion. Since $m = 5$ when $n = 4$, $\dfrac{m}{n} = \dfrac{5}{4} = \dfrac{m'}{18}$. Cross multiply and we have $4m' = 90$ or $m' = \dfrac{90}{4} = 22.5$.

If two quantities are proportional, you can always set up a proportion in this manner.

EXAMPLE 4: If a machine makes 3 yards of cloth in 2 minutes, how many yards of cloth will the machine make in 50 minutes?

The amount of cloth is proportional to the time the machine operates. Let y be the number of yards of cloth the machine makes in 50 minutes; then $\dfrac{2 \text{ minutes}}{50 \text{ minutes}} = \dfrac{3 \text{ yards}}{y \text{ yards}}$, so $\dfrac{2}{50} = \dfrac{3}{y}$. Cross multiply, and you have $2y = 150$, so $y = 75$. Therefore, the machine makes 75 yards of cloth in 50 minutes.

Since a ratio is a number, the units must cancel; so put the numbers which measure the same quantity in the same ratio.

> *Any two units of measurement of the same quantity are directly proportional.*

EXAMPLE 5:   How many ounces are there in $4\frac{3}{4}$ pounds?

Let x be the number of ounces in $4\frac{3}{4}$ pounds. Since there are 16 ounces in a pound, $\dfrac{x \text{ ounces}}{16 \text{ ounces}} = \dfrac{4\frac{3}{4} \text{ pounds}}{1 \text{ pound}}$. Cross multiply to get $x = 16 \cdot 4\frac{3}{4} = 16 \cdot \dfrac{19}{4} = 76$; so $4\frac{3}{4}$ pounds = 76 ounces.

You can always change units by using a proportion. You should know the following measurements:

LENGTH:	1 foot = 12 inches
	1 yard = 3 feet
AREA:	1 square foot = 144 square inches
	1 square yard = 9 square feet
TIME:	1 minute = 60 seconds
	1 hour = 60 minutes
	1 day = 24 hours
	1 week = 7 days
	1 year = 52 weeks
VOLUME:	1 quart = 2 pints
	1 gallon = 4 quarts
WEIGHT:	1 ounce = 16 drams
	1 pound = 16 ounces
	1 ton = 2000 pounds

EXAMPLE 6:   On a map, it is $2\frac{1}{2}$ inches from Harrisburg to Gary. The actual distance from Harrisburg to Gary is 750 miles. What is the actual distance from town A to town B if they are 4 inches apart on the map?

Let d miles be the distance from A to B; then $\dfrac{2\frac{1}{2} \text{ inches}}{4 \text{ inches}} = \dfrac{750 \text{ miles}}{d \text{ miles}}$. Cross multiply and we have $\left(2\frac{1}{2}\right) d = 4 \times 750 = 3{,}000$, so $d = \dfrac{2}{5} \times 3{,}000 = 1{,}200$. Therefore, the distance from A to B is 1,200 miles. Problems like this one are often called scale problems.

Two variables, a and b, are *indirectly proportional* if they satisfy a relationship of the form $k = ab$, where k is a number. So the average speed of a car and the time it takes the car to travel 300 miles are indirectly proportional, since $st = 300$ where s is the speed and t is the time.

EXAMPLE 7: m is indirectly proportional to n and $m = 5$ when $n = 4$. What is the value of m when $n = 18$?

Since m and n are indirectly proportional, $m \cdot n = k$, and $k = 5 \cdot 4 = 20$ because $m = 5$ when $n = 4$. Therefore, $18m = k = 20$, so $m = \dfrac{20}{18} = \dfrac{10}{9}$ when $n = 18$.

Other examples of indirect proportion are work problems (see Section II-3-3).

If two quantities are directly proportional, then when one increases, the other increases. If two quantities are indirectly proportional, when one quantity increases, the other decreases.

5–3

It is also possible to compare three or more numbers by a ratio. The numbers A, B, and C are in the ratio $2:4:3$ means $A:B = 2:4$, $A:C = 2:3$, and $B:C = 4:3$. The order of the terms is important. $A:B:C$ is read A is to B is to C.

EXAMPLE 1: What is the ratio of Tom's salary to Martha's salary to Anne's salary if Tom makes \$15,000, Martha makes \$12,000 and Anne makes \$10,000?

The ratio is $15,000:12,000:10,000$ which is the same as $15:12:10$. You can cancel a factor which appears in *every* term.

EXAMPLE 2: The angles of a triangle are in the ratio $5:4:3$; how many degrees are there in the largest angle?

The sum of the angles in a triangle is $180°$. If the angles are $a°$, $b°$, and $c°$, then $a + b + c = 180$, and $a:b:c = 5:4:3$. You could find b in terms of a, since $\dfrac{a}{b} = \dfrac{5}{4}$, and c in terms of a, since $\dfrac{a}{c} = \dfrac{5}{3}$, and then solve the equation for a.

A quicker method for this type of problem is:

(1) Add all the numbers, so $5 + 4 + 3 = 12$.
(2) Use each number as the numerator of a fraction whose denominator is the result of step (1), getting $\dfrac{5}{12}, \dfrac{4}{12}, \dfrac{3}{12}$.
(3) Each quantity is the corresponding fraction (from step 2) of the total.

Thus

$a = \dfrac{5}{12}$ of 180 or 75, $b = \dfrac{4}{12}$ of 180 or 60, and $c = \dfrac{3}{12}$ of 180 or 45.

So the largest angle is $75°$.

CHECK: $75:60:45 = 5:4:3$ and $75 + 60 + 45 = 180$.

II–6. Sequence and Progressions

6–1

A SEQUENCE is an ordered collection of numbers. For example, 2,4,6,8,10, . . . is a sequence. 2,4,6,8,10 are called the *terms* of the sequence. We identify the terms by their position in the sequence; so 2 is the first term, 8 is the 4th term and so on. The dots mean the sequence continues; you should be able to figure out the succeeding terms. In the example, the sequence is the sequence of even integers, and the next term after 10 would be 12.

EXAMPLE 1:   What is the eighth term of the sequence 1,4,9,16,25, . . . ?

Since $1^2 = 1, 2^2 = 4, 3^2 = 9$, the sequence is the sequence of squares of integers, so the eighth term is $8^2 = 64$.

Sequences are sometimes given by a rule which defines an entry (usually called the n-th entry) in terms of previous entries of the sequence.

EXAMPLE 2:   If a sequence is defined by the rule $a_n = (a_{n-1} - 3)^2$, what is a_4 (the fourth term of the sequence) if a_1 is 1?

Since a_1 is 1, a_2 is $(1 - 3)^2 = 2^2 = 4$. So a_3 is $(4 - 3)^2 = (1)^2 = 1$. Therefore, a_4 is $(1 - 3)^2 = 4$.

6–2

An *arithmetic progression* is a sequence of numbers with the property that the *difference* of any two consecutive numbers is always the same. The numbers $2, 6, 10, 14, 18, 22, \ldots$ constitute an arithmetic progression, since each term is 4 more than the term before it. 4 is called the common difference of the progression.

If d is the common difference and a is the first term of the progression, then the nth term will be $a + (n - 1)d$. So a progression with common difference 4 and initial term 5 will have $5 + 6(4) = 29$ as its 7th term. You can check your answer. The sequence would be $5,9,13,17,21,25,29, \ldots$ so 29 is the seventh term.

A sequence of numbers is called a *geometric progression* if the *ratio* of consecutive terms is always the same. So $3,6,12,24,48, \ldots$ is a geometric progression since $\frac{6}{3} = 2 = \frac{12}{6} = \frac{24}{12} = \frac{48}{24}, \ldots$. *The nth term of a geometric progression is ar^{n-1}* where a is the first term and r is the common ratio. If a geometric progression started with 2 and the common ratio was 3, then the fifth term should be $2 \cdot 3^4 = 2 \cdot 81 = 162$. The sequence would be $2,6,18,54,162, \ldots$ so 162 is indeed the fifth term of the progression.

We can quickly add up the first n terms of a geometric progression which starts with a and has common ratio r. *The formula for the sum of the first n terms is $\frac{ar^n - a}{r - 1}$* when $r \neq 1$. (If $r = 1$ all the terms are the same so the sum is na.)

EXAMPLE: Find the sum of the first 7 terms of the sequence $5,10,20,40, \ldots$.

Since $\frac{10}{5} = \frac{20}{10} = \frac{40}{20} = 2$, the sequence is a geometric sequence with common ratio 2. The first term is 5, so $a = 5$ and the common ratio is 2. The sum of the first seven terms means $n = 7$, thus the sum is

$$\frac{5 \cdot 2^7 - 5}{2 - 1} = 5(2^7 - 1) = 5(128 - 1) = 5 \cdot 127 = 635.$$

CHECK: The first seven terms are $5,10,20,40,80,160,320$, and $5 + 10 + 20 + 40 + 80 + 160 + 320 = 635$.

II–7. Inequalities

7–1

A number is positive if it is greater than 0, so 1, $\dfrac{1}{1000}$, and 53.4 are all positive numbers. Positive numbers are signed numbers whose sign is $+$. If you think of numbers as points on a number line (see Section I-6-1), positive numbers correspond to points to the right of 0.

A number is negative if it is less than 0. $-\dfrac{4}{5}$, -50, and $-.0001$ are all negative numbers. Negative numbers are signed numbers whose sign is $-$. Negative numbers correspond to points to the left of 0 on a number line.

0 is the only number which is neither positive nor negative.

$a > b$ means the number a is greater than the number b; that is, $a = b + x$ where x is a positive number. If we look at a number line, $a > b$ means a is to the right of b. $a > b$ can also be read as b is less than a, which is also written $b < a$. For example, $-5 > -7.5$ because $-5 = -7.5 + 2.5$ and 2.5 is positive.

The notation $a \le b$ means a is less than or equal to b, or b is greater than or equal to a. For example, $5 \ge 4$; also $4 \ge 4$. $a \ne b$ means a is not equal to b.

If you need to know whether one fraction is greater than another fraction, put the fractions over a common denominator and compare the numerators.

EXAMPLE: Which is larger, $\dfrac{13}{16}$ or $\dfrac{31}{40}$?

A common denominator is 80. $\dfrac{13}{16} = \dfrac{65}{80}$, and $\dfrac{31}{40} = \dfrac{62}{80}$; since $65 > 62$, $\dfrac{65}{80} > \dfrac{62}{80}$, so $\dfrac{13}{16} > \dfrac{31}{40}$.

7–2

Inequalities have certain properties which are similar to equations. We can talk about the left side and the right side of an inequality, and we can use algebraic expressions for the sides of an inequality. For example, $6x < 5x + 4$. A value for an unknown *satisfies an inequality*, if when you evaluate each side of the inequality the numbers satisfy the inequality. So if $x = 2$, then $6x = 12$ and $5x + 4 = 14$ and since $12 < 14$, $x = 2$ satisfies $6x < 5x + 4$. Two inequalities are equivalent if the same collection of numbers satisfies both inequalities.

The following basic principles are used in work with inequalities:

(A) Adding the same expression to *each* side of an inequality gives an equivalent inequality (written $a < b \leftrightarrow a + c < b + c$ where $\leftrightarrow$ means equivalent).
(B) Subtracting the same expression from *each* side of an inequality gives an equivalent inequality ($a < b \leftrightarrow a - c < b - c$).
(C) Multiplying or dividing *each* side of an inequality by the same *positive* expression gives an equivalent inequality ($a < b \leftrightarrow ca < cb$ for $c > 0$).

(D) Multiplying or dividing each side of an inequality by the same *negative* expression *reverses* the inequality ($a < b \leftrightarrow ca > cb$ for $c < 0$).

(E) If both sides of an inequality have the same sign, inverting both sides of the inequality *reverses* the inequality.

$$0 < a < b \leftrightarrow 0 < \frac{1}{b} < \frac{1}{a}$$

$$a < b < 0 \leftrightarrow \frac{1}{b} < \frac{1}{a} < 0$$

(F) If two inequalities are of the same type (both greater or both less), adding the respective sides gives the same type of inequality.

$$(a < b \text{ and } c < d, \text{ then } a + c < b + d)$$

Note that the inequalities are *not* equivalent.

(G) If $a < b$ and $b < c$ then a < c.

EXAMPLE 1: Find the values of x for which $5x - 4 < 7x + 2$.

Using principle (B) subtract $5x + 2$ from each side, so $(5x - 4 < 7x + 2) \leftrightarrow -6 < 2x$. Now use principle (C) and divide each side by 2, so $-6 < 2x \leftrightarrow -3 < x$.

So any x greater than -3 satisfies the inequality. It is a good idea to make a spot check. -1 is > -3; let $x = -1$ then $5x - 4 = -9$ and $7x + 2 = -5$. Since $-9 < -5$, the answer is correct for at least the particular value $x = -1$.

EXAMPLE 2: Find the values of a which satisfy $a^2 + 1 > 2a + 4$.

Subtract $2a$ from each side, so
$(a^2 + 1 > 2a + 4) \leftrightarrow a^2 - 2a + 1 > 4$.
$a^2 - 2a + 1 = (a - 1)^2$ so
$a^2 - 2a + 1 > 4 \leftrightarrow (a - 1)^2 > 2^2$.

We need to be careful when we take the square roots of inequalities. If $q^2 > 4$ and if $q > 0$, then $q > 2$; but if $q < 0$, then $q < -2$. We must look at two cases in example 2. First, if $(a - 1) \geq 0$ then

$(a - 1)^2 > 2^2 \leftrightarrow a - 1 > 2$ or $a > 3$.
If $(a - 1) < 0$ then $(a - 1)^2 > 2^2 \leftrightarrow a - 1 < -2 \leftrightarrow a < -1$.
So the inequality is satisfied if $a > 3$ or if $a < -1$.

CHECK: $(-2)^2 + 1 = 5 > 2(-2) + 4 = 0$, and $5^2 + 1 = 26 > 14 = 2 \cdot 5 + 4$.

Some inequalities are not satisfied by *any* real number. For example, since $x^2 \geq 0$ for all x, there is no real number x such that $x^2 < -9$.

You may be given an inequality and asked whether other inequalities follow from the original inequality. You should be able to answer such questions by using principles (A) through (G).

If there is any property of inequalities you can't remember, try out some specific numbers. If $x < y$, then what is the relation between $-x$ and $-y$? Since $4 < 5$ but $-5 < -4$, the relation is probably $-x > -y$, which is true by (D).

Probably the most common mistake is forgetting to reverse the inequalities if you multiply or divide by a negative number.

III. Geometry

III–1. Angles

1–1

If two straight lines meet at a point they form an *angle*. The point is called the *vertex* of the angle and the lines are called the *sides* or *rays* of the angle. The sign for angle is ∠ and an angle can be denoted in the following ways:

(A) ∠*ABC* where *B* is the vertex, *A* is a point on one side, and *C* a point on the other side.

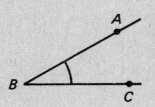

(B) ∠*B* where *B* is the vertex.

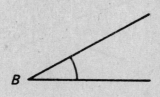

(C) ∠1 or ∠*x* where *x* or 1 is written inside the angle.

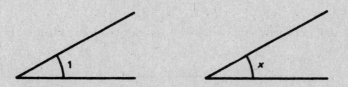

Angles are usually measured in degrees. We say that an angle equals *x* degrees, when its measure is *x* degrees. Degrees are denoted by °. An angle of 50 degrees is 50°. 60′ = 1°, 60″ = 1′ where ′ is read minutes and ″ is read seconds.

1–2

Two angles are *adjacent* if they have the same vertex and a common side and one angle is not inside the other.

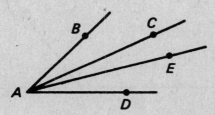

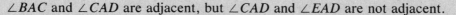

∠*BAC* and ∠*CAD* are adjacent, but ∠*CAD* and ∠*EAD* are not adjacent.

If two lines intersect at a point, they form 4 angles. The angles opposite each other are called *vertical* angles. $\angle 1$ and $\angle 3$ are vertical angles. $\angle 2$ and $\angle 4$ are vertical angles.

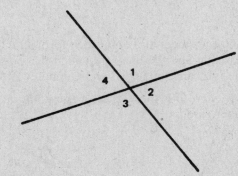

Vertical angles are equal,

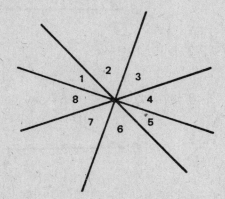

so $\angle 1 = \angle 5$, $\angle 2 = \angle 6$, $\angle 3 = \angle 7$, $\angle 4 = \angle 8$.

1–3

A straight angle is an angle whose sides lie on a straight line. *A straight angle equals 180°.*

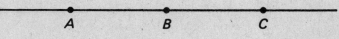

$\angle ABC$ is a straight angle.

If the sum of two adjacent angles is a straight angle, then the angles are *supplementary* and each angle is the supplement of the other.

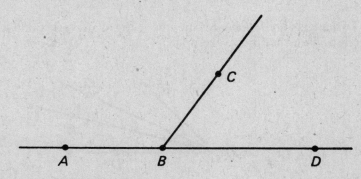

$\angle ABC$ and $\angle CBD$ are supplementary.

If an angle of $x°$ and an angle of $y°$ are supplements, then $x + y = 180$.

If two supplementary angles are equal, they are both *right angles*. A right angle is half of a straight angle. A right angle = 90°.

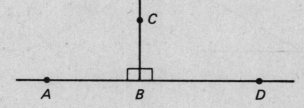

$\angle ABC = \angle CBD$ and they are both right angles. A right angle is denoted by ⌐. When 2 lines intersect and all four of the angles are equal, then each of the angles is a right angle.

If the sum of two adjacent angles is a right angle, then the angles are *complementary* and each angle is the complement of the other.

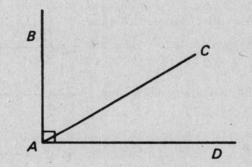

$\angle BAC$ and $\angle CAD$ are complementary.

If an angle of $x°$ and an angle of $y°$ are complementary, then $x + y = 90$.

EXAMPLE: If the supplement of angle x is three times as much as the complement of angle x, how many degrees is angle x?

Let d be the number of degrees in angle x; then the supplement of x is $(180 - d)°$, and the complement of x is $(90 - d)°$. Since the supplement is 3 times the complement, $180 - d = 3(90 - d) = 270 - 3d$ which gives $2d = 90$, so $d = 45$.

Therefore, angle x is 45°.

If an angle is divided into two equal angles by a straight line, then the angle has been *bisected* and the line is called the *bisector* of the angle.

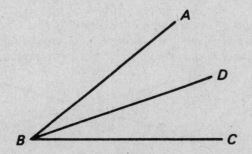

BD bisects $\angle ABC$; so $\angle ABD = \angle DBC$.

An *acute angle* is an angle less than a right angle. An *obtuse* angle is an angle greater than a right angle, but less than a straight angle.

∠1 is an acute angle, and ∠2 is an obtuse angle.

III–2. Lines

2–1

A line is understood to be a straight line. A line is assumed to extend indefinitely in both directions. *There is one and only one line between two distinct points.* There are two ways to denote a line:

(1) (A) by a single letter: l is a line;

(2) (B) by two points on the line: AB is a line.

A *line segment* is the part of a line between two points called *endpoints*. A line segment is denoted by its endpoints.

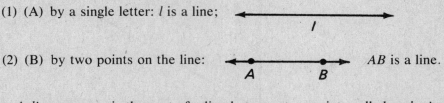

AB is a line segment. If a point P on a line segment is equidistant from the endpoints, then P is called the *midpoint* of the line segment.

P is the midpoint of AB if the length of $AP =$ the length of PB. Two line segments are equal if their lengths are equal; so $AP = PB$ means the line segment AP has the same length as the line segment PB. When a line segment is extended indefinitely in one direction, it is called a *ray*. A ray has one endpoint.

AB is a ray which has A as its endpoint.

2–2

P is a *point of intersection* of two lines if P is a point which is on both of the lines. *Two different lines cannot have more than one point of intersection,* because there is only one line between two points.

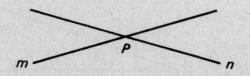

P is the point of intersection of m and n. We also say m and n intersect at P.

Two lines in the same plane are parallel if they do not intersect no matter how far they are extended.

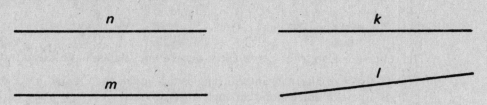

m and n are parallel, but k and l are not parallel since if k and l are extended they will intersect. Parallel lines are denoted by the symbol $\|$; so $m \parallel n$ means m is parallel to n.

If two lines are parallel to a third line, then they are parallel to each other.

If a third line intersects two given lines, it is called a *transversal*. A transversal and the two given lines form eight angles. The four inside angles are called *interior* angles. The four outside angles are called *exterior* angles. If two angles are on opposite sides of the transversal they are called *alternate* angles.

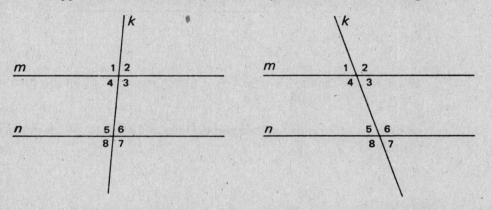

k is a transversal of the lines m and n. Angles 1, 2, 7, and 8 are the exterior angles, and angles 3, 4, 5, and 6 are the interior angles. $\angle 4$ and $\angle 6$ are an example of a pair of alternate angles. $\angle 1$ and $\angle 5$, $\angle 2$ and $\angle 6$, $\angle 3$ and $\angle 7$, and $\angle 4$ and $\angle 8$ are pairs of *corresponding* angles.

If two parallel lines are intersected by a transversal then:

    (1) Alternate interior angles are equal.
    (2) Corresponding angles are equal.
    (3) Interior angles on the same side of the transversal are supplementary.

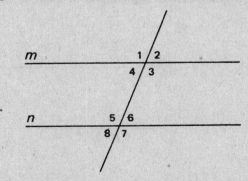

If we use the fact that vertical angles are equal, we can replace "interior" by "exterior" in (1) and (3).

m is parallel to *n* implies:

(1) $\angle 4 = \angle 6$ and $\angle 3 = \angle 5$
(2) $\angle 1 = \angle 5$, $\angle 2 = \angle 6$, $\angle 3 = \angle 7$ and $\angle 4 = \angle 8$
(3) $\angle 3 + \angle 6 = 180°$ and $\angle 4 + \angle 5 = 180°$

The reverse is also true. Let *m* and *n* be two lines which have *k* as a transversal.

(1) If a pair of alternate interior angles are equal, then *m* and *n* are parallel.
(2) If a pair of corresponding angles are equal, then *m* and *n* are parallel.
(3) If a pair of interior angles on the same side of the transversal are supplementary, then *m* is parallel to *n*.

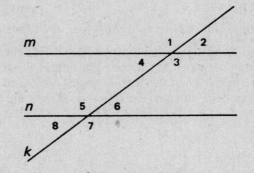

If $\angle 3 = \angle 5$, then $m \parallel n$. If $\angle 4 = \angle 6$ then $m \parallel n$. If $\angle 2 = \angle 6$ then $m \parallel n$. If $\angle 3 + \angle 6 = 180°$, then $m \parallel n$.

EXAMPLE: If *m* and *n* are two parallel lines and angle 1 is 60°, how many degrees is angle 2?

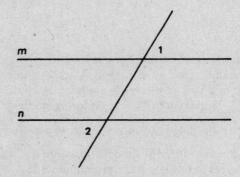

Let $\angle 3$ be the vertical angle equal to angle 2.

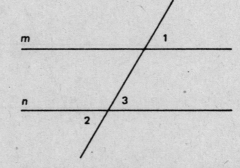

$\angle 3 = \angle 2$. Since *m* and *n* are parallel, corresponding angles are equal. Since $\angle 1$ and $\angle 3$ are corresponding angles, $\angle 1 = \angle 3$. Therefore, $\angle 1 = \angle 2$, and $\angle 2$ equals 60° since $\angle 1 = 60°$.

2–3

When two lines intersect and all four of the angles formed are equal, the lines are said to be *perpendicular*. If two lines are perpendicular, they are the sides of right angles whose vertex is the point of intersection.

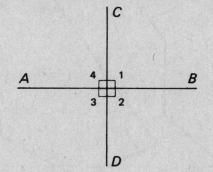

AB is perpendicular to CD, and angles 1, 2, 3, and 4 are all right angles. $\perp$ is the symbol for perpendicular; so $AB \perp CD$.

If two lines in a plane are perpendicular to the same line, then the two lines are parallel.

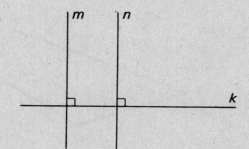

$m \perp k$ and $n \perp k$ imply that $m \parallel n$.

If *any one* of the angles formed when two lines intersect is a right angle, then the lines are perpendicular.

III–3. Polygons

A POLYGON is a closed figure in a plane which is composed of line segments which meet only at their endpoints. The line segments are called *sides* of the polygon, and a point where two sides meet is called a *vertex* (plural *vertices*) of the polygon.

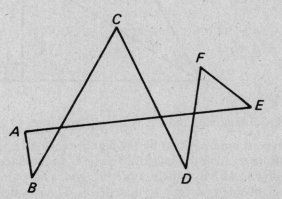

$ABCDEF$ is not a polygon since the line segments intersect at points which are not endpoints.

Some examples of polygons are:

A polygon is usually denoted by the vertices given in order.

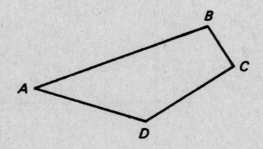

ABCD is a polygon.

A *diagonal* of a polygon is a line segment whose endpoints are nonadjacent vertices. The *altitude* from a vertex *P* to a side is the line segment with endpoint *P* which is perpendicular to the side.

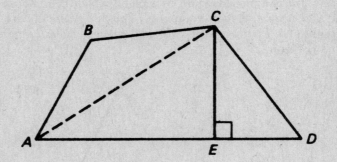

AC is a diagonal, and *CE* is the altitude from *C* to *AD*.

Polygons are classified by the number of angles or sides they have. A polygon with three angles is called a *triangle;* a four-sided polygon is a *quadrilateral;* a polygon with five angles is a *pentagon;* a polygon with six angles is a *hexagon;* an eight-sided polygon is an *octagon*. The number of angles is always equal to the number of sides in a polygon, so a six-sided polygon is a hexagon. The term *n*-gon refers to a polygon with *n* sides.

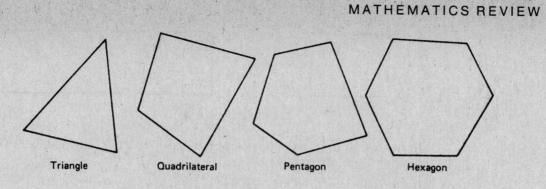

Triangle   Quadrilateral   Pentagon   Hexagon

If the sides of a polygon are all equal in length and if all the angles of a polygon are equal, the polygon is called a *regular* polygon.

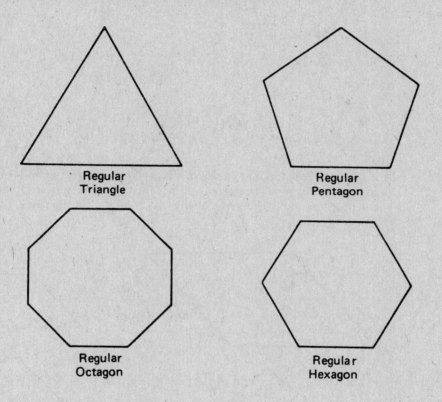

Regular
Triangle

Regular
Pentagon

Regular
Octagon

Regular
Hexagon

If the corresponding sides and the corresponding angles of two polygons are equal, the polygons are *congruent*. Congruent polygons have the same size and the same shape

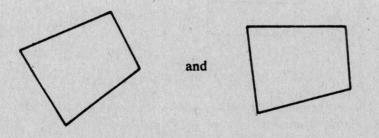

and

are congruent but

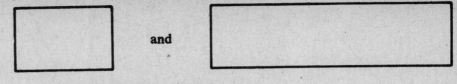

and

are not congruent.

In figures for problems on congruence, sides with the same number of strokes through them are equal.

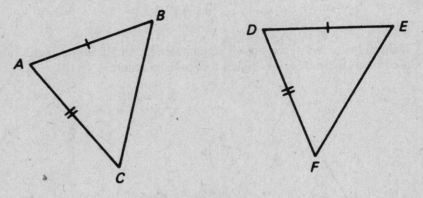

This figure indicates that $AB = DE$ and $AC = DF$.

If all the corresponding angles of two polygons are equal and the lengths of the corresponding sides are proportional, the polygons are said to be *similar*. Similar polygons have the same shape but need not be the same size.

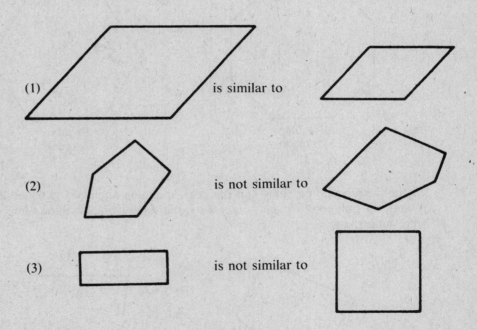

(1)   is similar to

(2)   is not similar to

(3)   is not similar to

In (3) the corresponding angles are equal, but the corresponding sides are not proportional.

The sum of all the angles of an n-gon is $(n - 2)180°$. So the sum of the angles in a hexagon is $(6 - 2)180° = 720°$.

III–4. **Triangles**

4–1

A TRIANGLE is a 3-sided polygon. If two sides of a triangle are equal, it is called *isosceles*. If all three sides are equal, it is an *equilateral* triangle. If all of the sides have different lengths, the triangle is *scalene*. When one of the angles in a triangle is a right angle, the triangle is a *right triangle*. If one of the angles is obtuse we have an *obtuse triangle*. If all the angles are acute, the triangle is an *acute triangle*.

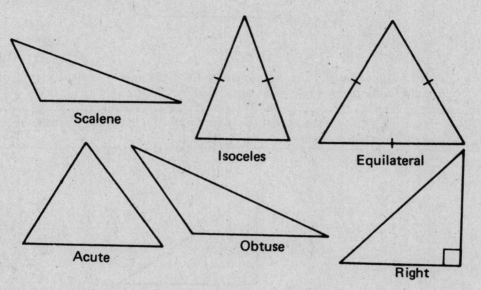

Scalene

Isoceles

Equilateral

Acute

Obtuse

Right

The symbol for a triangle is △; so △*ABC* means a triangle whose vertices are *A*, *B*, and *C*.

> *The sum of the angles in a triangle is 180°.*

The sum of the lengths of any two sides of a triangle must be longer than the remaining side.

If two angles in a triangle are equal, then the lengths of the sides opposite the equal angles are equal. If two sides of a triangle are equal, then the angles opposite the two equal sides are equal. In an equilateral triangle all the angles are equal and each angle = 60°. If each of the angles in a triangle is 60°, then the triangle is equilateral.

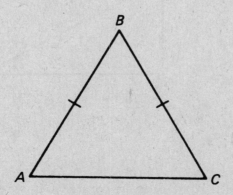

If $AB = BC$, then $\angle BAC = \angle BCA$.

If one angle in a triangle is larger than another angle, the side opposite the larger angle is longer than the side opposite the smaller angle. If one side is longer than another side, then the angle opposite the longer side is larger than the angle opposite the shorter side.

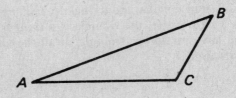

$AB > AC$ implies $\angle BCA > \angle ABC$.

In a right triangle, the side opposite the right angle is called the *hypotenuse*, and the remaining two sides are called *legs*.

The *Pythagorean Theorem* states that *the square of the length of the hypotenuse is equal to the sum of the squares of the lengths of the legs*.

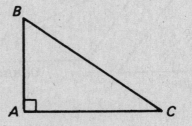

$(BC)^2 = (AB)^2 + (AC)^2$

If $AB = 4$ and $AC = 3$ then $(BC)^2 = 4^2 + 3^2 = 25$ so $BC = 5$. If $BC = 13$ and $AC = 5$, then $13^2 = 169 = (AB)^2 + 5^2$. So $(AB)^2 = 169 - 25 = 144$ and $AB = 12$.

If the lengths of the three sides of a triangle are, a, b, and c and $a^2 = b^2 + c^2$, then the triangle is a right triangle where a is the length of the hypotenuse.

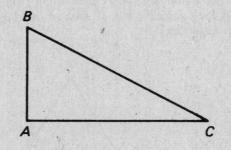

If $AB = 8$, $AC = 15$, and $BC = 17$, then since $17^2 = 8^2 + 15^2$, $\angle BAC$ is a right angle.

4–2

CONGRUENCE. Two triangles are congruent, if two pairs of corresponding sides and the corresponding *included* angles are equal. This is called *Side-Angle-Side* and is denoted by S.A.S.

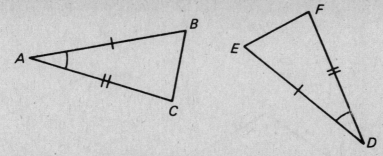

$AB = DE$, $AC = DF$ and $\angle BAC = \angle EDF$ imply that $\triangle ABC \cong \triangle DEF$. $\cong$ means congruent.

Two triangles are congruent if two pairs of corresponding angles and the corresponding *included* sides are equal: This is called *Angle-Side-Angle* or A.S.A.

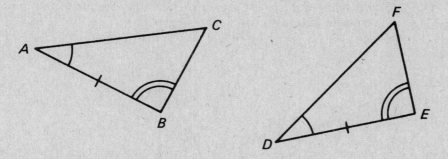

If $AB = DE$, $\angle BAC = \angle EDF$, and $\angle CBA = \angle FED$ then $\triangle ABC \cong \triangle DEF$.

If all three pairs of corresponding sides of two triangles are equal, then the triangles are congruent. This is called *Side-Side-Side* or S.S.S.

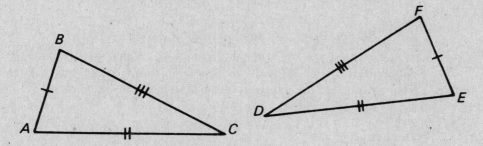

$AB = EF$, $AC = ED$, and $BC = FD$ imply that $\triangle ABC \cong \triangle EFD$.

Because of the Pythagorean Theorem, if any two corresponding sides of two right triangles are equal, the third sides are equal and the triangles are congruent.

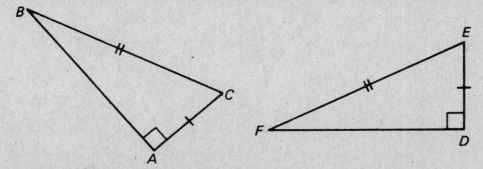

$AC = DE$ and $BC = EF$ imply $\triangle ABC \cong \triangle DFE$.

In general, if two corresponding sides of two triangles are equal, we cannot infer that the triangles are congruent.

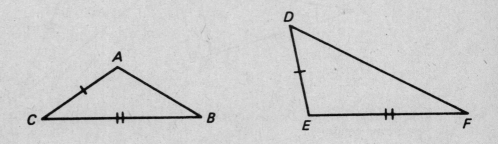

$AC = DE$ and $CB = EF$, but the triangles are not congruent.

If two sides of a triangle are equal, then the altitude to the third side divides the triangle into two congruent triangles.

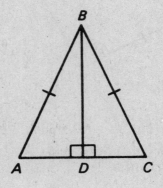

$AB = BC$ and $BD \perp AC$ imply $\triangle ADB \cong \triangle CDB$.

Therefore, $\angle ABD = \angle CBD$, so BD bisects $\angle ABC$. Since $AD = DC$, D is the midpoint of AC so BD is the median from B to AC. A *median* is the segment from a vertex to the midpoint of the side opposite the vertex.

EXAMPLE: $EF = ?$

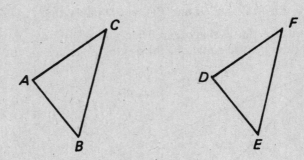

$AB = 4$, $AC = 4.5$ and $BC = 6$, $\angle BAC = \angle EDF$, $DE = 4$ and $DF = 4.5$

Since two pairs of corresponding sides (AB and DE, AC and DF) and the corresponding included angles ($\angle BAC$, $\angle EDF$) are equal, the triangles ABC and DEF are congruent by S.A.S. Therefore, $EF = BC = 6$.

4–3

Similarity. *Two triangles are similar if all three pairs of corresponding angles are equal.* Since the sum of the angles in a triangle is 180°, it follows that if two corresponding angles are equal, the third angles must be equal.

If you draw a line which passes through a triangle and is parallel to one of the sides of the triangle, the triangle formed is similar to the original triangle.

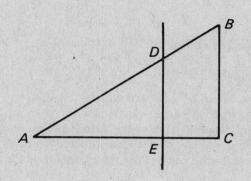

If $DE \parallel BC$ then $\triangle ADE \sim \triangle ABC$. The symbol $\sim$ means similar.

EXAMPLE: A man 6 feet tall casts a shadow 4 feet long; at the same time a flagpole casts a shadow which is 50 feet long. How tall is the flagpole?

The man with his shadow and the flagpole with its shadow can be regarded as the pairs of corresponding sides of two similar triangles.

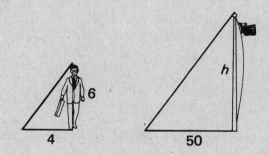

Let h be the height of the flagpole. Since corresponding sides of similar triangles are proportional, $\dfrac{4}{50} = \dfrac{6}{h}$. Cross multiply, getting $4h = 6 \cdot 50 = 300$; so $h = 75$. Therefore, the flagpole is 75 feet high.

III–5.   Quadrilaterals

A QUADRILATERAL is a polygon with four sides. The sum of the angles in a quadrilateral is 360°. If the opposite sides of a quadrilateral are parallel, the figure is a *parallelogram*.

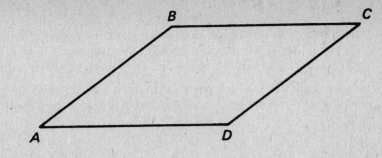

ABCD is a parallelogram.

In a parallelogram:

    (1) The opposite sides are equal.
    (2) The opposite angles are equal.
    (3) Any diagonal divides the parallelogram into two congruent triangles.
    (4) The diagonals bisect each other. (A line *bisects* a line segment if it intersects the segment at the midpoint of the segment.)

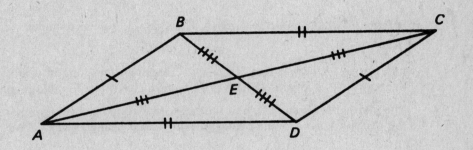

ABCD is a parallelogram.

    (1) $AB = DC$, $BC = AD$.
    (2) $\angle BCD = \angle BAD$, $\angle ABC = \angle ADC$.
    (3) $\triangle ABC \cong \triangle ADC$, $\triangle ABD \cong \triangle CDB$.
    (4) $AE = EC$ and $BE = ED$.

If *any* of the statements (1), (2), (3) and (4) are true for a quadrilateral, then the quadrilateral is a parallelogram.

If all of the sides of a parallelogram are equal, the figure is called a *rhombus*.

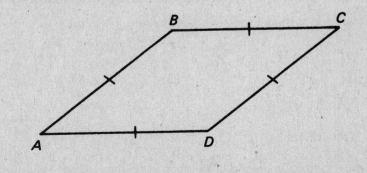

ABCD is a rhombus.

The diagonals of a rhombus are perpendicular.

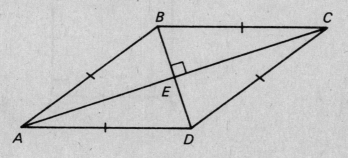

$BD \perp AC; \angle BEC = \angle CED = \angle AED = \angle AEB = 90°.$

If all the angles of a parallelogram are right angles, the figure is a *rectangle*.

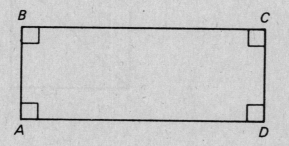

ABCD is a rectangle.

Since the sum of the angles in a quadrilateral is 360°, if *all* the angles of a quadrilateral are equal then the figure is a rectangle. The diagonals of a rectangle are equal. The length of a diagonal can be found by using the Pythagorean Theorem.

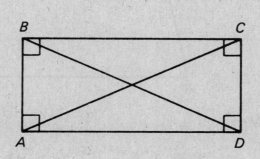

If *ABCD* is a rectangle, $AC = BD$ and $(AC)^2 = (AD)^2 + (DC)^2$.

If all the sides of a rectangle are equal, the figure is a *square*.

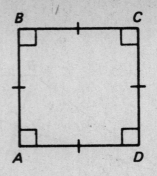

ABCD is a square.

If all the angles of a rhombus are equal, the figure is a square. The length of the diagonal of a square is $\sqrt{2}\,s$ where s is the length of a side.

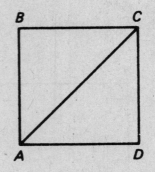

In square *ABCD*, $AC = (\sqrt{2})AD$.

A quadrilateral with two parallel sides and two sides which are not parallel is called a *trapezoid*. The parallel sides are called *bases*, and the nonparallel sides are called *legs*.

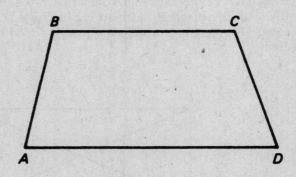

If *BC* ‖ *AD* then *ABCD* is a trapezoid; *BC* and *AD* are the bases.

III–6. Circles

A CIRCLE is a figure in a plane consisting of all the points which are the same distance from a fixed point called the *center* of the circle. A line segment from any point on the circle to the center of the circle is called a *radius* (plural: radii) of the circle. All radii of the same circle have the same length.

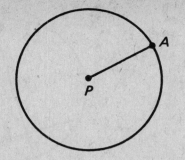

This circle has center *P* and radius *AP*.

A circle is denoted by a single letter, usually its center. Two circles with the same center are *concentric*.

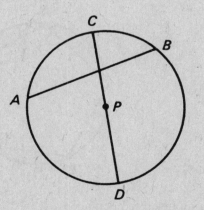

C and *D* are concentric circles.

A line segment whose endpoints are on a circle is called a *chord.* A chord which passes through the center of the circle is a *diameter*. *The length of a diameter is twice the length of a radius.* A diameter divides a circle into two congruent halves which are called *semicircles*.

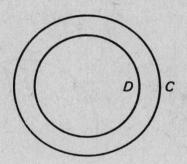

P is the center of the circle.
AB is a chord and *CD* is a diameter.

A diameter which is perpendicular to a chord bisects the chord.

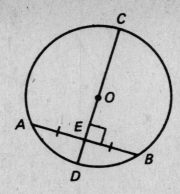

O is the center of this circle and $AB \perp CD$; then $AE = EB$.

If a line intersects a circle at one and only one point, the line is said to be a *tangent* to the circle. The point common to a circle and a tangent to the circle is called the *point of tangency*. The radius from the center to the point of tangency is perpendicular to the tangent.

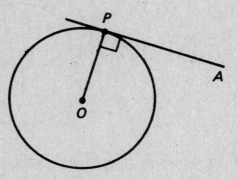

AP is tangent to the circle with center O. P is the point of tangency and $OP \perp PA$.

A polygon is *inscribed* in a circle if all of its vertices are points on the circle.

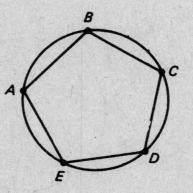

$ABCDE$ is an inscribed pentagon.

An angle whose vertex is a point on a circle and whose sides are chords of the circle is called an *inscribed angle*. An angle whose vertex is the center of a circle and whose sides are radii of the circle is called a *central angle*.

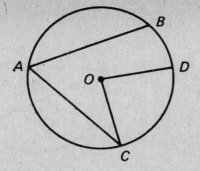

∠*BAC* is an inscribed angle.
∠*DOC* is a central angle.

An *arc* is a part of a circle.

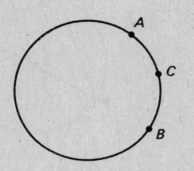

ACB is an arc. Arc *ACB* is written $\overset{\frown}{ACB}$.

If two letters are used to denote an arc, they represent the smaller of the two possible arcs. So $\overset{\frown}{AB} = \overset{\frown}{ACB}$.

An arc can be measured in degrees. The entire circle is 360°; thus an arc of 120° would be ⅓ of a circle.

A central angle is equal in measure to the arc it intercepts.

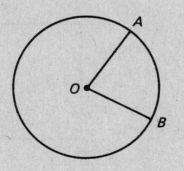

∠*AOB* = $\overset{\frown}{AB}$

An inscribed angle is equal in measure to ½ the arc it intercepts.

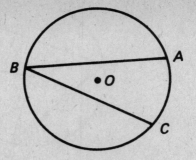

$\angle ABC = \frac{1}{2}\overset{\frown}{AC}$

An angle inscribed in a semicircle is a *right angle*.

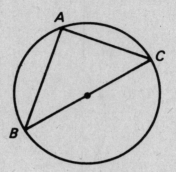

If BC is a diameter, then $\angle BAC$ is inscribed in a semicircle; so $\angle BAC = 90°$.

III–7. Area and Perimeter

7–1

The area A of a square equals s^2, where s is the length of a side of the square. Thus, $A = s^2$.

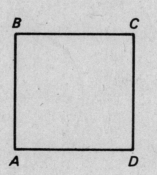

If $AD = 5$ inches, the area of square $ABCD$ is 25 square inches.

The area of a rectangle equals length times width; if L is the length of one side and W is the length of a perpendicular side, then the area $A = LW$.

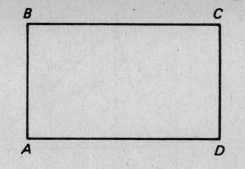

If $AB = 5$ feet and $AD = 8$ feet, then the area of rectangle $ABCD$ is 40 square feet.

The area of a parallelogram is base × height; $A = bh$, where b is the length of a side and h is the length of an altitude to that side.

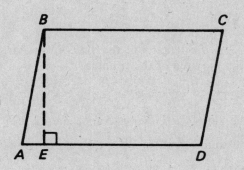

If $AD = 6$ yards and $BE = 4$ yards, then the area of the parallelogram $ABCD$ is $6 \cdot 4$ or 24 square yards.

The area of a trapezoid is the (average of the bases) × height. $A = [(b_1 + b_2)/2]h$ where b_1 and b_2 are the lengths of the parallel sides and h is the length of an altitude to one of the bases.

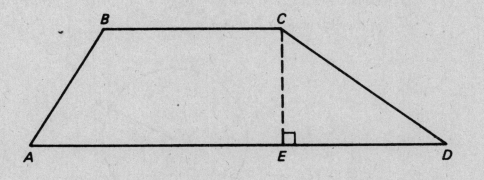

If $BC = 3$ miles, $AD = 7$ miles, and $CE = 2$ miles, then the area of trapezoid $ABCD$ is $[(3 + 7)/2] \cdot 2 = 10$ square miles.

The area of a triangle is $\frac{1}{2}$ (base × height); $A = \frac{1}{2} bh$, where b is the length of a side and h is the length of the altitude to that side.

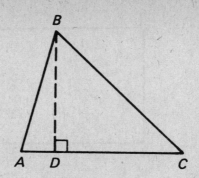

If AC = 5 miles and BD = 4 miles, then the area of the triangle is $\frac{1}{2}$ × 5 × 4 = 10 square miles.

Since the legs of a right triangle are perpendicular to each other, the area of a right triangle is one-half the product of the lengths of the legs.

EXAMPLE: If the lengths of the sides of a triangle are 5 feet, 12 feet, and 13 feet, what is the area of the triangle?

Since 5^2 + 12^2 = 25 + 144 = 169 = 13^2, the triangle is a right triangle and the legs are the sides with lengths 5 feet and 12 feet. Therefore, the area is $\frac{1}{2}$ × 5 × 12 = 30 square feet.

If we want to find the area of a polygon which is not of a type already mentioned, we break the polygon up into smaller figures such as triangles or rectangles, find the area of each piece, and add these to get the area of the given polygon.

The area of a circle is πr^2 where r is the length of a radius. Since $d = 2r$ where d is the length of a diameter, $A = \pi \left(\frac{d}{2}\right)^2 = \pi \frac{d^2}{4}$. π is a number which is approximately $\frac{22}{7}$ or 3.14; however, there is *no fraction which is exactly equal to π. π is called an irrational number*.

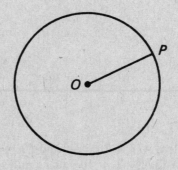

If OP = 2 inches, then the area of the circle with center O is $\pi 2^2$ or 4π square inches. The portion of the plane bounded by a circle and a central angle is called a *sector* of the circle.

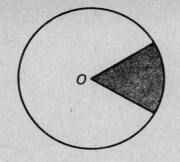

The shaded region is a sector of the circle with center O. The area of a sector with central angle $n°$ in a circle of radius r is $\dfrac{n}{360} \pi r^2$.

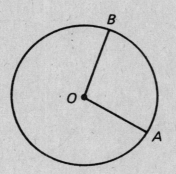

If $OB = 4$ inches and $\angle BOA = 100°$, then the area of the sector is $\dfrac{100}{360} \pi \cdot 4^2$

$= \dfrac{5}{18} \cdot 16\pi = \dfrac{40}{9} \pi$ square inches.

7–2

The *perimeter* of a polygon is the sum of the lengths of the sides.

EXAMPLE 1: What is the perimeter of a regular pentagon whose sides are 6 inches long?

A pentagon has 5 sides. Since the pentagon is regular, all sides have the same length which is 6 inches. Therefore, the perimeter of the pentagon is 5×6 which equals 30 inches or 2.5 feet.

The *perimeter of a rectangle is* $2(L + W)$ where L is the length and W is the width.

The *perimeter of a square is* $4s$ where s is the length of a side of the square.

The *perimeter of a circle* is called the *circumference* of the circle. The *circumference of a circle is* πd or $2\pi r$, where d is the length of a diameter and r is the length of a radius.

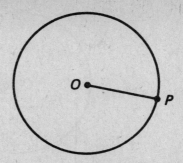

If O is the center of a circle and $OP = 5$ feet, then the circumference of the circle is $2 \times 5\pi$ or 10π feet.

The length of an arc of a circle is $(n/360)\,\pi d$ where the central angle of the arc is $n°$.

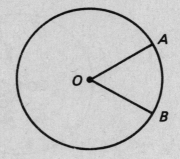

If O is the center of a circle where $OA = 5$ yards and $\angle AOB = 60°$, then the length of arc AB is $\dfrac{60}{360}\,\pi \times 10 = \dfrac{10}{6}\,\pi = \dfrac{5}{3}\,\pi$ yards.

EXAMPLE 2:   How far will a wheel of radius 2 feet travel in 500 revolutions? (Assume the wheel does not slip.)

The diameter of the wheel is 4 feet; so the circumference is 4π feet. Therefore, the wheel will travel $500 \times 4\pi$ or $2,000\pi$ feet in 500 revolutions.

III–8. Volume and Surface Area

8–1

The volume of a rectangular prism or box is length times width times height.

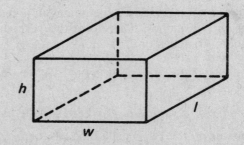

$$V = lwh$$

EXAMPLE 1:   What is the volume of a box which is 5 feet long, 4 feet wide, and 6 feet high?

The volume is 5 × 4 × 6 or 120 cubic feet.

If each of the faces of a rectangular prism is a congruent square, then the solid is a *cube*. The volume of a cube is the length of a side (or edge) cubed.

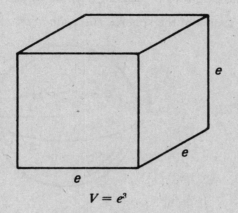

$$V = e^3$$

If the side of a cube is 4 feet long, then the volume of the cube is 4^3 or 64 cubic feet.

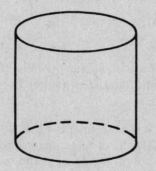

This solid is a circular cylinder. The top and the bottom are congruent circles. Most tin cans are circular cylinders. The volume of a circular cylinder is the product of the area of the circular base and the height.

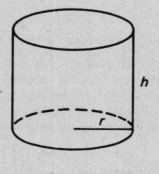

$$V = \pi r^2 h$$

EXAMPLE 2:   A circular pipe has a diameter of 10 feet. A gallon of oil has a volume of 2 cubic feet. How many gallons of oil can fit into 50 feet of the pipe?

Think of the 50 feet of pipe as a circular cylinder on its side with a height of 50 feet and a radius of 5 feet. Its volume is $\pi \cdot 5^2 \cdot 50$ or $1,250\pi$ cubic feet. Since a gallon of oil has a volume of 2 cubic feet, 50 feet of pipe will hold $1,250\pi/2$ or 625π gallons of oil.

A *sphere* is the set of points in space equidistant from a fixed point called the center. The length of a segment from any point on the sphere to the center is called the radius of the sphere. *The volume of a sphere of radius r is* $\frac{4}{3}\pi r^3$.

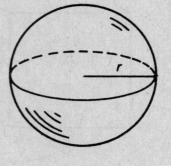

$$V = \frac{4}{3}\pi r^3$$

The volume of a sphere with radius 3 feet is $\frac{4}{3}\pi 3^3 = 36\pi$ cubic feet.

8–2

The surface area of a rectangular prism is $2LW + 2LH + 2WH$ where L is the length, W is the width, and H is the height.

EXAMPLE 1: If a roll of wallpaper covers 30 square feet, how many rolls are needed to cover the walls of a rectangular room 10 feet long by 8 feet wide by 9 feet high? There are no windows in the room.

We have to cover the surface area of the walls which equals $2(10 \times 9 + 8 \times 9)$ or $2(90 + 72)$ or 324 square feet. (Note that the product omits the area of the floor or the ceiling.) Since a roll covers 30 square feet, we need $\frac{324}{30} = 10\frac{4}{5}$ rolls.

The surface area of a cube is $6e^2$ where e is the length of an edge.

The area of the circular part of a cylinder is called the lateral area. The lateral area of a cylinder is $2\pi rh$, since if we unroll the circular part, we get a rectangle whose dimensions are the circumference of the circle and the height of the cylinder. The total surface area is the lateral surface area plus the areas of the circles on top and bottom, so the total surface area is $2\pi rh + 2\pi r^2$.

EXAMPLE 2: How much tin is needed to make a tin can in the shape of a circular cylinder whose radius is 3 inches and whose height is 5 inches?

The area of both the bottom and top is $\pi \cdot 3^2$ or 9π square inches. The lateral area is $2\pi \cdot 3 \cdot 5$ or 30π square inches. Therefore, we need $9\pi + 9\pi + 30\pi$ or 48π square inches of tin.

III–9. Coordinate Geometry

In coordinate geometry, every point in the plane is associated with an ordered pair of numbers called *coordinates*. Two perpendicular lines are drawn; the horizontal line is called the *x*-axis and the vertical line is called the *y*-axis. The point where the two axes intersect is called the *origin*. Both of the axes are number lines with the origin corresponding to zero (see I–6). Positive numbers on the *x*-axis are to the right of the origin, negative numbers to the left. Positive numbers on the *y*-axis are above the origin, negative numbers below the origin. The coordinates of a point *P* are (*x,y*) if *P* is located by moving *x* units along the *x*-axis from the origin and then moving *y* units up or down. *The distance along the x-axis is always given first.*

The numbers in parentheses are the coordinates of the point. Thus "*P* = (3,2)" means that the coordinates of *P* are (3,2). *The distance between the point with coordinates (x,y) and the point with coordinates (a,b) is* $\sqrt{(x - a)^2 + (y - b)^2}$. You should be able to answer most questions by using the distance formula.

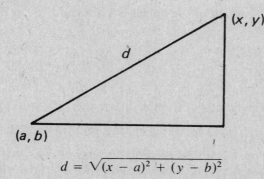

$$d = \sqrt{(x - a)^2 + (y - b)^2}$$

EXAMPLE: Is *ABCD* a parallelogram? *A* = (3,2), *B* = (1, −2), *C* = (−2,1), *D* = (1,5).

The length of *AB* is $\sqrt{(3 - 1)^2 + (2 - (-2))^2} = \sqrt{2^2 + 4^2} = \sqrt{20}$. The length of *CD* is $\sqrt{(-2 - 1)^2 + (1 - 5)^2} = \sqrt{(-3)^2 + (-4)^2} = \sqrt{25}$. Therefore, *AB* ≠ *CD*, so *ABCD* cannot be a parallelogram, since in a parallelogram the lengths of opposite sides are equal.

Geometry problems occur frequently in the data sufficiency questions. *If you are not provided with a diagram, draw one for yourself.* Think of any conditions which will help you answer the question; perhaps you can see how to answer a different question which will lead to an answer to the original question. It may help to draw in some diagonals, altitudes, or other auxiliary lines in your diagram.

IV. Tables and Graphs

IV–1. Tables

General Hints

(A) Make sure to look at the *entire* table or graph.

(B) Figure out what *units* the table or graph is using. Make sure to express your answer in the correct units.

(C) Look at the possible answers before calculating. Since many questions only call for an approximate answer, it may be possible to round off (see I–5), saving time and effort.

(D) Don't confuse decimals and percentages. If the units are percentages, then an entry of .2 means .2% which is equal to .002.

(E) In inference questions, only the information given can be used.

(F) See if the answer makes sense.

EXAMPLE: (Refer to the table on page 201.)

1. Ⓐ Ⓑ Ⓒ Ⓓ Ⓔ

1. What percent of the babies born in the U.S. in 1947 died before the age of 1 year?

(A) 3.22   (D) 32.2
(B) 4.7   (E) 47
(C) 26.7

To find a percentage, use the information given in the rate columns. The rate is given *per thousand*. In 1947 the rate was 32.2 per thousand which is $\dfrac{32.2}{1000}$ = .0322 or 3.22%. So the correct answer is (A). If you assumed incorrectly that the rate was per hundred, you would get the incorrect answer (D); if you looked in the wrong column you might get (B) or (E) as your answer.

2. Ⓐ Ⓑ Ⓒ Ⓓ Ⓔ

2. Which state had the most infant deaths in 1940?

(A) California   (D) Pennsylvania
(B) New Mexico   (E) Texas
(C) New York

INFANT DEATHS (UNDER 1 YEAR OF AGE) AND RATES PER 1,000 LIVE BIRTHS, BY STATES: 1940 TO 1950

STATE	NUMBER OF INFANT DEATHS					RATE PER 1,000 LIVE BIRTHS				
	1940	1947	1948	1949	1950	1940	1947	1948	1949	1950
United States	110,984	119,173	113,169	111,531	103,825	47.0	32.2	32.0	31.3	29.2
Alabama	3,870	3,301	3,228	3,345	3,044	61.5	37.5	37.8	39.6	36.8
Arizona	983	973	1,083	1,034	953	85.5	50.8	56.4	51.0	45.8
Arkansas	1,810	1,445	1,363	1,539	1,209	47.0	29.5	28.4	33.7	26.5
California	4,403	7,233	6,885	6,574	6,115	39.2	29.4	28.6	26.8	25.0
Colorado	1,270	1,234	1,267	1,153	1,167	60.4	37.5	38.4	35.1	34.4
Connecticut	868	1,150	1,026	943	886	34.0	25.2	24.3	23.1	21.8
Delaware	217	239	214	224	235	47.7	31.0	29.5	30.4	30.7
District of Columbia	554	691	531	576	603	49.3	31.9	25.5	29.1	30.4
Florida	1,818	2,285	2,103	2,088	2,078	53.8	38.2	35.3	33.8	32.1
Georgia	3,744	3,251	3,169	3,101	3,064	57.8	34.2	34.2	33.3	33.5
Idaho	506	478	481	431	434	42.9	29.4	29.8	27.0	27.1
Illinois	4,398	5,672	5,123	5,195	4,868	35.3	28.9	27.7	27.4	25.6
Indiana	2,595	2,949	2,760	2,746	2,520	42.1	30.6	29.8	29.1	27.0
Iowa	1,636	1,817	1,610	1,591	1,555	36.5	28.5	26.6	25.7	24.8
Kansas	1,106	1,251	1,151	1,136	1,130	38.3	28.1	26.9	25.9	25.7
Kentucky	3,387	2,971	3,073	3,139	2,616	53.1	37.1	39.8	41.2	34.9
Louisiana	3,268	2,773	2,779	2,810	2,639	64.3	37.2	37.9	37.2	34.6
Maine	810	853	706	713	650	53.2	35.7	32.0	32.5	30.9
Maryland	1,590	1,794	1,537	1,636	1,465	49.1	31.6	28.8	30.5	27.0
Massachusetts	2,458	3,027	2,613	2,347	2,240	37.5	28.1	26.8	24.5	23.3
Michigan	4,032	5,080	4,639	4,545	4,230	40.7	31.5	30.0	28.9	26.3
Minnesota	1,758	2,165	1,959	1,893	1,889	33.2	28.6	26.9	25.6	25.1
Mississippi	2,869	2,448	2,474	2,631	2,385	54.4	36.8	37.9	39.6	36.7
Missouri	2,885	2,929	2,585	2,563	2,510	46.9	32.5	30.3	30.0	29.2
Montana	537	484	461	457	441	46.5	32.1	30.7	29.7	28.2
Nebraska	792	894	835	761	796	36.0	27.8	26.8	24.1	25.0
Nevada	109	134	147	118	139	51.7	33.2	39.8	32.1	37.9
New Hampshire	341	399	361	333	282	40.9	30.1	29.1	27.9	24.5
New Jersey	2,121	2,965	2,585	2,534	2,467	35.5	27.9	26.5	26.0	25.2
New Mexico	1,488	1,379	1,438	1,408	1,211	100.6	67.9	70.1	65.1	54.8
New York	7,297	9,123	8,258	7,878	7,429	37.2	28.2	27.3	26.1	24.7
North Carolina	4,631	3,938	3,858	4,113	3,674	57.6	34.9	35.3	38.1	34.5
North Dakota	593	523	487	517	453	45.1	30.6	29.4	30.7	26.6
Ohio	4,744	5,817	5,693	5,315	4,990	41.4	29.5	30.5	28.1	26.8
Oklahoma	2,238	1,733	1,731	1,531	1,514	49.9	32.3	34.4	30.8	30.2
Oregon	585	895	897	869	812	33.2	24.7	25.5	24.6	22.5
Pennsylvania	7,404	7,741	6,442	6,567	6,126	44.7	31.1	28.4	29.2	27.6
Rhode Island	410	522	444	395	450	37.9	28.2	26.3	24.0	27.8
South Carolina	3,042	2,352	2,331	2,283	2,220	68.2	39.5	40.4	39.0	38.6
South Dakota	466	511	525	448	473	38.7	30.9	32.0	26.0	26.6
Tennessee	2,954	3,144	3,098	3,331	2,961	53.5	36.3	37.7	40.2	36.4
Texas	8,675	8,161	9,131	8,628	7,630	68.3	41.1	46.2	42.7	37.4
Utah	539	545	568	535	503	40.4	25.1	27.4	25.3	23.7
Vermont	309	303	271	301	221	44.5	31.2	28.9	32.4	24.5
Virginia	3,335	3,142	3,163	3,162	2,836	58.5	36.6	38.5	38.1	34.6
Washington	992	1,643	1,537	1,530	1,522	35.2	28.1	27.5	27.1	27.3
West Virginia	2,269	2,091	2,108	2,082	1,822	53.7	38.0	40.2	39.6	36.1
Wisconsin	2,046	2,476	2,148	2,202	2,121	37.3	29.5	26.3	26.5	25.7
Wyoming	232	249	293	280	247	44.7	34.0	39.5	37.4	32.5

Source: Department of Health, Education, and Welfare, Public Health Service, National Office of Vital Statistics; annual report, *Vital Statistics of the United States.*

Source: Statistical Abstract of the U.S. 1957

Look in the numbers column under 1940. Only Texas had more than 8,000 in 1940, so the correct answer is (E). New Mexico had a *higher rate,* but the question asked for the *highest amount. Make sure you answer the question which is asked.*

3. Ⓐ Ⓑ Ⓒ Ⓓ Ⓔ

3. Which of the following statements can be inferred from the table?

I. In 1950 less than ½₀ of the babies born in the U.S. died before the age of 1 year.
II. The number of infant deaths in the U.S. decreased from 1945 to 1950.
III. More than 5% of the infant deaths in the U.S. in 1950 occurred in California.
IV. The number of infant deaths in North America in 1950 was less than 150,000.

(A) I only
(B) II only
(C) I and III only
(D) I, III, IV only
(E) I, II, III, IV

Analysis:

Statement I can be inferred since $\frac{1}{20}$ of 1,000 = 50 which exceeds the rate per thousand of 29.2 in 1950.

Statement II can't be inferred since the table has no information about 1945. Infant deaths decreased between 1940 and 1950, but that doesn't mean they decreased between 1945 and 1950.

Statement III can be inferred from the table. The total number of infant deaths in 1950 was 103,825, and 6,115 occurred in California. A calculation of 6,115/103,825 could be made, but it is much quicker to find 5% of 103,825 which is 5,191. Since 6,115 is greater than 5,191, more than 5% of the infant deaths in the U.S. occurred in California.

Statement IV can't be inferred, because the table only gives information about the U.S. and there are other countries in North America.

So the correct answer is (C).

IV–2. **Circle Graphs**

CIRCLE GRAPHS are used to show how various sectors share in the whole. Circle graphs are sometimes called pie charts. Circle graphs usually give the percentage that each sector receives.

EXAMPLE: (Refer to the graph on page 203.)

1. Ⓐ Ⓑ Ⓒ Ⓓ Ⓔ

1. The amount spent on materials in 1960 was 120% of the amount spent on

(A) research in 1960
(B) compensation in 1960
(C) advertising in 1970
(D) materials in 1970
(E) legal affairs in 1960

When using circle graphs to find ratios of various sectors, don't find the amounts each sector received and then the ratio of the amounts. Find the *ratio of the percentages,* which is much quicker. In 1960, 18% of the expenditures were for materials. We want x where 120% of x = 18%; so x = 15%. Any category which received 15% of 1960 expenditures gives the correct answer, but only one of the five choices is correct. Here, the answer is (A) since research received 15% of the expenditure in 1960. Check the 1960 answers first since you need look only at the percentages, which can be done quickly. Notice that (C) is incorrect, since 15% of the expenditures for 1970 is different from 15% of the expenditures for 1960.

EXPENDITURES OF GENERAL INDUSTRIES
(by major categories)

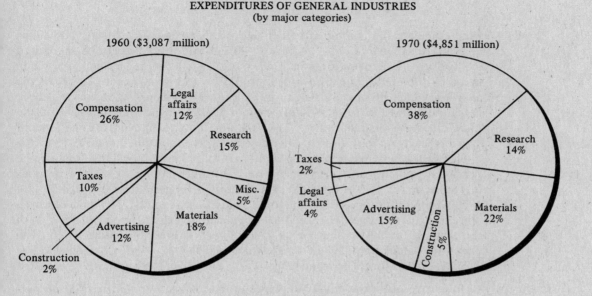

1960 ($3,087 million)

1970 ($4,851 million)

2. The fraction of the total expenditures for 1960 and 1970 spent on compensation was about   2. Ⓐ Ⓑ Ⓒ Ⓓ Ⓔ

(A) ⅕   (D) 3/7
(B) ¼   (E) ½
(C) ⅓

In 1960, 26% of $3,087 million was spent on compensation and in 1970 compensation received 38% of $4,851 million. The total expenditures for 1960 and 1970 are $(3,087 + 4,851) million. So the exact answer is [(.26)(3,087) + (.38)(4,851)]/(3,087 + 4,851). Actually calculating the answer, you will waste a lot of time. Look at the answers and think for a second.

We are taking a weighted average of 26% and 38%. To find a weighted average, we multiply each value by a weight and divide by the total of all the weights. Here 26% is given a weight of 3,087 and 38% a weight of 4,851. The following general rule is often useful in average problems: The average or weighted average of a collection of values can *never* be:

(1) less than the smallest value in the collection, or
(2) greater than the largest value in the collection.

Therefore, the answer to the question must be greater than or equal to 26% and less than or equal to 38%.

Since ⅕ = 20% and ¼ = 25%, which are both less than 26%, neither (A) nor (B) can be the correct answer. Since 3/7 = 42⁶/₇% and ½ = 50%, which are both greater than 38%, neither (D) nor (E) can be correct. Therefore, by elimination (C) is the correct answer.

3. Ⓐ Ⓑ Ⓒ Ⓓ Ⓔ

3. The amount spent in 1960 for materials, advertising, and taxes was about the same as

(A) ⁵⁄₄ of the amount spent for compensation in 1960
(B) the amount spent for compensation in 1970
(C) the amount spent on materials in 1970
(D) ⁵⁄₃ of the amount spent on advertising in 1970
(E) the amount spent on research and construction in 1970

First calculate the combined percentage for materials, advertising, and taxes in 1960. Since 18% + 12% + 10% = 40%, these three categories accounted for 40% of the expenditures in 1960. You can check the one answer which involves 1960 now. Since ⁵⁄₄ of 26% = 32.5%, (A) is incorrect. To check the answers which involve 1970, you must know the amount spent on the three categories above in 1960. 40% of 3,087 is 1234.8; so the amount spent on the three categories in 1960 was $1,234.8 million. You could calculate the amount spent in each of the possible answers, but there is a quicker way. Find the *approximate* percentage that 1,234.8 is of 4,851, and check this against the percentages of the answers. Since ¹²⁄₄₈ = ¼, the amount for the 3 categories in 1960 is about 25% of the 1970 expenditures. Compensation received 38% of 1970 expenditures, so (B) is incorrect. Materials received 22% and research and construction together received 19%; since advertising received 15%, ⁵⁄₃ of the amount for advertising yields 25%. So (D) is probably correct. You can check by calculating 22% of 4,851 which is 1,067.22, while 25% of 4,851 = 1,212.75. Therefore, (D) is correct.

In inference questions involving circle graphs, *do not compare different percentages*. Note in question 3 that the percentage of expenditures in 1960 for the three categories (40%) is *not equal* to 40% of the expenditures in 1970.

IV–3. Line Graphs

LINE GRAPHS are used to show how a quantity changes continuously. Very often the quantity is measured as time changes. If the line goes up, the quantity is increasing; if the line goes down, the quantity is decreasing; if the line is horizontal, the quantity is not changing. To measure the height of a point on the graph, use your pencil or a piece of paper (for example, the admission card to the exam) as a straight edge.

EXAMPLE: (Refer to the graph on page 205.)

1. Ⓐ Ⓑ Ⓒ Ⓓ Ⓔ

1. The ratio of productivity in 1967 to productivity in 1940 was about

(A) 1:4
(B) 1:3
(C) 3:1

(D) 4:1
(E) 9:1

In 1967 productivity had an index number of 400, and the index numbers are based on 1940 = 100. So the ratio is 400:100 = 4:1. Therefore, the answer is (D). [If you used (incorrectly) output or employment (instead of productivity) you would get the wrong answer (E) or (C); if you confused the order of the ratio you would have incorrectly answered (A).]

TRENDS IN INDUSTRIAL INVESTMENT, LABOUR PRODUCTIVITY, EMPLOYMENT AND OUTPUT, 1940 TO 1967

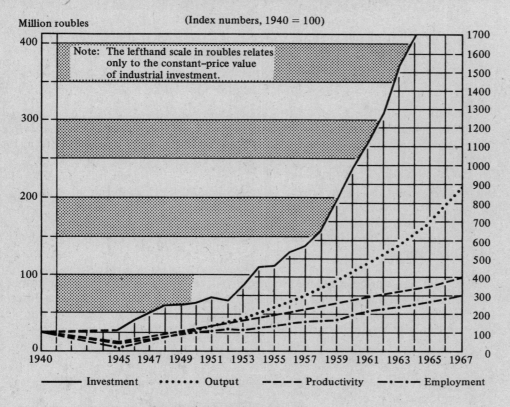

(Index numbers, 1940 = 100)

Million roubles

Note: The lefthand scale in roubles relates only to the constant–price value of industrial investment.

——— Investment   •••••• Output   – – – Productivity   —•—•— Employment

Source: United Nations Economics Bulletin for Europe

2. If 1 rouble = $3, then the constant-price value of industrial investment in 1959 was about   2. Ⓐ Ⓑ Ⓒ Ⓓ Ⓔ

(A) $1.9 million

(B) $200 million

(C) $420,000,000

(D) $570,000,000

(E) $570,000 million

In 1959, the value was about 190 million roubles. (It was a little below 200 million.) The answers are all in dollars, so multiply 190 by 3 to get $570 million or $570,000,000 (D). If you are not careful about units, you may answer (B) or (E), which are incorrect.

3. Employment was at its minimum during the years shown in   3. Ⓐ Ⓑ Ⓒ Ⓓ Ⓔ

(A) 1940

(B) 1943

(C) 1945

(D) 1953

(E) 1967

The minimum of a quantity displayed on a line graph is the lowest place on the line. Thus in 1945, (C), the minimum value of employment was reached.

4. Ⓐ Ⓑ Ⓒ Ⓓ Ⓔ

4. Between 1954 and 1965, output

(A) decreased by about 10%

(B) stayed about the same

(C) increased by about 200%

(D) increased by about 250%

(E) increased by about 500%

The line for output goes up between 1954 and 1965, so output increased between 1954 and 1965. Therefore, (A) and (B) are wrong. Output was about 200 in 1954 and about 700 in 1965, so the increase was 500. Since $\frac{500}{200} = 2.5 = 250\%$, the correct answer is (D).

IV–4. Bar Graphs

Quantities can be compared by the height or length of a bar in a bar graph. A bar graph can have either vertical or horizontal bars. You can compare different quantities or the same quantity at different times. Use your pencil or a piece of paper to compare bars which are not adjacent to each other.

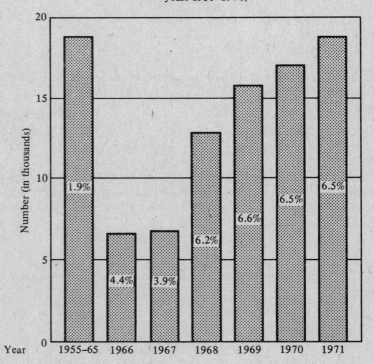

DISABILITY BENEFICIARIES REPORTED AS REHABILITATED
(number, as percent of all rehabilitated clients of state vocational rehabilitation agencies, years 1955–1971)

Source: Social Security Bulletin

EXAMPLE: (Refer to the graph on page 206.)

1. Between 1967 and 1971, the largest number of disability beneficiaries were 1. Ⓐ Ⓑ Ⓒ Ⓓ Ⓔ
reported as rehabilitated in the year

(A) 1967   (D) 1970
(B) 1968   (E) 1971
(C) 1969

The answer is (E) since the highest bar is the bar for 1971. The percentage of
disability beneficiaries out of all rehabilitated clients was higher in 1969, but
the *number* was lower.

2. Between 1955 and 1965, about how many clients were rehabilitated by state 2. Ⓐ Ⓑ Ⓒ Ⓓ Ⓔ
vocational rehabilitation agencies?

(A) 90,000   (D) 1,900,000
(B) 400,000   (E) 10,000,000
(C) 1,000,000

1.9% of those rehabilitated were disability beneficiaries, and there were about
19,000 disability beneficiaries rehabilitated. So if T is the total number rehabilitated, then 1.9% of T = 19,000 or .019T = 19,000. Thus T = 19,000/.019
= 1,000,000 and the answer is (C).

IV–5. Cumulative Graphs

You can compare several categories by a graph of the cumulative type. These
are usually bar or line graphs where the height of the bar or line is divided up
proportionately among different quantities.

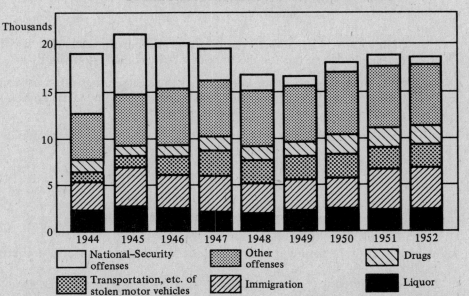

**FEDERAL PRISONERS RECEIVED FROM THE COURTS,
BY MAJOR OFFENSE GROUPS: YEARS 1944–1952**

Legend:
- National–Security offenses
- Transportation, etc. of stolen motor vehicles
- Other offenses
- Immigration
- Drugs
- Liquor

Source: Statistical Abstract of the U.S. 1953

EXAMPLE: (Refer to the graph on page 207.)

1. Ⓐ Ⓑ Ⓒ Ⓓ Ⓔ   **1.** In 1946, roughly what percent of the federal prisoners received from the courts were national-security offenders?

(A) 10   (D) 30
(B) 15   (E) 35
(C) 25

The total number of prisoners in 1946 was about 20,000, and national-security offenders accounted for the part of the graph from just above 15,000 to just above 20,000. Therefore, there were about 20,000 − 15,000 = 5,000 prisoners convicted of national-security offenses. Since 5,000/20,000 = ¼ = 25%, the correct answer is (C).

2. Ⓐ Ⓑ Ⓒ Ⓓ Ⓔ   **2.** Of the combined total for the four years 1947 through 1950, the largest number of offenders were in the category

(A) national-security offenses   (D) immigration
(B) other offenses   (E) liquor
(C) drugs

The correct answer is (B). Since other offenses had the most offenders in each year, that category must have the largest total number of offenders. [If you answered this question for the years 1944–1946, then (A) would be correct.]

3. Ⓐ Ⓑ Ⓒ Ⓓ Ⓔ   **3.** Which of the following statements can be inferred from the graph?

   I. The number of federal prisoners received from the courts decreased each year from 1946 to 1948.
   II. More than 40% of the prisoners between 1944 and 1952 came from the other offenses category.
   III. 2% of the federal prisoners received in 1952 were convicted on heroin charges.

(A) I only   (D) I and III only
(B) III only   (E) I, II, and III
(C) I and II only

Statement I is true, since the height of the bar for each year was lower than the height of the bar for the previous year in 1946, 1947, and 1948.

Statement II is not true. For most of the years, other offenses accounted for about 25–30%, and it never was more than 40% in any year. Therefore, it could not account for more than 40% of the total.

Statement III can not be inferred. There is a category of drug offenders, but there is no information about specific drugs.

So, the correct answer is (A).

REVIEW OF FORMULAS

(Numbers next to the formulas refer to the section of the Math Review where the formula is discussed.)

Interest = Amount × Time × Rate	I–4
Discount = Cost × Rate of Discount	I–4
Price = Cost × (100% − Rate of Discount)	I–4
$x = \dfrac{1}{2a}[-b \pm \sqrt{b^2 - 4ac}]$ (quadratic formula)	II–2

Distance = Rate × Time	II–3
$a^2 + b^2 = c^2$ when a and b are the legs and c is	III–4
the hypotenuse of a right triangle (Pythagorean Theorem)	
Diameter of a circle = 2 × Radius	III–6
Area of a square = s^2	III–7
Area of a rectangle = LW	III–7
Area of a triangle = ½bh	III–7
Area of a circle = πr^2	III–7
Area of a parallelogram = bh	III–7
Area of a trapezoid = ½$(b_1 + b_2)h$	III–7
Circumference of a circle = πd	III–7
Perimeter of a square = $4s$	III–7
Perimeter of a rectangle = $2(L + W)$	III–7
Volume of a box = lwh	III–8
Volume of a cube = e^3	III–8
Volume of a cylinder = $\pi r^2 h$	III–8
Volume of a sphere = $\frac{4}{3}\pi r^3$	III–8
Surface area of a box = $2LW + 2LH + 2WH$	III–8
Surface area of a cube = $6e^2$	III–8
Surface area of a cylinder = $2\pi rh + 2\pi r^2$	III–8
Distance between points (x,y) and (a,b) is $\sqrt{(x - a)^2 + (y - b)^2}$	III–9

Hints for Answering Mathematics Questions

1. Make sure you answer the question you are asked to answer.

2. Look at the answers before you start to work out a problem; you can save a lot of time.

3. Don't waste time on superfluous computations.

4. *Estimate* whenever you can to save time.

5. Budget your time so you can try all the questions. (Bring a watch.)

6. You probably won't be able to answer all the questions; don't waste time worrying about it.

7. Do all the problems you know how to work *before* you start to think about those that you can't answer in a minute or two.

8. If you skip a question, make sure you skip that number on the answer sheet.

9. Don't make extra assumptions on inference questions.

10. Work efficiently; don't waste time worrying during the test.

11. Make sure you express your answer in the units asked for.

12. On data sufficiency questions, don't do any more work than is necessary. (Don't solve the problem; you only have to know that the problem can be solved.)

Practice Exercises

The four exercises that follow will give you an indication of your ability to handle both mathematics and data sufficiency questions. The time for each practice mathematics exercise is 30 minutes. Scoring for each of the mathematics exercises may be interpreted as follows:

22–25   EXCELLENT
18–21+   GOOD
13–17+   FAIR
0–12+   POOR

Your score should be determined by counting the number of correct answers minus ¼ the number of incorrect answers.

MATHEMATICS
EXERCISE A

DIRECTIONS: Solve each of the following problems.
NOTE: A figure that appears with a problem is drawn as accurately as possible unless the words "Figure not drawn to scale" appear next to the figure. Numbers in this test are real numbers.

1. Ⓐ Ⓑ Ⓒ Ⓓ Ⓔ

1. In 1955, it cost $12 to purchase one hundred pounds of potatoes. In 1975, it cost $34 to purchase one hundred pounds of potatoes. The price of one hundred pounds of potatoes increased X dollars between 1955 and 1975 with X equal to:

(A) 1.20   (B) 2.20   (C) 3.40   (D) 22   (E) 34

2. Ⓐ Ⓑ Ⓒ Ⓓ Ⓔ

2. A house cost Ms. Jones C dollars in 1965. Three years later she sold the house for 25% more than she paid for it. She has to pay a tax of 50% of the gain. (The gain is the selling price minus the cost.) How much tax must Ms. Jones pay?

(A) $\frac{1}{24} C$ (B) $\frac{C}{8}$ (C) $\frac{1}{4} C$ (D) $\frac{C}{2}$ (E) .6C

3. Ⓐ Ⓑ Ⓒ Ⓓ Ⓔ

3. If the length of a rectangle is increased by 20%, and the width of the same rectangle is decreased by 20%, then the area of the rectangle

(A) decreases by 20%   (B) decreases by 4%   (C) is unchanged   (D) increases by 20%   (E) increases by 40%

Use the following graph for questions 4–7.

WORLDWIDE MILITARY EXPENDITURES

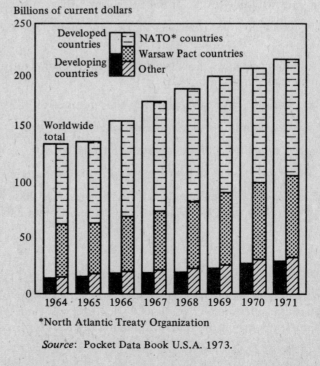

*North Atlantic Treaty Organization

Source: Pocket Data Book U.S.A. 1973.

4. Between 1964 and 1969, worldwide military expenditures

(A) increased by about 50%   (B) roughly doubled   (C) increased by about 150%
(D) almost tripled   (E) increased by 10%

5. The average yearly military expenditure by the developing countries between 1964 and 1971 was approximately how many billions of current dollars?

(A) 20   (B) 50   (C) 100   (D) 140   (E) 175

6. Which of the following statements can be inferred from the graph?

I. The NATO countries have higher incomes than the Warsaw Pact countries.
II. Worldwide military expenditures have increased each year between 1964 and 1971.
III. In 1972 worldwide military expenditures were more than 230 billion current dollars.

(A) I only   (B) II only   (C) I and II only   (D) II and III only   (E) I, II, and III

7. A speaker claims that the NATO countries customarily spend ⅓ of their combined incomes on military expenditures. According to the speaker, the combined incomes of the NATO countries (in billions of current dollars) in 1971 was about

(A) 100   (B) 200   (C) 250   (D) 350   (E) 500

8. 8% of the people eligible to vote are between 18 and 21. In an election 85% of those eligible to vote who were between 18 and 21 actually voted. In that election, people between 18 and 21 who actually voted were what percent of those people eligible to vote?

(A) 4.2   (B) 6.4   (C) 6.8   (D) 8   (E) 68

9. If n and p are both odd numbers, which of the following numbers *must* be an even number?

(A) $n + p$ (B) np (C) $np + 2$ (D) $n + p + 1$ (E) $2n + p$

10. It costs g cents a mile for gasoline and m cents a mile for all other costs to run a car. How many *dollars* will it cost to run the car for 100 miles?

(A) $\dfrac{g + m}{100}$ (B) $100g + 100m$ (C) $g + m$ (D) $g + .1m$ (E) g

11. What is the length of the line segment which connects A to B?

(A) $\sqrt{3}$ (B) 2   (C) $2\sqrt{2}$ (D) 4
(E) 8

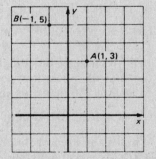

12. A cabdriver's income consists of his salary and tips. His salary is $50 a week. During one week his tips were $\dfrac{5}{4}$ of his salary. What fraction of his income for the week came from tips?

(A) $\dfrac{4}{9}$ (B) $\dfrac{1}{2}$ (C) $\dfrac{5}{9}$ (D) $\dfrac{5}{8}$ (E) $\dfrac{5}{4}$

Use the following table for questions 13–17.

INCOME (IN DOLLARS)	TAX (IN DOLLARS)
0– 4,000	1% of income
4,000– 6,000	40 + 2% of income over 4,000
6,000– 8,000	80 + 3% of income over 6,000
8,000–10,000	140 + 4% of income over 8,000
10,000–15,000	220 + 5% of income over 10,000
15,000–25,000	470 + 6% of income over 15,000
25,000–50,000	1,070 + 7% of income over 25,000

13. How much tax is due on an income of $7,500?

    (A) $75   (B) $80   (C) $125   (D) $150   (E) $225

14. Your income for a year is $26,000. You receive a raise so that next year your income will be $29,000. How much *more* will you pay in taxes next year if the tax rate remains the same?

    (A) $70   (B) $180   (C) $200   (D) $210   (E) $700

15. Joan paid $100 tax. If X was her income, which of the following statements is true?

    (A) $0 < X < 4,000$ (B) $4,000 < X < 6,000$ (C) $6,000 < X < 8,000$ (D) $8,000 < X < 10,000$ (E) $10,000 < X < 15,000$

16. The town of Zenith has a population of 50,000. The average income of a person who lives in Zenith is $3,700 per year. What is the total amount paid in taxes by the people of Zenith? Assume each person pays tax on $3,700.

    (A) $37   (B) $3,700   (C) $50,000   (D) $185,000   (E) $1,850,000

17. A person who has an income of $10,000 pays what percent (to the nearest percent) of his or her income in taxes?

    (A) 1   (B) 2   (C) 3   (D) 4   (E) 5

18. Given that x and y are real numbers, let $S(x,y) = x^2 - y^2$. Then $S(3, S(3,4)) =$

    (A) -40 (B) -7 (C) 40   (D) 49   (E) 56

19. Eggs cost 90¢ a dozen. Peppers cost 20¢ each. An omelet consists of 3 eggs and ¼ of a pepper. How much will the ingredients for 8 omelets cost?

    (A) $.90   (B) $1.30   (C) $1.80   (D) $2.20   (E) $2.70

20. It is 185 miles from Binghamton to New York City. If a bus takes 2 hours to travel the first 85 miles, how long must the bus take to travel the final 100 miles in order to average 50 miles an hour for the entire trip?

    (A) 60 min.   (B) 75 min.   (C) 94 min.   (D) 102 min.   (E) 112 min.

21. What is the area of this figure? `ABDC` is a rectangle and *BDE* is an isosceles right triangle.

    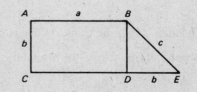

    (A) ab (B) ab^2 (C) $b\left(a + \dfrac{b}{2}\right)$

    (D) cab (E) $\dfrac{1}{2} bc$

22. If $2x + y = 5$ then $4x + 2y$ is equal to

    (A) 5   (B) 8   (C) 9   (D) 10   (E) none of these

23. In 1967, a new sedan cost $2,500; in 1975, the same type of sedan cost $4,800. The cost of that type of sedan has increased by what percent between 1967 and 1975?

(A) 48   (B) 52   (C) 92   (D) 152   (E) 192

24. What is the area of the square *ABCD*?

(A) 10   (B) 18   (C) 24   (D) 36
(E) 48

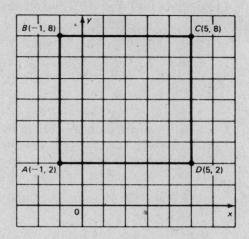

25. If $x + y = 6$ and $3x - y = 4$, then $x - y$ is equal to

(A) −1   (B) 0   (C) 2   (D) 4   (E) 6

MATHEMATICS
EXERCISE B

DIRECTIONS: Solve each of the following problems.
NOTE: A figure that appears with a problem is drawn as accurately as possible so as to provide information that may help in answering the question. Numbers in this test are real numbers.

Use the graphs below for questions 1–5.

WOMEN IN THE LABOR FORCE

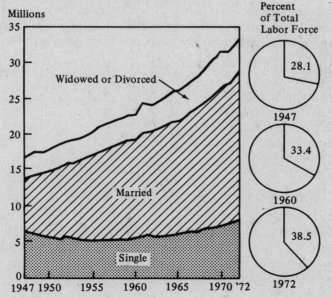
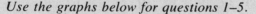
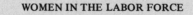

Source: Pocket Data Book U.S.A. 1973. Bureau of the Census.

1. The total labor force in 1960 was about *y* million with *y* equal to about

(A) 22   (B) 65   (C) 75   (D) 80   (E) 85

2. In 1947, the percentage of women in the labor force who were married was about

(A) 28   (B) 33   (C) 38   (D) 50   (E) 65

3. What was the first year when more than 20 million women were in the labor force?

(A) 1950   (B) 1953   (C) 1956   (D) 1958   (E) 1964

4. Between 1947 and 1972, the number of women in the labor force

(A) increased by about 50%   (B) increased by about 100%   (C) increased by about 150%   (D) increased by about 200%   (E) increased by about 250%

5. Which of the following statements about the labor force can be inferred from the graphs?

I. Between 1947 and 1957, there were no years when more than 5 million widowed or divorced women were in the labor force.
II. In every year between 1947 and 1972, the number of single women in the labor force has increased.
III. In 1965, women made up more than ⅓ of the total labor force.

(A) I only   (B) II only   (C) I and II only   (D) I and III only   (E) I, II, and III

6. If $\dfrac{x}{y} = \dfrac{2}{3}$ then $\dfrac{y^2}{x^2}$ is equal to

(A) $\dfrac{4}{9}$ (B) $\dfrac{2}{3}$ (C) $\dfrac{3}{2}$ (D) $\dfrac{9}{4}$ (E) $\dfrac{5}{2}$

7. In the figure, BD is perpendicular to AC. BA and BC have length a. What is the area of the triangle ABC?

(A) $2x\sqrt{a^2 - x^2}$ (B) $x\sqrt{a^2 - x^2}$
(C) $a\sqrt{a^2 - x^2}$ (D) $2a\sqrt{x^2 - a^2}$
(E) $x\sqrt{x^2 - a^2}$

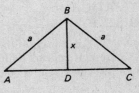

8. If two places are one inch apart on a map, then they are actually 160 miles apart. (The scale on the map is one inch equals 160 miles.) If Seaton is 2⅞ inches from Monroe on the map, how many miles is it from Seaton to Monroe?

(A) 3   (B) 27   (C) 300   (D) 360   (E) 460

9. In the accompanying diagram $ABCD$ is a rectangle. The area of isosceles right triangle $ABE = 7$, and $EC = 3(BE)$. The area of ABCD is

(A) 21   (B) 28   (C) 42   (D) 56   (E) 84

10. An automobile tire has two punctures. The first puncture by itself would make the tire flat in 9 minutes. The second puncture by itself would make the tire flat in 6 minutes. How long will it take for both punctures together to make the tire flat? (Assume the air leaks out at a constant rate.)

(A) $3\dfrac{3}{5}$ minutes   (B) 4 minutes   (C) $5\dfrac{1}{4}$ minutes   (D) $7\dfrac{1}{2}$ minutes   (E) 15 minutes

11. If n^3 is odd, which of the following statements are true?

I. n is odd.
II. n^2 is odd.
III. n^2 is even.

(A) I only   (B) II only   (C) III only   (D) I and II only   (E) I and III only

Use the table below for questions 12–15.

Participation in National Elections

Persons in millions. Civilian noninstitutional population as of Nov. 1. Based on post-election surveys of persons reporting whether or not they voted; differs from table 103 data which are based on actual vote counts.

Characteristic	1964 Persons of voting age	1964 Percent voted	1968 Persons of voting age	1968 Percent voted	1972 Persons of voting age	1972 Percent voted
Total	111	69	117	68	136	63
Male	52	72	54	70	64	64
Female	58	67	62	66	72	62
White	99	71	105	69	121	64
Negro and other	11	57	12	56	15	51
Negro	10	58	11	58	13	52
Region:						
North and West	78	75	82	71	94	66
South	32	57	35	60	43	55
Age:						
18–24 years	10	51	12	50	25	50
25–44 years	45	69	46	67	49	63
45–64	38	76	40	75	42	71
65 years and over	17	66	18	66	20	63

Source: U.S. Bureau of the Census.

12. Which of the following groups had the highest percentage of voters in 1968?

(A) 18–24 years (B) Female (C) South (D) 25–44 years (E) Male

13. In 1972, what percent (to the nearest percent) of persons of voting age were female?

(A) 52 (B) 53 (C) 62 (D) 64 (E) 72

14. In 1968, how many males of voting age voted?

(A) 37,440,000 (B) 37,800,000 (C) 42,160,000 (D) 62,000,000 (E) 374,400,000

15. Let X be the number (in millions) of persons of voting age in the range 25–44 years who lived in the North and West in 1964. Which of the following includes all possible values and only possible values of X?

(A) $0 \leq X \leq 45$ (B) $13 \leq X \leq 45$ (C) $13 \leq X \leq 78$ (D) $45 \leq X \leq 78$ (E) $75 \leq X \leq 78$

16. There are 50 students enrolled in Business 100. Of the enrolled students, 90% took the final exam. Two-thirds of the students who took the final exam passed the final exam. How many students passed the final exam?

(A) 30 (B) 33 (C) 34 (D) 35 (E) 45

17. If a is less than b, which of the following numbers is greater than a and less than b?

(A) $(a + b)/2$ (B) $(ab)/2$ (C) $b^2 - a^2$ (D) ab (E) $b - a$

18. In the figure, OR and PR are radii of circles. The length of OP is 4. If $OR = 2$, what is PR? PR is tangent to the circle with center O.

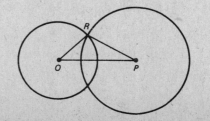

(A) 2 (B) $\dfrac{5}{2}$ (C) 3 (D) $2\sqrt{3}$ (E) $3\sqrt{2}$

19. A bus uses one gallon of gasoline to travel 15 miles. After a tune-up, the bus travels 15% farther on one gallon. How many gallons of gasoline (to the nearest tenth) will it take for the bus to travel 150 miles after a tune-up?

(A) 8.5 (B) 8.7 (C) 8.9 (D) 9.0 (E) 10.0

20. If $x + 2y = 4$ and $x/y = 2$, then x is equal to

(A) 0 (B) $\frac{1}{2}$ (C) 1 (D) $\frac{3}{2}$ (E) 2

Use the following table for questions 21–23.

	SPEED OF A TRAIN OVER A 3-HOUR PERIOD							
TIMED PERIOD *(in minutes)*	0	30	45	60	90	120	150	180
SPEED AT TIME *(in m.p.h.)*	40	45	47.5	50	55	60	65	70

21. How fast was the train traveling 2½ hours after the beginning of the timed period?

(A) 50 m.p.h. (B) 55 m.p.h. (C) 60 m.p.h. (D) 65 m.p.h. (E) 70 m.p.h.

22. During the three hours shown on the table the speed of the train

(A) increased by 25% (B) increased by 50% (C) increased by 75% (D) increased by 100% (E) increased by 125%

23. At time t measured in minutes after the beginning of the time period, which of the following gives the speed of the train in accordance with the table?

(A) $\frac{1}{6}t$ (B) $10t$ (C) $40 + t$ (D) $40 + \frac{1}{6}t$ (E) $40 + 10t$

24. It costs $1,000 to make the first thousand copies of a book and x dollars to make each subsequent copy. If it costs a total of $7,230 to make the first 8,000 copies of a book, what is x?

(A) .89 (B) .90375 (C) 1.00 (D) 89 (E) 90.375

25. If 16 workers can finish a job in three hours, how long should it take 5 workers to finish the same job?

(A) $3\frac{1}{2}$ hours (B) 4 hours (C) 5 hours (D) $7\frac{1}{16}$ hours (E) $9\frac{3}{5}$ hours

MATHEMATICS EXERCISE C

DIRECTIONS: Solve each of the following problems.
NOTE: A figure that appears with a problem is drawn as accurately as possible so as to provide information that may help in answering the question. Numbers in this test are real numbers.

1. A box contains 12 poles and 7 pieces of net. Each piece of net weighs .2 pounds; each pole weighs 1.1 pounds. The box and its contents together weigh 16.25 pounds. How much does the empty box weigh?

(A) 1.2 pounds (B) 1.65 pounds (C) 2.75 pounds (D) 6.15 pounds (E) 16 pounds

2. If $a + b + c + d$ is a positive number, a minimum of x of the numbers a, b, c, and d must be positive where x is equal to

(A) 0 (B) 1 (C) 2 (D) 3 (E) 4

3. Consider the accompanying diagram. Which of the following statements is true?

(A) $KM < KL$ (B) $KM < LM$ (C) $KL + LM < KM$
(D) $KL < LM$ (E) $KL > LM$

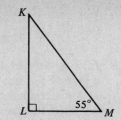

Use the graphs below for questions 4–6.

POPULATION CHARACTERISTICS

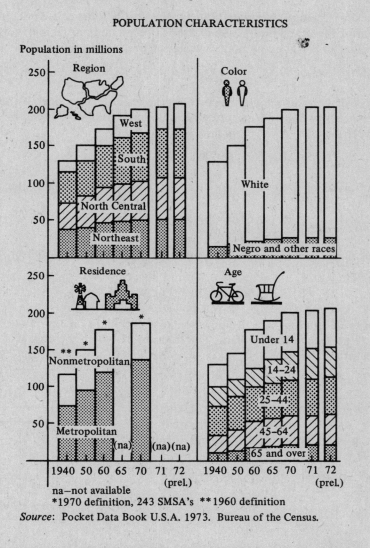

4. In 1970, the ratio of the population living in metropolitan areas to the population living in nonmetropolitan areas was approximately

(A) 1 to 2 (B) 2 to 3 (C) 7 to 5 (D) 3 to 2 (E) 2 to 1

5. In 1950, the age group which had the fewest people was

(A) under 14 (B) 14–24 (C) 25–44 (D) 45–64 (E) 65 and over

6. How many of the regions shown had a population increase of less than 5% between 1940 and 1972?

(A) 0 (B) 1 (C) 2 (D) 3 (E) 4

7. Which of the following numbers is the largest?

(A) $(2 + 2 + 2)^2$ (B) $[(2 + 2)^2]^2$ (C) $(2 \times 2 \times 2)^2$ (D) $2 + 2^2 + (2^2)^2$ (E) 4^3

8. In a survey of the town of Waso, it was found that 65% of the people surveyed watched the news on television, 40% read a newspaper, and 25% read a newspaper and watched the news on television. What percent of the people surveyed neither watched the news on television nor read a newspaper?

(A) 0%   (B) 5%   (C) 10%   (D) 15%   (E) 20%

9. A worker is paid d dollars an hour for the first 8 hours she works in a day. For every hour after the first 8 hours, she is paid c dollars an hour. If she works 12 hours in one day, what is her average hourly wage for that day?

(A) $(2d + c)/3$ (B) $8d + 4c$ (C) $(8d + 12c)/12$ (D) $(4d + 8c)/12$ (E) $d + (\frac{1}{3})c$

10. A screwdriver and a hammer currently have the same price. If the price of a screwdriver rises by 5% and the price of a hammer goes up by 3%, how much more will it cost to buy 3 screwdrivers and 3 hammers?

(A) 3%   (B) 4%   (C) 5%   (D) 8%   (E) 24%

11. If the radius of a circle is increased by 6%, then the area of the circle is increased by

(A) .36%   (B) 3.6%   (C) 6%   (D) 12.36%   (E) 36%

12. Given that a and b are real numbers, let $f(a,b) = ab$ and let $g(a) = a^2 + 2$. Then $f[3, g(3)] =$

(A) $3a^2 + 2$ (B) $3a^2 + 6$ (C) 27   (D) 29   (E) 33

13. A share of stock in Ace Enterprises cost D dollars on Jan. 1, 1975. One year later, a share increased to Q dollars. The fraction by which the cost of a share of stock has increased in the year is

(A) $(Q - D)/D$ (B) $(D - Q)/Q$ (C) D/Q (D) Q/D (E) $(Q - D)/Q$

14. $ABCD$ is a square, $EFGH$ is a rectangle. $AB = 3$, $EF = 4$, $FG = 6$. The area of the region outside of $ABCD$ and inside $EFGH$ is

(A) 6   (B) 9   (C) 12   (D) 15   (E) 24

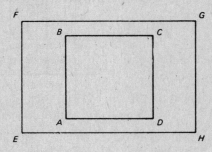

Use the table below for questions 15–17.

	% OF PROTEIN	% OF CARBOHYDRATES	% OF FAT	COST PER 100 GRAMS
FOOD A	10	20	30	$1.80
FOOD B	20	15	10	$3.00
FOOD C	20	10	40	$2.75

15. If you purchase x grams of Food A, y grams of Food B, and z grams of Food C, the cost will be

(A) $(\frac{9}{5}x + 3y + \frac{11}{4}z)\textcent$ (B) $\$(\frac{9}{5}x + 3y + \frac{11}{4}z)$ (C) $\$(1.8x + 3z + 2.75y)$ (D) $(3x + 1.8y + 2.75z)\textcent$ (E) $\$(x + y + z)$

16. Which of the following diets would supply the most grams of protein?

(A) 500 grams of A   (B) 250 grams of B   (C) 350 grams of C   (D) 150 grams of A and 200 grams of B   (E) 200 grams of B and 200 grams of C

17. All of the following diets would supply at least 75 grams of fat. Which of the diets costs the least?

(A) 200 grams of A, 150 grams of B   (B) 500 grams of B, 100 grams of A
(C) 200 grams of C   (D) 150 grams of A, 100 grams of C
(E) 300 grams of A

18. CD is parallel to EF. $AD = DF$, $CD = 4$, and $DF = 3$. What is EF?

(A) 4   (B) 5   (C) 6   (D) 7   (E) 8

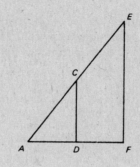

19. Which of the following fractions is the largest?

(A) $\dfrac{5}{6}$ (B) $\dfrac{11}{14}$ (C) $\dfrac{12}{15}$ (D) $\dfrac{17}{21}$ (E) $\dfrac{29}{35}$

20. How much simple interest will $2,000 earn in 18 months at an annual rate of 6%?

(A) $120   (B) $180   (C) $216   (D) $1,800   (E) $2,160

21. If $x + y > 5$ and $x - y > 3$, then which of the following gives all possible values of x and only possible values of x?

(A) $x > 3$ (B) $x > 4$ (C) $x > 5$ (D) $x < 5$ (E) $x < 3$

22. If the average (or arithmetic mean) of 6 numbers is 4.5, what is the sum of the numbers?

(A) 4.5   (B) 24   (C) 27   (D) 30   (E) cannot be determined

23. A silo is filled to capacity with W pounds of wheat. Rats eat r pounds a day. After 25 days, what percentage of the silo's capacity have the rats eaten?

(A) $25r/W$ (B) $25r/100W$ (C) $2,500(r/W)$ (D) r/W (E) $r/25W$

24. If $x^2 + 2x - 8 = 0$, then x is either -4 or

(A) -2 (B) -1 (C) 0   (D) 2   (E) 8

25. The interest charged on a loan is p dollars per $1,000 for the first month and q dollars per $1,000 for each month after the first month. How much interest will be charged during the first three months on a loan of $10,000?

(A) $30p$ (B) $30q$ (C) $p + 2q$ (D) $20p + 10q$ (E) $10p + 20q$

DATA SUFFICIENCY
EXERCISE

We have included one data sufficiency exercise to give you practice in answering this type of problem. The time allotted for this practice exercise is 18 minutes. Scoring may be interpreted as follows:

13–15	EXCELLENT
10–12+	GOOD
7–9+	FAIR
0–6+	POOR

Determine your score by counting the number of correct answers minus ¼ the number of incorrect answers. Before starting this practice exercise, refer to the strategy for answering data sufficiency questions as outlined on pages 16–17 of this book.

DIRECTIONS: Each of the following problems has a question and two statements which are labeled (1) and (2). Use the data given in (1) and (2) together with other available information (such as the number of hours in a day, the definition of *clockwise*, mathematical facts, etc.) to decide whether the statements are *sufficient* to answer the question. Then fill in space

(A) if you can get the answer from (1) alone but not from (2) alone;

(B) if you can get the answer from (2) alone but not from (1) alone;

(C) if you can get the answer from (1) and (2) together, although neither statement by itself suffices;

(D) if statement (1) alone suffices *and* statement (2) alone suffices;

(E) if you cannot get the answer from statements (1) and (2) together, but need even more data.

All numbers used in this section are real numbers. A figure given for a problem is intended to provide information consistent with that in the question, but not necessarily with the additional information contained in the statements.

1. Find the value of the expression $x^3y - (x^3/y)$.

   (1) $x = 2$
   (2) $y = 1$

2. If x is a two-digit number (so $x = ba$ with b and a digits), what is the last digit a of x?

   (1) The number $3x$ is a three-digit number whose last digit is a.
   (2) The digit a is less than 7.

3. Is the number $N/3$ an odd integer? (You may assume that $N/3$ is an integer.)

   (1) $N = 3K$ where K is an integer.
   (2) $N = 6J + 3$ where J is an integer.

4. How many families in Jaytown own exactly two phones?

   (1) 150 families in Jaytown own at least one telephone.
   (2) 45 families in Jaytown own at least three telephones.

5. Is the line *PQ* parallel to the line *SR*?

    (1) $w = q$
    (2) $y = z$

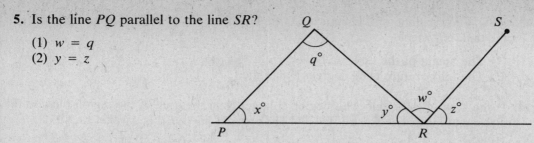

6. What is the value of $x^3 - y^3$?

    (1) $x^6 - y^6 = 0$
    (2) $y = 0$

7. How much does John weigh? Tim weighs 200 pounds.

    (1) Tim's weight plus Moe's weight is equal to John's weight.
    (2) John's weight plus Moe's weight is equal to twice Tim's weight.

8. Which triangle, *ADE* or *AEC*, has the larger area? *ABCD* is a rectangle.

    (1) *DE* is longer than *EC*.
    (2) *AC* is longer than *AE*.

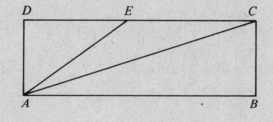

9. *ABCDEFGH* is a cube. What is the length of the line segment *AG*?

    (1) The length of the line segment *AB* is 4 inches.
    (2) The area of the square *BCGH* is 16 square inches.

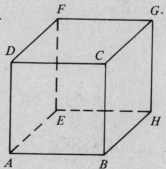

10. Is the integer *K* an odd integer?

    (1) $K = 3M$ where *M* is an integer.
    (2) $K = 6J$ where *J* is an integer.

11. What was the value of the sales of the ABC Company in 1980?

    (1) The sales of the ABC Company increased by \$100,000 each year from 1970 to 1980.
    (2) The value of the sales of the ABC Company doubled between 1970 and 1980.

12. Is *x* greater than 2? (You may assume *y* is not equal to zero.)

    (1) (x/y) is greater than 2.
    (2) $(1/y)$ is less than 1.

13. How many gallons of a chemical can be stored in a cylindrical tank if the radius of the tank is 15 feet?

(1) The height of the tank is 20 feet.
(2) The temperature is 60 degrees Fahrenheit.

14. Is the area of the circle with center O larger than the area of the region outside the circle and inside the square $ABCD$? The straight line OEF is parallel to AB.

(1) $OE < (1/4)AB$
(2) $EF < (1/4)AB$

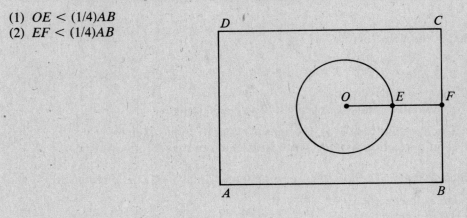

15. If $x^6 - y^6 = 0$, what is the value of $x^3 - y^3$?

(1) x is positive.
(2) y is greater than 1.

Answers

The letter following each question number is the correct answer. The numbers in parentheses refer to the sections of this chapter which explain the necessary mathematics principles. A more detailed explanation of all answers follows.

Mathematics Exercise A

1. **D** (I-1)
2. **B** (I-4)
3. **B** (III-7, I-4)
4. **A** (IV-4, IV-5, I-4)
5. **A** (IV-4, I-7)
6. **B** (IV-4)
7. **D** (IV-4, I-2)
8. **C** (I-4)
9. **A** (I-1)
10. **C** (II-1)
11. **C** (III-9, I-8)
12. **C** (I-2)
13. **C** (I-4)
14. **D** (I-4)
15. **C** (I-4)
16. **E** (I-7, I-4)
17. **B** (I-4, I-5)
18. **A** (II-1)
19. **D** (I-2)
20. **D** (II-3)
21. **C** (III-7, II-1, I-8)
22. **D** (II-2)
23. **C** (I-4)
24. **D** (III-9, III-7)
25. **A** (II-2)

Mathematics Exercise C

1. **B** (I-3)
2. **B** (II-7, I-6)
3. **E** (III-4)
4. **E** (IV-5, II-5)
5. **E** (IV-5)
6. **A** (IV-5)
7. **B** (I-8)
8. **E** (II-4)
9. **A** (I-7, II-1)
10. **B** (I-4)
11. **D** (III-7)
12. **E** (II-1)
13. **A** (I-2)
14. **D** (III-7)
15. **A** (II-1)
16. **E** (I-4)
17. **E** (IV-1)
18. **E** (III-4)
19. **A** (I-1, I-2, III-7)
20. **B** (I-4)
21. **B** (II-7)
22. **C** (I-7)
23. **C** (I-4)
24. **D** (II-1, II-2)
25. **E** (II-1)

Mathematics Exercise B

1. **B** (IV-2, IV-3)
2. **D** (IV-3)
3. **C** (IV-3)
4. **B** (IV-3)
5. **A** (IV-3)
6. **D** (I-8)
7. **B** (III-4, III-7)
8. **E** (II-5)
9. **D** (III-7)
10. **A** (II-3)
11. **D** (I-1)
12. **E** (IV-1)
13. **B** (IV-1)
14. **B** (IV-1)
15. **B** (IV-1, II-7)
16. **A** (I-4, I-2)
17. **A** (II-7)
18. **D** (III-6, III-4)
19. **B** (I-4)
20. **E** (II-2)
21. **D** (IV-1)
22. **C** (IV-1)
23. **D** (II-1)
24. **A** (II-2)
25. **E** (II-3)

Data Sufficiency Exercise

1. **(B)**
2. **(E)**
3. **(B)**
4. **(E)**
5. **(A)**
6. **(C)**
7. **(C)**
8. **(A)**
9. **(D)**
10. **(B)**
11. **(C)**
12. **(E)**
13. **(E)**
14. **(A)**
15. **(C)**

Explanation of Answers

Mathematics Exercise A

1. **D** The price increased by $34 - 12 = 22$ dollars.

2. **B** She sold the house for 125% of C or $\frac{5}{4}C$. Thus, the gain is $\frac{5}{4}C - C = \frac{C}{4}$. She must pay a tax of 50% of $\frac{C}{4}$ or $\frac{1}{2}$ of $\frac{C}{4}$. Therefore, the tax is $\frac{C}{8}$. Notice that the three years has nothing to do with the problem. Sometimes a question contains unnecessary information.

3. **B** The area of a rectangle is length times width. Let L and W denote the original length and width. Then the new length is $1.2L$ and the new width is $.8W$. Therefore, the new area is $(1.2L)(.8W) = .96LW$ or 96% of the original area. So the area has decreased by 4%.

4. **A** In 1964 military expenditures were about 140 billion and by 1969 they had increased to about 200 billion. $\frac{60}{140} = \frac{3}{7}$ which is almost 50%. By using a straight edge, you may see that the bar for 1969 is about half again as long as the bar for 1964.

5. **A** Since the developing countries' military expenditures for every year were less than 30 billion, choice A is the only possible answer. Notice that by reading the possible answers first, you save time. You don't need the exact answer.

6. **B** I cannot be inferred since the graph indicates *only* the dollars spent on military expenditures, not the percent of income and not total income. II is true since each bar is higher than the previous bar to the left. III cannot be inferred since the graph gives no information about 1972. So only statement II can be inferred from the graph.

7. **D** In 1971 the NATO countries spent over 100 billion and less than 150 billion on military expenditures. Since this was $\frac{1}{3}$ of their combined incomes the combined income is between 300 billion and 450 billion. Thus choice D must be the correct answer.

8. **C** Voters between 18 and 21 who voted are 85% of the 8% of eligible voters. Thus, $(.08)(.85) = .068$, so 6.8% of the eligible voters were voters between 18 and 21 who voted.

9. **A** Odd numbers are of the form $2x + 1$ where x is an integer. Thus if $n = 2x + 1$ and $p = 2k + 1$, then $n + p = 2x + 1 + 2k + 1 = 2x + 2k + 2$ which is even. Using $n = 3$ and $p = 5$, all the other choices give an odd number. In general, if a problem involves odd or even numbers, try using the fact that odd numbers are of the form $2x + 1$ and even numbers of the form $2y$ where x and y are integers.

10. **C** To run a car 100 miles will cost $100(g + m)$ cents. Divide by 100 to convert to dollars. The result is $g + m$.

11. **C** Using the distance formula, the distance from A to B is $\sqrt{(1 - (-1))^2 + (3 - 5)^2} = \sqrt{4 + 4} = \sqrt{8} = \sqrt{4 \times 2} = \sqrt{4}\sqrt{2} = 2\sqrt{2}$. You have to be able to simplify $\sqrt{8}$ in order to obtain the correct answer.

12. **C** Tips for the week were $\frac{5}{4} \cdot 50$ so his total income was $50 + \frac{5}{4}(50) = \frac{9}{4}(50)$.

Therefore, tips made up $\frac{5/4(50)}{9/4(50)} = \frac{5/4}{9/4} = \frac{5}{9}$ of his income. *Don't* waste time figuring out the total income and the tip income. You can use the time to answer other questions.

13. **C** 7,500 is in the 6,000–8,000 bracket so the tax will be 80 + 3% of the income over 6,000. Since 7,500 − 6,000 = 1,500, the income over 6,000 is 1,500. 3% of 1,500 = (.03)(1,500) = 45, so the tax is 80 + 45 = 125.

14. **D** The tax on 26,000 is 1,070 + 7% of (26,000 − 25,000). Thus, the tax is 1,070 + 70 = 1,140. The tax on 29,000 is 1.070 + 7% of (29,000 − 25,000). Thus, the tax on 29,000 is 1,070 + 280 = 1,350. Therefore, you will pay 1,350 − 1,140 = $210 more in taxes next year. A faster method is to use the fact that the $3,000 raise is income over 25,000, so it will be taxed at 7%. Therefore, the tax on the extra $3,000 will be (.07)(3,000) = 210.

15. **C** If income is less than 6,000, then the tax is less than 80. If income is greater than 8,000, then the tax is greater than 140. Therefore, if the tax is 100, the income must be between 6,000 and 8,000. You *do not* have to calculate her exact income.

16. **E** Each person pays the tax on $3,700 which is 1% of 3,700 or $37. Since there are 50,000 people in Zenith, the total taxes are (37)(50,000) = $1,850,000.

17. **B** The tax on 10,000 is 220, so taxes are $\frac{220}{10,000} = .022 = 2.2\%$ of income. 2.2% is 2% after rounding to the nearest percent.

18. **A** $S(3,4) = 3^2 - 4^2 = 9 - 16 = -7$. Therefore, $S(3,S(3,4)) = S(3,-7) = 3^2 - (-7)^2 = 9 - 49 = -40$.

19. **D** 8 omelets will use $8 \cdot 3 = 24$ eggs and $8 \cdot \frac{1}{4} = 2$ peppers. Since 24 is two dozen, the cost will be $(2)(90¢) + (2)(20¢) = 220¢$ or $2.20.

20. **D** In order to average 50 m.p.h. for the trip, the bus must make the trip in $\frac{185}{50} = 3\frac{7}{10}$ hours which is 222 minutes. Since 2 hours or 120 minutes were needed for the first 85 miles, the final 100 miles must be completed in 222 − 120 which is 102 minutes.

21. **C** The area of a rectangle is length times width so the area of *ABDC* is ab. The area of a triangle is one half of the height times the base. Since *BDE* is an isosceles right triangle, the base and height both are equal to b. Thus, the area of *BDE* is $\frac{1}{2}b^2$. Therefore, the area of the figure is $ab + \frac{1}{2}b^2$ which is equal to $b\left(a + \frac{b}{2}\right)$. You have to express your answer as one of the possible answers, so you need to be able to simplify.

22. **D** Since $4x + 2y$ is equal to $2(2x + y)$ and $2x + y = 5$, $4x + 2y$ is equal to $2(5)$ or 10.

23. **C** The cost has increased by $4,800 minus $2,500 or $2,300 between 1967 and 1975. So the cost has increased by $\frac{2,300}{2,500}$ which is .92 or 92%. Answer (E) is incorrect. The price in 1975 is 192% of the price in 1967, but the *increase* is 92%.

24. **D** The distance from $(-1, 2)$ to $(5, 2)$ is 6. (You can use the distance formula or just count the blocks in this case.) The area of a square is the length of a side squared, so the area is 6^2 or 36.

25. **A** Since $x + y = 6$ and $3x - y = 4$, we may add the two equations to obtain $4x = 10$, or $x = 2.5$. Then, because $x + y = 6$, y must be 3.5. Therefore, $x - y = -1$.

Mathematics Exercise B

1. **B** In 1960 women made up 33.4% or about ⅓ of the labor force. The line graph shows there were about 22 million women in the labor force in 1960. So the labor force was about 3(22) or 66 million. The closest answer among the choices is 65 million.

2. **D** In 1947, there were about 16 million women in the labor force, and about 14 − 6 or 8 million of them were married. Therefore, the percentage of women in the labor force who were married is $\frac{8}{16}$ or 50%.

3. **C** Look at the possible answers first. You can use your pencil and admission card as straight edges.

4. **B** In 1947, there were about 16 million women in the labor force. By 1972 there were about 32 million. Therefore, the number of women doubled which is an increase of 100%. (Not of 200%.)

5. **A** I is true since the width of the band for widowed or divorced women was never more than 5 million between 1947 and 1957. II is false since the number of single women in the labor force decreased from 1947 to 1948. III cannot be inferred since there is no information about the total labor force or women as a percent of it in 1965. Thus, only I can be inferred.

6. **D** If $\frac{x}{y}$ is $\frac{2}{3}$, then $\frac{y}{x}$ is $\frac{3}{2}$. Since $\left(\frac{y}{x}\right)^2$ is equal to $\frac{y^2}{x^2}$, $\frac{y^2}{x^2}$ is $\left(\frac{3}{2}\right)^2$ or $\frac{9}{4}$.

7. **B** The area of a triangle is $\frac{1}{2}$ altitude times base. Since BD is perpendicular to AC, x is the altitude. Using the Pythagorean theorem, $x^2 + (AD)^2 = a^2$ and $x^2 + (DC)^2 = a^2$. Thus, $AD = DC$, and $AD = \sqrt{a^2 - x^2}$. So the base is $2\sqrt{a^2 - x^2}$. Therefore, the area is $\frac{1}{2}(x)(2\sqrt{a^2 - x^2})$ which is choice B.

8. **E** $1 : 160 :: 2\frac{7}{8} : x$. $x = 2\frac{7}{8}(160)$. $2\frac{7}{8}$ is $\frac{23}{8}$ so the distance from Seton to Monroe is $\frac{23}{8}(160) = 460$ miles.

9. **D** Let $EF = FG = GC$. Therefore, $BE = EF = FG = GC$. Draw perpendiculars EH, FI, GJ. Draw diagonals HF, IG, JC. The 8 triangles are equal in area since they each have the same altitude (AB or DC) and equal bases (BE, EF, FG, GC, AH, HI, IJ, JD). Since the area of $ABE = 7$, the area of $ABCD = (8)(7)$ or 56.

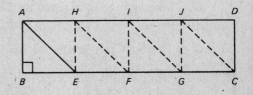

10. **A**   In each minute the first puncture will leak $\frac{1}{9}$ of the air and the second puncture will leak $\frac{1}{6}$ of the air. Together $\frac{1}{9} + \frac{1}{6} = \frac{5}{18}$. So $\frac{5}{18}$ of the air will leak out in each minute. In $\frac{18}{5}$ or $3\frac{3}{5}$ minutes the tire will be flat.

11. **D**   Since an even number times any number is even, and n times n^2 is odd, neither n nor n^2 can be even. Therefore, n and n^2 must both be odd for n^3 to be odd. I and II are true, and III is false.

12. **E**   Look in the fourth column.

13. **B**   In 1972 there were 72 million females out of 136 million persons of voting age. $\frac{72}{136} = .529$ which is 53% to the nearest percent.

14. **B**   In 1968, 70% of the 54 million males of voting age voted, and $(.7)(54,000,000) = 37,800,000$.

15. **B**   Since 78 million persons of voting age lived in the North and West in 1964, and there were 65 million persons of voting age not in the 25–44 year range, there must be at least $78 - 65 = 13$ million people in the North and West in the 25–44 year range. X must be greater than or equal to 13. Since there were 45 million people of voting age in the 25–44 year range, X must be less than or equal to 45.

16. **A**   90% of 50 is 45, so 45 students took the final. $\frac{2}{3}$ of 45 is 30. Therefore, 30 students passed the final.

17. **A**   The average of two different numbers is always between the two. If $a = 2$ and $b = 3$, then $b^2 - a^2 = 5$, $ab = 6$, and $b - a = 1$ so C, D, and E must be false. If $a = \frac{1}{2}$ and $b = 1$, then $(ab)/2 = \frac{1}{4}$, so B is also false.

18. **D**   Since the radius to the point of tangency is perpendicular to the tangent OR must be perpendicular to PR. Therefore, ORP is a right triangle, and $(PO)^2 = (OR)^2 + (PR)^2$. Then, $(PR)^2 = (PO)^2 - (OR)^2$. Thus, $(PR)^2 = 4^2 - 2^2$, and $PR = \sqrt{16 - 4} = \sqrt{12} = \sqrt{4}\sqrt{3} = 2\sqrt{3}$.

19. **B**   After the tune-up, the bus will travel $(1.15)(15) = 17.25$ miles on a gallon of gas. Therefore, it will take $(150) \div (17.25) = 8.7$ (to the nearest tenth) gallons of gasoline to travel 150 miles.

20. **E**   If $x/y = 2$, then $x = 2y$, so $x + 2y = 2y + 2y = 4y$. But $x + 2y = 4$, so $4y = 4$, or $y = 1$. Since $x = 2y$, x must be 2.

21. **D**   2½ hours is 150 minutes.

22. **C**   The train's speed increased by $70 - 40$ which is 30 miles per hour. 30/40 is 75%.

23. **D**   When $t = 0$, the speed is 40, so A and B are incorrect. When $t = 180$, the speed is 70, so C and E are incorrect. Choice D gives all the values which appear in the table.

24. **A**   The cost of producing the first 8,000 copies is $1,000 + 7,000x$. $1,000 + 7,000x = \$7,230$. Therefore, $7,000x = 6230$ and $x = .89$.

25. **E**   Assume all workers work at the same rate unless given different information. Since 16 workers take 3 hours, each worker does $\frac{1}{48}$ of the job an hour. Thus, the 5 workers will finish $\frac{5}{48}$ of the job each hour. $\frac{5}{48}x = \frac{48}{48}$. It will take $\frac{48}{5} = 9\frac{3}{5}$ hours for them to finish the job.

Mathematics Exercise C

1. **B** The 12 poles weigh (12)(1.1) = 13.2 pounds and the 7 pieces of net weigh 7(.2) = 1.4 pounds, so the contents of the box weigh 13.2 + 1.4 = 14.6 pounds. Therefore, the box by itself must weigh 16.25 − 14.6 = 1.65 pounds.

2. **B** If all the numbers were not positive, then the sum could not be positive so A is incorrect. If a, b, and c were all −1 and d were 5, then $a + b + c + d$ would be positive so C, D, and E are incorrect.

3. **E** Since the measure of angle M is 55°, the measure of angle K is 35°. Therefore, $KL > LM$ since the larger side is opposite the larger angle.

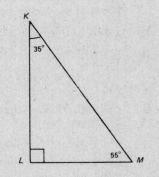

4. **E** The population in metropolitan areas in 1970 was about 140 million, and the population in nonmetropolitan areas was about 210 − 140 or 70 million. Therefore, the ratio was about 140 to 70 or 2 to 1.

5. **E** Compare the segments of the second bar under "age."

6. **A** All regions increased by at least 10%. Compare the segments of the first bar with those of the last bar under "Region."

7. **B** Choice A gives 6^2 or 36. Choice B gives 4^4 or 256. Choice C is 8^2 or 64. Choice D is 2 + 4 + 16 or 22. Choice E is 4^3 or 64.

8. **E** Since 25% read the newspaper and watched the news on television and 40% read the newspaper, 40% − 25% or 15% read the newspaper but did not watch the news on television. Thus 65% + 15% or 80% read the newspaper or watched the news on television, so 100% − 80% or 20% neither read the newspaper nor watched the news on television.

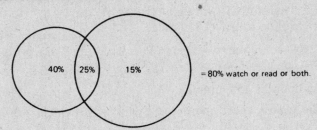

65 % watch TV.   40% read newspapers.
100% − 80% = 20% neither watch nor read.

9. **A** For the first 8 hours, she is paid a total of $8d$. For the final 4 hours (12 − 8), she is paid $4c$. Therefore, her total pay is $8d + 4c$. To find the average hourly pay, divide by 12. To find the correct answer among the choices, you have to reduce the fraction. Divide the numerator by four and the denominator by four.

10. **B** If the price of one screwdriver increases by 5%, then the price of three screwdrivers increases by 5% (not 15%). The percentage change is the same regardless of the number sold. Since a screwdriver and a hammer currently cost the same, the screwdrivers and the hammers each cost one half of the total price. So one half of the total is increased by 5%. The other half is increased by 3%. Therefore, the total price is increased by ½ (5%) + ½ (3%) = 4%.

11. **D** After the radius is increased by 6%, the radius will be 1.06 times the original radius. Since the area of a circle is πr^2, the new area will be $\pi(1.06r)^2 = \pi(1.1236r^2)$ or $1.1236\pi r^2$. Thus, the area has been increased by .1236 or by 12.36%.

12. **E** Since $g(a) = a^2 + 2$, $g(3)$ is $3^2 + 2$ or 11. So $f[3,g(3)]$ is $f(3,11) = 3 \times 11$ or 33.

13. **A** The difference in the price is $Q - D$. So the fraction by which it has increased is $(Q - D)/D$. Note that the denominator is the *original* price.

14. **D** Since $ABCD$ is a square, the area of $ABCD$ is 3^2 or 9. The area of the rectangle $EFGH$ is *length* times *width* or $4 \times 6 = 24$. Thus, the area outside the square and inside the rectangle is $24 - 9$ or 15.

15. **A** The cost of food A is $1.80 per hundred grams or 1.8¢ a gram, so x grams cost $(1.8x)$¢ or $(9/5)x$¢. Each gram of food B costs 3¢ so y grams of food B will cost $3y$¢. Each gram of food C costs 2.75¢ or $11/4$¢; thus, z grams of food C will cost $(11/4)z$¢. Therefore, the total cost is $[(9/5)x + 3y + (11/4)z]$¢.

16. **E** Since food A is 10% protein, 500 grams of food A will supply 50 grams of protein. Food B is 20% protein so 250 grams of food B will supply 50 grams of protein. 350 grams of food C will supply 70 grams of protein. 150 grams of food A and 200 grams of food B will supply $15 + 40 = 55$ grams of protein. 200 grams of food B and 200 grams of food C will supply $40 + 40$ or 80 grams of protein. Choice E supplies the most protein.

17. **E** The diet of choice A will cost $2(\$1.80) + (3/2)(\$3) = \$3.60 + \$4.50 = \$8.10$. Choice B will cost $5(\$3) + \$1.80 = \$16.80$. Choice C costs $2(\$2.75) = \$5.50$. Choice D costs $(3/2)(\$1.80) + \$2.75 = \$2.70 + \$2.75 = \$5.45$. The diet of Choice E costs $3(\$1.80)$ or 5.40 so Choice E costs the least.

18. **E** Since CD is parallel to EF, the triangles ACD and AEF are similar. Therefore, corresponding sides are proportional. So CD is to EF as AD is to AF. Since $AD = DF$, AD/AF is ½. Therefore, EF is twice CD or 8.

19. **A** You need to find a common denominator for the fractions. One method is to multiply all the denominators. A quicker method is to find the least common multiple of the denominators. Since $6 = 3 \times 2$, $14 = 2 \times 7$, $15 = 3 \times 5$, $21 = 3 \times 7$, and $35 = 5 \times 7$, the least common multiple is $2 \times 3 \times 5 \times 7 = 210$. 5/6 is 175/210, 11/14 is 165/210, 12/15 is 168/210, 17/21 is 170/210, and 29/35 is 174/210. So 5/6 is the largest.

20. **B** 18 months is 3/2 of a year. Interest = Amount × Time × Rate. ($2,000) $(3/2)(.06) = \$180$.

21. **B** If $x + y > 5$ and $x - y > 3$, then, since both inequalities are of the same type, the corresponding sides can be added to obtain $2x > 8$ or $x > 4$.

22. **C** The average of 6 numbers is the sum of the numbers divided by 6. Thus, the sum of the numbers is the average multiplied by 6 or 4.5×6 which is 27.

23. **C** After 25 days the rats have eaten $25r$ pounds of wheat. So $(25r)/W$ is the fraction of the capacity eaten by the rats. To change this to percent, multiply by 100. $(25r)/W \times 100 = 2500(r/W)$.

24. **D** Factor $x^2 + 2x - 8$ into $(x + 4)(x - 2)$. If x is either -4 or 2, $x^2 + 2x - 8 = 0$, and D is the correct answer.

25. **E** The interest on the $10,000 for the first month will be $10p$. For the next 2 months the interest will be $20q$. The total interest is $10p + 20q$.

Data Sufficiency Exercise

(Refer to pages 16–17 for an explanation of the strategy used in solving the following problems.)

1. **B** If STATEMENT (1) is true, then $x^3y - (x^3/y)$ is equal to $8y - (8/y)$, but the value of y is needed to find the value of the expression. Therefore, (1) alone is not sufficient. So the answer to question I is NO, and the only possible choices are B, C, or E.

   If STATEMENT (2) alone is true, then $x^3y - (x^3/y)$ is equal to $x^3 1 - (x^3/1)$, which is equal to 0. Therefore, (2) alone is sufficient, and the answer to question II is YES. So the correct choice is B.

   This problem illustrates the need to be careful. You might quickly infer that a value for x and a value for y are both needed and INCORRECTLY answer C. To understand the problem, you need to simplify the expression by factoring out an x^3 from each term. So $x^3y - (x^3/y)$ is equal to $x^3(y - (1/y))$, which is equal to 0 if $x = 0$ or if $y - (1/y) = 0$. Thus, the expression's value is determined if $x = 0$ or if $y = 1$; otherwise, you need both a value for x and a value for y.

2. **E** If STATEMENT (1) is true, then since $x = ba$, $3x = 3(10b + a) = 30b + 3a$. Now, because b is multiplied by 10 in the expression for $3x$, the final digit of $3x$ must be the final digit of $3a$. Since a is a digit, $0 \le a \le 9$, which implies $0 \le 3a \le 27$. So for the last digit of $3a$ to be equal to a, $3a$ must equal a or $10 + a$ or $20 + a$. If $a = 3a$, then $a = 0$. If $10 + a = 3a$, then $10 = 2a$ or $a = 5$. If $20 + a = 3a$, then $20 = 2a$ or $a = 10$, but since 10 is not a digit this is not possible. So if (1) is true, then a is 0 or 5, and (1) alone is not sufficient. Thus the answer to question I is NO, and the only possible choices are B, C, or E.

   Now since 26 and 25 are both two-digit numbers whose last digits are less than 7, STATEMENT (2) alone is not sufficient. So the answer to question II is NO, and the only possible choices are C or E. Also, since (2) does not allow us to choose between 0 and 5, STATEMENTS (1) and (2) together are not sufficient, so the correct choice is E.

   Many people would be able to see that STATEMENT (2) alone would be insufficient but might not be able to decide whether (1) is sufficient. You can use the strategy to make an intelligent guess. Since (2) alone is not sufficient, the answer to question II on the decision tree is NO. Since choices B and D need an answer of YES to II, the only possible choices are A, C, or E. Since you can eliminate two choices, it is worthwhile to guess.

3. **B** STATEMENT (1) alone is not sufficient since then $N/3 = (3K)/3 = K$. Now if $K = 1$, then $N/3 = 1$, which is odd, but if $K = 2$, then $N/3 = 2$, which is even. So the answer to question I is NO, and the only possible choices are B, C, or E.

   STATEMENT (2) alone is sufficient since then $N/3 = (6J + 3)/3 = 2J + 1$, which is always odd since J is an integer. So the answer to question II is YES, and the correct choice is B.

4. **E** If you use STATEMENTS (1) and (2) together, you can deduce that $150 - 45 = 105$ families own at least one telephone and less than three telephones. However, since this is the total of families with one phone and families with two phones, we cannot find the number of families with exactly two phones. So (1) and (2) together are not sufficient. Thus, the answer to question III is NO, and the correct choice is E.

5. **A** Since w and q are alternate interior angles, if STATEMENT (1) is true then PQ is parallel to SR. So (1) alone is sufficient. Thus, the answer to question I is YES and the only possible choices are A and D.

STATEMENT (2) alone is not sufficient since the line RS can be moved so that y is still equal to z but PQ and RS are not parallel. (See the diagram below.)

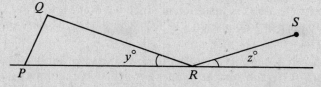

Therefore, the answer to question II is NO, and the correct choice is A.

6. C   If STATEMENT (1) alone is true, then since $x^6 - y^6$ can be factored into $(x^3 + y^3)(x^3 - y^3)$, either $x^3 + y^3 = 0$ or $x^3 - y^3 = 0$. So (1) alone is not sufficient, and the answer to question I is NO. Thus, the only possible choices are B, C, or E.

STATEMENT (2) alone is insufficient since if $y = 0$, then $x^3 - y^3 = x^3$, and we have no value for x. So the answer to question II is NO, and the only possible choices are C or E.

If (1) and (2) are both true, then we can deduce that x and y must both be equal to zero, which is sufficient. Thus, the answer to question III is YES, and the correct choice must be C.

7. C   Let J, M, and T stand for the weights of John, Moe, and Tim respectively. We need to find J and we know $T = 200$. STATEMENT (1) gives the equation $200 + M = J$, but since we don't know M, (1) alone is not sufficient.

STATEMENT (2) alone gives the equation $J + M = 2T = 400$, and since we don't know M, (2) alone is insufficient.

However, if we use STATEMENTS (1) and (2) together, then we have two linear equations in two unknowns, which we know can be solved to find J and M. NOTE: Don't waste time actually solving the equations. You only have to decide if there is enough information to answer the question; you don't have to compute the actual answer.

8. A   Since the area of a triangle is (1/2) (altitude) (base) and since both triangles have DA as an altitude, if the base (DE) of triangle ADE is larger than the base (EC) of triangle AEC, then the area of ADE is larger than the area of AEC. So STATEMENT (1) alone is sufficient, and the answer to question I is YES.

STATEMENT (2) alone is not sufficient since for any point E between D and C (2) will be true, but, depending on whether E is closer to D or C, a different triangle will have the larger area. So the answer to question II is NO, and the correct choice is A.

9. D   By using the distance formula (Pythagorean theorem) you could find the length of AG if you knew the lengths of AH and GH (or if you knew the lengths of AC and CG or many other combinations). If you knew the lengths of AB and BH, then you could find the length of AH. Thus, it is sufficient to know the lengths of AB, BH, and GH. Since $ABCDEFGH$ is a cube, AB, BH, and GH all have the same length since they are all edges of the cube. So it is sufficient to know the length of an edge of the cube. Now STATEMENTS (1) and (2) are equivalent since the area of a square face of the cube is 16 if and only if the length of an edge is 4. Therefore, (1) alone and (2) alone are sufficient, and the correct choice is D.

Notice that, if you knew that (1) and (2) are equivalent, then the only possible choices are D or E, so you *can* make an intelligent guess.

10. B   STATEMENT (2) alone is sufficient since if (2) is true, then $K = 2(3J)$, which means that K is even. Note this is sufficient to answer the question even though the answer is NO.

STATEMENT (1) alone is not sufficient since if M is even, then K is even, but if M is odd, then K is odd.

11. **C** STATEMENT (1) alone is insufficient since we don't know the sales for any year. Thus, the answer to question I is NO. Therefore, the only possible choices are B, C, or E.

STATEMENT (2) alone is not sufficient since we don't know the value of the sales in 1970. So the answer to question III is NO, and the only possible choices are C and E.

Using (1), we can calculate the change in sales from 1970 to 1980, and then by using (2), we can find the value of the sales in 1980. Therefore, the answer to question III is YES, and the correct choice is C.

12. **E** Since $x = 3$, $y = 1$, and $x = 1$, $y = (1/3)$ both make STATEMENT (1) true, (1) alone is not sufficient. So the answer to question I is NO, and the only possible choices are B, C, or E.

STATEMENT (2) alone is obviously not sufficient since it gives no information about x. Thus, the answer to question II is NO, and the only possible choices are C or E. (NOTE: Even if you can't answer question I for this problem, you should be able to answer question II, and you would be able to guess either A, C, or E.)

Now if y were positive, we could use STATEMENT (2) to deduce that $y > 1$ and then (1) would imply that $x > 2$. However, negative values of y can also satisfy (2) (for example, $y = -1$) and then (1) would have solutions with $x < 2$. So (1) and (2) together are not sufficient, and the answer to question III is NO. Thus the correct choice is E.

13. **E** (1) alone is insufficient since it will allow you to find the volume of the tank, but there is no information about how many cubic feet a gallon of the chemical occupies. So the only choices are B, C, or E.

Since STATEMENT (2) does not give any information about the space needed by a gallon of the chemical, statements (1) and (2) together are not sufficient, and the correct choice must be E.

14. **A** The area of the circle plus the area of the region outside the circle and inside the square is equal to the area of the square, which is $(AB)^2$. Thus if you can determine whether one area is larger (or smaller) than $(1/2)AB^2$, that is sufficient.

STATEMENT (1) alone is sufficient since the area of the circle is $\pi(OE)^2$, and if (1) holds, then $\pi(OE)^2 < \pi((1/4)AB)^2 = \pi (1/16)AB^2$. But since $\pi/16$ is less than $(1/2)$, we can answer the question. So the answer to question I is YES, and the only possible choices are A or D.

STATEMENT (2) alone is not sufficient since (2) does not give any information about the radius of the circle. Note you might think that $OE + EF = (1/2)AB$; however, that requires the additional information that O is also the center of the square, which is NOT given. So the answer to question II is NO, and the correct choice is A.

15. **C** The key to solving this problem is to relate $x^3 - y^3$ to the information $x^6 - y^6 = 0$. If you think of $x^6 - y^6$ as $(x^3)^2 - (y^3)^2$, then you can factor the equation into $(x^3 - y^3) (x^3 + y^3) = 0$. So if $x^3 + y^3$ is not zero, then $x^3 - y^3$ must be zero. Thus STATEMENTS (1) and (2) together are sufficient because they imply that $x^3 + y^3$ is greater than zero.

However, (1) alone or (2) alone is not sufficient because since the cube of a negative number is negative we could have $x^3 + y^3$ equal zero, and then the value of $x^3 - y^3$ may not be determined. For example, $x = 1$, $y = 1$ and $x = 1$, $y = -1$ show (1) alone is not sufficient, and $x = 2$, $y = 2$ and $x = -2$, $y = 2$ show (2) alone is not sufficient.

Answer Sheet—Sample Test 1

Section I
Reading Comprehension

1. Ⓐ Ⓑ Ⓒ Ⓓ Ⓔ
2. Ⓐ Ⓑ Ⓒ Ⓓ Ⓔ
3. Ⓐ Ⓑ Ⓒ Ⓓ Ⓔ
4. Ⓐ Ⓑ Ⓒ Ⓓ Ⓔ
5. Ⓐ Ⓑ Ⓒ Ⓓ Ⓔ
6. Ⓐ Ⓑ Ⓒ Ⓓ Ⓔ
7. Ⓐ Ⓑ Ⓒ Ⓓ Ⓔ
8. Ⓐ Ⓑ Ⓒ Ⓓ Ⓔ
9. Ⓐ Ⓑ Ⓒ Ⓓ Ⓔ
10. Ⓐ Ⓑ Ⓒ Ⓓ Ⓔ
11. Ⓐ Ⓑ Ⓒ Ⓓ Ⓔ
12. Ⓐ Ⓑ Ⓒ Ⓓ Ⓔ
13. Ⓐ Ⓑ Ⓒ Ⓓ Ⓔ
14. Ⓐ Ⓑ Ⓒ Ⓓ Ⓔ
15. Ⓐ Ⓑ Ⓒ Ⓓ Ⓔ
16. Ⓐ Ⓑ Ⓒ Ⓓ Ⓔ
17. Ⓐ Ⓑ Ⓒ Ⓓ Ⓔ
18. Ⓐ Ⓑ Ⓒ Ⓓ Ⓔ
19. Ⓐ Ⓑ Ⓒ Ⓓ Ⓔ
20. Ⓐ Ⓑ Ⓒ Ⓓ Ⓔ
21. Ⓐ Ⓑ Ⓒ Ⓓ Ⓔ
22. Ⓐ Ⓑ Ⓒ Ⓓ Ⓔ
23. Ⓐ Ⓑ Ⓒ Ⓓ Ⓔ
24. Ⓐ Ⓑ Ⓒ Ⓓ Ⓔ
25. Ⓐ Ⓑ Ⓒ Ⓓ Ⓔ

Section II
Problem Solving

1. Ⓐ Ⓑ Ⓒ Ⓓ Ⓔ
2. Ⓐ Ⓑ Ⓒ Ⓓ Ⓔ
3. Ⓐ Ⓑ Ⓒ Ⓓ Ⓔ
4. Ⓐ Ⓑ Ⓒ Ⓓ Ⓔ
5. Ⓐ Ⓑ Ⓒ Ⓓ Ⓔ
6. Ⓐ Ⓑ Ⓒ Ⓓ Ⓔ
7. Ⓐ Ⓑ Ⓒ Ⓓ Ⓔ
8. Ⓐ Ⓑ Ⓒ Ⓓ Ⓔ
9. Ⓐ Ⓑ Ⓒ Ⓓ Ⓔ
10. Ⓐ Ⓑ Ⓒ Ⓓ Ⓔ
11. Ⓐ Ⓑ Ⓒ Ⓓ Ⓔ
12. Ⓐ Ⓑ Ⓒ Ⓓ Ⓔ
13. Ⓐ Ⓑ Ⓒ Ⓓ Ⓔ
14. Ⓐ Ⓑ Ⓒ Ⓓ Ⓔ
15. Ⓐ Ⓑ Ⓒ Ⓓ Ⓔ
16. Ⓐ Ⓑ Ⓒ Ⓓ Ⓔ
17. Ⓐ Ⓑ Ⓒ Ⓓ Ⓔ
18. Ⓐ Ⓑ Ⓒ Ⓓ Ⓔ
19. Ⓐ Ⓑ Ⓒ Ⓓ Ⓔ
20. Ⓐ Ⓑ Ⓒ Ⓓ Ⓔ

Section III
Analysis of Situations

1. Ⓐ Ⓑ Ⓒ Ⓓ Ⓔ
2. Ⓐ Ⓑ Ⓒ Ⓓ Ⓔ
3. Ⓐ Ⓑ Ⓒ Ⓓ Ⓔ
4. Ⓐ Ⓑ Ⓒ Ⓓ Ⓔ
5. Ⓐ Ⓑ Ⓒ Ⓓ Ⓔ
6. Ⓐ Ⓑ Ⓒ Ⓓ Ⓔ
7. Ⓐ Ⓑ Ⓒ Ⓓ Ⓔ
8. Ⓐ Ⓑ Ⓒ Ⓓ Ⓔ
9. Ⓐ Ⓑ Ⓒ Ⓓ Ⓔ
10. Ⓐ Ⓑ Ⓒ Ⓓ Ⓔ
11. Ⓐ Ⓑ Ⓒ Ⓓ Ⓔ
12. Ⓐ Ⓑ Ⓒ Ⓓ Ⓔ
13. Ⓐ Ⓑ Ⓒ Ⓓ Ⓔ
14. Ⓐ Ⓑ Ⓒ Ⓓ Ⓔ
15. Ⓐ Ⓑ Ⓒ Ⓓ Ⓔ
16. Ⓐ Ⓑ Ⓒ Ⓓ Ⓔ
17. Ⓐ Ⓑ Ⓒ Ⓓ Ⓔ
18. Ⓐ Ⓑ Ⓒ Ⓓ Ⓔ
19. Ⓐ Ⓑ Ⓒ Ⓓ Ⓔ
20. Ⓐ Ⓑ Ⓒ Ⓓ Ⓔ
21. Ⓐ Ⓑ Ⓒ Ⓓ Ⓔ
22. Ⓐ Ⓑ Ⓒ Ⓓ Ⓔ
23. Ⓐ Ⓑ Ⓒ Ⓓ Ⓔ
24. Ⓐ Ⓑ Ⓒ Ⓓ Ⓔ
25. Ⓐ Ⓑ Ⓒ Ⓓ Ⓔ
26. Ⓐ Ⓑ Ⓒ Ⓓ Ⓔ
27. Ⓐ Ⓑ Ⓒ Ⓓ Ⓔ
28. Ⓐ Ⓑ Ⓒ Ⓓ Ⓔ
29. Ⓐ Ⓑ Ⓒ Ⓓ Ⓔ
30. Ⓐ Ⓑ Ⓒ Ⓓ Ⓔ
31. Ⓐ Ⓑ Ⓒ Ⓓ Ⓔ
32. Ⓐ Ⓑ Ⓒ Ⓓ Ⓔ
33. Ⓐ Ⓑ Ⓒ Ⓓ Ⓔ
34. Ⓐ Ⓑ Ⓒ Ⓓ Ⓔ
35. Ⓐ Ⓑ Ⓒ Ⓓ Ⓔ

Section IV
Data Sufficiency

1. Ⓐ Ⓑ Ⓒ Ⓓ Ⓔ
2. Ⓐ Ⓑ Ⓒ Ⓓ Ⓔ
3. Ⓐ Ⓑ Ⓒ Ⓓ Ⓔ
4. Ⓐ Ⓑ Ⓒ Ⓓ Ⓔ
5. Ⓐ Ⓑ Ⓒ Ⓓ Ⓔ
6. Ⓐ Ⓑ Ⓒ Ⓓ Ⓔ
7. Ⓐ Ⓑ Ⓒ Ⓓ Ⓔ
8. Ⓐ Ⓑ Ⓒ Ⓓ Ⓔ
9. Ⓐ Ⓑ Ⓒ Ⓓ Ⓔ
10. Ⓐ Ⓑ Ⓒ Ⓓ Ⓔ
11. Ⓐ Ⓑ Ⓒ Ⓓ Ⓔ
12. Ⓐ Ⓑ Ⓒ Ⓓ Ⓔ
13. Ⓐ Ⓑ Ⓒ Ⓓ Ⓔ
14. Ⓐ Ⓑ Ⓒ Ⓓ Ⓔ
15. Ⓐ Ⓑ Ⓒ Ⓓ Ⓔ
16. Ⓐ Ⓑ Ⓒ Ⓓ Ⓔ
17. Ⓐ Ⓑ Ⓒ Ⓓ Ⓔ
18. Ⓐ Ⓑ Ⓒ Ⓓ Ⓔ
19. Ⓐ Ⓑ Ⓒ Ⓓ Ⓔ
20. Ⓐ Ⓑ Ⓒ Ⓓ Ⓔ
21. Ⓐ Ⓑ Ⓒ Ⓓ Ⓔ
22. Ⓐ Ⓑ Ⓒ Ⓓ Ⓔ
23. Ⓐ Ⓑ Ⓒ Ⓓ Ⓔ
24. Ⓐ Ⓑ Ⓒ Ⓓ Ⓔ
25. Ⓐ Ⓑ Ⓒ Ⓓ Ⓔ

Section V
Writing Ability

1. Ⓐ Ⓑ Ⓒ Ⓓ Ⓔ
2. Ⓐ Ⓑ Ⓒ Ⓓ Ⓔ
3. Ⓐ Ⓑ Ⓒ Ⓓ Ⓔ
4. Ⓐ Ⓑ Ⓒ Ⓓ Ⓔ
5. Ⓐ Ⓑ Ⓒ Ⓓ Ⓔ
6. Ⓐ Ⓑ Ⓒ Ⓓ Ⓔ
7. Ⓐ Ⓑ Ⓒ Ⓓ Ⓔ
8. Ⓐ Ⓑ Ⓒ Ⓓ Ⓔ
9. Ⓐ Ⓑ Ⓒ Ⓓ Ⓔ
10. Ⓐ Ⓑ Ⓒ Ⓓ Ⓔ
11. Ⓐ Ⓑ Ⓒ Ⓓ Ⓔ
12. Ⓐ Ⓑ Ⓒ Ⓓ Ⓔ
13. Ⓐ Ⓑ Ⓒ Ⓓ Ⓔ
14. Ⓐ Ⓑ Ⓒ Ⓓ Ⓔ
15. Ⓐ Ⓑ Ⓒ Ⓓ Ⓔ
16. Ⓐ Ⓑ Ⓒ Ⓓ Ⓔ
17. Ⓐ Ⓑ Ⓒ Ⓓ Ⓔ
18. Ⓐ Ⓑ Ⓒ Ⓓ Ⓔ
19. Ⓐ Ⓑ Ⓒ Ⓓ Ⓔ
20. Ⓐ Ⓑ Ⓒ Ⓓ Ⓔ
21. Ⓐ Ⓑ Ⓒ Ⓓ Ⓔ
22. Ⓐ Ⓑ Ⓒ Ⓓ Ⓔ
23. Ⓐ Ⓑ Ⓒ Ⓓ Ⓔ
24. Ⓐ Ⓑ Ⓒ Ⓓ Ⓔ
25. Ⓐ Ⓑ Ⓒ Ⓓ Ⓔ

Section VI
Analysis of Situations

1. Ⓐ Ⓑ Ⓒ Ⓓ Ⓔ
2. Ⓐ Ⓑ Ⓒ Ⓓ Ⓔ
3. Ⓐ Ⓑ Ⓒ Ⓓ Ⓔ
4. Ⓐ Ⓑ Ⓒ Ⓓ Ⓔ
5. Ⓐ Ⓑ Ⓒ Ⓓ Ⓔ
6. Ⓐ Ⓑ Ⓒ Ⓓ Ⓔ
7. Ⓐ Ⓑ Ⓒ Ⓓ Ⓔ
8. Ⓐ Ⓑ Ⓒ Ⓓ Ⓔ
9. Ⓐ Ⓑ Ⓒ Ⓓ Ⓔ
10. Ⓐ Ⓑ Ⓒ Ⓓ Ⓔ
11. Ⓐ Ⓑ Ⓒ Ⓓ Ⓔ
12. Ⓐ Ⓑ Ⓒ Ⓓ Ⓔ
13. Ⓐ Ⓑ Ⓒ Ⓓ Ⓔ
14. Ⓐ Ⓑ Ⓒ Ⓓ Ⓔ
15. Ⓐ Ⓑ Ⓒ Ⓓ Ⓔ
16. Ⓐ Ⓑ Ⓒ Ⓓ Ⓔ
17. Ⓐ Ⓑ Ⓒ Ⓓ Ⓔ
18. Ⓐ Ⓑ Ⓒ Ⓓ Ⓔ
19. Ⓐ Ⓑ Ⓒ Ⓓ Ⓔ
20. Ⓐ Ⓑ Ⓒ Ⓓ Ⓔ
21. Ⓐ Ⓑ Ⓒ Ⓓ Ⓔ
22. Ⓐ Ⓑ Ⓒ Ⓓ Ⓔ
23. Ⓐ Ⓑ Ⓒ Ⓓ Ⓔ
24. Ⓐ Ⓑ Ⓒ Ⓓ Ⓔ
25. Ⓐ Ⓑ Ⓒ Ⓓ Ⓔ
26. Ⓐ Ⓑ Ⓒ Ⓓ Ⓔ
27. Ⓐ Ⓑ Ⓒ Ⓓ Ⓔ
28. Ⓐ Ⓑ Ⓒ Ⓓ Ⓔ
29. Ⓐ Ⓑ Ⓒ Ⓓ Ⓔ
30. Ⓐ Ⓑ Ⓒ Ⓓ Ⓔ
31. Ⓐ Ⓑ Ⓒ Ⓓ Ⓔ
32. Ⓐ Ⓑ Ⓒ Ⓓ Ⓔ
33. Ⓐ Ⓑ Ⓒ Ⓓ Ⓔ
34. Ⓐ Ⓑ Ⓒ Ⓓ Ⓔ
35. Ⓐ Ⓑ Ⓒ Ⓓ Ⓔ

Section VII
Writing Ability

1. Ⓐ Ⓑ Ⓒ Ⓓ Ⓔ
2. Ⓐ Ⓑ Ⓒ Ⓓ Ⓔ
3. Ⓐ Ⓑ Ⓒ Ⓓ Ⓔ
4. Ⓐ Ⓑ Ⓒ Ⓓ Ⓔ
5. Ⓐ Ⓑ Ⓒ Ⓓ Ⓔ
6. Ⓐ Ⓑ Ⓒ Ⓓ Ⓔ
7. Ⓐ Ⓑ Ⓒ Ⓓ Ⓔ
8. Ⓐ Ⓑ Ⓒ Ⓓ Ⓔ
9. Ⓐ Ⓑ Ⓒ Ⓓ Ⓔ
10. Ⓐ Ⓑ Ⓒ Ⓓ Ⓔ
11. Ⓐ Ⓑ Ⓒ Ⓓ Ⓔ
12. Ⓐ Ⓑ Ⓒ Ⓓ Ⓔ
13. Ⓐ Ⓑ Ⓒ Ⓓ Ⓔ
14. Ⓐ Ⓑ Ⓒ Ⓓ Ⓔ
15. Ⓐ Ⓑ Ⓒ Ⓓ Ⓔ
16. Ⓐ Ⓑ Ⓒ Ⓓ Ⓔ
17. Ⓐ Ⓑ Ⓒ Ⓓ Ⓔ
18. Ⓐ Ⓑ Ⓒ Ⓓ Ⓔ
19. Ⓐ Ⓑ Ⓒ Ⓓ Ⓔ
20. Ⓐ Ⓑ Ⓒ Ⓓ Ⓔ
21. Ⓐ Ⓑ Ⓒ Ⓓ Ⓔ
22. Ⓐ Ⓑ Ⓒ Ⓓ Ⓔ
23. Ⓐ Ⓑ Ⓒ Ⓓ Ⓔ
24. Ⓐ Ⓑ Ⓒ Ⓓ Ⓔ
25. Ⓐ Ⓑ Ⓒ Ⓓ Ⓔ

Section VIII
Problem Solving

1. Ⓐ Ⓑ Ⓒ Ⓓ Ⓔ
2. Ⓐ Ⓑ Ⓒ Ⓓ Ⓔ
3. Ⓐ Ⓑ Ⓒ Ⓓ Ⓔ
4. Ⓐ Ⓑ Ⓒ Ⓓ Ⓔ
5. Ⓐ Ⓑ Ⓒ Ⓓ Ⓔ
6. Ⓐ Ⓑ Ⓒ Ⓓ Ⓔ
7. Ⓐ Ⓑ Ⓒ Ⓓ Ⓔ
8. Ⓐ Ⓑ Ⓒ Ⓓ Ⓔ
9. Ⓐ Ⓑ Ⓒ Ⓓ Ⓔ
10. Ⓐ Ⓑ Ⓒ Ⓓ Ⓔ
11. Ⓐ Ⓑ Ⓒ Ⓓ Ⓔ
12. Ⓐ Ⓑ Ⓒ Ⓓ Ⓔ
13. Ⓐ Ⓑ Ⓒ Ⓓ Ⓔ
14. Ⓐ Ⓑ Ⓒ Ⓓ Ⓔ
15. Ⓐ Ⓑ Ⓒ Ⓓ Ⓔ
16. Ⓐ Ⓑ Ⓒ Ⓓ Ⓔ
17. Ⓐ Ⓑ Ⓒ Ⓓ Ⓔ
18. Ⓐ Ⓑ Ⓒ Ⓓ Ⓔ
19. Ⓐ Ⓑ Ⓒ Ⓓ Ⓔ
20. Ⓐ Ⓑ Ⓒ Ⓓ Ⓔ

FIVE

FIVE SAMPLE GMATs WITH ANSWERS AND ANALYSIS

Sample Test 1

Section I   Reading Comprehension

TIME: 30 minutes

DIRECTIONS: This part contains three reading passages. You are to read each one carefully. When answering the questions, you *will* be allowed to refer back to the passages. The questions are based on what is *stated* or *implied* in each passage. You have thirty minutes to complete this section.

Passage 1:

These huge waves wreak terrific damage when they crash on the shores of distant lands or continents. Under a perfectly sunny sky and from an apparently calm sea, a wall of water may break twenty or thirty feet high over beaches and waterfronts, crushing houses and drowning unsuspecting residents and bathers in
(5)   its path.

How are these waves formed? When a submarine earthquake occurs, it is likely to set up a tremendous amount of shock, disturbing the quiet waters of the deep ocean. This disturbance travels to the surface and forms a huge swell in the ocean many miles across. It rolls outward in all directions, and the water lowers in the
(10)   center as another swell looms up. Thus, a series of concentric swells are formed similar to those made when a coin or small pebble is dropped into a basin of water. The big difference is in the size. Each of the concentric rings of basin water traveling out toward the edge is only about an inch across and less than a quarter of an inch high. The swells in the ocean are sometimes nearly a mile wide and rise
(15)   to several multiples of ten feet in height.

Many of us have heard about these waves, often referred to by their Japanese name of "tsunami." For ages they have been dreaded in the Pacific, as no shore has been free from them. An underwater earthquake in the Aleutian Islands could start a swell that would break along the shores and cause severe damage in the
(20)   southern part of Chile in South America. These waves travel hundreds of miles an hour, and one can understand how they would crash as violent breakers when caused to drag in the shallow waters of a coast.

(25)   Nothing was done about tsunamis until after World War II. In 1947 a particularly bad submarine earthquake took place south of the Aleutian Islands. A few hours later, people bathing in the sun along the quiet shores of Hawaii were dashed to death and shore-line property became a mass of shambles because a series of monstrous, breaking swells crashed along the shore and drove far inland. Hundreds of lives were lost in this catastrophe, and millions upon millions of dollars' worth of damage was done.

(30)   Hawaii (at that time a territory) and other Pacific areas then asked the U.S. Coast and Geodetic Survey to attempt to forecast these killer waves. With the blessing of the government, the Coast and Geodetic Survey initiated a program in 1948 known as the Seismic Seawave Warning System, using the earthquake-monitoring facilities of the agency, together with the world seismological data (35) center, to locate submarine earthquakes as soon as they might occur. With this information they could then tell how severe a submarine earthquake was and could set up a tracking chart, with the center over the area of the earthquake, which would show by concentric time belts the rate of travel of the resulting wave. This system would indicate when and where, along the shores of the Pacific, the swells (40) caused by the submarine earthquakes would strike.

1. One surprising aspect of the waves discussed in the passage is the fact that they

(A) are formed in concentric patterns
(B) often strike during clear weather
(C) arise under conditions of cold temperature
(D) are produced by deep swells
(E) may be forecast scientifically

2. The waves discussed in the passage often strike

(A) along the coasts of the Aleutian Islands
(B) in regions outside the area monitored by the Coast and Geodetic Survey
(C) at great distances from their place or origin
(D) at the same time as the occurrence of earthquakes
(E) in areas outside the Pacific region

3. It is believed that the waves are caused by

(A) seismic changes
(B) concentric time belts
(C) atmospheric conditions
(D) underwater earthquakes
(E) storms

4. The normal maximum width of the waves is approximately

(A) five feet
(B) ten feet
(C) one mile
(D) five miles
(E) thirty miles

5. The U.S. Coast and Geodetic Survey set up a program to

  I. Prevent submarine earthquakes
  II. Locate submarine earthquakes
  III. Determine the severity of submarine earthquakes

(A) I only
(B) III only
(C) I and II only
(D) II and III only
(E) I, II, and III

6. Nothing was done about the waves until

(A) deaths occurred
(B) the outbreak of World War II
(C) a solution was found
(D) millions of dollars worth of damage was incurred in Hawaii
(E) large areas in Chile were devastated

7. The movement of the waves has been measured at a speed of

(A) 30 miles an hour
(B) 40 miles an hour
(C) 50 miles an hour
(D) 100 miles an hour
(E) more than a hundred miles an hour

8. According to the passage, the waves occur most frequently in the area of

(A) the Eastern U.S. seaboard
(B) the Pacific
(C) Argentina
(D) Western Europe
(E) Asia

9. Given present wave-tracking systems, scientists can forecast all of the following *except*

(A) the severity of underwater earthquakes
(B) the wave's rate of travel
(C) when a wave will strike
(D) where a wave will strike
(E) the height of the wave

Passage 2:

This passage was written in 1972.

The United States economy made progress in reducing unemployment and moderating inflation. On the international side, this year was much calmer than last. Nevertheless, continuing imbalances in the pattern of world trade contributed to intermittent strains in the foreign exchange markets. These strains intensified to
(5) crisis proportions, precipitating a further devaluation of the dollar.

The domestic economy expanded in a remarkably vigorous and steady fashion. . . . The resurgence in consumer confidence was reflected in the higher proportion of incomes spent for goods and services and the marked increase in consumer willingness to take on installment debt. A parallel strengthening in business
(10) psychology was manifested in a stepped-up rate of plant and equipment spending and a gradual pickup in outlays for inventory. Confidence in the economy was also reflected in the strength of the stock market and in the stability of the bond market. . . . For the year as a whole, consumer and business sentiment benefited from rising public expectations that a resolution of the conflict in Vietnam was in
(15) prospect and that East-West tensions were easing.

The underpinnings of the business expansion were to be found in part in the stimulative monetary and fiscal policies that had been pursued. Moreover, the restoration of sounder liquidity positions and tighter management control of production efficiency had also helped lay the groundwork for a strong expansion. In
(20) addition, the economic policy moves made by the President had served to renew optimism on the business outlook while boosting hopes that inflation would be brought under more effective control. Finally, of course, the economy was able to grow as vigorously as it did because sufficient leeway existed in terms of idle men and machines.

(25)   The United States balance of payments deficit declined sharply. Nevertheless, by any other test, the deficit remained very large, and there was actually a substantial deterioration in our trade account to a sizable deficit, almost two thirds of which was with Japan. . . . While the overall trade performance proved disappointing, there are still good reasons for expecting the delayed impact of

(30)   devaluation to produce in time a significant strengthening in our trade picture. Given the size of the Japanese component of our trade deficit, however, the outcome will depend importantly on the extent of the corrective measures undertaken by Japan. Also important will be our own efforts in the United States to fashion internal policies consistent with an improvement in our external balance.

(35)   The underlying task of public policy for the year ahead—and indeed for the longer run—remained a familiar one: to strike the right balance between encouraging healthy economic growth and avoiding inflationary pressures. With the economy showing sustained and vigorous growth, and with the currency crisis highlighting the need to improve our competitive posture internationally, the em-

(40)   phasis seemed to be shifting to the problem of inflation. The Phase Three program of wage and price restraint can contribute to dampening inflation. Unless productivity growth is unexpectedly large, however, the expansion of real output must eventually begin to slow down to the economy's larger run growth potential if generalized demand pressures on prices are to be avoided. Indeed, while the

(45)   unemployment rates of a bit over five percent were still too high, it seems doubtful whether the much lower rates of four percent and below often cited as appropriate definitions of full employment do in fact represent feasible goals for the United States economy—unless there are improvements in the structure of labor and product markets and public policies influencing their operation. There is little

(50)   doubt that overall unemployment rates can be brought down to four percent or less, for a time at least, by sufficient stimulation of aggregate demand. However, the resultant inflationary pressures have in the past proved exceedingly difficult to contain.

10. The passage was most likely published in a

(A) popular magazine
(B) general newspaper
(C) science journal
(D) financial journal
(E) textbook

11. Confidence in the economy was expressed by all of the following except

(A) a strong stock market
(B) a stable bond market
(C) increased installment debt
(D) increased plant and equipment expenditures
(E) rising interest rates

12. During the year in question, public confidence in the economy resulted in part from which of the following occurrences?

  I. Possible peace in Vietnam
 II. Reduction in East-West tensions
III. An entente with China

(A) I only
(B) III only
(C) I and II only
(D) II and III only
(E) I, II, and III

13. According to the author, business expansion for the period under review was caused largely by

(A) stimulative monetary and fiscal policies
(B) rising interest rates
(C) increased foreign trade
(D) price and wage controls
(E) implementation of the Phase Three program

14. Most of the trade deficit in the balance of payments was attributed to trade with which country?

(A) United Kingdom
(B) Japan
(C) Germany
(D) France
(E) Saudi Arabia

15. Part of the public policy task, as outlined in the passage, is to

(A) cut consumer spending
(B) prevent balance of payments deficits
(C) devalue the dollar
(D) avoid inflationary pressures
(E) increase the balance of trade

16. The Phase Three program contained

(A) higher income taxes
(B) reduced government spending
(C) devaluation of the dollar
(D) productivity measures
(E) wage and price controls

17. The passage states that the unemployment rate at the time the article was written was

(A) 6 percent
(B) a little over 5 percent
(C) 5 percent
(D) a little over 4 percent
(E) 4 percent

Passage 3:

Literature is at once the most intimate and the most articulate of the arts. It cannot impart its effect through the senses or the nerves as the other arts can; it is beautiful only through the intelligence; it is the mind speaking to the mind; until it has been put into absolute terms, of an invariable significance, it does not exist at all. It cannot awaken this emotion in one, and that in another; if it fails to express precisely the meaning of the author, if it does not say *him*, it says nothing, and is nothing. So that when a poet has put his heart, much or little, into a poem, and sold it to a magazine, the scandal is greater than when a painter has sold a picture to a patron, or a sculptor has modelled a statue to order. These are artists less articulate and less intimate than the poet; they are more exterior to their work; they are less personally in it; they part with less of themselves in the dicker. It does not change the nature of the case to say that Tennyson and Longfellow and Emerson sold the poems in which they couched the most mystical messages their genius was charged to bear mankind. They submitted to the conditions which none can escape; but that does not justify the conditions, which are none the less the conditions of hucksters because they are imposed upon poets. If it will serve to make my meaning a little clearer, we will suppose that a poet has been crossed in love, or has suffered some real sorrow, like the loss of a wife or child. He pours out his broken heart in verse that shall bring tears of sacred sympathy from his readers, and an editor pays him a hundred dollars for the right of bringing his verse to their notice. It is perfectly true that the poem was not written for these dollars, but it is perfectly true that it was sold for them. The poet must use his emotions to pay his provision bills; he has no other means; society does not propose to pay his bills for him. Yet, and at the end of the ends, the unsophisticated witness finds the transaction ridiculous, finds it repulsive, finds it shabby. Somehow he knows that if our huckstering civilization did not at every moment violate the eternal fitness of things, the poet's song would have been given to the world, and the poet would have been cared for by the whole human brotherhood, as any man should be who does the duty that every man owes it.

The instinctive sense of the dishonor which money-purchase does to art is so strong that sometimes a man of letters who can pay his way otherwise refuses pay for his work, as Lord Byron did, for a while, from a noble pride, and as Count Tolstoy has tried to do, from a noble conscience. But Byron's publisher profited by a generosity which did not reach his readers; and the Countess Tolstoy collects the copyright which her husband foregoes; so that these two eminent instances of protest against business in literature may be said not to have shaken its money basis. I know of no others; but there may be many that I am culpably ignorant of. Still, I doubt if there are enough to affect the fact that Literature is Business as well as Art, and almost as soon. At present business is the only human solidarity; we are all bound together with that chain, whatever interests and tastes and principles separate us.

18. The author implies that writers are

   (A) incompetent businessmen
   (B) not sufficiently paid for their work
   (C) greedy
   (D) hucksters
   (E) profiting against their will

19. A possible title that best expresses the meaning of the passage would be

   (A) *The Man of Letters as a Man of Business*
   (B) *Literature and the Arts*
   (C) *Progress in Literature*
   (D) *Poets and Writers*
   (E) *The State of the Arts*

20. The author laments the fact that Tennyson, Longfellow, and Emerson

   (A) wrote mystical poems
   (B) had to sell their poetry
   (C) were not appreciated in their time
   (D) were prolific poets
   (E) wrote emotional poetry

21. The passage states that authors such as Tennyson "submitted to the conditions which none can escape." What conditions is the author of the passage referring to?

   (A) An unappreciative audience
   (B) A materialistic society
   (C) The fact that writers had to sell their work to survive
   (D) Authors wrote for an esoteric audience
   (E) Authors wrote what the public wanted

22. According to the author, Lord Byron

(A) refused payment for his work
(B) combined business with literature
(C) did not copyright his work
(D) was well known in the business community
(E) founded a school for aspiring writers

23. The author of the passage implies that

(A) society should subsidize artists and writers
(B) writers should rebel against the business system
(C) more writers should follow the example set by Lord Byron
(D) writers should only accept remuneration that will provide them with a basic standard of living
(E) writers should not attempt to change society

24. The author of the passage proposes that writers and artists

(A) make the best out of a bad situation
(B) attempt to induce society to change its values
(C) withhold their work until they gain recognition
(D) adopt the principles of commercialism
(E) adopt the value system of society

25. By accepting payment for works of literature or art, its creators are

I. writing and painting solely for monetary gain
II. justifying the practice of art
III. exchanging their work for remuneration

(A) I only
(B) III only
(C) I and II only
(D) II and III only
(E) I, II, and III

If there is still time remaining, you may review the questions in this section only.
You may not turn to any other section of the test.

Section II   Problem Solving

TIME: 30 minutes

DIRECTIONS: Solve each of the following problems; then indicate the correct answer on the answer sheet. [On the actual test you will be permitted to use any space available on the examination paper for scratch work.]

NOTE: A figure that appears with a problem is drawn as accurately as possible so as to provide information that may help in answering the question. Numbers in this test are real numbers.

1. A trip takes 6 hours to complete. After traveling ¼ of an hour, 1⅜ hours, and 2⅓ hours, how much time does one need to complete the trip?

   (A) 2¹¹/₁₂ hours
   (B) 2 hours, 2½ minutes
   (C) 2 hours, 5 minutes
   (D) 2⅛ hours
   (E) 2 hours, 7½ minutes

2. If a stock average was 500 points at the beginning of a week and 400 points at the end of the same week, by what percent has it decreased during the week?

   (A) 20
   (B) 22
   (C) 25
   (D) 27
   (E) 30

3. A car wash can wash 8 cars in 18 minutes. At this rate, how many cars can the car wash wash in 3 hours?

   (A) 13
   (B) 40.5
   (C) 80
   (D) 125
   (E) 405

4. If the ratio of the areas of 2 squares is 2:1, then the ratio of the perimeters of the squares is

   (A) 1:2
   (B) 1:$\sqrt{2}$
   (C) $\sqrt{2}$:1
   (D) 2:1
   (E) 4:1

5. In Leesville, 70% of the cars have whitewall tires and 25% of the cars are air-conditioned. If 20% of the cars are air-conditioned and have whitewall tires, what percentage of the cars have neither air-conditioning nor whitewall tires?

   (A) 5
   (B) 10
   (C) 15
   (D) 20
   (E) 25

6. A company issued 100,000 shares of stock. In 1970, each share of stock was worth $122.50. In 1973, each share of the stock was worth $111.10. How much less were the 100,000 shares worth in 1973 than in 1970?

   (A) $114,000
   (B) $1,100,040
   (C) $1,140,000
   (D) $114,000,000
   (E) $1,140,000,000

7. A worker's daily salary varies each day. In one week he worked five days. His daily salaries were $51.90, $52.20, $49.80, $51.50, and $50.60. What was his average daily wage for the week?

(A) $50.80
(B) $51.20
(C) $51.50

(D) $51.60
(E) $255.00

8. A borrower pays 18% interest per year on the first $600 he borrows and 17% per year on the part of the loan in excess of $600. How much interest will the borrower pay on a loan of $6,000 for 1 year?

(A) $926
(B) $1,020
(C) $1,026

(D) $1,080
(E) $1,126

9. If $3x - 2y = 8$, then $4y - 6x$ is:

(A) -16
(B) -8
(C) 8

(D) 16
(E) none of these

10. It costs 10¢ a kilometer to fly and 12¢ a kilometer to drive. If you travel 200 kilometers, flying x kilometers of the distance and driving the rest, then the cost of the trip in dollars is

(A) 20
(B) 24
(C) $24 - 2x$

(D) $24 - .02x$
(E) $2,400 - 2x$

11. If two identical rectangles R_1 and R_2 form a square when placed next to each other, and the length of R_1 is x times the width of R_1, then x is

(A) 1
(B) ½
(C) ⁵⁄₄

(D) 2
(E) 3

12. If the area of a square increases by 69%, then the side of the square increases by

(A) 13%
(B) 30%
(C) 39%

(D) 69%
(E) 130%

13. A used car dealer sells a car for $1,380 and makes a 20% profit. How much did the car cost the dealer?

(A) $1,100
(B) $1,120
(C) $1,150

(D) $1,180
(E) $1,560

14. If $x < z$ and $x < y$, which of the following statements are always true? Assume $x \geq 0$.

    I. $y < z$
   II. $x < yz$
  III. $2x < y + z$

(A) only I
(B) only II
(C) only III
(D) II and III only
(E) I, II, and III

Use the following table for questions 15–17.

Distribution of Work Hours in a Factory

Numbers of Workers		Number of Hours Worked
20		45–50
15		40–44
25		35–39
16		30–34
4		0–29
80	TOTAL	3,100

15. What percentage of workers worked 40 or more hours?

(A) 18.75   (D) 40
(B) 25   (E) 43.75
(C) 33⅓

16. The number of workers who worked from 40 to 44 hours is x times the number who worked up to 29 hours, where x is

(A) $^{15}/_{16}$ (D) 5
(B) 3¾   (E) 6¼
(C) 4

17. Which of the following statements can be inferred from the table?

    I. The average number of hours worked per worker is less than 40.
   II. At least 3 worked more than 48 hours.
  III. More than half of all the workers worked more than 40 hours.

(A) I only
(B) II only
(C) I and II only
(D) I and III only
(E) I, II, and III

18. A truck traveling at 70 miles per hour uses 30% more gasoline to travel a certain distance than it does when it travels at 50 miles per hour. If the truck can travel 19.5 miles on a gallon of gasoline at 50 miles per hour, how far can the truck travel on 10 gallons of gasoline at a speed of 70 miles per hour?

(A) 130   (D) 175
(B) 140   (E) 195
(C) 150

19. $\frac{2}{5} + \frac{1}{3} = \frac{x}{30}$, where x is

(A) 4

(B) 7

(C) 11

(D) 16

(E) 22

20. How many squares with sides ½ inch long are needed to cover a rectangle which is 4 feet long and 6 feet wide?

(A) 24

(B) 96

(C) 3,456

(D) 13,824

(E) 14,266

If there is still time remaining, you may review the questions in this section only.
You may not turn to any other section of the test.

Section III   Analysis of Situations

TIME: 30 minutes

DIRECTIONS: Read the following passages. After you have completed each one, you will be asked to answer questions that involve determining the importance of specific factors included in the passage. When answering questions, you may consult the passage.

Passage 1:

The success of the Abco Corporation in the investment-conscious country of Frieland was recently the subject of a government inquiry. Frieland is a developing country about the size of New York State with a population of ten million people. It has a small but growing industrial base, and several multinational business concerns have established manufacturing plants in various parts of the country.

Government policy in Frieland has traditionally favored foreign investment. Leaders of all political parties have been virtually unanimous in their belief that foreign investment in Frieland would contribute to speeding that country's economic development, a major priority of both the ruling coalition and opposition parties. Of special interest to the government were those industries that exported a significant share of their total output. Since Frieland had a relatively small population, there was a limit to the amount of goods that could be produced for the local market. Also, the government did not want to encourage foreign investors to compete with local industry, even though new industries might alleviate the already high unemployment rate.

A final reason for encouraging export-intensive industries was to earn badly needed foreign exchange. Frieland had a chronic deficit in its balance of trade; that is, its imports were regularly greater than its exports. This meant that it had to use scarce foreign exchange to pay for the growing deficit. Therefore, Frieland welcomed potential investors that would promise to export a significant share of their total output. So when executives of Abco Corporation proposed to establish a shoe manufacturing plant which would be export-intensive, it received ready approval from the government.

Government support for the enterprise was given not only because of the promise to export, but also because of the high unemployment rate in the country. However, approval was given despite the fact that there was at the time surplus shoe production in Frieland, most factories having large excess capacities and underworked labor forces. It was known that Abco had promised the government, among other things, to (1) employ hundreds of workers, (2) reduce the price of shoes by some 30 percent, and (3) export more than half its output.

In return for these promises, Abco received the following concessions from the government:

(1) Land was given the company on a lease basis for a period of 99 years, rent-free.
(2) A government-owned contracting firm built the factory at low subsidized prices.
(3) The company received loans at very low interest rates for an extended period of time. These loans could be renewed at company request at lower than the prevailing market interest rate.
(4) The government trained workers at the plant at no expense to the company.

Production commenced one year after the first equipment arrived at the new plant. It took another half year to properly train the new work force to operate the sophisticated equipment which was introduced. After the "running in" period, production continued smoothly for about a year until a labor dispute occurred. It appeared that management wanted to dismiss about 10 percent of the work force owing to what a company spokesman called "a temporary slack in demand" for Abco's products. The labor union representing the company's work force refused to accept any reduction in the work force and threatened a strike if workers were terminated. After some discussion, union representatives agreed that the company might be justified in laying off some workers, but nowhere near the 10 percent figure that management desired. At any rate, the union claimed that the company must first submit its request to a joint union-management grievance committee which was authorized under the current labor agreement to deal with such disputes. Management acquiesced to the union demand. After several days of bargaining, an agreement was worked out whereby Abco would be allowed to terminate most part-time workers, amounting to only one percent of the total work force. Although the agreement brought about a temporary solution to the current problem, labor-management relations at Abco continued to be strained, as management was convinced that more workers were redundant than the union cared to admit.

After another six months, it became apparent that what management had termed "a temporary slack in demand" was in reality a failure of the company to sell the quantity of shoes that had been forecast before production began. Actual sales never reached the target quantity, and, as a result, the company lost $1 million in each of its first two years of operation. The American representatives on the board of directors—who constituted a majority—voted to terminate the company's operations in Frieland. Shortly after the vote, bankruptcy hearings began.

Because Abco was located in an underdeveloped area of the country, the government was worried about the political ramifications if production ceased. The company employed 500 workers, and quite a few shopkeepers were dependent upon their patronage. When government representatives asked Abco management what could be done to keep the company operating, they received the following answer. Management was willing to continue production if the government granted the company an additional five-million-dollar loan on favorable terms. If the government could not grant such a loan, then another alternative was to purchase the company from Abco at a "reasonable" price.

The government was in a dilemma. On the one hand, it was concerned about the political consequences if Abco should continue the bankruptcy proceedings. On the other hand, if it granted the loan, it might be setting a precedent for any other company that was in financial difficulties. Moreover, there was a certain risk involved in lending the money to a company in bad shape. The government appointed a special committee to investigate the financial condition of Abco and decide the issue.

One month later, the committee submitted its report. The major finding was that Abco had not kept any of its original promises to the government. For one thing, Abco's shoe prices were no lower than those of any of its competitors. As for exports, not only had the company failed to reach its promised goal of 50 percent, but as of the bankruptcy hearings, its exports for a five-year period only amounted to 5 percent of total output. In light of these developments, the government felt that it had to make a quick decision in the Abco affair in such a way as to avoid criticism from the opposition.

DIRECTIONS: The questions that follow relate to the preceding passage. Evaluate, in terms of the passage, each of the items given. Then select your answer from one of the following classifications, and blacken the corresponding space on the answer sheet.

(A) A MAJOR OBJECTIVE in making the decision: one of the goals sought by the decision maker

(B) A MAJOR FACTOR in making the decision: an aspect of the problem, specifically mentioned in the passage, that fundamentally affects and/or determines the decision

(C) A MINOR FACTOR in making the decision: a less important element bearing on or affecting a Major Factor, rather than a Major Objective directly.

(D) A MAJOR ASSUMPTION in making the decision: a projection or supposition arrived at by the decision maker before considering the factors and alternatives

(E) AN UNIMPORTANT ISSUE in making the decision: an item lacking significant impact on, or relationship to, the decision

1. Ability of Abco to survive if the five-million-dollar loan was granted

2. High unemployment in Frieland

3. Dependence of shopkeepers on the existence of Abco

4. Government investment incentives granted to Abco

5. Status of Frieland as a developing country

6. Continued operation of Abco

7. Training of workers at no expense to Abco

8. Strained worker-management relations at Abco

9. Export potential of Abco

10. Political philosophy of the opposition party

11. Need for a quick decision by the government as to whether to grant the loan requested by Abco

12. Availability of government funds needed to support Abco

13. Prevention of layoffs of workers at Abco

14. Political consequence of an Abco bankruptcy

15. Frieland's small population

16. Increasing foreign exchange reserves

17. Surplus shoe production

18. Reduction of shoe prices

Passage 2:

In early 1957 the Conway Clock Company was considering the introduction of a new line of electric clocks in an effort to increase unit sales and thereby utilize a greater percentage of its production facilities. The new line would be sold under the brand name Concord and would be marketed in direct competition with the lower-priced models of the regular Conway line. While the total market for clocks had increased in recent years, Conway's unit sales had remained relatively constant. The company's sales manager felt that one way to increase sales was to introduce a line of non-fair-traded clocks.[1]

The Conway Company had been producing a line of quality household clocks for almost a century. Throughout its existence the company had maintained an excellent reputation for the production of quality clocks. Many of its first clocks were known to be still operating in satisfactory fashion. Some were even considered family heirlooms.

In 1955 the Conway Company produced a line consisting of eight basic models. In 1956, however, four new models were added, making a total of twelve models of electric and mechanical clocks sold under the Conway name. Of these, two were alarm clocks, three were table model occasional clocks, and seven were wall clocks. Each model was produced in several different colors, with black, brown, and red the most popular ones. Styles ranged from traditional to ultramodern. The company employed a full-time designer and emphasized style in its dealer and consumer promotions.

The clock market was considered to be highly competitive. The industry was comprised of a number of firms, most of which were small or medium size. The giant in the field was General Electric with its Telechron line of electric clocks. The smaller firms sold either on a price or quality-of-workmanship basis. These firms usually produced a relatively small number of models and changed styles frequently. Conway was one of the medium-sized companies with about 5 percent of the industry's sales. The company's share of the market had been greater during the late 1920's and early 1930's, but the increase in the number of firms selling inexpensive electric clocks had cut into the company's share substantially. Because of an expanding market, however, Conway's unit sales had remained relatively constant since 1945. Dollar sales of Conway clocks approximated $7 million in 1956. The increase in dollar sales which had taken place since World War II was due almost entirely to changes in Conway's prices.

The Conway Company employed salesmen who sold to 300 distributors, most of whom were jewelry wholesalers. These wholesalers sold to over 14,000 retail outlets, of which 80 percent were jewelry stores and the rest department stores. The bulk of the company's sales to department stores was accounted for by 60 to 70 large stores. Each of the company's salesmen had about 20 large retail accounts to which he sold direct. If an outlet which had been served by one of the wholesalers was sold direct by a Conway salesman, the outlet was billed through the wholesaler so that the latter received its margin.

---

[1] The company had enforced resale price maintenance or fair trade on its regular line of clocks. Resale price maintenance is a procedure whereby a manufacturer is permitted in some states to establish, by contract, a minimum retail price below which retailers may not sell its products.

To back up the efforts of the salesmen, the company budgeted about $250,000 annually for advertising. About 70 percent was spent on consumer advertising and the remainder on trade advertising. Most of the consumer advertisements were placed in magazines, although some radio spots were used. The advertisements stressed the up-to-date styling and quality of the Conway clocks.

Conway clocks were priced at retail from $8.95 to $59.50, but most of the sales were in the $29 to $39 price range. The company established a policy of resale price maintenance for the Conway line to protect the small dealer. This policy was policed largely by examining dealer advertisements and collecting information from trade sources. If a dealer sold Conway merchandise at less than the fair-traded price, Conway issued a warning to the dealer. If a second violation occurred within a year, Conway sought a court injunction against the dealer to prevent future violations. Actually, Conway had little difficulty in maintaining its retail prices. The company did, however, face growing price competition from small clock manufacturers who frequently offered large credit jewelers and discount houses a special price for a volume order.

TABLE 1

EXAMPLE OF A COMPARABLE PRICE STRUCTURE ON CONWAY AND CONCORD CLOCKS

Price	Conway Model No. 102* (Fair Traded)	Concord Model No. C102 (Not Fair Traded)	
		Lots of 1–24	Lots of 25 or More
List	$10.95	$10.95	$10.95
To dealer	7.23	6.68	5.97
To distributor	5.59	5.25	4.50

* No quantity discounts offered on this model.

The new line of clocks under consideration in 1957 would be sold under the Concord brand and would consist solely of two electric alarm clocks and three electric wall models. The styles for these five models would be obtained from (1) previously discontinued Conway models, (2) new models developed especially for Concord, or (3) modified current Conway models, usually "stripped" versions. These clocks would have suggested list prices ranging from $6.95 to $14.95. These prices would be identical to the prices charged for the comparable Conway models. However, the Concord line would *not* be fair traded and the price to dealers would be less. (See Table 1 for a price schedule.) It was expected that many retailers would sell the Concord line at considerably less than the list price.

The only advertising planned for the Concord line was some illustrated price lists for use by company salesmen and distributors, point-of-purchase signs, display racks, and consumer handouts for use by retailers. This material would be free to distributors and dealers. It was thought that many of the retailers handling the Conway line would also handle the Concord models. It was expected that the quality of the Conway models would be used as a selling point by both distributors and retailers. It was hoped that additional cut-price outlets, such as credit jewelers, large drug chain outlets, and discount houses, would be interested in the new line.

DIRECTIONS: The questions that follow relate to the preceding passage. Evaluate, in terms of the passage, each of the items given. Then select your answer from one of the following classifications, and blacken the corresponding space on the answer sheet.

(A) A MAJOR OBJECTIVE in making the decision: one of the goals sought by the decision maker

(B) A MAJOR FACTOR in making the decision: an aspect of the problem, specifically mentioned in the passage, that fundamentally affects and/or determines the decision

(C) A MINOR FACTOR in making the decision: a less important element bearing on or affecting a Major Factor, rather than a Major Objective directly

(D) A MAJOR ASSUMPTION in making the decision: a projection or supposition arrived at by the decision maker before considering the factors and alternatives

(E) AN UNIMPORTANT ISSUE in making the decision: an item lacking significant impact on, or relationship to, the decision

19. The selling by wholesalers to 14,000 retail outlets

20. Utilization of excess capacity

21. Conway's declining market share

22. Conway's 100 years in business

23. The placement of most consumer ads in magazines

24. Consumer acceptance of the new line

25. Competition from small manufacturers

26. Selling new line to discount houses

27. Need to increase unit sales

28. Reputation of Conway

29. Resale price maintenance

30. Protection of the small dealer

31. Importance of styling

32. Sales to department stores

33. Existing retailers to sell Concord models

34. Checking dealer advertisements

35. Growing price competition

If there is still time remaining, you may review the questions in this section only.
You may not turn to any other section of the test.

Section IV Data Sufficiency

TIME: 30 minutes

DIRECTIONS: Each of the following problems has a question and two statements which are labeled (1) and (2). Use the data given in (1) and (2) together with other available information (such as the number of hours in a day, the definition of *clockwise*, mathematical facts, etc.) to decide whether the statements are *sufficient* to answer the question. Then fill in space

(A) if you can get the answer from (1) alone but not from (2) alone;

(B) if you can get the answer from (2) alone but not from (1) alone;

(C) if you can get the answer from (1) and (2) together, although neither statement by itself suffices;

(D) if statement (1) alone suffices *and* statement (2) alone suffices;

(E) if you cannot get the answer from statements (1) and (2) together, but need even more data.

All numbers used in this section are real numbers. A figure given for a problem is intended to provide information consistent with that in the question, but not necessarily with the additional information contained in the statements.

1. Are two triangles congruent?

   (1) Both triangles are right triangles.
   (2) Both triangles have the same perimeter.

2. Is x greater than zero?

   (1) $x^4 - 16 = 0$
   (2) $x^3 - 8 = 0$

3. If both conveyer belt A and conveyer belt B are used, they can fill a hopper with coal in one hour. How long will it take for conveyer belt A to fill the hopper without conveyer belt B?

   (1) Conveyer belt A moves twice as much coal as conveyer belt B.
   (2) Conveyer belt B would take 3 hours to fill the hopper without belt A.

4. A fly crawls around the outside of a circle once. A second fly crawls around the outside of a square once. Which fly travels further?

   (1) The diagonal of the square is equal to the diameter of the circle.
   (2) The fly crawling around the circle took more time to complete his journey than the fly crawling around the square.

5. How much did it cost the *XYZ* Corporation to insure its factory from fire in 1972?

   (1) It cost $5,000 for fire insurance in 1971.
   (2) The total amount the corporation spent for fire insurance in 1970, 1971, and 1972 was $18,000.

6. Is y larger than 1?

   (1) y is larger than 0.
   (2) $y^2 - 4 = 0$.

7. A worker is hired for 6 days. He is paid $2 more for each day of work than he was paid for the preceding day of work. How much was he paid for the first day of work?

   (1) His total wages for the 6 days were $150.
   (2) He was paid 150% of his first day's pay for the sixth day.

8. A car originally sold for $3,000. After a month, the car was discounted $x\%$, and a month later the car's price was discounted $y\%$. Is the car's price after the discounts less than $2,600?

   (1) $y = 10$
   (2) $x = 15$

9. What is the value of a?

   (1) $a = f$
   (2) $a = b$

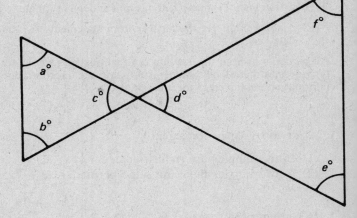

10. In triangle ABC, find z if $AB = 5$ and $y = 40$.

    (1) $BC = 5$
    (2) The bisector of angle B is perpendicular to AC.

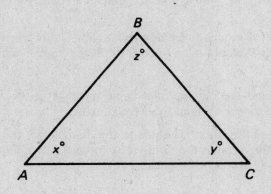

11. How much cardboard will it take to make an open cubical box with no top?

    (1) The area of the bottom of the box is 4 square feet.
    (2) The volume of the box is 8 cubic feet.

12. How many books are on a bookshelf?

    (1) The total weight of all the books on the bookshelf is 40 pounds.
    (2) The average weight of the books on the bookshelf is 2.5 pounds.

13. Is the figure *ABCD* a rectangle?

(1) $x = 90$
(2) $AB = CD$

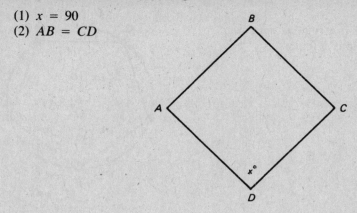

14. A sequence of numbers is given by the rule $a_n = (a_{n-1})^2$. What is a_5?

(1) $a_1 = -1$
(2) $a_3 = 1$

15. How much is John's weekly salary?

(1) John's weekly salary is twice as much as Fred's weekly salary.
(2) Fred's weekly salary is 40% of the total of Chuck's weekly salary and John's weekly salary.

16. Find $x + 2y$.

(1) $x + y = 4$
(2) $2x + 4y = 12$

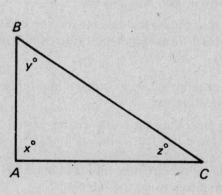

17. Is angle *BAC* a right angle?

(1) $x = 2y$
(2) $y = 1.5z$

18. Is x greater than y?

(1) $x = 2k$
(2) $k = 2y$

19. How much profit did Toyland make selling 65 dolls if each doll cost $8?

(1) The amount the dolls sold for was $750.
(2) The dolls cost $7 each last year.

20. 50% of the people in Teetown have blue eyes and blond hair. What percent of the people in Teetown have blue eyes but do not have blond hair?

(1) 70% of the people in Teetown have blond hair.
(2) 60% of the people in Teetown have blue eyes.

21. The pentagon *ABCDE* is inscribed in the circle with center *O*. How many degrees is angle *ABC*?

    (1) The pentagon *ABCDE* is a regular pentagon.
    (2) The radius of the circle is 5 inches.

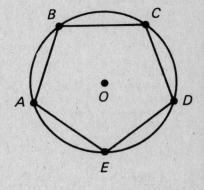

22. What is the area of the circle with center *O*? (*AB* and *DE* are straight lines)

    (1) *DE* = 5 inches
    (2) *AB* = 7 inches

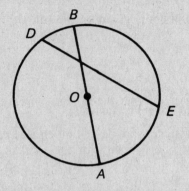

23. What is the taxable income of the Kell family in 1973? The taxable income of the Kell family in 1971 was $10,000.

    (1) The Kell family had taxable income of $12,000 in 1972.
    (2) The total taxable income of the Kell family for the three years 1971, 1972, and 1973 was $34,000.

24. A piece of string 6 feet long is cut into three smaller pieces. How long is the longest of the three pieces?

    (1) Two pieces are the same length.
    (2) One piece is 3 feet, 2 inches long.

25. If a group of 5 craftsmen take 3 hours to finish a job, how long will it take a group of 4 apprentices to do the same job?

    (1) An apprentice works at ⅔ the rate of a craftsman.
    (2) The 5 craftsmen and the 4 apprentices working together will take 1²²⁄₂₃ hours to finish the job.

If there is still time remaining, you may review the questions in this section only.
You may not turn to any other section of the test.

Section V Writing Ability

TIME: 30 minutes

DIRECTIONS: This test consists of a number of sentences, in each of which some part or the whole is underlined. Each sentence is followed by five alternative versions of the underlined portion. Select an alternative you consider both most correct and most effective according to the requirements of standard written English. Answer A is the same as the original version; if you think the original version is best, select answer A.

In considering the answer choices, be attentive to matters of grammar, diction, and syntax, as well as clarity, precision, and fluency. Do not select an answer which alters the meaning of the original sentence.

1. If he was to decide to go to college, I, for one, would recommend that he plan to go to Yale.

   (A) If he was to decide to go to college,
   (B) If he were to decide to go to college,
   (C) Had he decided to go to college,
   (D) In the event that he decides to go to college,
   (E) Supposing he was to decide to go to college,

2. Except for you and I, everyone brought a present to the party.

   (A) Except for you and I, everyone brought
   (B) With exception of you and I, everyone brought
   (C) Except for you and I, everyone had brought
   (D) Except for you and me, everyone brought
   (E) Except for you and me, everyone had brought

3. When one reads the poetry of the seventeenth century, you find a striking contrast between the philosophy of the Cavalier poets such as Suckling and the attitude of the Metaphysical poets such as Donne.

   (A) When one reads the poetry of the seventeenth century, you find
   (B) When you read the poetry of the seventeenth century, one finds
   (C) When one reads the poetry of the seventeenth century, he finds
   (D) If one reads the poetry of the 17th century, you find
   (E) As you read the poetry of the 17th century, one finds

4. Because of his broken hip, John Jones has not and possibly never will be able to run the mile again.

   (A) has not and possibly never will be able to run
   (B) has not and possibly will never be able to run
   (C) has not been and possibly never would be able to run
   (D) has not and possibly never would be able to run
   (E) has not been able to run and possibly never will be able to run

5. Had I realized how close I was to failing, I would not have gone to the party.

   (A) Had I realized how close
   (B) If I would have realized
   (C) Had I had realized how close
   (D) When I realized how close
   (E) If I realized how close

6. Having finished the marathon in record-breaking time, <u>the city awarded him its Citizen's Outstanding Performance Medal</u>.

   (A) the city awarded him its Citizen's Outstanding Performance Medal
   (B) the city awarded the Citizen's Outstanding Performance Medal to him
   (C) he was awarded the Citizen's Outstanding Performance Medal by the city
   (D) the Citizen's Outstanding Performance Medal was awarded to him
   (E) he was awarded by the city with the Citizen's Outstanding Performance Medal

7. <u>The football team's winning it's first game of the season</u> excited the student body.

   (A) The football team's winning it's first game of the season
   (B) The football team having won it's first game of the season
   (C) The football team's having won it's first game of the season
   (D) The football team's winning its first game of the season
   (E) The football team winning it's first game of the season

8. Anyone interested in the use of computers can learn much <u>if you have access to</u> a Radio Shack TRS-80 or a Pet Microcomputer.

   (A) if you have access to
   (B) if he has access to
   (C) if access is available to
   (D) by access to
   (E) from access to

9. <u>No student had ought to be put into a situation where</u> he has to choose between his loyalty to his friends and his duty to the class.

   (A) No student had ought to be put into a situation where
   (B) No student had ought to be put into a situation in which
   (C) No student should be put into a situation where
   (D) No student ought to be put into a situation in which
   (E) No student ought to be put into a situation where

10. <u>Being a realist,</u> I could not accept his statement that supernatural beings had caused the disturbance.

    (A) Being a realist,
    (B) Since I am a realist,
    (C) Being that I am a realist,
    (D) Being as I am a realist,
    (E) Realist that I am,

11. The reason <u>I came late to class today is because</u> the bus broke down.

    (A) I came late to class today is because
    (B) why I came late to class today is because
    (C) I was late to school today is because
    (D) that I was late to school today is because
    (E) I came late to class today is that

12. I have <u>to make dinner, wash the dishes, do my homework, and then relaxing</u>.

    (A) to make dinner, wash the dishes, do my homework, and then relaxing
    (B) to make dinner, washing the dishes, do my homework, and then relax
    (C) to make dinner, wash the dishes, doing my homework and then relaxing
    (D) to prepare dinner, wash the dishes, do my homework, and then relaxing
    (E) to make dinner, wash the dishes, do my homework, and then relax

13. The climax occurs when he asks who's in the closet.

    (A) occurs when he asks who's
    (B) is when he asks whose
    (C) occurs when he asks whose
    (D) is when he asks who'se
    (E) occurs when he asked who's

14. The grocer hadn't hardly any of those kind of canned goods.

    (A) hadn't hardly any of those kind
    (B) hadn't hardly any of those kinds
    (C) had hardly any of those kind
    (D) had hardly any of those kinds
    (E) had scarcely any of those kind

15. Having stole the money, the police searched the thief.

    (A) Having stole the money, the police searched the thief.
    (B) Having stolen the money, the thief was searched by the police.
    (C) Having stolen the money, the police searched the thief.
    (D) Having stole the money, the thief was searched by the police.
    (E) Being that he stole the money, the police searched the thief.

16. The child is neither encouraged to be critical or to examine all the evidence for his opinion.

    (A) neither encouraged to be critical or to examine
    (B) neither encouraged to be critical nor to examine
    (C) either encouraged to be critical or to examine
    (D) encouraged either to be critical nor to examine
    (E) not encouraged either to be critical or to examine

17. The process by which the community influence the actions of its members is known as social control.

    (A) influence the actions of its members
    (B) influences the actions of its members
    (C) had influenced the actions of its members
    (D) influences the actions of their members
    (E) will influence the actions of its members

18. To be sure, there would be scarcely no time left over for other things if school children would have been expected to have considered all sides of every matter on which they hold opinions.

    (A) would have been expected to have considered
    (B) should have been expected to have considered
    (C) were expected to consider
    (D) will be expected to have been considered
    (E) were expected to be considered

19. Depending on skillful suggestion, argument is seldom used in advertising.

    (A) Depending on skillful suggestion, argument is seldom used in advertising.
    (B) Argument is seldom used by advertisers, who depend instead on skillful suggestion.
    (C) Skillfull suggestion is depended on by advertisers instead of argument.
    (D) Suggestion, which is more skillful, is used in place of argument by advertisers.
    (E) Instead of suggestion, depending on argument is used by skillful advertisers.

20. When this war is over, no nation will either be isolated in war or peace.

   (A) either be isolated in war or peace
   (B) be either isolated in war or peace
   (C) be isolated in neither war nor peace
   (D) be isolated either in war or in peace
   (E) be isolated neither in war or peace

21. Each will be within trading distance of all the others and will be able to strike them.

   (A) within trading distance of all the others and will be able to strike them
   (B) near enough to trade with and strike all the others
   (C) trading and striking the others
   (D) within trading and striking distance of all the others
   (E) able to strike and trade with all the others

22. Examining the principal movements sweeping through the world, it can be seen that they are being accelerated by the war.

   (A) Examining the principal movements sweeping through the world, it can be seen
   (B) Having examined the principal movements sweeping through the world, it can be seen
   (C) Examining the principal movements sweeping through the world can be seen
   (D) Examining the principal movements sweeping through the world, we can see
   (E) It can be seen examining the principal movements sweeping through the world

23. However many mistakes have been made in our past, the tradition of America, not only the champion of freedom but also fair play, still lives among millions who can see light and hope scarcely anywhere else.

   (A) not only the champion of freedom but also fair play,
   (B) the champion of not only freedom but also of fair play,
   (C) the champion not only of freedom but also of fair play,
   (D) not only the champion but also freedom and fair play,
   (E) not the champion of freedom only, but also fair play,

24. In giving expression to the play instincts of the human race, new vigor and effectiveness are afforded by recreation to the body and to the mind.

   (A) new vigor and effectiveness are afforded by recreation to the body and to the mind
   (B) recreation affords new vigor and effectiveness to the body and to the mind
   (C) there are afforded new vigor and effectiveness to the body and to the mind
   (D) by recreation the body and mind are afforded new vigor and effectiveness
   (E) the body and the mind afford new vigor and effectiveness to themselves by recreation

25. Play being recognized as an important factor in improving mental and physical health and thereby reducing human misery and poverty.

   (A) Play being recognized as
   (B) By recognizing play as
   (C) Their recognizing play as
   (D) Recognition of it being
   (E) Play is recognized as

If there is still time remaining, you may review the questions in this section only.
You may not turn to any other section of the test.

Section VI   Analysis of Situations

TIME: 30 minutes

DIRECTIONS: Read the following passages. After you have completed each one, you will be asked to answer either one or two sets of questions that involve determining the importance of specific factors included in the passage. When answering questions, you may consult the passage.

Passage 1:

Mr. Ed Krim, a building contractor by profession, met with an old friend, Mr. Sam Sims, a marketing consultant. Mr. Krim was excited about a business opportunity and wanted to obtain Sims's evaluation of its prospects. Posturemat, a small company producing foam rubber mattresses, was in financial trouble, and its owners were anxious to sell it. The company had been established some twenty years, but its market share had steadily declined over the last five years. Since Mr. Krim had no previous experience in the mattress business, he requested that his friend find out what he could about the company.

Mr. Sims first analyzed the company's resources. Its best resource was its product and brand name. Foam rubber mattresses are made of imported latex and are extremely firm, unlike synthetic rubber mattresses made of polyurethane. However, synthetics are much cheaper than foam rubber mattresses. Latex mattresses are known for their orthopedic and anti-allergic qualities, among others. The Posturemat brand name had very nearly become a generic term for all types of rubber mattresses. Posturemat, however, was the only latex mattress produced locally.

Apart from a superior product, the company had few resources. Its equipment, while satisfactory, was old and had been fully depreciated. It operated in leased premises on a year-to-year basis, although the landlord was willing to conclude a long-term agreement on favorable terms. On the other hand, the company's labor force was experienced and dedicated and its production manager had more than ten years' experience in latex manufacturing.

Mr. Joe Caspi, president of the company, was past seventy years old and was anxious to retire. He had tried to retire previously, but had failed to train a successor. Apart from Fred Lefko, the sales manager, no one else shared responsibility for marketing or administration. Fred Lefko let Sam Sims know that if the company were sold, he had no intention of remaining. Lefko had eighteen years' experience in the mattress industry, including twelve years with Posturemat. If Lefko left the company, Krim might be hard pressed to find a suitable replacement. This was another issue that Sam Sims would have to study.

Posturemat's financial position was precarious. The company was heavily in debt and its line of credit fully extended. There was some question as to whether the company would be able to purchase enough latex to keep production going, but Mr. Caspi assured Sam Sims that the company had a bank letter of credit to purchase an additional three months' supply.

It spite of Mr. Caspi's optimism, the fact was that his company had steadily lost market share. Once the dominant mattress manufacturer, with fifty percent of the local market, its market share had declined to less than ten percent. Mr. Caspi attributed this decline to inroads made by spring mattress manufacturers, who had only begun production five years ago. Spring mattresses now accounted for seventy percent of the total market, Caspi's company ten percent, with the remaining twenty percent shared by a number of small plants producing synthetic rubber mattresses. Spring mattresses had some attributes similar to those of foam rubber, such as orthopedic qualities. They were less costly to manufacture, but sold to the consumer at about the same price as Posturemat mattresses.

Because of Posturemat's financial difficulties, it ceased advertising in newspapers and on radio. Little if any advertising had been done in other media over the past five years. As a result, retailers were reluctant to handle the product line. By contrast, two of the larger spring mattress manufacturers had advertised heavily in the mass media. One of these manufacturer's products was sold exclusively by the largest furniture chain in the country. During his study of the mattress market, a number of retailers had expressed the opinion to Mr. Sims that a whole generation of young people were largely unaware of Posturemat products because of the lack of advertising. One retailer was quoted as saying: "It is true that older people remember Posturemat, but these mattresses last for almost twenty years. The big market is not the replacement market, but sales generated by family formation. Thousands of young couples get married every year, and every marriage means another mattress sale. But these young people only see advertisements for spring mattresses. It is obviously easier for my salesman to sell a mattress which his customers have seen in countless advertisements than one which is relatively unknown."

Sims was aware of the fact that if Posturemat was ever to regain some of its lost market share, it would have to launch a major advertising program to educate young adults about the important attributes found in its products. A major question that needed an immediate answer was: "To what extent are people aware of Posturemat mattresses and their attributes?" Other questions involved the attitudes of people toward foam rubber mattresses in general and how these attitudes compared to those toward spring mattresses. Mr. Sims ordered a market research survey to obtain answers to his questions. In brief, the study revealed that a large segment of the population over twenty-five years of age was aware of Posturemat mattresses and had favorable attitudes toward their attributes. About three-quarters of these people expressed a preference for foam rubber mattresses for their children (by contrast with other mattresses for their own use). Awareness among younger segments of the population of the attributes of foam rubber mattresses in general, and of Posturemat in particular, was very low. Few young people expressed an intention to buy foam rubber mattresses.

On the basis of the preliminary research results, Krim was optimistic that he could turn the company around. In support of his belief, he cited the recognition of the company among a significant portion of the population, and the fact that they would buy a Posturemat for their children. He believed that once retailers became aware that new management had taken over the company, they would be willing to stock the product. Krim was aware that the research findings were not always in agreement with his conclusions. However, the finding that young people were relatively unaware of Posturemat did not seem to worry him. He felt that a well-designed advertising program would convince many people to buy a foam rubber mattress, rather than any competing type. Moreover, the introduction of a new management team would instill confidence among Posturemat's bankers. Credit lines would be increased, thereby improving the company's financial position. However, before making a final decision as to whether to purchase Posturemat, Mr. Krim waited for Sam Sims's final report and recommendations.

DIRECTIONS: The questions that follow relate to the preceding passage. Evaluate, in terms of the passage, each of the items given. Then select your answer from one of the following classifications, and blacken the corresponding space on the answer sheet.

(A) A MAJOR OBJECTIVE in making the decision: one of the goals sought by the decision maker

(B) A MAJOR FACTOR in making the decision: an aspect of the problem, specifically mentioned in the passage, that fundamentally affects and/or determines the decision

(C) A MINOR FACTOR is making the decision: a less important element bearing on or affecting a Major Factor, rather than a Major Objective directly

(D) A MAJOR ASSUMPTION in making the decision: a projection or supposition arrived at by the decision maker before considering the factors and alternatives

(E) AN UNIMPORTANT ISSUE in making the decision: an item lacking significant impact on, or relationship to, the decision

1. Public awareness of the high quality of Posturemat mattresses

2. Joe Caspi's marketing ability

3. The anti-allergic qualities of Posturemat mattresses

4. Attitude of older consumers towards Posturemat mattresses

5. Willingness of retailers to stock Posturemat products in the future

6. Need to import latex rubber

7. Posturemat's present market share

8. Sam Sims's recommendations

9. Posturemat leased its premises

10. Plausibility of changing consumer attitudes through advertising

11. Orthopedic qualities of Posturemat mattresses

12. Use of polyurethane in the production of synthetic mattresses

13. Lefko's intention to leave Posturemat

14. Age of Posturemat's manufacturing equipment

15. Likelihood that credit lines could be increased

16. Caspi's explanation for loss of market share

Passage 2:

In 1956 officials of the Grace Fabri-Tool Company, manufacturers of special tools and presses for working with laminated plastic sheets[1] such as Formica, Micarta, and Textolite, were considering possible changes in the company's distribution channels. From the company's founding in 1953, it had sold through laminated plastics distributors. Sales increased rapidly from the start, but profits were not satisfactory. This condition resulted from the difficulties encountered by distributors in providing adequate field service.

In 1942 Mr. Robert Grace had first realized the difficulties that Formica presented to the fabricator. While working in his father's shop, he was often given the job of cutting Formica and bonding it to plywood, and in time he developed considerable skill in handling the plastic material.

After serving in the armed forces and attending college, Mr. Grace decided to put his knowledge of Formica to good advantage. He persuaded the Formica Company to hire him to travel all over the country to show fabricators and cabinetmakers improved methods of cutting and forming Formica sheets. As a demonstrator, Mr. Grace arranged meetings for distributors. Typically such a meeting would attract 50 to 500 people from the cabinet shops and woodworking and plastic-fabricating plants in the distributor's area. Each meeting lasted about two hours and was generally held in a hotel in which a shop had

---

[1] Laminated plastic sheets were made of specially processed papers impregnated with resins and then cured under intense heat and pressure. The layers were then fused into sheets usually about 1/16 inch thick. These sheets were bonded to plywood and hardboard and used as a surface material on many types of domestic, commercial, and industrial furniture and furnishings. One of the most popular applications in the home was for kitchen counter tops.

been set up for temporary use by Mr. Grace. Distributors found that a large number of their customers and prospective customers attended these meetings because most of them had little experience in working with laminated plastic sheets and were in need of aid. Following such a meeting, it was not uncommon for a distributor to experience a 30 to 35 percent increase in Formica sales.

After two years as a Formica demonstrator, Grace felt that Formica could be fabricated more efficiently if special tools and presses were available for that purpose. The officials of the company encouraged Grace to find someone to design and produce such tools and presses, but no manufacturer was interested in his idea. Therefore, Grace decided to form his own company to design and sell the tools and presses. After completing the designs in his own workshop, he engaged a tool manufacturer to produce them.

Grace Fabri-Tool Company was formed in 1953 and was the first to introduce a line of tools for working laminated plastic sheets, but Stanley and Porter-Cable were quick to follow. Even though specially made for working plastic sheets, these tools could also be used with other materials, including wood.

The principal types of operation used in working laminated plastic sheets were sawing, drilling, routing, beveling, bonding, and forming. While all these operations except forming could be performed with ordinary shop tools, field experience indicated that carbide-tipped tools, such as those made by Grace, gave better results and lasted longer. However, such tools were about twice as expensive as ordinary carpenter's tools. Representative of the tools were the routing and trimming fixtures. The average price of the tools was about $15.

Grace Fabri-Tool Company also sold bonding and forming presses; the least expensive model initially sold for $1,650. The Grace Thermofast vacuum press used a heat process which saved a great deal of time over the conventional cold-pressure method of bonding plastic sheets (or other material such as wood veneer) to a second surface. Field tests indicated that the Grace press could complete in six minutes a bond that would require several hours using the cold-pressure method.

Forming presses were used to shape sheets of plastic in more than one plane. For example, in place of a flat plastic-covered kitchen counter top, it was not uncommon for a designer to specify an extension of the plastic sheet up the back wall and down over the front edge, or a slight ridge along the front edge of the counter top to prevent water from running off. Forming sheets in this manner required special presses which, because of their cost, could be purchased only by the large fabricators, who consequently did the bulk of this kind of work either on their own account or on a custom basis for smaller firms. Initially it was felt that the presses could be installed and operated with a minimum of instruction and would require virtually no service.

Mr. Grace was particularly fortunate in that the Formica Company continued to use his services, on an independent contractor basis, for a period of about five months after he had formed his own company. Under this arrangement he continued as a demonstrator of Formica, but was paid according to the number of demonstrations made, rather than on a straight salary basis. This arrangement subsidized his selling efforts on behalf of his own products and brought him into direct contact with prospective distributors and final users of his products. He estimated that this support was worth $10,000–$12,000 and that it was instrumental in assuring the success of the firm at a critical stage.

In view of the above arrangement, Mr. Grace decided to sell his products through laminated plastic sheet distributors. He sent letters to 50 of them with the result that 40 sent in orders. They gave the company representation in most parts of the country.

Laminated plastic sheet distributors generally sold only plastic sheets, plywood, adhesives, and seam-fillers. However, some had taken on noncompeting items to serve their customers better. Many of the customers of the distributors were relatively unacquainted with the problems of working with laminated plastic sheets and welcomed any information or tools that would help them. As a result, the Grace Fabri-Tools were added to their lines by many distributors. Not only were they better able to service their customers' needs, but it was possible for their salesmen to call on customers with something new to talk about.

Distributor interest in Grace tools continued, since for some time a new tool was added to the line almost every month. Distributors' salesmen thus had a steady stream of new items to talk about as they called on their customers. As the number of new tools increased, the need for additional ones decreased and in time the company ran out of ideas. This caused distributors' salesmen to lose their special interest in the Grace tools.

Prior to late 1955, distributors aggressively sought business. However, the demand for plastic sheets became so great after that time that distributors took most of their salesmen off the road and had them use the telephone to take orders. Even with this arrangement distributors' sales of plastic sheets increased as much as 30 percent in a year. But the sale of Grace products suffered from the lack of selling effort. Distributors spent most of their time taking orders for plastic sheets and trying to fill them. The search for funds to finance their operations became a major problem. This situation continued into 1956. However, there were some indications that it might again become necessary for distributors to get out and sell.

Sales of the Grace Company amounted to $60,000 during the last six months of 1953. The following year they rose to $350,000 and in 1955 reached $455,000. Despite the sales increases, profits suffered as a result of field service costs. The company, belatedly recognizing the need for field service on the presses and the inadequacy of distributors in this respect, leaned over backwards to remedy the situation.

By 1955 distributors found that service demands and complaints from buyers of presses were a problem. The buyer looked to the distributor to keep the press running. Yet the distributor usually had no facilities, and Grace was inadequately prepared to meet the service needs which developed. This situation resulted in long delays in completing service calls. Distributors had in the past been able to adjust customers' complaints on the spot inasmuch as they involved small tools, adhesives, plywood, and plastic sheets. Defects in these products could be detected easily, and when necessary, the product could be replaced out of stock at a small cost. This was not possible, however, with a machine costing several thousand dollars and normally shipped by the manufacturer to the customer.

Flatbed presses were originally priced at $1,650 on the assumption that service and repairs under the warranty would be a trivial expense to the company. Actual experience, however, indicated that claims made under the company's warranty could not be handled by letter or telephone and that satisfactory handling incurred expenses ranging from $200 to $300 per press. Moreover, redesign of the presses increased manufacturing costs from $400 to $500 per press. In setting a new price, the company decided to set it high enough to recover the added manufacturing costs and the estimated cost of delivering, installing the equipment, training operators, and handling service and repairs under the warranty. The new price was established at $2,975. Many distributors felt that at this price the item was too expensive to handle. Some made no effort to sell it but continued to sell the smaller tools. Others voluntarily dropped the Grace products.

With the adoption of the new installation and service policy it became necessary for the company to reconsider its distribution channels. Moreover, the desire to achieve broader distribution and more aggressive selling increased the need for reassessing existing channels.

Distributors' discounts were cut from 20 percent to 10 percent of list price, except in those cases where the distributor was able and willing to handle, install, and service presses and to train operators. A discount was allowed anyone who bought for resale. However, no discounts were allowed on direct sales by the company to users, no matter how large. It was reasoned that a user would buy only what he required whether or not quantity discounts were allowed.

In 1956 the management felt that manufacturers' representatives, together with the remaining distributors, would provide the desired coverage and selling effort. In investigating this possibility some difficulty was encountered in locating representatives who were regularly calling on prospective buyers of Grace products and who were not selling competing items. In some cases agents not calling upon potential buyers of Grace products were willing to do so and asked for the Grace line.

The representatives under consideration carried various other products. Several handled automotive items, one handled kitchen cabinets and appliances, another handled noncompeting electronic gluing equipment, and one with a very large territory was willing to handle Grace products exclusively. Some representatives for laminated plastic sheets also expressed interest in taking on Grace products. A representative was paid a 10 percent commission on all shipments of tools or presses destined for his area, even those resulting from distributor effort. However, if a representative obtained an order for shipment into the territory of another representative, the commission was to be split. The Grace Fabri-Tool Company management recognized that from 12 to 18 months would be required before a representative could be expected to develop his territory.

> DIRECTIONS: The questions that follow relate to the preceding passage. Evaluate, in terms of the passage, each of the items given. Then select your answer from one of the following classifications, and blacken the corresponding space on the answer sheet.
>
> (A) A MAJOR OBJECTIVE in making the decision: one of the goals sought by the decision maker
>
> (B) A MAJOR FACTOR in making the decision: an aspect of the problem, specifically mentioned in the passage, that fundamentally affects and/or determines the decision
>
> (C) A MINOR FACTOR in making the decision: a less important element bearing on or affecting a Major Factor, rather than a Major Objective directly
>
> (D) A MAJOR ASSUMPTION in making the decision: a projection or supposition arrived at by the decision maker before considering the factors and alternatives
>
> (E) AN UNIMPORTANT ISSUE in making the decision: an item lacking significant impact on, or relationship to, the decision

17. Total cost of a Grace press

18. Adoption of a new service policy

19. Adoption of a new distribution channel

20. Working in his father's shop

21. Service expenses of $400 to $500 per press

22. Lack of selling effort

23. Desire for expanded distribution

24. Complaints from buyers

25. Possibility that manufacturers' representatives would expand coverage

26. The press being too expensive for distributors to handle

27. Cutting of distributors' discounts

28. Difficulty in finding distributors

29. The fact that some prospective representatives carried appliances

30. Easy detection of defects in Fabri-Tools

31. Delays in completing service calls

32. Lack of distributor facilities

33. Level of distributor discounts

34. Arrangement of meetings for distributors

35. Likelihood of buying regardless of quantity discounts

If there is still time remaining, you may review the questions in this section only.
You may not turn to any other section of the test.

Section VII   Writing Ability

TIME: **30 minutes**

DIRECTIONS: This test consists of a number of sentences, in each of which some part or the whole is underlined. Each sentence is followed by five alternative versions of the underlined portion. Select the alternative you consider both most correct and most effective according to the requirements of standard written English. Answer A is the same as the original version; if you think the original version is best, select answer A.

In considering the answer choices, be attentive to matters of grammar, diction, and syntax, as well as clarity, precision, and fluency. Do not select an answer which alters the meaning of the original sentence.

1. John wanted to have gone to the movies.

   (A) wanted to have gone
   (B) had wanted to have gone
   (C) wanted to go
   (D) wanted to have went
   (E) had wanted to have went

2. Knowing the cost of the Space Shuttle program, its breakdown caused the director much irritation.

   (A) Knowing the cost of the Space Shuttle program, its breakdown caused the director much irritation.
   (B) Knowing the cost of the Space Shuttle program. Its breakdown caused the director much irritation.
   (C) Knowing the cost of the Space Shuttle program, the director was greatly irritated by its breakdown.
   (D) By knowing the cost of the Space Shuttle program, its breakdown greatly irritated the director.
   (E) Knowledge of the cost of the Space Shuttle program: its breakdown greatly irritated the director.

3. In this particular job we have discovered that to be diligent is more important than being bright.

   (A) to be diligent is more important than being bright
   (B) for one to be diligent is more important than being bright
   (C) diligence is more important than brightness
   (D) being diligent is more important than to be bright
   (E) by being diligent is more important than being bright

4. On their return, they not only witnessed the sinking ship but the amazing escape of the passengers.

   (A) not only witnessed the sinking ship but the
   (B) not only witnessed the sinking ship, but the
   (C) did not only witness the sinking ship, but also the
   (D) witnessed not only the sinking ship but the
   (E) witnessed the sinking ship and also the

5. No one but him could have told them that the thief was I.

   (A) him could have told them that the thief was I
   (B) he could have told them that the thief was I
   (C) he could have told them that thief was me
   (D) him could have told them that the thief was me
   (E) he could have told them the thief was me

6. Either you transfer the data which was demanded or file a report explaining why you did not submit the overall annual figures.

   (A) Either you transfer the data which was demanded
   (B) You either transfer the data, which was demanded,
   (C) You either transfer the data which were demanded
   (D) Either you transfer the data, which was demanded,
   (E) Either you transfer the data, which were demanded,

7. On entering the stadium, cheers greeted them as a sign of universal approval of their great achievement.

   (A) On entering the stadium, cheers greeted them
   (B) On entering the stadium, they were greeted by cheers
   (C) While entering the stadium, cheers greeted them
   (D) On entering the stadium cheers greeted them
   (E) On entering the stadium: cheers greeted them

8. The set of propositions which was discussed by the panel have been published in the society journal.

   (A) which was discussed by the panel have
   (B) which were discussed by the panel have
   (C) that was discussed by the panel has
   (D) which were discussed by the panel has
   (E) which was discussed, by the panel, has

9. In a great amount of the requests, there have been very few that the staff could deal with efficiently.

   (A) In a great amount of the requests, there have been very few
   (B) Out of the great amount of the requests, there have been very little
   (C) In a great amount of the requests, there has been very few
   (D) In a great number of the requests, there have been very few
   (E) Of the great number of requests, there have been very few

10. They decided to honor Mr. Wilson, who <u>will be president of the club for ten years next Tuesday</u>.

    (A) will be president of the club for ten years next Tuesday
    (B) shall have been president of the club for ten years next Tuesday
    (C) next Tuesday will have been president of the club for ten years
    (D) next Tuesday has been president of the club for ten years
    (E) had been president of the club for ten years next Tuesday

11. After a careful evaluation of the circumstances surrounding the incident, we decided that we <u>neither have the authority nor</u> the means to cope with the problem.

    (A) neither have the authority nor
    (B) neither have authority or
    (C) have neither the authority nor
    (D) have neither the authority or
    (E) have not either the authority nor

12. <u>Everyone of us have understood that without him helping us</u> we would not have succeeded in our program over the past six months.

    (A) Everyone of us have understood that without him helping us
    (B) Everyone of us has understood that without his helping us
    (C) Everyone of us have understood that without his help
    (D) Everyone of us has understood that without him helping us
    (E) Every single one of us have understood that without him helping us

13. On the African continent, the incidence of vitamin <u>deficiencies correlates positively with</u> the level of solar radiation.

    (A) deficiencies correlates positively with
    (B) deficiencies correlate positively with
    (C) deficiencies, correlate positively with,
    (D) deficiencies correlate positively to
    (E) deficiencies correlates positively to

14. <u>A thoroughly frightened child was seen by her cowering in the corner of the room.</u>

    (A) A thoroughly frightened child was seen by her cowering in the corner of the room.
    (B) Cowering in the corner of the room a thoroughly frightened child was seen by her.
    (C) She saw, cowering in the corner of the room, a thoroughly frightened child.
    (D) A thoroughly frightened child, cowering in the corner of the room, was seen by her.
    (E) She saw a thoroughly frightened child who was cowering in the corner of the room.

15. <u>If they would have taken greater care</u> in the disposal of the nuclear waste, the disaster would not have occurred.

    (A) If they would have taken greater care
    (B) Unless they took greater care
    (C) Had they not taken greater care
    (D) If they had taken greater care
    (E) If they took greater care

16. <u>Neither the judge nor I am ready to announce who the winner is.</u>

    (A) Neither the judge nor I am ready to announce who the winner is.
    (B) Neither the judge nor I are ready to announce who the winner is.
    (C) Neither the judge nor I are ready to announce who is the winner.
    (D) Neither the judge nor I am ready to announce who is the winner.
    (E) Neither I or the judge are ready to announce who is the winner.

17. After adequate deliberation, the council <u>can see scarcely any valid reason for its</u> reviewing the request.

    (A) can see scarcely any valid reason for its
    (B) can not see scarcely any valid reason for its
    (C) can see any valid reason scarcely for its
    (D) can see scarcely any valid reason for it's
    (E) can scarcely see any valid reason for it's

18. Knowing little algebra, <u>it was difficult to solve the problem</u>.

    (A) it was difficult to solve the problem
    (B) the problem was difficult to solve
    (C) I found it difficult to solve the problem
    (D) the solution to the problem was difficult to solve
    (E) solving the problem was difficult

19. If she <u>were I, she would have accepted the prize if she had</u> won it.

    (A) were I, she would have accepted the prize if she had
    (B) was I, she would have accepted the prize if she would have
    (C) was I, she would have accepted the prize if she had
    (D) were I, she would have accepted the prize if she would have
    (E) were me, she would have accepted the prize if she had

20. We expect help <u>in providing adequate facilities and ample funds from everybody</u> in order to advance this vital program.

    (A) in providing adequate facilities and ample funds from everybody
    (B) in the provision of adequate facilities and ample funds from everybody
    (C) in providing adequate facilities and funds from everyone
    (D) with facilities and funds from everyone
    (E) from everybody in providing adequate facilities and ample funds

21. From the moment he took public office, his actions have <u>been loaded with significance and filled with worth</u>.

    (A) been loaded with significance and filled with worth
    (B) been significant and worthwhile
    (C) become loaded with significance and worth
    (D) to be loaded with significance and filled with worth
    (E) been actions of significance and worth

22. After several days' tour, we became convinced that <u>the climate of this deserted island was like Florida in winter</u>.

  (A) the climate of this deserted island was like Florida in winter
  (B) the climate of this deserted island was like that of Florida in winter
  (C) the climate of this desert Island was like Florida in winter
  (D) the climate of this deserted island in winter was like Florida
  (E) the climate of this desert island was as Florida in winter

23. The students have always had <u>a most sincere interest and admiration for</u> the important work of Professor Jakobsen.

  (A) a most sincere interest and admiration for
  (B) a most sincere interest in and admiration for
  (C) mostly a sincere interest and admiration for
  (D) a most sincere interest, and admiration for
  (E) a most sincere interest and an admiration for

24. I might have provided a happier <u>ending if I was the author of that novel</u>.

  (A) ending if I was the author of that novel
  (B) ending, if I were the author of that novel
  (C) ending. If I were the author of that novel
  (D) ending if I had been the author of that novel
  (E) ending, if I had to be the author of that novel

25. Last night, our guest lecturer spoke about the methods of controlling population growth, <u>the dangers involved in manipulating nature, and how to calculate</u> potential change in species' size.

  (A) the dangers involved in manipulating nature, and how to calculate
  (B) the dangers involved in manipulating nature and in calculating
  (C) how to manipulate nature, and how to calculate
  (D) the dangers involved in manipulating nature, and the method of calculating
  (E) how to manipulate nature and to calculate

If there is still time remaining, you may review the questions in this section only.
You may not turn to any other section of the test.

Section VIII   Problem Solving

TIME: 30 minutes

DIRECTIONS: Solve each of the following problems; then indicate the correct answer on the answer sheet. [On the actual test you will be permitted to use any space available on the examination paper for scratch work.]

NOTE: A figure that appears with a problem is drawn as accurately as possible so as to provide information that may help in answering the question. Numbers in this test are real numbers.

Use the following graphs for questions 1–3.

AVERAGE ANNUAL RECEIPTS AND OUTLAYS OF U.S. GOVERNMENT 1967–1970 IN PERCENTAGE

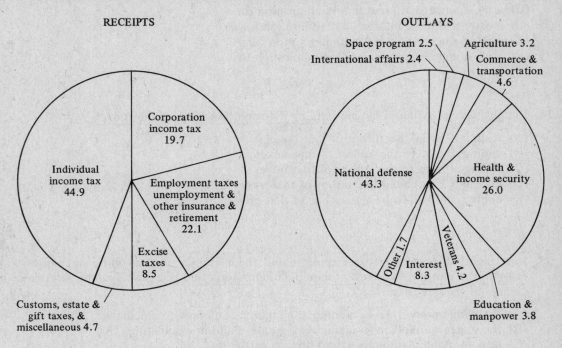

1. If the annual average receipts from the corporation income tax during the years 1967–1970 equal x, then the average annual receipts during this period were about

   (A) $\dfrac{x}{4}$

   (B) x^2

   (C) $3x$

   (D) $5x$

   (E) x^5

2. The average annual combined outlay for veterans, education and manpower, and health and income security was roughly what fraction of the average annual outlays?

   (A) ¼

   (B) ⅓

   (C) ⅖

   (D) ½

   (E) ⅔

3. If ⅝ of the average annual outlays for agriculture was spent in the western U.S., what percentage of average annual outlays was spent on agriculture in the western U.S.?

   (A) ⅝

   (B) 1

   (C) 1¼

   (D) 2

   (E) 3.2

4. The next number in the geometric progression 5,10,20 . . . is

(A) 25　　　　　　　　　　　　(D) 40
(B) 30　　　　　　　　　　　　(E) 50
(C) 35

5. Eggs cost 8¢ each. If the price of eggs increases by ⅛, how much will a dozen eggs cost?

(A) 90¢　　　　　　　　　　　(D) $1.12
(B) $1.08　　　　　　　　　　(E) $1.18
(C) $1.10

6. A trapezoid *ABCD* is formed by adding the isosceles right triangle *BCE* with base 5 inches to the rectangle *ABED* where *DE* is *t* inches. What is the area of the trapezoid in square inches?

(A) $5t + 12.5$　　　　　　　(D) $(t + 5)^2$
(B) $5t + 25$　　　　　　　　(E) $t^2 + 25$
(C) $2.5t + 12.5$

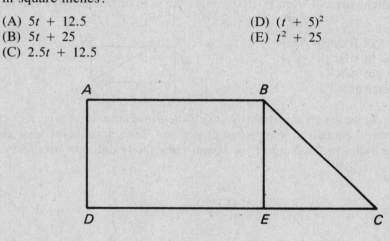

7. A manufacturer of jam wants to make a profit of $75 when he sells 300 jars of jam. It costs 65¢ each to make the first 100 jars of jam and 55¢ each to make each jar after the first 100. What price should he charge for the 300 jars of jam?

(A) $75　　　　　　　　　　　(D) $240
(B) $175　　　　　　　　　　(E) $250
(C) $225

8. A farmer walks around the outside of a rectangular field at a constant speed. It takes him twice as long to walk the length of the field as it takes him to walk the width of the field. If he walked 300 yards when he walked around the field, what is the area of the field in square yards?

(A) 5,000　　　　　　　　　　(D) 25,000
(B) 15,000　　　　　　　　　(E) 30,000
(C) 20,000

9. A company makes a profit of 7% selling goods which cost $2,000; it also makes a profit of 6% selling a machine which cost the company $5,000. How much total profit did the company make on both transactions?

(A) $300　　　　　　　　　　(D) $440
(B) $400　　　　　　　　　　(E) $490
(C) $420

10. If $\dfrac{x}{y} = \dfrac{3}{z}$, then $9y^2$ equals

(A) $\dfrac{x^2}{9}$

(B) x^3z

(C) x^2z^2

(D) $3x^2$

(E) $\left(\dfrac{1}{9}\right)x^2z^2$

11. The operation * applied to a number gives as its result 10 subtracted from twice the number. What is *(*9)?

(A) -11

(B) 6

(C) 8

(D) 9

(E) 36

12. *ABCD* is a rectangle. The length of *BE* is 4 and the length of *EC* is 6. The area of triangle *BEA* plus the area of triangle *DCE* minus the area of triangle *AED* is

(A) 0

(B) .4 of the area of triangle *AEB*

(C) .5 of the area of triangle *AED*

(D) .5 of the area of *ABCD*

(E) cannot be determined

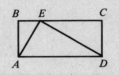

13. 36 identical chairs must be arranged in rows with the same number of chairs in each row. Each row must contain at least three chairs and there must be at least three rows. A row is parallel to the front of the room. How many different arrangements are possible?

(A) 2

(B) 4

(C) 5

(D) 6

(E) 10

14. Which of the following solids has the largest volume? (*Figures are not drawn to scale.*)

I. A cylinder of radius 5 mm and height 11 mm
(volume of a cylinder is $\pi r^2 h$)

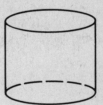

II. A sphere of radius 6mm
(volume of a sphere is $\dfrac{4}{3}\,\pi r^3$)

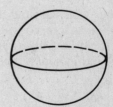

III. A cube with edge of 9mm
(volume of a cube is e^3)

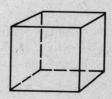

(A) I

(B) II

(C) III

(D) I and II

(E) II and III

15. If .2% of x is .03, then x is

(A) 150

(B) $66\frac{2}{3}$

(C) 15

(D) $6\frac{2}{3}$

(E) 1.5

16. A pension fund has a total of $1 million invested in stock of the ABC Company and bonds of the DEF Corporation. The ABC stock yields 12% in cash each year, and the DEF bonds pay 10% in cash each year. The pension fund received a total of $115,000 in cash from ABC stock and DEF bonds last year. How much money was invested in ABC stock?

(A) $750,000.00

(B) $600,000.00

(C) $500,000.00

(D) $333,333.33

(E) $250,000.00

17. The ratio of chickens to pigs to horses on a farm can be expressed as the triple ratio 20:4:6. If there are 120 chickens on the farm, then the number of horses on the farm is

(A) 4

(B) 6

(C) 24

(D) 36

(E) 60

18. If $x^2 - y^2 = 15$ and $x + y = 3$, then $x - y$ is

(A) -3

(B) 0

(C) 3

(D) 5

(E) cannot be determined

19. Tom's salary is currently $35,000. When Tom was hired 5 years ago, his salary was $10,000. By what percentage has Tom's salary increased since he was hired?

(A) $28\frac{4}{7}$

(B) 40

(C) 50

(D) 250

(E) 350

20. What is the area of the shaded region? The radius of the outer circle is a and the radius of each of the circles inside the large circle is $\frac{a}{3}$.

(A) 0

(B) $\left(\frac{1}{3}\right)\pi a^2$

(C) $\left(\frac{2}{3}\right)\pi a^2$

(D) $\left(\frac{7}{9}\right)\pi a^2$

(E) $\left(\frac{8}{9}\right)\pi a^2$

If there is still time remaining, you may review the questions in this section only.
You may not turn to any other section of the test.

Answers

Section I   Reading Comprehension

1. (B)	8. (B)	15. (D)	22. (A)
2. (C)	9. (E)	16. (E)	23. (A)
3. (D)	10. (D)	17. (B)	24. (A)
4. (C)	11. (E)	18. (E)	25. (B)
5. (D)	12. (C)	19. (A)	
6. (D)	13. (A)	20. (B)	
7. (E)	14. (B)	21. (C)	

Section II   Problem Solving

(Numbers in parentheses indicate the section in the Mathematics Review where material concerning the question is discussed.)

1. (B) (I-2)	6. (C) (I-3)	11. (D) (III-5)	16. (B) (II-2)
2. (A) (I-4)	7. (B) (I-7)	12. (B) (III-7, I-4)	17. (A) (IV-1)
3. (C) (II-5)	8. (C) (I-4)	13. (C) (I-4)	18. (C) (I-4, II
4. (C) (II-5,III-7)	9. (A) (II-2)	14. (C) (II-7)	19. (E) (I-2)
5. (E) (II-4)	10. (D) (II-1)	15. (E) (I-4)	20. (D) (III-7)

Section III   Analysis of Situations

1. (D)	11. (D)	21. (B)	31. (B)
2. (B)	12. (D)	22. (C)	32. (C)
3. (C)	13. (A)	23. (E)	33. (D)
4. (E)	14. (B)	24. (D)	34. (E)
5. (E)	15. (E)	25. (B)	35. (B)
6. (A)	16. (A)	26. (D)	
7. (E)	17. (E)	27. (A)	
8. (B)	18. (D)	28. (B)	
9. (B)	19. (E)	29. (B)	
10. (E)	20. (A)	30. (A)	

Section IV   Data Sufficiency

1. (E)	8. (B)	15. (E)	22. (B)
2. (B)	9. (E)	16. (B)	23. (C)
3. (D)	10. (D)	17. (C)	24. (B)
4. (A)	11. (D)	18. (E)	25. (D)
5. (E)	12. (C)	19. (A)	
6. (C)	13. (E)	20. (B)	
7. (D)	14. (D)	21. (A)	

Section V — Writing Ability

1. (B)	8. (B)	15. (B)	22. (D)
2. (D)	9. (D)	16. (E)	23. (C)
3. (C)	10. (A)	17. (B)	24. (B)
4. (E)	11. (E)	18. (C)	25. (E)
5. (A)	12. (E)	19. (B)	
6. (C)	13. (A)	20. (D)	
7. (D)	14. (D)	21. (D)	

Section VI — Analysis of Situations

1. (B)	11. (C)	21. (C)	31. (B)
2. (E)	12. (E)	22. (B)	32. (C)
3. (C)	13. (B)	23. (A)	33. (E)
4. (C)	14. (E)	24. (B)	34. (E)
5. (D)	15. (D)	25. (D)	35. (D)
6. (E)	16. (B)	26. (B)	
7. (B)	17. (B)	27. (E)	
8. (B)	18. (B)	28. (B)	
9. (E)	19. (A)	29. (C)	
10. (D)	20. (E)	30. (E)	

Section VII — Writing Ability

1. (C)	8. (D)	15. (D)	22. (B)
2. (C)	9. (E)	16. (A)	23. (B)
3. (C)	10. (C)	17. (A)	24. (D)
4. (D)	11. (C)	18. (C)	25. (D)
5. (A)	12. (B)	19. (A)	
6. (C)	13. (A)	20. (E)	
7. (B)	14. (C)	21. (B)	

Section VIII — Problem Solving

(Numbers in parentheses indicate the section in the Mathematics Review where material concerning the question is discussed.)

1. (D) (IV-2)	6. (A) (III-7)	11. (B) (II-1, 3)	16. (A) (II-2)
2. (B) (IV-2)	7. (E) (II-3)	12. (A) (III-7)	17. (D) (II-5)
3. (D) (IV-2)	8. (A) (III-7)	13. (C) (I-1)	18. (D) (II-1, 2)
4. (D) (II-6)	9. (D) (I-4)	14. (B) (III-8)	19. (D) (I-4)
5. (B) (I-2)	10. (C) (II-5, I-8)	15. (C) (I-3, 4, II-2)	20. (D) (III-7)

Analysis

Section I   Reading Comprehension

1. **(B)** See paragraph 1: "Under a perfectly sunny sky and from an apparently calm sea . . ." None of the other answer choices is particularly surprising.

2. **(C)** See the first sentence of the passage: ". . . distant lands or continents."

3. **(D)** See paragraph 2, line 1: "How are these waves formed? When a submarine earthquake occurs. . . ."

4. **(C)** See paragraph 2: "The swells in the ocean are sometimes nearly a mile wide. . . ."

5. **(D)** See paragraph 5: ". . . the Coast and Geodetic Survey initiated a program . . . to locate submarine earthquakes [and] tell how severe a submarine earthquake was. . . ."

6. **(D)** See paragraph 4.

7. **(E)** See paragraph 3: "These waves travel hundreds of miles an hour. . . ."

8. **(B)** See paragraph 3.

9. **(E)** All are mentioned in paragraph 5, except for the height of the wave.

10. **(D)** This is clearly a passage dealing with the economy and economic policy. Note that (E) is too vague; an *economic policy* textbook might have been a correct answer.

11. **(E)** All of the others are given in paragraph 2.

12. **(C)** See paragraph 2: ". . . consumer and business sentiment benefited from rising public expectations that a resolution of the conflict in Vietnam was in prospect and that East-West tensions were easing."

13. **(A)** See paragraph 3, line 1: "The underpinnings of the business expansion were to be found in part in the stimulative monetary and fiscal policies that had been pursued."

14. **(B)** See paragraph 4: ". . . there was actually a substantial deterioration in our trade account to a sizable deficit, almost two thirds of which was with Japan."

15. **(D)** See paragraph 5, lines 1–3: Only (D) was mentioned.

16. **(E)** See paragraph 5, sentence 3: "The Phase Three program of wage and price restraint can contribute to dampening inflation."

17. **(B)** See paragraph 5: ". . . the unemployment rates of a bit over 5 percent . . ."

18. **(E)** This expression is found throughout the passage, e.g.: in paragraph 1: ". . . when a poet has put his heart . . . into a poem, and sold it to a magazine, the scandal is greater. . . ."

19. **(A)** The passage treats the problem of the poet or writer who must "sell" his works to survive; therefore he acts like a businessman.

20. **(B)** See paragraph 1: They sold their poetry, i.e., ". . . submitted to the conditions which none can escape."

21. **(C)** See paragraph 1: ". . . the poem was not written for these dollars, but it is perfectly true that it was sold for them."

22. **(A)** See paragraph 2: Lord Byron refused payment for his work (although others gained monetarily from it).

23. **(A)** This is implied in paragraph 1: ". . . the poet would have been cared for by the whole human brotherhood, as any man should be who does the duty that every man owes it."

24. **(A)** The author proposes that until society changes its value system (which he does not foresee) the artist and writer must compromise as best they can with the existing system without, however, debasing their work.

25. **(B)** See paragraph 1: Exchanging their work for money does not mean that it was "written for these dollars," even though it was "sold for them." Moreover, the act of selling for gain "does not justify the conditions" or reality of the situation.

Section II   Problem Solving

1. **(B)** The time needed to complete the trip is $\left(6 - \frac{1}{4} - 1\frac{3}{8} - 2\frac{1}{3}\right)$ hours. This equals $6 - (1 + 2) - \left(\frac{1}{4} + \frac{3}{8} + \frac{1}{3}\right) = 3 - \frac{6 + 9 + 8}{24} = 3 - \frac{23}{24} = 2\frac{1}{24} = 2$ hours $2\frac{1}{2}$ minutes.

2. **(A)** The average has decreased by $500 - 400$ or 100 points during the week, so the percentage of decrease is 100/500 or 20%.

3. **(C)** Since there are 180 minutes in 3 hours, then $\frac{x}{8} = \frac{180}{18}$, where x is the number of cars washed in 3 hours. Therefore, $x = 8 \times 10 = 80$.

4. **(C)** If s and t denote the sides of the two squares, then $s^2 : t^2 = 2 : 1$, or $\frac{s^2}{t^2} = \frac{2}{1}$. Thus $\left(\frac{s}{t}\right)^2 = \frac{2}{1}$ and $\frac{s}{t} = \frac{\sqrt{2}}{1}$. Since the ratio of the perimeters is $4s : 4t = s : t$, (C) is the correct answer.

5. **(E)** The Venn diagram indicates the answer immediately. The region outside both circles denotes neither whitewall tires nor air-conditioning.

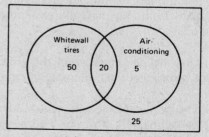

6. **(C)** Each share was worth $122.50 - 111.10 or $11.40 less in 1973 than it was in 1970. Therefore, the 100,000 shares were worth 100,000 × $11.40 or $1,140,000 less in 1973 than in 1970.

7. **(B)** Add up the daily wages to get the total wages for the week. $51.90 + 52.20 + 49.80 + 51.50 + 50.60 = $256.00. Divide $256.00 by 5 to get the average daily wage, $51.20.

8. **(C)** The interest on the first $600 is (.18) ($600) or $108 for a year. There is $5,400 of the loan in excess of $600; so he must pay (.17)(5,400) or $918 interest for the year on the $5,400. Therefore, the interest for one year will be $108 + $918 or $1,026.

9. **(A)** $4y - 6x = -2(3x - 2y) = -2(8) = -16$.

10. **(D)** Since the total distance is 200 kilometers, of which you fly x kilometers, you drive $(200 - x)$ kilometers. Therefore, the cost is $10x + (200 - x)12$, which is $10x - 12x + 2400$ or $2400 - 2x$ cents. The answer in dollars is obtained by dividing by 100, which is $(24 - .02x)$ dollars.

11. **(D)** Since the sides of the square equal the length of the rectangles, which is twice the width, the length of R_1 is 2 times its width.

12. **(B)** If A_1 denotes the increased area and A the original area, then $A_1 = 1.69A$, since A_1 is A increased by 69%. Thus, $s_1^2 = A_1 = 1.69A = 1.69s^2$, where s_1 is the increased side and s the original side. Since the square root of 1.69 is 1.3, we have $s_1 = 1.3s$ so s is increased by .3 or 30%.

13. **(C)** Since the dealer made a profit of 20%, he sold the car for 120% of what the car cost. Thus, if C is the cost of the car, 120% of $C = $1,380 or $(\%)C = $1,380. Therefore, $C = \%$ of $1,380, which is $1,150.

14. **(C)** STATEMENT I is not always true. For example, 1 is less than 5 and 1 is less than 6, but 6 is not less than 5.

   STATEMENT II is not always true, since ⅜ < ½ and ⅜ < ⅔ but ⅜ is not less than (½) (⅔) = ⅓.

   Since STATEMENT III is always true, (C) is the correct answer.

15. **(E)** The total number of workers is 80, and 35 of them work 40 or more hours. Therefore, ³⁵⁄₈₀ = .4375 = 43.75%.

16. **(B)** 15 people worked 40 to 44 hours, and 4 worked up to 29 hours. So $4x = 15$, which means $x = ¹⁵⁄₄ = 3¾$.

17. **(A)** STATEMENT I can be inferred, since the average number of hours worked is $\frac{3100}{80} = 38\frac{3}{4}$ which is less than 40.

STATEMENT II cannot be inferred, since there is no information about the number of workers who worked over 48 hours.

STATEMENT III is not true, since there are only 35 workers who worked 40 or more hours.

18. **(C)** The truck uses 30% more gasoline to travel the same distance at 70 mph than it does at 50 mph. Therefore, the truck requires 130% of a gallon of gasoline, which is 1.3 gallons, to travel 19.5 miles at 70 mph. So the truck will travel $(10/1.3)(19.5)$ or 150 miles on 10 gallons of gas at 70 mph.

19. **(E)** Convert ⅖ and ⅓ into fractions with denominators of 30. Since ⅖ = ¹²⁄₃₀ and ⅓ = ¹⁰⁄₃₀, ⅖ + ⅓ = ¹²⁄₃₀ + ¹⁰⁄₃₀ = ²²⁄₃₀, and x is equal to 22.

20. **(D)** The area of the rectangle is $4 \times 6 = 24$ square feet. Since 1 square foot is 144 square inches, the area of the rectangle is 3,456 square inches. Each square has an area of $(½)^2$ or ¼ square inches. Therefore, the number of squares needed = $3,456 \div ¼ = 3,456 \times 4 = 13,824$.

Section III   Analysis of Situations

1. **(D)** A *Major Assumption* of the government is that Abco will stay in business if the loan is granted.

2. **(B)** High unemployment in the country is a *Major Factor*, because it is a primary consideration in the decision as to whether to approve the additional loan.

3. **(C)** The dependence of shopkeepers on the existence of Abco is a *Minor Factor* in the government's weighing of the loan decision. Although not crucial in itself, the fact that shopkeepers may be harmed by an Abco bankruptcy helps to sway the government towards a decision to grant the loan.

4. **(E)** Investment incentives (concessions) were an important factor in Abco's decision to establish a plant in Frieland, but they do not figure in the government's decision as to whether to make the loan.

5. **(E)** The fact that Frieland is a developing country is not a consideration in the selection of an alternative course of action, nor is it a major assumption made by a decision maker.

6. **(A)** Finding a way to keep Abco operating is the *Major Objective* of the government, for both economic and political reasons.

7. **(E)** The initial training of workers at government expense has no bearing on the present decision.

8. **(B)** Poor worker-management relations is a *Major Factor* in the government's decision concerning the loan. It raises the problem of whether the company can become an economically viable institution.

9. **(B)** One of the government's economic policy goals is to increase exports. It is committed to supporting those companies that can contribute to this goal. Therefore, the export potential of Abco is a *Major Factor* in the decision, supporting the alternative of granting the company further financial support.

10. **(E)** There is nothing in the passage to suggest that the political *philosophy* of the opposition party is a consideration in the government's decision as to whether to make an additional loan. Of course, the political *consequence* (question 14) is important.

11. **(D)** The existence of a deadline ("a quick decision") is mentioned in the passage. The government *believes* that a quick decision is necessary to avoid criticism from the opposition. However, there are no facts cited to support this contention.

12. **(D)** The key word is "availability." No facts are mentioned to indicate that sufficient government funds are actually available to assist Abco.

13. **(A)** One *Major Objective* of the government is to prevent increased unemployment.

14. **(B)** The political consequence of Abco's pending bankruptcy is a *Major Factor* in the government's consideration of whether to grant the additional loan.

15. **(E)** The size of the population has no weight in the consideration of any decision alternative.

16. **(A)** Frieland encouraged investment in industries that would export most of their total output, so that the country could earn badly needed foreign exchange. Increasing foreign exchange reserves was a *Major Objective* of the government.

17. **(E)** According to the passage, government approval for an Abco factory was given "despite the fact that there was . . . surplus shoe production in Frieland." Apparently, the government chose to overlook the fact of overemployment in the shoe industry in their decision to grant approval to Abco.

18. **(D)** Abco had promised the government, among other things, to reduce shoe prices by 30 percent. This estimate was a projection supplied by management and was a *Major Assumption* of government decision makers.

19. **(E)** This fact was not related to a major decision or objective of the decision maker.

20. **(A)** The company had excess capacity and its utilization was a *Major Objective*.

21. **(B)** Although Conway's unit sales had remained constant, its share of total market had declined. Therefore, management decided to introduce a new line to increase both sales and market share.

22. **(C)** This is clearly a *Minor Factor*, having no direct influence on the company's objective.

23. **(E)** The placing of advertising is an *Unimportant Issue* not directly related to the problem.

24. **(D)** No information is given to substantiate management's *assumption* that the proposed line will be accepted by consumers.

25. **(B)** Growing price competition from small clock manufacturers led Conway management to decide on a new line which would be sold to dealers at a lower price than the existing line.

26. **(D)** Key words in the passage are "expected" and "hoped." That the line would be bought by these dealers was a *Major Assumption*.

27. **(A)** A *Major Objective* of management was to increase sales.

28. **(B)** Conway's reputation was very good. Because smaller manufacturers competed on either a price or a quality basis, reputation is an important factor to be considered.

29. **(B)** The fact that Conway's present line could not be discounted prevented the company from reaching a segment of the market that desired cheaper clocks. This was a *Major Factor* in the decision to market a line that would be discounted.

30. **(A)** Protecting the small dealer (against price competition) would have to be considered as an objective because it is the reason for the adoption of resale price maintenance.

31. **(B)** Styling was an important factor in the decision to market a new line of clocks. First, styling was important to maintain Conway's reputation for high quality. Second, styles were changed frequently by the industry. Third, advertising stressed up-to-date styling, an attribute of importance to consumers.

32. **(C)** Sales to department stores amounted to 20 percent of total wholesale sales (paragraph 5) and represented 60 to 70 out of 14,000 retail outlets. Therefore, sales to department stores is a *Minor Factor*.

33. **(D)** Conway management "thought" that existing retailers would also sell the Concord models. This supposition was considered in management's decision to market the new line of clocks.

34. **(E)** Conway policed dealer advertisements to make sure they were maintaining suggested price schedules. The mechanics of policing was not a factor related to the decision to market a new line.

35. **(B)** Growing price competition for small clock manufacturers was a major reason that management considered marketing a lower-priced line of clocks.

Section IV   Data Sufficiency

1. **(E)** A triangle with sides of lengths 3, 4, and 5 is a right triangle since $3^2 + 4^2 = 5^2$, and its perimeter is 12. A triangle with sides of lengths 2, 4⅘, and 5⅕ also has a perimeter of 12. And

since $2^2 + (4\frac{4}{5})^2 = (5\frac{1}{5})^2$, it too is a right triangle. Therefore, two triangles can satisfy STATEMENTS (1) and (2) yet not be congruent. On the other hand, any pair of congruent right triangles satisfy STATEMENTS (1) and (2). Thus, STATEMENTS (1) and (2) together are not sufficient to answer the question.

2. **(B)** $x^3 - 8 = 0$ has only $x = 2$ as a real solution. And 2 is greater than 0, so STATEMENT (2) alone is sufficient.

Since $x = 2$ and $x = -2$ are both solutions of $x^4 - 16 = 0$, STATEMENT (1) alone is not sufficient.

3. **(D)** STATEMENT (1) is sufficient since it implies that conveyer belt A loads $\frac{2}{3}$ of the hopper while conveyer belt B loads only $\frac{1}{3}$ with both working. Since conveyer belt A loads $\frac{2}{3}$ of the hopper in a hour, it will take $1 \div \frac{2}{3}$ or $1\frac{1}{2}$ hours to fill the hopper by itself.

STATEMENT (2) is also sufficient since it implies that conveyer belt B fills $\frac{1}{3}$ of the hopper in 1 hour. Thus, conveyer belt A loads $\frac{2}{3}$ in one hour, and that means conveyer belt A will take $1\frac{1}{2}$ hours by itself.

4. **(A)** The first fly will travel a distance equal to the circumference of the circle which is π times the diameter. The second fly will travel $4s$ where s is the length of a side. Since the diagonal of a square has length $\sqrt{2}s$, the second fly will travel $4/\sqrt{2}$ times the diagonal of the square. Therefore, (1) alone is sufficient, since $4/\sqrt{2} = 4\sqrt{2}/2 = 2\sqrt{2}$ which is less than π. (2) alone is not sufficient, since one fly might have crawled faster than the other.

5. **(E)** Using (1) and (2) together, it is only possible to determine the total amount paid for fire insurance in 1970 and 1972. Since no relation is given between the amounts paid in 1970 and 1972, there is not enough information to determine the cost in 1972.

6. **(C)** (2) alone is not sufficient since both $y = 2$ and $y = -2$ satisfy $y^2 - 4 = 0$. (1) alone is not sufficient, since $\frac{1}{2}$ is larger than 0 but less than 1 while 3 is larger than 0 and larger than 1. The only solution of $y^2 - 4 = 0$ which is larger than 0 is 2 which is larger than 1. Therefore, (1) and (2) are sufficient.

7. **(D)** Let x be the amount he was paid the first day. Then he was paid $x + 2$, $x + 4$, $x + 6$, $x + 8$, and $x + 10$ dollars for the succeeding days. (1) alone is sufficient, since the total he was paid is $(6x + 30)$ dollars, and we can solve $6x + 30 = 150$ (to find that he was paid \$20 for the first day). (2) alone is also sufficient. He was paid $\$(x + 10)$ on the sixth day, so (2) means that $(1.5)x = x + 10$ (which is the same as $x = 20$).

8. **(B)** Since 85% of \$3,000 is \$2,550, (2) alone is sufficient. (1) alone is not sufficient, since if x were 5% (1) would tell us the price of the car is less than \$2,600. But if x were 1%, (1) would imply that the price of the car is greater than \$2,600.

9. **(E)** Vertical angles are equal, so $c = d$. Since the sum of the angles in a triangle is 180°, $a + b + c = d + e + f$ which means $a + b = e + f$. If we use (1) and (2), we have $a + a = e + a$ so $e = a$. And we know the triangles are similar. However this does not give any information about the value of a, since any two similar triangles can be made to satisfy conditions (1) and (2). Therefore, (1) and (2) together are not sufficient.

10. **(D)** (1) alone is sufficient since $BC = AB$ implies $x = y = 40$. Since the sum of the angles in a triangle is 180°, z must equal 100. (2) alone is sufficient. Let D be the point where the bisector of angle B meets AC. Then according to (2), triangle BDC is a right triangle. Since angle y is 40°, the remaining angle in triangle BDC is 50° and equals $\frac{1}{2}z$, so $z = 100$.

11. **(D)** Since there are a bottom and 4 sides, each a congruent square, the amount of cardboard needed will be $5e^2$ where e is the length of an edge of the box. So we need to find e. (1) alone is sufficient. Since the area of the bottom is e^2, (1) means $e^2 = 4$ with $e = 2$ feet. (2) alone is also sufficient. Since the volume of the box is e^3, (2) means $e^3 = 8$ and $e = 2$ feet.

12. **(C)** The average weight of the books is the total weight of all the books divided by the number of books on the shelf. Thus (1) and (2) together are sufficient. (Solve $2.5 = \frac{40}{x}$ for x, the number of books on the shelf.) (1) alone is not sufficient, nor is (2) alone sufficient.

13. **(E)** If *ABCD* has the pairs of opposite sides equal and each angle is 90°, then it is a rectangle. But there are many quadrilaterals which have two opposite sides equal with one angle a right angle. For example, the figure has $AB = DC$ and $x = 90$, but it is not a rectangle. Therefore, (1) and (2) together are insufficient.

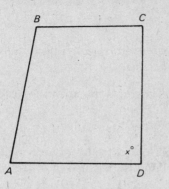

14. **(D)** (2) alone is sufficient, since if $a_3 = 1$ then $a_4 = (a_3)^2 = 1^2 = 1$; then $a_5 = (a_4)^2 = 1^2 = 1$. (1) alone is also sufficient. If $a_1 = -1$ then $a_2 = (a_1)^2 = 1$, and $a_3 = (a_2)^2 = 1$, but $a_3 = 1$ is given by (2) which we know is sufficient.

15. **(E)** Let *J*, *F* and *C* stand for the weekly salaries of John, Fred, and Chuck. (1) says $J = 2F$ and (2) says $F = .4(C + J)$. Since there is no information given about the values of *C* or *F*, we cannot deduce the value of *J*. Therefore, (1) and (2) together are insufficient.

16. **(B)** STATEMENT (2) alone is sufficient. $2x + 4y = 2(x + 2y)$, so if $2x + 4y = 12$ then $2(x + 2y) = 12$ and $x + 2y = 6$.

STATEMENT (1) alone is insufficient. If you only use STATEMENT (1) then you can get $x + 2y = x + y + y = 4 + y$ but there is no information on the value of *y*.

17. **(C)** Since the sum of the angles in a triangle is 180°, $x + y + z = 180$. Using STATEMENT (1) alone we have $2y + y + z = 3y + z = 180$, which is insufficient to determine *y* or *z*.

Using STATEMENT (2) alone we have $x + 1.5z + z = x + 2.5z = 180$, which is not sufficient to determine *x* or *z*.

However, if we use both STATEMENTS (1) and (2) we obtain $3y + z = 4.5z + z = 5.5z = 180$, so $z = \frac{2}{11}$ of 180. Now $y = \frac{3}{2}$ of *z*, so $y = \frac{3}{11}$ of 180, and $x = \frac{6}{11}$ of 180. Therefore, angle *BAC* is not a right angle and STATEMENTS (1) and (2) are sufficient.

18. **(E)** Since STATEMENT (1) only describes *x* and STATEMENT (2) only describes *y* both are needed to get an answer. Using STATEMENT (2), STATEMENT (1) becomes $x = 2k = 2 \cdot 2y = 4y$, so $x = 4y$. However, this is not sufficient, since if $y = -1$ then $x = -4$ and -4 is less than -1, but if $y = 1$ then $x = 4$ and *x* is greater than *y*.

19. **(A)** If each doll costs $8, then 65 dolls will cost $8 \times 65 = 520. Using STATEMENT (1), the profit is selling price minus cost $= $750 - $520 = 230, so STATEMENT (1) alone is sufficient.

STATEMENT (2) alone is not sufficient since you need to know what price the dolls sell for to find the profit.

20. **(B)** STATEMENT (2) alone is sufficient. 60% of the people have blue eyes and 50% of the people have blue eyes and blond hair, so 60% − 50% = 10% of the people have blue eyes but do not have blond hair.

STATEMENT (1) alone is not sufficient. Using STATEMENT (1) alone we can only find out how many people have blond hair and do not have blue eyes, in addition to what is given.

21. **(A)** The sum of the angles of the pentagon is 540°. (The sum of the angles of a polygon with *n* sides which is inscribed in a circle is $(n - 2)180°$.) STATEMENT (1) alone is sufficient. If the polygon is regular, all angles are equal and so angle *ABC* is $\frac{1}{5}$ of 540° or 108°.

STATEMENT (2) alone is insufficient because the radius of the circle does not give any information about the angles of the pentagon.

22. **(B)** The area of a circle is πr^2, where *r* is the radius of the circle. Since *O* is a point on the line *AB*, *AB* is a diameter of the circle. Therefore, since a radius is one half of a diameter, the radius of the circle is 3.5 inches. Thus, STATEMENT (2) alone is sufficient.

STATEMENT (1) alone is insufficient since there is no relation between *DE* and the radius.

23. **(C)** Using STATEMENT (2) alone we have $10,000 + x + y = $34,000$, where *x* is the taxable income for 1972 and *y* is the taxable income for 1973. So STATEMENT (2) alone is not sufficient.

STATEMENT (1) alone is not sufficient since no relation is given between taxable income in 1972 and 1973.

STATEMENTS (1) and (2) together give the equation $10,000 + $12,000 + y = $34,000, which means y = $12,000, where y is the taxable income for 1973.

24. **(B)** STATEMENT (2) alone is sufficient. 3 feet 2 inches is more than half of 6 feet so the piece of string 3 feet 2 inches long must be longer than the other 2 pieces put together.

STATEMENT (1) alone is insufficient. There is not enough information to find the length of *any* of the three pieces of string.

25. **(D)** Let *r* be the fraction of the job the 4 apprentices finish in 1 hour. Then ¹⁄ᵣ is the amount of time in hours that it will take the 4 apprentices to finish the job. So it is sufficient to find *r*. The group of 5 craftsmen finishes ⅓ of the job per hour, so each craftsman does ¹⁄₁₅ of the job per hour.

STATEMENT (1) alone is sufficient. An apprentice will do ⅔ of ¹⁄₁₅ = ²⁄₄₅ of the job per hour, so r = ⁸⁄₄₅.

STATEMENT (2) alone is sufficient. The craftsmen and the apprentices together will finish ⅓ + r of the job per hour. Since it takes them 1²²⁄₂₃ hours to finish the job, (⅓ + r) (⁴⁵⁄₂₃) = 1 which can be solved for r.

Section V   Writing Ability

1. **(B)** This corrects the misuse of the subjunctive.

2. **(D)** This corrects the error in the case of the pronoun. Choice E corrects the error in case but introduces an error in tense.

3. **(C)** The improper use of the pronouns *one* and *you* is corrected in Choice C.

4. **(E)** The omission of the past participle *been* is corrected in Choice E.

5. **(A)** No error.

6. **(C)** This corrects the dangling participle

7. **(D)** Misuse of word. The pronoun is *its*.

8. **(B)** This corrects the unnecessary switch in the pronouns, *anyone—you*.

9. **(D)** This corrects the error in tense and in the use of adjective or adverbial clauses.

10. **(A)** No error.

11. **(E)** *The reason is that* is preferable to *The reason is because*.

12. **(E)** This corrects the error in parallel structure.

13. **(A)** No error.

14. **(D)** This corrects the double negative (*hadn't hardly*) and the misuse of *those* with *kind*.

15. **(B)** This corrects the dangling participle and the misuse of *stole* for *stolen*.

16. **(E)** This question involves two aspects of correct English. *Neither* should be followed by *nor*; *either* by *or*. Choices A and D are, therefore, incorrect. The words *neither . . . nor* and *either . . . or* should be placed before the two items being discussed—*to be critical* and *to criticize*. Choice E meets both requirements.

17. **(B)** This question tests agreement. Agreement between subject and verb and pronoun and antecedent are both involved. *Community* (singular) needs a singular verb, *influences*. Also, the pronoun which refers to *community* should be singular (*its*). Choice B is best.

18. **(C)** *Would have been expected* is incorrect as a verb in a clause introduced by the conjunction *if*. *Had been expected* or *were expected* is preferable. *To have considered* does not follow correct sequence of tense and should be changed to *to consider*. Choice E changes the thought of the sentence and is illogical. Choice C is best.

19. **(B)** As presented, the sentence contains a dangling participle, *depending*. Choice B corrects this error. The other choices change the emphasis presented by the author.

20. **(D)** This question is similar to question 16. *Either . . . or* should precede the two choices offered (*in war* and *in peace*.).

21. **(D)** This phrase expresses the thought more compactly than the other four choices.

22. **(D)** Choices A and B are incorrect because of the dangling participle. Choice C is incoherent. Choice E also has a dangling phrase.

23. **(C)** Parallel structure requires that *not only . . . but also* immediately precede the words they limit.

24. **(B)** Given a choice, most authorities recommend the use of the active voice whenever possible. Thus, *affords* in Choice B is stronger than *are afforded* in Choices A, C, and D. The meaning of the sentence is changed in Choice E.

25. **(E)** This is an incomplete sentence or fragment. The sentence needs a verb to establish a principle clause. Choice E provides the verb (*is recognized*) and presents the only complete sentence in the group.

Section VI   Analysis of Situations

1. **(B)** A primary consideration in Mr. Krim's decision as to whether to buy the firm is the degree of public awareness of the company's products, since this will help determine the company's chances for future success.

2. **(E)** Caspi's marketing ability is not important to Krim's decision to buy the company, since Caspi will retire if the company is sold.

3. **(C)** While not crucial in itself, this feature of Posturemat mattresses is one of the strengths of the product and so of the company as a whole.

4. **(C)** This is a *Minor Factor*, since older consumers play only a small role in determining the present and future success of the company.

5. **(D)** Krim's assumption about retailers' attitudes is contrary to the facts given in the passage. Only if Posturemat launches an aggressive advertising campaign may retailers' attitudes change. But this is an assumption, not a fact.

6. **(E)** The importation of latex is not an issue in the decision as to whether to buy the company.

7. **(B)** Posturemat's declining market share is a *Major Factor* in the decision as to whether to buy the company. The issue is whether the decline can be halted and reversed.

8. **(B)** Although Krim had a preconceived notion of whether to buy the company, he nevertheless has asked Sims to prepare a marketing analysis upon which he will base his final decision.

9. **(E)** The ownership of the premises is not critical to the success of the firm or its viability as an enterprise.

10. **(D)** That attitudes toward foam rubber mattresses can be changed by advertising is an assumption of Mr. Krim not supported by any facts cited in the passage.

11. **(C)** The advantage or attribute of orthopedic qualities in particular is a *Minor Factor* in the decision as to whether to buy the company. The *overall* quality of Posturemat (including other attributes) would constitute a *Major Factor*.

12. **(E)** The fact that synthetic mattresses are made of polyurethane does not influence the selection of an alternative, and is related to neither a major objective nor an assumption of the decision maker.

13. **(B)** The passage states that Lefko handled the sales force of Posturemat. If he leaves, Krim will not have a single experienced manager to handle marketing and sales. Therefore, Krim must weigh the impact that Lefko's leaving would have on the management of the firm. It is, therefore, a *Major Factor*.

14. **(E)** The age of the machinery does not mean that the equipment was obsolete or useless (see paragraph 3). Therefore, the condition does not directly influence any of the decision alternatives.

15. **(D)** Krim *felt* that introduction of a new management team would instill confidence in the firm and allow for increased credit (see the last paragraph). However, no evidence is presented in the passage to support his feeling.

16. **(B)** Caspi attributed Posturemat's loss in market share to the competition of spring mattresses, which had "similar attributes" and were "less costly to manufacture, but sold at about the same price as Posturemat. . . ." Whether Posturemat would in the future successfully compete against these conditions is a *Major Factor* in the decision to buy the company.

17. **(B)** The total cost of a press was a *Major Factor* in the determination of the new price and distribution channels.

18. **(B)** Adoption of a new service policy was a *Major Factor* in the consideration of distribution channel alternatives.

19. **(A)** Adoption of a new distribution channel was a major outcome or goal sought by Mr. Grace.

20. **(E)** Working in his father's shop lacked any impact on the consideration of a new distribution channel.

21. **(C)** The price of a new press was comprised of manufacturing cost, and the costs of delivery, instruction, training, and service. Service expenses were only one consideration in the pricing and channel selection decisions.

22. **(B)** The lack of selling effort on the part of Grace's present distributors was a *Major Factor* in the decision to select a new distribution channel.

23. **(A)** Note the key word "desire." The desire for broader distribution is an outcome sought by the decision maker.

24. **(B)** Note the word "complaints." Complaints from buyers were one of several factors contributing to the outcome sought, a new distribution channel.

25. **(D)** Note the key word "possibility." Management "felt that manufacturers' representatives . . . would provide the desired coverage. . . ." The question deals with an opinion or belief. This *assumption* is important to the decision because it is related to a major advantage of a channel alternative.

26. **(B)** Although the passage states that distributors "felt" the price was high, it is not an assumption. It is explicitly stated that some distributors dropped Grace products, while others made no effort to sell them because of the high price.

27. **(E)** The fact that discounts were cut is mentioned in the passage. However, there is nothing in the passage to suggest that this action played a significant role in the decision process.

28. **(B)** The difficulty in finding representatives who were regularly calling on prospective buyers of Grace products was a major consideration in a decision alternative (to use manufacturers' representatives extensively).

29. **(C)** The fact that some prospective representatives carried appliances is a narrower consideration within the more important consideration of whether they carried competing products.

30. **(E)** Defects in Fabri-Tools was not an issue in any alternative course of action considered by Grace management.

31. **(B)** Delays in completing service calls was a major issue in the consideration to select a new distribution system.

32. **(C)** Lack of distributor facilities was one of the factors contributing to delays in completing service calls. Lack of facilities alone is not a major issue. The major issue is the resulting effect, i.e., delays in completing service calls.

33. **(E)** Although one might assume that the issue of distributor discounts is an important one, it does not appear to significantly influence the consideration of an alternative course of action on the part of a decision maker.

34. **(E)** In the past, Mr. Grace earned income for his company by arranging meetings for distributors. More recently, that effort does not play a role in Mr. Grace's decision making.

35. **(D)** It is stated in the passage that "no discounts were allowed on direct sales by the company to users, no matter how large." The decision was taken because it "was reasoned" that a quantity discount would not induce buyers to purchase more than they need.

Section VII   Writing Ability

1. **(C)** The sequence of tenses is incorrect. According to the meaning of the sentence, John's wanting comes *before*, not *after*, John's going.

2. **(C)** The participle *knowing* should be followed by *director*, the noun it modifies.

3. **(C)** Parallelism: a similar form is required on either side of the comparison.

4. **(D)** They did witness two things, *not only the sinking ship* but the *escape* as well.

5. **(A)** *But* meaning *except* is always followed by the objective pronoun, and the copula *was* takes the subjective *I*.

6. **(C)** *Either . . . or* connect *transfer* and *file*. *Data* here is plural and requires the verb *were*.

7. **(B)** A participial phrase at the beginning of a sentence must be followed by the word it modifies.

8. **(D)** The *set has been* published, while the *propositions* (individually) *were* discussed.

9. **(E)** *Requests* as a countable noun requires *number*, whereas only *a few* of them could be dealt with.

10. **(C)** The future perfect tense is required here, since the action continues from the past into the future (*next Tuesday*).

11. **(C)** *Neither . . . nor* apply to *authority* and *means* and must precede them directly.

12. **(B)** *Everyone* is singular and requires the singular *has*. The preposition *without* requires the gerund *helping* preceded by the possessive *his*.

13. **(A)** The *incidence* (singular) *correlates*. The preposition *with* is correct.

14. **(C)** This is a suspenseful sentence since what *She saw* is held off to the very last word in the sentence. Also, an active verb, *saw*, is preferable to the passive *was seen*.

15. **(D)** The correct form of the past conditional requires the past perfect in the conditional clause: *had taken*.

16. **(A)** In *neither . . . nor* constructions, the verb is matched to the noun or pronoun that immediately precedes it. The sentence is not a question, and thus does not become inverted.

17. **(A)** *Scarcely* applies to the *valid reason* and thus must precede it directly. *Scarcely*, having a negative connotation, does not require a negation of the verb.

18. **(C)** This answer provides the correct subject (*I*) modified by the verbal *knowing*.

19. **(A)** No error. The sequence of tenses requires that the past perfect tense be used in the conditional clause *if she had won it*. Also, *I* is required after a form of the verb *to be*.

20. **(E)** *Everybody* is expected to help. The sense demands that *from everybody* be placed in the general position. *In the provision of* makes the sentence unnecessarily bulky.

21. **(B)** The original sentence is too wordy.

22. **(B)** The *climate* can only be compared to another climate.

23. **(B)** *Interest in* a subject and *admiration for* it: the prepositions must remain.

24. **(D)** This is a past conditional and requires the past perfect in the conditional clause. There is no punctuation before the *if*.

25. **(D)** Parallel structure demands a list of noun phrases: *the methods, the dangers,* and *the method*.

Section VIII   Problem Solving

1. **(D)** The corporation income tax accounted for 19.7% of all average annual receipts for the years 1967–1970. Since 19.7% is about 20% or $\frac{1}{5}$, the average annual receipts were about 5 times the average annual receipts from the corporation income tax. Therefore, the answer is $5x$.

2. **(B)** Veterans received 4.2%, education and manpower 3.8%, and health and income security 26% of the average annual outlays; so together the three categories received 4.2% + 3.8% + 26% or 34%. Since $\frac{1}{3}$ is $33\frac{1}{3}$%, 34% is roughly $\frac{1}{3}$.

3. **(D)** Since $\frac{5}{8}$ of 3.2% = 5 × .4% = 2.0%, the correct answer is (D).

4. **(D)** $\frac{10}{5} = 2 = \frac{20}{10}$, so the ratio of successive terms of the progression is 2. Therefore, the term which follows 20 is 2 times 20 or 40.

5. **(B)** Since ⅛ of 8¢ is 1¢, each egg will cost 8¢ + 1¢ or 9¢ after the price has increased. The price of a dozen eggs will be 12 × 9¢ or $1.08.

6. **(A)** The area of trapezoid ABCD equals the area of rectangle ABED, which is $t \times 5$ (since $BE = BC = 5$), plus the area of triangle BEC, which is $\frac{(5 \times 5)}{2}$. The answer is thus $5t + 12.5$.

7. **(E)** The selling price of the jars should equal cost + $75. The cost of making 300 jars = $(100)65¢ + (200)55¢ = \$65 + \$110 = \$175$. So the selling price should be $175 + $75 or $250.

8. **(A)** Since it takes twice as long to walk the length as the width, $l = 2w$ where l is the length and w the width. The perimeter equals $2l + 2w = 3l = 300$ yards, so the length is 100 yards and the width is 50 yards. Therefore, the area is $50 \times 100 = 5{,}000$ square yards.

9. **(D)** The company's profit $= (2{,}000)(.07) + (5{,}000)(.06) = \$140 + \$300 = \$440$.

10. **(C)** Since $\frac{x}{y} = \frac{3}{z}$, $xz = 3y$ and $9y^2 = (3y)^2$; so $9y^2 = (xz)^2 = x^2z^2$.

11. **(B)** *9 is 10 subtracted from twice 9, or 2(9) − 10. So *9 is $18 - 10 = 8$. Thus *(*9) will be *8. *8 is 10 subtracted from twice 8, or $16 - 10 = 6$. Therefore 6 is the correct answer.

12. **(A)** The area of a triangle is 1/2 the base times the altitude. Since ABCD is a rectangle, the triangles AED, BEA, and CDE all have the same altitude (AB). The base of AED is AD, which is equal to the base of ABE (BE) plus the base of CDE (EC). So the area of ABE plus the area of CDE is equal to the area of AED. Therefore, subtracting the area of ADE from the sum of the areas of ABE and CDE gives a result of 0.

13. **(C)** Let c be the number of chairs in a row and r be the number of rows. Since each row must have the same number of chairs, c times r must equal 36. We need to know how many ways we can write 36 as a product of two integers each greater than or equal to three, since each way to write 36 corresponds to an acceptable arrangement of the room. (c must be greater than or equal to 3 since each row must contain at least 3 chairs. In the same way, r must be greater than or equal to 3 because there must

be at least 3 rows.) Writing 36 as a product of primes, we obtain $36 = 2 \times 18 = 2 \times 2 \times 9 = 2 \times 2 \times 3 \times 3$. So 36 can be written as 1×36, 2×18, 3×12, 4×9, 6×6, 9×4, 12×3, 18×2, and 36×1. Of these possibilities, 5 (3×12, 4×9, 6×6, 9×4, and 12×3) satisfy the requirements. Therefore, there are 5 arrangements.

14. **(B)** Volume of the cube is $9 \times 9 \times 9 = 729$ cubic mm. The sphere has volume $\frac{4}{3}\pi 6 \times 6 \times 6 = 288\pi$. Since π is greater than 3, 288π is greater than 729. The volume of the cylinder is $5 \times 5 \times 11 \pi = 275\pi$. So the sphere has the largest volume.

You can save a lot of time in this problem if you do not change π to a decimal and then multiply the answers out.

15. **(C)** Change the percentage to a decimal to compute. Since .2% is .002, you know that .002x = .03. So x is $\frac{.03}{.002} = \frac{30}{2} = 15$.

16. **(A)** Let s be the amount invested in ABC stock and b be the amount invested in DEF bonds. Then $s + b = 1{,}000{,}000$ and $.12s + .10b = 115{,}000$. Solve $s + b = 1{,}000{,}000$ for b and you get $b = 1{,}000{,}000 - s$. Now substitute this into the second equation. The result is $.12s + .10(1{,}000{,}000 - s) = .12s - .10s + 100{,}000 = 115{,}000$. So $.02s = 15{,}000$, which gives $s = 15{,}000/.02$. Therefore, $s = \$750{,}000$.

17. **(D)** A triple ratio is a compact way of expressing three ratios. So the ratio of chickens to pigs to horses, $20:4:6$, means that the ratio of chickens to pigs is $20:4$ and the ratio of pigs to horses is $4:6$ and the ratio of chickens to horses is $20:6$. Thus for every 20 chickens there are 6 horses. So if there are 120 chickens, there are x horses where x satisfies the proportion $\frac{120}{20} = \frac{x}{6}$. Cross multiplying gives $20x = 720$ or $x = 36$. You can check the answer by seeing that the ratio of chickens to horses is $120:36$, which is the same ratio as $20:6$.

18. **(D)** $x^2 - y^2$ be factored into $(x + y)(x - y)$. So if $x + y$ is equal to 3, then $x^2 - y^2 = 15$ is equivalent to $3(x - y) = 15$. Dividing each side of the equation by 3, we obtain $x - y = \frac{15}{3} = 5$.

19. **(D)** His salary has increased by $35,000 − $10,000 = $25,000. So his salary has increased by $\dfrac{\$25,000}{\$10,000} = 2.5 = 250\%$. The question asks for the percentage of increase. His current salary is 350% of his starting salary, but his salary has not increased by $35,000. Notice that the period of 5 years has nothing to do with the correct solution.

20. **(D)** The area of a circle is π times the square of the radius of the circle. So the area of the large circle is πa^2, and the area of each of the interior circles is $\pi\left(\dfrac{a}{3}\right)^2 = \left(\dfrac{1}{9}\right)\pi a^2$. Since there are two interior circles the shaded region has area equal to $\pi a^2 - 2\left(\left(\dfrac{1}{9}\right)\pi a^2\right) = \left(1 - \dfrac{2}{9}\right)\pi a^2 = \left(\dfrac{7}{9}\right)\pi a^2$.

Evaluating Your Score

Tabulate your score for each section of Sample Test 1 according to the directions on pages 4–5 and record the results in the Self-scoring Table below. Then find your rating for each score on the Self-scoring Scale and record it in the appropriate blank.

Self-scoring Table

SECTION	SCORE	RATING
1		
2		
3		
4		
5		
6		
7		
8		

Self-scoring Scale

RATING

SECTION	POOR	FAIR	GOOD	EXCELLENT
1	0–12+	13–17+	18–21+	22–25
2	0–9+	10–13+	14–17+	18–20
3	0–17+	18–24+	25–31+	32–35
4	0–12+	13–17+	18–21+	22–25
5	0–12+	13–17+	18–21+	22–25
6	0–17+	18–24+	25–31+	32–35
7	0–12+	13–17+	18–21+	22–25
8	0–9+	10–13+	14–17+	18–20

Study again the Review sections covering material in Sample Test 1 for which you had a rating of FAIR or POOR. Then go on to Sample Test 2.

To obtain an approximation of your GMAT score see page 5.

Answer Sheet—Sample Test 2

Section I Reading Comprehension	Section III Problem Solving		Section VI Problem Solving	
1. Ⓐ Ⓑ Ⓒ Ⓓ Ⓔ	1. Ⓐ Ⓑ Ⓒ Ⓓ Ⓔ	28. Ⓐ Ⓑ Ⓒ Ⓓ Ⓔ	1. Ⓐ Ⓑ Ⓒ Ⓓ Ⓔ	28. Ⓐ Ⓑ Ⓒ Ⓓ Ⓔ
2. Ⓐ Ⓑ Ⓒ Ⓓ Ⓔ	2. Ⓐ Ⓑ Ⓒ Ⓓ Ⓔ	29. Ⓐ Ⓑ Ⓒ Ⓓ Ⓔ	2. Ⓐ Ⓑ Ⓒ Ⓓ Ⓔ	29. Ⓐ Ⓑ Ⓒ Ⓓ Ⓔ
3. Ⓐ Ⓑ Ⓒ Ⓓ Ⓔ	3. Ⓐ Ⓑ Ⓒ Ⓓ Ⓔ	30. Ⓐ Ⓑ Ⓒ Ⓓ Ⓔ	3. Ⓐ Ⓑ Ⓒ Ⓓ Ⓔ	30. Ⓐ Ⓑ Ⓒ Ⓓ Ⓔ
4. Ⓐ Ⓑ Ⓒ Ⓓ Ⓔ	4. Ⓐ Ⓑ Ⓒ Ⓓ Ⓔ	31. Ⓐ Ⓑ Ⓒ Ⓓ Ⓔ	4. Ⓐ Ⓑ Ⓒ Ⓓ Ⓔ	31. Ⓐ Ⓑ Ⓒ Ⓓ Ⓔ
5. Ⓐ Ⓑ Ⓒ Ⓓ Ⓔ	5. Ⓐ Ⓑ Ⓒ Ⓓ Ⓔ	32. Ⓐ Ⓑ Ⓒ Ⓓ Ⓔ	5. Ⓐ Ⓑ Ⓒ Ⓓ Ⓔ	32. Ⓐ Ⓑ Ⓒ Ⓓ Ⓔ
6. Ⓐ Ⓑ Ⓒ Ⓓ Ⓔ	6. Ⓐ Ⓑ Ⓒ Ⓓ Ⓔ	33. Ⓐ Ⓑ Ⓒ Ⓓ Ⓔ	6. Ⓐ Ⓑ Ⓒ Ⓓ Ⓔ	33. Ⓐ Ⓑ Ⓒ Ⓓ Ⓔ
7. Ⓐ Ⓑ Ⓒ Ⓓ Ⓔ	7. Ⓐ Ⓑ Ⓒ Ⓓ Ⓔ	34. Ⓐ Ⓑ Ⓒ Ⓓ Ⓔ	7. Ⓐ Ⓑ Ⓒ Ⓓ Ⓔ	34. Ⓐ Ⓑ Ⓒ Ⓓ Ⓔ
8. Ⓐ Ⓑ Ⓒ Ⓓ Ⓔ	8. Ⓐ Ⓑ Ⓒ Ⓓ Ⓔ	35. Ⓐ Ⓑ Ⓒ Ⓓ Ⓔ	8. Ⓐ Ⓑ Ⓒ Ⓓ Ⓔ	35. Ⓐ Ⓑ Ⓒ Ⓓ Ⓔ
9. Ⓐ Ⓑ Ⓒ Ⓓ Ⓔ	9. Ⓐ Ⓑ Ⓒ Ⓓ Ⓔ		9. Ⓐ Ⓑ Ⓒ Ⓓ Ⓔ	
10. Ⓐ Ⓑ Ⓒ Ⓓ Ⓔ	10. Ⓐ Ⓑ Ⓒ Ⓓ Ⓔ		10. Ⓐ Ⓑ Ⓒ Ⓓ Ⓔ	
11. Ⓐ Ⓑ Ⓒ Ⓓ Ⓔ	11. Ⓐ Ⓑ Ⓒ Ⓓ Ⓔ		11. Ⓐ Ⓑ Ⓒ Ⓓ Ⓔ	
12. Ⓐ Ⓑ Ⓒ Ⓓ Ⓔ	12. Ⓐ Ⓑ Ⓒ Ⓓ Ⓔ		12. Ⓐ Ⓑ Ⓒ Ⓓ Ⓔ	
13. Ⓐ Ⓑ Ⓒ Ⓓ Ⓔ	13. Ⓐ Ⓑ Ⓒ Ⓓ Ⓔ		13. Ⓐ Ⓑ Ⓒ Ⓓ Ⓔ	
14. Ⓐ Ⓑ Ⓒ Ⓓ Ⓔ	14. Ⓐ Ⓑ Ⓒ Ⓓ Ⓔ		14. Ⓐ Ⓑ Ⓒ Ⓓ Ⓔ	
15. Ⓐ Ⓑ Ⓒ Ⓓ Ⓔ	15. Ⓐ Ⓑ Ⓒ Ⓓ Ⓔ		15. Ⓐ Ⓑ Ⓒ Ⓓ Ⓔ	
16. Ⓐ Ⓑ Ⓒ Ⓓ Ⓔ	16. Ⓐ Ⓑ Ⓒ Ⓓ Ⓔ		16. Ⓐ Ⓑ Ⓒ Ⓓ Ⓔ	
17. Ⓐ Ⓑ Ⓒ Ⓓ Ⓔ	17. Ⓐ Ⓑ Ⓒ Ⓓ Ⓔ		17. Ⓐ Ⓑ Ⓒ Ⓓ Ⓔ	
18. Ⓐ Ⓑ Ⓒ Ⓓ Ⓔ	18. Ⓐ Ⓑ Ⓒ Ⓓ Ⓔ		18. Ⓐ Ⓑ Ⓒ Ⓓ Ⓔ	
19. Ⓐ Ⓑ Ⓒ Ⓓ Ⓔ	19. Ⓐ Ⓑ Ⓒ Ⓓ Ⓔ		19. Ⓐ Ⓑ Ⓒ Ⓓ Ⓔ	
20. Ⓐ Ⓑ Ⓒ Ⓓ Ⓔ	20. Ⓐ Ⓑ Ⓒ Ⓓ Ⓔ		20. Ⓐ Ⓑ Ⓒ Ⓓ Ⓔ	
21. Ⓐ Ⓑ Ⓒ Ⓓ Ⓔ				
22. Ⓐ Ⓑ Ⓒ Ⓓ Ⓔ				
23. Ⓐ Ⓑ Ⓒ Ⓓ Ⓔ				
24. Ⓐ Ⓑ Ⓒ Ⓓ Ⓔ				
25. Ⓐ Ⓑ Ⓒ Ⓓ Ⓔ				

Section II Reading Comprehension	Section IV Analysis of Situations	Section V Data Sufficiency	Section VII Analysis of Situations	Section VIII Writing Ability
1. Ⓐ Ⓑ Ⓒ Ⓓ Ⓔ	1. Ⓐ Ⓑ Ⓒ Ⓓ Ⓔ	1. Ⓐ Ⓑ Ⓒ Ⓓ Ⓔ	1. Ⓐ Ⓑ Ⓒ Ⓓ Ⓔ	1. Ⓐ Ⓑ Ⓒ Ⓓ Ⓔ
2. Ⓐ Ⓑ Ⓒ Ⓓ Ⓔ	2. Ⓐ Ⓑ Ⓒ Ⓓ Ⓔ	2. Ⓐ Ⓑ Ⓒ Ⓓ Ⓔ	2. Ⓐ Ⓑ Ⓒ Ⓓ Ⓔ	2. Ⓐ Ⓑ Ⓒ Ⓓ Ⓔ
3. Ⓐ Ⓑ Ⓒ Ⓓ Ⓔ	3. Ⓐ Ⓑ Ⓒ Ⓓ Ⓔ	3. Ⓐ Ⓑ Ⓒ Ⓓ Ⓔ	3. Ⓐ Ⓑ Ⓒ Ⓓ Ⓔ	3. Ⓐ Ⓑ Ⓒ Ⓓ Ⓔ
4. Ⓐ Ⓑ Ⓒ Ⓓ Ⓔ	4. Ⓐ Ⓑ Ⓒ Ⓓ Ⓔ	4. Ⓐ Ⓑ Ⓒ Ⓓ Ⓔ	4. Ⓐ Ⓑ Ⓒ Ⓓ Ⓔ	4. Ⓐ Ⓑ Ⓒ Ⓓ Ⓔ
5. Ⓐ Ⓑ Ⓒ Ⓓ Ⓔ	5. Ⓐ Ⓑ Ⓒ Ⓓ Ⓔ	5. Ⓐ Ⓑ Ⓒ Ⓓ Ⓔ	5. Ⓐ Ⓑ Ⓒ Ⓓ Ⓔ	5. Ⓐ Ⓑ Ⓒ Ⓓ Ⓔ
6. Ⓐ Ⓑ Ⓒ Ⓓ Ⓔ	6. Ⓐ Ⓑ Ⓒ Ⓓ Ⓔ	6. Ⓐ Ⓑ Ⓒ Ⓓ Ⓔ	6. Ⓐ Ⓑ Ⓒ Ⓓ Ⓔ	6. Ⓐ Ⓑ Ⓒ Ⓓ Ⓔ
7. Ⓐ Ⓑ Ⓒ Ⓓ Ⓔ	7. Ⓐ Ⓑ Ⓒ Ⓓ Ⓔ	7. Ⓐ Ⓑ Ⓒ Ⓓ Ⓔ	7. Ⓐ Ⓑ Ⓒ Ⓓ Ⓔ	7. Ⓐ Ⓑ Ⓒ Ⓓ Ⓔ
8. Ⓐ Ⓑ Ⓒ Ⓓ Ⓔ	8. Ⓐ Ⓑ Ⓒ Ⓓ Ⓔ	8. Ⓐ Ⓑ Ⓒ Ⓓ Ⓔ	8. Ⓐ Ⓑ Ⓒ Ⓓ Ⓔ	8. Ⓐ Ⓑ Ⓒ Ⓓ Ⓔ
9. Ⓐ Ⓑ Ⓒ Ⓓ Ⓔ	9. Ⓐ Ⓑ Ⓒ Ⓓ Ⓔ	9. Ⓐ Ⓑ Ⓒ Ⓓ Ⓔ	9. Ⓐ Ⓑ Ⓒ Ⓓ Ⓔ	9. Ⓐ Ⓑ Ⓒ Ⓓ Ⓔ
10. Ⓐ Ⓑ Ⓒ Ⓓ Ⓔ	10. Ⓐ Ⓑ Ⓒ Ⓓ Ⓔ	10. Ⓐ Ⓑ Ⓒ Ⓓ Ⓔ	10. Ⓐ Ⓑ Ⓒ Ⓓ Ⓔ	10. Ⓐ Ⓑ Ⓒ Ⓓ Ⓔ
11. Ⓐ Ⓑ Ⓒ Ⓓ Ⓔ	11. Ⓐ Ⓑ Ⓒ Ⓓ Ⓔ	11. Ⓐ Ⓑ Ⓒ Ⓓ Ⓔ	11. Ⓐ Ⓑ Ⓒ Ⓓ Ⓔ	11. Ⓐ Ⓑ Ⓒ Ⓓ Ⓔ
12. Ⓐ Ⓑ Ⓒ Ⓓ Ⓔ	12. Ⓐ Ⓑ Ⓒ Ⓓ Ⓔ	12. Ⓐ Ⓑ Ⓒ Ⓓ Ⓔ	12. Ⓐ Ⓑ Ⓒ Ⓓ Ⓔ	12. Ⓐ Ⓑ Ⓒ Ⓓ Ⓔ
13. Ⓐ Ⓑ Ⓒ Ⓓ Ⓔ	13. Ⓐ Ⓑ Ⓒ Ⓓ Ⓔ	13. Ⓐ Ⓑ Ⓒ Ⓓ Ⓔ	13. Ⓐ Ⓑ Ⓒ Ⓓ Ⓔ	13. Ⓐ Ⓑ Ⓒ Ⓓ Ⓔ
14. Ⓐ Ⓑ Ⓒ Ⓓ Ⓔ	14. Ⓐ Ⓑ Ⓒ Ⓓ Ⓔ	14. Ⓐ Ⓑ Ⓒ Ⓓ Ⓔ	14. Ⓐ Ⓑ Ⓒ Ⓓ Ⓔ	14. Ⓐ Ⓑ Ⓒ Ⓓ Ⓔ
15. Ⓐ Ⓑ Ⓒ Ⓓ Ⓔ	15. Ⓐ Ⓑ Ⓒ Ⓓ Ⓔ	15. Ⓐ Ⓑ Ⓒ Ⓓ Ⓔ	15. Ⓐ Ⓑ Ⓒ Ⓓ Ⓔ	15. Ⓐ Ⓑ Ⓒ Ⓓ Ⓔ
16. Ⓐ Ⓑ Ⓒ Ⓓ Ⓔ	16. Ⓐ Ⓑ Ⓒ Ⓓ Ⓔ	16. Ⓐ Ⓑ Ⓒ Ⓓ Ⓔ	16. Ⓐ Ⓑ Ⓒ Ⓓ Ⓔ	16. Ⓐ Ⓑ Ⓒ Ⓓ Ⓔ
17. Ⓐ Ⓑ Ⓒ Ⓓ Ⓔ	17. Ⓐ Ⓑ Ⓒ Ⓓ Ⓔ	17. Ⓐ Ⓑ Ⓒ Ⓓ Ⓔ	17. Ⓐ Ⓑ Ⓒ Ⓓ Ⓔ	17. Ⓐ Ⓑ Ⓒ Ⓓ Ⓔ
18. Ⓐ Ⓑ Ⓒ Ⓓ Ⓔ	18. Ⓐ Ⓑ Ⓒ Ⓓ Ⓔ	18. Ⓐ Ⓑ Ⓒ Ⓓ Ⓔ	18. Ⓐ Ⓑ Ⓒ Ⓓ Ⓔ	18. Ⓐ Ⓑ Ⓒ Ⓓ Ⓔ
19. Ⓐ Ⓑ Ⓒ Ⓓ Ⓔ	19. Ⓐ Ⓑ Ⓒ Ⓓ Ⓔ	19. Ⓐ Ⓑ Ⓒ Ⓓ Ⓔ	19. Ⓐ Ⓑ Ⓒ Ⓓ Ⓔ	19. Ⓐ Ⓑ Ⓒ Ⓓ Ⓔ
20. Ⓐ Ⓑ Ⓒ Ⓓ Ⓔ	20. Ⓐ Ⓑ Ⓒ Ⓓ Ⓔ	20. Ⓐ Ⓑ Ⓒ Ⓓ Ⓔ	20. Ⓐ Ⓑ Ⓒ Ⓓ Ⓔ	20. Ⓐ Ⓑ Ⓒ Ⓓ Ⓔ
21. Ⓐ Ⓑ Ⓒ Ⓓ Ⓔ	21. Ⓐ Ⓑ Ⓒ Ⓓ Ⓔ	21. Ⓐ Ⓑ Ⓒ Ⓓ Ⓔ	21. Ⓐ Ⓑ Ⓒ Ⓓ Ⓔ	21. Ⓐ Ⓑ Ⓒ Ⓓ Ⓔ
22. Ⓐ Ⓑ Ⓒ Ⓓ Ⓔ	22. Ⓐ Ⓑ Ⓒ Ⓓ Ⓔ	22. Ⓐ Ⓑ Ⓒ Ⓓ Ⓔ	22. Ⓐ Ⓑ Ⓒ Ⓓ Ⓔ	22. Ⓐ Ⓑ Ⓒ Ⓓ Ⓔ
23. Ⓐ Ⓑ Ⓒ Ⓓ Ⓔ	23. Ⓐ Ⓑ Ⓒ Ⓓ Ⓔ	23. Ⓐ Ⓑ Ⓒ Ⓓ Ⓔ	23. Ⓐ Ⓑ Ⓒ Ⓓ Ⓔ	23. Ⓐ Ⓑ Ⓒ Ⓓ Ⓔ
24. Ⓐ Ⓑ Ⓒ Ⓓ Ⓔ	24. Ⓐ Ⓑ Ⓒ Ⓓ Ⓔ	24. Ⓐ Ⓑ Ⓒ Ⓓ Ⓔ	24. Ⓐ Ⓑ Ⓒ Ⓓ Ⓔ	24. Ⓐ Ⓑ Ⓒ Ⓓ Ⓔ
25. Ⓐ Ⓑ Ⓒ Ⓓ Ⓔ	25. Ⓐ Ⓑ Ⓒ Ⓓ Ⓔ	25. Ⓐ Ⓑ Ⓒ Ⓓ Ⓔ	25. Ⓐ Ⓑ Ⓒ Ⓓ Ⓔ	25. Ⓐ Ⓑ Ⓒ Ⓓ Ⓔ
	26. Ⓐ Ⓑ Ⓒ Ⓓ Ⓔ		26. Ⓐ Ⓑ Ⓒ Ⓓ Ⓔ	
	27. Ⓐ Ⓑ Ⓒ Ⓓ Ⓔ		27. Ⓐ Ⓑ Ⓒ Ⓓ Ⓔ	

Sample Test 2

Section I   Reading Comprehension

TIME: 30 minutes

DIRECTIONS: This part contains three reading passages. You are to read each one carefully. When answering the questions, you *will* be allowed to refer back to the passages. The questions are based on what is *stated* or *implied* in each passage. You have thirty minutes to complete this section.

Passage 1:

The following passage was written in 1964.

The main burden of assuring that the resources of the federal government are well managed falls on relatively few of the five million men and women whom it employs. Under the department and agency heads there are 8,600 political, career, military, and foreign service executives—the top managers and professionals—
(5)   who exert major influence on the manner in which the rest are directed and utilized. Below their level there are other thousands with assignments of some managerial significance, but we believe that the line of demarcation selected is the best available for our purposes in this attainment.

In addition to Presidential appointees in responsible posts, the 8,600 include the
(10)   three highest grades under the Classification Act; the three highest grades in the postal field service; comparable grades in the foreign service; general officers in the military service; and similar classes in other special services and in agencies or positions excepted from the Classification Act.

There is no complete inventory of positions or people in federal service at this
(15)   level. The lack may be explained by separate agency statutes and personnel systems, diffusion among so many special services, and absence of any central point (short of the President himself) with jurisdiction over all upper-level personnel of the government.

This Committee considers establishment and maintenance of a central inventory
(20)   of these key people and positions to be an elementary necessity, a first step in improved management throughout the Executive Branch.

Top Presidential appointees, about 500 of them, bear the brunt of translating the philosophy and aims of the current administration into practical programs. This group includes the secretaries and assistant secretaries of cabinet departments,
(25)   agency heads and their deputies, heads and members of boards and commissions with fixed terms, and chiefs and directors of major bureaus, divisions, and services. Appointments to many of these politically sensitive positions are made on recommendation by department or agency heads, but all are presumably responsible to Presidential leadership.

(30)   One qualification for office at this level is that there be no basic disagreement with Presidential political philosophy, at least so far as administrative judgments and actions are concerned. Apart from the bi-partisan boards and commissions, these men are normally identified with the political party of the President, or are sympathetic to it, although there are exceptions.

(35)   There are four distinguishable kinds of top Presidential appointees, including:

—Those whom the President selects at the outset to establish immediate and effective control over the government (e.g., Cabinet secretaries, agency heads, his own White House staff and Executive Office Personnel).

(40)   —Those selected by department and agency heads in order to establish control within their respective organizations (e.g.—assistant secretaries, deputies, assistants to, and major line posts in some bureaus and divisions).

—High-level appointees who—though often requiring clearance through political or interest group channels, or both—must have known scientific or technical competence (e.g.—the Surgeon General, the Commissioner of Educa-

(45)   tion).

—Those named to residual positions traditionally filled on a partisan patronage basis.

(50)   These appointees are primarily regarded as policy makers and overseers of policy execution. In practice, however, they usually have substantial responsibilities in line management, often requiring a thorough knowledge of substantive agency programs.

1. According to the passage, about how many top managerial professionals work for the federal government?

(A) five million
(B) two million
(C) twenty thousand
(D) nine thousand
(E) five hundred

2. No complete inventory exists of positions in the three highest levels of government service because

(A) no one has bothered to count them
(B) computers cannot handle all the data
(C) separate agency personnel systems are used
(D) the President has never requested such information
(E) the Classification Act prohibits such a census

3. Top Presidential appointees have as their central responsibility the

(A) prevention of politically motivated interference with the actions of their agencies
(B) monitoring of government actions on behalf of the President's own political party
(C) translation of the aims of the administration into practical programs
(D) investigation of charges of corruption within the government
(E) maintenance of adequate controls over the rate of government spending

4. One exception to the general rule that top Presidential appointees must be in agreement with the President's political philosophy may be found in

(A) most cabinet-level officers
(B) members of the White House staff
(C) bi-partisan boards and commissions
(D) those offices filled on a patronage basis
(E) offices requiring scientific or technical expertise

5. Applicants for Presidential appointments are usually identified with or are members of

(A) large corporations
(B) the foreign service
(C) government bureaus
(D) academic circles
(E) the President's political party

6. Appointees that are selected directly by the President include

(A) U.S. marshals and attorneys
(B) military officers
(C) agency heads
(D) assistant secretaries
(E) congressional committee members

7. Appointees usually have to possess expertise in

(A) line management
(B) military affairs
(C) foreign affairs
(D) strategic planning
(E) constitutional law

8. According to the passage, Presidential appointees are regarded primarily as

(A) political spokesmen
(B) policy makers
(C) staff managers
(D) scientific or technical experts
(E) business executives

9. Appointees selected by department and agency heads include

(A) military men
(B) cabinet secretaries
(C) deputy secretaries
(D) diplomats
(E) residual position holders

Passage 2:

The first and decisive step in the expansion of Europe overseas was the conquest of the Atlantic Ocean. That the nation to achieve this should be Portugal was the logical outcome of her geographical position and her history. Placed on the extreme margin of the old, classical Mediterranean world and facing the untraversed ocean,
(5) Portugal could adapt and develop the knowledge and experience of the past to meet the challenge of the unknown. Some centuries of navigating the coastal waters of Western Europe and Northern Africa had prepared Portuguese seamen to appreciate the problems which the Ocean presented and to apply and develop the methods necessary to overcome them. From the seamen of the Mediterranean, particularly
(10) those of Genoa and Venice, they had learned the organization and conduct of a mercantile marine, and from Jewish astronomers and Catalan mapmakers the rudiments of navigation. Largely excluded from a share in Mediterranean commerce at a time when her increasing and vigorous population was making heavy demands on her resources, Portugal turned southwards and westwards for opportunities of
(15) trade and commerce. At this moment of national destiny it was fortunate for her that in men of the calibre of Prince Henry, known as the Navigator, and King John II she found resolute and dedicated leaders.

(20)

(25)

(30)

(35)

The problems to be faced were new and complex. The conditions for navigation and commerce in the Mediterranean were relatively simple, compared with those in the western seas. The landlocked Mediterranean, tideless and with a climatic regime of regular and well-defined seasons, presented few obstacles to sailors who were the heirs of a great body of sea lore garnered from the experiences of many centuries. What hazards there were, in the form of sudden storms or dangerous coasts, were known and could be usually anticipated. Similarly the Mediterranean coasts, though they might be for long periods in the hands of dangerous rivals, were described in sailing directions or laid down on the portolan charts drawn by Venetian, Genoese and Catalan cartographers. Problems of determining positions at sea, which confronted the Portuguese, did not arise. Though the Mediterranean seamen by no means restricted themselves to coastal sailing, the latitudinal extent of the Mediterranean was not great, and voyages could be conducted from point to point on compass bearings; the ships were never so far from land as to make it necessary to fix their positions in latitude by astronomical observations. Having made a landfall on a bearing, they could determine their precise position from prominent landmarks, soundings or the nature of the sea bed, after reference to the sailing directions or charts.

(40)

(45)

By contrast, the pioneers of ocean navigation faced much greater difficulties. The western ocean which extended, according to the speculations of the cosmographers, through many degrees of latitude and longitude, was an unknown quantity, but certainly subjected to wide variations of weather and without known bounds. Those who first ventured out over its waters did so without benefit of sailing directions or traditional lore. As the Portuguese sailed southwards, they left behind them the familiar constellations in the heavens by which they could determine direction and the hours of the night, and particularly the pole-star from which by a simple operation they could determine their latitude. Along the unknown coasts they were threatened by shallows, hidden banks, rocks and contrary winds and currents, with no knowledge of convenient shelter to ride out storms or of very necessary watering places. It is little wonder that these pioneers dreaded the thought of being forced on to a lee shore or of having to choose between these inshore dangers and the unrecorded perils of the open sea.

10. Before the expansion of Europe overseas could take place

   (A) vast sums of money had to be raised
   (B) an army had to be recruited
   (C) the Atlantic Ocean had to be conquered
   (D) ships had to be built
   (E) seamen had to be trained

11. One of Portugal's leaders, known as the Navigator, was in reality

   (A) Christopher Columbus
   (B) King John II
   (C) a Venetian
   (D) Prince Henry
   (E) Prince Paul

12. Portugal was adept at exploring unknown waters because she possessed all of the following except

   (A) a navy
   (B) past experience
   (C) experienced navigators
   (D) experienced mapmakers
   (E) extensive trade routes

13. In addition to possessing the necessary resources for exploration, Portugal was the logical country for this task because of her

(A) wealth
(B) navigational experience
(C) geographical position
(D) prominence
(E) ability

14. The Portuguese learned navigational methods and procedures from all of the following except

(A) Jews
(B) Catalans
(C) Genoese
(D) Venetians
(E) Aegeans

15. Mediterranean seamen generally kept close to shore because

(A) they were afraid of pirates
(B) they feared being forced to a lee shore
(C) they lacked navigational ability
(D) they feared running into storms
(E) the latitudinal extent of the Mediterranean was not great

16. Hazards such as sudden storms and dangerous coasts were

(A) predictable risks
(B) unknown risks
(C) unknown to the area
(D) a major threat to exploration
(E) no threat to navigation

17. Sailing close to the coast enabled seamen to

(A) reach their destination faster
(B) navigate without sailing directions
(C) determine their positions from landmarks
(D) determine their longitude and latitude
(E) avoid dangerous shoals

Passage 3:

I decided to begin the term's work with the short story since that form would be the easiest for [the police officers], not only because most of their reading up to then had probably been in that genre, but also because a study of the reaction of people to various situations was something they relied on in their daily work. For instance, they had to be able to predict how others would react to their directives and interventions before deciding on their own form of action; they had to be able to take in the details of a situation quickly and correctly before intervening. No matter how factual and sparse police reports may seem to us, they must make use of a selection of vital detail, similar to that which a writer of a short story has to make.

This was taught to me by one of my students, a captain, at the end of the term. I had begun the study of the short story by stressing the differences between a factual report, such as a scientist's or a policeman's report, and the presentation of a creative writer. While a selection of necessary details is involved in both, the officer must remain neutral and clearly try to present a picture of the facts, while the artist usually begins with a preconceived message or attitude which is then transmitted through the use of carefully selected details of action described in words intended to provoke associations and emotional reactions in the reader. Only at the end of the term did the captain point out to me that he and his men also try to evaluate the events they describe and that their description of a sequence of events must of necessity be structured and colored by their understanding of what has taken place.

The policemen's reactions to events and characters in the stories were surprisingly unprejudiced. . . . They did not object to writers whose stories had to do with their protagonist's rebellion against society's accepted values. Nor did stories in which the strong father becomes the villain and in which our usual ideals of manhood are turned around offend them. The many hunters among my students readily granted the message in those hunting tales in which sensitivity triumphs over male aggressiveness, stories that show the boy becoming a man because he *fails* to shoot the deer, goose, or catbird. The only characters they did object to were those they thought unrealistic. As the previous class had done, this one also excelled in interpreting the ways in which characters reveal themselves, subtly manipulate and influence each other; they, too, understood how the story usually saves its insight, its revelation, for the end.

This almost instinctive grasp of the writing of fiction was revealed when the policemen volunteered to write their own short stories. . . . They not only took great pains with plot and character, but with style and language. The stories were surprisingly well written, revealing an understanding of what a solid short story must contain: the revelation of character, the use of background description and language to create atmosphere and mood, the need to sustain suspense and yet make each event as it occurs seem natural, the insight achieved either by the characters in the story or the reader or both. They tended to favor surprise endings. Some stories were sheer fantasies, or derived from previous reading, films, or television shows. Most wrote stories, obviously based on their own experiences, that revealed the amazing distance they must put between their personal lives and their work, which is part of the training for being a good cop. These stories, as well as their discussions of them, showed how coolly they judged their own weaknesses as well as the humor with which they accepted some of the difficulties or injustices of existence. Despite their authors' unmistakable sense of irony and awareness of corruption, these stories demonstrated how clearly, almost naively, these policemen wanted to continue to believe in some of the so-called American virtues—that courage is worth the effort and will be admired; that hard work will be rewarded; that life is somehow good; and that, despite the weariness, boredom, and occasional ugliness and danger, despite all their dislike of most of their routine and despite their own occasional grousing and complaints, they somehow did like being cops; that life, even in a chaotic and violent world, is worth it after all.

18. Compared to the artist, the policeman is

   (A) a man of action, not words
   (B) factual and not fanciful
   (C) neutral and not prejudiced
   (D) stoic and not emotional
   (E) aggressive and not passive

19. Policemen reacted to story events and characters

   (A) like most other people
   (B) according to a policeman's stereotyped image
   (C) like dilettantes
   (D) unrealistically
   (E) without emotion

20. To which sort of characters did policemen object?

    I. Unrealistic
   II. Emotional
 III. Sordid

  (A) I only
  (B) II only
  (C) I and II only
  (D) II and III only
  (E) I, II, and III

21. According to the passage, a short story should contain

  (A) elegant prose
  (B) suspense
  (C) objectivity
  (D) real-life experiences
  (E) irony

22. The instructor chose the short story because

    I. it was easy for the students
   II. students had experience with it
 III. students would enjoy it

  (A) I only
  (B) II only
  (C) I and II only
  (D) II and III only
  (E) I, II, and III

23. Like writers, policemen must

  (A) analyze situations
  (B) behave coolly
  (C) have an artistic bent
  (D) intervene quickly
  (E) attend college

24. According to the passage, most policemen wrote stories about

  (A) films
  (B) previous reading
  (C) American history
  (D) their work
  (E) politics

25. According to the author, policemen view their profession as

  (A) full of corruption
  (B) worth the effort
  (C) full of routine
  (D) poorly paid
  (E) dangerous but adventuresome

If there is still time remaining, you may review the questions in this section only.
You may not turn to any other section of the test.

Section II   Reading Comprehension

TIME: 30 minutes

DIRECTIONS: This part contains two reading passages. You are to be read each one carefully. When answering the questions, you *will* be able to refer to the passages. The questions are based on what is *stated* or *implied* in each passage. You have thirty minutes to complete this section.

Passage 1:

In the past, American colleges and universities were created to serve a dual purpose—to advance learning and to offer a chance to become familiar with bodies of knowledge already discovered to those who wished it. To create and to impart, these were the hallmarks of American higher education prior to the most recent,
(5)   tumultuous decades of the twentieth century. The successful institution of higher learning had never been one whose mission could be defined in terms of providing vocational skills or as a strategy for resolving societal problems. In a subtle way Americans believed postsecondary education to be useful, but not necessarily of immediate use. What the student obtained in college became beneficial in later
(10)   life—residually, without direct application in the period after graduation.

Another purpose has now been assigned to the mission of American colleges and universities. Institutions of higher learning—public or private—commonly face the challenge of defining their programs in such a way as to contribute to the service of the community.

(15)   This service role has various applications. Most common are programs to meet the demands of regional employment markets, to provide opportunities for upward social and economic mobility, to achieve racial, ethnic, or social integration, or more generally to produce "productive" as compared to "educated" graduates. Regardless of its precise definition, the idea of a service-university has won ac-
(20)   ceptance within the academic community.

One need only be reminded of the change in language describing the two-year college to appreciate the new value currently being attached to the concept of a service-related university. The traditional two-year college has shed its pejorative "junior" college label and is generally called a "community" college, a clearly
(25)   value-laden expression representing the latest commitment in higher education. Even the doctoral degree, long recognized as a required "union card" in the academic world, has come under severe criticism as the pursuit of learning for its own sake and the accumulation of knowledge without immediate application to a professor's classroom duties. The idea of a college or university that performs a
(30)   triple function—communicating knowledge to students, expanding the content of various disciplines, and interacting in a direct relationship with society—has been the most important change in higher education in recent years.

This novel development is often overlooked. Educators have always been familiar with those parts of the two-year college curriculum that have a "service"
(35)   or vocational orientation. Knowing this, otherwise perceptive commentaries on American postsecondary education underplay the impact of the attempt of colleges and universities to relate to, if not resolve, the problems of society. Whether the subject under review is student unrest, faculty tenure, the nature of the curriculum, the onset of collective bargaining, or the growth of collegiate bureaucracies, in
(40)   each instance the thrust of these discussions obscures the larger meaning of the emergence of the service-university in American higher education. Even the highly regarded critique of Clark Kerr, currently head of the Carnegie Foundation, which

set the parameters of academic debate around the evolution of the so-called "multiversity," failed to take account of this phenomenon and the manner in which
(45) its fulfillment changed the scope of higher education. To the extent that the idea of "multiversity" centered on matters of scale—how big is too big? how complex is too complex?—it obscured the fundamental question posed by the service-university: what is higher education supposed to do? Unless the commitment to what Samuel Gould has properly called the "communiversity" is clearly articu-
(50) lated, the success of any college or university in achieving its service-education functions will be effectively impaired. . . .

The most reliable report about the progress of Open Admissions became available at the end of August, 1974. What the document showed was that the dropout rate for all freshmen admitted in September, 1970, after seven semesters, was
(55) about 48 percent, a figure that corresponds closely to national averages at similar colleges and universities. The discrepancy between the performance of "regular" students (those who would have been admitted into the four-year colleges with 80% high school averages and into the two-year units with 75%) and Open Admissions freshmen provides a better indication of how the program worked. Taken
(60) together the attrition rate (from known and unknown causes) was 48 percent, but the figure for regular students was 36 percent while for Open Admissions categories it was 56 percent. Surprisingly, the statistics indicated that the four-year colleges retained or graduated more of the Open Admissions students than the two-year colleges, a finding that did not reflect experience elsewhere. Not sur-
(65) prisingly, perhaps, the figures indicated a close relationship between academic success defined as retention or graduation and high school averages. Similarly, it took longer for the Open Admissions students to generate college credits and graduate than regular students, a pattern similar to national averages. The most important statistics, however, relate to the findings regarding Open Admissions
(70) students, and these indicated as a projection that perhaps as many as 70 percent would not graduate from a unit of the City University.

1. The dropout rate among regular students in Open Admissions was approximately

(A) 35%
(B) 45%
(C) 55%
(D) 65%
(E) 75%

2. According to the passage, in the past it was *not* the purpose of American higher education to

(A) advance learning
(B) solve societal problems
(C) impart knowledge
(D) train workers
(E) prepare future managers

3. One of the recent, important changes in higher education relates to

(A) student representation on college boards
(B) faculty tenure requirements
(C) curriculum updates
(D) service-education concepts
(E) cost constraints

4. It was estimated that what percentage of Open Admissions students would fail to graduate from City University?

(A) 40%
(B) 50%
(C) 60%
(D) 70%
(E) 80%

5. According to the passage, the two-year college may be described as

   I. a junior college
  II. service-oriented
 III. a community college

(A) I only
(B) II only
(C) I and II only
(D) II and III only
(E) I, II, and III

6. The service role of colleges aims to

(A) improve services
(B) gain acceptance among educators
(C) serve the community
(D) provide skills for future use
(E) make graduates employable

7. The attrition rate for Open Admissions students was greater than the rate for regular students by what percent?

(A) 10%
(B) 20%
(C) 36%
(D) 40%
(E) 46%

8. Clark Kerr failed to take account of

(A) the "communiversity"
(B) collegiate bureacracies
(C) faculty tenure
(D) the service-university
(E) Open Admissions

9. The *average* attrition rate for regular and Open Admissions students was

(A) 36%
(B) 46%
(C) 56%
(D) 75%
(E) 92%

Passage 2:

    "The United States seems totally indifferent to our problems," charges French Foreign Minister Claude Cheysson, defending his Government's decision to defy President Reagan and proceed with construction of the Soviet gas pipeline. West German Chancellor Helmut Schmidt endorsed the French action and sounded a
(5)   similar note. Washington's handling of the pipeline, he said, has "cast a shadow

over relations" between Europe and the United States, "damaging confidence as regards future agreements."

(10) But it's not just the pipeline that has made a mockery of Versailles. Charges of unfair trade practices and threats of retaliation in a half-dozen industries are flying back and forth over the Atlantic—and the Pacific, too—in a worrisome crescendo. Businessmen, dismayed by the long siege of sluggish economic growth that has left some 30 million people in the West unemployed, are doing what comes naturally: pressuring politicians to restrain imports, subsidize exports, or both. Steelmakers in Bonn and Pittsburgh want help; so do auto makers in London and (15) Detroit, textile, apparel and shoe manufacturers throughout the West and farmers virtually everywhere.

Democratic governments, the targets of such pressure, are worried about their own political fortunes and embarrassed by their failure to generate strong growth and lower unemployment. The temptation is strong to take the path of least re-(20) sistance and tighten up on trade—even for a Government as devoted to the free market as Ronald Reagan's. In the past 18 months, Washington, beset by domestic producers, has raised new barriers against imports in autos, textiles and sugar. Steel is likely to be next. Nor is the United States alone. European countries, to varying degrees, have also sought to defend domestic markets or to promote (25) exports through generous subsidies. . . .

The upcoming meeting, to consider trade policy for the 1980's, is surely well timed. "It has been suggested often that world trade policy is 'at a crossroads'—but such a characterization of the early 1980's may be reasonably accurate," says C. Fred Bergsten, a former Treasury official in the Carter Administration, now (30) director of a new Washington think tank, the Institute for International Economics.

The most urgent question before the leaders of the industrial world is whether they can change the fractious atmosphere of this summer before stronger protective measures are actually put in place. So far, Mr. Bergsten, says, words have outweighed deeds. The trade picture is dismal. World trade reached some $2 trillion (35) a year in 1980 and hasn't budged since. In the first half of this year, Mr. Bergsten suspects that trade probably fell as the world economy stayed flat. But, according to his studies, increased protectionism is not the culprit for the slowdown in trade—at least not yet. The culprit instead is slow growth and recession, and the resulting slump in demand for imports. . . .

(40) But there are fresh problems today that could be severely damaging. Though tariffs and outright quotas are low after three rounds of intense international trade negotiations in the past two decades—new trade restraints, often bound up in voluntary agreements between countries to limit particular imports, have sprouted in recent years like mushrooms in a wet wood. Though the new protectionism is (45) more subtle than the old-fashioned variety, it is no less damaging to economic efficiency and, ultimately, to prospects for world economic growth.

A striking feature is that the new protectionism has focused on the same limited sectors in most of the major industrial countries—textiles, steel, electronics, footwear, shipbuilding and autos. Similarly, it has concentrated on supply from Japan (50) and the newly industrialized countries.

When several countries try to protect the same industries, the dealings become difficult. Take steel. Since 1977, the European Economic Community has been following a plan to eliminate excess steel capacity, using bilateral import quotas along the way to soften the blow to the steelworkers. The United States, responding (55) to similar pressure at home and to the same problem of a world oversupplied with steel, introduced a "voluntary" quota system in 1969, and, after a brief period of no restraint, developed a complex trigger price mechanism in 1978.

10. According to the passage, a "new protectionism" is evidenced by

    (A) bilateral import quotas
    (B) political suasion
    (C) lower than market prices
    (D) abrogating agreements
    (E) increased product standards

11. Increased protectionism has been caused by

    (A) the "cold war"
    (B) United States economic policy
    (C) increased unemployment
    (D) a breakdown in international law
    (E) a growth in cartels

12. A slowdown in world trade has been caused by

    (A) protectionism
    (B) slower population growth
    (C) less trade with Communist countries
    (D) economic recession
    (E) increased oil prices

13. The U.S. Government has increased barriers to the import of

    (A) autos, textiles, and sugar
    (B) autos, textiles, and steel
    (C) autos, electronics, and steel
    (D) shoes, textiles, and sugar
    (E) shoes, textiles, and steel

14. The best possible theme for the passage would be

    (A) "Reagan Administration's Economic Policies"
    (B) "International Trade Agreements in the 1960's"
    (C) "Tokyo Round of Trade Negotiations"
    (D) "A Perilous Time for World Trade"
    (E) "Problems and Prospects for World Exports"

15. In recent years, trade between nations has been constrained by

    (A) voluntary agreements limiting imports
    (B) rhetoric expressed by labor leaders
    (C) misalignment among world currencies
    (D) the free international exchange of goods
    (E) restrictive monetary and fiscal policies

16. While imports are restrained by barriers, exports are encouraged through

    (A) bargaining   (D) advertising
    (B) lowering prices   (E) dealing
    (C) subsidies

17. A means to increase steel capacity in the European Economic Community has been the use of

    (A) voluntary quotas   (D) trigger prices
    (B) bilateral quotas   (E) restraints
    (C) voluntary and bilateral quotas

Passage 3:

It is indisputable that in order to fulfill its many functions, water should be clean and biologically valuable. The costs connected with the provision of biologically valuable water for food production with the maintenance of sufficiently clean water, therefore, are primarily production costs. Purely "environmental" costs
(5) seem to be in this respect only costs connected with the safeguarding of cultural, recreational and sports functions which the water courses and reservoirs fulfill both in nature and in human settlements.

The pollution problems of the atmosphere resemble those of the water only partly. So far, the supply of air has not been deficient as was the case with water,
(10) and the dimensions of the air-shed are so vast that a number of people still hold the opinion that air need not be economized. However, scientific forecasts have shown that the time may be already approaching when clear and biologically valuable air will become problem No. 1.

Air being ubiquitous, people are particularly sensitive about any reduction in
(15) the quality of the atmosphere, the increased contents of dust and gaseous exhalations, and particularly about the presence of odors. The demand for purity of atmosphere, therefore, emanates much more from the population itself than from the specific sectors of the national economy affected by a polluted or even biologically aggressive atmosphere.

(20) The households' share in atmospheric pollution is far bigger than that of industry which, in turn, further complicates the economic problems of atmospheric purity. Some countries have already collected positive experience with the reconstruction of whole urban sectors on the basis of new heating appliances based on the combustion of solid fossil fuels; estimates of the economic consequences of such
(25) measures have also been put forward.

In contrast to water, where the maintenance of purity would seem primarily to be related to the costs of production and transport, a far higher proportion of the costs of maintaining the purity of the atmosphere derives from environmental considerations. Industrial sources of gaseous and dust emissions are well known
(30) and classified; their location can be accurately identified, which makes them controllable. With the exception, perhaps, of the elimination of sulphur dioxide, technical means and technological processes exist which can be used for the elimination of all excessive impurities of the air from the various emissions.

Atmospheric pollution caused by the private property of individuals (their dwell-
(35) ings, automobiles, etc.) is difficult to control. Some sources such as motor vehicles are very mobile, and they are thus capable of polluting vast territories. In this particular case, the cost of anti-pollution measures will have to be borne, to a considerable extent, by individuals, whether in the form of direct costs or indirectly in the form of taxes, dues, surcharges, etc.

(40) The problem of noise is a typical example of an environmental problem which cannot be solved passively, i.e., merely by protective measures, but will require the adoption of active measures, i.e., direct interventions at the source. The costs of a complete protection against noise are so prohibitive as to make it unthinkable even in the economically most developed countries. At the same time it would not
(45) seem feasible, either economically or politically, to force the population to carry the costs of individual protection against noise, for example, by reinforcing the sound insulation of their homes. A solution of this problem probably cannot be found in the near future.

18. According to the passage, the population at large

   (A) is unconcerned about air pollution controls
   (B) is especially aware of problems concerning air quality and purity

(C) regards water pollution as more serious than air pollution
(D) has failed to recognize the economic consequences of pollution
(E) is unwilling to make the sacrifices needed to ensure clean air

19. Scientific forecasts have shown that clear and biologically valuable air

(A) is likely to remain abundant for some time
(B) creates fewer economic difficulties than does water pollution
(C) may soon be dangerously lacking
(D) may be beyond the capacity of our technology to protect
(E) has already become difficult to obtain

20. According to the passage, which of the following contributes *most* to atmospheric pollution?

(A) industry
(B) production
(C) households
(D) mining
(E) waste disposal

21. The costs involved in the maintenance of pure water are determined primarily by

I. production costs
II. transport costs
III. research costs

(A) I only (B) III only (C) I and II only (D) II and III only (E) I, II, and III

22. According to the passage, atmospheric pollution caused by private property is

(A) easy to control
(B) impossible to control
(C) difficult to control
(D) decreasing
(E) negligible

23. According to the passage, the problem of noise can be solved through

I. Active measures
II. Passive measures
III. Tax levies

(A) I only
(B) III only
(C) I and II only
(D) II and III only
(E) I, II, and III

24. According to the passage, the costs of some anti-pollution measures will have to be borne by individuals because

(A) individuals contribute to the creation of pollution
(B) governments do not have adequate resources
(C) industry is not willing to bear its share
(D) individuals are more easily taxed than producers
(E) individuals demand production, which causes pollution

25. Complete protection against noise

(A) may be forthcoming in the near future
(B) is impossible to achieve
(C) may have prohibitive costs
(D) is possible only in developed countries
(E) has been achieved in some countries

If there is still time remaining, you may review the questions in this section only.
You may not turn to any other section of the test.

Section III   Problem Solving

TIME: 30 minutes

DIRECTIONS: Solve each of the following problems; then indicate the correct answer on the answer sheet. [On the actual test you will be permitted to use any space available on the examination paper for scratch work.]

NOTE: A figure that appears with a problem is drawn as accurately as possible so as to provide information that may help in answering the question. Numbers in this test are real numbers.

1. A borrower pays 6% interest on the first $500 he borrows and 5½% on the part of the loan in excess of $500. How much interest will the borrower have to pay on a loan of $5,500?

   (A) $275
   (B) $280
   (C) $302.50

   (D) $305
   (E) $330

2. If $2x - y = 4$, then $6x - 3y$ is

   (A) 4
   (B) 6
   (C) 8

   (D) 10
   (E) 12

3. The next number in the arithmetical progression 5, 11, 17, . . . is

   (A) 18
   (B) 22
   (C) 23

   (D) 28
   (E) 33

Use the following graph for questions 4–6.

INSTALLED CAPACITY OF ELECTRIC UTILITY GENERATING PLANTS 1920–1952

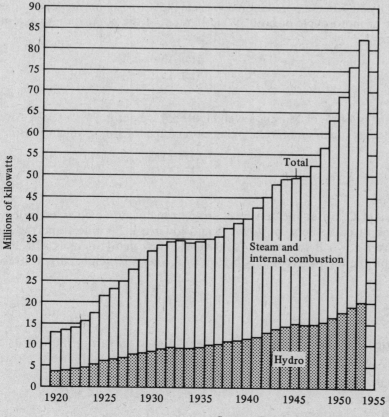

Source: Federal Power Commission

4. In what year did the installed capacity first exceed 50 million kilowatts?

(A) 1939
(B) 1944
(C) 1945
(D) 1947
(E) 1950

5. In 1952, the installed capacity of steam and internal combustion plants was about x times the installed capacity of the hydro plants where x is

(A) ½
(B) 1
(C) 2
(D) 3
(E) 4

6. Which of the following statements about the installed capacity of electric utility generating plants between 1920 and 1952 can be inferred from the graph?

 I. In the period 1930–39, there was less of an increase in capacity than in either of the periods 1920–1929 or 1940–1949.
 II. More than ⅕ of the capacity in 1925 was produced by hydro plants.
 III. The increase in capacity in kilowatts between 1945 and 1952 was greater than the increase between 1925 and 1945.

(A) I only
(B) II only
(C) I and III only
(D) II and III only
(E) I, II, and III

7. A warehouse has 20 packers. Each packer can load ⅛ of a box in 9 minutes. How many boxes can be loaded in 1½ hours by all 20 packers?

(A) 1¼
(B) 10¼
(C) 12½
(D) 20
(E) 25

8. In Motor City 90% of the population own a car, 15% own a motorcycle, and everybody owns a car or motorcycle or both. What percent of the population own a motorcycle but not a car?

(A) 5
(B) 8
(C) 9
(D) 10
(E) 15

9. Jim's weight is 140% of Marcia's weight. Bob's weight is 90% of Lee's weight. Lee weighs twice as much as Marcia. What percentage of Jim's weight is Bob's weight?

(A) 64²⁄₇
(B) 77⁷⁄₉
(C) 90
(D) 128⁴⁄₇
(E) 155⁵⁄₉

10. Towns A and C are connected by a straight highway which is 60 miles long. The straight-line distance between town A and town B is 50 miles, and the straight-line distance from town B to town C is 50 miles. How many miles is it from town B to the point on the highway connecting towns A and C which is closest to town B?

(A) 30
(B) 40
(C) $30\sqrt{2}$
(D) 50
(E) 60

11. A chair originally cost $50.00. The chair was offered for sale at 108% of its cost. After a week the price was discounted 10% and the chain was sold. The chair was sold for

(A) $45.00
(B) $48.60
(C) $49.00
(D) $49.50
(E) $54.00

12. A worker is paid x dollars for the first 8 hours he works each day. He is paid y dollars per hour for each hour he works in excess of 8 hours. During one week he works 8 hours on Monday, 11 hours on Tuesday, 9 hours on Wednesday, 10 hours on Thursday, and 9 hours on Friday. What is his average daily wage in dollars for the five-day week?

(A) $x + \dfrac{7}{5}y$

(B) $2x + y$

(C) $\dfrac{5x + 8y}{5}$

(D) $x + 2y$

(E) $5x + 7y$

13. A club has 8 male and 8 female members. The club is choosing a committee of 6 members. The committee must have 3 male and 3 female members. How many different committees can be chosen?

(A) 112,896
(B) 3,136
(C) 720

(D) 112
(E) 9

14. A motorcycle costs $2,500 when it is brand new. At the end of each year it is worth ⅘ of what it was at the beginning of the year. What is the motorcycle worth when it is 3 years old?

(A) $1,000
(B) $1,200
(C) $1,280

(D) $1,340
(E) $1,430

Use the following table for questions 15–17.

Type of vehicle	Cost of fuel for 200-mile trip
Automobile	$15
Motorcycle	$ 5
Bus	$20
Truck	$50
Airplane	$70

15. What is the cost of fuel for a 120-mile trip by automobile?

(A) $5
(B) $9
(C) $12

(D) $15
(E) $30

16. If the wages of a bus driver for a 200-mile trip are $70, and the only costs for a bus are the fuel and the driver's wages, how much should a bus company charge to charter a bus and driver for a 200-mile trip in order to obtain 120% of the cost?

(A) $24
(B) $90
(C) $94

(D) $104
(E) $108

17. If 3 buses, 4 automobiles, 2 motorcycles, and one truck each make a 200-mile trip, what is the average fuel cost per vehicle?

(A) $5
(B) $15
(C) $18

(D) $20
(E) $24

18. If $x + 2y = 2x + y$, then $x - y$ is equal to

(A) 0

(B) 2

(C) 4

(D) 5

(E) cannot be determined

19. 15% of the families in state x have an income of $25,000 or more. $\frac{2}{3}$ of the families with income of $25,000 or more in state x own a boat. What fraction of the families own a boat and have an income of $25,000 or more in state x?

(A) $\frac{1}{15}$

(B) $\frac{1}{12}$

(C) $\frac{1}{10}$

(D) $\frac{4}{21}$

(E) $\frac{9}{40}$

20. If the angles of a triangle are in the ratio $1:2:2$, then the triangle

(A) is isosceles

(B) is obtuse

(C) is a right triangle

(D) is equilateral

(E) has one angle greater than 80°

If there is still time remaining, you may review the questions in this section only.
You may not turn to any other section of the test.

Section IV   Analysis of Situations

TIME: **30 minutes**

DIRECTIONS: Read the following passages. After you have completed each one, you will be asked to answer questions that involve determining the importance of specific factors included in the passage. When answering questions, you may consult the passage.

Passage 1:

Bill Kamil was director of Tibland's national lottery. The lottery had been established twenty years before to raise funds for health, education, and welfare projects. It was owned by the state and supervised by a board of directors selected from among leading businessmen, professional people such as lawyers and educators, and government officials. Throughout its history, lottery sales had increased faster than the annual growth of population and about 20 percent faster than the annual rate of inflation. However, during the last two years, sales—while increasing—had grown at a decreasing rate. Kamil was concerned that, should this trend continue, sales would soon level off, or even decrease. He therefore called a meeting of his staff, including Fred Fishman, Marketing Manager; Arnold Fox, Operations Manager; and Ron Davis, Statistician. Fishman was responsible for the lottery program, changes in prizes, new products, pricing policy, and advertising. Fox was responsible for the distribution of lottery tickets to dealers, collection of ticket sales, and the maintenance of sales booths. Davis's main duties involved preparing monthly statistical reports on lottery sales and data analysis.

Tibland's lottery consisted of three games. The most widely played of the three was a weekly game. All the participant had to do was purchase a ticket printed with a five-digit number. Every Monday a lottery was held wherein a computer selected the winning numbers at random. In a second game, the participant checked a series of numbers in boxes printed on a standard form. He or she might choose a birthdate, his or her children's ages, or any random series of numbers. Winning numbers were also selected at random by a computer. The third game was an instant lottery. Participants scraped off the foil on part of a card which revealed a series of numbers, symbols, or pictures, depending upon the game. Winning tickets were those that contained four of a kind (first prize), three of a kind (second prize), or two of a kind (third prize).

Top on the agenda of Kamil's staff meeting was a discussion of how sales of all lottery games could be increased. Kamil especially drew the staff's attention to a sales report prepared by Ron Davis.

Lottery Sales
(100,000 units of local currency)

Year	Weekly	Lottery Lotto	Instant	Total Sales
1961	38	—	—	38
1966	111	—	—	111
1971	136	31	—	167
1976	278	174	—	452
1977	356	233	—	589
1978	467	351	78	896
1979	616	494	142	1,252
1980	822	623	140	1,585

The report showed that total lottery sales in monetary units had increased every year. However, the rate of increase had declined since 1978. Ron Davis pointed out that Lotto sales had tapered off more than those of the weekly lottery. Instant lottery sales had actually declined slightly in 1980, and early sales returns for 1981 showed a similar downward trend. In all three games, the *number* of tickets sold had declined. If the trend continued, lottery sales growth in real terms (discounted for inflation) would be negative.

Kamil requested his staff to suggest alternative courses of action that would result in (1) an *annual* increase in the sales of all three games of not less than 30 percent, (2) a ten-percent increase in the number of tickets sold, and (3) the introduction of four new instant games every year. The following discussion ensued.

Fishman: Stagnating lottery sales are owing to bad publicity surrounding the introduction of the instant game in 1978. Initially, there were many buyers who even waited on long lines to purchase tickets. Media coverage of this frantic period was extensive, but negative. Rather than emphasize the positive aspects of the lottery, the news media pointed out that most of the purchasers seemed to be members of the lower social classes. We must do all we can to stimulate sales among upper income groups.

Fox: It wasn't the media that lowered sales, but simply that the initial enthusiasm wore off. Prizes are much smaller in the instant lottery compared to the weekly, even though the ticket prices of both are nearly the same. Participants feel that they are not getting their money's worth from the instant game.

Davis: There may be a third factor. Many people who were regular purchasers of weekly lottery tickets tried the instant game. Those who were disappointed with the instant game may have stopped purchasing other lottery games as well. This would explain the decrease in the number of tickets sold.

Fishman: An increase in sales of all lottery games can be made possible by, first, attracting new buyers, and, second, increasing the rate of purchase of existing buyers.

According to a recent survey, the "non buyers" of most lottery games are mainly upper-income, professional people. We can best reach these people through a direct-mail campaign. One possibility is to sell them ticket subscriptions. Instead of buying one or a few tickets at a time of a single lottery, we should offer them a half year's subscription to the weekly lottery. Subscriptions can be paid for through the mail, at great convenience to the consumer.

Fox: Subscriptions might be the answer to the weekly lottery, but they will not work for the instant and Lotto games. Moreover, a six-month subscription would cost $52. Not enough people will pay such a sum in advance. Costs for printing special tickets and circulating them through the mail would be greater than the costs of our present distribution method.

Davis: We want to reach upper-income groups; they will be willing to pay for the convenience of subscribing to a series of lotteries in advance, without having to purchase tickets at a retail outlet. Present buyers who do not choose to subscribe may continue to purchase tickets at retail locations.

Fishman: Subscriptions sales work well in Germany and a few other European countries. I do not believe there is any difference between purchases in those countries and Tibland. People buy lottery tickets for two reasons: for the fun of playing, and to fulfill some sort of dream that only a large sum of money can make real. These motives are universal.

Fox: Subscriptions may induce non-buyers to purchase lottery tickets, but sales of the instant game and Lotto will not increase. We must increase advertising expenditures by at least fifty percent to stimulate sales. I have been in this business for twenty years. Based on my experience, advertising has always been the key to sales.

Davis: We have to operate within a budget. We do not have sufficient resources to undertake a subscription campaign, while at the same time increasing advertising expenditures by fifty percent. We may also be criticized by consumer councils for spending so much of our income on advertising, rather than allocating it to public projects.

Fishman: Let's consider trying to increase sales by making the games more attractive. For instance, we could immediately institute a plan to introduce new instant games every six weeks. The Lotto game could also be improved by adding a consolation prize. These changes would do more to stimulate sales than an increase in advertising. It is the product that counts, not the advertising.

DIRECTIONS: The questions that follow relate to the preceding passage. Evaluate, in terms of the passage, each of the items given. Then select your answer from one of the following classifications, and blacken the corresponding space on the answer sheet.

(A) A MAJOR OBJECTIVE in making the decision: one of the goals sought by the decision maker

(B) A MAJOR FACTOR in making the decision: an aspect of the problem, specifically mentioned in the passage, that fundamentally affects and/or determines the decision

(C) A MINOR FACTOR in making the decision: a less important element bearing on or affecting a Major Factor, rather than a Major Objective directly

(D) A MAJOR ASSUMPTION in making the decision: a projection or supposition arrived at by the decision maker before considering the factors and alternatives

(E) AN UNIMPORTANT ISSUE in making the decision: an item lacking significant impact on, or relationship to, the decision

1. Fox's years of experience in the lottery business

2. Increasing the number of lottery games

3. Stagnating lottery sales

4. Cost of an advertising campaign

5. Increasing lottery sales by 30 percent

6. Number of tickets likely to be sold under each alternative

7. Predominance of members of the lower classes among purchasers of instant lottery tickets

8. Existence of lotteries in Tibland for the past twenty years

9. Printing costs for subscription tickets

10. Similarity of motives of purchasers of lottery tickets in Tibland and in Europe

11. Likelihood of stimulating sales through advertising

12. Attracting new buyers of lotteries

13. Amount of money available in the budget

14. Cost of proposed subscriptions to the weekly lottery game

15. Socio-economic status of members of the board of directors

16. Holding a lottery every Monday

17. Paying for subscriptions in advance

18. Selecting winning numbers at random

Passage 2:

Len Hibert was given the task of formulating compensation policy for overseas managers for a multinational firm operating in several Latin American countries and Europe. His company is a major manufacturer of heavy industrial equipment that has been operating in foreign markets for over 40 years. Like many early export-oriented companies, most of the international business was export with no manufacturing abroad. In recent years, the company orientation and attitudes toward the foreign operation have shifted drastically; they now have manufacturing in six different countries and the international portion of their business accounts for well over 50 percent of their annual profits. The company philosophy toward International has been shifting away from viewing the international portion as export only and trying to organize into a multinational company. This shift in philosophy and the importance of the international division has placed greater emphasis on the type and function of the international manager sent abroad. While the company has effectively utilized the typical "expatriate freewheeler" to represent them abroad (although mavericks in thier management style, they have proved to be extremely effective for the company), it is now becoming more evident that there is a need for a different type of person to spend a shorter period of time abroad. Most host countries have changed their policies toward foreigners working in their countries from relatively liberal permission to operate at many levels to increasingly more restrictive policies. For example, many of the Latin American countries will not permit foreign personnel when there are qualified nationals to fulfill the tasks. The only exception is that a U.S. citizen will be given a work permit for three or four yours to train a national replacement. Even in Europe, it is becoming more and more politically astute to hire nationals. For the company this has meant sending fewer people to represent their worldwide operations abroad, and further, that those who are sent abroad must be extremely capable, understand the total operation, and be effective teachers. The "right man" to go abroad is the same person with the same qualifications who would be in demand in the domestic operation as well.

The company has, historically, provided the typical inducements for moving abroad: cost of living allowances, depending on the country, from 20 percent to 30 percent of the base salary; paid vacations on an annual basis back to the United States; schooling allowances for children back in the States or in private schools; and all moving expenses including complete household furnishings. Despite such inducements there have been some real problems with prospective people the company has wanted to send abroad. Many of them center around the family. Over the years, the personnel director has kept a record of some of the typical complaints and questions raised when executives have been asked to go abroad. For example, "Will you keep up supplied with baby food in Columbia [Colombia]? You mean to pay only 20 percent premium for the sacrifice of leaving the United States? My daughter could live at home while she attends college; will you bring her back to the States and pay her living expenses? Will you pay my way back to see my own doctor if it's necessary? Will you move my new outboard cruiser? Will you move my mother-in-law, who lives with us, to Buenos Aires too?" While these questions may not seem relevant to an outsider, to the individual raising the questions they are important. It has been felt that these kinds of issues are critical in the initial decision to go abroad and are also quite important as reasons why executives return ahead of schedule. An article in *Business Week* tends to sum up the kinds of problems Len is facing.

COMPENSATION FOR OVERSEAS EXECUTIVES TOO MUCH OR TOO LITTLE?[1]

Today, serving a hitch overseas for the company is required of almost anyone wanting company advancement. Many problems arise in sending the executive overseas, but one of the most critical is compensation. Some feel that the overseas executive or expatriate is overcompensated; others feel that, considering the sacrifice, he is undercompensated. You be the judge.

On the plus side, a man of 28 to 45 (the usual age range of overseas appointees) generally gets a boost in his career: higher pay, broader responsibilities. Major companies are sending their top-ranking younger men abroad, not employees they want to "bury."

Says a Chase Manhattan Bank executive: "A man is smart to have some overseas time if he really wants to move up the ladder." About 80 percent of those Chase sends abroad are sent for career development. The same holds for a growing number of big and medium-size international outfits. The usual hitch lasts from two to five years. And the man most apt to benefit from it is the middle manager. He will probably get control over a whole local operation. That lets him prove his general managerial ability. And, if he is successful, he returns home with higher status. A younger man is smart to go for experience—even without more pay.

A far less attractive deal involves going overseas for an indeterminate period to train a national for a job abroad. This missionary must return home to discover that a former equal has stepped above him. Usually, of course, a man over 50 goes abroad only to fill a high-ranking spot. Some big companies now provide added incentive; they allow foreign service men to retire early (often at 60) with varying retirement benefits.

The big gamble is not so much age and the assignment. It's how well a man's wife and children will adjust to the relocation. There's likely to be at least moderate strain—and there are plenty of cases where relocation has broken up marriages. Even a move to Western Europe can be difficult. "People who have strong family ties back home are poor risks," says a Jersey Standard personnel executive. Some self-examination is a must, say the pros. But too often this is ignored by the man eager to push ahead. Says one old hand in the international field: "If you're just trying to get away from it all, forget about going abroad. Your problems will magnify."

As a rule, you won't get a contract for an overseas hitch (and it's best not to push for one). But there are some things you will want to nail down. You should expect a foreign service premium of 15 percent to 25 percent above your base salary. This is what many of the larger outfits are paying. Note that the cost of living abroad can be higher than in the United States. For example, it may cost up to $200 a month more to rent a comparable house in Europe than in the United States. "Making a profit on a tour abroad doesn't work these days," says one pro, "except in a place like Nairobi,"

Moving expenses should be paid, too. This may mean $5,000 to $6,000 (non-taxable) for moving your family to Western Europe. In addition, many companies will pay $800 to $1,000 per child per year for school expenses abroad. Some pay for one round trip a year for a college-age son or daughter studying in the United States. Quite a few companies will even help you in your search for a school and pay exceptional costs such as high tutoring fees in remote areas.

As an example,

a typical United States executive assigned in Brussels might receive in addition to his base salary: (1) a 10 percent to 25 percent premium; (2) a cost-of-living allowance of several hundred dollars a month; and (3) housing allowance which permits him to live in the best Brussels suburb at about the same cost as a more modest house at home. He drives a European sports car while his wife makes do with the American sedan the company shipped overseas for him. His children attend the best local private schools when they would have gone to public schools at home. His social circle includes some of the top business, professional, and government people in the country. His wife is able to visit some of the finest museums, concerts, and lectures in the world—if she can find time away from an active social life. And yet they both complain to their friends in the local expatriate community, to local management, and to company headquarters that they are being vastly undercompensated, are deeply unhappy, and feel that the company has done them an injustice.[2]

Len's company's compensation program is not too different from the ones discussed in the article above. His company has also had several executives return from foreign assignments within six to eight months, and in most cases after returning they have left the company. Some were not considered a loss, but there were at least one or two whom the company did not want to lose. While this has not been a major problem, certainly Len's immediate superior feels that part of the reason why some executives have returned before their assignments were up was the arm twisting done to get them to accept the assignment. They were not really enthusiastic about going abroad in the first place but felt obligated, and further, they were not properly prepared to face the cultural shock involved.

There is some indication that companies are cutting fringe benefits. There are several reasons for this—living conditions abroad are not as bad today as they once were, companies' philosophies have changed to the extent that advancement to higher executive positions requires involvement in the foreign operations, and there is a general feeling that there is no need to pay extra just for going overseas and doing an accepted part of a job. The *Wall Street Journal* reported that Hewlett-Packard Company has moved to eliminate cost-of-living allowances, phase out their housing subsidies, and eliminate their yearly educational allowance of up to 1,250 dollars per child. Standard Oil of California has decided to cut its premiums to U.S. executives in Venezuela from the current 28 percent to about 17 percent. IBM and DuPont are also considering reduction of their extras. While reduction of extras is occurring among some, an extensive survey by the Conference Board taken in 1974 of 267 of the largest U.S.-based international corporations showed the following: 84 percent paid their American officials abroad a premium for foreign service; 81 percent paid cost-of-living allowances for what was perceived as the higher cost of maintaining an American standard of living abroad; and 72 percent gave housing subsidies.

---

[2] Reprinted from J. Vivian, "Expatriate Executives: Overpaid but Undercompensated," *Columbia Journal of World Business*. January–February 1968, pp. 29–40. Copyright © 1968 by the Trustees of Columbia University.

Another problem that many companies are having and that Len's company faces as it expands is how to deal effectively with the returning executive. In the past, the company has been able to absorb all of its returning personnel in meaningful positions at headquarters. However, as policies and changes mentioned above lead to a larger turnover in foreign executive personnel, management needs to consider the effective integration of these executives in meaningful positions when they return to the U.S. The cultural shock experienced by returning executives is a problem.

A recent study of repatriated executives from 25 international companies suggests some of the problems of integrating returning executives into regular company operations. The men interviewed were between the ages of 30 and 45, married, with an average of 3 children, and they had spent from 2 to 6 years abroad. Many had left their jobs for positions with other companies shortly after returning from abroad. The principal reason given for leaving was dissatisfaction with their new domestic assignments.

In general, most of the executives were alienated from their companies and the reasons cited were: (1) the nature of the new domestic assignment was too disagreeable; (2) the location of the domestic assignment was unacceptable to the returnee; (3) salary and fringe benefits to which the individual and his family had become accustomed while on foreign assignment were lost; and (4) the skills and experience acquired could be marketed more to the individual's advantage either domestically or internationally through another company. Finally, there were several individuals who complained of unfair discriminatory practice by the company in dealing with their objections and grievances.[3]

The findings of this study were supported by a recent incident involving a financial officer of Len's company who had been stationed in Western Europe. The Browns lived in Paris where he was responsible for overseeing the financial operations of the company in six European countries. He and his family had enjoyed their five-year stay in Paris and had become accustomed to French culture and the higher level of living there. Their children had been enrolled in private schools outside of Paris and liked the more relaxed pace of European life. The company ordered him back to the U.S. since it wanted to provide foreign experience for another executive. A new company policy of calling back executives after a four-year assignment had recently been initiated. This policy was considered necessary to provide foreign experience for as many key personnel as possible. Brown was the first to be affected.

He was ordered back to Chicago as assistant to the Vice President of Finance. In this position he had much less responsibility and authority than he had had in the European post where he reported directly to the President of European operations. As a consequence, he found his new job strange and certainly less challenging. Even though his salary had not been reduced, he was not happy in Chicago. In his European job he had operated in a number of different capacities and become very familiar with the entire European operation. He felt that the company did not appreciate him and was not effectively using his experience gained as a key European financial officer. In addition to his dissatisfaction, the lifestyle in Chicago was substantially different than that in Paris, and his whole family was upset about having to move back to the States. In fact, one daughter stayed in Europe to complete her education since she had received most of her education there and didn't want to transfer to U.S. schools. After about six months in Chicago, Brown quit and went to work with a competitor.

Part of Len's task is to determine if the new policy of rotating key personnel in foreign assignments should continue to be followed, and if so how to avoid losing men like Brown. There is no doubt that top management was upset about losing Brown, whom they considered to have been a definite asset to the organization.

Not only is there no simple solution to repatriating executives, but Len must also deal with the negative aspects of sending men abroad because of the hardships of moving and

---

[3] For an interesting report on this problem see J. Alex Murray, "International Personnel Repatriation: Cultural Shock in Reverse," *MSU Business Topics*, Summer 1973, pp. 59–66.

the cost of maintaining an American style of living standard abroad at today's prices. See the table for some indication of the cost of living in different parts of the world.

Cost of Living Indexes and Apartment Rents for
Selected Major Business Centers

City	Index* (New York = 100)	3-Room Apt.† Furnished (monthly)
Tokyo	130.4	$755–1,132
Frankfurt	110.1	$324–405
Zurich	106.1	$363–495
Geneva	105.3	$330–462
Brussels	100.1	$214–348
New York	100.0	$300–500
Amsterdam	92.3	$259–370
Athens	86.7	$235–370
London	82.4	$341–585
Rome	79.4	$209–296
Madrid	76.5	$270–540
São Paulo	68.0	$299–498

* The following categories of living expenses are included: shopping basket (retail food products and non-alcoholic beverages), alcoholic beverages, household supplies and operations (cleaning supplies, laundry and dry cleaning charges), personal care products, tobacco, utilities, clothing and footwear, domestic help, recreation and entertainment (TV rental fees, nightclub entertainment, theatre/concerts, cinema, dinner at a fashionable restaurant, subscription to English-language newspaper) and transportation.
† Cost of 3-bedroom apartment (living room, dining room, kitchen, bedrooms) near center of city.
Source: "Selected Cost of Living Indexes Abroad," *Sales Management*, January 7, 1974, pp. 83–85.

Further, when Len read about the abductions in South America of U.S. executives, it was hard to believe that there wouldn't be more resistance to moving abroad, especially if the outstanding man he wants to assign abroad can see that he has as much opportunity in the States as he would have by moving. There is no doubt, however, that the trend is to keep the number of Americans overseas as low as possible and to eventually reduce the number in relation to business volume as rapidly as possible while at the same time giving as many as possible international experience. Thus the men who go to foreign operations almost always are picked for special knowledge and are expected to train nationals to replace them; this means Len must send his best. His task is to devise a policy to help solve the immediate problems as well as those he can anticipate in the future. This policy may entail recommendations for specific changes in organization and methods of control. Hopefully, the new policy will help motivate his executives to go overseas and provide him with the best possible talent abroad, talent the company will be able to effectively utilize once they return to the United States.

DIRECTIONS: The questions that follow relate to the preceding passage. Evaluate, in terms of the passage, each of the items given. Then select your answer from one of the following classifications, and blacken the corresponding space on the answer sheet.

(A) A MAJOR OBJECTIVE in making the decision: one of the goals sought by the decision maker

(B) A MAJOR FACTOR in making the decision: an aspect of the problem, specifically mentioned in the passage, that fundamentally affects and/or determines the decision

(C) A MINOR FACTOR in making the decision: a less important element bearing on or affecting a Major Factor, rather than a Major Objective directly

(D) A MAJOR ASSUMPTION in making the decision: a projection or supposition arrived at by the decision maker before considering the factors and alternatives

(E) AN UNIMPORTANT ISSUE in making the decision: an item lacking significant impact on, or relationship to, the decision

19. Determining compensation policy for overseas managers

20. Production of heavy industrial equipment

21. Organizing into a multinational company

22. Location of overseas executives

23. Cost of renting a house in Europe

24. Cost of living abroad

25. Selecting personnel for overseas assignments

26. Problem of integrating returning executives

27. Disadvantages of rotating key personnel in foreign assignments

28. Number of countries in which Hibert's company operates

29. Operating abroad for over 40 years

30. Company philosophy

31. Host country policies toward foreign employees

32. Kidnappings in South America

33. Motivating executives to go overseas

34. Cultural shock experienced by expatriates

35. The Browns' living in Paris

If there is still time remaining, you may review the questions in this section only.
You may not turn to any other section of the test.

Section V   Data Sufficiency

TIME: 30 minutes

DIRECTIONS: Each of the following problems has a question and two statements which are labeled (1) and (2). Use the data given in (1) and (2) together with other available information (such as the number of hours in a day, the definition of *clockwise*, mathematical facts, etc.) to decide whether the statements are *sufficient* to answer the question. Then fill in space

(A) if you can get the answer from (1) alone but not from (2) alone;

(B) if you can get the answer from (2) alone but not from (1) alone;

(C) if you can get the answer from (1) and (2) together, although neither statement by itself suffices;

(D) if statement (1) alone suffices *and* statement (2) alone suffices;

(E) if you cannot get the answer from statements (1) and (2) together, but need even more data.

All numbers used in this section are real numbers. A figure given for a problem is intended to provide information consistent with that in the question, but not necessarily with the additional information contained in the statements.

1. Is x greater than y?

   (1) $3x = 2k$
   (2) $k = y^2$

2. Is *ABCD* a parallelogram?

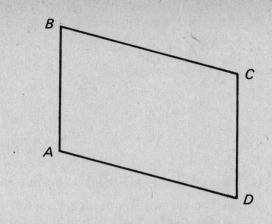

  (1) *AB* = *CD*
  (2) *AB* is parallel to *CD*

3. What was Mr. Smith's combined income for the years 1965–1970? In 1965 he made $10,000.

  (1) His average yearly income for the years 1965–1970 was $12,000.
  (2) In 1970, his income was $20,000.

4. How much profit did Walker's Emporium make selling dresses?

  (1) Each dress cost $10.
  (2) 600 dresses were sold.

5. *k* is a positive integer. Is *k* a prime number?

  (1) No integer between 2 and $\sqrt{k}$ inclusive divides *k* evenly.

  (2) No integer between 2 and $\dfrac{k}{2}$ inclusive divides *k* evenly, and *k* is greater than 5.

6. The towns *A*, *B*, and *C* lie on a straight line. *C* is between *A* and *B*. The distance from *A* to *B* is 100 miles. How far is it from *A* to *C*?

  (1) The distance from *A* to *B* is 25% more than the distance from *C* to *B*.
  (2) The distance from *A* to *C* is ¼ of the distance from *C* to *B*.

7. Is *AB* perpendicular to *CD*?

  (1) *AC* = *BD*
  (2) *x* = *y*

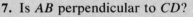

8. What is the value of $x - y$?

  (1) $x + 2y = 6$
  (2) $x = y$

9. The number of eligible voters is 100,000. How many eligible voters voted?

  (1) 63% of the eligible men voted.
  (2) 67% of the eligible women voted.

10. If $z = 50$, find the value of x.

(1) $RS \neq ST$
(2) $x + y = 60$

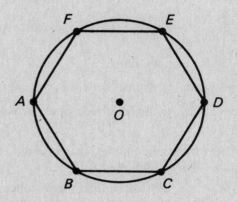

11. How much was the original cost of a car which sold for $2,300?

(1) The car was sold for a discount of 10% from its original cost.
(2) The sales tax was $150.

12. The hexagon *ABCDEF* is inscribed in the circle with center *O*. What is the length of *AB*?

(1) The radius of the circle is 4 inches.
(2) The hexagon is a regular hexagon.

13. How many rolls of wallpaper are necessary to cover the walls of a room whose floor and ceiling are rectangles 12 feet wide and 15 feet long?

(1) A roll of wallpaper covers 20 square feet.
(2) There are no windows in the walls.

14. What is the average daily wage of a worker who works five days? He made $80 the first day.

(1) The worker made a total of $400 for the first four days of work.
(2) The worker made 20% more each day then he did on the previous day.

15. Is *ABC* a right triangle? $AB = 5$; $AC = 4$.

(1) $BC = 3$
(2) $AC = CD$

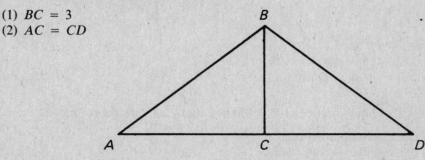

16. Did the price of energy rise last year?

(1) If the price of energy rose last year, then the price of food would rise this year.
(2) The price of food rose this year.

17. How much was a certain Rembrandt painting worth in January 1971?

(1) In January 1977 the painting was worth $2,000,000.
(2) Over the ten years 1968–1977 the painting increased in value by 10% each year.

18. A sequence of numbers $a_1, a_2, a_3, \ldots$ is given by the rule $a_n{}^2 = a_{n+1}$. Does 3 appear in the sequence?

(1) $a_1 = 2$
(2) $a_3 = 16$

19. Is AB greater than AC?

(1) $z > x$
(2) $AC > AD$

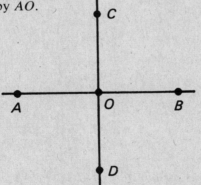

20. x and y are integers that are both less than 10. Is x greater than y?

(1) x is a multiple of 3.
(2) y is a multiple of 2.

21. Is $\dfrac{1}{x}$ greater than $\dfrac{1}{y}$?

(1) x is greater than 1.
(2) x is less than y.

22. AB intersects CD at point O. Is AB perpendicular to CD? $AC = AD$.

(1) Angle CAD is bisected by AO.
(2) $BC = AD$

23. Plane X flies at r miles per hour from A to B. Plane Y flies at S miles per hour from B to A. Both planes take off at the same time. Which plane flies at a faster rate? Town C is between A and B.

(1) C is closer to A than it is to B.
(2) Plane X flies over C before plane Y.

24. What is the value of $x + y$?

(1) $2x + y = 4$
(2) $x + 2y = 5$

25. What is the area of the circular section *AOB*?
    A and *B* are points on the circle which has
    O as its center.

    (1) Angle *AOB* = 36°
    (2) *OB* = *OA*

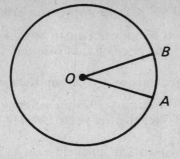

If there is still time remaining, you may review the questions in this section only.
You may not turn to any other section of the test.

Section VI   Problem Solving

TIME: **30 minutes**

DIRECTIONS: Solve each of the following problems; then indicate the correct answer on the answer sheet. [On the actual test you will be permitted to use any space available on the examination paper for scratch work.]
NOTE: A figure that appears with a problem is drawn as accurately as possible so as to provide information that may help in answering the question. Numbers in this test are real numbers.

1. If a car travels at a constant rate of 60 miles per hour, how long will it take to travel 255 miles?

   (A) 3¾ hours   (D) 4¼ hours
   (B) 4 hours   (E) 4½ hours
   (C) 4⅛ hours

2. A car currently travels 15 miles on a gallon of gas but after a tune-up the car will use only ¾ as much gas as it does now. How many miles will the car travel on a gallon of gas after the tune-up?

   (A) 15   (D) 18⅔
   (B) 16½   (E) 20
   (C) 17½

3. Successive discounts of 20% and 15% are equal to a single discount of

   (A) 30%   (D) 35%
   (B) 32%   (E) 36%
   (C) 34%

Use the following graphs for questions 4–7.

PER CAPITA PERSONAL HEALTH CARE EXPENDITURES

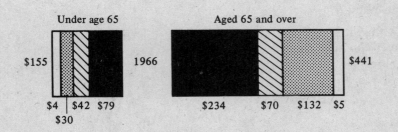

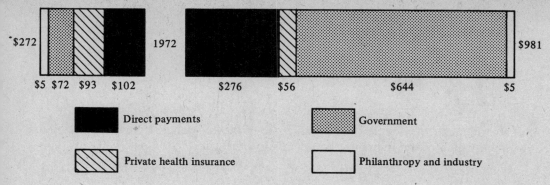

$272 — $5 $72 $93 $102

1972 — $276 $56 $644 $5 — $981

Direct payments

Government

Private health insurance

Philanthropy and industry

Source: Social Security Bulletin

4. If there were about 20 million people 65 and over in 1966, how much did the govenment spend on personal health care for people aged 65 and over in 1966?

(A) $26 million
(B) $264 million
(C) $2 billion
(D) $2.640 billion
(E) $3.6 billion

5. Between 1966 and 1972, the per capita amount spent by the government on personal health care for those under age 65 increased by $x\%$ where x is

(A) 100
(B) 120
(C) 140
(D) 220
(E) 240

6. In 1972, the fraction contributed by philanthropy and industry towards expenditures for personal health care for those aged 65 and over was about

(A) $\frac{1}{500}$
(B) $\frac{1}{196}$
(C) $\frac{1}{99}$
(D) $\frac{1}{88}$
(E) $\frac{2}{101}$

7. Which of the following statements about expenditures for personal health care between 1966 and 1972 can be inferred from the graphs?

  I. The total amount spent for those aged 65 and over in 1972 was more than 3 times as much as the total amount spent on those under 65.
  II. Between 1966 and 1972, the amount spent per capita by those aged 65 and over increased in each of the four categories (direct payments, government, private health insurance, philanthropy).
  III. The government paid more than ½ of the amount of expenditures for those aged 65 and over in 1972.

(A) I only
(B) II only
(C) III only
(D) I and III only
(E) II and III only

8. Oranges cost $1.00 for a crate containing 20 oranges. If oranges are sold for 6¢ each, what percent of the selling price is the profit?

(A) 5%
(B) 10%
(C) 16⅔%
(D) 20%
(E) 25%

9. A hen lays 7½ dozen eggs during the summer. There are 93 days in the summer and it costs $10 to feed the hen for the summer. How much does it cost in food for each egg produced?

(A) 10¢
(B) 11⅑¢
(C) 12³/₁₃¢

(D) 13¹/₁₃¢
(E) 15¢

10. If the diameter of a circle has length d, the radius has length r, and the area equals a, then which of the following statements is (are) true?

I. $a = \pi d^2$
II. $d = 2r$
III. $\dfrac{a}{d} = \pi\dfrac{r}{2}$

(A) only II
(B) I and II only
(C) I and III only
(D) II and III only
(E) I, II, and III

11. If hose A can fill up a tank in 20 minutes, and hose B can fill up the same tank in 15 minutes, how long will it take for the hoses together to fill up the tank?

(A) 5 minutes
(B) 7½ minutes
(C) 8⁴/₇ minutes

(D) 9²/₇ minutes
(E) 12 minutes

12. If 5 men take 2 hours to dig a ditch, how long will it take 12 men to dig the ditch?

(A) 45 minutes
(B) 50 minutes
(C) 54 minutes

(D) 60 minutes
(E) 84 minutes

Use the following table for questions 13–15.

Car Production at Plant T for One Week in 1960

	Number of cars produced	Total daily wages
MONDAY	900	$30,000
TUESDAY	1200	$40,000
WEDNESDAY	1500	$52,000
THURSDAY	1400	$50,000
FRIDAY	1000	$32,000

13. What was the average number of cars produced per day for the week shown?

(A) 1,000
(B) 1,140
(C) 1,180

(D) 1,200
(E) 1,220

14. What was the average cost in wages per car produced for the week?

(A) $25
(B) $26
(C) $29

(D) $32
(E) $34

15. Which of the following statements about the production of cars and the wages paid for the week can be inferred from the table?

I. ¼ of the cars were produced on Wednesday.
II. More employees came to the plant on Friday than on Monday.
III. ⅖ of the days accounted for ½ the wages paid for the week.

(A) I only
(B) II only
(C) I and II only
(D) I and III only
(E) I, II, and III

16. A train travels from Cleveland to Toledo in 2 hours and 10 minutes. If the distance from Cleveland to Toledo is 150 miles, then the average speed of the train is about

(A) 60 mph
(B) 66 mph
(C) 69 mph
(D) 72 mph
(E) 75 mph

17. If $x > 2$ and $y > -1$, then

(A) $xy > -2$
(B) $-x < 2y$
(C) $xy < -2$
(D) $-x > 2y$
(E) $x < 2y$

18. What is the area of the rectangle $ABCD$, if the length of AC is 5 and the length of AD is 4?

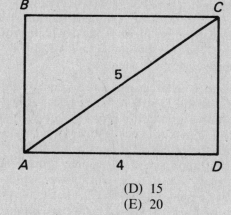

(A) 3
(B) 6
(C) 12
(D) 15
(E) 20

19. If electricity costs k¢ an hour, heat \$$d$ an hour, and water w¢ an hour, how much will all three cost for 12 hours?

(A) $12(k + d + w)$¢
(B) \$$(12k + 12d + 12w)$
(C) \$$(k + 100d + w)$
(D) $\$\left(12k + \dfrac{12d}{100} + 12w \right)$
(E) $\$(.12k + 12d + .12w)$

20. If $x = y = 2z$ and $x \cdot y \cdot z = 256$, then x equals

(A) 2
(B) $2\sqrt[3]{2}$
(C) 4
(D) $4\sqrt[3]{2}$
(E) 8

If there is still time remaining, you may review the questions in this section only.
You may not turn to any other section of the test.

Section VII   Analysis of Situations

TIME: 30 minutes

DIRECTIONS: Read the following passages. After you have completed each one, you will be asked to answer questions that involve determining the importance of specific factors included in the passage. When answering questions, you may consult the passage.

Passage 1:

In 1967 Mr. Ed Carswell, a chemical engineer, began experimenting in his spare time with a new method for processing fresh orange juice. By 1970, he had perfected the process to such an extent that he was ready to begin production in a small way. His process enabled him to extract 18 percent more juice from oranges than was typically extracted by a pressure juicer of the type currently used in cafes. His process also removed some of the bitterness which got into the juice from the peelings when oranges were squeezed with out peeling them.

Since many of the better quality restaurants preferred to serve fresh orange juice instead of canned or frozen juice, Mr. Carswell believed he could find a ready market for his product. Another appeal of his product would be that he could maintain more consistent juice flavor than haphazard restaurant juicing usually produced.

Mr. Carswell patented the process and then started production. Since his capital was limited, he began production in a small building which previously had been a woodworking shop. With the help of his brother, Mr. Carswell marketed the juice through local restaurants. The juice was distributed in glass jugs, which proved to be rather expensive because of high breakage. The new product was favorably accepted by the public, however, and the business proved to be a success.

Mr. Carswell began to receive larger and more frequent orders from his customers and their business associates. In 1972, he quit his regular job in order to devote full time to his juice business. He soon reached his capacity because of his inability to personally cover a larger area with his pickup truck. Advertising was on a small scale because of limited funds. Faced with the problems of glass jug breakage and limited advertising and distribution, Mr. Carswell approached a regional food distributor for a solution. Mr. Carswell was offered a plan whereby the distributor would advertise and distribute the product on the basis of 25 percent of gross sales. The distributor would assist Mr. Carswell in securing a loan from the local bank to expand production.

Before he had an opportunity to contact the bank to borrow money, Mr. Carswell was introduced to Mr. Bernie Lubo, a plastics engineer, who produced plastic containers. Mr. Carswell mentioned his own problems in the expansion of his business. Mr. Lubo wanted to finance expanded juice production with the understanding that plastic containers would be used for marketing the orange juice. He would lend the money interest free, but he was to receive 40 percent of the net profits for the next ten years. Distribution and advertising were to be done through a local broker for 25 percent of gross sales. The principal on Mr. Lubo's invested money was to be repaid by Mr. Carswell on a basis of 10 percent of his share of the profits. Mr. Lubo was to retain an interest in the profits of the firm until the loan was repaid, or at least for ten years.

Mr. Carswell's current sales were 10,000 gallons of juice a month. If distribution could be expanded, sales could be doubled, given the potential demand. Of the possible total sales of 20,000 a month, about 75 percent would be sold to large restaurants and the remainder to small cafeterias and luncheonettes. As soon as the juice was bottled in plastic containers, sales could also be made to household consumers. Mr. Carswell was very optimistic that sales to the final consumer through retail shops would succeed. Some initial contacts were made with a local franchiser of drive-in dairy shops. The franchiser was sure that he could sell 4,000 gallons a month through his outlets.

Mr. Carswell also calculated his potential profits. His goal was to increase sales while at the same time earning a 10 percent rate of return on his prior capital investment in equipment and other assets. The present value of Mr. Carswell's investment was $250,000. Of this sum, machinery and equipment were valued at $100,000; real estate was worth $50,000 and his patent and know-how were valued at $100,000. On the basis of this evaluation, Mr. Carswell desired a return of $25,000 above salaries and other expenses after the first year of operation.

Both the regional distributor and Mr. Bernie Lubo believed that Mr. Carswell's sales could be increased to 15,000 gallons of juice per month by the end of the first year of expanded operations. However, the extent to which production could be expanded to meet demand depended on the availability of plastic containers (which would be supplied at factory cost under Mr. Lubo's proposal), and additional machinery. Increased market coverage would be obtained under both the regional food distributor and Lubo proposals. The critical deciding factor, as Mr. Carswell understood, was which plan would maximize his return on investment beyond the minimum figure of 10 percent.

DIRECTIONS: The questions that follow relate to the preceding passage. Evaluate, in terms of the passage, each of the items given. Then select your answer from one of the following classifications, and blacken the corresponding space on the answer sheet.

   (A) A MAJOR OBJECTIVE in making the decision: one of the goals sought by the decision maker

   (B) A MAJOR FACTOR in making the decision: an aspect of the problem, specifically mentioned in the passage, that fundamentally affects and/or determines the decision

   (C) A MINOR FACTOR in making the decision: a less important element bearing on or affecting a Major Factor, rather than a Major Objective directly

   (D) A MAJOR ASSUMPTION in making the decision: a projection or supposition arrived at by the decision maker before considering the factors and alternatives

   (E) AN UNIMPORTANT ISSUE in making the decision: an item lacking significant impact on, or relationship to, the decision

1. Cost of securing a loan

2. High breakage rate of glass jugs

3. Expansion of the business

4. Continued demand by the public for Carswell's orange juice

5. Availability of an interest-free loan

6. Possibility of doubling sales through expanded distribution

7. Current valuation of Carswell's real estate

8. Previous use of Mr. Carswell's building as a woodworking shop

9. Ten percent return on investment

10. Plausibility of monthly sales of 4,000 gallons in dairy shops

11. Small scale of current advertising

12. Availability of a loan from a local rather than a national bank

13. Sale of juice to cafeterias

14. Value of patent held by Mr. Carswell
15. Mr. Carswell's current level of sales
16. Carswell's background in chemical engineering
17. Carswell's processing method
18. Cost of plastic containers

Passage 2:

National Office Machines of Dayton, Ohio, manufacturers of cash registers, EDP equipment, adding machines, and other small office equipment, has recently (March, 1970) entered into a joint venture with Nippon Cash Machines of Tokyo, Japan. National Office Machines (N.O.M.) had domestic sales of over _____ million dollars in 1969 and foreign sales of nearly _____ million. Besides the United States, they operate in most of Western Europe, the Mideast, and some parts of the Far East. In the past, they have had no significant sales or sales force in Japan although they were represented there by a small trading company until a few years ago. In the United States they are one of the leaders in their field and are considered to have one of the most successful and aggressive sales forces found in the this highly competitive industry.

Nippon Cash Machines (N.C.M.) is an old-line cash register manufacturing company organized in 1872. At one time, they were the major manufacturer of cash register equipment in Japan but they have been losing ground since 1950 even though they produce perhaps the best cash register in Japan. Sales in 1969 were _____ yen (280 yen = 1 U.S. dollar), a 15 percent decrease over sales in 1968. The fact that they produce only cash registers is one of their major problems; the merger with N.O.M. will give them much-needed breadth in their product offerings. Another hoped-for strength to be gained from the joint venture is managerial leadership, which they sorely need.

There are 14 Japanese companies which have products that compete with Nippon, plus several foreign giants such as IBM, National Cash Register, Burroughs of the United States, and Sweda Machines of Sweden. Nippon has a small sales force of 21 men, most of whom have been with the company since shortly after World War II and a few since pre-World War II days. These salesmen have been responsible for selling to Japanese trading companies and to a few large purchasers of equipment.

Part of the joint venture agreement was doubling the sales force within a year, with N.O.M. responsible for hiring and training the new salesmen, who must all be young, college-trained Japanese nationals. The agreement also allowed for U.S. personnel in supervisory positions for an indeterminate period of time and retaining the current Nippon sales force.

One of the many sales management problems facing the Nippon/American Business Machines Corporation (N.A.B.M.C.—the name of the new joint venture) was what sales compensation plan to use, i.e., should they follow the Japanese tradition of straight salary and guaranteed employment until death with no incentive program, or the U.S. method (very successful for N.O.M. in the United States) of commissions and various incentives based on sales performance, with the ultimate threat of being fired if sales quotas continuously go unfilled.

The immediate response to the problem might well be one of using the tried and true U.S. compensation methods, since they have worked so well in the United States and are perhaps the kind of changes needed and expected from the U.S. management. N.O.M.

management is convinced that salesmen selling their kinds of products in a competitive market must have strong incentives in order to produce. In fact, N.O.M. had experimented on a limited basis in the United States with straight salary about 10 years ago and it was a "bomb." Unfortunately the problem is considerably more complex than it appears on the surface.

One of the facts to be faced by N.O.M. management is the traditional labor-management relations and employment systems which exist in Japan. The roots of the system go back to Japan's feudal era, when a serf promised a lifetime of service to his lord in exchange for a lifetime of protection. By the start of the country's industrial revolution in the 1880s, an unskilled worker pledged to remain with a company all his useful life if the employer would teach him the new mechanical arts. The tradition of spending a lifetime with a single employer survives today mainly because most workers like it that way. There is little chance of being fired, pay raises are regular, and there is a strict order of job-protecting seniority.

Japanese workers at larger companies still are protected from out-right dismissal by union contracts and an industrial tradition that some personnel specialists believe has the force of law. Under this tradition, a worker can be dismissed after an initial trial period only for gross cause, such as theft or some other major infraction. As long as the company remains in business he isn't discharged, or even furloughed, simply because there isn't enough work to be done.

Besides the guarantee of employment for life, the typical Japanese worker receives many fringe benefits from the company. Just how paternalistic the typical Japanese firm can be is illustrated by a statement from the Japanese Ministry of Foreign Affairs which gives the example of "A," a male worker who is employed in a fairly representative company in Tokyo:

To begin with, A lives in a house provided by his company, and the rent he pays is amazingly low when compared with average city rents. His daily trips between home and factory are paid by the company. A's working hours are from 9 A.M. to 5 P.M. with a break for lunch which he usually takes in the company restaurant at a very cheap price. He often brings back to his wife food, clothing, and other miscellaneous articles that he buys at the company store at a discount ranging from 10 percent to 30 percent below city prices. The company store even supplies furniture, refrigerators, and television sets on an installment basis, for which, if necessary, A can obtain a loan from the company almost free of interest.

In case of illness, A is given free medical treatment in the company hospital, and if his indisposition extends over a number of years, the company will continue paying almost his full salary. The company maintains lodges at seaside or mountain resorts, where A can spend the holidays or an occasional weekend with the family at moderate prices. . . . It must also be remembered that when A reaches retirement age (usually 55) he will receive a lump sum retirement allowance or a pension, either of which will assure him a relatively stable living for the rest of his life.[1]

Even though "A" is only an example of a typical employee, a salesman can expect the same treatment. Job security is such an expected part of everyday life that no attempt is made to motivate the Japanese salesman in the same manner as in the United States; as a consequence, selling traditionally has been primarily an order-taking job. Except for the fact that sales work offers some travel, entry to outside executive offices, the opportunity to entertain, and similar side benefits, it provides a young man with little other incentive to surpass his basic quotas and drum up new business. The traditional Japanese bonuses (which normally amount to about two or four months' salary over the year) are no larger for salesmen than any other functional job in the company.

As a key executive in a Mitsui-affiliated engineering firm put it recently: "The typical salesman in Japan isn't required to have any particular talent." In return for meeting sales

---

[1] "Japan's Paternalistic Employment System Is Changing in Face of Tight Labor Market," *The Wall Street Journal*, March 27, 1967, p. 6. Reprinted by permission of *The Wall Street Journal*, © Dow Jones & Company, Inc. (1967). All Rights Reserved.

quotas, most Japanese salesmen draw a modest monthly salary, sweetened about twice a year by bonuses. Manufacturers of industrial products generally pay no commission or other incentives to boost their businesses.

Besides the problem of motivation, a foreign company faces other strange customs when trying to put together and manage a sales force. Class systems and the Japanese distribution system with its penchant for reciprocity put strain on the creative talents of the best sales managers, as Simmons, the U.S. bedding manufacturer, was quick to learn. One Simmons executive explains:

> We had no idea of the workings of the class system. Hiring a good man from the lower classes, for instance, could be a disaster. If he called on a client of a higher class, there was a good chance the client would be insulted. There is also a really big difference in language among the classes.[2]

In the field, Simmons found itself stymied by the bewildering realities of Japanese marketing, especially the traditional distribution system which operates on a philosophy of reciprocity that goes beyond mere business to the core of the Japanese character. It's involved with "on," the notion that regards a favor or any kind as a debt that must be repaid. To "wear" another's "on" in business and then turn against him is to lose face, abhorrent to most Japanese. Thus, the owner of large Western-style apartments, hotels, or developments will buy his beds from the supplier to whom he owes a favor, no matter what the competition offers.

In small department and other retail stores, where most items are handled on consignment, the bond with the supplier is even stronger. Consequently, all sales outlets are connected in a complicated web that runs from the largest supplier, with a huge national force, to the smallest local distributor, with a handful of door-to-door salesmen. The system is self-perpetuating and all but impossible to crack from the outside.

However, there is some change in attitude taking place as both workers and companies start discarding traditions for the job mobility common in the United States. Skilled workers are willing to bargain on the strength of their experience in an open labor market in an effort to get higher wages or better job opportunities; in the United States it's called "shopping around." And a few companies are showing willingness to lure workers away from other concerns. A number of companies are also plotting on how to rid themselves of some of the "deadwood" workers accumulated as a result of promotions by strict seniority.

Toyo Rayon Company, Japan's largest producer of synthetic fibers, says it will start reevaluating all its senior employees every five years with the implied threat that those who don't measure up to the company's expectations will have to accept reassignment and possibly demotion; some may even be asked to resign. A chemical engineering and construction firm is planning to ask all its employees over 42 to negotiate a new contract with the company every two years. Pay raises and promotions will go to those the company wants to keep. For those who think they are worth more than the company is willing to pay, the company will offer "retirement" with something less than the $15,000 lump-sum payment that the average Japanese worker receives when he reaches 55.

And a few U.S. companies operating in Japan are also experimenting with incentive plans. Nitta and Company, a belting manufacturer and Japanese distributor for Chesterton Packing and Seal Company, was persuaded by Chesterton to set up a travel plan incentive for salesmen who topped their regular sales quotas. Unorthodox as the idea was for Japan, Nitta went along and, the first year, special one-week trips to Far East holiday spots like Hong Kong, Taiwan, Manila, and Macao were inaugurated. Nitta's sales of Chesterton products jumped 212 percent and this year sales are up 60 percent over 1968.

---

[2] "Simmons in Japan, No Bed of Roses," *Sales Management*, August 1, 1967, pp. 27–29. Reprinted by permission from Sales & Marketing Management magazine. Copyright 1967.

Last April, Nitta took the full step toward an American-style sales program. Under Chesterton's guidance, the company eliminated bonuses and initiated a sales commission plan.

When the first quarterly commission checks were mailed last June, the top salesmen found they had earned an average of $550 per month each, compared to original basic salaries of about $100 a month.

At first, Nitta's management had resisted any form of incentive program for its personnel, arguing that it would "disrupt" all normal business operations of the company. The virtually instantaneous success of the travel incentives in motivating previously plodding sales performances into an enthusiastic burst of initiative has prompted Nitta to consider installing some form of incentive and/or commission sales plan for its extensive non-Chesterton operations. The company is one of the largest manufacturers of industrial belting in Japan.

IBM also has made a move toward chucking the traditional Japanese sales system (i.e., salary plus bonus but no incentives). For about a year it has been working with a combination which retains the semi-annual bonus while adding commission payments on the sales over pre-set quotas.

"It's difficult to apply a straight commission system in selling computers because of the complexities of the product," an IBM-Japan official said. "Our salesmen don't get big commissions because other employees would be jealous." To head off possible ill-feeling, therefore, some non-selling IBM employees receive monetary incentives.

Most Japanese companies seem reluctant to follow IBM's and Nitta's example because they have their doubts about directing older salesmen to go beyond their usual order-taking role. High-pressure tactics are not well accepted here, and sales channels are often pretty well set by custom and long practice (e.g., a manufacturer normally deals with one trading company, which in turn sells only to customers A, B, C, and D). A salesman or trading company, for that matter, is not often encouraged to go after customer Z and get him away from a rival supplier.

Japanese companies also consider non-sales employees a tough problem to handle. With salesmen deprived of the "glamour" status often accorded by many top managements in the United States, even Nitta executives admit they have a ticklish problem in explaining how salesmen—who are considered to be just another key working group in the company with no special status—rate incentive pay and special earning opportunities.[3]

The Japanese market is becoming more competitive and there is real fear on the part of N.O.M. executives that the traditional system just won't work in a competitive market. On the other hand, the proponents of the incentive system agree that the system really has not been tested over long periods or even very adequately, since it has only been applied in a growing market. In other words, was it the incentive system which caused the successes achieved by the companies or was it market growth? Especially is there doubt since other companies following the traditional method of compensation and employee relations have also had sales increases during the same period.

The problem is further complicated for Nippon/American because they will have both new and old salesmen. The young Japanese seem eager to accept the incentive method but older men are hesitant. How do you satisfy both since you must, by agreement, retain all the sales staff? Another very critical problem lies with the nonsales employees; traditionally, all employees on the same level are treated equally whether sales, production, or staff. How do you encourage competitive, aggressive salesmanship in a market unfamiliar to such tactics, and how do you compensate salesmen in such a manner to promote more aggressive selling in the face of tradition-bound practices of paternalistic company behavior?

---

[3] "How to Put New Hustle into a Japanese Salesman," *Business Abroad*, November 27, 1967, pp. 33–34. Reprinted with permission.

DIRECTIONS: The questions that follow relate to the preceding passage. Evaluate, in terms of the passage, each of the items given. Then select your answer from one of the following classifications, and blacken the corresponding space on the answer sheet.

(A) A MAJOR OBJECTIVE in making the decision: one of the goals sought by the decision maker

(B) A MAJOR FACTOR in making the decision: an aspect of the problem, specifically mentioned in the passage, that fundamentally affects and/or determines the decision

(C) A MINOR FACTOR in making the decision: a less important element bearing on or affecting a Major Factor, rather than a Major Objective directly

(D) A MAJOR ASSUMPTION in making the decision: a projection or supposition arrived at by the decision maker before considering the factors and alternatives

(E) AN UNIMPORTANT ISSUE in making the decision: an item lacking significant impact on, or relationship to, the decision

19. Motivating Japanese salesmen

20. Using U.S. compensation methods in Japan

21. Labor-management relations

22. Job security of Japanese workers

23. Retaining the current Nippon sales force

24. Doubling the sales force

25. The establishment of Nippon in 1872

26. Determining a sales compensation plan

27. Differences in American and Japanese fringe benefits

28. Understanding the Japanese class system

29. The reevaluation of senior employees by Toyo Rayon

30. Regular pay raises in Japan

31. Expanding N.C.M.'s product line

32. Selling to Japanese trading companies

33. Improving N.C.M.'s management

34. The traditional compensation system not working in a competitive market

35. N.O.M.'s aggressive sales force

If there is still time remaining, you may review the questions in this section only.
You may not turn to any other section of the test.

Section VIII   Writing Ability

TIME: 30 minutes

DIRECTIONS: This test consists of a number of sentences, in each of which some part or the whole is underlined. Each sentence is followed by five alternative versions of the underlined portion. Select the alternative you consider both most correct and most effective according to the requirements of standard written English. Answer A is the same as the original version; if you think the original version is best, select answer A.

In considering the answer choices, be attentive to matters of grammar, diction, and syntax, as well as clarity, precision, and fluency. Do not select an answer which alters the meaning of the original sentence.

1. <u>Although I calculate that he will be here</u> any minute, I cannot wait much longer for him to arrive.

   (A) Although I calculate that he will be here
   (B) Although I reckon that he will be here
   (C) Because I calculate that he will be here
   (D) Although I think that he will be here
   (E) Because I am confident that he will be here

2. <u>The fourteen-hour day not only has been reduced</u> to one of ten hours but also, in some lines of work, to one of eight or even six.

   (A) The fourteen-hour day not only has been reduced
   (B) Not only the fourteen-hour day has been reduced
   (C) Not the fourteen-hour day only has been reduced
   (D) The fourteen-hour day has not only been reduced
   (E) The fourteen-hour day has been reduced not only

3. The trend toward a decrease is further evidenced in the longer weekend <u>already</u> given to employees in many business establishments.

   (A) already
   (B) all ready
   (C) allready
   (D) ready
   (E) all in all

4. <u>Using it wisely,</u> leisure promotes health, efficiency, and happiness.

   (A) Using it wisely,
   (B) If used wisely,
   (C) Having used it wisely,
   (D) Because it is used wisely,
   (E) Because of usefulness,

5. Americans are learning that their concept of a research worker, <u>toiling alone in his laboratory and who discovers miraculous cures</u> has been highly idealized and glamorized.

   (A) toiling alone in his laboratory and who discovers miraculous cures
   (B) toiling in his laboratory by himself and discovers miraculous cures
   (C) toiling alone in his laboratory to discover miraculous cures,
   (D) who toil alone in the laboratory and discover miraculous cures
   (E) toiling in his laboratory to discover miraculous cures by himself

6. <u>We want the teacher to be him</u> who has the best rapport with the students.

   (A) We want the teacher to be him
   (B) We want the teacher to be he
   (C) We want him to be the teacher
   (D) We desire that the teacher be him
   (E) We anticipate that the teacher will be him

7. <u>If he were to win the medal,</u> I for one would be disturbed.

   (A) If he were to win the medal,
   (B) If he was to win the medal,
   (C) If he wins the medal,
   (D) If he is the winner of the medal,
   (E) In the event that he wins the medal,

8. The scouts were told <u>to take an overnight hike, pitch camp, prepare dinner, and that they should be in bed by 9 p.m.</u>

   (A) to take an overnight hike, pitch camp, prepare dinner, and that they should be in bed by 9 p.m.
   (B) to take an overnight hike, to pitch camp, to prepare dinner, and that they should be in bed by 9 p.m.
   (C) to take an overnight hike, pitch camp, prepare dinner, and be in bed by 9 p.m.
   (D) to take an overnight hike, pitching camp, preparing dinner and going to bed by 9 p.m.
   (E) to engage in an overnight hike, pitch camp, prepare dinner, and that they should be in bed by 9 p.m.

9. The dean informed us that the <u>applicant had not and never will be accepted by the college because of his high school record.</u>

   (A) applicant had not and never will be accepted by the college because of his high school record
   (B) applicant had not and never would be accepted by the college because of his high school record
   (C) applicant had not been and never will be excepted by the college because of his high school record
   (D) applicant had not been and never would be excepted by the college because of his high school record
   (E) applicant had not been and never would be accepted by the college because of his high school record

10. The <u>government's failing to keep it's pledges</u> will earn the distrust of all the other nations in the alliance.

   (A) government's failing to keep it's pledges
   (B) government failing to keep it's pledges
   (C) government's failing to keep its pledges
   (D) government failing to keep its pledges
   (E) governments failing to keep their pledges

11. Her brother along with her parents <u>insist</u> that she remain in school.

   (A) insist
   (B) insists
   (C) are insisting
   (D) were insisting
   (E) have insisted

12. Most students like to read <u>these kind of books</u> during their spare time.

    (A) these kind of books
    (B) these kind of book
    (C) this kind of book
    (D) this kinds of books
    (E) those kind of books

13. <u>She not only was competent but also friendly</u> in nature.

    (A) She not only was competent but also friendly
    (B) Not only was she competent but friendly also
    (C) She not only was competent but friendly also
    (D) She was not only competent but also friendly
    (E) She was not only competent but friendly also

14. In the normal course of events, <u>John will graduate high school and enter</u> college in two years.

    (A) John will graduate high school and enter
    (B) John will graduate from high school and enter
    (C) John will be graduated from high school and enter
    (D) John will be graduated from high school and enter into
    (E) John will have graduated high school and enter

15. With the exception of <u>Frank and I, everyone in the class finished</u> the assignment before the bell rang.

    (A) Frank and I, everyone in the class finished
    (B) Frank and me, everyone in the class finished
    (C) Frank and me, everyone in the class had finished
    (D) Frank and I, everyone in the class had finished
    (E) Frank and me everyone in the class finished

16. Many middle-class individuals find that they cannot obtain good medical attention, <u>despite they need it badly</u>.

    (A) despite they need it badly
    (B) despite they badly need it
    (C) in spite of they need it badly
    (D) however much they need it
    (E) therefore, they need it badly

17. During the winter of 1973, Americans <u>discovered the need to conserve energy and attempts were made to meet the crisis</u>.

    (A) discovered the need to conserve energy and attempts were made to meet the crisis
    (B) discovered the need to conserve energy and that the crisis had to be met
    (C) discovered the need to conserve energy and attempted to meet the crisis
    (D) needed to conserve energy and to meet the crisis
    (E) needed to conserve energy and attempts were made to meet the crisis

18. When one eats in this restaurant, you often find that the prices are high and that the food is poorly prepared.

    (A) When one eats in this restaurant, you often find
    (B) When you eat in this restaurant, one often finds
    (C) As you eat in this restaurant, you often find
    (D) If you eat in this restaurant, you often find
    (E) When one ate in this restaurant, he often found

19. Ever since the bombing of Cambodia, there has been much opposition from they who maintain that it was an unauthorized war.

    (A) from they who maintain that it was an unauthorized war
    (B) from they who maintain that it had been an unauthorized war
    (C) from those who maintain that it was an unauthorized war
    (D) from they maintaining that it was unauthorized
    (E) from they maintaining that it had been unauthorized

20. John was imminently qualified for the position because he had studied computer programming and how to operate an IBM machine.

    (A) imminently qualified for the position because he had studied computer programming and how to operate an IBM machine
    (B) imminently qualified for the position because he had studied computer programming and the operation of an IBM machine
    (C) eminently qualified for the position because he had studied computer programming and how to operate an IBM machine
    (D) eminently qualified for the position because he had studied computer programming and the operation of an IBM machine
    (E) eminently qualified because he had studied computer programming and how to operate an IBM machine

21. I am not to eager to go to this play because it did not get good reviews.

    (A) I am not to eager to go to this play because it did not get good reviews.
    (B) Because of its poor reviews, I am not to eager to go to this play.
    (C) Because of its poor revues, I am not to eager to go to this play.
    (D) I am not to eager to go to this play because the critics did not give it good reviews.
    (E) I am not too eager to go to this play because of its poor reviews.

22. It was decided by us that the emphasis would be placed on the results that might be attained.

    (A) It was decided by us that the emphasis would be placed on the results that might be attained.
    (B) We decided that the emphasis would be placed on the results that might be attained.
    (C) We decided to emphasize the results that might be attained.
    (D) We decided to emphasize the results we might attain.
    (E) It was decided that we would place emphasis on the results that might be attained.

23. May I venture to say that I think this performance is the most superior I have ever heard.

    (A) May I venture to say that I think this performance is the most superior
    (B) May I venture to say that this performance is the most superior
    (C) May I say that this performance is the most superior
    (D) I think this performance is superior to any
    (E) This performance is the most superior of any

24. <u>Completing the physical examination, the tonsils were found to be diseased.</u>

    (A) Completing the physical examination, the tonsils were found to be diseased.
    (B) Having completed the physical examination, the tonsils were found to be diseased.
    (C) When the physical examination was completed, the tonsils were found to be diseased.
    (D) The physical examination completed, the tonsils were found to be diseased.
    (E) The physical examination found that the tonsils were diseased.

25. Today this is a totally different world <u>than we have seen</u> in the last decade.

    (A) than we have seen
    (B) from what we have seen
    (C) from what we seen
    (D) than what we seen
    (E) then we have seen

If there is still time remaining, you may review the questions in this section only.
You may not turn to any other section of the test.

Answers

Section I — Reading Comprehension

1. (D)	8. (B)	15. (E)	22. (C)
2. (C)	9. (C)	16. (A)	23. (A)
3. (C)	10. (C)	17. (C)	24. (D)
4. (C)	11. (D)	18. (C)	25. (B)
5. (E)	12. (E)	19. (A)	
6. (C)	13. (C)	20. (A)	
7. (A)	14. (E)	21. (B)	

Section II — Reading Comprehension

1. (A)	8. (D)	15. (A)	22. (C)
2. (B)	9. (B)	16. (C)	23. (C)
3. (D)	10. (A)	17. (B)	24. (A)
4. (D)	11. (C)	18. (B)	25. (C)
5. (D)	12. (D)	19. (C)	
6. (E)	13. (A)	20. (C)	
7. (B)	14. (D)	21. (C)	

Section III — Problem Solving

(Numbers in parentheses indicate the section in the Mathematics Review where material concerning the question is discussed.)

1. (D) (I-4)	6. (E) (IV-4)	11. (B) (I-4)	16. (E) (I-4)
2. (E) (II-2)	7. (E) (II-5)	12. (A) (II-3)	17. (C) (I-7)
3. (C) (II-6)	8. (D) (II-4)	13. (B) (II-4)	18. (A) (II-2)
4. (D) (IV-4)	9. (D) (II-2, I-4)	14. (C) (II-6)	19. (C) (I-2, 4)
5. (D) (IV-4)	10. (B) (III-4)	15. (B) (II-5)	20. (A) (III-4)

Section IV — Analysis of Situations

1. (E)	10. (D)	19. (A)	28. (E)
2. (A)	11. (D)	20. (E)	29. (E)
3. (B)	12. (A)	21. (B)	30. (B)
4. (C)	13. (B)	22. (B)	31. (B)
5. (A)	14. (C)	23. (C)	32. (D)
6. (B)	15. (E)	24. (B)	33. (A)
7. (D)	16. (E)	25. (A)	34. (B)
8. (E)	17. (B)	26. (C)	35. (E)
9. (C)	18. (E)	27. (B)	

Section V   Data Sufficiency

1. (E)	8. (B)	15. (A)	22. (A)
2. (C)	9. (E)	16. (E)	23. (E)
3. (A)	10. (E)	17. (C)	24. (C)
4. (E)	11. (A)	18. (D)	25. (E)
5. (D)	12. (C)	19. (A)	
6. (D)	13. (E)	20. (E)	
7. (B)	14. (B)	21. (C)	

Section VI   Problem Solving

(Numbers in parentheses indicate the section in the Mathematics Review where material concerning the question is discussed.)

1. (D) (II-3)	6. (B) (IV-5)	11. (C) (II-3)	16. (C) (II-3)
2. (E) (I-2)	7. (C) (IV-5)	12. (B) (II-3)	17. (B) (II-7)
3. (B) (I-4)	8. (C) (I-4)	13. (D) (IV-1, I-7)	18. (C) (III-4, 7)
4. (D) (IV-5)	9. (B) (I-2)	14. (E) (IV1, I-7)	19. (E) (II-3)
5. (C) (IV-5)	10. (D) (III-6, 7)	15. (D) (IV-1)	20. (E) (II-2, I-8)

Section VII   Analysis of Situations

1. (B)	10. (D)	19. (A)	28. (B)
2. (B)	11. (B)	20. (D)	29. (E)
3. (A)	12. (E)	21. (B)	30. (C)
4. (D)	13. (C)	22. (C)	31. (A)
5. (B)	14. (E)	23. (B)	32. (E)
6. (D)	15. (C)	24. (A)	33. (A)
7. (C)	16. (E)	25. (E)	34. (D)
8. (E)	17. (B)	26. (A)	35. (E)
9. (A)	18. (C)	27. (C)	

Section VIII   Writing Ability

1. (D)	8. (C)	15. (C)	22. (D)
2. (E)	9. (E)	16. (D)	23. (D)
3. (A)	10. (C)	17. (C)	24. (E)
4. (B)	11. (B)	18. (C)	25. (B)
5. (C)	12. (C)	19. (C)	
6. (B)	13. (D)	20. (D)	
7. (A)	14. (B)	21. (E)	

Analysis

Section I   Reading Comprehension

1. **(D)** Note that the question asks "about how many," which requires an approximate figure. Of all the alternative answers, (D) comes closest to the 8,600 employees given in paragraph 1.

2. **(C)** See paragraph 3, lines 1 and 2.

3. **(C)** See paragraph 5, line 1: "Top Presidential appointees, . . . bear the brunt of translating the philosophy and aims of the current administration into practical programs."

4. **(C)** See paragraph 6, sentence 2.

5. **(E)** See paragraph 6, last line.

6. **(C)** See paragraph 7: "Those whom the president selects . . ." and following.

7. **(A)** See paragraph 8: ". . . they usually have substantial responsibilities in line management. . . ."

8. **(B)** Paragraph 8, line 1: "These appointees are primarily regarded as policy makers. . . ."

9. **(C)** See paragraph 7: "Those selected by department and agency heads . . ." and following.

10. **(C)** See paragraph 1, line 1: "The first and decisive step in the expansion of Europe overseas was the conquest of the Atlantic Ocean."

11. **(D)** See paragraph 1, line 15: ". . . in men of the calibre of Prince Henry, known as the Navigator. . . ."

12. **(E)** In paragraph 1, the sentence containing the statement "Portugal could adapt and develop the knowledge and experience of the past to meet the challenge of the unknown . . . ," meets answer (B); also in this paragraph there is mention of experienced Portuguese seamen and a mercantile marine (A), rudiments of navigation (C), and mapmakers (D). Since extensive trade routes are never mentioned, the correct answer is (E).

13. **(C)** Portugal was the logical nation for this task because of her "geographical position and her history." Wealth (A) and navigational experience (B) are resources in context with the question, while (D) and (E) are vague.

14. **(E)** See paragraph 1.

15. **(E)** See paragraph 2, line 28: Seamen kept close to shore because ". . . the latitudinal extent of the Mediterranean was not great, and voyages could be conducted from point to point on compass bearings," not because of the other reasons given in the question.

16. **(A)** See paragraph 2, line 22: ". . . hazards . . . in the form of sudden storms or dangerous coasts, were known and could be usually anticipated."

17. **(C)** See paragraph 2, line 31: "Having made a landfall on a bearing, they could determine their precise position from prominent landmarks. . . ."

18. **(C)** The correct answer is given in paragraph 2. The policeman must be neutral and present the facts, while the "artist usually begins with a preconceived message or attitude . . . ," i.e., prejudiced. While artists are "emotional," no mention is made that policemen are stoic (D).

19. **(A)** The writer explains that the policemen's reactions were "surprisingly unprejudiced." The rest of paragraph 3 explains that policemen reacted to story events and characters according to alternative (A).

20. **(A)** The only characters that policemen objected to were unrealistic. See paragraph 3.

21. **(B)** Only "suspense" was given in the passage (in paragraph 4).

22. **(C)** Alternatives I and II may be found in the first paragraph.

23. **(A)** Policemen must "also try to evaluate the events they describe. . . ." The "also" refers to artists and writers. See paragraph 2, and also paragraph 1: ". . . they had to be able to take in the details of a situation quickly. . . ."

24. **(D)** Policemen wrote about their work. See paragraph 4.

25. **(B)** Alternative (B) sums up their feeling. Corruption and routine were mentioned as minor annoyances. The issues of pay and adventure were not mentioned. See paragraph 4.

Section II   Reading Comprehension

1. **(A)** The dropout rate on average for all Open Admissions students was 48%; for regular students, 36%; and for Open Admissions categories, 56% (lines 59–62).

2. **(B)** See paragraph 1: "The successful institution of higher learning had never been one whose mission could be defined in terms of providing vocational skills or . . . resolving societal problems." This is the sort of question that must be read carefully; it asks for an answer that is *not* among the alternatives given in the passage.

3. **(D)** The idea that a university must relate to the problems of society is given in paragraphs 2, 3, and 5.

4. **(D)** See the last sentence.

5. **(D)** The two-year college is described in paragraph 4 as a "service-related" and "community" college. It is no longer called a "junior" college.

6. **(E)** The idea of the service-oriented college is to produce "productive" students and, as stated in the third paragraph, to provide programs "to meet the demands of regional employment markets, . . ." i.e., to make graduates employable.

7. **(B)** The attrition rate for Open Admissions students was 56 percent, and that for regular students 36 percent, a difference of 20 percent. See lines 61–62.

8. **(D)** The phrase "this phenomenon" in line 44 refers to the preceding discussion of the service-university, and not just to the "multiversity."

9. **(B)** The attrition rate for Open Admissions students was 56 percent and for regular students, 36 percent. The average of 56 percent and 36 percent is 48 percent. See lines 59–62.

10. **(A)** See the example of steel in the last two paragraphs.

11. **(C)** Increased barriers to trade—protectionism—have been caused by recession and unemployment. See paragraph 2.

12. **(D)** See line 36: ". . . trade probably fell as the world economy stayed flat."

13. **(A)** See lines 21–22: ". . . Washington . . . has raised new barriers against imports in autos, textiles and sugar."

14. **(D)** Alternatives (B) and (E) can be eliminated since the subject of the passage is not trade agreements or world exports (trade, of course, includes imports as well). Alternative (A) is not plausible, because the passage does not emphasize "domestic" but rather international economic policy. The "Tokyo Round," (C), was not mentioned in the passage. Alternative (D) certainly reflects the passage, which is pessimistic about the future of world trade.

15. **(A)** See lines 42–43: ". . . new trade restraints, often bound up in voluntary agreements . . . to limit particular imports . . ."

16. **(C)** Exports are promoted through subsidies. See lines 24–25.

17. **(B)** Bilateral quotas were used by the European Economic Community. See the last paragraph.

18. **(B)** See paragraph 3, sentence 1: ". . . people are particularly sensitive about any reduction in the quality of the atmosphere. . . ."

19. **(C)** This is implied in paragraph 2.

20. **(C)** See paragraph 4: "The households' share in atmospheric pollution is far bigger than that of industry. . . ." The key word in the question is "most."

21. **(C)** Both production *and* transportation costs are important. Although paragraph 1 states that the costs of maintaining clean water are "primarily" production costs, paragraph 5 states that this problem is "related to the costs of production and transport . . ."

22. **(C)** See paragraph 6, line 1: "Atmospheric pollution caused by the private property of individuals . . . is difficult to control."

23. **(C)** See paragraph 7: both active and passive resources. No mention is made of levying taxes.

24. **(A)** See paragraph 6: "*In this particular case*, the cost of anti-pollution measures will have to be borne, to a considerable extent, by individuals. . . ." "In this particular case" refers to the situation also described in the paragraph where pollution is caused by the private property of individuals.

25. **(C)** See paragraph 7: While noise abatement is not impossible to achieve, the "costs of a complete protection against noise are so prohibitive. . . ."

Section III   Problem Solving

1. **(D)** Since he pays 6% on the first $500, this equals (.06)(500) or $30 interest on the first $500. He is borrowing $5,500 which is $5,000 in excess of the first $500. Thus, he also pays 5½% of $5,000, which is (.055)(5,000) or $275.00. Therefore, the total interest is $305.

2. **(E)** $6x - 3y$ is $3(2x - y)$. Since $2x - y = 4$, $6x - 3y = 3 \cdot 4$ or 12.

3. **(C)** The progression is arithmetic and $11 - 5 = 6 = 17 - 11$, so every term is 6 more than the previous team. Therefore, the next term after 17 is $17 + 6$ or 23.

4. **(D)** The bar was above 50 in 1947.

5. **(D)** In 1952, hydro plants had about 21 million kilowatts, while the total capacity was about 84 million kilowatts. Therefore, the capacity of the steam and internal combustion plants in 1952 was about $(84 - 21)$ or 63 million kilowatts. Since $\frac{63}{21} = 3$, x is 3.

6. **(E)** STATEMENT I is true since the graph is almost horizontal between 1930 and 1939, whereas it rises between 1920 and 1929 and between 1940 and 1949.

Since the total capacity in 1925 was less than 25 million kilowatts and the capacity of the hydro plants in 1925 was more than 5 million kilowatts, STATEMENT II can be inferred.

STATEMENT III is also true. Between 1925 and 1945, the capacity went from about 22 million to about 50 million kilowatts, which is an increase of about 28 million kilowatts. However, the capacity in 1925 was about 83 million kilowatts, so the increase between 1945 and 1952 was about 33 million kilowatts.

Therefore, STATEMENTS I, II, and III can all be inferred from the graph.

7. **(E)** Since each packer loads ⅛ of a box in 9 minutes, the 20 packers will load ²⁰⁄₈, or 2½ boxes in 9 minutes. There are 90 minutes in 1½ hours; so the 20 packers will load $10 \times 2\frac{1}{2}$ or 25 boxes in 1½ hours.

8. **(D)** The entire population can be divided into three nonoverlapping parts: owns both a car and a motorcyle, owns a car but not a motorcycle, and owns a motorcycle but not a car. If we denote these categories by A, B, and C respectively, we know that $A + B + C = 100\%$. Also, since $A + B$ consists of all the people who own a car, we have $A + B = 90\%$. Therefore, C must be 10%. But C is the category of people who own a motorcycle but do not own a car.

9. **(D)** To do computations, change percentages to decimals. Let J, M, B, and L stand for Jim's, Marcia's, Bob's, and Lee's respective weights. Then we know $J = 1.4M$, $B = .9L$, and $L = 2M$. We need to know B as a percentage of J. Since $B = .9L$ and $L = 2M$, we have $B = .9 (2M) = 1.8M$. $J = 1.4M$ is equivalent to $M = (1/(1.4))J$. So $B = 1.8M = 1.8(1/(1.4))J = (1²⁄₇)J$. Converting 1²⁄₇ to a percentage, we have $1²⁄₇ = 1.28⁴⁄₇ = 128⁴⁄₇\%$, so (D) is the correct answer.

10. **(B)** The towns can be thought of as the vertices of a triangle.

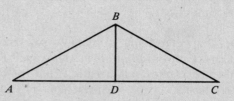

Since the distance from A to B is equal to the distance from B to C, the triangle is isosceles. The point D on AC which is closest to B is the point on AC such that BD is perpendicular to AC. (If BD were not perpendicular to AC, then there would be a point on AC closer to B than D; in the picture, E is closer to B than D is.)

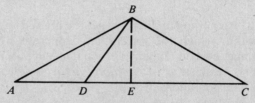

So the triangles ABD and CBD are right triangles with two corresponding sides equal. Therefore ABD is congruent to CBD. Thus $AD = DC$, and since AC is 60, AD must be 30. Since ABD is a right triangle with hypotenuse 50 and another side $= 30$, the remaining side (BD) must be 40.

11. **(B)** Since 108% of $50 = (1.08)(50) = \$54$, the chair was offered for sale at \$54.00. It was sold for 90% of \$54 since there was a 10% discount. Therefore, the chair was sold for $(.9)(\$54)$ or \$48.60.

12. **(A)** Here's a table of the hours worked:

	Mon.	Tues.	Wed.	Thurs.	Fri.	Wages for week
	8	8	8	8	8	$5x$
excess over 8 hrs	0	3	1	2	1	$(0 + 3 + 1 + 2 + 1)y = 7y.$

The average daily wage equals $\dfrac{(5x + 7y)}{5}$, or $x + \dfrac{7}{5}y$.

13. **(B)** There are 8 choices for the first female, then 7 choices for the second female, and 6 choices for the third female on the committee. So there are $8 \times 7 \times 6$ different ways to pick the three females in order. However, if member A is chosen first, then member B, then member C, the same three females are chosen as when C

is followed by A and B is chosen last. In fact, the same three members can be chosen in $3 \times 2 \times 1$ different orders. So to find the number of different groups of 3 females, DIVIDE $8 \times 7 \times 6$ by $3 \times 2 \times 1$ to obtain 56.

In the same way, there are $8 \times 7 \times 6 = 336$ ways to choose the three males in order, but any group of three males can be put in order $3 \times 2 \times 1 = 6$ different ways. So there are $336/6 = 56$ different groups of three males. Therefore, there are $56 \times 56 = 3,136$ different committees of 3 males and 3 females.

14. **(C)** Let x_n be what the motorcycle is worth after n years. Then we know $x_0 = \$2,500$ and $x_{n+1} = \frac{4}{5} \times x_n$. So $x_1 = \frac{4}{5} \times 2,500$, which is \$2,000. x_2 is $\frac{4}{5} \times 2,000$, which is 1,600, and finally x_3 is $\frac{4}{5} \times 1,600$, which is 1,280. Therefore, the motorcycle is worth \$1,280 at the end of three years.

OR

$x_3 = \frac{4}{5}x_2 = \frac{4}{5}(\frac{4}{5}x_1) = (\frac{4}{5})(\frac{4}{5})(\frac{4}{5}x_0) = \frac{64}{125}x_0.$
$(\frac{64}{125})2500 = 1280.$

15. **(B)** Since 120 miles is $\frac{3}{5}$ of 200 miles, it should cost $\frac{3}{5}$ of \$15 to travel 120 miles by automobile. Therefore, the cost is \$9.

16. **(E)** Since the only costs are \$20 for fuel and \$70 for the driver's wages, the total cost is \$90. Therefore, the company should charge 120% of \$90, which is $(1.2)(\$90)$ or \$108.

17. **(C)** The total fuel cost will be $3 \cdot 20 + 4 \cdot 15 + 2 \cdot 5 + 1 \cdot 50$, which is \$180. Since there are 10 vehicles, the average fuel cost is $180/10$ or \$18 per vehicle.

18. **(A)** Since $x + 2y = 2x + y$, we can subtract $x + 2y$ from each side of the equation and the result is $0 = x - y$.

19. **(C)** $\frac{2}{3}$ of the 15% of the families with income over \$25,000 own boats. Since $\frac{2}{3}$ of 15% = 10%, $\frac{1}{10}$ of the families own boats and have an income of \$25,000 or more.

20. **(A)** The angles are in the ratio of $1:2:2$, so 2 angles are equal to each other, and both are twice as large as the third angle of the triangle. Since a triangle with two equal angles must have the sides opposite equal, the triangle is isosceles. (Using the fact that the sum of the angles of a triangle is 180°, you can see that the angles of the triangle are 72°, 72° and 36°, so only (A) is true.)

Section IV   Analysis of Situations

1. **(E)** Fox's twenty years experience have no significant impact on the decision as to how to increase lottery sales.

2. **(A)** Increasing the number of instant lottery games was a *Major Objective* of Kamil, aimed at boosting lottery sales. *Increasing* the number of games, therefore, was an outcome sought.

3. **(B)** Note the word "stagnating." Stagnation is certainly not an outcome sought; rather, it is a condition which must be changed. The leveling off of lottery sales is a *Major Factor* in the decision process, since it forces the lottery directors to search for means of reversing this trend.

4. **(C)** The cost of the advertising campaign, while a factor in the decision, was limited to only one of the alternatives considered in the decision as to how to increase lottery sales.

5. **(A)** Increasing sales of lottery games by at least 30 percent was a major outcome desired by Kamil.

6. **(B)** The number of tickets to be sold was a *Major Factor* associated with all decision alternatives. In paragraph 4, the situation is described. In other parts of the passage, decision alternatives such as subscriptions, increasing the number of instant games (to sell more tickets), and the introduction of consolation prizes for the Lotto, all deal with increasing the *number* of tickets sold.

7. **(D)** Fishman raised the issue that members of the lower classes were the main purchasers of instant game tickets. Although this contention appeared in the press, management had no definite evidence that non-buyers were from the upper income groups. It is possible that there were lottery ticket buyers from upper-income groups and middle-income groups as well.

8. **(E)** The long history of lottery sales in Tibland has no bearing on any of the decision alternatives.

9. **(C)** The printing costs of special tickets is a *Minor Factor*. It is only one element in the *overall cost* of the decision alternative to issue subscriptions. The other element is circulation cost. The entire cost of introducing subscriptions would be a *Major Factor*.

10. **(D)** Fishman *believed* that the purchasing behavior of lottery buyers in Europe and Tibland was similar. No facts were presented to support his contention.

11. **(D)** That advertising stimulates sales must be taken as an *assumption* in this case. The argument for more advertising is put forward by Fox, based on his "experience." He did not present any facts to show, for example, that when advertising expenditures increased, sales increased, or some similar, clearly demonstrable relationship.

12. **(A)** Attracting new buyers is one of the outcomes desired by the decision makers. See paragraph 9.

13. **(B)** According to the passage, the limited budget within which the lottery must operate would make certain expensive schemes impossible. This restriction is a *Major Factor* in selecting a decision alternative.

14. **(C)** Cost of the subscriptions is a major determinant of whether consumers will purchase them and therefore a factor in management's decision as to whether to offer the product. It is a *Minor Factor* since it relates only to one alternative.

15. **(E)** The type of people serving on the board of directors is not an element in the decision making process.

16. **(E)** The fact that lotteries were run every Monday was an *Unimportant Issue* and had no bearing on any decision alternative.

17. **(B)** A major consideration of whether to adopt the alternative of subscriptions is whether enough people would be willing to pay in advance. Fox thought not, while Davis and Fishman believed in the affirmative.

18. **(E)** While winning numbers were selected at random by computer, this fact was an *Unimportant Issue* in the decision consideration.

19. **(A)** Determining compensation policy for overseas executives is an outcome desired by Len Hibert.

20. **(E)** The fact that the company produces industrial equipment does not influence the selection of an alternative course of action.

21. **(B)** As Len's company becomes more international, more emphasis has been placed on the "type and functions" of its managers sent abroad. This importance is a *Major Factor* in determining a compensation program (a major objective).

22. **(B)** The country in which an executive will be located is a major issue in determining what his compensation will be. For example, the cost-of-living is different according to location (see the table in the passage), and executives may have to be compensated accordingly.

23. **(C)** The cost of renting a house in Europe is only one of several factors that determine the total cost of living abroad, which is a Major Factor.

24. **(B)** The cost-of-living abroad is a major determinant of an overseas executive's compensation package.

25. **(A)** In addition to determining a compensation plan, Len Hibert was responsible for selecting the "right" sort of person for overseas assignments. See the last paragraph.

26. **(C)** Returning executives "into regular company operations" is a problem. One of the causes of the problem was that the salary and benefits that the overseas executive had enjoyed were lost when he returned for domestic assignment. However, dissatisfaction with domestic salary is only one of the causes of the problem. The problem, of course, is related to the question of whether the policy of rotating key personnel in foreign assignments should continue.

27. **(B)** The disadvantages of rotating key personnel in foreign assignments are major considerations in the decision to maintain the policy. See the discussion of Mr. Brown's case in the passage.

28. **(E)** Hibert's company has manufacturing facilities in six countries. The *number* of countries is not a consideration in any alternative course of action. It is not the number of firms that is important, but rather the fact that the company has become multinational.

29. **(E)** The fact that the company has operated abroad for over 40 years is an *Unimportant Issue*. The time period is not a consideration in any decision alternative.

30. **(B)** The company philosophy of becoming more international in thought as well as in practice has created a demand for a different sort of manager. This philosophy is a *Major Factor* that affects the decision as to employee recruiting, selection, and compensation.

31. **(B)** Most host countries are becoming increasingly restrictive in their policies toward foreigners working in their countries. This is a *Major Factor* that affects the decision as to employee selection, since employees will be expected to train nationals to replace them.

32. **(D)** Increased abductions of American executives in South America led Hibert to assume that the trend would cause more resistance by personnel to work in that area.

33. **(A)** Given the mounting dissatisfaction of managers to accept overseas assignments, a *Major Objective* of Len Hibert is to formulate a new policy that will motivate key talent to fill positions abroad.

34. **(B)** A major problem in the integration of returning managers is the extent to which they experienced cultural shock abroad. The extent of this shock is a *Major Factor* to be considered in the decision to assign a returning manager to a position in the home company.

35. **(E)** The fact that the Browns lived in Paris was an *Unimportant Issue*. What was important, however, was the experience the Brown family had integrating into French society and subsequently readjusting to the lifestyle in Chicago after Brown's transfer back to the States.

Section V   Data Sufficiency

1. **(E)**
   Since STATEMENT (1) describes only x and STATEMENT (2) describes only y, both are needed to get an answer. Using STATEMENT (2), STATEMENT (1) becomes $3x = 2k = 2y^2$, so $x = \frac{2y^2}{3}$. However, this is not sufficient, since if $y = -1$ then $x = \frac{2}{3}$ and x is greater than y, but if $y = 1$ then again $x = \frac{2}{3}$ but now x is less than y.

   Therefore, STATEMENTS (1) and (2) together are not sufficient.

2. (C)

ABCD is a parallelogram if *AB* is parallel to *CD* and *BC* is parallel to *AD*. STATEMENT (2) tells you that *AB* is parallel to *CD*, but this is not sufficient since a trapezoid has only one pair of opposite sides parallel. Thus, STATEMENT (2) alone is not sufficient.

STATEMENT (1) alone is not sufficient since a trapezoid can have the two nonparallel sides equal.

However, using STATEMENTS (1) and (2) together we can deduce that *BC* is parallel to *AD*, since the distance from *BC* to *AD* is equal along two different parallel lines.

3. (A)

STATEMENT (1) alone is sufficient. The average is the combined income for 1965–1970 divided by 6 (the number of years). Therefore, the combined income is 6 times the average yearly income.

STATEMENT (2) alone is not sufficient since there is no information about his income for the years 1966–1969.

4. (E)

To find the profit, we must know the selling price of the dress as well as it cost. STATEMENTS (1) and (2) together are not sufficient, since there is no information about the selling price of the dresses.

5. (D)

k is a prime if none of the integers 2,3,4, . . . up to *k* − 1 divide *k* evenly. STATEMENT (1) alone is sufficient since if *k* is not a prime then $k = (m)(n)$ where *m* and *n* must be integers less than *k*. But this means either *m* or *n* must be less than or equal to $\sqrt{k}$, since if *m* and *n* are both larger than $\sqrt{k}$, $(m)(n)$ is larger than $(\sqrt{k})(\sqrt{k})$ or *k*. So STATEMENT (1) implies *k* is a prime.

STATEMENT (2) alone is also sufficient, since if $k = (m)(n)$ and *m* and *n* are both larger than $\frac{k}{2}$, than $(m)(n)$ is greater than $\frac{k^2}{4}$; but $\frac{k^2}{4}$ is greater than *k* when *k* is larger than 5. Therefore, if no integer between 2 and $\frac{k}{2}$ inclusive divides *k* evenly, then *k* is a prime.

6. (D)

Since we are given the fact that 100 miles is the distance from *A* to *B*, it is sufficient to find the distance from *C* to *B*. This is so, because 100 minus the distance from *C* to *B* is the distance from *A* to *C*. STATEMENT (1) says that 125% of the distance from *C* to *B* is 100 miles. Thus, we can find the distance from *C* to *B*, which is sufficient. Since the distance from *A* to *C* plus the distance from *C* to *B* is the distance from *A* to *B*, we can use STATEMENT (2) to set up the equation 5 times the distance from *A* to *C* equals 100 miles.

Therefore, STATEMENTS (1) and (2) are each sufficient.

7. (B)

STATEMENT (1) alone is not sufficient. If the segment *AC* is moved further away from the segment *BD*, then the angles *x* and *y* will change. So STATEMENT (1) does not ensure that *CD* and *AB* are perpendicular.

STATEMENT (2) alone is sufficient. Since *AB* is a straight line, $x + y$ equals 180. Thus, if $x = y$, *x* and *y* both equal 90 and *AB* is perpendicular to *CD*. So the correct answer is (B).

8. (B)

STATEMENT (2) alone is sufficient, since $x = y$ implies $x - y = 0$.

STATEMENT (1) alone is not sufficient. An infinite number of pairs satisfy STATEMENT (1), for example, $x = 2$, $y = 2$, for which $x - y = 0$, or $x = 4$, $y = 1$, for which $x - y = 3$.

9. (E)

Since there is no information on how many of the eligible voters are men or how many are women, STATEMENTS (1) and (2) together are not sufficient.

10. (E)

We need to find the measure of angle *PSR* or of angle *PST*. Using STATEMENT (2), we can find angle *PTR*, but STATEMENT (1) does not give any information about either of the angles needed.

11. (A)

STATEMENT (1) is sufficient since it means 90% of the original cost is $2,300. Thus, we can solve the equation for the original cost.

STATEMENT (2) alone is insufficient, since it gives no information about the cost.

12. (C)
Draw the radii from O to each of the vertices. These lines divide the hexagon into six triangles. STATEMENT (2) says that all the triangles are congruent since each of their pairs of corresponding sides is equal. Since there are 360° in a circle, the central angle of each triangle is 60°. And, since all radii are equal, each angle of the triangle equals 60°. Therefore, the triangles are equilateral, and AB is equal to the radius of the circle. Thus, if we assume STATEMENT (1), we know the length of AB. Without STATEMENT (1), we can't find the length of AB.

Also, STATEMENT (1) alone is not sufficient, since AB need not equal the radius unless the hexagon is regular.

13. (E)
We need to know the area of the walls. To find the area of the walls, we need the distance from the floor to the ceiling. Since neither STATEMENT (1) nor (2) gives any information about the height of the room, together they are not sufficient.

14. (B)
STATEMENT (2) alone is sufficient, since we know $80 was the amount the worker made the first day. We can use STATEMENT (2) to find his pay for each day thereafter and then find the average daily wage.

STATEMENT (1) alone is not sufficient, since there is no way to find out how much the worker made on the fifth day.

15. (A)
STATEMENT (1) alone is sufficient. Since $3^2 + 4^2 = 5^2$, ABC is a right triangle by the Pythagorean theorem.

STATEMENT (2) alone is not sufficient since you can choose a point D so that $AC = CD$ for *any* triangle ABC.

16. (E) (1) and (2) are not sufficient. The price of food could rise for other reasons besides the price of energy rising.

17. (C) (1) alone is obviously insufficient. To use (2) you need to know what the painting was worth at some time between 1968 and 1977. So (2) alone is insufficient, but by using (1) and (2) together you can figure out the worth of the painting in January 1971.

18. (D) (1) alone is sufficient since the rule enables you to compute all successive values once you know a_1. Also the rule and (1) tell you that the numbers in the sequence will always increase. Thus since $a_2 = 4$, 3 will never appear. In the same way, by using (2) and the rule for the sequence you can determine that $a_2 = 4$ and a_1 is 2 or -2, so the reasoning used above shows that 3 will never appear.

19. (A) (1) alone is sufficient. If $z > x$ then the side opposite angle ABC is larger than the side opposite angle ACB. (2) alone is insufficient since D can be anywhere between B and C, so you can't decide whether AD is larger or smaller than AB.

20. (E) If $x = 9$ and $y = 8$, then (1) and (2) would be true and $x > y$. However, if $x = 6$ and $y = 8$, (1) and (2) would still be true although $x < y$.

21. (C)
STATEMENT (2) alone is not sufficient. -1 is less than 2 and $\frac{1}{-1}$ is less than ½ but 1 is less than 2 and $\frac{1}{1}$ is greater than ½.

STATEMENT (1) alone is insufficient since there is no information about y.

STATEMENTS (1) and (2) together imply that x and y are both greater than 1 and for two positive numbers x and y, if x is less than y then $\frac{1}{x}$ is greater than $\frac{1}{y}$.

22. (A)
STATEMENT (1) alone is sufficient. Since angle CAD is bisected by AO, the triangles AOD and AOC are congruent by side-angle-side ($AO = AO$). Therefore, angle AOD = angle AOC. Since the sum of the angles is 180° (CD is a straight line) the two angles are right angles and AB is $\perp CD$.

STATEMENT (2) alone is insufficient. We can choose B so that $BC = AD$ whether or not $AB \perp CD$.

23. (E)
Since C is closer to A, if plane X is flying faster than plane Y it will certainly fly over C before plane Y. However, if plane X flies slower than plane Y, and C is very close to A, plane X would still fly over C before plane Y does. Thus, STATEMENTS (1) and (2) together are not sufficient.

24. **(C)**

STATEMENT (1) gives $x + y = 4 - x$ and since there is no further information about x, STATEMENT (1) alone is insufficient.

STATEMENT (2) alone is also insufficient because STATEMENT (2) only implies $x + y = 5 - y$. However, if you multiply STATEMENT (2) by -2 and add it to STATEMENT (1), the result is $-3y = -6$ or $y = 2$. So $x + y = 5 - 2 = 3$. Therefore, STATEMENTS (1) and (2) together are sufficient and (C) is the answer.

25. **(E)**

Since the area of a circle is πr^2, the area of the circular section AOB is the fraction $x/360$ times πr^2, where angle $AOB = x°$. (There are $360°$ in the entire circle.) Using STATEMENT (1), we know $x = 36$ so $(x/360)\pi r^2 = \frac{1}{10}\pi r^2$. However, STATEMENT (1) gives no information about the value of r, so STATEMENT (1) alone is insufficient.

STATEMENT (2) gives no information about the value of r, so STATEMENTS (1) and (2) together are insufficient.

Section VI   Problem Solving

1. **(D)** The car travels at 60 mph; so the time to travel 255 miles is $\frac{255}{60}$ hours. Since $\frac{255}{60} = 4\frac{15}{60} = 4\frac{1}{4}$, it takes $4\frac{1}{4}$ hours.

2. **(E)** After the tune-up, the car will travel 15 miles on $\frac{3}{4}$ of a gallon of gas. So it will travel $\frac{15}{3/4}$ or $\frac{4}{3} \times 15$ or 20 miles on one gallon of gas.

3. **(B)** The price after a discount of 20% is 80% of P, the original price. After another 15% discount, the price is 85% of 80% of P or $(.85)(.80)$ P, which equals $.68P$. Therefore, after the successive discounts, the price is 68% of what it was originally, which is the same as a single discount of 32%.

4. **(D)** Since the government spent $132 per capita on personal health care for people aged 65 and over in 1966, the total expenditure by the government was $(20)(132)$ million, which is $2,640 million, or $2.640 billion.

5. **(C)** In 1966, the government spent $30 per capita on people under 65; by 1972 the per capita amount for those under 65 was $72. Therefore, the increase was $42. Since $\frac{42}{30} = 1.4 = 140\%$, the correct answer is (C).

6. **(B)** In 1972, philanthropy and industry contributed $5 out of the $981 per capita spent on personal health care for those aged 65 and over. Therefore, the fraction is $\frac{5}{981}$, which is about $\frac{5}{980} = \frac{1}{196}$.

7. **(C)**

STATEMENT I cannot be inferred since the graph gives only per capita amounts. The total amount will also depend on the number of people in each group.

STATEMENT II is false since private health insurance decreased from $70 to $56 per capita.

STATEMENT III is true since $644 is more than ½ of $981.

Therefore, only STATEMENT III can be inferred from the graphs.

8. **(C)** Since there are 20 oranges in a crate, a crate of oranges is sold for $20 \times 6¢$ or $1.20. A crate of oranges costs $1.00; so the profit on a crate is $1.20 - 1.00 or $.20. Therefore, the rate of profit $= \frac{.20}{1.20} = \frac{1}{6} = 16\frac{2}{3}\%$.

9. **(B)** $7\frac{1}{2}$ dozen is $\frac{15}{2} \times 12 = 90$, so during the summer the hen lays 90 eggs. The food for the summer costs $10, so the cost in food per egg is $\frac{\$10}{90} = \frac{\$1}{9} = 11\frac{1}{9}¢$.

10. **(D)**

STATEMENT I is not true since the diameter is not equal to the radius and the area of the circle is πr^2.

STATEMENT II is true since the length of a diameter is twice the length of a radius.

STATEMENT III is true since $a = \pi r^2 = \pi r(d/2) = \pi(r/2)d$. Therefore, $a/d = \pi(r/2)$.

Therefore, only STATEMENTS II and III are true.

11. **(C)** Since hose A takes 20 minutes to fill the tank, it fills up $\frac{1}{20}$ of the tank each minute. Since hose B fills up the tank in 15 minutes, it fills up $\frac{1}{15}$ of the tank each minute. Therefore, hose A and hose B together will fill up $\frac{1}{20} + \frac{1}{15}$ or $\frac{3+4}{60}$ or $\frac{7}{60}$ of the tank each minute. Thus, it will take $\frac{60}{7}$ or $8\frac{4}{7}$ minutes to fill the tank.

12. **(B)** If T is the amount of time it takes for 12 men to dig the ditch, then $T = \frac{5}{12}$ of $2 = \frac{5}{6}$ of an hour. Therefore, the 12 men will take 50 minutes.

13. **(D)** The total number of cars produced was 900 + 1200 + 1500 + 1400 + 1000 or 6,000. So the average per day is $\frac{6,000}{5}$ or 1,200 cars per day.

14. **(E)** There were 6,000 cars produced and the total wages paid for the week was ($30,000 + $40,000 + $52,000 + $50,000 + $32,000) or $204,000. Therefore, the average cost in wages per car $= \frac{\$204,000}{6,000} = \$34$.

15. **(D)**

STATEMENT I is true since the total number of cars produced was 6,000 and ¼ of 6,000 is 1,500.

STATEMENT II cannot be inferred since there are no data about the number of employees. If some employees are paid more than others, there may be fewer employees present who receive higher wages.

STATEMENT III is true since $102,000 was paid on Wednesday and Thursday and $102,000 is ½ of the weekly total of $204,000.

Therefore, only STATEMENTS I and III can be inferred from the graph.

16. **(C)** The train travels 150 miles in 2 hours and 10 minutes which is $2\frac{1}{6}$ hours. Therefore, the average speed is $\frac{150}{2\frac{1}{6}} = 150 \times \frac{6}{13} = \frac{900}{13} = 69\frac{3}{13}$ or about 69 miles per hour.

17. **(B)** Since $x > 2$, then $-x < -2$; but $y > -1$ implies $2y > -2$. Therefore, $-x < -2 < 2y$ so $-x < 2y$. None of the other statements is always true. (A) is false if x is 5 and $y = -\frac{1}{2}$; (C) is false if $x = 3$ and $y = -\frac{1}{2}$; (D) is false if $x = 3$ and $y = 3$, and (E) is false if $x = 3$ and $y = -\frac{1}{2}$.

18. **(C)** Since $ABCD$ is rectangle, all its angles are right angles. The area of a rectangle is length times width; and the length of AD is 4. Using the Pythagorean theorem we have $4^2 + (\text{width})^2 = 5^2$, so the $(\text{width})^2$ is $25 - 16 = 9$. Therefore, the width is 3, and the area is $4 \times 3 = 12$.

19. **(E)** The electricity costs $12k¢$ for 12 hours, the heat costs $12d$ for 12 hours, and the water costs $12w¢$ for 12 hours. So the total is $12k¢ + \$12d + 12w¢$ or $\$.12k + \$12d + \$.12w$ which is $\$(.12k + 12d + .12w)$.

20. **(E)** Since $x = 2z$ and $y = 2z$, $x \cdot y \cdot z = (2z)(2z)(z) = 4z^3$; but $x \cdot y \cdot z = 256$ so $4z^3 = 256$. Therefore, $z^3 = 64$ and z is 4; so $x = 8$.

Section VII   Analysis of Situations

1. **(B)** The cost of securing a loan is a *Major Factor* in making the decision.

2. **(B)** *Major Factor*. The breakage of glass jugs was a consideration in the decision to expand sales.

3. **(A)** Business expansion is clearly the *Major Objective* of Mr. Carswell.

4. **(D)** Continued public acceptance of the product is a *Major Assumption* which has led Mr. Carswell to want to expand his business.

5. **(B)** The availability of the loan was a *Major Factor* in the decision as to whether to accept Mr. Lubo's offer.

6. **(D)** The possibility of doubling his sales was a *Major Assumption* of Mr. Carswell, not an objective.

7. **(C)** Mr. Carswell's total investment was valued at $250,000, of which $50,000 was real estate. Real estate, then, was only one element in the total investment evaluation.

8. **(E)** The *previous* use of the building was of no importance to the present operation or to the decision to expand.

9. **(A)** Receiving a 10 percent rate of return is a *Major Objective* of Mr. Carswell.

10. **(D)** The franchiser was *sure* that 4,000 gallons of juice could be sold monthly through drive-in dairy shops. This figure is an estimate not substantiated by any facts cited in the passage.

11. **(B)** *Major Factor*. Mr. Carswell could advertise only on a small scale owing to lack of funds. In order to expand his business, Mr. Carswell would have to increase his advertising.

12. **(E)** The specific *source* of a business loan was an *Unimportant Issue* to Mr. Carswell.

13. **(C)** *Minor Factor*. Only 25 percent of total expected sales would be made through cafeterias.

14. **(E)** Mr. Carswell's patent—while important to protect his process—was only one part of the overall value of his business.

15. **(C)** Mr. Carswell's current sales served only as a baseline as far as expansion was concerned. Of far more importance to his decision to expand were potential sales and the expected rate of return on his investment.

16. **(E)** Carswell's background as a chemical engineer is not a consideration in any alternative course of action. It is an *Unimportant Issue*.

17. **(B)** Carswell's new method for processing orange juice had advantages over existing methods: (1) 18 percent more efficiency, (2) improved taste and flavor. Another advantage was the patent protection. The improved method was a *Major Factor* in a decision to expand operations.

18. **(C)** The *supply* of plastic containers was a major consideration because without them production could not be expanded, nor could sales be made to household consumers. The cost of the containers is a *Minor Factor*, affecting supply.

19. **(A)** The *Major Objective* of management is to devise a plan whereby Japanese salesmen can be better motivated to sell more. This is evidenced by the fact that the Japanese company's sales had declined by 15 percent before the merger.

20. **(D)** American management was "convinced" that strong incentives would motivate Japanese salesmen. Although some companies in Japan had instituted such systems successfully, the Japanese experience was mixed, and company management believed that "the system really has not been tested . . . very adequately. . . ." (See the next to last paragraph.)

21. **(B)** The structure of labor-management relations in Japan is a major consideration in any decision to change the *status quo*.

22. **(C)** Job security is but one factor of the Japanese employment structure, so it is a *Minor Factor* in the decision process.

23. **(B)** Part of the joint-venture agreement stipulates that the Nippon sales force be maintained. This could be a major issue in management's consideration of a compensation plan.

24. **(A)** Doubling the sales force within a year was a major objective of management. See paragraph 4.

25. **(E)** The establishment date of Nippon was not an issue considered by a decision maker.

26. **(A)** Determining a sales compensation plan for Japanese salesmen was an outcome desired by management. See paragraph 5.

27. **(C)** The subject of this question is "Differences . . ." and this relates to only one issue of a compensation-fringe benefits plan, so it is a *Minor Factor*.

28. **(B)** It would be impossible for management to hire salesmen or to determine a compensation plan without understanding the class system. Since this understanding is crucial to the success or failure of a Major Objective, it is a *Minor Factor*.

29. **(E)** Toyo's reevaluation of its senior employees does not significantly influence a decision maker's consideration.

30. **(C)** Regular pay raises is one of the factors that comprise the Japanese employment structure, so it is a *Major Factor*.

31. **(A)** N.C.M. produced only cash registers. One of the reasons for the merger with N.O.M. was to expand and improve N.O.M.'s product depth. So, the product line expansion is a *Major Objective*.

32. **(E)** The fact that N.C.M. sold to trading companies was not a particular consideration in an alternative course of action. It is an *Unimportant Issue*.

33. **(A)** Another Major Objective of the merger was to improve N.C.M.'s management ability.

34. **(D)** N.O.M. executives feared that the traditional Japanese compensation system would not work in a more competitive marketplace. However, this was a *Major Assumption* on their part.

35. **(E)** That N.O.M.'s sales force was aggressive was not an issue. The consideration was how to motivate *Japanese* salesmen to become more aggressive.

Section VIII   Writing Ability

1. **(D)** Do not use *calculate* or *reckon* when you mean *think*.

2. **(E)** Since the words *but also* precede a phrase, *to one of eight or even six*, the words *not only* should precede a phrase, *to one of ten hours*. This error in parallel structure is corrected in choice E.

3. **(A)** *Already* is an adverb; *all ready* is an adjectival construction. *Allready* is a misspelling. Choices D and E do not convey the thought of the sentence.

4. **(B)** One way of correcting a dangling participle is to change the participial phrase to a clause. Choices B and D substitute clauses for the phrase. However, choice D changes the meaning of the sentence.

5. **(C)** In the underlined phrase, we find two modifiers of worker—*toiling* and *who discovers.* . . . The first is an adjective and the second a clause. This results in an error in parallel structure. Choice C corrects this by eliminating one of the modifiers of *worker*. Choice E does the same thing but creates a change in the thought of the

sentence. Choice D corrects the error in parallel structure but introduces an error in agreement between subject and verb—*who* (singular) and *toil* (plural).

6. **(B)** "He" is the subject of the sentence which takes who as the relative pronoun.

7. **(A)** No error.

8. **(C)** This choice does not violate parallel structure.

9. **(E)** The omission of an important word (*been*) is corrected in choice E. *Excepted* (which means to *exclude*) is the wrong word to use in this sentence.

10. **(C)** Choice C corrects errors in the possessive form of *government* (needed before a verbal noun) and *it*.

11. **(B)** This corrects the error in agreement: *Her brother . . . insists*.

12. **(C)** This is also an error in agreement: *Kind* is singular and requires a singular modifier (*this*).

13. **(D)** This choice eliminates the error in parallel structure.

14. **(B)** The correct idiom is *graduate form*. The active case is preferred to the passive used in choice C. Choice D adds an unnecessary word, *into*.

15. **(C)** This corrects the two errors in this sentence—the error in case (*me* for *I*) and the error in tense (*had finished* for *finished*).

16. **(D)** *Despite* should be used as a preposition, not as a word joining clauses.

17. **(C)** This corrects the lack of parallel structure.

18. **(C)** This was an unnecessary shift of pronoun. Do not shift from *you* to *one*. Choice D changes the meaning unnecessarily.

19. **(C)** The demonstrative pronoun *those* is needed here—*from those* (persons).

20. **(D)** Choice D corrects the error in diction and the error in parallel structure.

21. **(E)** Choice E corrects the misuse of the word *too*.

22. **(D)** Active verbs are preferred to passive verbs.

23. **(D)** The phrase *May I venture to say that* is unnecessary, as is *most* before *superior*.

24. **(E)** This answer eliminates the misplaced modifier, *completing*, and the passive verb, *were found*.

25. **(B)** The correct idiom is *different from*.

Evaluating Your Score

Tabulate your score for each section of Sample Test 2 according to the directions on pages 4–5 and record the results in the Self-scoring Table below. Then find your rating for each score on the Self-scoring Scale and record it in the appropriate blank.

Self-scoring Table

SECTION	SCORE	RATING
1		
2		
3		
4		
5		
6		
7		
8		

Self-scoring Scale

RATING

SECTION	POOR	FAIR	GOOD	EXCELLENT
1	0–12+	13–17+	18–21+	22–25
2	0–12+	13–17+	18–21+	22–25
3	0–9+	10–13+	14–17+	18–20
4	0–17+	18–24+	25–31+	32–35
5	0–12+	13–17+	18–21+	22–25
6	0–9+	10–13+	14–17+	18–20
7	0–17+	18–24+	25–31+	32–35
8	0–12+	13–17+	18–21+	22–25

Study again the Review sections covering material in Sample Test 2 for which you had a rating of FAIR or POOR. Then go on to Sample Test 3.

To obtain an approximation of your actual GMAT score, see page 5.

Answer Sheet—Sample Test 3

Section I
Reading Comprehension

1. Ⓐ Ⓑ Ⓒ Ⓓ Ⓔ
2. Ⓐ Ⓑ Ⓒ Ⓓ Ⓔ
3. Ⓐ Ⓑ Ⓒ Ⓓ Ⓔ
4. Ⓐ Ⓑ Ⓒ Ⓓ Ⓔ
5. Ⓐ Ⓑ Ⓒ Ⓓ Ⓔ
6. Ⓐ Ⓑ Ⓒ Ⓓ Ⓔ
7. Ⓐ Ⓑ Ⓒ Ⓓ Ⓔ
8. Ⓐ Ⓑ Ⓒ Ⓓ Ⓔ
9. Ⓐ Ⓑ Ⓒ Ⓓ Ⓔ
10. Ⓐ Ⓑ Ⓒ Ⓓ Ⓔ
11. Ⓐ Ⓑ Ⓒ Ⓓ Ⓔ
12. Ⓐ Ⓑ Ⓒ Ⓓ Ⓔ
13. Ⓐ Ⓑ Ⓒ Ⓓ Ⓔ
14. Ⓐ Ⓑ Ⓒ Ⓓ Ⓔ
15. Ⓐ Ⓑ Ⓒ Ⓓ Ⓔ
16. Ⓐ Ⓑ Ⓒ Ⓓ Ⓔ
17. Ⓐ Ⓑ Ⓒ Ⓓ Ⓔ
18. Ⓐ Ⓑ Ⓒ Ⓓ Ⓔ
19. Ⓐ Ⓑ Ⓒ Ⓓ Ⓔ
20. Ⓐ Ⓑ Ⓒ Ⓓ Ⓔ
21. Ⓐ Ⓑ Ⓒ Ⓓ Ⓔ
22. Ⓐ Ⓑ Ⓒ Ⓓ Ⓔ
23. Ⓐ Ⓑ Ⓒ Ⓓ Ⓔ
24. Ⓐ Ⓑ Ⓒ Ⓓ Ⓔ
25. Ⓐ Ⓑ Ⓒ Ⓓ Ⓔ

Section II
Problem Solving

1. Ⓐ Ⓑ Ⓒ Ⓓ Ⓔ
2. Ⓐ Ⓑ Ⓒ Ⓓ Ⓔ
3. Ⓐ Ⓑ Ⓒ Ⓓ Ⓔ
4. Ⓐ Ⓑ Ⓒ Ⓓ Ⓔ
5. Ⓐ Ⓑ Ⓒ Ⓓ Ⓔ
6. Ⓐ Ⓑ Ⓒ Ⓓ Ⓔ
7. Ⓐ Ⓑ Ⓒ Ⓓ Ⓔ
8. Ⓐ Ⓑ Ⓒ Ⓓ Ⓔ
9. Ⓐ Ⓑ Ⓒ Ⓓ Ⓔ
10. Ⓐ Ⓑ Ⓒ Ⓓ Ⓔ
11. Ⓐ Ⓑ Ⓒ Ⓓ Ⓔ
12. Ⓐ Ⓑ Ⓒ Ⓓ Ⓔ
13. Ⓐ Ⓑ Ⓒ Ⓓ Ⓔ
14. Ⓐ Ⓑ Ⓒ Ⓓ Ⓔ
15. Ⓐ Ⓑ Ⓒ Ⓓ Ⓔ
16. Ⓐ Ⓑ Ⓒ Ⓓ Ⓔ
17. Ⓐ Ⓑ Ⓒ Ⓓ Ⓔ
18. Ⓐ Ⓑ Ⓒ Ⓓ Ⓔ
19. Ⓐ Ⓑ Ⓒ Ⓓ Ⓔ
20. Ⓐ Ⓑ Ⓒ Ⓓ Ⓔ

Section III
Analysis of Situations

1. Ⓐ Ⓑ Ⓒ Ⓓ Ⓔ
2. Ⓐ Ⓑ Ⓒ Ⓓ Ⓔ
3. Ⓐ Ⓑ Ⓒ Ⓓ Ⓔ
4. Ⓐ Ⓑ Ⓒ Ⓓ Ⓔ
5. Ⓐ Ⓑ Ⓒ Ⓓ Ⓔ
6. Ⓐ Ⓑ Ⓒ Ⓓ Ⓔ
7. Ⓐ Ⓑ Ⓒ Ⓓ Ⓔ
8. Ⓐ Ⓑ Ⓒ Ⓓ Ⓔ
9. Ⓐ Ⓑ Ⓒ Ⓓ Ⓔ
10. Ⓐ Ⓑ Ⓒ Ⓓ Ⓔ
11. Ⓐ Ⓑ Ⓒ Ⓓ Ⓔ
12. Ⓐ Ⓑ Ⓒ Ⓓ Ⓔ
13. Ⓐ Ⓑ Ⓒ Ⓓ Ⓔ
14. Ⓐ Ⓑ Ⓒ Ⓓ Ⓔ
15. Ⓐ Ⓑ Ⓒ Ⓓ Ⓔ
16. Ⓐ Ⓑ Ⓒ Ⓓ Ⓔ
17. Ⓐ Ⓑ Ⓒ Ⓓ Ⓔ
18. Ⓐ Ⓑ Ⓒ Ⓓ Ⓔ
19. Ⓐ Ⓑ Ⓒ Ⓓ Ⓔ
20. Ⓐ Ⓑ Ⓒ Ⓓ Ⓔ
21. Ⓐ Ⓑ Ⓒ Ⓓ Ⓔ
22. Ⓐ Ⓑ Ⓒ Ⓓ Ⓔ
23. Ⓐ Ⓑ Ⓒ Ⓓ Ⓔ
24. Ⓐ Ⓑ Ⓒ Ⓓ Ⓔ
25. Ⓐ Ⓑ Ⓒ Ⓓ Ⓔ
26. Ⓐ Ⓑ Ⓒ Ⓓ Ⓔ
27. Ⓐ Ⓑ Ⓒ Ⓓ Ⓔ
28. Ⓐ Ⓑ Ⓒ Ⓓ Ⓔ
29. Ⓐ Ⓑ Ⓒ Ⓓ Ⓔ
30. Ⓐ Ⓑ Ⓒ Ⓓ Ⓔ
31. Ⓐ Ⓑ Ⓒ Ⓓ Ⓔ
32. Ⓐ Ⓑ Ⓒ Ⓓ Ⓔ
33. Ⓐ Ⓑ Ⓒ Ⓓ Ⓔ
34. Ⓐ Ⓑ Ⓒ Ⓓ Ⓔ
35. Ⓐ Ⓑ Ⓒ Ⓓ Ⓔ

Section IV
Data Sufficiency

1. Ⓐ Ⓑ Ⓒ Ⓓ Ⓔ
2. Ⓐ Ⓑ Ⓒ Ⓓ Ⓔ
3. Ⓐ Ⓑ Ⓒ Ⓓ Ⓔ
4. Ⓐ Ⓑ Ⓒ Ⓓ Ⓔ
5. Ⓐ Ⓑ Ⓒ Ⓓ Ⓔ
6. Ⓐ Ⓑ Ⓒ Ⓓ Ⓔ
7. Ⓐ Ⓑ Ⓒ Ⓓ Ⓔ
8. Ⓐ Ⓑ Ⓒ Ⓓ Ⓔ
9. Ⓐ Ⓑ Ⓒ Ⓓ Ⓔ
10. Ⓐ Ⓑ Ⓒ Ⓓ Ⓔ
11. Ⓐ Ⓑ Ⓒ Ⓓ Ⓔ
12. Ⓐ Ⓑ Ⓒ Ⓓ Ⓔ
13. Ⓐ Ⓑ Ⓒ Ⓓ Ⓔ
14. Ⓐ Ⓑ Ⓒ Ⓓ Ⓔ
15. Ⓐ Ⓑ Ⓒ Ⓓ Ⓔ
16. Ⓐ Ⓑ Ⓒ Ⓓ Ⓔ
17. Ⓐ Ⓑ Ⓒ Ⓓ Ⓔ
18. Ⓐ Ⓑ Ⓒ Ⓓ Ⓔ
19. Ⓐ Ⓑ Ⓒ Ⓓ Ⓔ
20. Ⓐ Ⓑ Ⓒ Ⓓ Ⓔ
21. Ⓐ Ⓑ Ⓒ Ⓓ Ⓔ
22. Ⓐ Ⓑ Ⓒ Ⓓ Ⓔ
23. Ⓐ Ⓑ Ⓒ Ⓓ Ⓔ
24. Ⓐ Ⓑ Ⓒ Ⓓ Ⓔ
25. Ⓐ Ⓑ Ⓒ Ⓓ Ⓔ

Section V
Writing Ability

1. Ⓐ Ⓑ Ⓒ Ⓓ Ⓔ
2. Ⓐ Ⓑ Ⓒ Ⓓ Ⓔ
3. Ⓐ Ⓑ Ⓒ Ⓓ Ⓔ
4. Ⓐ Ⓑ Ⓒ Ⓓ Ⓔ
5. Ⓐ Ⓑ Ⓒ Ⓓ Ⓔ
6. Ⓐ Ⓑ Ⓒ Ⓓ Ⓔ
7. Ⓐ Ⓑ Ⓒ Ⓓ Ⓔ
8. Ⓐ Ⓑ Ⓒ Ⓓ Ⓔ
9. Ⓐ Ⓑ Ⓒ Ⓓ Ⓔ
10. Ⓐ Ⓑ Ⓒ Ⓓ Ⓔ
11. Ⓐ Ⓑ Ⓒ Ⓓ Ⓔ
12. Ⓐ Ⓑ Ⓒ Ⓓ Ⓔ
13. Ⓐ Ⓑ Ⓒ Ⓓ Ⓔ
14. Ⓐ Ⓑ Ⓒ Ⓓ Ⓔ
15. Ⓐ Ⓑ Ⓒ Ⓓ Ⓔ
16. Ⓐ Ⓑ Ⓒ Ⓓ Ⓔ
17. Ⓐ Ⓑ Ⓒ Ⓓ Ⓔ
18. Ⓐ Ⓑ Ⓒ Ⓓ Ⓔ
19. Ⓐ Ⓑ Ⓒ Ⓓ Ⓔ
20. Ⓐ Ⓑ Ⓒ Ⓓ Ⓔ
21. Ⓐ Ⓑ Ⓒ Ⓓ Ⓔ
22. Ⓐ Ⓑ Ⓒ Ⓓ Ⓔ
23. Ⓐ Ⓑ Ⓒ Ⓓ Ⓔ
24. Ⓐ Ⓑ Ⓒ Ⓓ Ⓔ
25. Ⓐ Ⓑ Ⓒ Ⓓ Ⓔ

Section VI
Problem Solving

1. Ⓐ Ⓑ Ⓒ Ⓓ Ⓔ
2. Ⓐ Ⓑ Ⓒ Ⓓ Ⓔ
3. Ⓐ Ⓑ Ⓒ Ⓓ Ⓔ
4. Ⓐ Ⓑ Ⓒ Ⓓ Ⓔ
5. Ⓐ Ⓑ Ⓒ Ⓓ Ⓔ
6. Ⓐ Ⓑ Ⓒ Ⓓ Ⓔ
7. Ⓐ Ⓑ Ⓒ Ⓓ Ⓔ
8. Ⓐ Ⓑ Ⓒ Ⓓ Ⓔ
9. Ⓐ Ⓑ Ⓒ Ⓓ Ⓔ
10. Ⓐ Ⓑ Ⓒ Ⓓ Ⓔ
11. Ⓐ Ⓑ Ⓒ Ⓓ Ⓔ
12. Ⓐ Ⓑ Ⓒ Ⓓ Ⓔ
13. Ⓐ Ⓑ Ⓒ Ⓓ Ⓔ
14. Ⓐ Ⓑ Ⓒ Ⓓ Ⓔ
15. Ⓐ Ⓑ Ⓒ Ⓓ Ⓔ
16. Ⓐ Ⓑ Ⓒ Ⓓ Ⓔ
17. Ⓐ Ⓑ Ⓒ Ⓓ Ⓔ
18. Ⓐ Ⓑ Ⓒ Ⓓ Ⓔ
19. Ⓐ Ⓑ Ⓒ Ⓓ Ⓔ
20. Ⓐ Ⓑ Ⓒ Ⓓ Ⓔ

Section VII
Data Sufficiency

1. Ⓐ Ⓑ Ⓒ Ⓓ Ⓔ
2. Ⓐ Ⓑ Ⓒ Ⓓ Ⓔ
3. Ⓐ Ⓑ Ⓒ Ⓓ Ⓔ
4. Ⓐ Ⓑ Ⓒ Ⓓ Ⓔ
5. Ⓐ Ⓑ Ⓒ Ⓓ Ⓔ
6. Ⓐ Ⓑ Ⓒ Ⓓ Ⓔ
7. Ⓐ Ⓑ Ⓒ Ⓓ Ⓔ
8. Ⓐ Ⓑ Ⓒ Ⓓ Ⓔ
9. Ⓐ Ⓑ Ⓒ Ⓓ Ⓔ
10. Ⓐ Ⓑ Ⓒ Ⓓ Ⓔ
11. Ⓐ Ⓑ Ⓒ Ⓓ Ⓔ
12. Ⓐ Ⓑ Ⓒ Ⓓ Ⓔ
13. Ⓐ Ⓑ Ⓒ Ⓓ Ⓔ
14. Ⓐ Ⓑ Ⓒ Ⓓ Ⓔ
15. Ⓐ Ⓑ Ⓒ Ⓓ Ⓔ
16. Ⓐ Ⓑ Ⓒ Ⓓ Ⓔ
17. Ⓐ Ⓑ Ⓒ Ⓓ Ⓔ
18. Ⓐ Ⓑ Ⓒ Ⓓ Ⓔ
19. Ⓐ Ⓑ Ⓒ Ⓓ Ⓔ
20. Ⓐ Ⓑ Ⓒ Ⓓ Ⓔ
21. Ⓐ Ⓑ Ⓒ Ⓓ Ⓔ
22. Ⓐ Ⓑ Ⓒ Ⓓ Ⓔ
23. Ⓐ Ⓑ Ⓒ Ⓓ Ⓔ
24. Ⓐ Ⓑ Ⓒ Ⓓ Ⓔ
25. Ⓐ Ⓑ Ⓒ Ⓓ Ⓔ

Section VIII
Critical Reasoning

1. Ⓐ Ⓑ Ⓒ Ⓓ Ⓔ
2. Ⓐ Ⓑ Ⓒ Ⓓ Ⓔ
3. Ⓐ Ⓑ Ⓒ Ⓓ Ⓔ
4. Ⓐ Ⓑ Ⓒ Ⓓ Ⓔ
5. Ⓐ Ⓑ Ⓒ Ⓓ Ⓔ
6. Ⓐ Ⓑ Ⓒ Ⓓ Ⓔ
7. Ⓐ Ⓑ Ⓒ Ⓓ Ⓔ
8. Ⓐ Ⓑ Ⓒ Ⓓ Ⓔ
9. Ⓐ Ⓑ Ⓒ Ⓓ Ⓔ
10. Ⓐ Ⓑ Ⓒ Ⓓ Ⓔ
11. Ⓐ Ⓑ Ⓒ Ⓓ Ⓔ
12. Ⓐ Ⓑ Ⓒ Ⓓ Ⓔ
13. Ⓐ Ⓑ Ⓒ Ⓓ Ⓔ
14. Ⓐ Ⓑ Ⓒ Ⓓ Ⓔ
15. Ⓐ Ⓑ Ⓒ Ⓓ Ⓔ
16. Ⓐ Ⓑ Ⓒ Ⓓ Ⓔ
17. Ⓐ Ⓑ Ⓒ Ⓓ Ⓔ
18. Ⓐ Ⓑ Ⓒ Ⓓ Ⓔ
19. Ⓐ Ⓑ Ⓒ Ⓓ Ⓔ
20. Ⓐ Ⓑ Ⓒ Ⓓ Ⓔ

Sample Test 3

Section I   Reading Comprehension

TIME: 30 minutes

DIRECTIONS: This part contains three reading passages. You are to read each one carefully. When answering the questions, you *will* be allowed to refer back to the passages. The questions are based on what is *stated* or *implied* in each passage. You have thirty minutes to complete this section.

Passage 1:

With Friedrich Engels, Karl Marx in 1848 published the *Communist Manifesto,* calling upon the masses to rise and throw off their economic chains. His maturer theories of society were later elaborated in his large and abstruse work *Das Capital.* Starting as a non-violent revolutionist, he ended life as a major social theorist

(5)   more or less sympathetic with violent revolution, if such became necessary in order to change the social system which he believed to be frankly predatory upon the masses.

On the theoretical side, Marx set up the doctrine of surplus value as the chief element in capitalistic exploitation. According to this theory, the ruling classes no

(10)   longer employed military force primarily as a means to plundering the people. Instead, they used their control over employment and working conditions under the bourgeois capitalistic system for this purpose, paying only a bare subsistence wage to the worker while they appropriated all surplus values in the productive process. He further taught that the strategic disadvantage of the worker in industry

(15)   prevented him from obtaining a fairer share of the earnings by bargaining methods and drove him to revolutionary procedures as a means to establishing his economic and social rights. This revolution might be peacefully consummated by parliamentary procedures if the people prepared themselves for political action by mastering the materialistic interpretation of history and by organizing politically for

(20)   the final event. It was his belief that the aggressions of the capitalist class would eventually destroy the middle class and take over all their sources of income by a process of capitalistic absorption of industry—a process which has failed to occur in most countries.

With minor exceptions, Marx's social philosophy is now generally accepted by

(25)   leftwing labor movements in many countries, but rejected by centrist labor groups, especially those in the United States. In Russia and other Eastern European countries, however, Socialist leaders adopted the methods of violent revolution because of the opposition of the ruling classes. Yet, many now hold that the present Communist regime in Russia and her satellite countries is no longer a proletarian

(30)   movement based on Marxist social and political theory, but a camouflaged imperialistic effort to dominate the world in the interest of a new ruling class.

It is important, however, that those who wish to approach Marx as a teacher should not be "buffaloed" by his philosophic approach. They are very likely to in these days, because those most interested in propagating the ideas of Marx, the

(35)   Russian Bolsheviks, have swallowed down his Hegelian philosophy along with his science of revolutionary engineering, and they look upon us irreverent peoples

who presume to meditate social and even revolutionary problems without making our obeisance to the mysteries of Dialectic Materialism, as a species of unredeemed and well-nigh unredeemable barbarians. They are right in scorning our ignorance of the scientific ideas of Karl Marx and our indifference to them. They are wrong in scorning our distaste for having practical programs presented in the form of systems of philosophy. In that we simply represent a more progressive intellectual culture than that in which Marx received his education—a culture farther emerged from the dominance of religious attitudes.

(40)

1. According to the passage, the chief element in Marx's analysis of capitalist exploitation was the doctrine of

(A) just wages
(B) the price system
(C) surplus value
(D) predatory production
(E) subsistence work

2. *Das Capital* differs from the *Communist Manifesto* in that it

(A) was written with the help of Friedrich Engels
(B) retreated from Marx's earlier revolutionary stance
(C) expressed a more fully developed form of Marxist theory
(D) denounced the predatory nature of the capitalist system
(E) expressed sympathy for the plight of the middle class

3. According to the passage, Marx ended his life

I. a believer in non-violent revolution
II. accepting violent revolution
III. a major social theorist

(A) I only
(B) III only
(C) I and III only
(D) II and III only
(E) Neither I, II, nor III

4. The author suggests that the present Communist regime in Russia may best be categorized as a(n)

(A) proletarian movement
(B) social government
(C) imperialistic state
(D) revolutionary government
(E) social democracy

5. Marx's social philosophy is now generally accepted by

(A) centrist labor groups
(B) most labor unions
(C) left-wing labor unions
(D) only those in Communist countries
(E) only those in Russia

6. It can be concluded that the author of the passage is

(A) sympathetic to Marx's ideas
(B) unsympathetic to Marx's ideas
(C) uncritical of Marx's interpretation of history
(D) a believer in Hegelian philosophy
(E) a Leninist-Marxist

7. Which of the following classes did Marx believe should control the economy?

(A) The working class   (D) The lower class
(B) The upper class   (E) The capitalist class
(C) The middle class

8. According to Marx, a social and economic revolution could take place through

   I. parliamentary procedures
  II. political action
III. violent revolution

(A) I only
(B) III only
(C) I or II only
(D) II or III only
(E) I, II, or III

Passage 2:

The basic character of our governmental and political institutions conditions the federal budgetary system. The working relationships between branches, and between the elements within each branch, are intricate, subtle, and in continuous change—affected by partisan politics, personalities, social forces, and public
(5)   opinion. A few landmark stages in the evolution of the present system provide perspective.

In 1789 Alexander Hamilton, as the first Secretary of the Treasury, affirmed and successfully established a position of strong executive leadership in matters of public finance. His proposals on revenues, banking, and the assumption of prior
(10) debts of both national and state governments were based on his philosophy that federal fiscal policies should be designed to encourage economic growth. However, Hamilton's successors, and the Presidents under whom they served, did not follow his concept of executive responsibility for "plans of finance."

Partly through default, Congress took charge of all phases of fiscal policy. At
(15) the outset, each chamber was so small that coherent initiative was possible. (The first House had some 60 members—about the number of its present Appropriations Committee.) Spending estimates, considered in Committee of the Whole in 1789, were later referred to the Committee on Ways and Means. In 1865 expenditures were assigned to a new Appropriations Committee while revenues remained with
(20) the Ways and Means Committee. In 1885 most spending proposals were subdivided among the legislative committees so that appropriation bills came to be handled by numerous committees (14 in the House and 15 in the Senate), each dealing directly with the departments. The presidential role was minimal.

By the turn of the century there was a clear need for reform in financial man-
(25) agement. At all levels of government, officials spent money on activities "as authorized by law" and in line with "appropriations" made by legislative bodies— usually after committee consideration. Other officials collected taxes and fees under various unrelated statutes. Such a system—or lack-of-system—worked within reason as long as governments had little to do. But as government activities
(30) grew, becoming more technical and closely interrelated, this lack-of-system bogged down.

Several factors played a part in the eventual breakthrough. In the first decade of the twentieth century, an "executive budget" came into successful use by some cities and states. President Taft's Commission on Efficiency and Economy pre-

(35) pared an illustrative federal budget which—while rejected by Congress—commanded broad public support. The more advanced methods developed by European governments came to American attention. World War I precipitated accounting chaos, with an aftermath of scandal. The need for new and better methods was established beyond dispute.

(40) The Budget and Accounting Act of 1921 placed direct responsibility for preparation and execution of the federal budget upon the President, making a unified federal budget possible for the first time. The Act set up two new organizational units, the General Accounting Office (GAO) and the Bureau of the Budget. GAO is headed by the Comptroller General, appointed by the President *with* Senate

(45) approval for a 15-year term, and is regarded as primarily a congressional rather than an executive resource. The Bureau, under a Director appointed by the President *without* Senate confirmation and serving at his pleasure, has from its inception been the President's chief reliance in budgetary and related matters.

9. Alexander Hamilton's philosophy was that federal fiscal policies should

   (A) be expansionary
   (B) encourage economic growth
   (C) be determined by Congress
   (D) encourage a balanced budget
   (E) be determined by the President

10. Hamilton's successors

   I. followed his economic philosophy of "plans of finance"
   II. followed his social philosophy
   III. did not follow his philosophy of strong executive leadership

   (A) I only
   (B) III only
   (C) I and II only
   (D) II and III only
   (E) I, II, and III

11. In the history of U.S. fiscal management, spending estimates were *first* considered by the

   (A) Committee of the Whole
   (B) Appropriations Committee
   (C) Ways and Means Committee
   (D) Commission on Efficiency and Economy
   (E) General Accounting Office

12. At the end of the nineteenth century, there was a need for

   (A) more restrained executive leadership
   (B) a new finance commission
   (C) more Congressional interest in finance
   (D) overall reform of financial management
   (E) creation of a new Appropriations committee

13. The "executive budget" was first used

   (A) by Alexander Hamilton
   (B) in the 19th century
   (C) in the first decade of the 20th century
   (D) by President Eisenhower
   (E) by President Truman

14. President Taft's federal budget was

(A) based on procedures used by some European governments
(B) enthusiastically accepted by Congress
(C) a partial cause of accounting chaos during World War I
(D) rejected by Congress
(E) vilified by the public

15. In 1921, the responsibility for preparation and execution of the federal budget fell upon the

(A) President
(B) Congress
(C) Bureau of the Budget
(D) House of Representatives
(E) Senate

16. All of the following are true about the Bureau of the Budget except

(A) its Director is appointed by the President
(B) it assists the President in budgetary matters
(C) its Director need not be approved by the Senate
(D) it was established in 1921
(E) its Director serves for a 15-year term

Passage 3:

In describing the Indians of the various sections of the United States at different stages in their history, some of the factors which account for their similarity amid difference can be readily accounted for, others are difficult to discern.

(5) The basic physical similarity of the Indians from Alaska to Patagonia is explained by the fact that they all came originally from Asia by way of the Bering Strait and the Aleutian Islands into Alaska and then southward. They came in different waves, the earliest around 25,000 years ago, the latest probably not long before America was discovered by Europeans. Because these people all came from Asia and were therefore drawn from the same pool of Asiatic people, they tended to
(10) look alike. But since the various waves of migration crossed into Alaska at widely separated times, there were differences among them in their physical characteristics.

There were also differences in cultural equipment. The earliest arrivals are known to science only through their simple tools of chipped stone and bone.
(15) Despite their limited technical equipment, some of the New Mexico Indians were very successful big game hunters. Twenty-five thousand years ago they were hunting the wooly mammoth, the giant bison, the ground sloth and the camel, all characteristic animals of the closing phases of the last ice age.

After their arrival from Asia in various waves across the Bering Strait, the early
(20) peoples in the Americas slowly spread southward into the vast empty spaces of the two continents. A group of people moving slowly down the Mackenzie River valley east of the Rockies into the general region of Southern Alberta, then eastward across the northern prairies reaching the wooded country around the upper Mississippi and the Western Great Lakes, then in a southeastward movement
(25) following the Mississippi valley until some final settlement was reached in the Gulf states, would encounter a wide variety of physical environments. At various stages of such wanderings they would have to evolve methods of coping with the cold, barren, tundra country of northern Canada; the prairies, cold, treeless but well stocked with large game; then later the completely different flora and fauna of the
(30) Minnesota-Wisconsin-Illinois area, thickly forested and well watered and providing an abundance of small game and wild vegetable foods; then the semi-tropical

character of the lower Mississippi country as they neared the Gulf of Mexico. Since such a migration would be spread over many centuries, the modification of whatever basic culture they had on their arrival from Asia would be very slow.
(35) Yet the end result would be completely different from their original culture. It would also be different from the final culture of a closely allied group who became separated from them early in their wanderings and whose movements led them into different types of country. In its final form, the culture of this second group would have little in common with that of the first except perhaps a continuing
(40) resemblance in language and in physical type.

17. According to the passage, Indians who migrated to what is now the United States originated in

(A) Asia
(B) Africa
(C) South America
(D) Alaska
(E) Patagonia

18. Physical differences among Indians who migrated to Alaska can be accounted for by the fact that they came

(A) from different places
(B) from different tribes
(C) at different times
(D) from different races
(E) to different places

19. It is estimated that Indians first came to what is now the United States about

(A) 5,000 years ago
(B) 10,000 years ago
(C) 15,000 years ago
(D) 25,000 years ago
(E) 50,000 years ago

20. The author is most interested in discussing the Indians'

(A) cultural background
(B) eating habits
(C) technical abilities
(D) migration patterns
(E) physical characteristics

21. According to the passage, the southernmost area reached by the earliest Indians was the

(A) northern prairies
(B) upper Mississippi
(C) Great Lakes
(D) Mackenzie River valley
(E) Gulf States

22. Particularly noted for their hunting prowess were the Indians of

(A) Mississippi
(B) Southern Alberta
(C) the Mackenzie River valley
(D) New Mexico
(E) the American prairies

23. What characteristics of Indian culture remained fairly stable despite the Indian migrations?

I. Language
II. Physical type
III. Technical abilities

(A) I only
(B) III only
(C) I and II only
(D) II and III only
(E) I, II, and III

24. Which animals were hunted by the Indians when they first migrated to the Americas?

   I. Bison
  II. Wooly mammoth
 III. Camel

(A) I only
(B) III only
(C) I and II only
(D) II and III only
(E) I, II, and III

25. The passage most likely was written by a(n)

(A) economist
(B) historian
(C) educator
(D) social scientist
(E) anthropologist

If there is still time remaining, you may review the questions in this section only.
You may not turn to any other section of the test.

Section II Problem Solving

TIME: 30 minutes

DIRECTIONS: Solve each of the following problems; then indicate the correct answer on the answer sheet. [On the actual test you will be permitted to use any space available on the examination paper for scratch work.]
NOTE: A figure that appears with a problem is drawn as accurately as possible so as to provide information that may help in answering the question. Numbers in this test are real numbers.

1. If 64% of the students in a class got a grade of C and there are 200 students in the class, how many students in the class received a grade of C?

(A) 64
(B) 118
(C) 124
(D) 128
(E) 164

2. If $2x + y = 10$ and $x = 3$, what is $x - y$?

(A) -4
(B) -1
(C) 0
(D) 1
(E) 7

3. If a worker can pack ⅙ of a carton of canned food in 15 minutes and there are 40 workers in a factory, how many cartons should be packed in the factory in 1⅔ hours?

(A) 33
(B) 40²⁄₉
(C) 43⁴⁄₉
(D) 44⁴⁄₉
(E) 45²⁄₃

4. Potatoes cost 15¢ a pound. If the price of 10 pounds of potatoes rises by 10%, how much will 10 pounds of potatoes cost?

(A) 17¢
(B) $1.50
(C) $1.60
(D) $1.65
(E) $1.75

5. A truck driver must complete a 180-mile trip in 4 hours. If he averages 50 miles an hour for the first three hours of his trip, how fast must he travel in the final hour?

(A) 30 mph
(B) 35 mph
(C) 40 mph
(D) 45 mph
(E) 50 mph

6. If a triangle has base B and the altitude of the triangle is twice the base, then the area of the triangle is

(A) $\frac{1}{2}AB$
(B) AB
(C) $\frac{1}{2}B^2$
(D) B^2
(E) $2B^2$

7. If the product of two numbers is 10 and the sum of the two number is 7, then the larger of the two numbers is

(A) -2
(B) 2
(C) 3
(D) $4\frac{1}{4}$
(E) 5

8. Oranges cost $\$x$ a bag for the first 100 bags a store buys from a wholesaler. All bags bought in addition to the first 100 get a discount of 10%. How much does it cost to buy 150 bags of oranges from the wholesaler?

(A) $100
(B) $140x$
(C) $145x$
(D) $150x$
(E) $100x + \$50$

9. If the lengths of the two sides of a right triangle adjacent to the right angle are 8 and 15 respectively, then the length of the side opposite the right angle is

(A) $\sqrt{258}$
(B) 15.8
(C) 16
(D) 17
(E) 17.9

10. It costs x¢ each to print the first 600 copies of a newspaper. It costs $\left(x - \dfrac{y}{10}\right)$¢ for every copy after the first 600. How much does it cost to print 1,500 copies of the newspaper?

(A) $1500x$¢
(B) $150y$¢
(C) $(1500x - 90y)$¢
(D) $\$(150x - 9y)$
(E) $\$15x$

11. Which of the following sets of values for w, x, y, and z respectively are possible if $ABCD$ is a parallelogram?

I. 50, 130, 50, 130
II. 60, 110, 70, 120
III. 60, 150, 50, 150

(A) I only
(B) II only
(C) I and II only
(D) I and III only
(E) I, II, and III

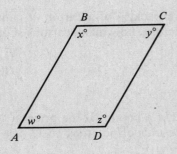

12. John weighs twice as much as Marcia. Marcia's weight is 60% of Bob's weight. Dave weighs 50% of Lee's weight. Lee weighs 190% of John's weight. Which of these 5 persons weighs the least?

(A) Bob
(B) Dave
(C) John
(D) Lee
(E) Marcia

13. The sum of 5 consecutive integers is 35. How many of the five consecutive integers are prime numbers?

(A) 0
(B) 1
(C) 2
(D) 3
(E) 4

14. Circle 1 has the same radius as circle 2. A is the center of circle 1, and B is the center of circle 2. Circle 1 and circle 2 meet only at C. ACB is a straight line segment of length 10. What is the length of DB if DA is perpendicular to AC?

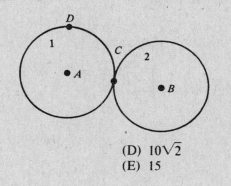

(A) 10
(B) $5\sqrt{5}$
(C) 11
(D) $10\sqrt{2}$
(E) 15

15. The assessed value of a house is $72,000. The assessed value is 60% of the market value of the house. If taxes are $3 for every $1,000 of the market value of the house, how much are the taxes on the house?

(A) $216
(B) $360
(C) $1,386
(D) $2,160
(E) $3,600

16. If the operation $*$ is defined by $*a = a^2 - 2$, then $*(*5)$ is

(A) 23
(B) 527
(C) 529
(D) 621
(E) 623

17. If $y/x = 1/3$ and $x + 2y = 10$, then x is

(A) 2
(B) 3
(C) 4
(D) 5
(E) 6

18. What is the area of the parallelogram *ABCD*? $A = (1, -1)$, $B = (2, 2)$, $C = (5, 2)$ and $D = (4, -1)$.

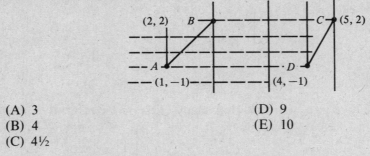

(A) 3

(B) 4

(C) 4½

(D) 9

(E) 10

19. The area of a rectangular field is 1,000 square yards. If the length of the field is *y* yards, then how many yards is the perimeter of the field?

(A) $y + 1,000/y$

(B) $2y + 1,000$

(C) $1,000$

(D) $2y + 1,000/y$

(E) $2y + 2,000/y$

20. The figure *ABCDEFGH* is a cube. $AB = 10$. What is the length of the line segment *AF*?

(A) 10

(B) $10\sqrt{2}$

(C) $10\sqrt{3}$

(D) 20

(E) $10\sqrt{5}$

If there is still time remaining, you may review the questions in this section only. You may not turn to any other section of the test.

Section III   Analysis of Situations

TIME: 30 minutes

DIRECTIONS: Read the following passages. After you have completed each one, you will be asked to answer questions that involve determining the importance of specific factors included in the passage. When answering questions, you may consult the passage.

Passage 1:

For the past two years, Bennett Joseph, head of the regional firm R and S Packing Company, had been seriously considering the use of U.S. government grade labeling for its high-quality canned fruits and vegetables. Having enjoyed an excellent reputation with the public under the trademark "Delish" for more than 30 years, these canned goods were known throughout the area by distributors and consumers alike as among the best.

The grade-labeling problems had come to the fore as the result of a new food super-market chain called *Gaynes*. The new chain, a national organization, was making a depth penetration in the region by spending a sizeable portion of its large advertising and promotion budget for pushing its own private brands of frozen and canned fruits and vegetables. Its advertising emphasized that the public could find both grade and descriptive labeling on each package and can. The descriptive labels listed the type of food, the can size, the number of servings per can, the net contents, and the name and address of the chain.

Joseph had always paid careful attention to the descriptive labeling on R and S products but had been most reluctant to commit the company to the use of grade labeling. Joseph's reluctance was supported by the company's advertising and promotion manager and the production boss, who believed with him that grade labeling could hardly bring out the fresh flavor and taste upon which the company prided itself and had been able to capture through its own special heating, processing, and canning techniques.

A factor that seriously concerned Joseph in the use of grade labels on canned fruits and vegetables was the possible use of a high grade on one of the grading characteristics to offset a low score on another. This method could hardly help R and S, whose pack was known by distributors and consumers alike to be much better even than the highest grades of its competitors.

While Joseph was pondering this problem, he mulled over what he had read about grade labeling. In the first place, grading and labeling of canned foods had been developed to protect and help the consumer. Through the Department of Agriculture, federal stan-dards had been set up for standardization, grading, and inspection work. To encourage voluntary use of these standards, the Department of Agriculture hired inspectors who carried out the federal inspection program at production periods. For canned fruits and vegetables, the grades were A, B, and C, which were based on such criteria as uniformity, succulence, and color—not flavor or food value.

Joseph certainly agreed that grade labeling could provide additional information for the consumer. R and S could also use it in company advertisements to supplement its own descriptive labels. But didn't everyone know about the taste and quality of R and S products? He also wondered what happened when a company using grade labeling saw the qualities of fruits and vegetables change from year to year. At one period, that quality might be high for most growers; it might also be low during another. Too, some factors that were very important in their effect on consumer choice could not be subjected to a grading discipline. For example, the range of individual tastes was impossible to stand-ardize. Certainly taste, Joseph felt, should be at least as important as the other, more tangible criteria used to grade canned goods.

Joseph's legal advisor pointed out that there was another aspect to the problem of grade labeling. He had been informed by colleagues employed at the Department of Commerce that while present use of standards was voluntary, such use might become mandatory in the not-too-distant future. His contacts explained that their information was based not on present government plans, but on possible Congressional legislation. The scenario went like this. Several consumer organizations were active in promoting "truth in la-beling" legislation. Their objective was the provision of more information on packaging so that consumers could make better decisions on what products to buy. Simply put, it was argued that consumers could not distinguish between competing products on the basis of present labeling requirements. Present labels contained only the manufacturer's name and address, the fact that the contents conformed to Federal Drug and Agriculture food standards, and net weight. No mandatory criteria existed for grade standards. Con-sumers could judge quality only on the basis of trial-and-error, by trying the product or by reading the advertised claims of competing brands. Government officials believed that if several of the larger consumer organizations combined efforts to lobby in Congress for passage of consumer legislation, there was an even chance that a "truth in labeling" law could be passed within a year.

Joseph weighed the findings of his legal advisor. He realized that, while taste was the ultimate criterion for choosing one brand over another, the *initial* choice of a particular brand could be influenced by product grade. Moreover, since R and S products were of the highest quality, they would undoubtedly carry the highest possible federal grades. Joseph was most concerned about the timing of a decision to accept product grading, which was at the present time still voluntary. Would it be to R and S's advantage to adopt a voluntary labeling program, or would it be better to wait until grading became mandatory for all processors? What advantages and disadvantages would result from taking a wait-and-see attitude, rather than immediately commencing a voluntary grading program?

Before Joseph completed his study of the problem, one of his leading competitors, Taam Foods, commenced a voluntary label standardization program. Joseph was worried about the possibility that some of Taam Foods' products might be designated grade A quality. Taam Foods could quickly exploit this advantage at the expense of R and S. Thus, grading had now become a competitive issue. Joseph felt that he had to make a quick decision one way or the other.

DIRECTIONS: The questions that follow relate to the preceding passage. Evaluate, in terms of the passage, each of the items given. Then select your answer from one of the following classifications, and blacken the corresponding space on the answer sheet.

(A) A MAJOR OBJECTIVE in making the decision: one of the goals sought by the decision maker

(B) A MAJOR FACTOR in making the decision: an aspect of the problem, specifically mentioned in the passage, that fundamentally affects and/or determines the decision

(C) A MINOR FACTOR in making the decision: a less important element bearing on or affecting a Major Factor, rather than a Major Objective directly

(D) A MAJOR ASSUMPTION in making the decision: a projection or supposition arrived at by the decision maker before considering the factors and alternatives

(E) AN UNIMPORTANT ISSUE in making the decision: an item lacking significant impact on, or relationship to, the decision

1. Establishment of a new supermarket chain

2. Mandatory standardization of food labeling practices

3. Effects on sales of grade labeling of R and S products

4. Federal food standards established by the Department of Agriculture

5. Maintaining the R and S brand image

6. Likelihood that grade labeling would become mandatory

7. Present label requirements established by law

8. Influence of consumer groups on government actions

9. Taam Foods' labels

10. The 30 years of experience behind R and S packing company

11. Superior taste of R and S products

12. Quality of R and S products

13. Variability of grade scores

14. Adoption of grade labeling by *Gaynes*

15. The use of grades A, B, and C for canned fruit

16. The federal inspection program

17. Grade labeling used in advertising

18. Advantages and disadvantages of not adopting grade labeling

Passage 2:

Source Perrier was one of the largest distributors of natural water drinks in France. By the early 1970s it was having difficulty in sustaining growth of its sales in France and looked to develop a market in the United States. Its American operation was headed by Bruce Nevins.

There were a number of conditions that made Nevins optimistic about the acceptance of Perrier water by American consumers. The most important of these was the growing diet-consciousness. Miller brewing had hit the market with phenomenal success a few years earlier with the introduction of Lite beer. Since cyclamates had been banned in soft drinks, producers had turned to saccharin which many people found distasteful. There was also no popular low-calorie drink that was considered chic to order. The use of the adjective "diet" simply announced that the drinker was encountering weight problems. If people could be persuaded that Perrier tasted good, then it could be a preferred low-calorie alternative.

Another trend was toward natural foods for health reasons. Even tap water and the 75 percent of bottled water that was processed from tap water had become suspect. In the process of purification, cancer-suspect chlorine derivatives were added to water. Furthermore, certain viruses, sodium, and heavy metals were still found in most purified water and soda water. Perrier came from natural springs, contained high calcium, no sodium, and no additives. It could be promoted as a natural drink with healthy properties even though some of the bubbles were lost when the water was removed from the springs and put back in during the bottling process.

A third factor was a growing U.S. preference for imports. This was apparent not only by noting the rising ratio of imports to gross national expenditures, but also by the acceptance of "foreignness." In terms of food, so-called gourmet restaurants, cookbooks, dinner clubs, ingredients, and wines were becoming commonplace, and French items were practically synonymous with the word gourmet. Perrier might successfully capitalize on these attitudes.

The marketing program for Great Waters of France really got underway in 1977. One of the first questions was in which part of the market to position Perrier. The three trends discussed above would clearly lead to different price, promotion, and distribution strategies because of facing different competitors in each segment. In order to go after the diet market segment, for example, Perrier would come face-to-face with Coca-Cola and Pepsi-Cola, who between them controlled 45 percent of the soft-drink market. These firms, along with the many others that competed for the remaining 55 percent of sales, fought vigorously in the market by keeping prices fairly low, advertising heavily, and clamoring for shelf space in the soft-drink section of supermarkets. The difficulty of competing in this segment is evident by the experience of Schweppes, which in spite of establishing U.S. bottling facilities and engaging in heavy marketing outlays had failed to get even 1 percent of the market. To compete in this mass market segment might also cause Perrier to lose the snob appeal it held among high-income buyers.

To compete in the natural or health foods segment would pit Perrier against other bottled water producers and various tonics that contained healthful additives. This was a very small market as compared with soft drinks. The 1976 sales of bottled water were $189 million of which 93 percent was from purified domestic still water. This was largely sold in five-gallon containers at low prices through home or commercial delivery. Less than 20 percent of bottled water was sold in retail stores, and there was little brand identification. To expand retail sales would probably mean concentrating on gaining shelf space in the health food sections of stores. Since bottled water sales were determined to be much more geographically concentrated than soft-drink sales, it would be far easier for Perrier to target its promotion and distribution for this segment. About 50 percent of sales, for example, were in California.

The gourmet market was the one to which Source Perrier had been selling for some 70 years. There were undoubtedly usage as well as distributional gaps in this market. The total sales of mineral water in 1976 were only $15 million. Primary demand might be increased and Perrier might be made more readily available through increased distribution to specialty stores and new distribution to the growing gourmet sections of supermarkets.

Perrier decided to hit the mass market by competing in the soft-drink market segment. One of the first problems that they had to overcome was the price of the product. Through massive distribution, they reasoned that the retail price could be cut about 30 percent. Even at that, the price was still about 50 percent higher than the average soft drink. This price was considered "rock bottom." The cost of transporting water across the Atlantic was expensive, resulting in an East Coast retail price in 1977 of 69 cents for a 23-ounce bottle. This included a retail gross margin of 27.6 percent as compared to 22.6 percent on soft drinks. Management reasoned that the higher margin would make supermarkets more willing to handle Perrier. A low margin was maintained by Perrier not only to become more price competitive with domestic soft drinks, but also to dissuade other European firms from exporting to the United States. To get people to pay what was still a high price, it was necessary to segment the soft-drink market differently than anyone had heretofore done—by aiming at an adult population and using the higher price to gain snob appeal.

Great Waters of France felt that distribution was the real key to success. A sales force of forty people, almost all of whom were formerly with soft-drink firms, were hired. Through a close examination of demographics, three cities were picked for the first expansion efforts. The cities (New York, San Francisco, and Los Angeles) were those with the largest penchant for imported food items. The company made a film designed to convey to distributors and supermarket chains that Perrier water had a long-term viability. The film showed that the springs had been popular as far back as 218 B.C. when Hannibal partook of the waters and that the present firm dates back to 1903, supplies 400 million bottles a year, and outsells the leading cola in Europe by 2 to 1. Perrier sought the most aggressive distributors for these first and subsequent market areas. These included soft-drink bottlers, alcoholic beverage distributors, and food brokers in different areas. It was essential that distributors be able to get supermarket space in the soft-drink sections, replenish stocks frequently, and set up point of purchase displays. One of the first distributors, Joyce Beverage Management, bought fifty-five trucks and hired 100 additional people to handle the Perrier account. In the introductory period, arrangements were made for secondary display stacks and in-store tastings. The company also gave cents-off coupons with purchases. Within a year, Perrier had moved from three to twenty major market areas. This was doubled in the second year.

For the big sales push, Perrier developed 11-ounce and 6.5-ounce bottles, the latter sold in multipacks. They also developed a modern logo on the bottles, later to be replaced by the original label design, which was more congruent with the old-world image that the firm wished to project. With initial distribution assured, it was necessary to get sufficient appeal so that the bottles on the shelves would be sold. In Europe the company could make therapeutic claims; however, the U.S. law was very strictly against this. In test marketing, Perrier tried such themes as "formerly heavy drinkers such as Richard Burton and Ed McMahon are now 'hooked' on Perrier," and "contains no sodium which causes heartburn." These were abandoned in favor of messages emphasizing its qualities as a natural thirst-quencher with no calories and no additives. Initial promotion was regional, relying heavily on the print media. Groups of food and beverage writers were invited for dinners and exhibitions so that they would write about Perrier. Marathons were sponsored so that the product would be associated both with "healthiness" and "thirst-quenching."

As distribution became national, Perrier got Orson Welles to give T.V. spots on network channels. The advertising budget was set high, $1 million, $2 million, and $7 million for respective fiscal years 1977, 1978, and 1979. Throughout this period, Perrier was able to maintain a snob appeal by getting tidbits in gossip columns about celebrities being seen sipping Perrier in the "right places."

Sales increased rapidly to 21 million bottles in 1977, 60 million in 1978, over 100 million in 1979, and over 200 million in 1980. The increase did not go unnoticed by either the media or by competitors. By 1979, a bottling executive said, "Everyone with water seeping from a rock is buying glass, slapping a label on it, and marketing a new bottled water." In the first quarter of 1979 alone, seven new bottled waters came on the market. Some of the old bottled spring water firms suddenly sought a larger share of the growing market. They promoted blind tasting comparisons to emphasize that American water was just as tasty as the imports. Nestlé's Deer Park brand made a challenge with a spring water priced 35–40 percent below Perrier. A Chicago firm, Hincley and Schmitt, introduced Premier in a bottle with a label that unashamedly copied Perrier. Its theme was, "let your guests *think* it's imported." Norton Simon's Canada Dry began repositioning its club soda to be more competitive with Perrier. SAMI, a market research group, reported 104 brands of bottled waters in its territory.*

In view of the increased competition from American companies, Nevins was forced to review his company's marketing strategy.

DIRECTIONS: The questions that follow relate to the preceding passage. Evaluate, in terms of the passage, each of the items given. Then select your answer from one of the following classifications, and blacken the corresponding space on the answer sheet.

(A) A MAJOR OBJECTIVE in making the decision: one of the goals sought by the decision maker

(B) A MAJOR FACTOR in making the decision: an aspect of the problem, specifically mentioned in the passage, that fundamentally affects and/or determines the decision

(C) A MINOR FACTOR in making the decision: a less important element bearing on or affecting a Major Factor, rather than a Major Objective directly

(D) A MAJOR ASSUMPTION in making the decision: a projection or supposition arrived at by the decision maker before considering the factors and alternatives

(E) AN UNIMPORTANT ISSUE in making the decision: an item lacking significant impact on, or relationship to, the decision

19. Perrier as a low-calorie alternative to soft drinks

20. Growing U.S. preference for imports

21. No sodium in Perrier water

22. Finding aggressive distributors

23. Diet-consciousness of Americans

24. The establishment of Perrier in 1903

---

* Data for the case were taken from: 1. James F. Clarity, "Perrier, the Snob's Drink, Soon to Come in Six Packs," *New York Times*, 27 April 1977, p. C1+ ; Louis Botto, "Straight from the Source," *New York Times Magazine*, 26 June 1977, pp. 68–72. 2. Roger B. May, "French Bottler Tries to Replace U.S. Pop With a Natural Fizz," *Wall Street Journal*, 12 April 1978, p. 1+ ; Maria Anna Ferrara, "Nestlé's Deer Park Challenges Perrier in New York Market," *Wall Street Journal*, 27 November 1978, p. 34; "Deep Chic," *Wall Street Journal*, 7 December 1979, p. 24. 3. Carolyn Pfaff, "Perrier Fortunes Rest on Whimsical Chief," *Advertising Age*, 14 April 1980, p. 66. 4. Peter C. DuBois, "Perrier Going Flat?" *Barron's*, 12 May 1980, p. 71. 5. "Perrier: Putting More Sparkle into Sales," *S & MM*, January 1979, pp. 16–17. 6. Bob Lederer and Martin Westerman, "How Perrier Became a Soft Drink," *Beverage World*, May 1979, pp. 37–45. 7. "Perrier: The Astonishing Success of an Appeal to Affluent Adults," *Business Week*, 22 January 1979, pp. 64–65. 8. "The Water Treatment," *Fortune*, 12 January 1981, p. 22.

25. Cutting the retail price by 30 percent

26. Perrier's success in France

27. Advantages of mineral water

28. Cost of shipping to the United States

29. Lagging growth of Perrier in France

30. Finding a market position for Perrier

31. Proportion of bottled water sold in five-gallon containers

32. Increased competition from American bottlers

33. Banning of cyclamates in soft drinks

34. Acceptance of "foreignness" by consumers

35. U.S. advertising legislation

If there is still time remaining, you may review the questions in this section only.
You may not turn to any other section of the test.

Section IV   Data Sufficiency

TIME: 30 minutes

DIRECTIONS: Each of the following problems has a question and two statements which are labeled (1) and (2). Use the data given in (1) and (2) together with other available information (such as the number of hours in a day, the definition of *clockwise*, mathematical facts, etc.) to decide whether the statements are *sufficient* to answer the question. Then fill in space

(A) if you can get the answer from (1) alone but not from (2) alone;

(B) if you can get the answer from (2) alone but not from (1) alone;

(C) if you can get the answer from (1) and (2) together, although neither statement by itself suffices;

(D) if statement (1) alone suffices *and* statement (2) alone suffices;

(E) if you cannot get the answer from statements (1) and (2) together, but need even more data.

All numbers used in this section are real numbers. A figure given for a problem is intended to provide information consistent with that in the question, but not necessarily with the additional information contained in the statements.

1. In triangle ABC, find x if $y = 40$.

   (1) $AB = BC$
   (2) $z = 100$

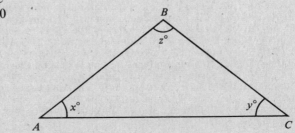

2. What is the area of the shaded part of the circle? *O* is the center of the circle.

(1) The radius of the circle is 4.
(2) *x* is 60.

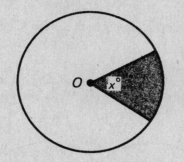

3. What was Mr. Kliman's income in 1970?

(1) His total income for 1968, 1969, and 1970 was $41,000.
(2) He made 20% more in 1969 than he did in 1968.

4. If *l* and *l'* are straight lines, find *y*.

(1) $x = 100$
(2) $z = 80$

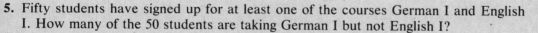

5. Fifty students have signed up for at least one of the courses German I and English I. How many of the 50 students are taking German I but not English I?

(1) 16 students are taking German I and English I.
(2) The number of students taking English I but not German I is the same as the number taking German I but not English I.

6. Is *ABCD* a square?

(1) $AD = AB$
(2) $x = 90$

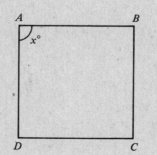

7. The *XYZ* Corporation has 7,000 employees. What is the average yearly wage of an employee of the *XYZ* Corporation?

(1) 4,000 of the employees are executives.
(2) The total amount the company pays in wages each year is $77,000,000.

8. Is $x > y$?

(1) $(x + y)^2 > 0$
(2) x is positive

9. What is the area of the shaded region if both circles have radius 4, and O and O' are the centers of the circles?

(1) The area enclosed by both circles is 29π.
(2) The line connecting O and O' is perpendicular to the line connecting B and C (B and C are the points where the two circles intersect).

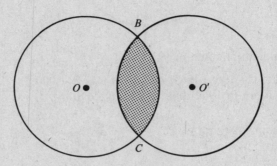

10. How long will it take to travel from A to B? It takes 4 hours to travel from A to B and back to A.

(1) It takes 25% more time to travel from A to B than it does to travel from B to A.
(2) C is midway between A and B, and it takes 2 hours to travel from A to C and back to A.

11. l, l', and k are straight lines. Are l and l' parallel?

(1) $x = y$
(2) $y = z$

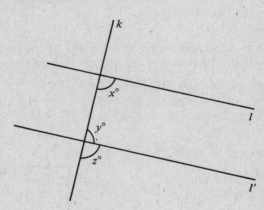

12. What is $x + y + z$?

(1) $x + y = 3$
(2) $x + z = 2$

13. How much cardboard will it take to make a rectangular box with a lid whose base has length 7 inches?

(1) The width of the box will be 5 inches.
(2) The height of the box will be 4 inches.

14. What is the profit on 15 boxes of detergent?

    (1) The cost of a crate of boxes of detergent is $50.

    (2) Each crate contains 100 boxes of detergent.

15. Which of the two figures, *ABCD* or *EFGH*, has the largest area?

    (1) The perimeter of *ABCD* is longer than the perimeter of *EFGH*.

    (2) *AC* is longer than *EG*.

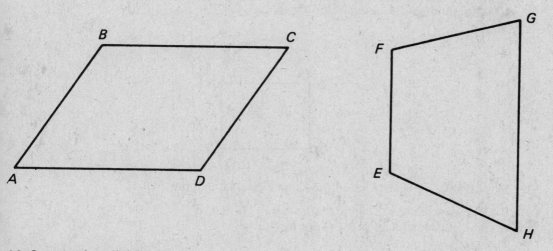

16. Is a number divisible by 9?

    (1) The number is divisible by 3.

    (2) The number is divisible by 27.

17. *PQRS* is a rectangle. The coordinates of the point *P* are (2,3). What is the area of *PQRS*?

    (1) The coordinates of the point *S* are (2,5).

    (2) The coordinates of the point *Q* are (6,3).

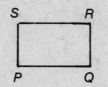

18. *ABCD* is a rectangle. Which region, *ABEF* or *CDFE*, has a larger area?

    (1) *BE* is longer than *FD*.

    (2) *BE* is longer than *CD*.

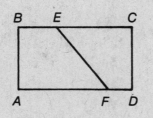

19. Is the integer *k* odd or even?

    (1) k^2 is odd.

    (2) $2k$ is even.

20. Does a car with 5 gallons of gas in its fuel tank have enough fuel to travel 100 miles?

    (1) The car travels 25 miles on one gallon of gas.
    (2) The car is driven at a speed of 50 miles per hour.

21. *ABCD* is a square.
BCO is a semicircle.
What is the area of *ABOCD*?

    (1) The length of *AC* is $4\sqrt{2}$.
    (2) The radius of the semicircle *BOC* is 2.

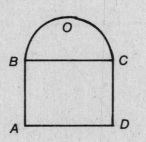

22. Do the points *P* and *Q* lie on the same circle with center (0,0)?

    (1) The coordinates of point *P* are (2,3).
    (2) The coordinates of point *Q* are (4,1).

23. Did ABC Company make a profit in 1980?

    (1) ABC Company made a profit in 1979.
    (2) ABC Company made a profit in 1981.

24. Is 2^n divisible by 8?

    (1) *n* is an odd integer.
    (2) *n* is an integer greater than 5.

25. Did the price of a bushel of soybeans increase during every week of 1980?

    (1) The price of a bushel of soybeans was $2 on Jan 1, 1980.
    (2) The price of a bushel of soybeans was $4 on Jan 1, 1981.

If there is still time remaining, you may review the questions in this section only.
You may not turn to any other section of the test.

Section V   Writing Ability

TIME: **30 minutes**

DIRECTIONS: This test consists of a number of sentences, in each of which some part or the whole is underlined. Each sentence is followed by five alternative versions of the underlined portion. Select the alternative you consider both most correct and most effective according to the requirements of standard written English. Answer A is the same as the original version; if you think the original version is best, select answer A.

In considering the answer choices, be attentive to matters of grammar, diction, and syntax, as well as clarity, precision, and fluency. Do not select an answer which alters the meaning of the original sentence.

1. <u>If we cooperate together by dividing up the work</u>, we shall be able to finish it quickly.

   (A) If we cooperate together by dividing up the work
   (B) If we cooperate by dividing up the work
   (C) If we cooperate together by dividing the work
   (D) If we cooperate by dividing up the work together
   (E) If we cooperate by dividing the work

2. <u>I think he approves my choice despite the fact I differ with him, granted the generation gap between us.</u>

   (A) I think he approves my choice despite the fact I differ with him, granted the generation gap between us.
   (B) Granted the generation gap between us, I think he approves my choice despite the fact I differ with him.
   (C) Despite the fact I differ with him, I think he approves my choice, granted the generation gap between us.
   (D) Despite the fact I differ with him, I think, granted the generation gap between us, he approves my choice.
   (E) Granted the generation gap between us, despite the fact that I differ with him, I think he approves by choice.

3. The vacationers <u>enjoyed swimming in the pool, bathing in the ocean, and, particularly, to snorkel</u> near the reef.

   (A) enjoyed swimming in the pool, bathing in the ocean, and, particularly, to snorkel
   (B) enjoyed swimming in the pool, to bathe in the ocean, and, particularly, to snorkel
   (C) enjoyed swimming in the pool, to bathe in the ocean, and, particularly snorkeling
   (D) enjoyed swimming in the pool, bathing in the ocean, and, particularly, snorkeling
   (E) enjoyed to swim in the pool, to bathe in the ocean, and, particularly, to snorkel

4. <u>Crossing the street, a car almost struck us.</u>

   (A) Crossing the street, a car almost struck us.
   (B) A car almost struck us, crossing the street.
   (C) As we crossed the street, a car almost struck us.
   (D) A car, crossing the street, almost struck us.
   (E) Having crossed the street, a car almost struck us.

5. <u>The theme of this novel is how money doesn't make you happy.</u>

   (A) The theme of this novel is how money doesn't make you happy.
   (B) The theme of this novel is that money doesn't make you happy.
   (C) In this novel, its theme is how money doesn't make you happy.
   (D) In this novel, that money doesn't make you happy is the theme.
   (E) In this novel, you are not made happy by money is the theme.

6. If some Americans <u>look at where they are going, it can be seen that our goal</u> is money.

    (A) look at where they are going, it can be seen that our goal
    (B) look back at where they are going, they see that their goal
    (C) look ahead to where they are going, it can be seen that their goal
    (D) look at where they are going, they can see our goal
    (E) look ahead to where they are going, they can see their goal

7. Mary, a girl with little talent for cooking, <u>enjoys preparing</u> pizza.

    (A) Mary, a girl with little talent for cooking, enjoys preparing
    (B) Mary is a girl who has little talent for cooking who enjoys to prepare
    (C) Mary is a girl with little talent for cooking and who enjoys preparing
    (D) Mary, who has little talent for cooking, enjoys to prepare
    (E) With little talent for cooking, Mary is a girl who enjoys to prepare

8. <u>My grandmother is the most remarkable person of all the persons I have ever met.</u>

    (A) My grandmother is the most remarkable person of all the persons I have ever met.
    (B) Of all the persons I have ever met, my grandmother is the most remarkable person.
    (C) Of all the persons I have ever met, the most remarkable person is my grandmother.
    (D) Of all the persons I have ever met, the most remarkable is my grandmother.
    (E) My grandmother, of all the persons I have ever met, is the most remarkable.

9. Start the motor, and <u>then you should remove the blocks.</u>

    (A) Start the motor, and then you should remove the blocks.
    (B) Start the motor and then remove the blocks.
    (C) Start the motor, then removing the blocks.
    (D) Start the motor, and then the blocks should be removed.
    (E) Starting the motor, the blocks should then be removed.

10. <u>He is a genius, although he is eccentric and wants recognition.</u>

    (A) He is a genius, although he is eccentric and wants recognition.
    (B) Although he is eccentric, he is a genius and wants recognition.
    (C) Although he is eccentric, he is a genius although he wants recognition.
    (D) His is a genius although he is eccentric and although he wants recognition.
    (E) Although he is eccentric and wants recognition, he is a genius.

11. <u>Every creditor feels that their claim is the most important thing</u> in the world.

    (A) Every creditor feels that their claim is the most important thing
    (B) Every creditor feels that his claim is the most important thing
    (C) Each and every creditor feels that their claim is the most important thing
    (D) Every creditor feels that their claims are the most important things
    (E) Every creditor feels that his claim is the more important thing

12. <u>The smaller firms sold either on a price or quality-of-workmanship basis.</u>

    (A) The smaller firms sold either on a price or quality-of-workmanship basis.
    (B) The smaller firms either sold on a price or quality-of-workmanship basis.
    (C) The smaller firms sold on either a price or a quality-of-workmanship basis.
    (D) The smaller firms sold on either a price or on a quality-of-workmanship basis.
    (E) Either the smaller firms sold on a price or on a quality-of-workmanship basis.

13. The matter was <u>referred back to committee since the solution to the problem was different from the one proposed earlier which was not practicable.</u>

   (A) referred back to committee since the solution to the problem was different from the one proposed earlier which was not practicable
   (B) referred to committee since the solution to the problem was different from the one proposed earlier which was not practicable
   (C) referred back to committee since the solution to the problem was different than the one proposed earlier which was not practical
   (D) referred to committee since the solution to the problem was different than the one proposed earlier which was not practicable
   (E) referred back to committee since the solution to the problem was different from the one proposed earlier which was not practical

14. <u>Irregardless of the consequences, the police officer was forbidden from making any pinches.</u>

   (A) Irregardless of the consequences, the police officer was forbidden from making any pinches.
   (B) Irregardless of the consequences, the police officer was forbidden from making any arrests.
   (C) Regardless of the consequences, the police officer was forbidden from making any arrests.
   (D) Irregardless of the consequences, the police officer was forbidden to make any pinches.
   (E) Regardless of the consequences, the police officer was forbidden to make any arrests.

15. <u>The book having been read carefully and extensive notes having been taken, Tom</u> felt confident about the test.

   (A) The book having been read carefully and extensive notes having been taken, Tom
   (B) Tom, who read the book carefully and having taken extensive notes
   (C) Reading the book carefully and taking extensive notes, Tom
   (D) Having read the book carefully and extensive notes having been taken, Tom
   (E) Because he had read the book carefully and had taken extensive notes, Tom

16. He has <u>not only violated the law, but also he has escaped punishment.</u>

   (A) not only violated the law, but also he has escaped punishment
   (B) violated not only the law, but also he has escaped punishment
   (C) violated not only the law, but he has escaped punishment also
   (D) not only violated the law, but also escaped punishment
   (E) not only violated the law, but has escaped punishment

17. Ideally, <u>the fan should be placed in a different room than</u> the one you want to cool.

   (A) the fan should be placed in a different room than
   (B) the fan had ought to be placed in a different room from
   (C) the fan should be placed in a different room from
   (D) the fan had ought to be placed in a different room than
   (E) you should place the fan in a different room than

18. After viewing both movies, <u>John agreed that the first one was the best of the two</u>.

   (A) John agreed that the first one was the best of the two
   (B) John agreed that the first was the best of the two
   (C) John agreed that the first one was the better of the two
   (D) John agreed that of the two the better one was the first
   (E) John agreed that the best of the two was the first

19. Poor product quality angers Bob, <u>who wonders if it is part of a strategy by manu-facturers</u>.

   (A) who wonders if it is part of a strategy by manufacturers
   (B) who wonders if manufacturers are part of the strategy
   (C) that wonders if it is part of a strategy by manufacturers
   (D) wondering if this is part of a strategy by manufacturers
   (E) who wonders if they are part of a strategy by manufacturers

20. He noted <u>the dog's soft hair, strong legs, and keen sense of smell</u>.

   (A) the dog's soft hair, strong legs, and keen sense of smell
   (B) the dog's soft hair, strong legs, and that his sense of smell was keen
   (C) the dog's soft hair, and that his legs were strong and sense of smell was keen
   (D) the dog's soft hair, and that his legs were strong and smell was keen
   (E) the dog's soft hair, keen smell and that his legs were strong

21. <u>Because of production cutbacks caused by termination of government contracts, the management announces that the services of some personnel will be dispensed with effective immediately.</u>

   (A) Because of production cutbacks caused by termination of government contracts, the management announces that the services of some personnel will be dispensed with effective immediately.
   (B) Because of decreased production caused by loss of government contracts, the management announces the immediate firing of some personnel.
   (C) Because of loss of government contracts causing lower production, the management will have to dispense with some personnel immediately.
   (D) Because of reduced production caused by the end of government contracts, some personnel will be dismissed immediately.
   (E) The services of some personnel will be dispensed with immediately because of production cutbacks and the end of government contracts.

22. <u>Having bowed our heads, the minister led</u> us in prayer.

   (A) Having bowed our heads, the minister led
   (B) After we bowed our heads, the minister led
   (C) After we bowed our heads, the minister leads
   (D) After we had bowed our heads, the minister led
   (E) Having bowed our heads, the minister leads

23. She <u>seldom ever wants to try and face the true facts</u>.

   (A) seldom ever wants to try and face the true facts
   (B) seldom ever wants to try and face the facts
   (C) seldom ever wants to try to face the facts
   (D) seldom wants to try and face the facts
   (E) seldom wants to try to face the facts

24. The new legislation <u>also provides $5 billion to finance solar energy projects and for conservation measures</u>.

   (A) also provides $5 billion to finance solar energy projects and for conservation measures

   (B) provides also $5 billion to finance solar energy projects and for conservation measures

   (C) also provides $5 billion in order to finance solar energy projects and for conservation measures

   (D) also provides $5 billion to finance solar energy projects and to carry out conservation measures

   (E) provides $5 billion for financing solar energy projects and to carry out conservation measures

25. The president's talk <u>was directed toward whomever was present</u>.

   (A) was directed toward whomever was present
   (B) was directed toward whoever was present
   (C) was directed at who was present
   (D) was directed at whomever was present
   (E) was directed towards whomever was present

*If there is still time remaining, you may review the questions in this section only.
You may not turn to any other section of the test.*

Section VI   Problem Solving

TIME: 30 minutes

DIRECTIONS: Solve each of the following problems; then indicate the correct answer on the answer sheet. [On the actual test you will be permitted to use any space available on the examination paper for scratch work.]

NOTE: A figure that appears with a problem is drawn as accurately as possible so as to provide information that may help in answering the question. Numbers in this test are real numbers.

1. If the side of a square increases by 40%, then the area of the square increases by

   (A) 16%   (D) 116%
   (B) 40%   (E) 140%
   (C) 96%

2. If 28 cartons of soda cost $21.00, then 7 cartons of soda should cost

   (A) $5.25   (D) $7.00
   (B) $5.50   (E) $10.50
   (C) $6.40

3. Plane P takes off at 2 A.M. and flies at a constant speed of x mph. Plane Q takes off at 3:30 A.M. and flies the same route as P but travels at a constant speed of y mph. Assuming that y is greater than x, how many hours after 3:30 A.M. will plane Q overtake plane P?

(A) $\frac{3}{2}x$ hrs.

(B) $\frac{3}{2}$ hrs.

(C) $\frac{3}{2y}$ hrs.

(D) $\frac{3}{2(y-x)}$ hrs.

(E) $\frac{3x}{2(y-x)}$ hrs.

4. A worker is paid $20 for each day he works, and he is paid proportionately for any fraction of a day he works. If during one week he works ⅛, ⅔, ¾, ⅓, and 1 full day, what are his total earnings for the week?

(A) $40.75
(B) $52.50
(C) $54

(D) $57.50
(E) $58.25

Use the following table for questions 5–6.

DISTRIBUTION OF TEST SCORES IN A CLASS

Number of Students	Number of Correct Answers
10	36 to 40
16	32 to 35
12	28 to 31
14	26 to 27
8	0 to 25

5. What percent of the class answered 32 or more questions correctly?

(A) 16⅔
(B) 20
(C) 26⅔

(D) 43⅓
(E) 52

6. The number of students who answered 28 to 31 questions correctly is x times the number who answered 25 or fewer correctly, where x is

(A) ⅔
(B) 1
(C) 3/2

(D) 7/4
(E) 2

7. If the product of 3 consecutive integers is 210, then the sum of the two smaller integers is

(A) 5
(B) 11
(C) 12

(D) 13
(E) 18

8. Cereal costs ⅓ as much as bacon. Bacon costs ¾ as much as eggs. Eggs cost what fraction of the cost of cereal?

(A) 5/12
(B) 5/4
(C) 5/3

(D) 12/5
(E) 4/5

9. A truck gets 15 miles per gallon of gas when it is unloaded. When the truck is loaded, it travels only 80% as far on a gallon of gas as when unloaded. How many gallons will the loaded truck use to travel 80 miles?

(A) 5⅓   (D) 6⅔
(B) 6   (E) 6¾
(C) 6⅓

10. If x and y are negative numbers, which of the following statements is (are) always true?

   I. $x - y$ is negative.
  II. $-x$ is positive
 III. $(-x)(-y)$ is positive.

(A) I only   (D) II and III only
(B) II only   (E) I and III only
(C) I and II only

11. Both circles have radius 4 and the area enclosed by both circles is 28π. What is the area of the shaded region?

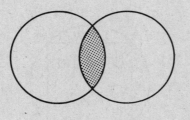

(A) 0   (D) $4\pi^2$
(B) 2π (E) 16π
(C) 4π

12. For each dollar spent by the sales department, the research department spends 20¢. For every $4 spent by the research department, the packing department spends $1.50. The triple ratio of the money spent by the sales department to the money spent by the research department to the money spent by the packing department can be expressed as

(A) $40:8:3$ (D) $4:1:5$
(B) $20:4:1$ (E) $2:1:5$
(C) $8:4:1$

13. $ABCD$ has area equal to 28. BC is parallel to AD. BA is perpendicular to AD. If BC is 6 and AD is 8, then what is CD?

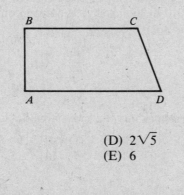

(A) $2\sqrt{2}$ (D) $2\sqrt{5}$
(B) $2\sqrt{3}$ (E) 6
(C) 4

14. A manufacturer prints books at a cost of $x each for the first thousand copies printed. The second thousand copies printed cost $.9x each. If it costs $3,264 to print 1,400 copies of a book, then x is

(A) 1.63
(B) 2.10
(C) 2.33

(D) 2.40
(E) 2.59

15. If X is an odd integer and Y is an even integer, which of the following statements is (are) always true?

   I. X + Y is odd.
  II. XY is odd.
 III. 2X + Y is even.

(A) I only
(B) III only
(C) I and III only

(D) II and III only
(E) I, II, and III

16. Find the area of the region inside the circle and outside the square ABCD. A, B, C, and D are all points on the circle, and the radius of the circle is 4.

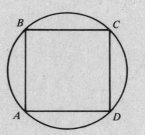

(A) 16π − 36
(B) 16(π − 2)
(C) 16(π − 1)

(D) 16π − 4
(E) 16π

17. *X is defined as the largest integer which is less than X. What is the value of (*3) + (*4) + (*4.5)?

(A) 9
(B) 10
(C) 11

(D) 11.5
(E) 12

18. Joan started work 2 years ago. Her starting salary was ½ of Mike's salary at that time. Each year since then Joan has received a raise of 5% in her salary and Mike has received a raise of 10% in his salary. What percentage (to the nearest percent) of Mike's current salary is Joan's current salary?

(A) 45
(B) 46
(C) 48

(D) 50
(E) 220

19. Which of the following integers has the most divisors?

(A) 88
(B) 91
(C) 95

(D) 99
(E) 101

20. The amount of fat in an ounce of food A plus the amount of protein in an ounce of food A is 100 grams. The amount of protein in an ounce of food A minus twice the amount of fat in an ounce of food A is 10 grams. How many grams of protein are there in an ounce of food A?

(A) 30   (D) 55
(B) 45   (E) 70
(C) 50

*If there is still time remaining, you may review the questions in this section only.
You may not turn to any other section of the test.*

Section VII   Data Sufficiency

TIME: 30 minutes

DIRECTIONS: Each of the following problems has a question and two statements which are labeled (1) and (2). Use the data given in (1) and (2) together with other available information (such as the number of hours in a day, the definition of *clockwise*, mathematical facts, etc.) to decide whether the statements are *sufficient* to answer the question. Then fill in space

(A) if you can get the answer from (1) alone but not from (2) alone;

(B) if you can get the answer from (2) alone but not from (1) alone;

(C) if you can get the answer from (1) and (2) together, although neither statement by itself suffices;

(D) if statement (1) alone suffices *and* statement (2) alone suffices;

(E) if you cannot get the answer from statements (1) and (2) together, but need even more data.

All numbers used in this section are real numbers. A figure given for a problem is intended to provide information consistent with that in the question, but not necessarily with the additional information contained in the statements.

1. What percentage is Y's salary of X's salary?

(1) X's salary is 80% of Z's salary.
(2) Y's salary is 120% of Z's salary.

2. How long will it be before ABC stock is worth $63 per share?

(1) ABC stock doubles in price every six months.
(2) ABC company pays dividends of $3 a share.

3. What is the value of $x + 2y$?

(1) $x + y - z = 10$
(2) $y + z = 4$

4. What is the sum of the three numbers x, y, and z?

(1) The average of x, y, and z is 12.
(2) $x = 3$, $y = 20$

5. Which angle is smaller, x or y?

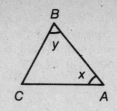

(1) $AB = BC$
(2) $x + y = 100°$

6. How much money did the Suppertime Theatre make from ticket sales? The theatre sells two kinds of tickets: reserved seat and general admission.

(1) The theatre made $2,000 from sales of reserved seats.
(2) The theatre sold 400 general admission tickets.

7. What is the value of $x + y$?

(1) $x = 50\%$ of y
(2) $2x + 2y = 6$

8. Does 3 evenly divide the integer x?

(1) 6 evenly divides x.
(2) 12 evenly divides x.

9. Are the lines l and m perpendicular?

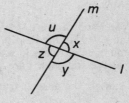

(1) $z = x$
(2) $u = y$

10. The expenses of the ABC corporation are each billed to one and only one of its three divisions: division A, division B, and division C. What percentage of the expenses of the ABC corporation were billed to division A?

(1) The expenses of division A are twice as much as the expenses of division B.
(2) The expenses of division B are the same as the expenses of division C.

11. The graph gives the distribution of expenses between Joe and Bill each month for their apartment. How much does Bill pay each month for the apartment?

(1) $x = 40$
(2) $y = 60$

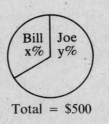

Total = $500

12. Is $\dfrac{x}{12} > \dfrac{y}{40}$?

(1) $10x > 3y$
(2) $12x < 4y$

13. What is the value of $x - y$?

(1) $x^2 - y^2 = 10$
(2) $x + y = 2$

14. In a survey of 100 people, 70 people owned a television or a telephone or both. If 30 people owned both a television and a telephone, which group of surveyed people is larger: those who own a television or those who own a telephone?

(1) 25 people own a television but do not own a telephone.
(2) 45 people own a telephone.

15. Which is larger, x or x^2?

(1) $x > 0$
(2) $x < 0$

16. Which line segment is longer, AB or CD?

(1) $x + y = 170$
(2) CB is longer than AD

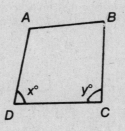

17. How many degrees Celsius is 100° Fahrenheit?

(1) degrees Celsius = 5/9 (degrees Fahrenheit) − 32)
(2) degrees Fahrenheit = 9/5 (degrees Celsius) + 32)

18. How much is Jane's salary?

(1) Jane's salary is 70% of John's salary.
(2) John's salary is 50% of Mary's salary.

19. What is the value of z? $z = x - (150\%$ of $y)$.

(1) $x = \dfrac{3}{2}y$
(2) $z = \sqrt{y}$

20. What is the length of AB?
The length of $AC = 5$.

(1) AC is perpendicular to CB.
(2) The length of CB is 12.

21. Is $x > 1$?

(1) $x + y = 2$
(2) $y < 0$

22. Is x positive?

(1) $x^2 + 3x - 4 = 0$
(2) $x > -2$

23. Can x, y, z be the lengths of the sides of a triangle?

(1) $x > y > z > 0$
(2) $x + y > z$

24. Is n the square of a positive integer k?

(1) $n = 4j^2$ with j an integer.
(2) $n^2 = A^2 + B^2$ with A, B integers.

25. Train Y leaves New York at 1 A.M. and travels east at a constant speed of y m.p.h. Train Z leaves New York at 2 A.M. and travels east at a constant speed of z m.p.h. Which train will travel farther by 4 A.M.?

(1) $y > z$
(2) $y = 1.2z$

If there is still time remaining, you may review the questions in this section only.
You may not turn to any other section of the test.

Section VIII Critical Reasoning

TIME: 30 minutes

DIRECTIONS: For each question, choose the best answer among the listed alternatives.

1. A politician wrote the following: "I realize there are some shortcomings to the questionnaire method. However, since I send a copy of the questionnaire to every home in the district, I believe the results are quite representative . . . I think the numbers received are so large that it is quite accurate even though the survey is not done scientifically."

The writer of the above statement makes which of the following assumptions:

(A) Most people who received the questionnaire have replied.
(B) Most people in the district live in homes.
(C) The questionnaire method of data collection is unscientific.
(D) The large number of replies means that a high proportion of those sampled have replied.
(E) A large, absolute number of replies is synonymous with accuracy.

2. In 1950, Transylvania earned $1 million in tourist revenue. By 1970, tourist revenue doubled and in 1980, it reached the sum of $4 million.

Each of the following, if true, may explain the trend in tourist revenue EXCEPT:

(A) The number of tourists has increased from 1950 to 1980.
(B) Average expenditure per tourist has increased.
(C) Average stay per tourist has increased.
(D) The number of total hotel rooms has increased.
(E) The average cost of tourist services has increased.

3. Donors are almost never offended by being asked too much (in fact, they are usually flattered). And if you ask for too much, your donor can always suggest a smaller amount. On the other hand, donors are frequently offended by being asked for too little. A common reaction is, "so that's all they think I'm worth."

The above statement assumes that:

(A) Donors are usually never asked enough.
(B) A good fund raiser will value the worth of the donor.
(C) It is worth the gamble to ask for large donations.
(D) Fund raisers often think that donors are incapable of giving much.
(E) Donors are seldom offended by fund raisers.

4. One major obligation of the social psychologist is to provide his own discipline, the other social sciences, and interested laymen with conceptual tools that will increase the range and the reliability of their understanding of social phenomena. Beyond that, responsible government officials are today turning more frequently to the social scientist for insights into the nature and solution of the problems with which they are confronted.

The above argument assumes that:

(A) Social psychologists must have a strong background in other sciences as well as their own.
(B) A study of social psychology should be a part of the curriculum of government officials.
(C) The social scientist has an obligation to provide the means by which social phenomena may be understood by others.
(D) Social phenomena are little understood by those outside the field of social psychology.
(E) A good social psychologist is obligated principally by the need to solve inter-disciplinary problems.

5. New problems require new solutions. And new problems arise with new populations and new technologies. The solutions of these problems require new institutions as well as new political, economic, and social mechanisms. Yet institutions and political and economic arrangements grow slowly and die slowly. Because old institutions die slowly, new institutions should be given every chance of success.

The writer of the above makes which of the following assumptions:

(A) New institutions are needed because old institutions are inefficient.
(B) New institutions are created in order to solve existing problems.
(C) As old institutions are phased out, new ones take their place.
(D) If there were no growth, old institutions would die more slowly.
(E) Socio-technological change requires new forms of institutional arrangements.

6. About 40 percent of American husbands think it is a good idea for wives with school age children to work outside the home. Only one out of ten German household heads approves of mothers working if school age children live at home. Every second American wife, and every third German wife with school age children has a job outside her home.

If the above is correct, which of the following must be true?

(A) More German than American wives work outside the home.
(B) Employment opportunities for American wives are greater than for German wives.
(C) German husbands have more conservative attitudes than American husbands.
(D) German husbands would seem to be less satisfied about working wives who have school age children than American husbands.
(E) German women have fewer children than American women.

7. Building codes required all public buildings constructed after 1980 to have reinforced-steel bomb shelters installed.

From which of the following can the statement above be inferred?

(A) Public buildings had to install reinforced-steel bomb shelters after 1980.
(B) No bomb shelters other than reinforced-steel shelters were installed in public buildings after 1980, but all public buildings constructed after 1980 were required to have bomb shelters.
(C) Some public buildings constructed before 1980 had installed bomb shelters.
(D) Bomb shelters were not required in public buildings before 1980, but some were installed voluntarily.
(E) Before 1980, public buildings had bomb shelters, but not necessarily made of reinforced-steel.

8. In 1950, the average child visited the dentist once a year, by 1970, the number of visits had increased to two. Today, the average child visits the dentist three times a year.

Each of the following, if true, could explain this trend EXCEPT:

(A) Dentist fees have declined over the period.
(B) Better home care of teeth has reduced the number of cavities.
(C) Dental care has become less painful.
(D) Parents are more aware of the importance of dental care.
(E) Tax benefits for deducting dental expenses have increased.

9. Attention is most often focused on net exports (exports less imports) because that figure measures the net effect of a nation's trade in goods and services with the rest of the world. In 1968, exports were 5.8 percent of GNP (Gross National Product) and in 1975, they were 6.8 percent.

If the information above is accurate, which of the following must be true?

(A) If GNP was constant from 1968 to 1975, net exports were almost three times greater in 1975 than in 1968.
(B) Exports were greater than imports in 1975, but not in 1968.
(C) Net exports increased from 1968 to 1975.
(D) In 1975, the increase in exports was nearly double that in 1968.
(E) In 1968, net exports were greater than in 1975.

10. Once a company has established an extensive sales network in a foreign market and therefore has achieved substantial sales, it seems that these markets should be treated in a very similar fashion to those in one's own country. It is therefore those countries where only initial sales and representation have been developed where marketing methods will have to differ from domestic activities.

The above statement assumes that:

(A) Sales networks can be the same in both foreign and domestic markets.
(B) Extensive sales networks are preferable to less developed ones.
(C) Some countries develop economically faster than others.
(D) Larger markets abroad are more adaptable to domestic marketing methods.
(E) A study of marketing should consider the adaptability of advertising campaigns in different countries.

11. The principal monetary policy objective is to reduce substantially the import surplus of the coming years while resuming economic growth. Realization of this goal entails a marked structural change of the economy, which can be brought about by freezing the standard of living (per capita private consumption plus public services) and restricting investments that do not further exports.

The writer of the above policy assumes that:

(A) Economic growth will result in a structural change of the economy.
(B) Only if people consume less can the economy grow.
(C) The import surplus can be reduced if investment is restricted.
(D) Only a structural change in the economy can substantially increase imports.
(E) People will have to be persuaded to give up consumption for the national good.

12. The most commonly cited explanation for nationalization of foreign companies is a change in government. Nationalization tends to cover a wide range of industries and is not selective by country of ownership.

The above statement assumes that:

(A) Defense-related, government-related, and natural resource industries are most likely to be nationalized.

(B) The process of nationalization is not limited to any particular industry or country.
(C) Nationalization of businesses is so widespread as to cause concern.
(D) Nationalization will not occur in countries with democratic governments.
(E) Sharing ownership with local nationals will forstall takeovers by foreign governments.

13. Equality of opportunity has long been prominent as a goal in many countries. In Europe and America there has also been advocacy of more equality of income — the results after taxes of what a person gets for his efforts and the yield of his property. Many western politicians believe this concept of equality should be implemented in developing countries in order to speed economic development.

Which of the following, if true, could weaken the argument above?

(A) In a poor society, total income is so low that if it were distributed equally, no one could save enough to provide resources for investment.
(B) Very large incomes may cause social dissension.
(C) The marginal dollars in the hands of people with large incomes provide less utility than those with lower incomes.
(D) High achievement in many societies is due to equality of incomes.
(E) Equality of opportunity is not necessarily synonymous with equality of income.

14. The balance of trade, i.e. exports minus imports, for most countries is calculated on a yearly basis, divided into quarters. A favorable balance is indicated by export revenue greater than import costs. The terms of trade, i.e. the ratio of export to import prices, is also calculated on a yearly basis. A ratio of 100 means that aggregate export earnings just equal aggregate import costs. Favorable terms are indicated by a ratio of more than 100. Euphoria's balance of trade worsened between 1980–1981, but its terms of trade improved.

If the above conditions are accurate, which of the following must be true?

(A) Euphoria paid more for aggregate imports in 1981 than in 1980.
(B) Between 1980 and 1981, Euphoria imported more than it exported, but earned more from its exports than it paid for its imports.
(C) Between 1980 and 1981, Euphoria exported more than it imported and earned more from its exports than it paid for its imports.
(D) Between 1980 and 1981, Euphoria exported more than it imported, but paid more for its imports than it earned from its exports.
(E) Euphoria earned more from aggregate exports in 1981 than in 1980.

15. A recent communique noted that China's foreign minister told officials in Italy that Beijing intends to maintain and extend its open-door policy to the West. The minister also said that China would continue with its program of political and economic changes despite a recent campaign against Western ideas and foreign aid.

The writer of the communique above makes which of the following assumptions?

(A) China's foreign minister asserts that internal change is a matter for only the Chinese to decide.
(B) Internal political and economic changes will not be tolerated.
(C) China's external relations with the West will continue despite turmoil at home.
(D) Internal changes in China will not follow Western models although foreign trade between them may continue.
(E) China's foreign minister does not realize that an open-door policy and rejection of Western ideas are mutually exclusive.

16. In 1985 there were 20 deaths from automobile accidents per 1,000 miles traveled. A total of 20,000 miles were traveled via automobiles in 1985. In the same year, 800 people died in airplane crashes and 400 people were killed in train disasters. A statistician concluded that it was more dangerous to travel by plane, train, and automobile, in that order.

Which of the following refutes the statistician's conclusion?

(A) There is no common denominator by which to compare the number of deaths resulting from each mode of travel.
(B) One year is insufficient to reach such a conclusion.
(C) More people travel by car than any other mode of transport, therefore, the probability of a car accident is greater.
(D) The number of plane flights and train trips is not stated.
(E) The probability of being killed in a train disaster and as a result of a car crash is the same.

17. From a letter to the commercial editor of a newspaper: Your article of January 9 drew attention to the large deficit in Playland's balance of payments that has worsened over the past three years. Yet, you favor the recent trade treaty signed between Playland and Workland. That treaty results in a lowering of our import duties that will flood us with Workland's goods. This will only exacerbate our balance of trade. How can you be in favor of the treaty?

Which of the following considerations would weaken the letter writer's argument?

(A) Import diversion versus import creation.
(B) Prices paid by importers versus prices paid by consumers.
(C) Economic goals versus political goals.
(D) Duties levied increase government revenue.
(E) Free trade versus protectionism.

18. In 1930, there were, on the average 10 deaths at birth (infant mortality) per 10,000 population. By 1940 there were 8.5, and by 1950, 7.0. Today there are 5.5 deaths at birth per 10,000 population, and it is anticipated that the downward trend will continue.

Each of the following, if true, would help to account for this trend EXCEPT:

(A) Medical care is more widespread and available.
(B) More effective birth control methods have been implemented.
(C) Sanitary conditions have improved.
(D) The number of pediatricians per 10,000 population has increased.
(E) Midwifery has declined in favor of medical doctors.

19. Product shipments of household appliances are expected to rise to $17 billion next year, an average annual increase of 8.0 percent over the past five years. The real growth rate, after allowing for probable price increases, is expected to be about 4.3 percent each year, resulting in shipments this year of $14 billion in 1987 dollars.

Each of the following, if true, could help to account for this trend EXCEPT:

(A) Increased consumer spending for durable products.
(B) Household formations have increased.
(C) Consumer disposable income has increased.
(D) The consumer price of electricity has decreased.
(E) Individual tax advantages have decreased.

20. Each year's increase or decrease in the trade deficit (merchandise imports greater than exports) is calculated in relation to the pevious year's. In 1976, imports of private vehicles were 10 percent higher than in 1975, while imports of vehicles including commercial vans was 15 percent higher than in 1975. That 15 percent increase was one and a half times the increase recorded in 1975.

If the information above is accurate, which of the following must be true?

(A) In 1976, the increase, if any, of commercial vehicle imports was smaller than the increase in imports of private vehicles.
(B) In 1976, the increase, if any, of commercial vehicle imports was greater than the increase in imports of private vehicles.
(C) In 1975, more commercial vehicles were imported than private vehicles.
(D) In 1975, more private vehicles were imported than commercial vehicles.
(E) The average number of private vehicles imported in 1975 declined.

Answers

Section I   Reading Comprehension

1. (C)	8. (E)	15. (A)	22. (D)
2. (C)	9. (B)	16. (E)	23. (C)
3. (D)	10. (B)	17. (A)	24. (E)
4. (C)	11. (A)	18. (C)	25. (E)
5. (C)	12. (D)	19. (D)	
6. (B)	13. (C)	20. (D)	
7. (A)	14. (D)	21. (E)	

Section II   Problem Solving

(Numbers in parentheses indicate the section in the Mathematics Review where material concerning the question is discussed.)

1. (D) (I-4)	6. (D) (III-7)	11. (A) (III-5)	16. (B) (I-8, II-1)
2. (B) (II-2)	7. (E) (II-2)	12. (E) (II-2)	17. (E) (II-2, 5)
3. (D) (II-3)	8. (C) (I-4)	13. (C) (I-1)	18. (D) (III-7, 9)
4. (D) (I-4)	9. (D) (III-4)	14. (B) (III-4, 6)	19. (E) (III-7)
5. (A) (II-3)	10. (C) (II-3)	15. (B) (I-3, 4)	20. (C) (III-8, 9)

Section III   Analysis of Situations

1. (B)	10. (E)	19. (A)	28. (B)
2. (C)	11. (C)	20. (B)	29. (B)
3. (B)	12. (B)	21. (C)	30. (A)
4. (C)	13. (B)	22. (A)	31. (E)
5. (A)	14. (B)	23. (B)	32. (B)
6. (D)	15. (E)	24. (E)	33. (C)
7. (E)	16. (E)	25. (D)	34. (C)
8. (C)	17. (C)	26. (E)	35. (B)
9. (B)	18. (B)	27. (B)	

Section IV   Data Sufficiency

1. (D)	8. (E)	15. (E)	22. (C)
2. (C)	9. (A)	16. (B)	23. (E)
3. (E)	10. (A)	17. (C)	24. (B)
4. (D)	11. (C)	18. (A)	25. (E)
5. (C)	12. (E)	19. (A)	
6. (E)	13. (C)	20. (A)	
7. (B)	14. (E)	21. (D)	

Section V   Writing Ability

1. (E)	8. (D)	15. (E)	22. (D)
2. (E)	9. (B)	16. (D)	23. (E)
3. (D)	10. (E)	17. (C)	24. (D)
4. (C)	11. (B)	18. (C)	25. (B)
5. (B)	12. (C)	19. (A)	
6. (E)	13. (B)	20. (A)	
7. (A)	14. (E)	21. (D)	

Section VI   Problem Solving

(Numbers in parentheses indicate the section in the Mathematics Review where material concerning the question is discussed.)

1. (C) (I-4, III-7)	6. (C) (II-3)	11. (C) (II-4, III-7)	16. (B) (III-7)
2. (A) (II-5)	7. (B) (I-1)	12. (A) (II-5)	17. (A) (II-1)
3. (E) (II-3)	8. (D) (I-2)	13. (D) (III-4, 7)	18. (B) (I-8, II-2)
4. (D) (I-2)	9. (D) (I-4)	14. (D) (II-2, 3)	19. (A) (I-1)
5. (D) (I-4)	10. (D) (I-6)	15. (C) (I-1)	20. (E) (II-2)

Section VII   Data Sufficiency

1. (C)	8. (D)	15. (B)	22. (C)
2. (E)	9. (E)	16. (E)	23. (E)
3. (C)	10. (C)	17. (D)	24. (A)
4. (A)	11. (D)	18. (E)	25. (D)
5. (C)	12. (A)	19. (A)	
6. (E)	13. (C)	20. (C)	
7. (B)	14. (D)	21. (C)	

Section VIII   Critical Reasoning

1. (E)	6. (D)	11. (E)	16. (A)
2. (D)	7. (B)	12. (B)	17. (A)
3. (C)	8. (B)	13. (A)	18. (B)
4. (C)	9. (A)	14. (B)	19. (E)
5. (E)	10. (D)	15. (D)	20. (B)

Analysis

Section I — Reading Comprehension

1. **(C)** See paragraph 2, line 1.

2. **(C)** See paragraph 1, sentence 2: "His maturer theories of society . . ."

3. **(D)** See paragraph 1: ". . . he ended life as a major social theorist . . . sympathetic with violent revolution. . . ."

4. **(C)** see paragraph 3: ". . . Russia . . . is no longer a proletarian movement . . . but a camouflaged imperialistic effort. . . ."

5. **(C)** See paragraph 3. Of course, it is accepted by those in (D) and (E), but also by those in (C).

6. **(B)** This can be deduced from the last paragraph.

7. **(A)** See paragraph 2.

8. **(E)** All these are mentioned in paragraph 1.

9. **(B)** See paragraph 2: ". . . fiscal policies should be designed to encourage economic growth."

10. **(B)** See paragraph 2: they did not.

11. **(A)** See paragraph 3: the Committee of the Whole.

12. **(D)** See paragraph 4, line 1.

13. **(C)** See paragraph 5: "In the first decade of the twentieth century, an 'executive budget' came into successful use. . . ."

14. **(D)** See paragraph 5: it was rejected.

15. **(A)** See paragraph 6, line 1: the responsibility was given by the Budget and Accounting Act of 1921.

16. **(E)** See paragraph 6: the Director of the Bureau of the Budget serves for an indefinite term.

17. **(A)** See paragraph 2.

18. **(C)** See paragraph 2: they came at different times.

19. **(D)** See paragraph 2.

20. **(D)** Paragraphs 2 and 4 especially mention the various points of migration which the Indians reached.

21. **(E)** See paragraph 4.

22. **(D)** See paragraph 3: ". . . the New Mexico Indians were very successful big game hunters."

23. **(C)** See the last line of paragraph 4.

24. **(E)** All these are given in paragraph 3.

25. **(E)** Certainly, alternatives (A) and (C) do not correspond to the contents of the passage, while (B) and (D) are too general. The main point in the passage is the migration of Indians, their cultures, and their acclimation to new surroundings. These subjects are in the domain of the anthropologist.

Section II — Problem Solving

1. **(D)** 64% of 200 is (.64)(200), which equals 128. Therefore, 128 students received a grade of C.

2. **(B)** Since $x = 3$, $2x + y = 6 + y$; so $6 + y = 10$ and $y = 4$. Therefore, $x - y = 3 - 4 = -1$.

3. **(D)** Since 15 minutes is $\frac{1}{4}$ of an hour, each worker can pack $4 \times \frac{1}{6}$ or $\frac{2}{3}$ of a case an hour. The factory has 40 workers, so they should pack $40 \times \frac{2}{3}$ or $\frac{80}{3}$ cases each hour. Therefore, in $1\frac{2}{3}$ or $\frac{5}{3}$ hours the factory should pack $\left(\frac{5}{3} \times \frac{80}{3} \right)$, which equals $\frac{400}{9}$ or $44\frac{4}{9}$ cases.

4. **(D)** If potatoes cost 15¢ a pound, then 10 pounds will cost $1.50. If the price increases by 10%, then 10 pounds of potatoes will cost 110% of $1.50, which is $1.65.

5. **(A)** Since the truck driver averaged 50 miles per hour for the first three hours, he traveled 3 × 50 or 150 miles during the first three hours. Since he needs to travel 180 − 150 miles in the final hour, he should drive at 30 mph.

6. **(D)** The area of a triangle is ½ the base times the altitude. The altitude is $2B$, so the area is $(\frac{1}{2})(B)(2B)$ or B^2.

7. **(E)** If we denote the two numbers by x and y, then $xy = 10$ and $x + y = 7$. Then x is $7 - y$ and $(7 - y)y = 7y - y^2 = 10$ or $y^2 - 7y + 10 = 0$. But $y^2 - 7y + 10 = (y - 5)(y - 2)$; so the two numbers are 5 and 2. The correct answer can be selected quickly by inspection of the choices.

8. **(C)** Since the first 100 bags cost $x each, the total cost of the first 100 bags is $100x. Since the remaining 50 bags are discounted 10%, each bag costs 90% of $x or $(.90)x$ and the 50 bags cost $45x. Thus, the total cost is $145x.

9. **(D)** According to the Pythagorean theorem, the length squared equals $8^2 + 15^2$, which is 289. So the length of the side opposite the right angle is 17.

10. **(C)** The first 600 copies cost a total of 600x¢. There are 1,500 − 600 or 900 copies after the first 600, each of which costs $\left(x - \frac{y}{10}\right)$¢; so the 900 copies cost $900\left(x - \frac{y}{10}\right)$¢, which equals $(900x - 90y)$¢. Therefore, the total cost is $(1500x - 90y)$¢.

11. **(A)** The sum of the angles of a parallelogram (which is 4-sided) must be $(4 - 2) 180° = 360°$. Since the sum of the values in III is 410, III cannot be correct. The sum of the numbers in II is 360, but in a parallelogram opposite angles must be equal so x must equal z and y must equal w. Since 60 is unequal to 70, II cannot be correct. The sum of the values in I is 360 and opposite angles will be equal, so I is correct.

12. **(E)** John weighs twice as much as Marcia, so John cannot weigh the least. Marcia's weight is less than Bob's weight, so Bob's weight is not the least. Dave's weight is ½ of Lee's weight, so Lee can't weigh the least. The only possible answers are Marcia or Dave. Let J, M, B, D, and L stand for the weights of John, Marcia, Bob, Dave, and Lee respectively. Then $D = .5L = .5(1.9)J$. So $D = .95J$. Since $J = 2M$, we know $M = .5J$. Therefore Marcia weighs the least.

13. **(C)** Since the sum of the integers is 35, the average is $35/5 = 7$. So the "middle" integer should be near 7. Since $5 + 6 + 7 + 8 + 9 = 35$, the five integers are 5, 6, 7, 8, and 9. 6 and 8 are not primes because they are divisible by 2; 9 is not a prime since it is divisible by 3. Only 5 and 7 are primes, so two of the five integers are primes.

14. **(B)** Since DA is perpendicular to AC, ABD is a right triangle. So the square of DB is equal to the square of AD plus the square of AB. We know AB is 10. AD is a radius of circle 1, and since ACB is a straight line and both circles have the same radii, ACB is equal to $AC + CB$. So 10 = twice the radius. Therefore, the radius is 5. Since AD is 5, we have $DB = \sqrt{100 + 25} = \sqrt{5} \times \sqrt{25} = 5\sqrt{5}$.

15. **(B)** First find the market value of the house. If M is the market value, then 60% of M is $72,000. So $.6M = \$72,000$, which means $M = \$72,000/.6 = \$120,000$. The tax rate is $3 for every $1,000 or .003. Therefore the taxes are $.003 \times \$120,000 = \$360$.

16. **(B)** First evaluate *5. Using the given rule, *5 is $(5 \times 5) - 2 = 25 - 2 = 23$. So *(*5) is *23, which is $(23 \times 23) - 2 = 529 - 2 = 527$.

17. **(E)** Since $y/x = 1/3$, cross multiply to obtain $x = 3y$. Substitute $x = 3y$ into $x + 2y = 10$ to get $3y + 2y = 5y = 10$. Therefore $y = 2$, so $x = 6$. You can check that $2/6 = 1/3$ and $6 + 2(2) = 10$, so you know your answer is correct.

18. **(D)** The area of a parallelogram is the altitude times the base. Since the bottom is part of the line $y = -1$ and the top is part of the line $y = 2$, an altitude is the distance between these two lines. This distance is $|2 - (-1)| = 3$. Since a base is the segment from $(1, -1)$ to $(4, -1)$, the base is $|4 - 1| = 3$. Therefore the area is $3 \times 3 = 9$.

19. **(E)** The perimeter of a rectangle is 2(length) + 2(width). Since we know the length is y, we need to find the width. The area of a rectangle

is (length) × (width). So the fact that the area is 1,000 square yards gives the equation y(width) = 1,000. Solving for the width, we get width = 1,000/y. Therefore the perimeter is $2y + 2(1,000/y) = 2y + 2,000/y$.

20. **(C)** Since the figure is a cube, $ADEH$ is a square whose sides have length 10. Therefore AE, which is a diagonal of the square, has length $\sqrt{10^2 + 10^2} = \sqrt{200}$. Since FE is perpendicular to AE, the triangle AEF is a right triangle. So AF squared is equal to the sum of the square of AE and the square of FE. Therefore $AF = \sqrt{200 + 10^2} = \sqrt{200 + 100} = \sqrt{300} = \sqrt{3} \times \sqrt{100} = 10\sqrt{3}$.

Section III   Analysis of Situations

1. **(B)** The establishment of a new supermarket chain in the R and S market area, and its use of grade labeling, was a *Major Factor* considered by Joseph in his decision as to whether to adopt the practice.

2. **(C)** The fact that the government's program would standardize grading was a *Minor Factor* related to the consideration of whether or not to adopt the practice.

3. **(B)** The effect of grade labeling on sales was a *Major Factor* considered by R and S in determining the consequences of the adoption of the future of the firm.

4. **(C)** Federal food standards were a *Minor Factor* in making the decision.

5. **(A)** In deciding whether to adopt grade labeling, Mr. Joseph's major consideration was what effect it would have on consumer acceptance of his products. Since R and S already enjoyed a high reputation, Joseph did not want to take any action that would jeopardize it.

6. **(D)** Joseph's legal advisor felt that grade labeling might become mandatory in the near future. It is clear from the passage that this was a matter of opinion only.

7. **(E)** Present label requirements, described in paragraph 7, were unimportant to Joseph's decision as to whether to adopt the government's voluntary program.

8. **(C)** Possible government legislation resulting from consumer pressure was a *Minor Factor* in Joseph's decision as to whether to adopt the voluntary labeling program.

9. **(B)** Taam Food's adoption of grading worried Joseph because of its possible competitive advantage.

10. **(E)** R and S Packing's experience was not a real consideration in any decision alternative.

11. **(C)** The superior flavor of R and S products was one aspect of the overall quality of the goods. Since the overall quality was a *Major Factor*, flavor was a *Minor Factor*.

12. **(B)** The quality of R and S products would largely determine their grade. The possibility of receiving a high grade was a major consideration in accepting the voluntary program.

13. **(B)** Joseph was concerned that one product might get a high grade on one characteristic which could be offset by a low grade on another. This consideration was a *Major Factor* in Joseph's decision to adopt grade labeling.

14. **(B)** *Gaynes* was making inroads in R and S's region by advertising heavily. *Gaynes* advertising emphasized the use of grade labeling. The passage mentions that "grade-labeling problems had come to the fore" as a result of *Gaynes's* decision. The adoption of grade labeling by *Gaynes* was a *Major Factor* in Joseph's consideration of the problem.

15. **(E)** The level of grades was not considered by a decision maker and was an *Unimportant Issue*.

16. **(E)** The sort of federal inspection program used by the Department of Agriculture was not a consideration in any decision alternative.

17. **(C)** Grade labeling as an advertising factor was secondary to its effect on consumer choice.

18. **(B)** The advantages and disadvantages of taking a "wait-and-see" strategy (although not all spelled out in the passage) were *Major Factors* in Joseph's decision process.

19. **(A)** Perrier management's marketing objective was to position the product as a "thirst-

quencher with no calories . . .'' (paragraph 9). Management also aimed the product at the mass market ''by competing in the soft-drink market segment'' (paragraph 7).

20. **(B)** Growing United States preference for imports (paragraph 3) was a major consideration in the decision to launch Perrier (i.e., its acceptance by Americans).

21. **(C)** Of all the qualities of Perrier, its therapeutic value was less valuable because of the inability to advertise it in the United States (paragraph 9).

22. **(A)** Since distribution was a key factor in the success of Perrier, finding aggressive distributors is a *Major Objective*.

23. **(B)** The growing diet-consciousness of Americans (paragraph 1) was a *Major Factor* in the decision to market Perrier in the United States.

24. **(E)** The year of Perrier's establishment has no bearing on an alternative course of action.

25. **(D)** Management ''reasoned'' that the retail price could be cut by 30 percent. The price could only be cut through a mass distribution policy, which is a major supposition on the part of management.

26. **(E)** Perrier's success in France did not influence the consideration of an alternative course of action in the United States.

27. **(B)** The advantages of mineral water (over other types of spring water, soft drinks, etc.) is a major consideration in the selection of an alternative course of action.

28. **(B)** The cost of shipping Perrier to the United States was a major consideration in the determination of the retail price of Perrier.

29. **(B)** A slowdown in the growth of Perrier sales in France was a *Major Factor* in the consideration to investigate the American market. See the introductory (italicized) paragraph.

30. **(A)** Once Perrier had decided to market in the United States, a *Major Objective* of management was finding what particular market in which to sell the product.

31. **(E)** While the marketing channels used in the sale of bottled water was a consideration, no attention was focused on the sort of containers used.

32. **(B)** After achieving initial success in the United States, Perrier was imitated by American bottlers (paragraph 10). The increased competition was a *Major Factor* in Perrier's review of its marketing strategy. See the final (italicized) paragraph.

33. **(C)** The banning of cyclamates in soft drinks was a *Minor Factor* that led producers to substitute saccharin (paragraph 1). The use of both products as sugar substitutes was due to the growing diet consciousness of consumers, a *Major Factor* in Perrier's decision to market in the United States.

34. **(C)** Acceptance of ''foreignness'' is a *Minor Factor* that affects the U.S. preference for imports, a *Major Factor* (paragraph 3).

35. **(B)** U.S. advertising legislation was a *Major Factor* in the consideration of advertising appeals, which was a *Major Objective*. For example, the passage states that in Europe Perrier could make therapeutic claims, but in the U.S. it could not, owing to the U.S. law (paragraph 9).

Section IV   Data Sufficiency

1. **(D)** (1) alone is sufficient, since if two sides of a triangle are equal, the angles opposite the equal sides are equal. Since $AB = BC$ then $x = y$, so $x = 40$. (2) alone is sufficient since the sum of the angles of a triangle is 180°. Therefore, if $z = 100$ and $y = 40$, x must equal $180 - 100 - 40 = 40$. Therefore, each statement alone is sufficient.

2. **(C)** (1) tells us the area of the circle is $\pi 4^2 = 16\pi$. Since there are 360° in the whole circle, (2) tells us that the shaded area is $60/360$ or $1/6$ of the area of the circle. Thus, using both (1) and (2), we can answer the question, but since we need both the radius of the circle and the value of x, neither of them alone is sufficient. Therefore, the answer is (C).

3. **(E)** Using (1) we can find the income for 1970 if we know the income for 1968 and 1969, but (1) gives no more information about the income for 1968 and 1969. If we also use (2) we can get the income in 1969 if we know the income for

1968, but we still can't determine the income for 1968. Therefore, both together are not sufficient.

4. **(D)** Since a straight line forms an angle of 180° and l' is a straight line, we know $x + y = 180$. If we use (1) we get $y = 80$, so (1) alone is sufficient. When two straight lines intersect, the vertical angles are equal. So $y = z$; thus if we use (2) we get $y = 80$. Therefore, (2) alone is sufficient. Thus, each statement alone is sufficient.

5. **(C)** In the figure, x denotes the number taking German I but not English I, and y the number taking English I but not German I. From (1) we know that $x + 16 + y = 50$; from (2), $x = y$. Neither statement alone can be solved for x, but both together are sufficient (and yield $x = 17$).

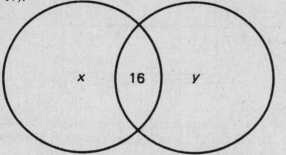

6. **(E)** (1) alone is not sufficient because it only says two sides are equal; in a square all four sides are equal. Even if we use (2) we don't know if $ABCD$ is a square since *all* angles have to be right angles in a square. Therefore, both statements together are insufficient.

7. **(B)** The average yearly wage per employee is the total amount of wages divided by the number of employees. So (2) alone is sufficient since it gives the total amount of wages and we are given the number of employees. (1) alone is not sufficient, since (1) by itself does not tell us the total wages. Therefore, the answer is (B).

8. **(E)** Since the square of any nonzero number is positive, (1) says $x + y \neq 0$ or $x \neq -y$. So (1) alone is not sufficient. If we also assume (2), we know only that x is positive and unequal to $-y$, not whether x is greater than or less than y. Thus (1) and (2) together are insufficient.

9. **(A)** Since the circles both have radius 4, the figure $OBO'C$ is a rhombus (each side is a radius) and the diagonals BC and OO' (of a rhombus) are perpendicular. So (2) does not give any new information, and is thus not sufficient

alone. (1) alone is sufficient. The area of each circle is 16π since the radius of each circle is 4. If there were no shaded area, the area enclosed by both circles would be $16\pi + 16\pi = 32\pi$. Since the area enclosed by both circles is 29π, the shaded area is $32\pi - 29\pi$ or 3π. So (1) alone is sufficient but (2) alone is insufficient.

10. **(A)** Let x be the time it takes to travel from A to B and let y be the time it takes to travel from B to A. We know $x + y = 4$. (1) says x is 125% of y or $x = \frac{5}{4}y$. So using (1) we have $x + \frac{5}{4}x = 4$ which we can solve for x. Thus, (1) alone is sufficient. (2) alone is not sufficient since we need information about the relation of x to y to solve the problem and (2) says nothing about the relation between x and y. Therefore, (1) alone is sufficient but (2) alone is insufficient.

11. **(C)** (1) alone is insufficient. If x and y were right angles, (1) would imply that l and l' are parallel, but if x and y are not right angles, (1) would imply that l and l' are not parallel. (2) alone is not sufficient since it gives information only about l' and says nothing about the relation of l and l'. (1) and (2) together give $x = z$ which means that l and l' are parallel. Therefore, (1) and (2) together are sufficient but neither alone is sufficient.

12. **(E)** If we use (1), we have $x + y + z = 3 + z$, but we have no information about z, so (1) alone is insufficient. If we use (2) alone, we have $x + y + z = y + 2$, but since we have no information about y, (2) alone is insufficient. If we use both (1) and (2), we obtain $x + y + z = y + 2 = 3 + z$. We can also add (1) and (2) to obtain $2x + y + z = 5$, but we can't find the value of $x + y + z$ without more information. So the answer is (E).

13. **(C)** We need to know the surface area of the box. Since each side is a rectangle, we know the surface area will be $2LW + 2LH + 2HW$ where H is the height of the box, L is the length, and W is the width. We are given that $L = 7$, so to answer the question we need H and W. Since (1) gives only the value of W and (2) gives only the value of H, neither alone is sufficient. But both (1) and (2) together are sufficient.

14. **(E)** The profit is the selling price minus the cost, so to answer the question we need to know both the selling price and the cost of 15 boxes of detergent. Since (1) and (2) give information only about the cost but no information about the selling price, both statements together are insufficient.

15. **(E)** (1) alone is not sufficient. A four-sided figure can have both larger perimeter and smaller area than another four-sided figure, or it could have larger perimeter and larger area. (2) alone is also insufficient since the length of one diagonal does not determine the area of a four-sided figure. (1) and (2) together are also insufficient, as shown by the figure.

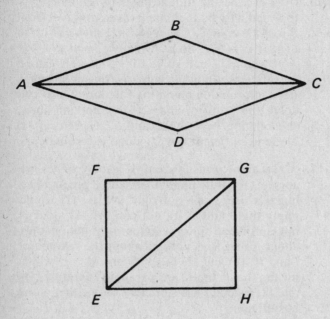

(1) and (2) are both satisfied and the area of EFGH is larger than ABCD. But (1) and (2) could still be satisfied and the area of ABCD be larger than the area of EFGH; so the answer is (E).

16. **(B)** Statement (1) alone is not sufficient, since 12 is divisible by 3 but 12 is not divisible by 9. Statement (2) alone is sufficient, since if a number is divisible by 27 then, because 27 = 9 × 3, the number must be divisible by 9.

17. **(C)** Statement (1) is not sufficient. (1) will let you figure out the length of the side SP; however, you need to know the length of SR or PQ to find the area. Statement (2) alone is not sufficient. (2) will allow you to find the length of PQ, but you also need to know the length of SP or RQ.

Statements (1) and (2) together are sufficient.

18. **(A)** Both regions ABEF and CDFE are trapezoids, so their area is given by the formula $a \left(\frac{1}{2}[b_1 + b_2]\right)$ where a is an altitude and b_1 and b_2 are the sides perpendicular to the altitude. Since ABCD is a rectangle, AB = CD, which means the altitudes are the same length

for each region. So it is sufficient to know whether BE + AF is larger than EC + FD.

Statement (1) alone is sufficient, since, if BE is larger than FD, then BC − BE, which is EC, must be smaller than AD − FD = AF. (AD = BC since ABCD is a rectangle.) So BE + AF is larger than EC + FD.

Statement (2) alone is not sufficient, since either region could be larger if BE is larger than CD (See figures).

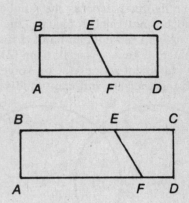

19. **(A)** The square of an even integer is always even. So if k^2 is odd, k can't be even. Therefore, k is odd and (1) alone is sufficient.

Statement (2) alone is not sufficient, since $2k$ is even for every integer k.

20. **(A)** Statement (1) alone is sufficient, since using (1) implies that the car can travel 125 miles using 5 gallons of fuel.

Statement (2) alone is not sufficient. The speed is not enough to determine how far the car can travel.

21. **(D)** The area of the region is the area of the square plus the area of the semicircle. So you must be able to determine the length of a side of the square and the length of the radius of the semicircle. Since the radius is ½ of BC, it is sufficient to determine either the radius or the length of a side of the square. Statement (1) alone is sufficient, since the diagonal of a square is $\sqrt{2}$ times the length of a side. Statment (2) alone is sufficient, since the length of a side of the square is twice the radius.

22. **(C)** Using statements (1) and (2), you can determine the distance from P to (0,0) and the distance from Q to (0,0). The distances are equal

if and only if P and Q are on the same circle with center $(0,0)$. Neither statement alone is sufficient, since you need to know both distances.

23. **(E)** Both statements together give no information about the year 1980.

24. **(B)** Since 2^n is n "copies" of 2 multiplied together, 2^n is divisible by 8 if and only if n is greater than or equal to 3. (This is because $8 = 2 \times 2 \times 2 = 2^3$). Therefore, (2) alone is sufficient.

Statement (1) alone is not sufficient, because there are odd numbers less than 3 (for example, 1) and odd numbers greater than 3.

25. **(E)** The fact that the price is higher at the end of the year than it was at the beginning of the year does not imply that the price rose every week during the year. The price could have gone up and down many times during the year.

Section V   Writing Ability

1. **(E)** Both *together* and *up* are unnecessary since their meaning is included in the words *cooperate* and *divide*.

2. **(E)** The important idea, *he approves my choice*, should be held to the end of the sentence. It should not be separated from *I think*, as it is the object of the verb *think*.

3. **(D)** Parallel structure requires the use of the gerund (verbal noun) as the object of the verb *enjoyed*: *swimming, bathing, snorkeling. Enjoy* should not be followed by an infinitive construction.

4. **(C)** The other choices all have misplaced modifiers.

5. **(B)** The clause *that money doesn't make you happy* is the predicate nominative of the verb *is. How* is inappropriate.

6. **(E)** The shift in pronouns from *they* to *our* is incorrect. The active verb *can see* is preferable to the passive verb *can be seen*. Also, one looks *ahead to* where one is going.

7. **(A)** No error.

8. **(D)** Suspense is created by holding *grandmother* to the end of the sentence. The word *person* does not have to be repeated.

9. **(B)** The two verbs should be parallel: *start* and *remove*.

10. **(E)** The key idea is that *he is a genius*. To create a suspenseful or periodic sentence, the writer should place *he is a genius* at the end of the sentence.

11. **(B)** The pronoun should agree in number with the noun to which it refers (*creditor/his*). *Most important* is correct here.

12. **(C)** The correlatives *either . . . or* should be placed as near as possible to the words with which they belong: *a price* and *a quality-of-workmanship basis*.

13. **(B)** *Referred back* is redundant. The prefix *re* means "back."

14. **(E)** *Irregardless* is not a word in current English usage. *Forbidden* requires an infinitive construction (forbidden *to make*). The word *pinch* is slang and should be avoided in writing.

15. **(E)** Active expressions are preferable to passive ones. The two subordinate reasons, reading and note-taking, should be preceded by *because*.

16. **(D)** The correlatives *not only . . . but also* should be placed near to the words with which they belong: *violated* and *escaped*.

17. **(C)** The correct idiom is *different from. Had ought* is not correct verb form.

18. **(C)** In sentences comparing two items, *-er* words are used. When comparing more than two items use *-est* words. Thus the correct form here is *better*. Choice D is more awkward in construction.

19. **(A)** No error. *Poor product quality* is singular, so the pronoun must also be singular—*it*. Choice B eliminates the pronoun and changes the meaning. Choice E uses a plural pronoun. Choice C uses an incorrect pronoun, *that*, in place of *who*. Choice D is awkward.

20. **(A)** No error. The phrases are all parallel: soft *hair*, strong *legs*, and keen *sense* of smell.

21. **(D)** The wordy main clause can be cut from fifteen words to six without any loss of meaning.

22. **(D)** *Having bowed our heads* is a dangling modifier. The act of bowing heads preceded the leading prayer, so the past perfect tense must be used.

23. **(E)** *Ever* and *true* are unnecessary. The infinitive *to try* is followed by *to*, not *and*.

24. **(D)** The sentence elements should be parallel: *to finance* and *to carry* are both infinitive constructions.

25. **(B)** The entire clause *whoever was present* is the object of the preposition *toward*; *whoever* is the subject of *was*. Therefore, *whomever*, which is in the objective case, is incorrect.

Section VI   Problem Solving

1. **(C)** If s is the original side of the square, then s^2 is the area of the original square. The side of the increased square is 140% of s or $(1.4)s$. Therefore, the area of the increased square is $(1.4s)^2$ or $1.96s^2$, which is 196% of the original area. Thus, the area has increased by 96%.

2. **(A)** If P is the price of 7 cartons, then $\frac{7}{28} = \frac{P}{21}$, so $P = \frac{1}{4}$ of \$21, which is \$5.25.

3. **(E)** Plane P will travel $\frac{3}{2}$ of an hour before Q takes off, so it will be $\frac{3x}{2}$ miles away at 3:30 A.M. Let t denote the number of hours after 3:30 A.M. it takes Q to overtake P. By then P has flown $tx + \frac{3x}{2}$ miles and Q has flown ty miles. We want the value of t, where $ty = tx + \frac{3x}{2}$, or $t(y - x) = \frac{3x}{2}$. Therefore, $t = \frac{3x}{2(y - x)}$.

4. **(D)** Note that $\left(\frac{2}{3} + \frac{1}{3}\right)$ equals 1 full day, and that $\left(\frac{1}{8} + \frac{3}{4}\right)$ is shy $\frac{1}{8}$ of being 1 full day. So he

works $2\frac{7}{8}$ days altogether.

$$\left(2\frac{7}{8}\right)(20) = \left(\frac{23}{8}\right)(20) = \frac{460}{8} = \$57.50.$$

5. **(D)** There were 26 (16 + 10) students who answered 32 or more questions correctly. Since the total number of students is 60, and $\frac{26}{60} = .43\frac{1}{3}$. So $43\frac{1}{3}\%$ of the class answered 32 or more questions correctly.

6. **(C)** 12 students had scores of 28 to 31, and 8 scores of 25 or less; so $8x = 12$ and $x = \frac{12}{8} = \frac{3}{2}$.

7. **(B)** The product of 3 consecutive integers is of the form $(x - 1)(x)(x + 1)$ and a good approximation to this is x^3. Since $6^3 = 216$, a good guess for x is 6. 6 is correct since $5 \times 6 \times 7 = 210$. Therefore, the sum of the two smaller integers is $5 + 6$ or 11.

8. **(D)** Let C, B, and E denote the cost of cereal, bacon, and eggs respectively. Then $C = \frac{1B}{3}$ and $B = \frac{5E}{4}$, or $E = \frac{4B}{5}$. Therefore, $E = \frac{4B}{5}$ and $B = 3C$; so we conclude that $E = \left(\frac{4}{5}\right)3C = \frac{12C}{5}$.

9. **(D)** Since 80% of 15 is 12, the loaded truck travels 12 miles on a gallon of gas. Therefore, it will use $\frac{80}{12}$ or $6\frac{8}{12}$ or $6\frac{2}{3}$ gallons of gas to travel 80 miles.

10. **(D)**
    Statement I is false since if $x = -5$ and $y = -6$, then $x - y = 1$, which is not negative.

    Statement II is true since $-$ a negative number is always a positive number.

    Statement III is true since $(-x)$ and $(-y)$ are both positive, and the product of two positive numbers is a positive number.

11. **(C)** Think of the area enclosed by both circles as three distinct sections. Then we want to

know the value of b. Since each circle has radius 4, the area of each circle is $\pi(4 \times 4) = 16\pi$. So $a + b = 16\pi$ and $b + c = 16\pi$ or $a + 2b + c = 32\pi$. The area enclosed by both circles is $a + b + c$, which must be equal to 28π. Now subtract $a + b + c = 28\pi$ from $a + 2b + c = 32\pi$ to obtain $b = 4\pi$.

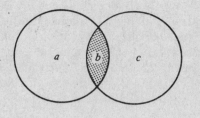

12. **(A)** Let S, R, and P be the respective amounts spent by the sales, research, and packing departments. Then $S:R$ is $1:.2$ and $R:P$ is $4:1.5$. In order to combine these into a triple ratio for $S:R:P$, we need to have the same number for R in both the ratios $S:R$ and $R:P$. If we multiply each term of the ratio $S:R$ by 20, we obtain $20:4$. Therefore we can express the triple ratio as $20:4:1.5$. However, this is not one of the given answers. If you multiply every term of a triple ratio by the same nonzero number, the triple ratio remains unchanged. So multiply each term by 2, and the triple ratio becomes $40:8:3$, which is (A).

13. **(D)** Let E be the point on AD such that CE is perpendicular to AD. Then CDE is a right triangle, and CD can be computed if we know CE and DE. Since EC and AB are perpendicular to the same line, $ABCE$ is a rectangle. So AE is equal to BC, which is 6. Therefore $ED = AD - AE = 8 - 6 = 2$. Since $ABCD$ is a trapezoid, its area is the average of AD and BC multiplied by an altitude. So $28 = (1/2)(6 + 8)$(altitude) means the altitude is $28/7 = 4$. Since CE is perpendicular to AD, CE is an altitude and so CE must equal 4. Finally, using the Pythagorean relation, we have $CD = \sqrt{4^2 + 2^2} = \sqrt{20} = \sqrt{4} \times \sqrt{5} = 2\sqrt{5}$.

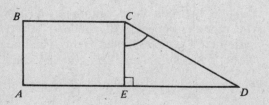

14. **(D)** The cost of 1,400 copies is the cost of the first 1,000 plus the cost of the next 400 copies. Each of the first 1,000 copies cost $\$x$, so the first 1,000 copies cost $\$1,000x$. The next 400 each cost $\$.9x$, so the next 400 copies will cost $\$(400)(.9x) = \$360x$. So the total cost of the 1,400 copies should be $\$1,000x + \$360x = \$1,360x$, which must equal $\$3,264$. Therefore, $x = 3,264/1,360 = 2.40$.

15. **(C)** An odd integer can be written as $2j - 1$ for some positive integer j, and an even integer can be written as $2k$ for some positive integer k. So let $x = 2j - 1$ and $y = 2k$. Then $x + y = 2j - 1 + 2k = 2(j + k) - 1$, which is odd. So I is true. Since $xy = (2j - 1)2k = 4jk - 2k = 2(2jk - k)$, xy is even and II is false. Finally, $2x + y$ is $2(2j - 1) + 2k = 4j - 2 + 2k = 2(2j - 1 + k)$, which is even. Therefore, III is true.

16. **(B)** The area of the region is the area of the circle minus the area of the square. Since the radius of the circle is 4, the area of the circle is $\pi(4 \times 4) = 16\pi$. Since $ABCD$ is a square, ABD is a right triangle with AB equal to AD. Since ABD is a right triangle, BD is a diameter of the circle, so BD equals 8. Therefore, $s^2 + s^2 = 8^2$ where s is the length of a side of the square. So $2s^2 = 64$ or $s^2 = 32$. Since s^2 is the area of the square, 32 is the area of the square. So the area of the region is $16\pi - 32 = 16(\pi - 2)$.

17. **(A)** Since $*X$ is the largest integer which is less than X, $*3$ is 2 (NOT 3). In the same way $*4$ is 3 and $*4.5$ is 4. So $(*3) + (*4) + (*4.5)$ equals $2 + 3 + 4 = 9$.

18. **(B)** Let JS and JC be Joan's starting and current salaries respectively. Let MS and MC be Mike's salary when Joan started and his current salary. We know $JS = .5MS$, and we want to find an equation relating JC and MC. Since Joan received a 5% raise each year, after 1 year her salary was $1.05JS$ and after 2 years her salary is $(1.05)(1.05)JS$. In the same way, we can see that Mike's current salary (MC) is $(1.10)(1.10)MS$. So $MC = (1.1)^2MS$. So $JC = (1.05)(1.05)JS = 1.1025JS = .5(1.1025)MS = (.55125)(1/(1.1)^2)MC = (.55125/1.21)MC$. Since we want the answer to the nearest percent, we must divide to three decimal places. So $.55125/1.21 = .455 = 46\%$ to the nearest percent.

19. **(A)** Since every integer has 1 and itself as divisors, we shall neglect these. Write each integer as a product of primes to determine its divisors.

So $88 = 2 \times 44 = 2 \times 2 \times 22 = 2 \times 2 \times 2 \times 11$. Therefore, the divisors of 88 are 2, 4, 8, 11, 22, and 44, for a total of 6. Since $91 = 7 \times 13$ and $95 = 5 \times 19$, they both have a total of 2 divisors. $99 = 3 \times 33 = 3 \times 3 \times 11$, so the divisors of 99 are 3, 9, 11, and 33, for a total of 4. 101 is a prime, so it has no divisors. (To see that 101 is a prime, you only have to see if primes less than $\sqrt{101}$, which is less than 11, divide 101.) Therefore, 88 has the most divisors.

20. **(E)** Let f and p be the amounts of fat and protein in an ounce of food A. Then we know that $f + p = 100$ and $p - 2f = 10$. So f is $100 - p$, and the second equation becomes $p - 2(100 - p) = p - 200 + 2p = 3p - 200 = 10$. So $3p = 210$ or $p = 70$.

Section VII   Data Sufficiency

1. **(C)** Using statement (1), you can set up an equation involving X's salary and Z's salary. Using statement (2), you can set up an equation involving Y's salary and Z's salary. Thus, using both (1) and (2), you can relate X's salary. You need both statements to solve the problem.

2. **(E)** If you knew what a share of ABC stock was worth, then using statement (1) you could decide when the stock would be worth $63. However, statement (2) does not give the needed information. Therefore, (1) and (2) together are not sufficient.

3. **(C)** If you add statements (1) and (2), you obtain $x + 2y = 14$. Since you don't know the value of z, statement (1) or (2) alone is insufficient.

4. **(A)** Since the average of the three numbers is their sum divided by 3, statement (1) alone is sufficient. Statement (2) alone is not sufficient.

5. **(C)** Statement (1) alone implies that angle $x =$ the angle opposite side AB.

   Statement (2) alone implies that the angle opposite side AB is 80°. So, using both, we can see that y is the smaller, but either statement alone is not sufficient.

6. **(E)** You need to know how much money was made from general admission ticket sales. Statements (2) only tells how many tickets were sold, not how much they cost.

7. **(B)** Statement (2) alone is sufficient, since $2x + 2y = 2(x + y)$. Generally you need to have two equations to solve for 2 unknowns. However, since $2x + 2y$ is a multiple of what you want, the extra equation, statement (1), is not needed.

8. **(D)** "3 evenly divides x" means $x = 3k$ for some integer k. Statement (1) alone is sufficient, since "6 evenly divides x" means $x = 6k$ for some integer k, so $x = 3(2k)$ and 3 evenly divides x. Statement (2) alone is sufficient since "12 evenly divides x" means $x = 12k$ for some integer k, so $x = 3(4k)$ and 3 divides x.

9. **(E)** When any two lines intersect, the vertical angles formed are equal. So for any pair of lines (perpendicular or non-perpendicular) statements (1) and (2) are true.

10. **(C)** The total of the percentage billed to A, the percentage billed to B, and the percentage billed to C is 100%. Using statement (1) and statement (2) together, you can set up an equation $A + \frac{1}{2}A + \frac{1}{2}A = 100$ and solve for A, where A is the percentage billed to A. If you use statement (1) alone or statement (2) alone, you can only get an equation that involves A and either B or C. So statement (1) alone is insufficient and statement (2) alone is insufficient.

11. **(D)** Statement (1) alone is sufficient, since it implies that Bill pays 40% of $500 each month. Statement (2) alone is sufficient, since $x + y = 100$.

   Therefore statement (1) and statement (2) are equivalent.

12. **(A)** To compare two fractions, the fractions must have the same denominator. The least common denominator for both fractions is 120. Using this fact, $\frac{x}{12} = \frac{10x}{120}$ and $\frac{y}{40} = \frac{3y}{120}$. So the relation between the fractions is the same as the relation between $10x$ and $3y$. Therefore statement (1) alone is sufficient. Statement (2) alone is not sufficient. Using $y = 13$ and $x = 4$, statement (2) is true and $\frac{x}{12}$ is greater than $\frac{y}{40}$. However, using $y = 10$ and $x = 2$, statement (2) is still true, but now $\frac{x}{12}$ is less than $\frac{y}{40}$.

13. **(C)** Since $x^2 - y^2 = (x + y)(x - y)$, statement (1) and statement (2) together are sufficient. Neither statement by itself is sufficient.

14. **(D)** The people can be divided into 3 distinct groups which do not overlap: A = people who own a television but do not own a telephone; B = people who own both a television and a telephone; C = people who own a telephone but do not own a television. You are given that the number of people in A plus the number of people in B plus the number of people in C equals 70. Furthermore, you know the number in B is 30. Since the groups you need to compare are those with a television (that is, those in A or B) and those with a telephone (that is, those in B or C), it is sufficient to know whether A or C has more members. By the above equations, if you know A, then you can determine C, and vice versa.

Statement (1) is sufficient, since it tells you how many people are in group A.

Statement (2) is sufficient, since it tells you how many people are in group B or in group C. Since there are 30 people in B, you can determine how many are in C. A Venn diagram is a useful way to visualize the information: A + B + C = 70.

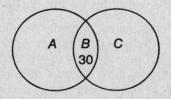

15. **(B)** Statement (2) alone is sufficient. If $x < 0$, then, since x^2 is always positive, x^2 is larger than x. Statement (1) alone is not sufficient. If x is > 1, then x^2 is larger, but if $0 < x < 1$, then x is larger. For example, if $x = 2$ then $x^2 = 4$, but if $x = \frac{1}{2}$ then $x^2 = \frac{1}{4}$.

16. **(E)** Statement (1) would imply that AB is shorter than CD if AD and CB were equal. However, even with statement (2) you can't deduce whether DC or AB is longer. If CB was "just a little bit" longer than AD, then CD would be longer, but if CB was "much" longer than AD, then AB would be longer than CD.

17. **(D)** Statement (1) alone is sufficient. Just use 100 for degrees Fahrenheit in the formula. Statement (2) alone is also sufficient, since the formula in statement (2) can be solved to give the formula of statement (1) which we know is sufficient.

18. **(E)** Statements (1) and (2) relate Jane's salary to other salaries, but none of those salaries is known. So statements (1) and (2) together are not sufficient.

19. **(A)** Statement (1) alone is sufficient because $\frac{3}{2}y$ is the same as 150% of y; thus statement (1) implies $z = 0$. Statement (2) alone is not sufficient, since you are given no value for y.

20. **(C)** Statement (1) means that the triangle ABC is a right triangle. So if two sides are known, the third side can be determined. Therefore, statements (1) and (2) together are sufficient. Statement (1) alone is not sufficient. You need to know the lengths of 2 sides, and you are only given one side.

Statement (2) alone is not sufficient. If you know the lengths of two sides but don't know an angle, you can't find the third side.

21. **(C)** Statements (1) and (2) together are sufficient.

Statement (1) alone is not sufficient, since it only relates x to y. Statement (2) alone is not sufficient since without (1) x and y are not related.

22. **(C)** Statement (1) alone is not sufficient. (1) implies x is equal to either -4 or 1.

Statement (2) alone is not sufficient, since there are positive numbers greater than -2 and negative numbers greater than -2.

Statements (1) and (2) together are sufficient, since the only possible value is 1.

23. **(E)** Statements (1) and (2) together are not sufficient. If $x = 10$, $y = 6$, and $z = 2$, then (1) and (2) are true, but since $6 + 2$ is not greater than 10, x, y, and z can't be the lengths of the sides of a triangle.

24. **(A)** Statement (1) alone is sufficient, since (1) implies that n is the square of $2j$.

Statement (2) alone is not sufficient. If $A = 3$, and $B = 4$, then $n^2 = 25$, so n, which is 5, is not the square of an integer.

25. **(D)** Statement (2) alone is sufficient. Since train Y travels for 3 hours and train Z travels for 2 hours, the distance train Y travels is $3y$, and the distance train Z travels is $2z$. Therefore, statement (1) alone is sufficient.

Section VIII   Critical Reasoning

1. **(E)** The politician assumes that a large, absolute number of replies means that the survey results are representative of the population (total homes in the district), even though a proportionately small number of replies may have resulted. Alternatives (A), (B), and (D) cannot be assumed from the statement. Alternative (C) is incorrect.

2. **(D)** The number of hotel rooms may be a function of the number of tourists and not vice versa. If average income per tourist did not increase over the time period, an increase in the number of tourists' (doubling every decade) total revenue would double (A). If the number of tourists did not double every decade, but average revenue per tourist doubled (B), total revenue would double. If the average stay per tourist increased, total revenue would increase (assuming that average revenue did not decrease) (C). If the average cost for, say, services, would have doubled during any ten year period, even assuming the same number of tourists and average revenue, total revenue would double. In short, any combination of increases in (A), (B), (C), and (E) could explain the doubling of tourist revenue in any ten year period.

3. **(C)** The assumption is that potential donors will be flattered by requests for large donations and frequently offended by requests for smaller amounts. Therefore, it is worth the gamble to start high — at worse the potential donor may decrease his gift. Alternatives (A), (B), and (D) are not assumptions made in the statement. Alternative (E) is partially correct: Donors are seldom offended if they are asked *too much* by fund raisers.

4. **(C)** The statement refers to the social psychologist's obligation to provide a wide range of people — those in his own discipline, other social scientists, laymen, and government officials — with the tools to understand social phenomena. Alternative (E) might be a correct assumption if it was not linked to inter-disciplinary problems. Alternatives (A), (B), and (D) are incorrect assumptions.

5. **(E)** New technologies and populations represent socio-technological change problems and require new mechanisms. The other alternatives are incorrect assumptions.

6. **(D)** is true. Forty percent of American husbands approve, while 50 percent of American wives work. Ten percent of German husbands approve, while 33 percent of German wives work. Therefore, the gap between German husbands' attitudes towards work and what their wives actually do is much greater than for American husbands and wives.

7. **(B)** Both statements may be inferred; if all public buildings constructed after 1980 were required to have reinforced-steel bomb shelters, then by definition, no bomb shelters other than reinforced-steel ones were installed after 1980. Alternative (A) is incorrect because it refers to *all* public buildings, i.e. those built before 1980. The statement mentions only those constructed *after* 1980.

8. **(B)** (A), (C), (D), and (E) should all encourage more visits to dentists. A decrease in the incidence of cavities should result in a decline of visits to dentists.

9. **(A)** The net export figure is measured in absolute terms, while the export and import figures are given as percents of GNP. Therefore, we may compare the trend in percentage terms and relate it to net exports (given in absolute terms) only as a proportion of GNP. If GNP remained constant over the period, we may compare only the percentage terms. Net exports/constant GNP in 1975 was 2.9 percent and in 1968, .3 percent.

10. **(D)** The assumption is that domestic marketing techniques may be transferable to only those markets that have substantial sales volume. The words "marketing methods" in the last sentence refer to the word "treated" in the first sentence.

11. **(E)** If the principal monetary policy is to be attained — reducing the import surplus while resuming economic growth — per-capita consumption will have to be frozen. Thus, consumers will have to be persuaded to give up consumption to further national economic goals. The assumption is that people will be willing to put a halt to growth in their standard of living.

12. **(B)** Even though nationalization is thought to be caused by changes in government, it is not "selective" by country and covers a wide range of industries.

13. **(A)** If the idea is to speed economic development, then there is place for an argument for inequality of income. In lower income countries, investment by local entrepreneurs is possible only because of income inequality (the wealthy have excess income which they invest).

14. **(B)** Terms of trade is a relative term. Euphoria's terms of trade improved, meaning that aggregate export earnings were greater than aggregate import costs (a ratio of more than 100).

15. **(D)** While (A) may be inferred, (D) better summarizes the minister's assertion. In this case,

"open-door policy" may signify increased trade since ideas and foreign aid are ruled out. There is no proof for (E), while (B) and (C) may not be inferred from the communique.

6. **(A)** Note that the casualty figure for automobile deaths is given as the ratio of number of deaths to miles traveled. In order to make a comparison with other modes of transport, the same denominator (miles traveled) would have to be used.

7. **(A)** If the treaty results in increased Workland exports to Playland at the expense of local producers (import creation), Playland's balance of payments will show a larger deficit. If however, increased Workland exports to Playland merely replace imports from other countries (import diversion), the trade balance will not change. Alternative (C) is a second best consideration, i.e. that political objectives supersede economic goals. The remaining alternatives have no bearing on Playland's balance of trade.

8. **(B)** There is no association between birth control and infant mortality. Birth control can prevent pregnancies but not death after birth.

19. **(E)** If tax advantages (deductions, etc.) decrease, less disposable income is available for spending. All other alternatives explain why total shipments of appliances has increased.

20. **(B)** First, the increase in imports of both types of vehicles was one and a half times greater in 1976 than in 1975. That means that there was a 10 percent increase in the import of both types of vehicles in 1975. Likewise, if the increase for 1976 of private vehicles was 10 percent, then the increase in 1975 was 6.7 percent. Therefore, the difference in import increases for both types of vehicles between 1975 and 1976 is 5 percent and for private vehicles, 3.3 percent. So, the relative increase in the imports of commercial vehicles was greater than for private vehicles:

	Both Types	Private
1975	10%	6.7%
1976	15%	10.0%
Increase	5%	3.3%

Evaluating Your Score

Tabulate your score for each section of Sample Test 3 according to the directions o
pages 4–5 and record the results in the Self-scoring Table below. Then find your ratin
for each score on the Self-scoring Scale and record it in the appropriate blank.

Self-scoring Table

SECTION	SCORE	RATING
1		
2		
3		
4		
5		
6		
7		
8		

Self-scoring Scale
RATING

SECTION	POOR	FAIR	GOOD	EXCELLENT
1	0–12 +	13–17 +	18–21 +	22–25
2	0–9 +	10–13 +	14–17 +	18–20
3	0–17 +	18–24 +	25–31 +	32–35
4	0–12 +	13–17 +	18–21 +	22–25
5	0–12 +	13–17 +	18–21 +	22–25
6	0–9 +	10–13 +	14–17 +	18–20
7	0–12 +	13–17 +	18–21 +	22–25
8	0–9 +	10–13 +	14–17 +	18–20

Study again the Review sections covering material in Sample Test 3 for which you ha
a rating of FAIR or POOR. Then go on to Sample Test 4.

To obtain an approximation of your actual GMAT score see page 5.

Answer Sheet—Sample Test 4

Section I
Reading Comprehension

1. Ⓐ Ⓑ Ⓒ Ⓓ Ⓔ
2. Ⓐ Ⓑ Ⓒ Ⓓ Ⓔ
3. Ⓐ Ⓑ Ⓒ Ⓓ Ⓔ
4. Ⓐ Ⓑ Ⓒ Ⓓ Ⓔ
5. Ⓐ Ⓑ Ⓒ Ⓓ Ⓔ
6. Ⓐ Ⓑ Ⓒ Ⓓ Ⓔ
7. Ⓐ Ⓑ Ⓒ Ⓓ Ⓔ
8. Ⓐ Ⓑ Ⓒ Ⓓ Ⓔ
9. Ⓐ Ⓑ Ⓒ Ⓓ Ⓔ
10. Ⓐ Ⓑ Ⓒ Ⓓ Ⓔ
11. Ⓐ Ⓑ Ⓒ Ⓓ Ⓔ
12. Ⓐ Ⓑ Ⓒ Ⓓ Ⓔ
13. Ⓐ Ⓑ Ⓒ Ⓓ Ⓔ
14. Ⓐ Ⓑ Ⓒ Ⓓ Ⓔ
15. Ⓐ Ⓑ Ⓒ Ⓓ Ⓔ
16. Ⓐ Ⓑ Ⓒ Ⓓ Ⓔ
17. Ⓐ Ⓑ Ⓒ Ⓓ Ⓔ
18. Ⓐ Ⓑ Ⓒ Ⓓ Ⓔ
19. Ⓐ Ⓑ Ⓒ Ⓓ Ⓔ
20. Ⓐ Ⓑ Ⓒ Ⓓ Ⓔ
21. Ⓐ Ⓑ Ⓒ Ⓓ Ⓔ
22. Ⓐ Ⓑ Ⓒ Ⓓ Ⓔ
23. Ⓐ Ⓑ Ⓒ Ⓓ Ⓔ
24. Ⓐ Ⓑ Ⓒ Ⓓ Ⓔ
25. Ⓐ Ⓑ Ⓒ Ⓓ Ⓔ

Section II
Problem Solving

1. Ⓐ Ⓑ Ⓒ Ⓓ Ⓔ
2. Ⓐ Ⓑ Ⓒ Ⓓ Ⓔ
3. Ⓐ Ⓑ Ⓒ Ⓓ Ⓔ
4. Ⓐ Ⓑ Ⓒ Ⓓ Ⓔ
5. Ⓐ Ⓑ Ⓒ Ⓓ Ⓔ
6. Ⓐ Ⓑ Ⓒ Ⓓ Ⓔ
7. Ⓐ Ⓑ Ⓒ Ⓓ Ⓔ
8. Ⓐ Ⓑ Ⓒ Ⓓ Ⓔ
9. Ⓐ Ⓑ Ⓒ Ⓓ Ⓔ
10. Ⓐ Ⓑ Ⓒ Ⓓ Ⓔ
11. Ⓐ Ⓑ Ⓒ Ⓓ Ⓔ
12. Ⓐ Ⓑ Ⓒ Ⓓ Ⓔ
13. Ⓐ Ⓑ Ⓒ Ⓓ Ⓔ
14. Ⓐ Ⓑ Ⓒ Ⓓ Ⓔ
15. Ⓐ Ⓑ Ⓒ Ⓓ Ⓔ
16. Ⓐ Ⓑ Ⓒ Ⓓ Ⓔ
17. Ⓐ Ⓑ Ⓒ Ⓓ Ⓔ
18. Ⓐ Ⓑ Ⓒ Ⓓ Ⓔ
19. Ⓐ Ⓑ Ⓒ Ⓓ Ⓔ
20. Ⓐ Ⓑ Ⓒ Ⓓ Ⓔ

Section III
Analysis of Situations

1. Ⓐ Ⓑ Ⓒ Ⓓ Ⓔ
2. Ⓐ Ⓑ Ⓒ Ⓓ Ⓔ
3. Ⓐ Ⓑ Ⓒ Ⓓ Ⓔ
4. Ⓐ Ⓑ Ⓒ Ⓓ Ⓔ
5. Ⓐ Ⓑ Ⓒ Ⓓ Ⓔ
6. Ⓐ Ⓑ Ⓒ Ⓓ Ⓔ
7. Ⓐ Ⓑ Ⓒ Ⓓ Ⓔ
8. Ⓐ Ⓑ Ⓒ Ⓓ Ⓔ
9. Ⓐ Ⓑ Ⓒ Ⓓ Ⓔ
10. Ⓐ Ⓑ Ⓒ Ⓓ Ⓔ
11. Ⓐ Ⓑ Ⓒ Ⓓ Ⓔ
12. Ⓐ Ⓑ Ⓒ Ⓓ Ⓔ
13. Ⓐ Ⓑ Ⓒ Ⓓ Ⓔ
14. Ⓐ Ⓑ Ⓒ Ⓓ Ⓔ
15. Ⓐ Ⓑ Ⓒ Ⓓ Ⓔ
16. Ⓐ Ⓑ Ⓒ Ⓓ Ⓔ
17. Ⓐ Ⓑ Ⓒ Ⓓ Ⓔ
18. Ⓐ Ⓑ Ⓒ Ⓓ Ⓔ
19. Ⓐ Ⓑ Ⓒ Ⓓ Ⓔ
20. Ⓐ Ⓑ Ⓒ Ⓓ Ⓔ
21. Ⓐ Ⓑ Ⓒ Ⓓ Ⓔ
22. Ⓐ Ⓑ Ⓒ Ⓓ Ⓔ
23. Ⓐ Ⓑ Ⓒ Ⓓ Ⓔ
24. Ⓐ Ⓑ Ⓒ Ⓓ Ⓔ
25. Ⓐ Ⓑ Ⓒ Ⓓ Ⓔ
26. Ⓐ Ⓑ Ⓒ Ⓓ Ⓔ
27. Ⓐ Ⓑ Ⓒ Ⓓ Ⓔ
28. Ⓐ Ⓑ Ⓒ Ⓓ Ⓔ
29. Ⓐ Ⓑ Ⓒ Ⓓ Ⓔ
30. Ⓐ Ⓑ Ⓒ Ⓓ Ⓔ
31. Ⓐ Ⓑ Ⓒ Ⓓ Ⓔ
32. Ⓐ Ⓑ Ⓒ Ⓓ Ⓔ
33. Ⓐ Ⓑ Ⓒ Ⓓ Ⓔ
34. Ⓐ Ⓑ Ⓒ Ⓓ Ⓔ
35. Ⓐ Ⓑ Ⓒ Ⓓ Ⓔ

Section IV
Data Sufficiency

1. Ⓐ Ⓑ Ⓒ Ⓓ Ⓔ
2. Ⓐ Ⓑ Ⓒ Ⓓ Ⓔ
3. Ⓐ Ⓑ Ⓒ Ⓓ Ⓔ
4. Ⓐ Ⓑ Ⓒ Ⓓ Ⓔ
5. Ⓐ Ⓑ Ⓒ Ⓓ Ⓔ
6. Ⓐ Ⓑ Ⓒ Ⓓ Ⓔ
7. Ⓐ Ⓑ Ⓒ Ⓓ Ⓔ
8. Ⓐ Ⓑ Ⓒ Ⓓ Ⓔ
9. Ⓐ Ⓑ Ⓒ Ⓓ Ⓔ
10. Ⓐ Ⓑ Ⓒ Ⓓ Ⓔ
11. Ⓐ Ⓑ Ⓒ Ⓓ Ⓔ

12. Ⓐ Ⓑ Ⓒ Ⓓ Ⓔ
13. Ⓐ Ⓑ Ⓒ Ⓓ Ⓔ
14. Ⓐ Ⓑ Ⓒ Ⓓ Ⓔ
15. Ⓐ Ⓑ Ⓒ Ⓓ Ⓔ
16. Ⓐ Ⓑ Ⓒ Ⓓ Ⓔ
17. Ⓐ Ⓑ Ⓒ Ⓓ Ⓔ
18. Ⓐ Ⓑ Ⓒ Ⓓ Ⓔ
19. Ⓐ Ⓑ Ⓒ Ⓓ Ⓔ
20. Ⓐ Ⓑ Ⓒ Ⓓ Ⓔ
21. Ⓐ Ⓑ Ⓒ Ⓓ Ⓔ
22. Ⓐ Ⓑ Ⓒ Ⓓ Ⓔ
23. Ⓐ Ⓑ Ⓒ Ⓓ Ⓔ
24. Ⓐ Ⓑ Ⓒ Ⓓ Ⓔ
25. Ⓐ Ⓑ Ⓒ Ⓓ Ⓔ

Section V
Writing Ability

1. Ⓐ Ⓑ Ⓒ Ⓓ Ⓔ
2. Ⓐ Ⓑ Ⓒ Ⓓ Ⓔ
3. Ⓐ Ⓑ Ⓒ Ⓓ Ⓔ
4. Ⓐ Ⓑ Ⓒ Ⓓ Ⓔ
5. Ⓐ Ⓑ Ⓒ Ⓓ Ⓔ
6. Ⓐ Ⓑ Ⓒ Ⓓ Ⓔ
7. Ⓐ Ⓑ Ⓒ Ⓓ Ⓔ
8. Ⓐ Ⓑ Ⓒ Ⓓ Ⓔ
9. Ⓐ Ⓑ Ⓒ Ⓓ Ⓔ
10. Ⓐ Ⓑ Ⓒ Ⓓ Ⓔ
11. Ⓐ Ⓑ Ⓒ Ⓓ Ⓔ
12. Ⓐ Ⓑ Ⓒ Ⓓ Ⓔ
13. Ⓐ Ⓑ Ⓒ Ⓓ Ⓔ
14. Ⓐ Ⓑ Ⓒ Ⓓ Ⓔ
15. Ⓐ Ⓑ Ⓒ Ⓓ Ⓔ
16. Ⓐ Ⓑ Ⓒ Ⓓ Ⓔ
17. Ⓐ Ⓑ Ⓒ Ⓓ Ⓔ
18. Ⓐ Ⓑ Ⓒ Ⓓ Ⓔ
19. Ⓐ Ⓑ Ⓒ Ⓓ Ⓔ
20. Ⓐ Ⓑ Ⓒ Ⓓ Ⓔ
21. Ⓐ Ⓑ Ⓒ Ⓓ Ⓔ
22. Ⓐ Ⓑ Ⓒ Ⓓ Ⓔ
23. Ⓐ Ⓑ Ⓒ Ⓓ Ⓔ
24. Ⓐ Ⓑ Ⓒ Ⓓ Ⓔ
25. Ⓐ Ⓑ Ⓒ Ⓓ Ⓔ

Section VI
Analysis of Situations

1. Ⓐ Ⓑ Ⓒ Ⓓ Ⓔ
2. Ⓐ Ⓑ Ⓒ Ⓓ Ⓔ
3. Ⓐ Ⓑ Ⓒ Ⓓ Ⓔ
4. Ⓐ Ⓑ Ⓒ Ⓓ Ⓔ
5. Ⓐ Ⓑ Ⓒ Ⓓ Ⓔ
6. Ⓐ Ⓑ Ⓒ Ⓓ Ⓔ
7. Ⓐ Ⓑ Ⓒ Ⓓ Ⓔ
8. Ⓐ Ⓑ Ⓒ Ⓓ Ⓔ
9. Ⓐ Ⓑ Ⓒ Ⓓ Ⓔ
10. Ⓐ Ⓑ Ⓒ Ⓓ Ⓔ
11. Ⓐ Ⓑ Ⓒ Ⓓ Ⓔ
12. Ⓐ Ⓑ Ⓒ Ⓓ Ⓔ
13. Ⓐ Ⓑ Ⓒ Ⓓ Ⓔ
14. Ⓐ Ⓑ Ⓒ Ⓓ Ⓔ
15. Ⓐ Ⓑ Ⓒ Ⓓ Ⓔ
16. Ⓐ Ⓑ Ⓒ Ⓓ Ⓔ
17. Ⓐ Ⓑ Ⓒ Ⓓ Ⓔ
18. Ⓐ Ⓑ Ⓒ Ⓓ Ⓔ
19. Ⓐ Ⓑ Ⓒ Ⓓ Ⓔ
20. Ⓐ Ⓑ Ⓒ Ⓓ Ⓔ
21. Ⓐ Ⓑ Ⓒ Ⓓ Ⓔ
22. Ⓐ Ⓑ Ⓒ Ⓓ Ⓔ
23. Ⓐ Ⓑ Ⓒ Ⓓ Ⓔ
24. Ⓐ Ⓑ Ⓒ Ⓓ Ⓔ
25. Ⓐ Ⓑ Ⓒ Ⓓ Ⓔ
26. Ⓐ Ⓑ Ⓒ Ⓓ Ⓔ
27. Ⓐ Ⓑ Ⓒ Ⓓ Ⓔ
28. Ⓐ Ⓑ Ⓒ Ⓓ Ⓔ
29. Ⓐ Ⓑ Ⓒ Ⓓ Ⓔ
30. Ⓐ Ⓑ Ⓒ Ⓓ Ⓔ
31. Ⓐ Ⓑ Ⓒ Ⓓ Ⓔ
32. Ⓐ Ⓑ Ⓒ Ⓓ Ⓔ
33. Ⓐ Ⓑ Ⓒ Ⓓ Ⓔ
34. Ⓐ Ⓑ Ⓒ Ⓓ Ⓔ
35. Ⓐ Ⓑ Ⓒ Ⓓ Ⓔ

Section VII
Data Sufficiency

1. Ⓐ Ⓑ Ⓒ Ⓓ Ⓔ
2. Ⓐ Ⓑ Ⓒ Ⓓ Ⓔ
3. Ⓐ Ⓑ Ⓒ Ⓓ Ⓔ
4. Ⓐ Ⓑ Ⓒ Ⓓ Ⓔ
5. Ⓐ Ⓑ Ⓒ Ⓓ Ⓔ
6. Ⓐ Ⓑ Ⓒ Ⓓ Ⓔ
7. Ⓐ Ⓑ Ⓒ Ⓓ Ⓔ
8. Ⓐ Ⓑ Ⓒ Ⓓ Ⓔ
9. Ⓐ Ⓑ Ⓒ Ⓓ Ⓔ
10. Ⓐ Ⓑ Ⓒ Ⓓ Ⓔ
11. Ⓐ Ⓑ Ⓒ Ⓓ Ⓔ
12. Ⓐ Ⓑ Ⓒ Ⓓ Ⓔ
13. Ⓐ Ⓑ Ⓒ Ⓓ Ⓔ
14. Ⓐ Ⓑ Ⓒ Ⓓ Ⓔ
15. Ⓐ Ⓑ Ⓒ Ⓓ Ⓔ
16. Ⓐ Ⓑ Ⓒ Ⓓ Ⓔ
17. Ⓐ Ⓑ Ⓒ Ⓓ Ⓔ
18. Ⓐ Ⓑ Ⓒ Ⓓ Ⓔ
19. Ⓐ Ⓑ Ⓒ Ⓓ Ⓔ
20. Ⓐ Ⓑ Ⓒ Ⓓ Ⓔ
21. Ⓐ Ⓑ Ⓒ Ⓓ Ⓔ
22. Ⓐ Ⓑ Ⓒ Ⓓ Ⓔ
23. Ⓐ Ⓑ Ⓒ Ⓓ Ⓔ
24. Ⓐ Ⓑ Ⓒ Ⓓ Ⓔ
25. Ⓐ Ⓑ Ⓒ Ⓓ Ⓔ

Section VIII
Problem Solving

1. Ⓐ Ⓑ Ⓒ Ⓓ Ⓔ
2. Ⓐ Ⓑ Ⓒ Ⓓ Ⓔ
3. Ⓐ Ⓑ Ⓒ Ⓓ Ⓔ
4. Ⓐ Ⓑ Ⓒ Ⓓ Ⓔ
5. Ⓐ Ⓑ Ⓒ Ⓓ Ⓔ
6. Ⓐ Ⓑ Ⓒ Ⓓ Ⓔ
7. Ⓐ Ⓑ Ⓒ Ⓓ Ⓔ
8. Ⓐ Ⓑ Ⓒ Ⓓ Ⓔ
9. Ⓐ Ⓑ Ⓒ Ⓓ Ⓔ
10. Ⓐ Ⓑ Ⓒ Ⓓ Ⓔ
11. Ⓐ Ⓑ Ⓒ Ⓓ Ⓔ
12. Ⓐ Ⓑ Ⓒ Ⓓ Ⓔ
13. Ⓐ Ⓑ Ⓒ Ⓓ Ⓔ
14. Ⓐ Ⓑ Ⓒ Ⓓ Ⓔ
15. Ⓐ Ⓑ Ⓒ Ⓓ Ⓔ
16. Ⓐ Ⓑ Ⓒ Ⓓ Ⓔ
17. Ⓐ Ⓑ Ⓒ Ⓓ Ⓔ
18. Ⓐ Ⓑ Ⓒ Ⓓ Ⓔ
19. Ⓐ Ⓑ Ⓒ Ⓓ Ⓔ
20. Ⓐ Ⓑ Ⓒ Ⓓ Ⓔ

Sample Test 4

Section I   Reading Comprehension

TIME: 30 minutes

DIRECTIONS: This part contains three reading passages. You are to read each one carefully. When answering the questions, you will be allowed to refer back to the passages. The questions are based on what is *stated* or *implied* in each passage. You have thirty minutes to complete this section.

Passage 1:

The economic condition of the low-income regions of the world is one of the great problems of our time. Their progress is important to the high-income countries, not only for humanitarian and political reasons but also because rapid economic growth in the low income countries could make a substantial contribution to the expansion
(5)   and prosperity of the world economy as a whole.

The governments of most high-income countries have in recent years undertaken important aid programs, both bilaterally and multilaterally, and have thus demonstrated their interest in the development of low-income countries. They have also worked within the General Agreement on Tariffs and Trade (GATT) for greater
(10)   freedom of trade and, recognizing the special problems of low-income countries, have made special trading arrangements to meet their needs. But a faster expansion of trade with high-income countries is necessary if the low-income countries are to enjoy a satisfactory rate of growth.

This statement is therefore concerned with the policies of high-income countries
(15)   toward their trade with low-income countries. Our recommendations are based on the conviction that a better distribution of world resources and a more rational utilization of labor are in the general interest. A liberal policy on the part of high-income countries with respect to their trade with low-income countries will not only be helpful to the low-income countries but, when transitional adjustments have taken
(20)   place, beneficial to the high-income countries as well.

It is necessary to recognize however, that in furthering the development of low-income countries, the high-income countries can play only a supporting role. If development is to be successful, the main effort must necessarily be made by the people of the low-income countries. The high-income countries are, moreover, likely
(25)   to provide aid and facilitate trade more readily and extensively where the low-income countries are seen to be making sound and determined efforts to help themselves, and thus to be making effective use of their aid and trade opportunities.

It is, then, necessary that the low-income countries take full account of the lessons that have been learned from the experience of recent years, if they wish to achieve
(30)   successful development and benefit from support from high-income countries. Among the most important of these lessons are the following:

Severe damage has been done by inflation. A sound financial framework evokes higher domestic savngs and investment as well as more aid and investment from abroad. Budgetary and monetary discipline and a more efficient financial and fiscal
(35)   system help greatly to mobilize funds for investment and thereby decisively

influence the rate of growth. Foreign aid should also be efficiently applied to this end.

The energies of the people of low-income countries are more likely to be harnessed to the task of economic development where the policies of their governments aim
(40) to offer economic opportunity for all and to reduce excessive social inequalities.

Development plans have tended to concentrate on industrial investment. The growth of industry depends, however, on concomitant development in agriculture. A steady rise in producitivity on the farms, where in almost all low-income countries a majority of the labor force works, is an essential condition of rapid over-all growth.
(45) Satisfactory development of agriculture is also necessary to provide an adequate market for an expanding industrial sector and to feed the growing urban population without burdening the balance of payments with heavy food imports. Diminishing surpluses in the high-income countries underline the need for a faster growth of agricultural productivity in low-income countries. Success in this should, moreover,
(50) lead to greater trade in agricultural products among the low-income countries themselves as well as to increased exports of some agricultural products to the high-income countries.

There can be no doubt about the urgency of the world food problem. Adequate nourishment and a balanced diet are not only necessary for working adults but are
(55) crucial for the mental and physical development of growing children. Yet, in a number of low-income countries where the diet is already insufficient the production of food has fallen behind the increase in population. A continuation of this trend must lead to endemic famine. The situation demands strenuous efforts in the low-income countries to improve the production, preservation, and distribution of food
(60) so that these countries are better able to feed themselves.

1. The economic conditions of low-income countries are important to high-income countries because of

   I. economic reasons
  II. political reasons
 III. cultural reasons

  (A) I only
  (B) III only
  (C) I and II only
  (D) II and III only
  (E) I, II, and III

2. According to the passage, governments of most high-income countries have

  (A) not worked for freer trade with low-income countries
  (B) undertaken important aid programs for low-income countries
  (C) injected massive doses of capital into low-income countries
  (D) provided training programs for low-income country entrepreneurs
  (E) helped improve the educational systems of low-income countries

3. The major subject with which the passage is concerned is

  (A) trade policies of high-income countries towards low-income countries
  (B) foreign trade problems of low-income countries
  (C) fiscal and monetary problems of low-income countries
  (D) trade arrangements under the GATT organization
  (E) general economic problems of low-income countries

4. If low-income countries expect aid from high-income countries, they must do all of the following *except*

(A) spend the aid wisely
(B) put their own houses in order first
(C) learn from the experience of developed countries
(D) curb inflation
(E) de-emphasize agricultural development in favor of industrial growth

5. Which of the following is mentioned for its influence upon the rate of economic growth?

(A) an efficient financial and fiscal system
(B) a trade surplus
(C) a democratic government
(D) little reliance upon foreign aid
(E) a budgetary surplus

6. Industrial growth depends upon a parallel growth of the

(A) labor force
(B) agricultural system
(C) balance of payments
(D) urban population
(E) monetary system

7. The passage states that participation of high-income countries should be limited to

(A) 10 percent of their GNP
(B) a supporting role
(C) regulations stipulated by GATT
(D) what low-income countries can absorb
(E) monetary aid only

8. In order to better enlist the support of the population in economic development efforts, low-income countries should

(A) not accept more foreign aid than they can use
(B) budget the capital wisely
(C) reduce excessive social inequalities
(D) concentrate on commercial development
(E) establish agricultural communes

9. People will be motivated to work if they are offered

(A) social equality
(B) better working conditions
(C) more money
(D) shorter hours
(E) quality jobs

Passage 2:

In *Scholasticism and Politics*, written during World War II, Maritain expressed discouragement at the pessimism and lack of self-confidence characteristic of the Western democracies, and in the postwar world he joined enthusiastically in the resurgence of that confidence. While stopping short of asserting that democracy as a political system flowed directly from correct philosophical principles, he nonetheless dismissed Fascism and Communism as inherently irrational. Bourgeois individualism was, however, implicitly immoral and, by breaking down all sense of community and shared moral values, would inevitably end in some form of statism: order imposed from above. In *Integral Humanism* (1936) and later works, he developed a systematic critique of the prevailing modern political ideologies and argued that a workable political order, which might appropriately be democracy, depended on a correct understanding of human nature and of natural moral law.

Maritain became something of an Americanophile, seeking to counter not only what he regarded as European misconceptions about America but also the Americans' own self-deprecation. In *Reflections on America* (1958), he argued that Americans were not really materialistic but were the most idealistic people in the world, although theirs was an idealism often unformed and lacking in philosophical bases. America, he thought, offered perhaps the best contemporary prospect for the emergence of a truly Christian civilization, based not on governmental decree but on the gradual realization of Christian values on the part of a majority of the population. American saints were coming, he predicted.

But his postulation of a possible Christian civilization in America did not in any way temper his optimistic political liberalism—a facet of his thought which caused him to be held in suspicion by some of his fellow Catholics in the 1950s. The Dominican chaplain at Princeton, for example, refused to allow him to address the Catholic students. (One of the exquisite ironies of recent Catholic history was that Maritain in his last books was acerbically critical of secularizing priests, while the Dominican chaplain resigned from the priesthood and ended his days as a real estate salesman in Florida.)

No doubt in part because of Raïssa's background, Maritain had an enduring interest in anti-Semitism, which he analyzed and criticized in two books, and he was one of the principal influences in the effort to establish better Jewish-Catholic relations. Racism he regarded as America's most severe flaw. As early as 1958 he was praising Martin Luther King, Jr., and the Chicago neighborhood organizer Saul Alinsky.

Maritain and, to a lesser extent, Gilson provided the program for a bold kind of Catholic intellectuality—an appropriation of medieval thought for modern use, not so much a medieval revival as a demonstration of the perennial relevance of the medieval philosophical achievement. The modern mind was to be brought back to its Catholic roots, not by the simple disparagement of modernity or by emphasis on the subjective necessity of faith, but by a rigorous and demanding appeal to reason. In the process, Scholastic principles would be applied in new and often daring ways.

In the end the gamble failed. Despite promising signs in the 1940s, secular thinkers did not finally find the Scholastic appeal persuasive. And, as is inevitable when an intellectual community is dominated so thoroughly by a single system of thought, a restiveness was building up in Catholic circles. Although Maritain insisted that Thomism, because of the central importance it gave to the act of existence, was the true existentialism, Catholic intellectuals of the 1950s were attracted to the movement which more usually went by that name; and Gabriel Marcel, a Catholic existentialist of the same generation as Gilson and Maritain, was available to mediate between faith and anguish. Catholic colleges in America were hospitable to existentialist and phenomenological currents at a time when few secular institutions were, and what Catholics sought there was primarily a philosophy which was serious about the metaphysical questions of existence, yet not as rationalistic, rigid, and abstract as Scholasticism often seemed to be.

10. Maritain believed that Americans were

    I. materialistic
   II. idealistic
  III. self-deprecating

(A) I only   (D) II and III only
(B) II only   (E) I, II, and III
(C) I and II only

11. Maritain could be characterized as

(A) anti-Semitic
(B) materialistic
(C) a Catholic chaplain
(D) a historian
(E) a political liberal

12. Which of the following statements best exemplifies Maritain's belief?

(A) Democracy was an old-fashioned ideology.
(B) Democracy and Fascism were both imperfect.
(C) Democracy flowed from correct philosophical principles.
(D) Bourgeois individualism would end in statism.
(E) Fascism and Communism were just as bad.

13. Maritain's program for Catholic intellectuality may be expressed as

(A) a synthesis of modernity and tradition
(B) political liberalism
(C) Dominican Catholicism
(D) Scholastic reasoning
(E) medieval Catholic values

14. Scholasticism was not accepted by secular thinkers because it was too

I. rationalistic
II. secular
III. nationalistic

(A) I only
(B) II only
(C) I and II only
(D) II and III only
(E) I, II, and III

15. Maritain discussed political ideologies in his publication(s)

I. *Scholasticism and Politics*
II. *Integral Humanism*
III. *Reflections on America*

(A) I only
(B) II only
(C) I and II only
(D) II and III only
(E) I, II, and III

16. Catholic intellectuals of the 1950s were attracted to

(A) eclectic movements
(B) existentialism
(C) Scholastic principles
(D) neo-Scholasticism
(E) medieval philosophers

17. The most appropriate title for the passage is

(A) "Catholicism in America"
(B) "Catholicism and Scholasticism"
(C) "Christian Civilization and Politics"
(D) "Catholic Intellectual Renaissance"
(E) "Catholic Thought on Campus"

Passage 3:

Much as an electrical lamp transforms electrical energy into heat and light, the visual "apparatus" of a human being acts as a transformer of light into sight. Light projected from a source or reflected by an object enters the cornea and lens of the eyeball. The energy is transmitted to the retina of the eye whose rods and cones
(5) are activated.

The stimuli are transferred by nerve cells to the optic nerve and then to the brain. Man is a binocular animal, and the impressions from his two eyes are translated into sight—a rapid, compound analysis of the shape, form, color, size, position, and motion of the things he sees.

(10) Photometry is the science of measuring light. The illuminating engineer and designer employ photometric data constantly in their work. In all fields of application of light and lighting, they predicate their choice of equipment, lamps, wall finishes, colors of light and backgrounds, and other factors affecting the luminous and environmental pattern to be secured, in great part from data supplied
(15) originally by a photometric laboratory. Today, extensive tables and charts of photometric data are used widely, constituting the basis for many details of design.

Although the lighting designer may not be called upon to do the detailed work of making measurements or plotting data in the form of photometric curves and analyzing them, an understanding of the terms used and their derivation form
(20) valuable background knowledge.

The perception of color is a complex visual sensation, intimately related to light. The apparent color of an object depends primarily upon four factors: its ability to reflect various colors of light, the nature of the light by which it is seen, the color of its surroundings, and the characteristics and state of adaptation of the eye.

(25) In most discussions of color, a distinction is made between white and colored objects. White is the color name most usually applied to a material that diffusely transmits a high percentage of all the hues of light. Colors that have no hue are termed neutral or achromatic colors. They include white, off-white, all shades of gray, down to black.

(30) All colored objects selectively absorb certain wave-lengths of light and reflect or transmit others in varying degrees. Inorganic materials, chiefly metals such as copper and brass, reflect light from their *surfaces*. Hence we have the term "surface" or "metallic" colors, as contrasted with "body" or "pigment" colors. In the former, the light reflected from the surface is often tinted.

(35) Most paints; on the other hand, have body or pigment colors. In these, light is reflected from the surface without much color change, but the body material absorbs some colors and reflects others; hence, the diffuse reflection from the body of the material is colored but often appears to be overlaid and diluted with a "white" reflection from the glossy surface of the paint film. In paints and enamels, the
(40) pigment particles, which are usually opaque, are suspended in a vehicle such as oil or plastic. The particles of a dye, on the other hand, are considerably finer and may be described as coloring matter in solution. The dye particles are more often transparent or translucent.

18. Light projected from a source enters the eyeball through the

(A) cornea   (D) cones
(B) retina   (E) brain
(C) rods

19. Photometry is the science of

(A) studying sight
(B) color configurations
(C) light projection
(D) light and motion
(E) measuring light

20. According to the passage, lighting engineers need *not*

(A) plot photometric curves
(B) understand photometric techniques
(C) utilize photometric data
(D) have mathematical expertise
(E) be college graduates

21. The color black is an example of

(A) a surface color
(B) an organic color
(C) an achromatic color
(D) a diffuse color
(E) a pigment color

22. The reflection of light wave-lengths is accomplished by

(A) all colors
(B) selective colors
(C) surface colors
(D) achromatic colors
(E) pigment colors

23. Inorganic materials refect light from their

(A) hues
(B) body
(C) surface
(D) pigment
(E) compounds

24. Paint would be an example of a substance containing

(A) inorganic material
(B) surface colors
(C) body colors
(D) metallic colors
(E) enamels

25. The perception of color is

(A) a photometric phenomenon
(B) activated by the brain
(C) a complex visual sensation
(D) light reflected by a source
(E) energy transmitted from the retina

If there is still time remaining, you may review the questions in this part only.
You may not look at the passages or turn to any other section of the test.

Section II   Problem Solving

TIME: 30 minutes

DIRECTIONS: Solve each of the following problems; then indicate the correct answer on the answer sheet. [On the actual test you will be permitted to use any space available on the examination paper for scratch work.]

NOTE: A figure that appears with a problem is drawn as accurately as possible so as to provide information that may help in answering the question. Numbers in this test are real numbers.

1. If 32 students in a class are female and there are 18 male students in the class, what percentage of the class is female?

   (A) 32%
   (B) 36%
   (C) 56.25%
   (D) 64%
   (E) 72%

2. If $x + y = 2$ and $y = 5$ what is $x - y$?

   (A) -8
   (B) -5
   (C) -3
   (D) 2
   (E) 8

3. If a job takes 12 men 4 hours to complete, how long should it take 15 men to complete the job?

   (A) 2 hrs. 40 min.
   (B) 3 hrs.
   (C) 3 hrs. 12 min.
   (D) 3 hrs. 24 min.
   (E) 3 hrs. 30 min.

4. Apples cost 10¢ each. If the price of a dozen apples rises by 12%, how much will a dozen apples cost?

   (A) 12¢
   (B) $1.20
   (C) $1.32
   (D) $1.34
   (E) $1.36

5. How long must a driver take to drive the final 70 miles of a trip if he wants to average 50 miles an hour for the entire trip and during the first part of the trip he drove 50 miles in 1½ hours?

   (A) 54 min.
   (B) 1 hr.
   (C) 66 min.
   (D) 70 min.
   (E) 75 min.

Use the following table for questions 6–8.

MAJOR WAGE NEGOTIATIONS IN 1973

Month	Employer	Unions	Workers Covered
January	Popular Price Dresses	Ladies Garment Workers	59,950
February	N.J. Apparel Contractors	Ladies Garment Workers	27,050
March	Con Edison	Utility Workers	16,800
April	Goodyear	Rubber Workers	23,000
May	General Electric Co.	Electrical Workers (I.U.E.)	90,000
	Int. Paper Kraft Division	United Paperworkers, Electrical Brotherhood	11,500
	Nat. Skirt and Sportswear Assn. N.Y. Coat and Suit Assn.	Ladies Garment Workers	51,500
June	Westinghouse Electric	Electrical Workers (I.U.E.)	36,300
	Calif. Processors	Teamsters	56,550
	Nat. Master Freight	Teamsters	450,000
	Railroads	United Transportation Union	135,000
July	U.S. Postal Service	Postal Workers	600,000
September	Major Automobile Makers	Auto Workers	670,250
October	Mack Truck	Auto Workers	13,900
December	Budd	Auto Workers	19,200

Source: U.S. Dept. of Labor.

6. For how many months in 1973 are there major wage negotiations which involve fewer than 150,000 workers?

   (A) 4
   (B) 5
   (C) 6
   (D) 7
   (E) 8

7. How many of the workers involved in the major wage negotiations of 1973 had their wage negotiations handled by the Ladies Garment Workers Union?

   (A) 51,500
   (B) 87,000
   (C) 102,000
   (D) 130,000
   (E) 138,500

8. Which of the following unions represented the largest number of workers in the major wage negotiations of 1973?

   (A) Ladies Garment Workers
   (B) Meat Cutters
   (C) Teamsters
   (D) Postal Workers
   (E) Auto Workers

9. If a rectangle has length L and the width is one half of the length, then the area of the rectangle is

(A) L
(B) L^2
(C) $\frac{1}{2}L^2$
(D) $\frac{1}{4}L^2$
(E) $2L$

10. Eggs cost 50¢ a dozen for the first 100 dozen a store buys from a wholesaler and 47¢ a dozen for all those bought in addition to the first 100 dozen. How much does it cost to buy 150 dozen eggs from the wholesaler?

(A) $70.50
(B) $72.00
(C) $73.50
(D) $123.50
(E) $150.00

11. If the product of two numbers is 5 and one of the numbers is $\frac{1}{2}$, then the sum of the two numbers is

(A) $4\frac{1}{3}$
(B) $4\frac{2}{3}$
(C) $4\frac{5}{6}$
(D) $5\frac{1}{6}$
(E) $6\frac{1}{2}$

12. Which of the following sets of numbers can be used as the lengths of the sides of a triangle?

  I. [5,7,12]
 II. [2,4,10]
III. [5,7,9]

(A) I only
(B) III only
(C) I and II only
(D) I and III only
(E) II and III only

13. What is the next number in the arithmetic progression 2,5,8 . . . ?

(A) 7
(B) 9
(C) 10
(D) 11
(E) 12

14. A dealer owns a group of station wagons and motorcycles. If the number of tires (excluding spare tires) on the vehicles is 30 more than twice the number of vehicles, then the number of station wagons the dealer owns is

(A) 10
(B) 15
(C) 20
(D) 30
(E) 45

Use this graph for questions 15–17.

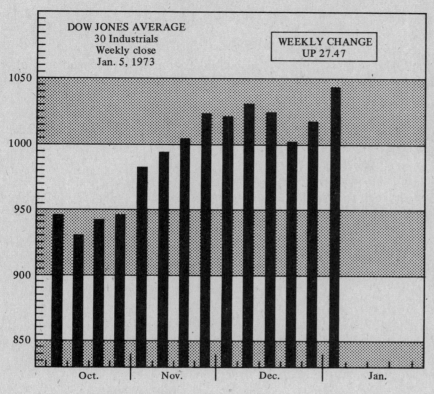

Source: Dow Jones & Company, Inc.

15. Between which two successive weeks (of those shown) did the average drop the most?

(A) first and second weeks in October
(B) fourth week in October and first week in November
(C) third and fourth weeks in November
(D) first and second weeks in December
(E) third and fourth weeks in December

16. What was the lowest value of the average during the time shown?

(A) 910
(B) 922
(C) 931

(D) 939
(E) 970

17. During how many weeks (of those shown) was the average close between 960 and 1,000?

(A) 2
(B) 3
(C) 4

(D) 5
(E) 6

18. If the two sides of a right triangle adjacent to the right angle are 5 and 12, then the third side of the triangle is

(A) 7   (D) 13
(B) 9   (E) 15
(C) 11

19. Rich sold his skis for $160.00 and his ski boots for $96.00. He made a profit of 20% on his boots and took a 10% loss on his skis. He ended up with a

(A) loss of $1.78
(B) loss of $1.50
(C) gain of $3.20
(D) gain of $7.53
(E) gain of $17.06

20. It costs 10¢ each to print the first 500 copies of a newspaper. It costs $(10 - x/50)$¢ each for every copy after the first 500. What is x if it cost $75.00 to print 1,000 copies of the newspaper?

(A) 2.5   (D) 250
(B) 100   (E) 300
(C) 25

If there is still time remaining, you may review the questions in this section only.
You may not turn to any other section of the test.

Section III   Analysis of Situations

TIME: 30 minutes

DIRECTIONS: Read the following passages. After you have completed each one, you will be asked to answer questions that involve determining the importance of specific factors included in the passage. When answering questions, you may consult the passage.

Passage 1:

The Parks Company, located in New York City, had engaged exclusively in the manufacture of baking powder in the seventy-five years since its founding. Sales were approximately $800,000 annually. The sales volume, measured in commodity units instead of dollars, had showed a decline of about 11 percent over the past decade. The company had a small office force and employed approximately 50 people in the production process, which was divided into (1) the mixing department, (2) the assembly department, and (3) the final inspection and packing department.

In 1935, distribution had been foreign as well as national. Forty years later, the sale of the product was confined to New England and the Middle Atlantic states. Mr. Andrew H. Pendler, the president, attributed this significant decrease in both market area and sales volume to high tariff rates, sterner competition, and trade dislocations caused by World War II.

Mr. Gordon Janis, the sales manager, after studying the market closely, arrived at a different set of reasons why sales had been dropping. In the first place, according to Janis, sales to commercial consumers had diminished to practically nothing. Many modern bakeries bought the necessary chemicals and manufactured their own baking powder. Secondly, the population had become urbanized. Formerly, when a larger portion of the citizenry was suburban, many housewives had done their own baking. People in cities were close to bakeries and other outlets where they could buy the finished product, and improved transportation had enabled fresh bakery products to be readily available at retail outlets. The third reason which Mr. Janis considered significant was the growing popularity of ready-mixes. The natural tendency of practically all human beings is to get as much as they can for a minimum of effort. Since ready-mixes did save housewives a good deal of labor, this type of product had been well received.

Mr. Janis believed that the company could not cope with the first two factors, and therefore his suggestion for increasing sales was to branch out and manufacture ready-mix baking products which would compare favorably with nationally-known brands. Management was particularly receptive to Janis's idea because production of ready-mixes would require only minor changes in personnel and the cost of additional machinery would be relatively small. Two additional machines were necessary, each costing approximately $10,000.

Mr. Pendler was determined to succeed in the marketing of the new products. He believed that a thorough market analysis was a prerequisite to making a final decision as to whether Janis's idea was commercially sound. Pendler wanted to know whether a small company like Parks could battle for a share of the ready-mix market against much bigger competitors. His concern centered on two key variables. First, he questioned the ability of his marketing people to develop a product which would be sufficiently differentiated from competitors' products. Parks would have to market a product which had some distinct advantage over competing products. This advantage could be in the form of an improvement over existing brands, for example, a mix that was easier to prepare. Second, a strong advertising campaign was necessary to enter the market with an unknown product. Potential consumers would have to be made aware of the new brand and its advantages. Pendler wanted to know how much such an advertising campaign would cost and whether the company had the financial resources to finance it.

Janis was given the task of preparing a marketing research report which would provide answers to Pendler's questions. Graduate students were hired to poll housewives as they entered supermarkets. Each student questioned a number of housewives about their purchases of ready-mixes, how frequently they used the products, what they liked and/or disliked about the mixes. Respondents were also asked to recall any advertising they remembered about ready-mixes. After about fifty interviews, Janis believed that he had collected enough information to reach certain conclusions.

Janis tabulated the research data and found the following trends. Most housewives said that they purchased ready-mixes and preferred to prepare their own cakes, rather than buy them from a bakery or supermarket. Housewives felt that ready-mixes were preferable to commercially-prepared cakes because of their freshness and economy. In particular, respondents liked the convenience of being able to bake a cake "in an emergency" if unexpected company came to visit. Other reasons mentioned for preferring ready-mixes were: "Tastes fresh," "modern thing to do," "my neighbors use it," and "I can choose some of the ingredients."

Few respondents using ready-mixes mentioned any dislikes. Some of the negative reactions mentioned were: "Lack of recipe variety," "my husband doesn't like them," and "all the mixes are the same."

Most of the housewives polled recalled seeing some advertising for ready-mixes during the last week. Half of the respondents recalled specific advertising themes of the major producers. Overall reaction to the advertising was favorable.

Examining the survey results, Janis concluded that Parks should market a ready-mix of its own. He reasoned that since consumer reaction was so favorable, there was room in the market for another brand. Janis recommended, however, that since the research did not reveal how Parks might differentiate its product from those already on the market, the best marketing strategy would be to charge a lower price than that of competing products. With a lower price, he asserted, Parks's ready-mix would sell well to the economy-minded housewife.

Advertising was a problem. It was clear that, given the relatively small marketing budget available to Janis, Parks could not emulate the sort of advertising campaign used by existing ready-mix manufacturers. Janis believed that if Parks would concentrate solely on the economy-minded market segment, advertising themes could be developed and a campaign launched within the company's budget constraints. Janis's report and conclusions were forwarded to Mr. Pendler. After a short deliberation, Pendler approved the ready-mix project.

Without further investigation, the manufacture of Parks's ready-mixes was started. After several months, ready-mix sales still amounted to less than 10 percent of gross sales, and 85 percent of ready-mix sales were in New York City. The entire position of the company was in jeopardy. Both Mr. Pendler and Mr. Janis were worried about the business, but neither seemed to know what to do.

DIRECTIONS: The questions that follow relate to the preceding passage. Evaluate, in terms of the passage, each of the items given. Then select your answer from one of the following classifications, and blacken the corresponding space on the answer sheet.

(A) A MAJOR OBJECTIVE in making the decision: one of the goals sought by the decision maker

(B) A MAJOR FACTOR in making the decision: an aspect of the problem, specifically mentioned in the passage, that fundamentally affects and/or determines the decision

(C) A MINOR FACTOR in making the decision: a less important element bearing on or affecting a Major Factor, rather than a Major Objective directly

(D) A MAJOR ASSUMPTION in making the decision: a projection or supposition arrived at by the decision maker before considering the factors and alternatives

(E) AN UNIMPORTANT ISSUE in making the decision: an item lacking significant impact on, or relationship to, the decision

1. Declining sales volume

2. New York City location of Parks Company

3. Production of a successful ready-mix baking product

4. Urbanization of the population

5. Increased world trade

6. Start-up costs for development of ready-mix product

7. Differentiation of Parks's ready-mix from competing products

8. Specific advertising themes recalled by shoppers being interviewed

9. $10,000 cost for one additional machine

10. Size of the office staff employed at Parks

11. Parks's ability to compete with bigger companies

12. Number of housewives interviewed for marketing survey

13. Modern bakeries' practice of producing their own baking powder

14. Financial resources of Parks

15. Cost of Parks's advertising campaign

16. High tariff rates

17. Parks's assembly department

18. Popularity of ready-mixes

Passage 2:

Sam Hoe's small furniture factory was doing more business than ever before and had a solid backlog of orders that ensured continuous production. Its profits, however, had not kept pace with production. Rising machinery, lumber, and hardware costs, higher wages, and higher operating expenses all combined to eat into profits. Mr. Hoe was concerned about this situation and had thought about raising prices on many of his products. This was not practical at the present, however, because the prices of most items had been increased within the last six months. Among various alternatives, he had considered opening an outlet to retail his own products.

The Hoe Company had been established when Sam's father had started a small woodworking shop in his garage twenty years before. When Sam had come into the business about five years later, the shop had been moved to a warehouse on the outskirts of town. At that time, much of the space was used for storage of materials and finished goods. Through the next ten years more and more of the storage area had been taken over for equipment and work space; therefore an additional storage building had been constructed next to the original building. The payroll had grown to twenty craftsmen, who were supervised by a production manager. Mr. Hoe and one bookkeeper did the purchasing, accounting, and sales work.

The shop, located in a city of 25,000 people, had begun on a special-order custom basis, selling mainly to local residents. Through the years a standard line of tables and chairs had been developed, which now accounted for 78 percent of sales. Most of the standard line furniture was sold through four wholesalers to retail furniture stores in a five-state area. Two outlets in the city, a department store and a large furniture showroom, bought directly from the factory. Although most orders for custom-made items came from within the state, a few came from states from all areas of the country.

In examining his sales and profit records for the past two years, Mr. Hoe found that while sales had increased steadily, profits showed only a very slight increase over the preceding year. Further study showed that while the sale of custom-made merchandise netted a consistently good profit, standard items, sold on a slimmer margin, lost money in some cases. Rising material costs and more rigid specifications, and demands from large retail purchasers had both contributed to the problem. Unfortunately, the number of orders for custom work had to be limited, for top craftsmen were in short supply and much of this work demanded highly skilled cabinetmakers.

Mr. Hoe believed that profits could be improved if the volume of standard furniture could be increased. Discussing the situation with his production manager, Mr. Hoe commented, "Lem, what would you think about opening a retail showroom here? The way I see it, our standard items are popular and almost sell themselves. There's plenty of room since we added the new building, and fixing up a nice-looking showroom shouldn't be too difficult or expensive. If we cut out the retailer's margin and split it between the customer and ourselves, we can cut prices—or hold them steady, anyway—and still make a decent profit." The retail showroom, Hoe explained, would not replace existing distribution channels, but rather complement them. The showroom could be located in the factory, thereby saving delivery and rental costs.

Another idea that Hoe raised was the possibility of increasing the number of retail stores that carried the Hoe Company's line. It was not suggested that furniture sales be extended geographically beyond the five states now served, but rather that a more intensive effort would be made to increase the number of retail outlets in these states. According to Hoe, this could be accomplished by adding more wholesalers, especially in the larger states.

Hoe's marketing manager, Norbert Ravis, agreed that the number of retail outlets should be increased by more intensive coverage of wholesalers or by adding additional wholesalers to the network. Norbert suggested that the company find a way to increase sales through moderate-sized retailers, rather than expand sales to department stores and large distributors. Norbert explained that although large retailers could order in bulk, the profit margin was lower. What was needed, according to Norbert, was a balance of sales between large and small retailers, with about three-fourths of total sales allocated to the smaller or moderate-sized retailer. To support his argument, Norbert supplied the following statistics: a standard set of a table and four chairs sold to a large department store earned a 25 percent profit to the factory. The same set sold to a small or moderate-sized retailer earned a 40 percent profit. Therefore, as far as Norbert was concerned, sales should be increased to smaller retailers only.

Sam Kander, Hoe's production manager, was worried about the production capabilities of the factory. With output reaching capacity, how could the marketing people plan for increased sales without taking into consideration the capacity of the plant? Even if an additional shift was added, the factory could only increase output by another 40 percent with existing machinery. Kander felt that the best way to increase sales would be to expand the custom-made merchandise. A special effort should be made to hire more cabinetmakers. Hoe could make a survey of the various vocational schools in the area to find young men who would work as apprentices in the factory. Demand was increasing for the sort of custom work that Hoe supplied. Moreover, custom work was the most profitable for the company.

Sam Hoe weighed all the alternatives. He came to the conclusion that increasing sales without improving profitability would be a waste of resources. He would have to determine which alternative would allow his company to grow, while at the same time contributing to profit improvement.

DIRECTIONS: The questions that follow relate to the preceding passage. Evaluate, in terms of the passage, each of the items given. Then select your answer from one of the following classifications, and blacken the corresponding space on the answer sheet.

(A) A MAJOR OBJECTIVE in making the decision: one of the goals sought by the decision maker

(B) A MAJOR FACTOR in making the decision: an aspect of the problem, specifically mentioned in the passage, that fundamentally affects and/or determines the decision

(C) A MINOR FACTOR in making the decision: a less important element bearing on or affecting a Major Factor, rather than a Major Objective directly

(D) A MAJOR ASSUMPTION in making the decision: a projection or supposition arrived at by the decision maker before considering the factors and alternatives

(E) AN UNIMPORTANT ISSUE in making the decision: an item lacking significant impact on or relationship to, the decision

19. Increased production costs incurred by Hoe's company

20. Increased demand for Hoe's furniture

21. Storage space needed by Hoe's company

22. Employment of 20 craftsmen in Hoe's factory

23. Opening of a retail showroom

24. Availability of skilled cabinetmakers

25. Improving profitability of Hoe's company

26. Number of states in which Hoe's furniture is sold

27. Ease of selling Hoe's standard furniture in an attached showroom

28. Addition of more retailers

29. Production capabilities of Hoe's factory

30. Direct sales to large retailers

31. Likelihood of recruiting apprentices through local schools

32. Rising hardware costs

33. Construction of a storage building

34. More intensive coverage of wholesalers

35. Production of more custom-made products

If there is still time remaining, you may review the questions in this section only.
You may not turn to any other section of the test.

Section IV   Data Sufficiency

TIME: 30 minutes

DIRECTIONS: Each of the following problems has a question and two statements which are labeled (1) and (2). Use the data given in (1) and (2) together with other available information (such as the number of hours in a day, the definition of *clockwise*, mathematical facts, etc.) to decide whether the statements are *sufficient* to answer the question. Then fill in space

(A) if you can get the answer from (1) alone but not from (2) alone;

(B) if you can get the answer from (2) alone but not from (1) alone;

(C) if you can get the answer from (1) and (2) together, although neither statement by itself suffices;

(D) if statement (1) alone suffices *and* statement (2) alone suffices;

(E) if you cannot get the answer from statements (1) and (2) together, but need even more data.

All numbers used in this section are real numbers. A figure given for a problem is intended to provide information consistent with that in the question, but not necessarily with the additional information contained in the statements.

1. A rectangular field is 40 yards long. Find the area of the field.

   (1) A fence around the outside of the field is 140 yards long.
   (2) The distance from one corner of the field to the opposite corner is 50 yards.

2. Is x greater than 0?

   (1) $x^3 + 1 = 0$
   (2) $x^2 - 1 = 0$

3. There are 450 boxes to load on a truck. A and B working independently but at the same time take 30 minutes to load the truck. How long should it take B working by himself to load the truck?

   (1) A loads twice as many boxes as B.
   (2) A would take 45 minutes by himself.

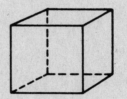

4. Is the above figure a cube?

   (1) The lengths of all edges are equal.
   (2) The angle between any two edges that meet is a right angle.

5. A car drives around a circular track once. A second car drives from point A to point B in a straight line. Which car travels farther?

   (1) The car driving around the circular track takes a longer time to complete its trip than the car traveling in a straight line.
   (2) The straight line from A to B is $1\frac{1}{2}$ times as long as the diameter of the circular track.

6. Find $x + y$

   (1) $x - y = 6$
   (2) $2x + 3y = 7$

7. Find the length of AC if AB has length 3 and x is 45.

   (1) $z = 45$
   (2) $y = 90$

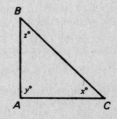

8. How much did it cost Mr. Jones to insure his car for the year 1971?

   (1) He spent $300.00 for car insurance in 1970.
   (2) The total amount he spent for car insurance in 1969, 1970, and 1971 was $905.00.

9. It costs 50 cents in tolls, 2 dollars in gas, and at least 1 dollar for parking to drive (round trip) from Utopia to Green Acres each day. The train offers a weekly ticket. Which is the cheaper way to travel per week?

   (1) The weekly train ticket costs 15 dollars.
   (2) Parking costs a total of 6 dollars.

10. Is *ABCD* a rectangle?

   (1) *AD* and *BC* bisect each other at *E*.
   (2) Angle *ACD* is 90°

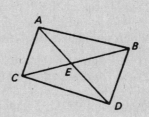

11. A worker is hired for five days. He is paid $5.00 more for each day of work than he was paid for the preceding day of work. What was the total amount he was paid for the five days of work?

   (1) He had made 50% of the total by the end of the third day.
   (2) He was paid twice as much for the last day as he was for the first day.

12. Is *y* larger than *x*?

   (1) $x + y = 2$
   (2) $\dfrac{x}{y} = 2$

13. Does a circle with diameter *d* have greater area than a square of side *s*?

   (1) $d < (\sqrt{2})s$
   (2) $d < s$

14. 5 apples cost 80 cents. How much will it cost to buy 10 apples and 3 oranges?

   (1) Oranges cost 6 for 50 cents.
   (2) 10 apples and 6 oranges cost $2.10.

15. A pair of skis originally cost $160. After a discount of *x*%, the skis were discounted *y*%. Do the skis cost less than $130 after the discounts?

   (1) $x = 20$
   (2) $y = 15$

16. What is the length of line segment *AB*? All lines that meet are perpendicular. *AJ*, *JI*, *HI*, *BC*, *FE*, *GF* and *DC* are each equal to *x*. *HG* and *DE* are each equal to *y*.

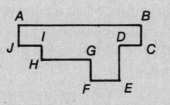

   (1) $y = 4$
   (2) $x = 2$

17. Is the angle c larger than 60°?

(1) $a + b$ is greater than c.
(2) a is greater than b which is greater than c.

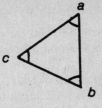

18. If a and b are both positive numbers, then which is larger, 2^a or 3^b?
    (1) a is greater than $2b$.
    (2) a is greater than or equal to $b + 3$.

19. Which number is the largest: a, b, or c?

(1) ab is greater than ac.
(2) ba is greater than bc.

20. Will the circle with center O fit inside the square $ABCD$?

(1) The diameter of the circle is less than a side of the square.
(2) The area of the circle is less than the area of the square.

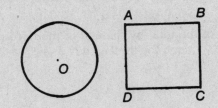

21. Is $xy < 0$?

(1) $\dfrac{1}{x} < \dfrac{1}{y}$
(2) $x > 0$

22. A square originally had sides with length s. The length of the side is increased by $x\%$. Did the area of the square increase by more than 10%?

(1) x is greater than 5.
(2) x is less than 10.

23. How much did the XYZ corporation make in 1970?

(1) The XYZ corporation made twice as much in 1970 as it did in 1969.
(2) The XYZ corporation made twice as much in 1971 as it did in 1970.

24. What is the value of x?

(1) $x - y = 6$
(2) $2x + 3y = 7$

25. How many books are on the bookshelf?

(1) The bookshelf is 12 feet long.
(2) The average weight of each book is 1.2 pounds.

If there is still time remaining, you may review the questions in this section only.
You may not turn to any other section of the test.

Section V   Writing Ability

TIME: 30 minutes

DIRECTIONS: This test consists of a number of sentences, in each of which some part or the whole is underlined. Each sentence is followed by five alternative versions of the underlined portion. Select the alternative you consider both most correct and most effective according to the requirements of standard written English. Answer A is the same as the original version; if you think the original version is best, select answer A.

In considering the answer choices, be attentive to matters of grammar, diction, and syntax, as well as clarity, precision, and fluency. Do not select an answer which alters the meaning of the original sentence.

1. More than any animal, the wolverine exemplifies the unbridled ferocity of "nature red in tooth and claw."

   (A) More than any animal
   (B) More than any other animal
   (C) More than another animal
   (D) Unlike any animal
   (E) Compared to other animals

2. In 1896, Henri Bequerel found that uranium salts emitted penetrating radiations similar to those which Roentgen produced only a year earlier with a gas discharge tube.

   (A) similar to those which Roentgen
   (B) like those which Roentgen
   (C) similar to those that Roentgen had
   (D) similar to them that Roentgen
   (E) similar to those Roentgen

3. Unless they reverse present policies immediately, the world may suffer permanent damage from the unregulated use of pesticides.

   (A) Unless they reverse present policies
   (B) Unless present policies are reversed
   (C) Unless present policies will be reversed
   (D) If it will not reverse present policies
   (E) If present policies will not be reversed

4. He interviewed several candidates who he thought had the experience and qualifications the position required.

   (A) who he thought
   (B) whom he thought
   (C) of whom he thought
   (D) he thought who
   (E) which he thought

5. The average citizen today is surprisingly knowledgeable about landmark court decisions concerning such questions as racial segregation, legislative appointment, prayer in the public schools, and whether a defendant has a right to counsel in a criminal prosecution.

   (A) whether a defendant has a right to counsel
   (B) if a defendant has a right to counsel
   (C) the right of a defendant to council
   (D) the right of a defendant to counsel
   (E) is a defendant entitled to counsel

6. The reason we are late is <u>due to the fact that the bus was delayed by heavy traffic</u>.

    (A) due to the fact that the bus was delayed by heavy traffic
    (B) because the bus was delayed by heavy traffic
    (C) that the bus was delayed by heavy traffic
    (D) due to the fact that heavy traffic delayed the bus
    (E) that the delay of our bus was caused by heavy traffic

7. Before starting a program of diet and exercise, <u>a consultation with your physician is advisable</u>.

    (A) a consultation with your physician is advisable
    (B) it is advisable to have a consultation with your physician
    (C) a physician's consultation is advisable
    (D) a consultation with your physician is necessary
    (E) you should consult your physician

8. The spraying of malathion in the infested areas is expected to eliminate the Mediterranean fruit fly, but the <u>effect that the chemical will have on human beings</u> is uncertain.

    (A) effect that the chemical will have on human beings
    (B) affect it will have on human beings
    (C) affect that the chemical will have on human beings
    (D) effect it would have on humans
    (E) affect by the chemical on human beings

9. The first of a number of receptions and testimonial dinners for the departing school superintendent <u>have been scheduled, with more events still</u> in the planning stage.

    (A) have been scheduled, with more events still
    (B) have been scheduled, and with more events still
    (C) has been scheduled, and with more events still
    (D) has been scheduled, with more events still
    (E) have been scheduled, and there is still more events

10. <u>If the Confederate Army would have carried the day at Gettysburg</u>, the history of America during the past century might have been profoundly altered.

    (A) If the Confederate Army would have carried the day at Gettysburg
    (B) Had the Confederate Army carried the day at Gettysburg
    (C) The Confederate Army having carried the day at Gettysburg
    (D) If the Confederate Army would have won at Gettysburg
    (E) If the Battle of Gettysburg would have been won by the Confederate Army

11. Economic conditions demand <u>that we not only cut wages and prices but also</u> reduce inflation-raised tax rates.

    (A) that we not only cut wages and prices but also
    (B) not only cutting wages and prices but also to
    (C) not only to cut wages and prices but also to
    (D) not only a cut in wages and prices but also to
    (E) not only to cut wages and prices but that we also

12. Legislative effectiveness, in theory, makes good sense; in actuality, however, <u>they are sometimes difficult to enforce</u>.

(A) they are sometimes difficult to enforce
(B) it is difficult to enforce them
(C) laws are sometimes difficult to enforce
(D) it is sometimes difficult to enforce laws
(E) this is sometimes difficult for them to enforce

13. <u>Fame as well as fortune were his goals</u> in life.

(A) Fame as well as fortune were his goals
(B) Fame as well as fortune was his goals
(C) Fame as well as fortune were his goal
(D) Fame and fortune were his goals
(E) Fame also fortune were his goals

14. Familiar with the terrain from previous visits, <u>the explorer's search for the abandoned mine site was a success</u>.

(A) the explorer's search for the abandoned mine site was a success
(B) the success of the explorer's search for the abandoned mine site was assured
(C) the explorer succeeded in finding the abandoned mine site
(D) the search by the explorer for the abandoned mine was successful
(E) the explorer in his search for the abandoned mine site was a success

15. <u>My plane was grounded for thirty minutes at Chicago, which made me miss</u> my connecting flight.

(A) My plane was grounded for thirty minutes at Chicago, which made me miss
(B) My plane was grounded for thirty minutes at Chicago, missing
(C) My plane was grounded for thirty minutes at Chicago, and because of that missed
(D) Because my plane was grounded for thirty minutes at Chicago, I missed
(E) Because my plane was grounded for thirty minutes at Chicago, it made me miss

16. During the first year that he and I were neighbors, our conversations turned frequently on the two cardinal points of poetry: the power of exciting the sympathy of the reader by a faithful adherence to the truth of nature and the <u>power to give</u> the interest of novelty by the modifying colors of imagination.

(A) power to give
(B) ability to give
(C) power to bestow
(D) ability to bestow
(E) power of giving

17. Modernization has gone hand in hand <u>and has offered incentives for such things as personal initiative and ambition, hard work, and resourcefulness</u>.

(A) and has offered incentives for such things as personal initiative and ambition, hard work, and resourcefulness
(B) with and has offered incentives for such things as personal initiative and ambition, hard work, and resourcefulness
(C) with and has offered incentives for such things as personal initiative and ambition, hard work, and the ability to be resourceful
(D) and has offered incentives such as personal initiative and ambition, hard work, and resourcefulness
(E) and is offering incentives for such things as personal initiative and ambition, hard work, and resourcefulness

18. A private corporation with only seven permanent employees launched a spacecraft made out of surplus rocket parts from a cattle ranch here today, ushering in what its promoters believe will be a new era of commercial exploitation of space technology.

   (A) A private corporation with only seven permanent employees launched a spacecraft made out of surplus rocket parts from a cattle ranch here today
   (B) Although it has only seven permanent employees, a private corporation launched a spacecraft made out of surplus rocket parts from a cattle ranch here today
   (C) From a cattle ranch here today, a private corporation with only seven permanent employees launched a spacecraft made out of surplus rocket parts
   (D) A private corporation with only seven permanent employees launched a spacecraft from a cattle ranch here today made out of surplus rocket parts
   (E) Made out of surplus rocket parts, a private corporation with only seven permanent employees launched a spacecraft from a cattle ranch here today

19. My objection to him taking part in this dispute is based on my belief that he is not a disinterested party.

   (A) My objection to him taking part in this dispute is based on my belief that he is not a disinterested party.
   (B) My objection to his taking part in this dispute is based on my belief that he is not a disinterested party.
   (C) My objection to him taking part in this dispute is based on my belief that he is not an uninterested party.
   (D) My objection to his taking part in this dispute is based on my belief that he is not an uninterested party.
   (E) I object to him taking part in this dispute because he is not a disinterested party.

20. Of the two candidates for this government position, Jason Harald is the most qualified because of his experience in the field.

   (A) most qualified because of
   (B) most qualified due to
   (C) more qualified due to
   (D) more qualified because of
   (E) most qualified as a result of

21. If anyone calls while we are in conference, tell them that I will return their call after the meeting.

   (A) them that I will return their call after the meeting
   (B) him or her that I will return their call after the meeting
   (C) them that I would return their call after the meeting
   (D) the person that I will return the call after the meeting
   (E) him or her that I would return the call after the meeting is over

22. Neither the earthquake or the subsequent fire was able to destroy the spirit of the city dwellers.

   (A) or the subsequent fire was
   (B) nor the subsequent fire were
   (C) or the subsequent fire were
   (D) nor the subsequent fire was
   (E) or the fire that occurred subsequently were

23. The Secretary of State reminded his listeners that this country <u>always has and always will try to honor</u> its commitments.

(A) always has and always will try to honor
(B) has always and will always try to honor
(C) always has tried and always will try to honor
(D) always has tried to honor and will always
(E) has always tried to honor and will always

24. Meanwhile, declining values for farm equipment and land—the collateral against which farmers borrow to get through the harvest season—<u>are going to force many lenders to tighten or deny</u> credit this spring.

(A) are going to force many lenders to tighten or deny
(B) is going to force many lenders to tighten or deny
(C) are the reason why many lenders will have to tighten or deny
(D) is the reason why many lenders will have to tighten or deny
(E) is going to force many lenders into tightening or denying

25. Tests show that catfish from Lake Apopka are safe to eat, even though they contain almost twice as much of the pesticide DDT this year <u>than they did</u> in 1982.

(A) than they did
(B) more than they did
(C) as they did
(D) than they had contained
(E) than they contained

If there is still time remaining, you may review the questions in this section only.
You may not turn to any other section of the test.

Section VI   Analysis of Situations

TIME: 30 minutes

DIRECTIONS: Read the following passages. After you have completed each one, you will be asked to answer questions that involve determining the importance of specific factors included in the passage. When answering questions, you may consult the passage.

Passage 1:

The second day of Vespucci SpA's annual sales conference in Milan threatened to end in uproar. The business equipment manufacturer's 28 salesmen had received sales manager Guido Tulli's proposal to re-assign them to new territories with angry condemnation.

Explaining the reasons behind the drastic measures, Tulli had reminded the salesmen that the company was suffering from declining sales and had a serious cash flow problem. This was mainly due to slow payments by customers. Accounts receivable were increasing at an alarming rate, he had told them.

Under Tulli's plan, the company's top salesmen were to be switched from the areas with high sales to areas that currently yielded low sales. He had explained that this would mean that the more experienced salesmen could concentrate on building up sales in the less productive regions. The less experienced salesmen could easily handle the well-developed territories.

Some of the firm's leading salesmen immediately started to object. "I have spent years building up my territory," one of them protested. "I do not see why I should have to start all over again in a new region."

Tulli pointed out that he felt that the firm's best salesmen were being wasted in these well-developed sales regions. "You are simply going to well-established customers and taking orders," he argued.

An experienced salesman contested this view, observing that he had greatly increased sales in his territory the previous year by persuading existing customers to expand the amount of their orders in business stationery.

This supported his view, retorted Tulli, that the salesmen in the well-established territories were becoming stale, and were failing to uncover new customers. "This is only natural," he added. "When I was promoted to the sales manager, I was amazed at how successful my successor was in getting new orders in my old territory. The company badly needs your experience to develop the weaker regions."

Another experienced salesman asked whether the new plan would mean that salesmen would get an extra bonus or higher commission rates for establishing new accounts. Tulli began to explain why he thought this was impractical, when he was interrupted by one of the younger salesmen who had been sitting at the back of the room quietly fuming. He told Tulli that he felt completely demotivated by the proposal to remove them from the undeveloped territories.

Tulli tried to reassure the young salesman that the company did not regard them as failures. The changes were being made simply because the company was having difficulties, and needed to boost sales quickly, he pointed out.

Tulli swallowed hard before announcing another new policy he knew was likely to upset the gathered salesmen. "The management board has also decided that in future sales commissions will be paid quarterly and only on those orders for which payments have been received from customers," he announced nervously. "As from today it will be your responsibility to raise the subject of slow payments with customers. Moreover, no new orders will be accepted from customers until all overdue payments are received."

This was too much for the salesmen to take and the meeting erupted into a noisy uproar. "Why shouldn't we be paid for orders we have succeeded in getting?" demanded one salesman furiously. "It is not our job to collect debts," protested another. "This contravenes our employment contract," shouted yet another.

The salesmen were all talking agitatedly at once when Tulli decided to close the proceedings for that day. He rushed to a nearby hotel where group managing director Leon Cavello was staying overnight. He was due to address the conference the following morning.

"Our proposals have met with even more hostility than we expected," Tulli told Cavello, relating how the meeting had broken up in disorder. "I'm afraid you will have a hard time of it tomorrow convincing them that the proposals are in everybody's interest. But I don't think we can dodge the issue now. We have to tackle it while we have them all together."

Cavello nodded gravely. His first inclination was to proceed with the proposals whether or not the salesmen approved. On the other hand, he reflected, salesmen are the key to a company's success. It might be unwise to impose a new system on them without their consent.

Cavello convinced Tulli that his plan, presented during the day at the sales meeting, could not be implemented because of the unequivocal opposition of the salesmen. A compromise plan had to be worked out. Tulli and Cavello worked long into the night putting together a plan which they believed would be acceptable to most of the salesmen and in harmony with the company's objectives.

Tulli suggested assigning quotas to salesmen in existing territories rather than shifting successful salesmen from high-sales territories. "By assigning quotas, we can measure individual performance and motivate salesmen towards a predetermined level of achievement. Annual quotas based on expected sales also help in planning production, inventory, and working capital needs. Shifting salesmen is easier under a quota system because quotas can be easily adjusted to reflect the area's potential. If a low-yielding territory has low sales potential, the quota would be relatively lower than in a high-yielding, high-potential territory."

Cavello agreed that a quota system might be the solution to their sales problem. However, quotas had some disadvantages. "Companies sometimes set lower quotas for less able salesmen, but this can be demoralizing. Better salesmen will feel that they are being discriminated against. They will not give their best effort under such a plan." Tulli insisted that a quota system would work. "We need to find a plan which will motivate our best as well as our younger, less experienced salesmen."

Cavello summarized the available options. The first option was a straight commission plan. No matter how much sales a salesman produced over his quota, he would earn the same commission rate. A second possibility was a combination of salary and commissions. "Salesmen drawing even nominal salaries tend to think as company men and they have less reason to resist sales plan changes that are justified in terms of goals." Cavello further pointed out that special incentives could be offered under such a plan, such as a new account bonus or higher commission rates for sales over 100% of quota. "By offering such incentives," Cavello added, "salesmen in less productive regions would be motivated to spend more time in building new accounts."

Tulli agreed that both options suggested by Cavello might be accepted by the salesmen. "But," he asked, "are these options better for the company than the ones I proposed today?"

DIRECTIONS: The questions that follow relate to the preceding passage. Evaluate, in terms of the passage, each of the items given. Then select your answer from one of the following classifications, and blacken the corresponding space on the answer sheet.

(A) A MAJOR OBJECTIVE in making the decision: one of the goals sought by the decision maker

(B) A MAJOR FACTOR in making the decision: an aspect of the problem, specifically mentioned in the passage, that fundamentally affects and/or determines the decision

(C) A MINOR FACTOR in making the decision: a less important element bearing on or affecting a Major Factor, rather than a Major Objective directly

(D) A MAJOR ASSUMPTION in making the decision: a projection or supposition arrived at by the decision maker before considering the factors and alternatives

(E) AN UNIMPORTANT ISSUE in making the decision: an item lacking significant impact on, or relationship to, the decision

1. Vespucci SpA's declining sales

2. Vespucci's accounts receivable problem

3. Vespucci's Italian location

4. Improved cash flow

5. Ease with which salesmen may be shifted under a quota system

6. Development of new customers

7. Late payments by customers

8. Ability of top salesmen to succeed in any territory

9. Assignment of quotas to salesmen

10. Flexibility in setting quotas at either high or low levels

11. Measurement of salesmen's individual performances

12. Likelihood that salesmen will accept Cavello's options

13. Disadvantages of sales quotas

14. Tulli's experience in dealing with salesmen

15. Number of salesmen working for Vespucci

16. Motivation of Vespucci salesmen

17. Planning production, inventory, and working capital

18. Rejection of Tulli's plan by salesmen

Passage 2:

Mr. Mark Davidson is the Vice-President and General Manager of the International Division of the Doltry Mining Company. His chief responsibility is choosing investment opportunities for the company, which has recently been investigating different sites for the establishmet of a new mining facility. Doltry has been trying to adopt a global planning strategy whereby the enterprise makes its major business decisions of allocating limited resources by considering global opportunities and alternatives as well as future global consequences. For each project, all possible alternatives are to be sorted out and compared as to profitability potential and consequences for achieving the firm's goals. The decision should not be biased as to which country is chosen, but rather, should rest on the site's potential of profitability to the company.

In order to insure a clear, unbiased opinion, some precautions were taken. One of the major safeguards Doltry used was the replacement of the names of the countries with letters. Another safeguard implemented was to limit the amount of information given on the countries Davidson was required to choose from. Furthermore, Davidson's choices only included the three countries that Doltry felt were most viable.

Unknown to Davidson, the first alternative given, Country A, was his home country, the United States. Country B was described as a lesser developed country, and Country C was described as an advanced country.

The information given on Country A include a sizeable deficit in the current account balance. This deficit was caused, in major part, by changes in operating performance, specifically owing to the deteriorating merchandise trade. Eventually, imports had exceeded exports; thereby, a major earnings contributor was eliminated. The reason cited for this change was increased foreign competition in export markets. Other factors in the current account included services and interest income from abroad. These factors were positive—i.e., earnings exceeded payments. However, the net earnings have not been large enough to offset the deficit in the merchandise account.

Another factor even more important was the country's weak liquidity position. Foreigners questioned whether this trend would ever reverse itself. They feared Country A might not be able to meet its obligations upon demand. On a more positive note, assets still exceeded liabilities.

Mr. Davidson was further given some information on Country A's political risk. Expropriation in Country A was seldomly enacted and when it had been, adequate compensation was provided. There were few political forces hostile toward foreign enterprise. Corruption and scandal seemed abnormally high in recent years. Only a limited amount of nationalistic philosophy was observed.

In the past ten years, there were no examples of armed conflict. For the most part, law enforcement was effective. Political uncertainty was minimal, as most citizens felt fairly confident with their government. Internal violence has been minimal. There have been few armed uprisings or assassinations. While police and internal security forces are strong, they are rarely used.

Country A has experienced a small but consistent growth pattern in gross national product per capita for the last seven years. Energy consumption has been increasing quite rapidly. There is one basic language in Country A, which is used by most people, even though many nationalities coexist in this country.

Extensive political competition exists and is encouraged. Legislative effectiveness, in theory, makes good sense; in actuality, however, the laws are difficult to enforce. There have been few constitutional changes in recent years. There is a set routine with regard to changing the head of state; however, some deviations have occurred. Mr. Davidson believed that Country A was a good political and economic risk.

Mr. Davidson's second alternative was Country B, a less developed country (LDC). The balance of payments information given Davidson had been obtained from the central bank. Country B's financial situation as indicated by its balance of payments was analyzed first. Data were only available for the past three years. These data showed an extremely high deficit for the first year, slightly lower the second year, and substantially lower the third year. SEE CHART BELOW. This deficit was caused by the development process which Country B was in the middle of. Davidson thought that, although Country B's current account was in deficit, imports were being used for industrialization. This growth process was a sign of strength.

Current Account Balance
For Country B
In Millions of Dollars

Year 1	Year 2	Year 3
−1,028	−986	−684

For an LDC, the balance of payments data were relatively favorable. However, political risks still had to be considered. Analyzing political risks gave some insight into Country B. There were little political turmoil and no recorded takeovers of private enterprises. The possibility of expropriation was believed to be nonexistent in the near future because of the lack of mining technology and capital available in Country B. Fear of future nationalistic feelings and a conviction that natural resource endowments should be exploited for the welfare of the residents of Country B, rather than for private profit, are shared by all managers of extractive industries there. It is believed that Country B would not have sufficient skills in the techniques of mining for approximately six years. Thus, fear of expropriation would not be present for this time period. Growth in gross national product per capita was extremely high. Energy consumption per capita, however, was relatively low.

As a result of the need for capital and technology, Country B would welcome foreign investment. Latent hostility would be minimal. Political stability was strengthened by the fact that a common goal was present.

Measures of societal conflict and government processes were considered by Davidson as indicators of the political climate. Public unrest and internal violence were barely existent. There were no irregular changes in heads of state ever recorded. These were positive indications of stability. Davidson also recommended that Doltry consider investing in Country B.

Finally, Country C, considered an advanced country, was analyzed. The balance of payments statistics were quite impressive. The current account surplus was increasing rapidly and approaching one billion dollars. If Country C were a company, it would be very profitable. Exports have exceeded imports for the past nine years.

Liquidity was not a problem in Country C. There was a good amount of capital in long-term investments. The country never had trouble paying its debts on time and, therefore, never accumulated much interest costs. One of the country's top priorities was to pay debts as soon as they were due. Country C also appeared to be in an excellent position for a loan, should it need one.

The problems of Country C lie in the instability of the government. Country C's recent political independence has contributed greatly to this problem. The lack of experienced political leadership has created considerable turmoil. This lack is due to the fact that there are many small parties. There is ineffective law enforcement, and this can adversely affect production, communication, and transportation.

There have been numerous reports of public unrest. Violent rioting and many organized demonstrations have created an uneasy feeling among the citizens. Internal violence has included three assassinations in the past five years. Limited security forces have certainly been one of the main causes of Country C's problems.

Legislative ineffectiveness in both the enactment stage and the carrying-out stage has done further damage to the country. The lack of a constitution and the irregular changes in heads of state have made Country C unstable. Although Country C has a strong economy, its political instability led Davidson to submit a negative recommendation as an investment opportunity.

DIRECTIONS: The questions that follow relate to the preceding passage. Evaluate, in terms of the passage, each of the items given. Then select your answer from one of the following classifications, and blacken the corresponding space on the answer sheet.

(A) A MAJOR OBJECTIVE in making the decision: one of the goals sought by the decision maker

(B) A MAJOR FACTOR in making the decision: an aspect of the problem, specifically mentioned in the passage, that fundamentally affects and/or determines the decision

(C) A MINOR FACTOR in making the decision: a less important element bearing on or affecting a Major Factor, rather than a Major Objective directly

(D) A MAJOR ASSUMPTION in making the decision: a projection or supposition arrived at by the decision maker before considering the factors and alternatives

(E) AN UNIMPORTANT ISSUE in making the decision: an item lacking significant impact on, or relationship to, the decision

19. Global planning strategy

20. Country A's deteriorating merchandise trade balance

21. Expropriation in Country A

22. Country A's liquidity position

23. Country A's political risk

24. Only one language in Country A

25. Country A, a good political risk

26. Likelihood of expropriation in Country B

27. Country B, a Less Developed Country

28. Country B's balance of payments position

29. Measures of societal conflict

30. Changes in heads of state

31. Selecting investment opportunities

32. Instability of Country C's government

33. Number of political parties in Country C

34. The fact that Country A was Davidson's home country

35. The number of political parties

If there is still time remaining, you may review the questions in this section only.
You may not turn to any other section of the test.

Section VII   Data Sufficiency

TIME: 30 minutes

DIRECTIONS: Each of the following problems has a question and two statements which are labeled (1) and (2). Use the data given in (1) and (2) together with other available information (such as the number of hours in a day, the definition of *clockwise*, mathematical facts, etc.) to decide whether the statements are *sufficient* to answer the question. Then fill in space

(A) if you can get the answer from (1) alone but not from (2) alone;

(B) if you can get the answer from (2) alone but not from (1) alone;

(C) if you can get the answer from (1) and (2) together, although neither statement by itself suffices;

(D) if statement (1) alone suffices *and* statement (2) alone suffices;

(E) if you cannot get the answer from statements (1) and (2) together, but need even more data.

All numbers used in this section are real numbers. A figure given for a problem is intended to provide information consistent with that in the question, but not necessarily with the additional information contained in the statements.

1. k is an integer. Is k divisible by 8?

   (1) k is divisible by 4.
   (2) k is divisible by 16.

2. How much is the average salary of the 30 assembly workers? The foreman is paid a salary of $12,000.

(1) The total salary paid to the 30 assembly workers and the foreman is $312,000.
(2) The foreman's salary is 120% of the average salary of the 30 assembly workers.

3. How far is it from town *A* to town *B*? Town *C* is 12 miles east of town *A*.

(1) Town *C* is south of town *B*.
(2) It is 9 miles from town *B* to town *C*.

4. How many vinyl squares with sides 5 inches long will be needed to cover the rectangular floor of a room?

(1) The floor is 10 feet long.
(2) The floor is 5 feet wide.

5. Mary must work 15 hours to make in wages the cost of a set of luggage. How many dollars does the set of luggage cost?

(1) Jim must work 12 hours to make in wages the cost of the set of luggage.
(2) Jim's hourly wage is 125% of Mary's hourly wage.

6. What is the value of *x*?

(1) $\dfrac{x}{y} = 3$
(2) $x - y = 9$

7. Is *DE* parallel to *AB*?

(1) $CD = DA$
(2) $CE = EB$

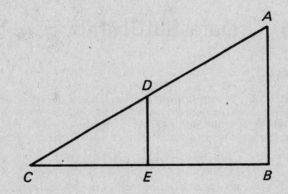

8. How many of the numbers *x* and *y* are positive? Both *x* and *y* are less than 20.

(1) *x* is less than 5.
(2) $x + y = 24$

9. What is the value of *x*? $PS = SR$.

(1) $y = 30$
(2) $PQ = QR$

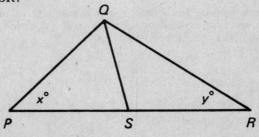

10. How much does the first volume of a 5-volume work weigh?

(1) The first 3 volumes weigh 4 pounds.
(2) The second, third and fourth volumes weigh a total of 3½ pounds.

11. How much wood will it take to make a rectangular box with a top?

(1) The area of the bottom is 4 square feet.
(2) The area of one side is 6 square feet.

12. A sequence of numbers is given by the rule $a_n = a_{n-1} + 2$. Is a_{10} an even integer?

(1) a_1 is an even integer.
(2) a_9 is 24.

13. Which side of triangle ABC is the longest? $y = 40°$.

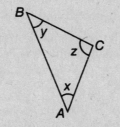

(1) $z > y$
(2) $x = 40°$

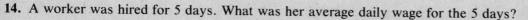

14. A worker was hired for 5 days. What was her average daily wage for the 5 days?

(1) She was paid a total of $500 for the 5 days.
(2) She earned $100 the first day and $100 the last day.

15. If $x = k$, is the expression $x^3 + ax^2 + bx$ equal to zero?

(1) $a = 0$
(2) $-b = k^2$

16. A crate of oranges costs $1.00. What percentage of the cost of an orange is the selling price of an orange?

(1) The oranges are sold for 6¢ each.
(2) There are 20 oranges in a crate.

17. What is the area of rectangle $ABCD$?

(1) $AC = 5$
(2) $AB = 4$

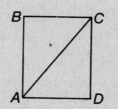

18. Is $xy < 0$?

(1) $x > 2$
(2) $y > -1$

19. Which is larger, a^b or b^a? $a > 0$ and $b > 0$.

(1) $a = 1$
(2) $b > 2$

20. Is x greater than y?

(1) $xy = 5$
(2) $x/y = 2$

21. *ABCD* is a square. What is the area of the triangle *ABE*?

    (1) $AB = 10$
    (2) $CE = DE$

22. Is x greater than y?

    (1) $x = 2y$
    (2) $x = y + 2$

23. A group of 49 consumers were offered a chance to subscribe to 3 magazines: A, B, and C. 38 of the consumers subscribed to at least one of the magazines. How many of the 49 consumers subscribed to exactly two of the magazines?

    (1) Twelve of the 49 consumers subscribed to all three of the magazines.
    (2) Twenty of the 49 consumers subscribed to magazine A.

24. Is k an odd integer?

    (1) k is divisible by 3.
    (2) The square root of k is an integer divisible by 3.

25. Which of the four numbers w, x, y, and z is the largest?

    (1) The average of w, x, y, and z is 25.
    (2) The numbers w, x, and y are each less than 24.

If there is still time remaining, you may review the questions in this section only.
You may not turn to any other section of the test.

Section VIII   Problem Solving

TIME: 30 minutes

DIRECTIONS: Solve each of the following problems; then indicate the correct answer on your answer sheet. [On the actual exam you will be permitted to use any space available on the examination paper for scratch work.]
NOTE: A figure that appears with a problem is drawn as accurately as possible unless the words "figure not drawn to scale" appear next to the figure.
Numbers in this test are real numbers.

1. The amount of coal necessary to heat a home cost $53.00 in 1972 and will increase at the rate of 15% a year. The amount of oil necessary to heat the same home cost $45.00 in 1972 but will increase at the rate of 20% a year. In 1974 which of the following methods would heat the home for the cheapest price?

    (A) Use of only coal
    (B) Use of only oil
    (C) Use of coal or oil since they cost the same amount
    (D) Use of oil for 8 months and coal for 4 months
    (E) Use of coal for 8 months and oil for 4 months

2. If the side of a square increases by 30%, then its area increases by

(A) 9%
(B) 30%
(C) 60%
(D) 69%
(E) 130%

3. Train Y leaves New York at 1 A.M. and travels east at an average speed of x mph. If train Z leaves New York at 2 A.M. and travels east, at what average rate of speed will train Z have to travel in order to catch train Y at exactly 5:30 A.M.?

(A) $\frac{5}{6}x$

(B) $\frac{9}{8}x$

(C) $\frac{6}{5}x$

(D) $\frac{9}{7}x$

(E) $\frac{3}{2}x$

Use this graph for question 4.

ANTIPOLLUTION FUNDING DURING THE 70s
(cost in billions of dollars for 1971–1980)

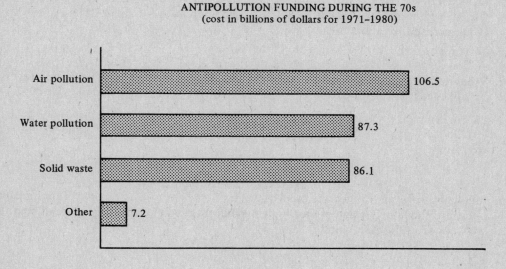

4. The ratio of air pollution funding to water pollution funding is about

(A) 2 to 1
(B) 3 to 2
(C) 6 to 5
(D) 5 to 6
(E) 2 to 3

5. If 30 boxes of pencils cost a total of $5.10, then 4 boxes of pencils should cost

(A) 52¢
(B) 68¢
(C) 78¢
(D) 85¢
(E) 93¢

6. A worker is paid r dollars for each hour he works up to 8 hours a day. For any time worked over 8 hours he is paid at the rate of $(1.5)r$ dollars an hour. The total amount of dollars the worker will earn if he works 11 hours in a day is

(A) $(4.5)r$
(B) $(5.5)r$
(C) $(9.25)r$
(D) $(11)r$
(E) $(12.5)r$

7. If the product of 3 consecutive integers is 120, then the sum of the integers is

(A) 9
(B) 12
(C) 14

(D) 15
(E) 18

Use the table below for questions 8 and 9.

Grants from the *XYZ* Foundation	1971	1972
Colleges	5.2	4.9
Medical research	3.1	3.5
Other	1.7	1.8
Total	10.0	10.2

8. Medical research grants between 1971 and 1972

(A) decreased by 4%
(B) stayed about the same
(C) increased by about 10%

(D) increased by about 13%
(E) increased by about 21%

9. What percentage of the total grants of the *XYZ* Foundation for both years was received by colleges?

(A) 49.8
(B) 50
(C) 50.2

(D) 50.5
(E) 51

10. Mechanics are paid twice the hourly wage of salesmen. Custodial workers are paid one-third the hourly wage of mechanics. What fraction of the hourly wage of custodial workers are salesmen paid?

(A) ⅓
(B) ½
(C) ⅔

(D) 4/3
(E) 3/2

11. If x and y are negative, then which of the following statements is (are) always true?

I. $x + y$ is positive
II. xy is positive
III. $x - y$ is positive

(A) I only
(B) II only
(C) III only

(D) I and III only
(E) II and III only

12. An unloaded truck travels 10 miles on a gallon of gas. When the same truck is loaded it travels only 85% as far on a gallon of gas. How many gallons (to the nearest hundredth) of gas will the loaded truck use to travel 50 miles?

(A) 5
(B) 5.67
(C) 5.88

(D) 6.02
(E) 6.3

13. If $8a = 6b$ and $3a = 0$ then

(A) a and b are equal   (D) $a = 6$ and $b = 8$

(B) $a = 6$

(C) $\dfrac{b}{a} = \dfrac{4}{3}$ (E) $\dfrac{a}{b} = \dfrac{3}{4}$

14. A horse can travel at the rate of 5 miles per hour for the first two hours of a trip. After the first two hours the horse's speed drops to 3 miles per hour. How many hours will it take the horse to travel 20 miles?

(A) 4   (B) 5   (C) 5⅓   (D) 5½   (E) 5⅔

Use the following table for question 15.

THE BUDGET DOLLAR

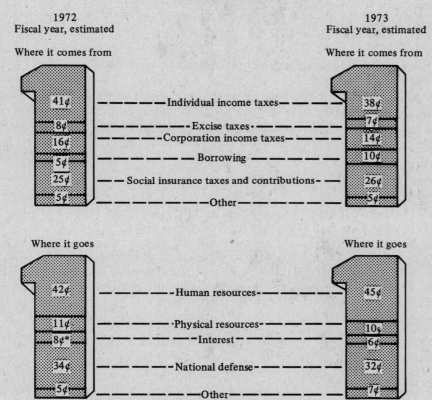

*Excludes interest paid to trust funds

©1973 by the New York Times Company. Reprinted by permission.

15. Which of the following statements can be inferred from the graph?

  I. The amount of money collected from excise taxes declined from 1972 to 1973.

 II. The government will borrow twice as much money in 1973 as it did in 1972.

III. Of the total amount of income in 1972 and 1973, 15% came from Corporation Income Taxes.

(A) None

(B) III only

(C) I and II only

(D) II and III only

(E) I, II, and III

16. If the ratio of the radii of two circles is 3 to 2, then the ratio of the areas of the two circles is

(A) 2 to 3 (D) 9 to 4
(B) 3 to 4 (E) 3 to 2
(C) 4 to 9

17. -5 times (-4) is

(A) -20 (D) -54
(B) 54 (E) -5
(C) 20

18. If $\dfrac{1}{x} < \dfrac{1}{y}$ then

(A) $x > y$
(B) x and y are negative
(C) x and y are positive
(D) $x < y$
(E) none of the preceding statements follows

19. A manufacturer of boxes wants to make a profit of x dollars. When he sells 5,000 boxes it costs 5¢ a box to make the first 1,000 boxes and then it costs y¢ a box to make the remaining 4,000 boxes. What price in dollars should he charge for the 5,000 boxes?

(A) $5,000 + 1,000y$
(B) $5,000 + 1,000y + 100x$
(C) $50 + 10y + x$
(D) $5,000 + 4,000y + x$
(E) $50 + 40y + x$

20. A clothing manufacturer has determined that she can sell 100 suits a week at a selling price of $200 each. For each rise of $4 in the selling price she will sell 2 less suits a week. If she sells the suits for x each, how many dollars a week will she receive from sales of the suits?

(A) $x^2/2$ (D) $150x - x^2/4$
(B) $200 - x/2$ (E) $200x - x^2/2$
(C) $50x + x^2/4$

If there is still time remaining, you may review the questions in this section only.
You may not turn to any other section of the test.

Answers

Section I Reading Comprehension

1.	**(C)**	8.	**(C)**	15.	**(C)**	22.	**(A)**
2.	**(B)**	9.	**(A)**	16.	**(B)**	23.	**(C)**
3.	**(A)**	10.	**(D)**	17.	**(D)**	24.	**(C)**
4.	**(E)**	11.	**(E)**	18.	**(A)**	25.	**(C)**
5.	**(A)**	12.	**(D)**	19.	**(E)**		
6.	**(B)**	13.	**(E)**	20.	**(A)**		
7.	**(B)**	14.	**(A)**	21.	**(C)**		

Section II Problem Solving

(Numbers in parentheses indicate the section in the Mathematics Review where material concerning the question is discussed.)

1.	**(D)** (I-4)	6.	**(E)** (IV-1)	11.	**(C)** (II-2)	16.	**(C)** (IV-4)
2.	**(A)** (II-2)	7.	**(E)** (IV-1)	12.	**(B)** (III-4)	17.	**(A)** (IV-4)
3.	**(C)** (II-3)	8.	**(E)** (IV-1)	13.	**(D)** (II-6)	18.	**(D)** (III-4)
4.	**(D)** (I-4)	9.	**(C)** (III-7)	14.	**(B)** (II-2, 3)	19.	**(A)** (I-4)
5.	**(A)** (II-3)	10.	**(C)** (II-2, 3)	15.	**(E)** (IV-4)	20.	**(D)** (II-3)

Section III Analysis of Situations

1.	**(B)**	11.	**(D)**	21.	**(E)**	31.	**(D)**
2.	**(E)**	12.	**(E)**	22.	**(E)**	32.	**(C)**
3.	**(A)**	13.	**(C)**	23.	**(A)**	33.	**(E)**
4.	**(B)**	14.	**(B)**	24.	**(B)**	34.	**(A)**
5.	**(E)**	15.	**(B)**	25.	**(A)**	35.	**(D)**
6.	**(B)**	16.	**(C)**	26.	**(E)**		
7.	**(A)**	17.	**(E)**	27.	**(D)**		
8.	**(E)**	18.	**(C)**	28.	**(A)**		
9.	**(C)**	19.	**(B)**	29.	**(B)**		
10.	**(E)**	20.	**(B)**	30.	**(E)**		

Section IV Data Sufficiency

1.	**(D)**	8.	**(E)**	15.	**(A)**	22.	**(A)**
2.	**(A)**	9.	**(A)**	16.	**(D)**	23.	**(E)**
3.	**(D)**	10.	**(C)**	17.	**(B)**	24.	**(C)**
4.	**(C)**	11.	**(D)**	18.	**(A)**	25.	**(E)**
5.	**(B)**	12.	**(C)**	19.	**(E)**		
6.	**(C)**	13.	**(B)**	20.	**(A)**		
7.	**(D)**	14.	**(D)**	21.	**(C)**		

Section V   Writing Ability

1. (B)	8. (A)	15. (D)	22. (D)
2. (C)	9. (D)	16. (E)	23. (C)
3. (B)	10. (B)	17. (B)	24. (A)
4. (A)	11. (A)	18. (C)	25. (C)
5. (D)	12. (C)	19. (B)	
6. (C)	13. (D)	20. (D)	
7. (E)	14. (C)	21. (D)	

Section VI   Analysis of Situations

1. (B)	11. (A)	21. (C)	31. (A)
2. (B)	12. (D)	22. (B)	32. (B)
3. (E)	13. (B)	23. (B)	33. (C)
4. (A)	14. (E)	24. (E)	34. (E)
5. (C)	15. (E)	25. (D)	35. (C)
6. (A)	16. (A)	26. (D)	
7. (C)	17. (C)	27. (E)	
8. (D)	18. (B)	28. (B)	
9. (A)	19. (A)	29. (B)	
10. (E)	20. (C)	30. (C)	

Section VII   Data Sufficiency

1. (B)	8. (B)	15. (C)	22. (B)
2. (D)	9. (C)	16. (C)	23. (E)
3. (C)	10. (E)	17. (C)	24. (E)
4. (C)	11. (E)	18. (E)	25. (C)
5. (E)	12. (D)	19. (C)	
6. (C)	13. (B)	20. (E)	
7. (C)	14. (A)	21. (A)	

Section VIII   Problem Solving

(Numbers in parentheses indicate the section in the Mathematics Review where material concerning the question is discussed.)

1. (B) (I-4)	6. (E) (II-3)	11. (B) (I-6)	16. (D) (III-7, II-5)
2. (D) (III-7)	7. (D) (I-1)	12. (C) (I-2)	17. (C) (I-6)
3. (D) (II-3)	8. (D) (IV-1)	13. (A) (I-2, II-2)	18. (E) (II-7)
4. (C) (IV-3, II-5)	9. (B) (IV-1)	14. (C) (II-3)	19. (E) (I-4, II-3)
5. (B) (II-5)	10. (E) (II-3)	15. (A) (IV-2)	20. (E) (II-1, 3)

Analysis

Section I   Reading Comprehension

1. **(C)** See the second sentence of paragraph 1.

2. **(B)** Paragraph 2: ". . . governments of most high-income countries have in recent years undertaken important aid programs. . . ."

3. **(A)** See paragraphs 3 and 4 especially.

4. **(E)** Choices (A) and (D) are all mentioned. See paragraphs 4, 6, 7, and 8.

5. **(A)** Paragraph 6: ". . . a more efficient financial and fiscal system help[s] greatly to mobilize funds for investment" and following.

6. **(B)** See paragraph 8, the section which states that industrial growth depends upon agricultural productivity.

7. **(B)** See paragraphs 2 and especially 4: ". . . high-income countries can play only a supporting role."

8. **(C)** See paragraph 7: "The energies of the people . . . are more likely to be harnessed . . . where . . . governments aim . . . to reduce excessive social inequalities."

9. **(A)** The answer is implied in paragraph 7.

10. **(D)** Answers were idealistic (II) and self-deprecating (III), but *not* materialistic. See paragraph 2.

11. **(E)** Maritain was a political liberal (paragraph 3), not anti-Semitic (paragraph 4) nor materialstic (the "not really materialistic" reference was to the Americans—paragraph 2). There was no mention of his being a chaplain, nor can it be inferred that he was a historian.

12. **(D)** Alternatives (A) and (B) were not mentioned. In paragraph 1 the passage states that Maritain "stopped short" of stating that democracy flowed from correct philosophical principles (C). While he believed that both Communism and Fascism were irrational, no statement or inference is made of their morality (E). (D) is mentioned in paragraph 1.

13. **(E)** Catholic intellectuality was expressed as a "demonstration of the perennial relevance of the medieval philosophical achievement." See paragraph 5.

14. **(A)** Only *rationalistic* is given (in the last paragraph) among the reasons why Scholasticism was not accepted by secular thinkers.

15. **(C)** While the term "political ideologies" is mentioned in paragraph 1 in a discussion of *Integral Humanism*, it is clear that the same topic was examined in *Scholasticism and Politics*.

16. **(B)** See paragraph 6: ". . . Catholic intellectuals . . . were attracted to the movement which more usually went by that name; . . ."—i.e., existentialism.

17. **(D)** While the locus of the passage is America (A), the major theme of the passage focuses on philosophy and is stated in paragraph 5 in the reference to "Catholic intellectuality," not just Catholic thought on campus (E). Alternative (B) is too narrow. The correct answer is (D).

18. **(A)** See paragraph 1: "Light projected from a source . . . enters the cornea and lens of the eyeball."

19. **(E)** See paragraph 3, line 1.

20. **(A)** See lines 16–17: ". . . lighting designer may not be called upon to do . . . photometric curves. . . ."

21. **(C)** See paragraph 6: "Colors that have no hue are termed neutral or achromatic colors. They include . . . black."

22. **(A)** See paragraph 7: "All colored objects selectively absorb certain wave-lengths of light and reflect. . . ."

23. **(C)** See paragraph 7.

24. **(C)** See line 33: "Most paints . . . have body or pigment colors."

25. **(C)** See paragraph 5, line 1.

Section II   Problem Solving

1. **(D)** There are 50 students in the class. Since $\frac{32}{50} = .64$, females make up 64% of the class.

2. **(A)** Since y is 5 and $x + y = 2$, $x + 5 = 2$. Add -5 to each side of the equation to obtain $x = -3$. Therefore, $x - y = -3 - (5) = -8$.

3. **(C)** Since 15 is ⁵⁄₄ of 12, it takes 15 men only ⁴⁄₅ as long as 12 men to do the job, ⁴⁄₅ of 4 = 3⅕ hours, or 3 hrs. 12 min.

4. **(D)** The new price of apples is $(1.12)10¢ = 11.2¢$ each. Therefore, a dozen apples will cost $12(11.2)¢ = 134.4¢ = \$1.34$.

5. **(A)** The total length of the trip will be 120 miles. Hence to average 50 mph for the trip, he must take 2.4 hrs. total traveling time. Since he has already traveled for 1.5 hrs., he must complete the trip in $2.4 - 1.5$ or .9 hrs. or 54 min.

6. **(E)** Jan., Feb., March, April, Aug., Oct., Nov., and Dec. Notice that some months did not appear on the table since there were no major wage negotiations during those months. These months had less than 150,000 workers involved in major wage negotiations so they must be counted.

7. **(E)** The wage negotiations will involve 87,000 in Jan. and Feb., and 51,500 in May. So the total is 138,500.

8. **(E)** The Auto Workers have one agreement involving 670,250. This agreement by itself makes their coverage the largest.

9. **(C)** Area = length times width = $(L)(\frac{1}{2}L) = \frac{1}{2}L^2$.

10. **(C)** The first 100 dozen cost $(100)(50¢) = \$50$. Since the total purchase is 150 dozen, the last 50 dozen cost 47¢ each. So the total cost is $\$50.00 + 50(47¢) = \$50.00 + \$23.50 = \$73.50$.

11. **(C)** Let x be the unknown number. Then $\left(\frac{3}{2}\right)x = 5$; so $x = (5)\left(\frac{2}{3}\right) = \frac{10}{3}$. The sum of the two numbers is $x + \frac{3}{2} = \frac{10}{3} + \frac{3}{2} = \frac{29}{6} = 4\frac{5}{6}$.

12. **(B)** The length of any side of a triangle must be less than the sum of the lengths of the other two sides. Since $5 + 7 = 12$ and 10 is greater than $2 + 4$, I and II cannot be the sides of a triangle. $5 + 7$ is greater than 9, $5 + 9$ is greater than 7, and $7 + 9$ is greater than 5. Therefore, there is a triangle whose sides have lengths of 5, 7, and 9.

13. **(D)** $2 + 3 = 5$ and $5 + 3 = 8$, so the next number is $8 + 3$ or 11.

14. **(B)** Each station wagon has 4 tires and each motorcycle has 2 tires. Let x be the number of station wagons and let y be the number of motorcycles. Then $4x + 2y$ is the total number of tires which must equal $2(x + y) + 30$. Thus, $4x + 2y = 2x + 2y + 30$ yielding $4x = 2x + 30$ with $2x = 30$ or $x = 15$.

15. **(E)** (B), (C), (D) are wrong since the average rose. The drop was roughly 15 pts. between the first and second weeks in October compared to about 25 pts. between the third and fourth weeks in December.

16. **(C)** The week with lowest value was the second week in October. (Each notch between 900 and 950 indicates 5 pts.)

17. **(A)** The average closed between 960 and 1,000 only at the end of the first and second weeks of November.

18. **(D)** The square of the hypotenuse, the side opposite the right angle, equals $(5)^2 + (12)^2$ or $25 + 144$ or 169. So the length of the side opposite the right angle is $\sqrt{169}$ or 13.

19. **(A)** Price = (cost)(rate). Let x be the original cost of the skis. Then $\$160 = x(.9)$, so $x = \$177.78$. Let y be the original cost of the boots;

then $96 = y(1.2)$, so $y = \$80$. So he made $96 - \$80 = \$16$ on the boots and lost $177.78 - \$160 = \$17.78$ on the skis. Therefore, he lost $1.78.

20. **(D)** The cost in cents of printing 1000 copies equals $500(10) + (1000 - 500)\left(10 - \dfrac{x}{50}\right) = 5000 + 500\left(10 - \dfrac{x}{50}\right)$. Therefore, $7500 = 5000 + 5000 - 10x$, $10x = 2500$, and $x = 250$.

Section III   Analysis of Situations

1. **(B)** Declining sales volume was a symptom of the company's problem; therefore, it is a *Major Factor* requiring a decision as to how the decline can be corrected.

2. **(E)** Company location had no direct bearing on the issues discussed in the passage.

3. **(A)** The production of profitable ready-mixes is the *Major Objective* of management. Whether or not the decision was a correct one can be discerned by the reader; nevertheless, this is the direction in which management decided to go.

4. **(B)** The urbanization of the population, leading to the consumption of commercially baked food products, was a *Major Factor* in management's decision to manufacture a home-baking product.

5. **(E)** The increase in world trade had no direct bearing on the company's problem. As management saw it, an increase in *tariff rates* abroad had caused a decline in their overseas sales.

6. **(B)** The relatively low start-up cost was a *Major Factor* considered in the decision to produce ready-mixes. The passage states that management was "particularly receptive" to the idea of marketing a ready-mix partly because the cost of additional personnel and machinery was relatively small.

7. **(A)** Mr. Pendler raised the issue (in paragraph 5) of whether his company could develop a product that would be differentiated from competitors' products. Product differentiation was a *Major Objective*.

8. **(E)** Mr. Pendler was concerned with the cost of an advertising campaign, not primarily with its content. Although housewives were asked to recall advertising themes, the responses were not used by Mr. Pendler or Mr. Janis either in decision-making or in formulating recommendations. Therefore, the recall of advertising themes is an *Unimportant Issue*.

9. **(C)** The cost of a machine is a *Minor Factor*, whereas the *total* start-up cost is the *Major Factor*.

10. **(E)** An *Unimportant Issue*. The size of Parks's office staff was not a consideration in any decision alternative.

11. **(D)** The decision to produce ready-mixes shows that management concluded that Parks could compete with much bigger firms. This conclusion is a *Major Assumption* not supported by the facts in the passage. Mr. Pendler raised two conditions that had to be met for a "go" decision. First, Parks's product had to be differentiated from those of its competitors. The research did not reveal *how* Parks could differentiate its product. Second, the advertising campaign had to be of a magnitude that would promote market entry. Nothing was mentioned about the *magnitude* decided upon; only the target audience was determined (the economy-minded segment). To conclude, management's decision to market the product was apparently based more on intuition than on facts.

12. **(E)** Nothing in the passage suggests that any special significance should be attached to the *number* of persons interviewed in the marketing survey.

13. **(C)** A *Minor Factor*. According to Mr. Janis, one of the reasons for declining sales of Parks's baking powder was the fact that modern bakeries were producing their own powder. The *Major Factor* in the decision to produce ready-mixes was the declining sales of baking powder, not the reasons that caused it.

14. **(B)** A major consideration of Mr. Pendler was whether Parks had sufficient resources to undertake an advertising program large enough to enable the company to enter the market with its new product. The cost of the campaign, weighed against the available resources to finance it, was a *Major Factor* in the decision to produce the ready-mix.

452 • FIVE SAMPLE GMATs WITH ANSWERS AND ANALYSIS

15. **(B)** A *Major Factor* for the same reason as in question 14. Here the emphasis is on *cost*, rather than the other side of the equation—the financing of the campaign.

16. **(C)** According to Pendler, high tariff rates were one of three factors that caused a decrease in sales volume (a *Major Factor*). Therefore, the tariff was a *Minor Factor*.

17. **(E)** Parks's assembly department was not a consideration in any decision alternative and was therefore an *Unimportant Issue*.

18. **(C)** According to Janis, sales of baking powder had decreased owing to three factors, one of which was the growing popularity of ready-mixes. Since the popularity of ready-mixes was part of a *Major Factor*, it was a *Minor Factor*.

19. **(B)** The major decision to be made by Sam Hoe is whether to open a retail showroom for the sale of his custom line. He felt that this strategy might be a solution to his major problem of a declining profit position caused by higher costs. Therefore, the fact of higher production costs was a *Major Factor* in making his decision.

20. **(B)** The increased demand for furniture which Sam Hoe had experienced was a *Major Factor* leading him to consider opening a retail showroom.

21. **(E)** Storage space is an *Unimportant Issue* in making the decision; it bears no direct relation to the manufacture and sale of furniture in this problem.

22. **(E)** Mr. Hoe's workshop employed 20 craftsmen but this fact wouldn't affect the opening of a showroom. It is an *Unimportant Issue*.

23. **(A)** Sam's major decision is whether to open a retail showroom or not. This is the *Major Objective*. See the explanation to question 21.

24. **(B)** The scarcity of cabinetmakers limited Mr. Hoe's output of custom-built furniture and therefore was a *Major Factor* in his contemplation of how to increase the profitability of his standard furniture line.

25. **(A)** Improving the profitability of the firm was one of Sam Hoe's primary objectives.

26. **(E)** The number of states in which the company sells its products was an *Unimportant Issue* in the consideration of the decision alternatives.

27. **(D)** Sam Hoe believed that his standard furniture items "are popular and almost sell themselves." However, this contention is not buttressed by facts in the passage.

28. **(A)** Adding more retailers was an objective of Hoe and Norbert Ravis.

29. **(B)** The capacity of Hoe's plant to produce additional amounts of furniture was a *Major Factor* in the alternative course of action to increase sales.

30. **(E)** No special importance was attached to the fact that sales were made directly to a department store and a large retail furniture showroom (see paragraph 3).

31. **(D)** This is a *Major Assumption* because no definite facts were cited to demonstrate that skilled apprentices were actually available.

32. **(C)** Hardware costs—among other costs—were part of production costs (a *Major Factor*). Since hardware costs affected production costs, they were a *Minor Factor*.

33. **(E)** The existing storage building had an insignificant relationship to a decision alternative and was an *Unimportant Issue*. While production space was a consideration, no mention was made of the importance of storage to a decision alternative.

34. **(A)** A *Major Objective* was increasing the number of retail stores selling Hoe's products.

35. **(D)** Kander "felt" that sales could be increased by expanding custom-made merchandise. This was a *Major Assumption* not buttressed by any facts.

Section IV   Data Sufficiency

1. **(D)** Area = (length)(width) = 40(width). So to find the area we must know the width. The perimeter of a rectangle is twice (length +

width). (1) tells us the perimeter equals 140 yds. Since the length is 40 yds, the width is 30 yds, so (1) is sufficient. If we connect 2 opposite corners of the field, then it is divided into 2 right triangles where the side opposite the right angle has length 50 and one of the other sides has length 40. Since $(40)^2 +$ (width)$^2 = (50)^2$ the width is 30, and (2) is sufficient by itself.

2. **(A)** Statement (1) is $x^3 + 1 = 0$, which means $x^3 = -1$; the only solution to this equation is -1. So x is not greater than 0. Therefore, (1) alone is sufficient. Statement (2) says $x^2 - 1 = 0$ or $x^2 = 1$. There are two possible solutions to this equation, one positive and the other negative. So (2) by itself is not sufficient.

3. **(D)** Statement (1) is sufficient since it implies that A loaded 300 boxes in 30 minutes and B loaded 150 boxes. So B should take 90 minutes to load the 450 boxes by himself. (2) is also sufficient since it implies A loads 10 boxes per minute; hence A loads 300 boxes in 30 minutes, and by the above argument we can deduce that B will take 90 minutes.

4. **(C)** A cube is a solid with 6 faces, all of which are congruent squares and any two faces that intersect are perpendicular. Statement (1) is not sufficient since a solid with 2 of the faces as diamonds (rhombus) is not a cube but does satisfy (1) . Statement (2) is not sufficient since a solid with 2 or 4 of the faces as congruent rectangles is not a cube . But (1) and (2) together mean that each face is a congruent square.

5. **(B)** The first car will travel a distance equal to the circumference of the circle, which is π times the diameter. Since π is greater than $1\frac{1}{2}$, (2) is sufficient. (1) is not sufficient since one car might have traveled at a faster rate than the other.

6. **(C)** Statement (1) tells us only that $x = 6 + y$, so it is not sufficient. In the same way (2) alone will give only one of the unknowns in terms of the other. However, if we use both (1) and (2), we obtain a system of two equations which can be solved for x and y.

7. **(D)** Since we know that the sum of the angles in a triangle is $180°$ and that $x = 45$, (1) implies (2) and (2) implies (1). Either one is sufficient, since if $z = 45$, then $x = z$ and the sides opposite the equal angles are equal. Hence $AC = AB = 3$.

8. **(E)** Using (1) and (2) together it is possible to determine only the total paid in 1969 and 1971. No relation is given between the amounts paid in 1969 and 1971; thus there is not enough information to determine the cost in 1971.

9. **(A)** It costs $10 in gas, $2.50 in the tolls, and at least $5 in parking to drive each week. So driving costs at least $17.50 a week. (1) is sufficient. Without information on the price of the train ticket we cannot compare the two methods, so (2) is not sufficient.

10. **(C)** Statement (1) is not sufficient since the diagonals of *any* parallelogram bisect each other. Statement (2) is not sufficient since the other angles of the figure do not have to be right angles. However, (1) and (2) together are sufficient. Statement (1) implies the figure is a parallelogram. In a parallelogram, opposite angles are equal and the sum of all four angles must be $360°$. Thus, if one of the angles in a parallelogram is $90°$, all of the angles are right angles and the parallelogram is a rectangle.

11. **(D)** Let x be the amount he was paid on the first day; then he was paid $x + 5$, $x + 10$, $x + 15$, and $x + 20$ for the remaining days of work. The total amount he was paid is $5x + 50$. Thus if we can find x, we can find the total amount he was paid. Statement (1) is sufficient since after 3 days his total pay was $x + x + 5 + x + 10$ or $3x + 15$; this is equal to $\frac{1}{2}(5x + 50)$. So $3x + 15 = 2.5(x) + 25$ which implies $x = 20$. Statement (2) is sufficient since he was paid $x + 20$ on the last day and so $x + 20 = 2x$ which implies $x = 20$.

Remember that to answer the question it is not necessary to actually *solve* the equations given in statements 1 and 2. You only have to know that they will give you an equation which can be solved for x. Don't bother to actually solve the problem since you only have a limited amount of time to work all the questions in this section.

12. **(C)** Statement (1) alone is not sufficient since $x = 3$, $y = -1$, and $x = -1$, $y = 3$ satisfy $x + y = 2$. Statement (2) alone is not sufficient since $x = 2$, $y = 1$ and $x = -2$, $y = -1$ satisfy (2). However, since (2) says $x = 2y$, using (1) $x + y = 2y + y = 2$ we see that $y = \frac{2}{3}$ and $x = \frac{4}{3}$. So (1) and (2) together are sufficient.

13. **(B)** Area of the circle is $\pi r^2 = \pi\left(\dfrac{d}{2}\right)^2 = \dfrac{\pi}{4}d^2$ and the area of the square is s^2. Statement (2) is sufficient. $d < s$ implies $d^2 < s^2$ and $\dfrac{\pi}{4}$ is less than 1. So $\dfrac{\pi}{4}d^2 < d^2 < s^2$. (Note that since d and s are both positive $d \leq s$ does imply $d^2 < s^2$.) However, if $d < \sqrt{2}s$ then $d^2 < 2s^2$ so $\dfrac{\pi}{4}d^2 < \dfrac{\pi}{2}s^2$. But $\dfrac{\pi}{2}$ is larger than 1, so the area of the circle could be larger or smaller than s^2. Thus (1) alone is not sufficient.

14. **(D)** 10 apples will cost $1.60. Hence if we can discover the cost of three oranges we can solve the problem. Statement (1) is sufficient since (1) implies 3 oranges will cost 25¢. Statement (2) is also sufficient since we know 10 apples cost $1.60; thus (2) implies (1) which we know to be sufficient.

15. **(A)** Since 80% of $160 = $128, we know that after the first discount the skis cost less than $130. Any further discount will only lower the price. So (1) alone is sufficient. Statement (2) alone is not sufficient since if x were 10%, (2) would tell us the price was less than $130; but if x were 1%, (2) would imply that the price was greater than $130.

16. **(D)** Since $AB = JI + HG + FE + DC$, if we knew the lengths of JI, HG, FE, and DC we could find the length of AB. So we need to know both what x is and what y is. Since $DE = IH + GF$, $y = 2x$. Thus, either (1) alone or (2) alone is sufficient.

17. **(B)** Statement (1) alone is not sufficient. If $a = 70°$, $b = 25°$ and $c = 85°$, statement (1) would be true; however, if $a = 90°$, $b = 45°$, and $c = 45°$, statement (1) would also be true.

Statement (2) alone is sufficient. Since we know that the sum of the angles in a triangle is 180°, the smallest angle is always less than or equal to 60°. Notice that statement (2) gives enough information to answer the question, but the answer is *no*. Don't confuse answering a question with answering a question affirmatively.

18. **(A)** Statement (1) alone is sufficient. If a is greater than $2b$, then 2^a is greater than $2^{2b} = (2^2)^b = 4^b$, and 4^b is greater than 3^b.

Statement (2) alone is not sufficient. If $b = 1$, then a could be 4 and 2^a would be greater than 3^b; however, if $b = 6$ and $a = 9$ then $2^a = 512$ and this is not greater than $3^b = 729$.

19. **(E)** If $a = 3$, $b = 2$, and $c = 1$, then statements (1) and (2) are both true, but if $a = 2$, $b = 3$, and $c = 1$, statements (1) and (2) are still true.

20. **(A)** Statement (1) alone is sufficient. Statement (2) is not sufficient. If the radius of the circle were $\sqrt{\pi}$ then the area of the circle would be $\pi r^2 = \pi^2$, but the diameter of the circle would be $2\sqrt{\pi}$, which is greater than π. So the circle could not fit inside a square with side of length π, although the area of the square would be π^2.

21. **(C)** Statement (1) alone is not sufficient. x could be negative or positive with y positive and (1) would be true.

Statement (2) alone is not sufficient, since it gives no information about y.

Statements (1) and (2) together are sufficient. If $x > 0$ then (1) implies y is > 0, so $xy > 0$.

22. **(A)** Statement (1) alone is sufficient. If x is greater than 5, then the area must increase by more than 10%, since $(1.05s)^2 = 1.1025(s^2)$.

Statement (2) alone is not sufficient. If x is 1 then the area increases by less than 10%. However, if x is 9, then the area increases by more

23. **(E)** Statements (1) and (2) together are not sufficient. You are only given comparisons between years.

24. **(C)** Statement (1) tells us only that $x = 6 + y$, so it is not sufficient. In the same way, statement (2) alone will give only one of the unknowns in terms of the other. However, if we use both (1) and (2), we obtain a system of two equations which can be solved for x and y.

25. **(E)** Statement (1) would be sufficient if there were information about the width of each book. Since statement (2) only gives information about the *weight* of each book, both statements together are not sufficient.

Section V   Writing Ability

1. **(B)** Choice (B) includes the necessary word *other*, which makes the comparison correct. Choice (D) changes the meaning of the sentence by its implication that the wolverine is *not* an animal.

2. **(C)** The past perfect tense *had produced* is required in this sentence to show that Roentgen's work preceded that of Bequerel.

3. **(B)** Choice (A) suffers from the use of the ambiguous pronoun *they*. It is not clear whom *they* is supposed to refer to. The use of the future tense in choices (C), (D), and (E) is incorrect.

4. **(A)** Choice (A) is correct because the subject of the verb *had* must be *who*, not *whom*. *Which* in choice (E) should not be used to refer to a person.

5. **(D)** Choices (A), (B), and (E) violate the principle of parallel structure—that parts of a sentence parallel in meaning should be parallel in structure. The nouns *segregation*, *appointment*, and *prayer* should be followed by the noun *right*, rather than a clause. Choice (C) incorrectly uses *council* (an advisory or legislative body) for *counsel* (a lawyer).

6. **(C)** *Due to* in choices (A) and (D) should not be used as a substitute for *because of*. The phrase *the reason is that* (C) is preferable to *the reason is because* (B). Choice (E) is unnecessarily wordy.

7. **(E)** Choice (E) best indicates the doer of the action in the sentence.

8. **(A)** *Effect* is correct. *Affect*—choices (B), (C), and (E)—should never be used as a noun. *Humans* in choice (D) should not be used for *human beings*; also the verb tense *would have* is incorrect.

9. **(D)** Choices (A), (B), and (E) have an error in agreement: the plural verb *have been scheduled* should be the singular *has been scheduled*, because its subject, *first*, is singular. The word *and* in choices (B) and (C) is unnecessary.

10. **(B)** The *if* clause with which the sentence begins expresses a condition contrary to fact and therefore requires the subjunctive mood. Choice (B) provides the necessary subjunctive. Choice (C) changes the meaning of the sentence.

11. **(A)** Choices (B), (D), and (E) do not maintain parallel structure. The infinitive *to cut* cannot be an object of *demand*, as in choice (C); a noun clause like the one in choice (A) corrects this error.

12. **(C)** The antecedent of the pronoun *they* should be stated, not merely implied in the sentence, or a noun should be substituted in its place; choice (C) makes clear that *laws*, not *legislative effectiveness*, are what *they* referred to.

13. **(D)** In the original sentence, the subject is *fame*, a singular noun. Therefore, the verb should also be singular. This eliminates choices (A) and (C). In choice (B), *goals* should be *goal*. The word *also* in choice (E) should not be used as a conjunction.

14. **(C)** In choices (A), (B), and (D), the modifier *familiar* is dangling. The wording in choice (E) suggests that the explorer was a success, whereas the original sentence states that the search was a success—a somewhat different meaning. Choice (C) corrects the error and retains the original meaning of the sentence.

15. **(D)** In choices (A) and (E) the use of the pronoun *which* or *it* to refer to the preceding clause is incorrect (vague antecedent of pronoun error). Choice (D) corrects this. Choice (B) substitutes a dangling participial phrase, and choice (C) incorrectly says that the plane missed the connecting flight.

16. **(E)** This choice preserves the parallel structure of the sentence.

17. **(B)** The preposition *with* is needed to complete the phrase *has gone hand in hand with*. Choice (C) unnecessarily changes the single word *resourcefulness* to *the ability to be resourceful*.

18. **(C)** Choice (C) corrects the problem of the misplaced modifier.

19. **(B)** A pronoun preceding a gerund should be in the possessive case: *his taking part*. Choice (D) incorrectly substitutes *uninterested* (*indifferent*) for *disinterested* (*impartial*).

20. **(D)** The superlative *most* is incorrect here; when two are compared, *more* should be used. Choices (B) and (C) incorrectly substitute *due to* for *because of*. Choice (E) unnecessarily changes the wording.

21. **(D)** There is an error in agreement: The singular pronoun *anyone* requires a singular pronoun or noun. Although choice (B) corrects the first error (changes *them* to *his or her*), *their* should also have been changed. Choice (E) uses the wrong tense and unnecessarily adds words.

22. **(D)** The correct correlative conjunctions are *neither . . . nor*. The verb agrees with the noun that follows the correlative *nor*: *fire was*; therefore (B) is incorrect.

23. **(C)** The original sentence contains an improper ellipsis. The first verb (*has tried*) should not be cut short, because it is not in the same tense as the second one (*will try*).

24. **(A)** The original sentence is correct. The plural subject *values* requires the plural verb *are*. (C) is unnecessarily wordy.

25. **(C)** The correct expression is *as much as*.

Section VI   Analysis of Situations

1. **(B)** The company had two major problems. The first mentioned in the passage was declining sales. The only explanation found in the passage was that salesmen had not developed enough new customers. Declining sales was a *Major Factor* in Tulli's decision to reassign salesmen, although one can argue whether his decision was correct. The second problem was the factor of increasing accounts receivable, because of slow customer payments. The problem, in turn, was a symptom of declining sales.

2. **(B)** As pointed out above, increasing accounts receivables was a major company problem and was a *Major Factor* in Tulli's decision to reassign salesmen and to change the company's compensation policy.

3. **(E)** The nationality of the company is an *Unimportant Issue*.

4. **(A)** The cash shortage is the problem uppermost in management's considerations. This condition was the primary issue which led to the change in compensation policy and the reassignment of salesmen.

5. **(C)** As one of the advantages attached by Tulli to a quota system, this is a *Minor Factor* in the decision process.

6. **(A)** *Major Objective*. The development of new customers by both experienced and less experienced salesmen was an outcome desired by Tulli.

7. **(C)** *Minor Factor*. The cash flow problem was caused by slow payments by customers. See paragraph 2 and the answers to questions 1 and 5.

8. **(D)** *Major Assumption*. Under Tulli's plan, top salesmen were to be re-assigned from high to low-sales areas. The underlying assumption of Tulli was that these salesmen would succeed in low-sales territories as well. However, low sales in a territory may be more owing to a lack of potential in the territory, rather than to a lack of experience or skill on the part of the salesman.

9. **(A)** *Major Objective*. Tulli suggested assigning quotas to salesmen as a solution to the incentive problem. Cavello agreed in principle to Tulli's proposal and added some variations of his own as stated in paragraph 17ff.

10. **(E)** *Unimportant Issue*. The quota rate does not influence the decision as to whether to adopt a quota system. The issue is whether a quota system will motivate salesmen to produce more sales.

11. **(A)** Through a quota system the individual performance of salesmen can be measured. This is one of the outcomes desired by Tulli.

12. **(D)** *Major Assumption*. That salesmen will accept Cavello's options is a *belief* held by Tulli. See the last paragraph.

13. **(B)** *Major Factor*. The disadvantages of sales quotas were considered by Cavello as factors that could determine the success or failure of a possible course of action (the quota option).

14. **(E)** *Unimportant Issue.* Nothing is stated in the passage which relates Tulli's experience in dealing with salesmen to the decision process.

15. **(E)** *Unimportant Issue.* The number of salesmen—although mentioned in the passage—is unrelated to the decision process.

16. **(A)** A major prerequisite of the sales plan alternatives was that they must motivate both experienced and less experienced salesmen.

17. **(C)** Tulli's suggested plan of assigning quotas to salesmen in existing territories, rather than changing a salesman's territory, also had a side benefit. The additional benefit was that a quota system could help in planning production, inventory, and working capital needs. However, this benefit was a *Minor Factor* in the decision to adopt the plan, certainly subsidiary to the major consideration of the plan's effect on salesmen's performance and morale. See paragraph 16.

18. **(B)** Carvello concluded—and succeeded in convincing Tulli—that Tulli's reorganization plan would not be accepted by the salesmen. This was based not on mere conjecture or supposition, but on the hostility of the salesmen to the plan as demonstrated during the sales meeting. The rejection was a *Major Factor* in the decision to consider Carvello's options.

19. **(A)** Adoption of a global planning strategy is a *Major Objective* of Doltry Mining.

20. **(C)** A Major Factor in the consideration of whether to invest in Country A is the condition of its current account balance. Since merchandise is but one part or component of the current account deficit, it is a *Minor Factor*.

21. **(C)** Expropriation is one consideration of political risk and, therefore, a *Minor Factor*.

22. **(B)** Country A's liquidity position was a major consideration in Mr. Davidson's decision.

23. **(B)** Political risk is a major consideration in the investment decision.

24. **(E)** The reader is not told how language is considered or weighed in an alternative course of action. Therefore, it is an *Unimportant Issue.*

25. **(D)** Davidson's *belief* that Country A is a good political risk was based on little public unrest, political competition, and few constitutional changes of government.

26. **(D)** It was *believed* that the likelihood of expropriation in Country B was nonexistent. The key word in the question is "likelihood."

27. **(E)** It is not clear whether the fact that Country B is a less developed country (LDC) was a major or minor consideration by Davidson.

28. **(B)** Balance of payments data are a *Major Factor* in the investment decision by management.

29. **(B)** Measures of societal conflict were considered as indicators of the political climate.

30. **(C)** Changes in heads of state is one component of the governmental processes (a Major Factor).

31. **(A)** Davidson's goal or task was selecting investment opportunities.

32. **(B)** Country C's instability was a major consideration in Davidson's decision not to recommend investment there.

33. **(C)** The number of political parties in Country C is one component of political processes, a major factor.

34. **(E)** Since the identity of Country A was disguised, the fact that it was Davidson's home country did not play any part in the investment decision.

35. **(C)** The number of political parties is a function of political leadership. For example, it is mentioned in the passage (paragraph 16) that Country C has many small parties because of a lack of political leadership. This lack of leadership is a contributor to political instability—a *Major Factor* in an investment decision. Therefore, the *number* of political parties is part of a Major Factor and thus is a *Minor Factor.*

Section VII   Data Sufficiency

1. **(B)** An integer k is divisible by another integer m if $k = mr$, where r is an integer. So STATEMENT (1) implies $k = 4r$ for some integer

r. STATEMENT (1) alone is insufficient because 12 is divisible by 4 (4 · 3 = 12) but 12 is not divisible by 8.

STATEMENT (2) alone is sufficient. STATEMENT (2) implies that $k = 16r$ for some integer r, but since 16 = 8 · 2 that means $k = 8 · 2r$ and $2r$ is an integer, so k is divisible by 8.

2. **(D)** STATEMENT (1) is sufficient. Since the foreman's salary is $12,000, the total of the assembly workers' salaries is $300,000. Therefore, the average salary is $300,000 ÷ 30 = $10,000.

STATEMENT (2) is sufficient. If A is the average salary of the assembly workers, then 120% of A is $12,000. Therefore, A = $12,000 ÷ ⁶⁄₅ = $10,000.

3. **(C)** STATEMENT (2) alone is insufficient since you need to know what direction town B is from town C.

STATEMENT (1) alone is insufficient, since you need to know how far it is from town B to town C.

Using both STATEMENTS (1) and (2), A, B and C form a right triangle with legs of 9 miles and 12 miles. The distance from town A to town B is the hypotenuse of the triangle, so the distance from town A to town B is $\sqrt{9^2 + 12^2}$ = 15 miles.

4. **(C)** STATEMENTS (1) and (2) by themselves are insufficient since you need to know the area of the floor, and STATEMENT (1) only gives the length and STATEMENT (2) only gives the width. Using STATEMENTS (1) and (2) together, the area of the floor is 5 × 10 = 50 square feet. Since the area of each square is 5^2 = 25 square inches, each square has area ²⁵⁄₁₄₄ square feet. Therefore, the number of squares is 50 ÷ ²⁵⁄₁₄₄ = 288.

5. **(E)** STATEMENTS (1) and (2) only give relations between Mary's wages and Jim's wages and tell you the cost of the set of luggage in terms of hours of wages. Since there is no information about the value of the hourly wages in dollars, STATEMENTS (1) and (2) together are not sufficient.

6. **(C)** STATEMENT (1) alone implies $x = 3y$. Since there is no more information about y, STATEMENT (1) alone is insufficient.

STATEMENT (2) alone gives $x = 9 + y$ but there is no information about y, so STATEMENT (2) alone is not sufficient.

STATEMENTS (1) and (2) together are sufficient. If $x = 9 + y$ and $x = 3y$, then $3y = 9 + y$ which gives y = ⁹⁄₂, so x = (3)(⁹⁄₂) = ²⁷⁄₂.

7. **(C)** STATEMENT (1) alone is not sufficient since if CD equals DA, E can be any point on the line CB. By the same reasoning, since D could be any point on AC if (2) is true, (2) alone is not sufficient. However, if both (1) and (2) are true, then triangles CDE and CAB are similar, with the corresponding angles CED and CBA equal. Thus the transversal CB has equal corresponding angles with the lines DE and AB, so DE is parallel to AB. Thus (1) and (2) together are sufficient.

8. **(B)** If $x + y = 24$ then at least one of the numbers x or y is positive. If x is positive then $y = 24 - x$ and since x is less than 20, $24 - x = y$ is positive. The same argument shows that if y is positive so is x. Therefore, STATEMENT (2) alone is sufficient to show that both numbers are positive.

STATEMENT (1) alone is insufficient, since the fact that x is less than 5 does not tell whether x is positive and no information is given about y.

9. **(C)** STATEMENT (2) alone implies $x = y$ since equal sides have equal angles in a triangle. Since there is no information about y, STATEMENT (2) alone is insufficient.

STATEMENT (1) alone is insufficient since there is no relation between x and y without STATEMENT (2).

STATEMENTS (1) and (2) together imply $x = y = 30$, so STATEMENTS (1) and (2) together are sufficient.

10. **(E)** Denote by w_1 the weight of the first volume, by w_2 the weight of the second volume, by w_3 the weight of the third volume and by w_4 the weight of the fourth volume. STATEMENT (1) gives $w_1 + w_2 + w_3 = 4$ and STATEMENT (2) gives $w_2 + w_3 + w_4 = 3½$. Using STATEMENTS (1) and (2) you can obtain $w_1 - w_4$ = ½ so $w_1 = w_4 + ½$ but no other information is given about w_4. Therefore, STATEMENTS (1) and (2) together are insufficient.

11. **(E)** Since the box is rectangular, there are 4 sides which occur in 2 different pairs. Therefore, you can't determine the area of every side using statements (1) and (2).

12. **(D)** If any value of a_n is an even integer, then all succeeding values are even. (Any even integer + 2 is an even integer.) Since a_{10} appears after a_1 and a_9, both statement (1) alone and statement (2) alone are sufficient.

13. **(B)** STATEMENT (2) alone is sufficient. Statement (2) allows you to find the values of x, y, and z, and the largest side is opposite the largest angle.

    STATEMENT (1) alone is not sufficient. (1) implies that AB is longer than AC, but you have no information about BC.

14. **(A)** STATEMENT (1) alone is sufficient, since the average is the total divided by 5.

    STATEMENT (2) alone is not sufficient. There is no information about her wages for the three days she worked between the first and last day.

15. **(C)** STATEMENT (1) alone is not sufficient. The expression becomes $x^3 + bx = x(x^2 + b)$, but there is no relationship between the expression and k.

    STATEMENT (2) alone is not sufficient, since the roots of the expression will depend on the value of a.

    STATEMENTS (1) and (2) together make the expression $x^3 + ax^2 + bx$ into $x^3 - k^2x = x(x^2 - k^2)$, which is equal to zero when $x = k$.

16. **(C)** STATEMENT (2) is needed to find the cost of each orange and STATEMENT (1) is needed to know the selling price of an orange.

17. **(C)** Since the figure is a rectangle, ABC is a right triangle. Therefore, using STATEMENTS (1) and (2) you can find BC, which will enable you to compute the area.

    STATEMENT (2) alone is not sufficient, since BC could be any value without contradicting statement (2).

    STATEMENT (1) alone is not sufficient. If $AB = 4$ and $BC = 3$, then $AC = 5$, and the area is 12. However, if $AB = 1$ and $BC = \sqrt{24}$, then $AC = 5$, but the area is $\sqrt{24}$, which is not 12.

18. **(E)** STATEMENTS (1) and (2) together are not sufficient. If $x = 3$ and $y = -\frac{1}{2}$, then $xy = -\frac{3}{2}$. But if $x = 3$ and $y = 1$, then $xy = 3$.

19. **(C)** STATEMENT (1) reduces a^b to $1^b = 1$, and $b^a = b$.

    STATEMENT (2) then allows us to decide, since $b > 2$ implies $b > 1$.

    STATEMENT (2) alone is not sufficient. If $a = 1$ and $b = 3$, then $a^b = 1$ is less than $b^a = 3$. However, if $a = 3$ and $b = 4$, then $a^b = 81$, which is greater than $b^a = 64$.

20. **(E)** STATEMENT (2) implies $x = 2y$. This is not sufficient since if x is negative, then x will be less than y, but if x is positive, then x will be greater than y. If we also use STATEMENT (1), we obtain $(2y)y = 2y^2 = 5$, which has two solutions, one positive, the other negative. Thus, both statements together are not sufficient.

21. **(A)** Since $ABCD$ is a square, BC is an altitude of the triangle ABE and AB is a base of the triangle ABE. So if we know AB (which equals BC), we can determine the area. Thus STATEMENT (1) alone is sufficient.

    STATEMENT (2) alone is not sufficient since it does not give any information about the length of any line segment.

22. **(B)** STATEMENT (2) alone is obviously sufficient. STATEMENT (1) is not sufficient since $x = 2$ and $y = 1$ and $x = -2$ and $y = -1$ both satisfy STATEMENT (1).

23. **(E)** The number who subscribed to at least one magazine is the sum of the numbers who subscribed to exactly one, two, and three magazines. So $38 = N1 + N2 + N3$, where $N1$, $N2$, and $N3$ are the number who subscribed to 1, 2, and 3 magazines respectively. We need to find $N2$. STATEMENT (1) is not sufficient since it tells the value of $N3$, but $N1$ and $N2$ are still both unknown. Even if we also use STATEMENT (1), we cannot find $N2$ since we have no information about the number of subscribers to magazines B and C.

24. **(E)** STATEMENT (1) is insufficient since 9 (which is odd) and 6 (which is even) are both divisible by 3.

    STATEMENT (2) is also insufficient since 81 is odd and 36 is even. 81 and 36 are also both divisible by 3, so (1) and (2) together are still insufficient.

25. **(C)** STATEMENT (1) is insufficient since any of the four numbers could be the largest.

STATEMENT (2) alone is insufficient since z could be larger than 24 or it could be smaller than one of the numbers x, y, or w.

STATEMENT (1) and STATEMENT (2) together are sufficient. (1) implies that $w + x + y + z = 100$ or $z = 100 - w - x - y$. Now using (2), we can see that $100 - w - x - y$ is greater than $100 - 24 - 24 - 24 = 28$. So z must be the largest number.

Section VIII   Problem Solving

1. **(B)** The increase in cost between 1972 and 1973 is the product (cost in 1972) · (rate of increase). The cost in 1973 will be the cost in 1972 (1 + rate of increase). Also, the cost in 1974 will equal (cost in 1973) (1 + rate of increase) or (cost in 1972) (1 + rate of increase)^2. So the cost of coal for 1974 = \$(53)(1.15)^2 = \$(53)(1.32225) = \$70.09, and the cost of oil for 1974 = \$(45)(1.2)^2 = \$(45)(1.44) = \$64.80. Since oil is cheaper than coal, (D) and (E) are incorrect because replacing oil by coal for any amount of time raises the cost.

2. **(D)** Let s be the side of the original square. Since the side of the increased square is $1.3s$, the area of the increased square is $1.69(s^2)$. Therefore, the area has increased by $1.69(s^2) - s^2$ or by $.69(s^2)$ or 69%.

3. **(D)** By 5:30 A.M. train Y will have traveled $(4\frac{1}{2})x$ miles. So train Z must travel $(4\frac{1}{2})x$ miles in $3\frac{1}{2}$ hours. The average rate of speed necessary is $\frac{4\frac{1}{2}x}{3\frac{1}{2}}$ which equals $\frac{9/2x}{7/2}$ or $\frac{9}{7}x$.

4. **(C)** $(6)(18) = 108$ and $(5)(18) = 90$. To make quick estimates, check the amount funded for water pollution if air pollution received 100. For example, if the ratio were 3 to 2, water pollution would get only 66.7 billion dollars.

5. **(B)** Let x be the cost in dollars of 4 boxes of pencils. $\frac{4}{30} = \frac{x}{5.10}$, which means $x = \$\left(\frac{4}{30}\right)(5.10) = \$.68 = 68¢$.

6. **(E)** The amount the worker is paid for working T hours if T is larger than 8 is $8r + (T - 8)(1.5)r$. When $T = 11$, the worker will be paid $8r + 3(1.5)r = (12.5)r$.

7. **(D)** The product of three consecutive integers is of the form $x(x + 1)(x + 2)$. A good approximation to this is $(x + 1)^3$. Since $5^3 = 125$, a good guess is 4, 5, 6. This is correct because $(4)(5)(6) = 120$. The sum of these three numbers is 15.

8. **(D)** Medical research grants increased by .4 between 1971 and 1972. The fractional increase is $\frac{.4}{3.1}$. Since $\frac{.4}{3.2} = \frac{1}{8} = 12.5\%$, 13% is the best estimate.

9. **(B)** The total amount was 20.2 and the total amount the colleges received was 10.1. The colleges received $\frac{10.1}{20.2}$ or $\frac{1}{2}$ or 50%.

10. **(E)** Let M be the mechanic's hourly wage, C the custodial worker's hourly wage, and S the salesman's hourly wage. Then $M = 2S$, and $C = \frac{1}{3}M$ or $M = 3C$, hence $3C = 2S$, $S = \frac{3}{2}C$.

11. **(B)** Statement I is false since $(-1) + (-2) = -3$, and III is false since $(-2) - (-1) = -1$. But II is true since $(-x)(-y) = xy$, for all x and y.

12. **(C)** The loaded truck gets $(.85)10$ miles or 8. miles per gallon. The loaded truck will require $\frac{50}{8.5}$ or 5.88 (to the nearest hundredth) gallons to travel 50 miles.

13. **(A)** Since $3a = 0$, a must equal 0, which implies that $b = 0$. Note that $\frac{b}{a}$ and $\frac{a}{b}$ are not defined.

14. **(C)** The horse will travel 10 miles in the first two hours. The horse will take $\frac{10}{3}$ or $3\frac{1}{3}$ hours to travel the final 10 miles. So the total time is $5\frac{1}{3}$ hours.

15. **(A)** Statement I is false since the graph indicates only that the percentage of the total collected was less. (If the total in 1973 was much larger, the amount collected from excise taxes could have increased.) II is false since, again, the graph gives only percentages not amounts. III is false for the same reason.

16. **(D)** Let r_1 be the radius of the first circle and r_2 the radius of the second circle. Then $\dfrac{r_1}{r_2} = \dfrac{3}{2}$, so $r_1 = \left(\dfrac{3}{2}\right)r_2$, and $\pi(r_1)^2 = \pi\dfrac{9}{4}(r_2)^2$. Since the area of a circle is $\pi\,(\text{radius})^2$, then the ratio of the areas is 9 to 4.

17. **(C)** $(-5)(-4) = (5)(4)$.

18. **(E)** Let $x = -3$ and $y = 2$, then $\dfrac{1}{-3} < \dfrac{1}{2}$, so (A), (B), and (C) are false. Let $x = 3$ and y $= 2$; then $\dfrac{1}{3} < \dfrac{1}{2}$ so (D) is false. (E) is the only correct answer.

19. **(E)** The selling price of the boxes should equal x plus the cost. The cost in cents of making 5,000 boxes is $(1,000)5¢ + (4,000)y$ which equals $50 + 40y$ in dollars. So the selling price should be $50 + 40y + x$.

20. **(E)** The amount received from suit sales will be equal to the number of suits sold times the price of each suit. Since each suit is sold for x, we need to know how many suits will be sold. First we must compute the number of $4 price raises. Since $x - 200$ is the increase in price, $(x - 200)/4$ is the number of $4 increases. Thus the number of suits sold will decrease by $2(x - 200)/4$. Therefore, the number of suits sold will be $100 - 2(x - 200)/4 = 100 - x/2 + 100 = 200 - x/2$. So the amount received is $x(200 - x/2) = 200x - x^2/2$.

Evaluating Your Score

Tabulate your score for each section of Sample Test 4 according to the directions on pages 4–5 and record the results in the Self-scoring Table below. Then find your rating for each score on the Self-scoring Scale and record it in the appropriate blank.

Self-scoring Table

SECTION	SCORE	RATING
1		
2		
3		
4		
5		
6		
7		
8		

Self-scoring Scale

RATING

SECTION	POOR	FAIR	GOOD	EXCELLENT
1	0–12+	13–17+	18–21+	22–25
2	0–9+	10–13+	14–17+	18–20
3	0–17+	18–24+	25–31+	32–35
4	0–12+	13–17+	18–21+	22–25
5	0–12+	13–17+	18–21+	22–25
6	0–17+	18–24+	25–31+	32–35
7	0–12+	13–17+	18–21+	22–25
8	0–9+	10–13+	14–17+	18–20

Study again the Review sections covering material in Sample Test 4 for which you had a rank of FAIR or POOR. Then go on to Sample Test 5.

To obtain an approximation of your actual GMAT score see page 5.

Answer Sheet—Sample Test 5

Section I
Reading Comprehension
1. Ⓐ Ⓑ Ⓒ Ⓓ Ⓔ
2. Ⓐ Ⓑ Ⓒ Ⓓ Ⓔ
3. Ⓐ Ⓑ Ⓒ Ⓓ Ⓔ
4. Ⓐ Ⓑ Ⓒ Ⓓ Ⓔ
5. Ⓐ Ⓑ Ⓒ Ⓓ Ⓔ
6. Ⓐ Ⓑ Ⓒ Ⓓ Ⓔ
7. Ⓐ Ⓑ Ⓒ Ⓓ Ⓔ
8. Ⓐ Ⓑ Ⓒ Ⓓ Ⓔ
9. Ⓐ Ⓑ Ⓒ Ⓓ Ⓔ
10. Ⓐ Ⓑ Ⓒ Ⓓ Ⓔ
11. Ⓐ Ⓑ Ⓒ Ⓓ Ⓔ
12. Ⓐ Ⓑ Ⓒ Ⓓ Ⓔ
13. Ⓐ Ⓑ Ⓒ Ⓓ Ⓔ
14. Ⓐ Ⓑ Ⓒ Ⓓ Ⓔ
15. Ⓐ Ⓑ Ⓒ Ⓓ Ⓔ
16. Ⓐ Ⓑ Ⓒ Ⓓ Ⓔ
17. Ⓐ Ⓑ Ⓒ Ⓓ Ⓔ
18. Ⓐ Ⓑ Ⓒ Ⓓ Ⓔ
19. Ⓐ Ⓑ Ⓒ Ⓓ Ⓔ
20. Ⓐ Ⓑ Ⓒ Ⓓ Ⓔ
21. Ⓐ Ⓑ Ⓒ Ⓓ Ⓔ
22. Ⓐ Ⓑ Ⓒ Ⓓ Ⓔ
23. Ⓐ Ⓑ Ⓒ Ⓓ Ⓔ
24. Ⓐ Ⓑ Ⓒ Ⓓ Ⓔ
25. Ⓐ Ⓑ Ⓒ Ⓓ Ⓔ

Section II
Problem Solving
1. Ⓐ Ⓑ Ⓒ Ⓓ Ⓔ
2. Ⓐ Ⓑ Ⓒ Ⓓ Ⓔ
3. Ⓐ Ⓑ Ⓒ Ⓓ Ⓔ
4. Ⓐ Ⓑ Ⓒ Ⓓ Ⓔ
5. Ⓐ Ⓑ Ⓒ Ⓓ Ⓔ
6. Ⓐ Ⓑ Ⓒ Ⓓ Ⓔ
7. Ⓐ Ⓑ Ⓒ Ⓓ Ⓔ
8. Ⓐ Ⓑ Ⓒ Ⓓ Ⓔ
9. Ⓐ Ⓑ Ⓒ Ⓓ Ⓔ
10. Ⓐ Ⓑ Ⓒ Ⓓ Ⓔ
11. Ⓐ Ⓑ Ⓒ Ⓓ Ⓔ
12. Ⓐ Ⓑ Ⓒ Ⓓ Ⓔ
13. Ⓐ Ⓑ Ⓒ Ⓓ Ⓔ
14. Ⓐ Ⓑ Ⓒ Ⓓ Ⓔ
15. Ⓐ Ⓑ Ⓒ Ⓓ Ⓔ
16. Ⓐ Ⓑ Ⓒ Ⓓ Ⓔ
17. Ⓐ Ⓑ Ⓒ Ⓓ Ⓔ
18. Ⓐ Ⓑ Ⓒ Ⓓ Ⓔ
19. Ⓐ Ⓑ Ⓒ Ⓓ Ⓔ
20. Ⓐ Ⓑ Ⓒ Ⓓ Ⓔ

Section III
Analysis of Situations
1. Ⓐ Ⓑ Ⓒ Ⓓ Ⓔ
2. Ⓐ Ⓑ Ⓒ Ⓓ Ⓔ
3. Ⓐ Ⓑ Ⓒ Ⓓ Ⓔ
4. Ⓐ Ⓑ Ⓒ Ⓓ Ⓔ
5. Ⓐ Ⓑ Ⓒ Ⓓ Ⓔ
6. Ⓐ Ⓑ Ⓒ Ⓓ Ⓔ
7. Ⓐ Ⓑ Ⓒ Ⓓ Ⓔ
8. Ⓐ Ⓑ Ⓒ Ⓓ Ⓔ
9. Ⓐ Ⓑ Ⓒ Ⓓ Ⓔ
10. Ⓐ Ⓑ Ⓒ Ⓓ Ⓔ
11. Ⓐ Ⓑ Ⓒ Ⓓ Ⓔ
12. Ⓐ Ⓑ Ⓒ Ⓓ Ⓔ
13. Ⓐ Ⓑ Ⓒ Ⓓ Ⓔ
14. Ⓐ Ⓑ Ⓒ Ⓓ Ⓔ
15. Ⓐ Ⓑ Ⓒ Ⓓ Ⓔ
16. Ⓐ Ⓑ Ⓒ Ⓓ Ⓔ
17. Ⓐ Ⓑ Ⓒ Ⓓ Ⓔ
18. Ⓐ Ⓑ Ⓒ Ⓓ Ⓔ
19. Ⓐ Ⓑ Ⓒ Ⓓ Ⓔ
20. Ⓐ Ⓑ Ⓒ Ⓓ Ⓔ
21. Ⓐ Ⓑ Ⓒ Ⓓ Ⓔ
22. Ⓐ Ⓑ Ⓒ Ⓓ Ⓔ
23. Ⓐ Ⓑ Ⓒ Ⓓ Ⓔ
24. Ⓐ Ⓑ Ⓒ Ⓓ Ⓔ
25. Ⓐ Ⓑ Ⓒ Ⓓ Ⓔ
26. Ⓐ Ⓑ Ⓒ Ⓓ Ⓔ
27. Ⓐ Ⓑ Ⓒ Ⓜ Ⓔ
28. Ⓐ Ⓑ Ⓒ Ⓓ Ⓔ
29. Ⓐ Ⓑ Ⓒ Ⓓ Ⓔ
30. Ⓐ Ⓑ Ⓒ Ⓓ Ⓔ
31. Ⓐ Ⓑ Ⓒ Ⓓ Ⓔ
32. Ⓐ Ⓑ Ⓒ Ⓓ Ⓔ
33. Ⓐ Ⓑ Ⓒ Ⓓ Ⓔ
34. Ⓐ Ⓑ Ⓒ Ⓓ Ⓔ
35. Ⓐ Ⓑ Ⓒ Ⓓ Ⓔ

Section IV
Data Sufficiency
1. Ⓐ Ⓑ Ⓒ Ⓓ Ⓔ
2. Ⓐ Ⓑ Ⓒ Ⓓ Ⓔ
3. Ⓐ Ⓑ Ⓒ Ⓓ Ⓔ
4. Ⓐ Ⓑ Ⓒ Ⓓ Ⓔ
5. Ⓐ Ⓑ Ⓒ Ⓓ Ⓔ
6. Ⓐ Ⓑ Ⓒ Ⓓ Ⓔ
7. Ⓐ Ⓑ Ⓒ Ⓓ Ⓔ
8. Ⓐ Ⓑ Ⓒ Ⓓ Ⓔ
9. Ⓐ Ⓑ Ⓒ Ⓓ Ⓔ
10. Ⓐ Ⓑ Ⓒ Ⓓ Ⓔ
11. Ⓐ Ⓑ Ⓒ Ⓓ Ⓔ
12. Ⓐ Ⓑ Ⓒ Ⓓ Ⓔ
13. Ⓐ Ⓑ Ⓒ Ⓓ Ⓔ
14. Ⓐ Ⓑ Ⓒ Ⓓ Ⓔ
15. Ⓐ Ⓑ Ⓒ Ⓓ Ⓔ
16. Ⓐ Ⓑ Ⓒ Ⓓ Ⓔ
17. Ⓐ Ⓑ Ⓒ Ⓓ Ⓔ
18. Ⓐ Ⓑ Ⓒ Ⓓ Ⓔ
19. Ⓐ Ⓑ Ⓒ Ⓓ Ⓔ
20. Ⓐ Ⓑ Ⓒ Ⓓ Ⓔ
21. Ⓐ Ⓑ Ⓒ Ⓓ Ⓔ
22. Ⓐ Ⓑ Ⓒ Ⓓ Ⓔ
23. Ⓐ Ⓑ Ⓒ Ⓓ Ⓔ
24. Ⓐ Ⓑ Ⓒ Ⓓ Ⓔ
25. Ⓐ Ⓑ Ⓒ Ⓓ Ⓔ

Section V
Writing Ability
1. Ⓐ Ⓑ Ⓒ Ⓓ Ⓔ
2. Ⓐ Ⓑ Ⓒ Ⓓ Ⓔ
3. Ⓐ Ⓑ Ⓒ Ⓓ Ⓔ
4. Ⓐ Ⓑ Ⓒ Ⓓ Ⓔ
5. Ⓐ Ⓑ Ⓒ Ⓓ Ⓔ
6. Ⓐ Ⓑ Ⓒ Ⓓ Ⓔ
7. Ⓐ Ⓑ Ⓒ Ⓓ Ⓔ
8. Ⓐ Ⓑ Ⓒ Ⓓ Ⓔ
9. Ⓐ Ⓑ Ⓒ Ⓓ Ⓔ
10. Ⓐ Ⓑ Ⓒ Ⓓ Ⓔ
11. Ⓐ Ⓑ Ⓒ Ⓓ Ⓔ
12. Ⓐ Ⓑ Ⓒ Ⓓ Ⓔ
13. Ⓐ Ⓑ Ⓒ Ⓓ Ⓔ
14. Ⓐ Ⓑ Ⓒ Ⓓ Ⓔ
15. Ⓐ Ⓑ Ⓒ Ⓓ Ⓔ
16. Ⓐ Ⓑ Ⓒ Ⓓ Ⓔ
17. Ⓐ Ⓑ Ⓒ Ⓓ Ⓔ
18. Ⓐ Ⓑ Ⓒ Ⓓ Ⓔ
19. Ⓐ Ⓑ Ⓒ Ⓓ Ⓔ
20. Ⓐ Ⓑ Ⓒ Ⓓ Ⓔ
21. Ⓐ Ⓑ Ⓒ Ⓓ Ⓔ
22. Ⓐ Ⓑ Ⓒ Ⓓ Ⓔ
23. Ⓐ Ⓑ Ⓒ Ⓓ Ⓔ
24. Ⓐ Ⓑ Ⓒ Ⓓ Ⓔ
25. Ⓐ Ⓑ Ⓒ Ⓓ Ⓔ

Section VI
Critical Reasoning
1. Ⓐ Ⓑ Ⓒ Ⓓ Ⓔ
2. Ⓐ Ⓑ Ⓒ Ⓓ Ⓔ
3. Ⓐ Ⓑ Ⓒ Ⓓ Ⓔ
4. Ⓐ Ⓑ Ⓒ Ⓓ Ⓔ
5. Ⓐ Ⓑ Ⓒ Ⓓ Ⓔ
6. Ⓐ Ⓑ Ⓒ Ⓓ Ⓔ
7. Ⓐ Ⓑ Ⓒ Ⓓ Ⓔ
8. Ⓐ Ⓑ Ⓒ Ⓓ Ⓔ
9. Ⓐ Ⓑ Ⓒ Ⓓ Ⓔ
10. Ⓐ Ⓑ Ⓒ Ⓓ Ⓔ
11. Ⓐ Ⓑ Ⓒ Ⓓ Ⓔ
12. Ⓐ Ⓑ Ⓒ Ⓓ Ⓔ
13. Ⓐ Ⓑ Ⓒ Ⓓ Ⓔ
14. Ⓐ Ⓑ Ⓒ Ⓓ Ⓔ
15. Ⓐ Ⓑ Ⓒ Ⓓ Ⓔ
16. Ⓐ Ⓑ Ⓒ Ⓓ Ⓔ
17. Ⓐ Ⓑ Ⓒ Ⓓ Ⓔ
18. Ⓐ Ⓑ Ⓒ Ⓓ Ⓔ
19. Ⓐ Ⓑ Ⓒ Ⓓ Ⓔ
20. Ⓐ Ⓑ Ⓒ Ⓓ Ⓔ
21. Ⓐ Ⓑ Ⓒ Ⓓ Ⓔ
22. Ⓐ Ⓑ Ⓒ Ⓓ Ⓔ
23. Ⓐ Ⓑ Ⓒ Ⓓ Ⓔ
24. Ⓐ Ⓑ Ⓒ Ⓓ Ⓔ
25. Ⓐ Ⓑ Ⓒ Ⓓ Ⓔ

Section VII
Writing Ability
1. Ⓐ Ⓑ Ⓒ Ⓓ Ⓔ
2. Ⓐ Ⓑ Ⓒ Ⓓ Ⓔ
3. Ⓐ Ⓑ Ⓒ Ⓓ Ⓔ
4. Ⓐ Ⓑ Ⓒ Ⓓ Ⓔ
5. Ⓐ Ⓑ Ⓒ Ⓓ Ⓔ
6. Ⓐ Ⓑ Ⓒ Ⓓ Ⓔ
7. Ⓐ Ⓑ Ⓒ Ⓓ Ⓔ
8. Ⓐ Ⓑ Ⓒ Ⓓ Ⓔ
9. Ⓐ Ⓑ Ⓒ Ⓓ Ⓔ
10. Ⓐ Ⓑ Ⓒ Ⓓ Ⓔ
11. Ⓐ Ⓑ Ⓒ Ⓓ Ⓔ
12. Ⓐ Ⓑ Ⓒ Ⓓ Ⓔ
13. Ⓐ Ⓑ Ⓒ Ⓓ Ⓔ
14. Ⓐ Ⓑ Ⓒ Ⓓ Ⓔ
15. Ⓐ Ⓑ Ⓒ Ⓓ Ⓔ
16. Ⓐ Ⓑ Ⓒ Ⓓ Ⓔ
17. Ⓐ Ⓑ Ⓒ Ⓓ Ⓔ
18. Ⓐ Ⓑ Ⓒ Ⓓ Ⓔ
19. Ⓐ Ⓑ Ⓒ Ⓓ Ⓔ
20. Ⓐ Ⓑ Ⓒ Ⓓ Ⓔ
21. Ⓐ Ⓑ Ⓒ Ⓓ Ⓔ
22. Ⓐ Ⓑ Ⓒ Ⓓ Ⓔ
23. Ⓐ Ⓑ Ⓒ Ⓓ Ⓔ
24. Ⓐ Ⓑ Ⓒ Ⓓ Ⓔ
25. Ⓐ Ⓑ Ⓒ Ⓓ Ⓔ

Section VIII
Problem Solving
1. Ⓐ Ⓑ Ⓒ Ⓓ Ⓔ
2. Ⓐ Ⓑ Ⓒ Ⓓ Ⓔ
3. Ⓐ Ⓑ Ⓒ Ⓓ Ⓔ
4. Ⓐ Ⓑ Ⓒ Ⓓ Ⓔ
5. Ⓐ Ⓑ Ⓒ Ⓓ Ⓔ
6. Ⓐ Ⓑ Ⓒ Ⓓ Ⓔ
7. Ⓐ Ⓑ Ⓒ Ⓓ Ⓔ
8. Ⓐ Ⓑ Ⓒ Ⓓ Ⓔ
9. Ⓐ Ⓑ Ⓒ Ⓓ Ⓔ
10. Ⓐ Ⓑ Ⓒ Ⓓ Ⓔ
11. Ⓐ Ⓑ Ⓒ Ⓓ Ⓔ
12. Ⓐ Ⓑ Ⓒ Ⓓ Ⓔ
13. Ⓐ Ⓑ Ⓒ Ⓓ Ⓔ
14. Ⓐ Ⓑ Ⓒ Ⓓ Ⓔ
15. Ⓐ Ⓑ Ⓒ Ⓓ Ⓔ
16. Ⓐ Ⓑ Ⓒ Ⓓ Ⓔ
17. Ⓐ Ⓑ Ⓒ Ⓓ Ⓔ
18. Ⓐ Ⓑ Ⓒ Ⓓ Ⓔ
19. Ⓐ Ⓑ Ⓒ Ⓓ Ⓔ
20. Ⓐ Ⓑ Ⓒ Ⓓ Ⓔ

Sample Test 5

Section I   Reading Comprehension

TIME: 30 minutes

DIRECTIONS: This part contains four reading passages. You are to read each one carefully. When answering the questions, you *will* be allowed to refer back to the passages. The questions are based on what is *stated* or *implied* in each passage. You have thirty minutes to complete this section.

Passage 1:

A newly issued report reveals in facts and figures what should have been known in principle, that quite a lot of business companies are going to go under during the coming decade, as tariff walls are progressively dismantled. Labor and capital valued at $12 billion are to be made idle through the impact of duty-free imports.
(5)   As a result, 35,000 workers will be displaced. Some will move to other jobs and other departments within the same firm. Around 15,000 will have to leave the firm now employing them and work elsewhere.

The report is measuring exclusively the influence of free trade with Europe. The authors do not take into account the expected expansion of production over the
(10)   coming years. On the other hand, they are not sure that even the export predictions they make will be achieved. For this presupposes that a suitable business climate lets the pressure to increase productivity materialize.

There are two reasons why this scenario may not happen. The first one is that industry on the whole is not taking the initiatives necessary to adapt fully to the
(15)   new price situation it will be facing as time goes by.

This is another way of saying that the manufacturers do not realize what lies ahead. The government is to blame for not making the position absolutely clear. It should be saying that in ten years' time tariffs on all industrial goods imported from Europe will be eliminated. There will be no adjustment assistance for man-
(20)   ufacturers who cannot adapt to this situation.

The second obstacle to adjustment is not stressed in the same way in the report; it is the attitude of the service sector. Not only are service industries unaware that the Common Market treaty concerns them too, they are artificially insulated from the physical pressures of international competition. The manufacturing sector
(25)   has been forced to apply its nose to the grindstone for some time now, by the increasingly stringent import-liberalization program.

The ancillary services on which the factories depend show a growing indifference to their work obligations. They seem unaware that overmanned ships, underutilized container equipment in the ports, and repeated work stoppages slow the country's
(30)   attempts to narrow the trade gap. The remedy is to cut the fees charged by these services so as to reduce their earnings—in exactly the same way that earnings in industrial undertakings are reduced by the tariff reduction program embodied in the treaty with the European Community.

There is no point in dismissing 15,000 industrial workers from their present jobs
(35)   during the coming ten years if all the gain in productivity is wasted by costly

harbor, transport, financial, administrative and other services. The free trade treaty is their concern as well. Surplus staff should be removed, if need be, from all workplaces, not just from the factories. Efficiency is everybody's business.

1. The attitude of the report, as described in the passage, may best be expressed as

(A) harshly condemnatory, because industry is not more responsive to the business climate
(B) optimistic that government will induce industry to make needed changes
(C) critical of labor unions
(D) pessimistic that anything can be done to reduce the trade gap
(E) objective in assessing the influence of free trade on employment

2. What is the meaning of *free trade* in line 8?

(A) unlimited sale of goods in Europe
(B) trade on a barter basis
(C) the elimination of tariffs
(D) sale of price-discounted goods to European countries
(E) trade with only the so-called "free countries," i.e., Western Europe

3. It can be inferred that the term *adjustment assistance* in line 19 refers mainly to

(A) unemployment compensation
(B) some sort of financial assistance to manufacturers hurt by free trade
(C) help in relocating plants to Europe
(D) aid in reducing work stoppages
(E) subsidy payments to increase exports

4. The author's central recommendation seems to be that

(A) unemployment should be avoided at all costs
(B) redundant labor should be removed in all sectors
(C) government should control the service sector
(D) tariffs should not be lowered
(E) workers should be retrained

5. Which of the following titles best describes the content of the passage?

(A) *The Prospects of Free Trade*
(B) *Government Intervention in World Trade*
(C) *Trade with the Common Market*
(D) *What Lies Ahead?*
(E) *Unemployment and Adjustment Assistance*

6. Which of the following will occur because of duty-free imports?

  I. Twelve billion dollars of capital will be idled.
 II. Thirty-five thousand workers will be unemployed.
III. Fifteen thousand firms will face bankruptcy.

(A) I only
(B) II only
(C) I and II only
(D) II and III only
(E) I, II, and III

7. According to the passage, the government is responsible for

   (A) increasing tariffs
   (B) subsidizing exports
   (C) not explaining its position
   (D) adjustment assistance
   (E) overmanned ships

8. Tariffs will be reduced on

   (A) all manufactured goods
   (B) manufactured and agricultural goods
   (C) all goods
   (D) industrial goods
   (E) industrial and consumer goods

9. Which industries will be affected by tariff reductions?

   I. Services
   II. Manufacturing
   III. Extracting

   (A) I only
   (B) II only
   (C) I and II only
   (D) II and III only
   (E) I, II, and III

Passage 2:

The fundamental objectives of sociology are the same as those of science generally—discovery and explanation. To *discover* the essential data of social behavior and the connections among the data is the first objective of sociology. To *explain* the data and the connections is the second and larger objective. Science
(5)　makes its advances in terms of both of these objectives. Sometimes it is the discovery of a new element or set of elements that marks a major breakthrough in the history of a scientific discipline. Closely related to such discovery is the discovery of relationships of data that had never been noted before. All of this is, as we know, of immense importance in science. But the drama of discovery, in
10)　this sense, can sometimes lead us to overlook the greater importance of explanation of what is revealed by the data. Sometimes decades, even centuries, pass before known connections and relationships are actually explained. Discovery and explanation are the two great interpenetrating, interacting realms of science.

The order of reality that interests the scientists is the *empirical* order, that is,
15)　the order of data and phenomena revealed to us through observation or experience. To be precise or explicit about what is, and is not, revealed by observation is not always easy, to be sure. And often it is necessary for our natural powers of observation to be supplemented by the most intricate of mechanical aids for a given object to become "empirical" in the sense just used. That the electron is
20)　not as immediately visible as is the mountain range does not mean, obviously, that it is any less empirical. That social behavior does not lend itself to as quick and accurate description as, say, chemical behavior of gases and compounds does not mean that social roles, statuses, and attitudes are any less empirical than molecules and tissues. What is empirical and observable today may have been nonexistent
25)　in scientific consciousness a decade ago. Moreover, the empirical is often data *inferred* from direct observation. All of this is clear enough, and we should make

no pretense that there are not often shadow areas between the empirical and the nonempirical. Nevertheless, the first point to make about any science, physical or social, is that its world of data is the empirical world. A very large amount of
(30) scientific energy goes merely into the work of expanding the frontiers, through discovery, of the known, observable, empirical world.

From observation or discovery we move to *explanation*. The explanation sought by the scientist is, of course, not at all like the explanation sought by the theologian or metaphysician. The scientist is not interested—not, that is, in his role of sci-
(35) entist—in ultimate, transcendental, or divine causes of what he sets himself to explain. He is interested in explanations that are as empirical as the data themselves. If it is the high incidence of crime in a certain part of a large city that requires explanation, the scientist is obliged to offer his explanation in terms of factors which are empirically real as the phenomenon of crime itself. He does not
(40) explain the problem, for example, in terms of references to the will of God, demons, or original sin. A satisfactory explanation is not only one that is empirical, however, but one that can be stated in the terms of a *causal proposition*. Description is an indispensable point of beginning, but description is not explanation. It is well to stress this point, for there are all too many scientists, or would-be scientists, who
(45) are primarily concerned with data gathering, data counting, and data describing, and who seem to forget that such operations, however useful, are but the first step. Until we have accounted for the problem at hand, explained it causally by referring the data to some principle or generalization already established, or to some new principle or generalization, we have not explained anything.

10. According to the passage, scientists are not interested in theological explanations because

(A) scientists tend to be atheists
(B) theology cannot explain change
(C) theological explanations are not empirical
(D) theology cannot explain social behavior
(E) scientists are concerned primarily with data gathering

11. The major objective of the passage is to

(A) show that explanation is more important than discovery
(B) prove that sociology is a science
(C) explain the major objectives of sociology
(D) discuss scientific method
(E) describe social behavior

12. Which of the following statements best agrees with the author's position?

(A) Science is the formulation of unverified hypotheses.
(B) Explanation is inferred from data.
(C) Causation is a basis for explanation.
(D) Generalization is a prerequisite for explanation.
(E) Empiricism is the science of discovery.

13. Judging from the contents of the passage, the final step in a study of social behavior would be to

(A) discover the problem
(B) establish principles
(C) offer an explanation of the data by determining causation
(D) collect data
(E) establish generalizations

14. According to the passage, which of the following activities contribute to the advance of science?

   I. Finding data relationships
  II. Expanding the limits of the empirical
 III. Establishing ultimate causes of phenomena
  (A) I only   (B) II only   (C) I and II only
  (D) I and III only   (E) I, II, and III

15. The author's main point in the first paragraph may best be described by which of the following statements?

  (A) Science and sociology are interdisciplinary.
  (B) The first objective of sociology is discovery.
  (C) Discovery without explanation is meaningless.
  (D) Both discovery and explanation are fundamental to building a science.
  (E) It takes a long time before relationships of data are discovered.

16. According to the author, which of the following explanations would a scientist accept?

   I. Snow falls because angels are having a pillow fight.
  II. Suicide is caused by weak character.
 III. Babies weigh 20% more than the average weight of newborns if their mothers take a 2-hour nap every day during the last 3 months of pregnancy.

  (A) I only
  (B) II only
  (C) III only
  (D) II and III only
  (E) I, II, and III

17. The major objective of the second paragraph is

  (A) to show that electrons are empirical data
  (B) to show that science changes as time passes
  (C) to demonstrate the difference between chemistry and sociology
  (D) to explain how science expands the frontiers of the observable world
  (E) to explain what the term *empirical order* means

Passage 3:

A polytheist always has favorites among the gods, determined by his own temperament, age, and condition, as well as his own interest, temporary or permanent. If it is true that everybody loves a lover, then Venus will be a popular deity with all. But from lovers she will elicit special devotion. In ancient Rome, when a young
(5) couple went out together to see a procession or other show, they would of course pay great respect to Venus, when her image appeared on the screen. Instead of saying, "Isn't love wonderful?" they would say, "Great art thou, O Venus." In a polytheistic society you could tell a good deal about a person's frame of mind by the gods he favored, so that to tell a girl you were trying to woo that you
(10) thought Venus overrated was hardly the way to win her heart. But in any case, a lovesick youth or maiden would be spontaneously supplicating Venus.

The Greeks liked to present their deities in human form; it was natural to them to symbolize the gods as human beings glorified, idealized. But this fact is also capable of misleading us. We might suppose that the ancients were really wor-
(15) shipping only themselves; that they were, like Narcissus, beholding their own image in a pool, so that their worship was *anthropocentric* (man-centered) rather

than *theocentric* (god-centered). We are in danger of assuming that they were simply constructing the god in their own image. This is not necessarily so. The gods must always be symbolized in one form or another. To give them a human

(20) form is one way of doing this, technically called *anthropomorphism* (from the Greek *anthropos*, a man, and *morphé*, form). People of certain temperaments and within certain types of culture seem to be more inclined to it than are others. It is, however, more noticeable in others than in oneself, and those who affect to despise it are sometimes conspicuous for their addiction to it. A German once said

(25) an Englishman's idea of God is an Englishman twelve feet tall. Such disparagement of anthropomorphism occurred in the ancient world, too. The Celts, for instance, despised Greek practice in this matter, preferring to use animals and other such symbols. The Egyptians favored more abstract and stylized symbols, among which a well-known example is the solar disk, a symbol of Rà, the sun-god.

(30)   Professor C. S. Lewis tells of an Oxford undergraduate he knew who, priggishly despising the conventional images of God, thought he was overcoming anthropomorphism by thinking of the Deity as infinite vapor or smoke. Of course even the bearded-old-man image can be a better symbol of Deity than ever could be the image, even if this were psychologically possible, of an unlimited smog.

(35)   What is really characteristic of all polytheism, however, is not the worship of idols or humanity or forests or stars; it is, rather, the worship of innumerable *powers* that confront and affect us. The powers are held to be valuable in themselves; that is why they are to be worshipped. But the values conflict. The gods do not cooperate, so you have to play them off against each other. Suppose you

(40) want rain. You know of two gods, the dry-god who sends drought and the wet-god who sends rain. You do not suppose that you can just pray to the wet-god to get busy, and simply ignore the dry-god. If you do so, the latter may be offended, so that no matter how hard the wet-god tries to oblige you, the dry-god will do his best to wither everything. Because both gods are powerful you must take both

(45) into consideration, begging the wet-god to be generous and beseeching the dry-god to stay his hand.

18. It can be inferred from the passage that polytheism means a belief in

(A) Greek gods
(B) more than one god
(C) a god-centered world
(D) powerful deities
(E) infinite numbers of gods

19. The author's statement in lines 8–9 that ''you could tell a good deal about a person's frame of mind by the gods he favored'' means that

(A) those who believed in gods were superstitious
(B) worship was either anthropocentric or theocentric
(C) gods were chosen to represent a given way of life
(D) the way a person thinks depends on the power of deities
(E) in certain cultures, the gods served as representations of what people thought of themselves

20. It may be inferred from the passage that the author would most likely agree that ancient cultures

 I. symbolized their deities only in human form
 II. symbolized the gods in many forms
III. were mainly self-worshippers
(A) I only   (B) II only   (C) I and II only
(D) I and III only   (E) I, II, and III

21. The main point the author makes about anthropomorphism in lines 19–22 is that

(A) certain cultures are inclined to anthropomorphism
(B) those who demean anthropomorphism may themselves practice it
(C) the disparagement of anthropomorphism is common to both ancient and modern cultures
(D) the Germans tend to be more theocentric than the English
(E) anthropomorphism is a practice common to all cultures

22. It may be inferred from the last paragraph that polytheism entails

(A) a commonality of interests among the deities
(B) predictable consequences
(C) incoherence and conflict among the "powers"
(D) an orderly universe
(E) worshipping one god at a time

23. Which people worshipped animals?

(A) Romans
(B) Greeks
(C) Egyptians
(D) Celts
(E) Pagans

24. Anthropomorphism may be said to be symbolizing

(A) a deity in one's own image
(B) a human form
(C) any form
(D) both human and spiritual forms
(E) an abstract form

25. A polytheist

I. has favorite gods
II. simultaneously worships more than one god
III. lived in Greece

(A) I only
(B) II only
(C) I and II only
(D) II and III only
(E) I, II, and III

If there is still time remaining, you may review the questions in this section only.
You may not turn to any other section of the test.

Section II   Problem Solving

TIME: 30 minutes

DIRECTIONS: Solve each of the following problems; then indicate the correct answer on the answer sheet. [On the actual test you will be permitted to use any space available on the examination paper for scratch work.]
NOTE: A figure that appears with a problem is drawn as accurately as possible so as to provide information that may help in answering the questions. Numbers in this test are real numbers.

1. What is the next number in the geometric progression 4, 12, 36?

(A) 44
(B) 60
(C) 72
(D) 108
(E) 144

2. An angle of x degrees has the property that its complement is equal to ⅙ of its supplement where x is

(A) 30
(B) 45
(C) 60
(D) 63
(E) 72

3. If a company makes a profit of $250 on sales of $1,900, the profit was approximately what percentage of sales?

(A) 10%
(B) 12%
(C) 13%
(D) 15%
(E) 17%

4. Which of the following numbers is the least common multiple of the numbers 2, 3, 4, and 5?

(A) 12
(B) 24
(C) 30
(D) 40
(E) 60

5. In a certain town 40% of the people have brown hair, 25% have brown eyes, and 10% have both brown hair and brown eyes. What percentage of the people in the town have neither brown hair nor brown eyes?

(A) 35
(B) 40
(C) 45
(D) 50
(E) 55

6. If the altitude of a triangle increases by 5% and the base of the triangle increases by 7%, by what percent will the area of the triangle increase?

(A) 3.33%
(B) 5%
(C) 6%
(D) 12%
(E) 12.35%

7. A shipping firm charges 2¢ a pound for the first 20 pounds of package weight and 1.5¢ for each pound or fraction of a pound over 20 pounds of package weight. How much will it charge to ship a package which weighs 23½ pounds?

(A) 6¢
(B) 8¢
(C) 45¢
(D) 46¢
(E) 47¢

8. If paper costs 1¢ a sheet, and a buyer gets a 2% discount on all the paper he buys after the first 1,000 sheets, how much will it cost to buy 5,000 sheets of paper?

(A) $49.20
(B) $50.00
(C) $3,920.00
(D) $4,920.00
(E) $5,000.00

9. Tom's salary is 150% of John's salary. John's salary is 80% of Steve's salary. What is the ratio of Steve's salary to Tom's salary?

(A) 1 to 2
(B) 2 to 3
(C) 5 to 6
(D) 6 to 5
(E) 5 to 4

10. A driver is taking a 5-hour trip. If he travels 135 miles in the first 3 hours, how far will he have to drive in the final 2 hours in order to average 50 miles an hour for the entire trip?

(A) 50 miles
(B) 55 miles
(C) 110 miles

(D) 115 miles
(E) 165 miles

11. If it takes 50 workers 4 hours to dig a sewer, how long should it take 30 workers to dig the same sewer?

(A) 2 hrs., 24 min.
(B) 5 hrs., 12 min.
(C) 6 hrs., 12 min.

(D) 6 hrs., 20 min.
(E) 6 hrs., 40 min.

Use the following graph for questions 12–14.

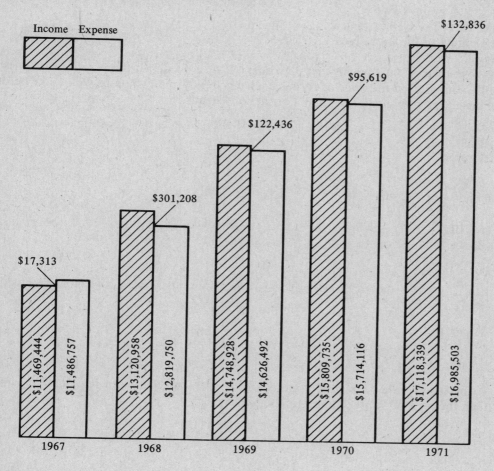

2. In what year was the profit (income minus expenses) the greatest?

(A) 1967
(B) 1968
(C) 1969

(D) 1970
(E) 1971

3. In how many of the years was the profit larger than in the preceding year?

(A) 0
(B) 1
(C) 2

(D) 3
(E) 4

14. Which of the following statements can be inferred from the graph?

    I. The company made a profit in all the years shown on the graph.
    II. The company's profit increased in every year between 1969 and 1971.
    III. The company's expenses increased in each year shown on the graph.

    (A) I only
    (B) II only
    (C) III only
    (D) I and III only
    (E) I, II, and III

15. If $x - 2$ is less than y then

    (A) x and y are positive
    (B) y is less than $x + 2$
    (C) y is greater than x
    (D) $y + 2$ is greater than x
    (E) none of the preceding

16. Wheat costs $2.00 a bushel and corn costs $2.62 a bushel. If the price of wheat rises 10% a month and the price of corn is unchanged, how many months will it take before a bushel of corn costs less than a bushel of wheat?

    (A) 2   (D) 5
    (B) 3   (E) 6
    (C) 4

17. If $\dfrac{1}{2} + \dfrac{1}{4} = \dfrac{x}{15}$, then x is

    (A) 10   (D) 13.75
    (B) 11.25   (E) 14
    (C) 12

18. If $x + y + z + w = 15$, then at least k of the numbers x, y, z, w must be positive where k is

    (A) 0   (D) 3
    (B) 1   (E) 4
    (C) 2

19. If the length of a rectangle is increased by 11% and the width remains the same, then the area of the rectangle is increased by

    (A) 11%   (D) 111%
    (B) 21%   (E) 121%
    (C) 110%

20. Which of the following figures has the largest area?

    I. A circle of radius $\sqrt{2}$.
    II. A equilateral triangle whose sides each have length 4.
    III. A triangle whose sides have lengths 3, 4, and 5.

    (A) I   (B) II   (C) III
    (D) I and II   (E) II and III

If there is still time remaining, you may review the questions in this section only. You may not turn to any other section of the test.

Section III   Analysis of Situations

TIME: 30 minutes

DIRECTIONS: Read the following passages. After you have completed each one, you will be asked to answer questions that involve determining the importance of specific factors included in the passage. When answering questions, you may consult the passage.

Passage 1:

Luigi Cappa was beginning to wonder what had made him give up a smoothly running job in New York to tackle what had turned out to be a baffling problem in southern Italy.

He was a U.S. citizen, and if he had stayed with his company he might have had a seat on the board within two years.

Then an uncle in Turin, in northern Italy, had written to Cappa, imploring him to come and run his printing plant near Palermo in Sicily, which produced transfer designs and other specialized printing, some of it for export.

Cappa was 28 years old, unmarried and ambitious. The offer had appealed to him in several ways.

First, there was the chance to be his own boss immediately. Second, there was the challenge, as Cappa saw it, of bringing U.S. know-how to the Italian family firm. Third, there was the satisfaction of returning as a man of some authority to the country where his own father had been born.

He was a believer in scientific management. He also believed that people everywhere are basically alike and will respond in about the same way to the carrot of cash rewards and the stick of firm leadership.

After only a few months in Palermo, he knew differently. Cappa's uncle had set up the plant five years previously with the active encouragement of the Italian government. But the 300-strong labor force still had no loyalty to the company from the distant north. The workers dreamed of orange groves rather than production targets.

Indeed, on one occasion Cappa had found a worker blissfully cleaning equipment from one of the printing machines in an orange grove near the plant. When he had ordered him back into the plant the man had looked astonished and replied: "Why should I work inside when I can do my job here?"

Productivity was very low. When Cappa had visited a local barber, who knew that he worked in the printing plant but did not know he was the boss, the man had said: "Sir, can you get me a job with the printing company so that I no longer have to work?"

As Cappa walked round the plant he saw plenty of modern machines. He also saw a workforce that yearned to be out in the sun, and wondered how he could get his employees to change their attitudes.

First, he tried using his personal appeal as an American-Italian. That did not work. He would have been more successful, he ruefully admitted to himself, had he been born in Palermo.

He instituted production committees, which were supposed to generate their own ideas on improving productivity. He worked at them very hard but they too were a dismal failure.

When managers sat on the committees the workers seemed struck dumb, failing to produce constructive ideas. Then, when Cappa gave the committee more autonomy to run its own affairs, the members used the time allocated for meetings to leave the factory and take a siesta outside.

Cappa decided that a bonus system relating pay directly to output was the only solution. At first the union opposed this, saying it was the kind of piecework they had been fighting against. Then, to Cappa's surprise, they gave in. He thought he had won a victory.

If so, it was a hollow one. The workers began demanding the bonus as a right, whether or not they had worked extra hours or produced more. When Cappa refused to pay, the workers went on strike.

Cappa felt that he was dealing with forces beyond his control, with people whom he could not fully understand.

"They just don't seem to want to participate," he wrote to a friend in New York. "If you give them the chance to run their own affairs, they take advantage of it. If you offer them a carrot, they eat half your arm as well. And if you wave a stick, they strike."

Cappa's friend replied that he should investigate the possibility of instituting a system of co-determination management. Co-determination management gives workers a part in making decisions within the firm in areas that are traditionally the prerogative of management. What the system amounts to—in practical terms—is that it allows workers to have some managerial authority in deciding corporate policy, and in some cases, objectives. Once a decision is made in principle to institute such a system, the next step is to work out just how much authority management is willing to share with the workers and in what policy areas.

Cappa decided to give co-determination a try as a last resort. Rather than dictate specific areas in which to implement co-determination, Cappa felt that it would be best to consult with workers' committees and then make a joint decision. At first, the workers expressed some interest in the plan, but when they asked Cappa to explain how the system would add to their pay, he was taken aback. Cappa tried to explain to the workers that they would gain decision-making authority, not only on the plant floor but in policy-making. He further explained that they would have some power to influence, for example, whether profits should be re-invested in the company, or distributed to shareholders. In reply, the workers' representatives said that they had no interest in having responsibility for managerial decisions because they had enough problems of their own. With that response, Cappa realized that his co-determination scheme had no chance of being accepted by the workers.

Cappa seemed to have reached a dead end. He could advise his uncle to concentrate production in Turin and get rid of the Palermo plant. But then he would have to return to the U.S. without a job and with a feeling of defeat.

Alternatively, Cappa could find a way of motivating his workers. But *how*, he asked himself for the thousandth time.

DIRECTIONS: The questions that follow relate to the preceding passage. Evaluate, in terms of the passage, each of the items given. Then select your answer from one of the following classifications, and blacken the corresponding space on the answer sheet.

(A) A MAJOR OBJECTIVE in making the decision: one of the goals sought by the decision maker

(B) A MAJOR FACTOR in making the decision: an aspect of the problem, specifically mentioned in the passage, that fundamentally affects and/or determines the decision

(C) A MINOR FACTOR in making the decision: a less important element bearing on or affecting a Major Factor, rather than a Major Objective directly

(D) A MAJOR ASSUMPTION in making the decision: a projection or supposition arrived at by the decision maker before considering the factors and alternatives

(E) AN UNIMPORTANT ISSUE in making the decision: an item lacking significant impact on, or relationship to, the decision

1. Location of company headquarters in northern Italy

2. Basic similarity of the motivations of people everywhere

3. Increasing the motivation of the Sicilian workers

4. Low worker productivity

5. Likelihood that higher pay would improve output

6. Cappa's U.S. citizenship

7. Degree of worker loyalty to the company

8. Usefulness of cash rewards in motivating employees

9. Desire of workers to run their own affairs

10. Relating pay to output

11. Quality of the machines used in the factory

12. Proximity of orange groves to the plant

13. Cappa's desire to meet with workers' committees before settling on a plan

14. Cappa's high degree of personal ambition

15. Power of the union to influence worker attitudes and behavior

16. Managing the Palermo printing plant

17. Cappa's chance to be his own boss

18. Producing transfer designs

Passage 2:

The Allied Industrial Rubber Company is a multinational corporation which is based in the United States with additional plants in Africa and Brazil. Sales have been increasing to levels exceeding one billion dollars. Production has gone up and the corporation itself is doing well. All plants concerned have responsible, intelligent management and employees so that labor relations, public relations, and basic operations have run smoothly. The plants in America and Africa are managed by Americans, while the plant in Brazil is managed by Brazilian nationals.

Allied had been conducting extensive economic scanning. This entailed the use of a standard economic measurement to provide a general comparison of the possibilities of different countries for setting up another firm. The firm had studied India for quite some time, and it was believed that India had the potential needed to become a site for an Allied plant. India had been considered because rubber is readily available and plentiful in supply, and is easily extracted. Jobs are scarce in India and thus cheap labor is available. The plant would offer a chance for many in the Indian population to better themselves and earn money from jobs supplied by the company.

After closer examination, the Allied Company decided to invest in India. After seven months the factory is nearing completion. It has already been decided that the labor force will be recruited from the native Indian population. Whether management-level positions will be filled by Americans or Indian nationals has not yet been decided.

Of course as with all foreign investments, requirements of the host country have to be considered and dealt with. Few regulations were laid out for the company to follow. No restrictions were specified as to the country from which managerial candidates would be selected. The consensus at Allied was that the majority of managerial jobs would be filled by either Indian nationals or American expatriates. It was decided that an even split would have the possibility of causing great internal conflict between management personnel. It is a well-known fact that European companies favor centralized control of operations by a select group of key executives. This gives precedence to a functionally orientated organizational structure. In the United States, on the other hand, companies favor a decentralized decision-making type of structure. However, in United States firms, there seem to be stricter control devices. However, whatever organization is selected, the company must remember that management must be amenable to the traditions and expectations of the labor force. If not, conflict may occur which will result in labor-management strife. Faced with the problem of how to select management, the Allied Industrial Rubber Company felt it was necessary to examine both the pros and the cons of hiring from either population. This was done through review of their two foreign plants in Africa and Brazil.

Allied's experience with American expatriate managers was examined first. Allied's African subsidiary, which has been operating successfully for the past six years, has Americans in key managerial positions. The pros of hiring Americans for managerial positions in Africa have been many. First and foremost, Allied has always felt more comfortable with American managers, because Allied is an American-based company. Another advantage has been that Allied has been able to transfer expatriate managers wherever and whenever necessary.

Hiring Americans has also been essential for the transfer and proper application of Allied technology. This has enabled Allied to receive maximum feedback from its plant. It has also provided a training ground for inexperienced, young executives. American expatriate managers have the advantage of gaining years of experience in a different and difficult environment. Also, by employing Americans, the company has eliminated the language barrier between subsidiary managers and those at the home base. Because of this, the geographic gap separating them has been narrowed. American expatriate managers seem to be more motivated and loyal. All of these qualifications are necessary for the successful operation of Allied. A final benefit of the use of expatriates has been elimination of the training sessions on company operations which these managers have already received in the United States.

Despite these advantages, there have been disadvantages to contend with. One major disadvantage has been the high costs of transferring Americans to Africa. Numerous incentives were necessary to lure them abroad. All costs of relocating were the firm's responsibility. The firm paid for transportation overseas, transportation while in Africa, housing, and domestic services, and provided a liberal expense account. In addition to this, managers were compensated by an increase in their base salary and a hardship premium.

An even bigger problem has been the cultural gap these managers and their families have experienced. Friends and relatives had to be left behind. Establishing new ties has been difficult because of the language barrier. There appears to be a higher rate of alcoholism, especially among the women, and rates of divorce also seem abnormally high. Furthermore, managers that returned to America had to take an unwelcome cut in salary. The managers remaining in Africa felt insecure with their position in the firm because of extended periods of time away from the home base.

Allied operations in Brazil have been relatively successful. Although Allied (Brazil) has been in operation for only four years, the use of Brazilian management has proved to be successful.

One of the major advantages of employing Brazilian managers has been the savings in costs through lower national salary levels. By offering salaries slightly above these low levels, Allied has succeeded in attracting brighter, more experienced people. On the average, this salary has been lower than what Allied would have had to pay an expatriate manager at the same level of expertise.

Through using Brazilian managers, Allied has eliminated the need for cross-cultural training and, of course, there is no language barrier between them and the other employees. These managers have also provided continuity of leadership for the past four years and presumably will do so for many more since the opportunity for advancement with the firm is very high.

Brazilians were hired not because the host country required that local nationals fill positions of importance, but mainly because there was a large pool of trained manpower. However, it was well known that the Brazilian government wanted local nationals to run the factory and was considering the adoption of national controls to achieve this goal. Therefore, Allied would not be affected if and when such legislation were to be enacted.

Hiring Brazilians, however, also has had disadvantages. Local managers require extensive training because of their lack of knowledge of Allied's technology, products, and managerial techniques. This training is costly, and several trainees left the company upon completion of the course. It was assumed that they used this training to obtain jobs elsewhere.

Allied was reluctant to transfer its technology to foreign employees, as this increased the potential for expropriation. Another fear concerned the vast differences in personal values. Most foreign employees cannot help but want to put the needs of their country first. Brazilians are no exception. Their lack of knowledge of and experience in other cultures leaves them ill prepared to work for multinational corporations. This may make them not always the best choice. However, they have run the Brazilian plant quite efficiently and effectively, and profit levels even exceed that of the African plant.

Given the experience of Allied with both expatriates and local nationals in the management of its plants in Africa and Brazil, management had to make a policy decision with regard to hiring in India.

DIRECTIONS: The questions that follow relate to the preceding passage. Evaluate, in terms of the passage, each of the items given. Then select your answer from one of the following classifications, and blacken the corresponding space on the answer sheet.

(A) A MAJOR OBJECTIVE in making the decision: one of the goals sought by the decision maker

(B) A MAJOR FACTOR in making the decision: an aspect of the problem, specifically mentioned in the passage, that fundamentally affects and/or determines the decision

(C) A MINOR FACTOR in making the decision: a less important element bearing on or affecting a Major Factor, rather than a Major Objective directly

(D) A MAJOR ASSUMPTION in making the decision: a projection or supposition arrived at by the decision maker before considering the factors and alternatives

(E) AN UNIMPORTANT ISSUE in making the decision: an item lacking significant impact on, or relationship to, the decision

19. Availability of rubber in India

20. Recruiting managers for working in India

21. Centralization of European company management

22. Respecting labor force traditions

23. High costs of transferring Americans abroad

24. Divorce rates of expatriate managers

25. Control methods in American firms

26. Indian government restrictions on the hiring of expatriates

27. Cost of transporting expatriates

28. Cultural problems overseas

29. Possibility of internal conflict

30. Allied's experience in Africa and Brazil

31. Eliminating the language barrier

32. Costs of housing expatriates

33. Longevity of the Brazilian operation

34. Cost of hiring Brazilian managers

35. Cross-cultural training in Brazil

If there is still time remaining, you may review the questions in this section only.
You may not turn to any other section of the test.

Section IV Data Sufficiency

TIME: 30 minutes

DIRECTIONS: Each of the following problems has a question and two statements which are labeled (1) and (2). Use the data given in (1) and (2) together with other available information (such as the number of hours in a day, the definition of *clockwise*, mathematical facts, etc.) to decide whether the statements are *sufficient* to answer the question. Then fill in space

(A) if you can get the answer from (1) alone but not from (2) alone;

(B) if you can get the answer from (2) alone but not from (1) alone;

(C) if you can get the answer from (1) and (2) together, although neither statement by itself suffices;

(D) if statement (1) alone suffices *and* statement (2) alone suffices;

(E) if you cannot get the answer from statements (1) and (2) together, but need even more data.

All numbers used in this section are real numbers. A figure given for a problem is intended to provide information consistent with that in the question, but not necessarily with the additional information contained in the statements.

1. *ABC* is a triangle inscribed in circle *AOCB*. Is *AC* a diameter of the circle *AOCB*?

   (1) Angle *ABC* is a right angle.
   (2) The length of *AB* is ¾ the length of *BC*.

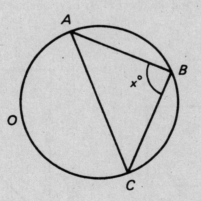

2. A cylindrical tank has a radius of 10 feet and its height is 20 feet. How many gallons of a liquid can be stored in the tank?

   (1) A gallon of the liquid occupies .13 cubic feet of space.
   (2) The diameter of the tank is 20 feet.

3. How many books are on the bookshelf?

   (1) The average weight of each book is 1.2 pounds.
   (2) The books and the bookshelf together weigh 34 pounds.

4. Is the triangle *ABC* congruent to the triangle *DEF*? *x* is equal to *y*.

   (1) *AB* is equal to *DE*.
   (2) *BC* is equal to *EF*.

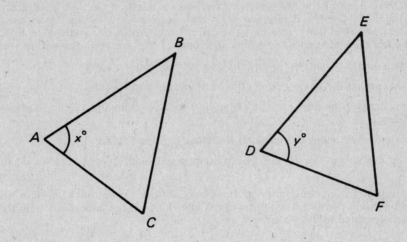

5. A plane flies over New York City. What is its speed in miles per hour?

   (1) The plane is flying in a circle.
   (2) The plane is flying at the speed of ⅑ mile per second.

6. Mr. Carpenter wants to build a room in the shape of a rectangle. The area of the floor will be 32 square feet. What is the length of the floor?

   (1) The length of the floor will be twice the width of the floor.
   (2) The width of the floor will be 4 feet less than the length of the floor.

7. Do the rectangle *ABCD* and the square *EFGH* have the same area?

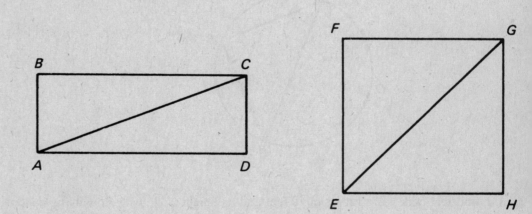

   (1) *AC* = *EG*, *AB* = ½ *EH*
   (2) The area of triangle *ABC* is not equal to the area of triangle *EFG*.

8. How much does Susan weigh?

   (1) Susan and Joan together weigh 250 pounds.
   (2) Joan weighs twice as much as Susan.

9. Two different holes, hole A and hole B, are put in the bottom of a full water tank. If the water drains out through the holes, how long before the tank is empty?

(1) If only hole A is put in the bottom, the tank will be empty in 24 minutes.
(2) If only hole B is put in the bottom, the tank will be empty in 42 minutes.

10. Find $x + y$

(1) $x - y = 6$
(2) $-2x + 2y = -12$

11. C is a circle with center D and radius 2. E is a circle with center F and radius R. Are there any points which are on both E and C?

(1) The distance from D to F is $1 + R$.
(2) $R = 3$.

12. Mr. Parker made $20,000 in 1967. What is Mr. Parker's average yearly income for the three years 1967 to 1969?

(1) He made 10% more in each year than he did in the previous year.
(2) His total combined income for 1968 and 1969 was $46,200.

13. Is angle ACB a right angle?

(1) $y = z$
(2) $(AC)^2 + (CB)^2 = (AB)^2$

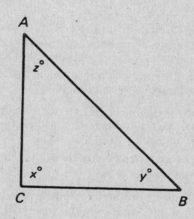

14. John and Paul are standing together on a sunny day. John's shadow is 10 feet long. Paul's shadow is 9 feet long. How tall is Paul?

(1) John is 6 feet tall.
(2) John is standing 2 feet away from Paul.

15. Is x greater than y?

(1) x^2 is greater than y^2
(2) $x + 3$ is greater than $y + 2$

16. A dozen eggs cost 90¢ in January 1980. Did a dozen eggs cost more than 90¢ in January 1981?

(1) In January 1980, the average worker had to work 5 minutes to pay for a dozen eggs.
(2) In January 1981, the average worker had to work 4 minutes to pay for a dozen eggs.

17. How many raffle tickets were sold if ticket sales brought in receipts of $10,000?

(1) Each ticket was sold for 25¢.
(2) 4000 books of tickets were sold.

18. What is the value of $\frac{x}{y}$? $x > 0$.

(1) $x = \frac{1}{4}y$
(2) $y = 400\%$ of x

19. What is the area of the circular sector AOB? A and B are points on the circle which has O as its center.

(1) Angle $AOB = 72°$.
(2) $OB = 4$

20. How many of the numbers x, y, and z are positive? x, y, and z are all less than 30.

(1) $x + y + z = 61$
(2) $x + y = 35$

21. How far is it from town A to town B? Town C is 15 miles west of town A.

(1) It is 10 miles from town B to town C.
(2) There is a river between town A and town B.

22. In 1980, the ratio of American cars sold to imported cars sold was 4 to 1. How many imported cars were sold in 1980?

(1) 6,000,000 American cars were sold in 1980.
(2) A total of 7,500,000 cars were sold in 1980.

23. What percentage of families in the state have annual incomes over $25,000 and own a sailboat?

(1) 28% of all the families in the state have an annual income over $25,000.
(2) 40% of the families in the state with an annual income over $25,000 own a sailboat.

24. What is the value of $x - y$?

(1) $x = 5$
(2) $x + 2y = 2x + y$

25. What is the radius of the circle with center O?

(1) The area of the circle is 25π.
(2) The area of the circle divided by the diameter of the circle is equal to π times $\frac{1}{2}$ of the radius of the circle.

If there is still time remaining, you may review the questions in this section only.
You may not turn to any other section of the test.

Section V   Writing Ability

DIRECTIONS: This test consists of a number of sentences, in each of which some part or the whole is underlined. Each sentence is followed by five alternative versions of the underlined portion. Select the alternative you consider both most correct and most effective according to the requirements of standard written English. Answer A is the same as the original version; if you think the original version is best, select answer A.

In considering the answer choices, be attentive to matters of grammar, diction, and syntax, as well as clarity, precision, and fluency. Do not select an answer which alters the meaning of the original sentence.

1. In her candid autobiography, the author discusses her early years, her desire to become an actress, and how she made her debut on the stage.

   (A) to become an actress, and how she made
   (B) that she become an actress, and how she made
   (C) to be come an actress, and
   (D) that she become an actress, and
   (E) that she become an actress and that she make

2. Government authorities predicted correctly that tremendous savings in the consumption of gasoline would be achieved if speeding was to be limited to 55 miles per hour.

   (A) speeding was to be limited to
   (B) motorists limited their speed to
   (C) speeding did not exceed
   (D) a motorist was to limit his speed to
   (E) speeding by motorists was to be limited to

3. The word processor has revolutionized office procedures more than any machine of modern times.

   (A) any machine
   (B) has any machine
   (C) any other machine
   (D) has any other machine
   (E) any other machine has

4. Bullied by his wife and intimidated by policemen and parking lot attendants alike, daydreaming about being a surgeon, a crack pistol shot, and so on, enable Walter Mitty to cope with the real world.

   (A) daydreaming about being a surgeon, a crack pistol shot, and so on, enable Walter Mitty to cope with the real world
   (B) daydreaming about being a surgeon, a crack pistol shot, and so on, enables Walter Mitty to cope with the real world
   (C) Walter Mitty reacts to the real world by his daydreams of being a surgeon, a crack pistol shot, and so on
   (D) Walter Mitty escapes from the real world by his daydreams of being a surgeon, a crack pistol shot, and so on
   (E) Walter Mitty is able to cope with the real world by daydreaming of being a surgeon, a crack pistol shot, and so on

5. The possibility of expropriation was believed to be unlikely in the near future <u>due to the lack of mining technology and</u> capital available in this small South American country.

   (A) due to the lack of mining technology and
   (B) because of the lack of mining technology and
   (C) because there was no mining technology and
   (D) because of the lack of mining technology and there was no
   (E) due to the lack of mining technology and there was no

6. <u>The owner of a Super-11 Food Store on Glen Avenue told police he was robbed of $7,500 in store receipts by a gunman wearing a ski mask as he was about to make a night deposit.</u>

   (A) The owner of a Super-11 food store on Glen Avenue told police he was robbed of $7,500 in store receipts by a gunman wearing a ski mask as he was about to make a night deposit.
   (B) Police said that the owner of a Super-11 Food Store on Glen Avenue was robbed of $7,500 in store receipts by a gunman wearing a ski mask as he was about to make a night deposit.
   (C) As he was about to make a night deposit, a gunman wearing a ski mask robbed him of $7,500 in store receipts, the owner of a Super-11 Food Store on Glen Avenue told police.
   (D) The owner of a Super-11 Food Store on Glen Avenue told police that, as he was about to make a night deposit, he was robbed of $7,500 in store receipts by a gunman wearing a ski mask.
   (E) As the owner of a Super-11 Food Store on Glen Avenue was about to make a night deposit, he told police that he was robbed of $7,500 in store receipts by a man wearing a ski mask.

7. The doctrine applies in Canada, where there <u>is a federal law and a provincial law that are each valid and</u> consistent.

   (A) is a federal law and a provincial law that are each valid and
   (B) are a federal law and a provincial law that are each valid and
   (C) are a federal law and a provincial law both of which are each valid and
   (D) is a federal law and a provincial law both of which are each valid and
   (E) are a federal law and a provincial law that are each valid or

8. Former Postal Service employees who believe they <u>may be affected</u> by this settlement should contact their last place of USPS employment, the department advised.

   (A) may be affected
   (B) may be effected
   (C) will have been affected
   (D) will be effected
   (E) will have been effected

9. Blake is among the very few individuals <u>who critics regard as genuinely significant in the history of both</u> art and literature.

   (A) who critics regard as genuinely significant in the history of both
   (B) whom critics regard as genuinely significant in the history of both
   (C) whom critics regard as genuinely significant both in the history of
   (D) who critics regard as genuinely significant both in the history of
   (E) who is regarded by critics as genuinely significant in the history of both

10. Many scientists are alarmed over the interest in such pseudo-scientific topics as ESP, flying saucers, and the occult, fearing that <u>this interest may herald a new dark age of gullibility, ignorance, and thinking in superstitious ways.</u>

(A) this interest may herald a new dark age of gullibility, ignorance, and thinking in superstitious ways

(B) it may herald a new dark age of gullibility, ignorance, and thinking in superstitious ways

(C) it may herald a new dark age of gullibility, ignorance, and superstition

(D) this interest may herald a new dark age of gullibility, ignorance, and superstition

(E) they may herald a new dark age of gullibility, ignorance, and superstition

11. <u>Having broken with Freud, Jung's later writings nevertheless bore signs of the continued</u> influence of Freudian doctrine and theories.

(A) Having broken with Freud, Jung's later writings nevertheless bore signs of the continued

(B) Since breaking with Freud, Jung's later writings nevertheless bore signs of the continued

(C) Although he had broken with Freud, in his later writings Jung nevertheless showed signs of the continued

(D) Having broken with Freud, Jung's later writings nevertheless bore signs of the continual

(E) Having broken with Freud, later writings by Jung nevertheless bore signs of the continued

12. That Giotto's paintings are significant in the history of the early Renaissance is undeniable, but Giotto <u>cannot scarcely be considered</u> the equal of such masters as Leonardo and Raphael.

(A) cannot scarcely be considered

(B) can scarcely be considered

(C) cannot hardly be considered

(D) cannot scarcely be considered to be

(E) isn't hardly to be considered

13. Although the theory of continental drift <u>was not widely accepted until the mid-twentieth century, the basic concept had been</u> described as early as 1620.

(A) was not widely accepted until the mid-twentieth century, the basic concept had been

(B) was not widely accepted until the mid-twentieth century, the basic concept was

(C) was not widely accepted until the mid-twentieth century, the basic concept has been

(D) had not been widely accepted until the mid-twentieth century, the basic concept has been

(E) had not been widely accepted until the mid-twentieth century, the basic concept was

14. The reason I am supporting Senator Blandings is <u>because her extensive background in foreign affairs has made her uniquely qualified for</u> a seat on this important sub-committee.

(A) because her extensive background in foreign affairs has made her uniquely qualified for

(B) that her extensive background in foreign affairs have made her uniquely qualified for

(C) that her extensive background in foreign affairs has made her uniquely qualified for

   (D) that her extensive background in foreign affairs has made her uniquely qualified to

   (E) because her extensive background in foreign affairs have made her uniquely qualified for

15. Even without any promotion of passenger service by Amtrak, there <u>has been sufficient numbers of passengers leaving and arriving at this station to warrant not only continuing the two daily stops here but also maintaining</u> the agent and station.

   (A) has been sufficient numbers of passengers leaving and arriving at this station to warrant not only continuing the two daily stops here but also maintaining

   (B) have been sufficient numbers of passengers leaving and arriving at this station to warrant not only continuing the two daily stops here but also maintaining

   (C) have been sufficient numbers of passengers leaving and arriving at this station not only to warrant continuing the two daily stops here but also maintaining

   (D) has been sufficient numbers of passengers leaving and arriving at this station to not only warrant continuing the two daily stops here but also maintaining

   (E) have been sufficient numbers of passengers leaving and arriving at this station to warrant not only continuing the two daily stops here but also to maintain

16. Fear of future nationalistic feelings and a conviction that natural resource endowments should be exploited for the welfare of the residents of the country, <u>rather than for private profit, are</u> shared by all managers of extractive industries there.

   (A) rather than for private profit, are

   (B) rather than for private profit, is

   (C) irregardless of private profit, are

   (D) as opposed to private profit, is

   (E) and not necessarily for private profit, is

17. The lieutenant reminded his men that <u>the only information to be given to the enemy if captured was each individual's name, rank, and serial number.</u>

   (A) the only information to be given to the enemy if captured was each individual's name, rank, and serial number

   (B) the only information to be given to the enemy if they were captured was each individual's name, rank, and serial number

   (C) the only information to be given to the enemy if captured were each individual's name, rank, and serial number

   (D) , if captured, the only information to be given to the enemy was each individual's name, rank, and what his serial number was

   (E) , if they were captured, the only information to be given to the enemy was each individual's name, rank, and serial number

18. Writing a beautiful sonnet is as much an achievement as <u>to finish</u> a 400-page novel.

   (A) to finish

   (B) it is to finish

   (C) finishing

   (D) if you finished

   (E) to have finished

19. Anyone interested in computer programming can find a job in contemporary industry <u>if you learn</u> the basic programming languages, such as COBOL and FORTRAN.

   (A) if you learn

   (B) if you will learn

   (C) if he would learn

   (D) by the study of

   (E) by studying

20. During the gasoline shortage of the 1970s caused by the actions of the OPEC nations, <u>the number of accidents on our highways decreased markedly</u>.

   (A) the number of accidents on our highways decreased markedly
   (B) the amount of accidents on our highways decreased markedly
   (C) there were less accidents on our highways
   (D) there were a fewer amount of accidents on our highways
   (E) they found there were many fewer accidents on our highways

21. <u>Being that only twenty-four states</u> have ratified the proposed amendment, we can assume that it will not be adopted.

   (A) Being that only twenty-four states
   (B) Since twenty-four states only
   (C) Being as only twenty-four states
   (D) Seeing as how only twenty-four states
   (E) Inasmuch as only twenty-four states

22. I have studied the works of George Bernard Shaw not only for their plots but <u>also because they are very witty</u>.

   (A) also because they are very witty
   (B) because they are also very witty
   (C) for their wit also
   (D) because they are very witty also
   (E) also for their wit

23. <u>The noise at the airport was deafening, which made conversation</u> difficult if not impossible.

   (A) The noise at the airport was deafening, which made conversation
   (B) The noise at the airport was deafening, and it made conversation
   (C) The deafening noise at the airport made conversation
   (D) The airport noise was deafening, which made conversation
   (E) The noise at the airport was deafening, conversation being

24. The majority of New Yorkers <u>have not been aware that one out of five English-speaking adults in the city lacks</u> critical reading and writing skills.

   (A) have not been aware that one out of five English-speaking adults in the city lacks
   (B) have not been aware that one out of five English-speaking adults in the city lack
   (C) has not been aware that one out of five English-speaking adults in the city lack
   (D) has not been aware that one out of five English-speaking adults in the city lacks
   (E) have not been aware that there are one out of five English-speaking adults in the city lacking

25. Inflation in the United States has not <u>and, we hope, never will reach</u> a rate of 20 percent a year.

   (A) and, we hope, never will reach
   (B) reached and, we hope, never will
   (C) and hopefully never will reach
   (D) reached and, we hope, never will reach
   (E) reached and hopefully never will

*If there is still time remaining, you may review the questions in this section only.
You may not turn to any other section of the test.*

Section VI   Critical Reasoning

TIME: 30 minutes

DIRECTIONS: For each question, choose the best answer among the listed alternatives.

1. The Black Death that reached Sicily in October 1347 from the ports of the Crimea traveled the same route as many slaves. Reflecting the rates of transportation of rats and fleas as well as of humans, the disease itself demonstrated the commercial integration of Western Europe. It arrived in England — having devastated France — in the summer of 1348, reached Sweden and Poland towards the end of 1349, and in the course of three years had infected the whole of the West with the exceptions of Bohemia and Hungary.

Which of the following statements best summarizes the above?

(A) The spread of the Black Death was caused by the commercial integration of Western Europe.
(B) The spread of the Black Death was caused by increasing rates of transportation.
(C) The spread of the Black Death was caused by the transportation of slaves.
(D) The spread of the Black Death was caused by the transportation of rats and fleas.
(E) The spread of the Black Death was caused by increasing contacts with the parts of the Crimea.

2. In almost all developing countries, the initial thrust of their respective trade policies was to foster domestic industries whose production would replace imports. This was a natural and logical strategy, given that import-substituting production could count on an existing known domestic demand, promised some mitigation of national economic dependence, and could be protected easily from external competition through high tariffs, quotas, or subsidies of various kinds.

Which of the following, if true, would weaken the strategy above?

(A) Domestic demand may be unknown.
(B) Quotas are more regressive than tariffs.
(C) Subsidies and import constraints keep domestic prices high and impose a burden on consumers.
(D) Fast economic growth fosters inequality of income.
(E) A protectionist policy may be beneficial to the developing country, but disliked by developing countries.

3. The 15th century was a period in which there was more reading and traveling than at any earlier period of the Middle Ages. The result was an increase of informed opinion, talk and discussion, and greater questioning over a wide range of topics, and the exchange stimulated by travel helped to modify the opinions of many different individuals. Despite the continuance of intolerance, persecution, and extremism, belief was growing in the agreement attainable through argument, in the power of books, and in peaceable persuasion.

Which of the following statements best summarizes the above?

(A) The 15th century is best characterized by intolerance, persecution, and extremism.
(B) The 15th century is best characterized as an age of doubting.
(C) In the 15th century, books were only available to those who traveled.
(D) The experience of books and travel brought new classes of people new confidence and new doubts.
(E) The 15th century was an age of peaceable persuasion.

4. The quantitative supply of labor (as well as its qualitative composition) depends on the following variables: the size of the population, its age-sex composition, marital structure, and participation rates in the labor force in accordance with these factors.

Each of the following, if true, could affect the supply of labor EXCEPT:

(A) Birth and death rates.
(B) Immigration and emigration.
(C) Educational level of the population.
(D) Number of employment agencies.
(E) Marital status of females.

5. In order to discourage present suburban growth patterns, which because of their low densities are uneconomic to service and wasteful of land and resources, land use policy studies should include research into innovative forms of high density, low-rise housing.

The above statement is a response to all of the following problems EXCEPT:

(A) The tendency to exclude light industry from residential areas means that people have to go outside their communities to seek work.
(B) The traditional practice of using land as a commodity rather than a resource has meant that the location of new communities is often solely governed by a developer's economic convenience.
(C) There is a lack of coordination between the planning and structure of communities and their relation to transportation networks.
(D) Present patterns of urban growth have squandered agricultural and rural lands.
(E) In houses designed for the standard family, there is a lack of inter and intra-unit privacy.

6. Over the last 20 years the rate of increase in total production in Workland has been second to none in the world. However, the growth is more modest when calculated per capita of total population. Over the last ten years progress has been much slower.

If the information above is accurate, which of the following must be true?

(A) Workland has a very large population.
(B) Productivity per capita has not grown as fast during the past ten years.
(C) Total production has increased faster than population growth.
(D) The birth rate has declined.
(E) The per capita production rate has not declined.

7. The earliest known proto-Eskimo are those of the Cape Denbigh Flint complex of northwestern Alaska. Denbigh people and their descendants were well equipped to survive in the Arctic. Their adaptive success is obvious in the speed with which they spread eastward across arctic Canada to northeast Greenland which they reached by 2000 B.C.

Which of the following, if true, would refute the above?

(A) The Cape Denbigh Flint complex dates back to 3000 B.C.
(B) The Vikings populated Greenland between 800 and 1100 A.D.
(C) Artifacts of early settlements in northeast Greenland date back further than artifacts found on Baffin Island.
(D) Denbigh origin lies in the Paleolithic and the Mesolithic periods of the Far East and in the early Neolithic period, say about 4000 B.C., of Siberia.
(E) The Denbigh people are known almost solely from their flint tools.

8. Harry Dyner was the Minister of Petroleum in a small oil-producing country. His country's oil exports were approximately 2 percent of total world oil sales. The Minister of Finance was anxious to maximize petroleum production and export to earn foreign exchange. Dyner, however, believed that increased sales would only drive down the world price of petroleum and lower his country's foreign exchange revenue.

Which of the following would best exemplify an error in Dyner's reasoning?

(A) Price of crude v. price of refined petroleum.
(B) Production goals v. financial goals.
(C) Individually produced supply v. aggregate supply on the market.
(D) Seasonal v. long-term supply.
(E) Long-term v. short-term demand.

9. There is no clear line between health and illness; it is easy to forget what it feels like to be really well and to get gradually used to often having a headache, feeling irritable, or tired. There is an unrecognized proportion of the population that has been tipped over the brink into ill health by ubiquitous contaminents.

Which of the following statements best describes the purpose of the above?

(A) The public must be encouraged to have regular medical examinations.
(B) The public must be warned to be aware of various physical and chemical hazards.
(C) The public must be warned to treat seriously such symptoms as headaches, irritability, and tiredness.
(D) The medical professional is not always capable of diagnosing illness.
(E) No one can really be sure if he is healthy or ill.

10. Administrators and executives are members of the most stable occupation.

The above statement, if true, could be a function of each of the following variables EXCEPT:

(A) Training and skills.
(B) Nature of the occupation.
(C) Status.
(D) Relatively high income.
(E) Rate of turnover.

11. By far the chief export in the 15th century was textiles. Among these, woolens and worsteds predominated; linens were far less important and silks played an insignificant part. Outside this group, the only important item in the first half of the century was corn, though the exports of fish, lead, and tin were by no means negligible.

Which of the following statements is correct given the above information?

(A) Corn, though not as important an export was still an important component of the export trade.
(B) Corn was nearly as important an export as linen.
(C) Silk was a valuable export in the 15th century.
(D) Fishing was a bigger industry than wool production in the 15th century.
(E) Nontextile items were one of the chief elements in the list of products exported in the 15th century.

12. Self-employment is found more often among men and women in the 25- to 44-year-old group than among their older or younger counterparts. Some 31 percent of the men and only 19 percent of the women who operate unincorporated businesses on a full-time basis completed four or more years of college. And while self-employed men are generally better educated than their wage-and-salary counterparts, the same cannot be said of self-employed women.

If the information above is accurate, which of the following must be true?

(A) Self-employed women are generally younger than self-employed men.
(B) Self-employed men are better educated than self-employed women.
(C) Women wage earners are better educated than men wage earners.
(D) Salaried men are younger then self-employed men.
(E) Self-employed men and women are better educated than wage-earning men and women.

13. Between 1940 and 1945 gasoline consumption in the U.S. dropped about 35 percent because of wartime rationing. In the same period, lung cancer in U.S. white males declined by approximately the same percentage. Between 1914 and 1950 lung cancer mortality increased nineteenfold and the rate of gasoline consumption increased at the same rate.

Which of the following facts, if true, would weaken the above argument?

(A) Between 1939 and 1949 lung cancer among urban blacks in the United States remained at the same level.
(B) The amount of lead in gasoline increased between 1916 and 1944.
(C) After 1950 gasoline consumption jumped.
(D) During World War II, people suffering from cancer were forbidden to drive.
(E) Women first began driving in large numbers between 1941 and 1951.

14. From 1920 to 1950, the amount of food production per worker and per hour increased twofold. From 1950 to 1980, food production per worker and per hour increased 1.3 times.

Each of the following, if true, could help to account for this trend EXCEPT:

(A) The number of farm workers increased.
(B) The use of mechanical technology in food production increased.
(C) Chemical fertilizers were more widely adopted in farming.
(D) The number of hours worked per unit of output decreased.
(E) Fewer workers were needed to produce the same unit of output.

15. "Some men are certainly tall, others are certainly not tall; but of intermediate men, we should say, 'tall'? Yes, I *think* so or no, I shouldn't be inclined to call him tall."

Which of the following most accurately reflects the intention of the writer of the above?

(A) Men intermediately tall, partake of "tallness" to a moderate degree.
(B) To call men tall who are not strikingly so must be to use the concept with undue imprecision.
(C) Every empirical concept has a degree of vagueness.
(D) There is really no need to be as indecisive as the writer of the above.
(E) Calling someone tall or short depends upon one's whim.

16. There are many reasons why individuals want to run their own businesses. Some foresee more personal satisfaction if they are successful in launching their own business, while others are interested mainly in the prospect of larger financial rewards. Since the late 1970s and early 1980s, tax regulations and other changes have encouraged increasing numbers of venture capitalists and entrepreneurs to start new enterprises. Since 1980, some one-half million new ventures have been started. Not all have succeeded, of course.

The above statement makes which of the following assumptions?

(A) Success in starting a new business depends in large part on sound financial planning.
(B) Social incentives motivate investors just as mush as financial rewards.
(C) Financial incentives are associated with new business starts.
(D) Most new business ventures succeed initially but fail later on.
(E) Venture capitalists are motivated by nonmonetary gains.

17. From the mint of Matthew Boulton in Birmingham there poured a stream of two penny pieces, pennies, halfpennies and other copper coins. Soon after these were issued in 1797, the price of copper began to rise and so the two penny pieces and penny pieces quickly disappeared into the melting pot.

Each of the following resulted from the above occurrence EXCEPT:

(A) Businessmen were forced to search the country for ready cash.
(B) Wages were paid in raw materials and manufactured goods.

(C) Expenditure increased as did employment.

(D) Gold was declared to be the sole standard and full legal tender.

(E) Incomes decreased.

18. The development of the American consumer might have been influenced by the tradition of the frontier, which made self-reliance necessary, as well as by the experience of immigration. The European consumer, on the other hand, might have been fashioned by the not-yet-forgotten experience of distinct classes and class rigidity, as well as by the former absence of geographical and occupational mobility.

The thesis above assumes that:

(A) European consumers are more experienced buyers than their counterparts in America.

(B) American consumers have not reached the sophistication of Europeans.

(C) Social class has a greater influence on consumer behavior in Europe than in America.

(D) A study of consumerism must take into consideration social class structure, tradition, acculturation, and mobility.

(E) Consumer behavior is not an exact science as evidenced by the lack of a definitive framework for understanding the differences between buyers in different countries.

19. Before the middle of the 14th century, there were no universities north of Italy, outside France and England. By the end of the 15th century, there were 23 universities in this region, from Louvain and Mainz to Rostock, Cracow, and Bratislava and the number of universities in Europe as a whole had more than doubled.

Which of the following statements is correct, given the above information?

(A) Until the age of university expansion in the 15th century, there were perhaps 11 universities in the whole of Europe.

(B) South of Italy there were 23 universities in the 14th century.

(C) In the 13th century, France and England were the only countries in Europe with universities.

(D) After the great age of university expansion in the 14th century, France and England were not the only northern European countries to have such centers of learning.

(E) Italy was the cradle of university expansion.

20. Between 1979 and 1983, the number of unincorporated business self-employed women increased five times faster than the number of self-employed men and more than three times faster than women wage-and-salary workers. Part-time self-employment among women increased more than full-time self-employment.

Each of the following, if true, could help to account for this trend EXCEPT:

(A) Owning a business affords flexibility to combine work and family responsibilities.

(B) The proportion of women studying business administration courses has grown considerably.

(C) There are more self-employed women than men.

(D) Unincorporated service industries have grown by 300 percent over the period; the ratio of women to men in this industry is three to one.

(E) The financial reward of having a second wage earner in the household has taken on increased significance.

21. The training of scientists should include more focused concern on the history of the sciences. The emphasis should be placed on how the accepted notions of physical, biological, and behavioral sciences have varied over time and how "facts" and "knowledge" were always relative to the preconceptions, assumptions, and paradigms that existed at a given time.

Which of the following problems would prompt the above advice?

(A) Discoveries or ideas that challenge the dominant, conceptual framework are not readily accepted.

(B) Some scientists fail to use precise experimental methods.

(C) Serious mistakes are made in the statistical analysis used in research reports.

(D) Specific personal attributes of the experimenter can affect the performance of subjects.

(E) Experimenters' expectancies or desires influence their subjects' responses.

22. Foreign investment is composed of direct investment transactions (investment in plant, equipment, and land) and securities investment transactions. Throughout the post-World War II period, net increases in U.S. direct investment in Europe (funds outflows) exceeded net new European direct investment in the U.S.

Each of the following, if true, could help to account for this trend EXCEPT:

(A) Land values in Europe were increasing at a faster rate than in the United States.

(B) Duties on imported goods in Europe were higher than those imposed by the United States.

(C) The cost of labor (wages) was consistently lower in Europe than in the United States.

(D) Labor mobility was much higher in the United States than in Europe.

(E) Corporate liquidity was lower in Europe than in the United States.

23. Social security law is an evolving law that tries as far as possible to reflect reality — to adjust to changes in and the needs of society.

Which of the following statements best summarizes the above?

(A) Legislation lags behind reality.

(B) Social security law gradually adapts itself to societal demands.

(C) A good social security system ought to reflect every change in social values.

(D) Changes in social conditions and needs imply the necessity for changes in social security legislation.

(E) We need to study social needs.

24. Opinion polls show that most Americans favor the idea of unpaid leave (up to 18 weeks) for working parents to care for newly born or seriously ill children. With a majority of mothers in the work force, including half of all new mothers, leaves of absence offer many parents a new opportunity to spend time with young children.

Which of the following, if true, would weaken the argument above?

(A) Parental leave is an option for those who choose it and accept its costs.

(B) Not everyone would take the full 18 weeks.

(C) Parental leave would reduce employee turnover and improve morale.

(D) Parental leave requires the hiring of temporary replacements and maintaining health insurance for those on leave.

(E) Raising children is not merely a private concern but also a social imperative.

25. Starting in 1955, all workers had to wear steel helmets if they were employed in the construction industry.

From which of the following can the statement above be properly inferred?

(A) No workers had to wear steel helmets before 1955, but all workers had to wear them after 1955.

(B) Construction industry workers were the first to be required to wear steel helmets.

(C) Construction industry workers had to wear steel helmets prior to 1955.

(D) Some workers may have worn steel helmets before 1955, but all construction workers were required to wear them beginning in 1955.

(E) Workers may have worn some type of helmet before 1955, but later all had to wear steel-type helmets.

If there is still time remaining, you may review the questions in this section only.
You may not turn to any other section of the test.

Section VII   Writing Ability

TIME: 30 minutes

DIRECTIONS: This test consists of a number of sentences, in each of which some part or the whole is underlined. Each sentence is followed by five alternative versions of the underlined portion. Select the alternative you consider both most correct and most effective according to the requirements of standard written English. Answer A is the same as the original version; if you think the original version is best, select answer A.

In considering the answer choices, be attentive to matters of grammar, diction, and syntax, as well as clarity, precision, and fluency. Do not select an answer which alters the meaning of the original sentence.

1. Since neither of the agencies had submitted the necessary documentation, each were required to reapply for the grant the following year.

   (A) each were required to reapply for the grant the following year
   (B) each were required, the following year, to reapply for the grant
   (C) each was required to reapply for the grant the following year
   (D) both were required to reapply, the following year, for the grant
   (E) it was required to reapply for the grant the following year

2. Stationary missile launching sites are frequently criticized by military experts on the ground that, in comparison to mobile units, they are the most vulnerable to preemptive attack.

   (A) they are the most
   (B) such sites are the most
   (C) they are rather
   (D) stationary sites are most
   (E) they are more

3. The qualities needed in a president are scarcely tested in today's political campaigns which call instead for showmanship, good looks, and being able to seem eloquent while saying nothing.

   (A) being able to seem eloquent
   (B) the ability to seem eloquent
   (C) having eloquence
   (D) a certain eloquence
   (E) that he seem eloquent

4. Anyone who would speak with authority on the poets of the Renaissance must have a broad acquaintance with the writers of classical antiquity.

   (A) Anyone who would speak
   (B) If one would speak
   (C) He which would speak
   (D) Anyone desirous for speaking
   (E) Those who have a wish to speak

5. Having chosen to demand an immediate vote on the issue, because of his belief that a sizable majority was within easy reach.

   (A) Having chosen to demand an immediate vote on the issue
   (B) An immediate vote on the issue having been demanded
   (C) He had chosen to demand an immediate vote on the issue
   (D) His demand had been for an immediate vote to be held on the issue
   (E) He had chosen that a vote on the issue should be held immediately

6. In its final report, the commission proposed, among other measures, that the legal drinking age be raised from eighteen to twenty-one.

   (A) that the legal drinking age be raised

(B) a rise of the legal drinking age
(C) that the legal drinking age should be raised
(D) raising the age of drinking legally
(E) to raise legally the drinking age

7. Since neither <u>her nor the Dean were willing</u> to veto the curriculum changes, they went into effect as of September 1.

(A) her nor the Dean were willing
(B) she nor the Dean was willing
(C) her nor the Dean wished
(D) she or the Dean was willing
(E) she nor the Dean were willing

8. A <u>broad range of opinions was represented between</u> the various members of the steering committee.

(A) A broad range of opinions was represented between
(B) A broad range of opinions were represented between
(C) A broad range of opinions had been held by
(D) A broad range of opinions was represented among
(E) Varying opinions were represented by

9. Undaunted by the political repercussions of his decision, <u>the new gasoline rationing plan was announced by the Governor</u> at the state office building last Friday.

(A) the new gasoline rationing plan was announced by the Governor
(B) the Governor's new gasoline rationing plan was announced
(C) the Governor made the announcement concerning the new gasoline rationing plan
(D) the new gasoline rationing plan of the Governor was announced
(E) the Governor announced the new gasoline rationing plan

10. Mario <u>had already swum five laps when I</u> jumped into the pool.

(A) had already swum five laps when I
(B) already swam five laps when I
(C) already swam five laps when I had
(D) had already swum five laps when I had
(E) had already swam five laps when I

11. Despite their avowed opposition to the strike, no one <u>from among the dozens of nonunion workers were willing</u> to cross the picket line.

(A) from among the dozens of nonunion workers were willing
(B) of the dozens of nonunion workers were willing
(C) was willing from among the dozens of nonunion workers
(D) from among the dozens of nonunion workers was willing
(E) from the dozens of nonunion workers were willing

12. According to one recent survey, gasoline economy, low price, <u>and safety have replaced</u> style and comfort as leading factors in the choice of a new car.

(A) and safety have replaced
(B) and safe driving have replaced
(C) and safety has replaced
(D) as well as safety has replaced
(E) along with safety have replaced

13. The poetry of George Herbert is regarded by many critics as <u>equal in quality, though less influential, than the work</u> of his more famous contemporary John Donne.

(A) equal in quality, though less influential, than the work
(B) equal in quality to, though less influential than, the work

    (C) qualitatively equal, though less influential than, that
    (D) equal in quality, though less influential, then the work
    (E) of equal quality, though of less influence, than that

14. If it is the present administration <u>whom we should blame</u> for the economic crisis, the first step toward a solution is to reject the incumbent at the polls this November.

    (A) whom we should blame
    (B) whom is to blame
    (C) who we should blame
    (D) who should be blamed
    (E) who one should blame

15. The assembly speaker has called for a shorter fall session of the legislature <u>in hopes that less amendments of a</u> purely symbolic nature will be proposed by the state's lawmakers.

    (A) in hopes that less amendments of a
    (B) hoping that fewer amendments that have a
    (C) in hopes that fewer amendments of a
    (D) in order that less amendments of a
    (E) in hope that fewer amendments of

16. <u>One of the costliest engineering projects ever undertaken, both public and private funds have been needed to support the space shuttle program.</u>

    (A) One of the costliest engineering projects ever undertaken, both public and private funds have been needed to support the space shuttle program.
    (B) One of the costliest engineering projects ever undertaken, support for the space shuttle program has come from both public and private funds.
    (C) The space shuttle program has been supported by both public and private funds, one of the costliest engineering projects ever undertaken.
    (D) From both public and private funds support has come for one of the costliest engineering projects ever undertaken; namely, the space shuttle program.
    (E) Both public and private funds have been needed to support the space shuttle program, one of the costliest engineering projects ever undertaken.

17. Parker's testimony made it clear that <u>he appointed Ryan before he had become aware</u> of Ryan's alleged underworld connections.

    (A) he appointed Ryan before he had become aware
    (B) he appointed Ryan before his awareness
    (C) he had appointed Ryan prior to his having become aware
    (D) his appointment of Ryan preceded awareness
    (E) he had appointed Ryan before becoming aware

18. <u>Despite its being smaller in size than are</u> conventional automobile engines, the new Alcock Engine can still deliver the horsepower needed for most short-distance city driving.

    (A) Despite its being smaller in size than are
    (B) In spite of its being smaller than
    (C) Although smaller than
    (D) Despite its size relative to
    (E) Though not comparable in size to

19. Seventy-four applications were received, <u>of whom the better were selected</u> for detailed review.

    (A) of whom the better were selected
    (B) from which were selected the better
    (C) the best of which were selected

(D) from whom were selected the best
(E) from which they selected the best

0. If the British government had had no fear of the increasing hostility of the Indian populace, Gandhi's nonviolent tactics would have availed little.

(A) If the British government had had no fear of
(B) If the British government did not fear
(C) Had the British government no fear
(D) If the British government did not have fear of
(E) Would the British government not have feared

1. The official imposition of "Lysenkoism" on Soviet biologists, with its chilling effects on scientists in countless related fields, illustrate vividly the dangers of government interference with science.

(A) illustrate vividly the dangers of government interference with science
(B) illustrate the dangers of government interference with science vividly
(C) illustrates vividly the dangers of government interference with science
(D) vividly illustrate the dangers of government interference with science
(E) vividly illustrates how dangerous can be government interference with science

2. Health care costs have been forced upward less by increases in the salaries of nurses, technicians, and other personnel than by increases in the amounts spent on diagnostic machinery and electronic equipment.

(A) than by increases in the amounts
(B) than the amounts
(C) but by increases in the amounts
(D) and more by increases in the amounts
(E) than by funds

3. The press secretary announced that neither himself nor the President would be available for questions until they had had more time to examine the report.

(A) neither himself nor the President would be
(B) neither he or the President was
(C) neither he nor the President would be
(D) he and the President will not be
(E) he nor the President would be

In routine cases, the Civilian Review Board receives all complaints about police misconduct, weighs the evidence and the seriousness of the charges, and then it decides whether a formal inquiry is needed.

(A) then it decides whether a formal inquiry is needed
(B) then decides if a formal inquiry would be needed
(C) then it decides whether to hold a formal inquiry
(D) then decides whether a formal inquiry is needed
(E) decides at that point if a formal inquiry is needed or not

Current scientific theory suggests that the dinosaurs were, in fact, one of the most spectacularly successful groups of organisms ever developed in the course of evolution.

(A) groups of organisms ever developed
(B) group of organisms that have been developed
(C) groups of organisms to ever be developed
(D) group of organisms to be developed
(E) groups of organism developed

If there is still time remaining, you may review the questions in this section only.
You may not turn to any other section of the test.

Section VIII   Problem Solving

TIME: 30 minutes

DIRECTIONS: Solve each of the following problems; then indicate the correct answer on your answer sheet. [On the actual exam you will be permitted to use any space available on the examination paper for scratch work.]

A figure that appears with a problem is drawn as accurately as possible unless the words "figure not drawn to scale" appear next to the figure.

Numbers in this test are real numbers.

1. Dictionaries weigh 6 pounds each and a set of encyclopedias weighs 75 pounds. 20 dictionaries are shipped in each box. 2 sets of encyclopedias are shipped in each box. A truck is loaded with 98 boxes of dictionaries and 50 boxes of encyclopedias. How much does the truck's load weigh?

   (A) 588 pounds
   (B) 7,500 pounds
   (C) 11,750 pounds
   (D) 19,260 pounds
   (E) 22,840 pounds

2. Mary is paid $600 a month on her regular job. During July in addition to her regular job, she makes $400 from a second job. Approximately what percentage of her annual income does Mary make in July? Assume Mary has no other income except the income mentioned above.

   (A) 8
   (B) 8⅓
   (C) 12½
   (D) 13
   (E) 14

3. If the area of a triangle with base S is equal to the area of a square with side S, then the altitude of the triangle is

   (A) ½S
   (B) S
   (C) $2S$
   (D) $3S$
   (E) $4S$

4. A train travels at an average speed of 20 mph through urban areas, 50 mph through suburban areas, and 75 mph through rural areas. If a trip consists of traveling half an hour through urban areas, 3½ hours through suburban areas, and 3 hours through rural areas, what is the train's average speed for the entire trip?

   (A) 50 mph
   (B) 53²⁄₇ mph
   (C) 54³⁄₇ mph
   (D) 58⁴⁄₇ mph
   (E) 59²⁄₇ mph

5. $(x - y)(y + 3)$ is equal to

   (A) $x^2 - 3y + 3$
   (B) $xy - 3y + y^2$
   (C) $xy - y^2 - 3y + 3x$
   (D) $xy - 3y + y^2 + 3x$
   (E) $y^2 - 3y + 3x - xy$

6. If $x < y$, $y < z$, and $z > w$, which of the following statements is always true?

   (A) $x > w$
   (B) $x < z$
   (C) $y = w$
   (D) $y > w$
   (E) $x < w$

7. What is the ratio of ⅔ to ⅝?

(A) ¼
(B) ¹⁰⁄₁₂
(C) ⁸⁄₁₅

(D) ²⁰⁄₆
(E) ²⁄₇

8. Of the numbers, 7, 9, 11, 13, 29, 33, how many are prime numbers?

(A) none
(B) 3
(C) 4

(D) 5
(E) all

9. A company issues 100,000 shares of stock. In 1960 each of the shares was worth $9.50. In 1970 each share was worth $13.21. How much more were the 100,000 shares worth in 1970 than in 1960?

(A) $37,000
(B) $37,010
(C) $37,100

(D) $371,000
(E) $371,100

10. A worker's daily salary varies each day. In one week he worked five days. His daily salaries were $40.62, $41.35, $42.00, $42.50, and $39.53. What was his average daily salary for the week?

(A) $40.04
(B) $40.89
(C) $41.04

(D) $41.20
(E) $206.00

11. One dozen eggs and ten pounds of apples are currently the same price. If the price of a dozen eggs rises by 10% and the price of apples goes up by 2%, how much more will it cost to buy a dozen eggs and ten pounds of apples?

(A) 2%
(B) 6%
(C) 10%

(D) 12%
(E) 12.2%

12. Find x when $x + y = 4$, and $2y = 6$.

(A) 1
(B) $\dfrac{3}{2}$
(C) -2

(D) -3
(E) -1

3. If 25 men can unload a truck in 1 hour and 30 minutes, how long should it take 15 men to unload the truck?

(A) 2 hours
(B) 2¼ hours
(C) 2⅓ hours

(D) 2½ hours
(E) 3 hours

4. A car gets 20 miles per gallon of gas when it travels at 50 miles per hour. The car gets 12% fewer miles to the gallon at 60 miles per hour. How far can the car travel at 60 miles per hour on 11 gallons of gas?

(A) 193.6 miles
(B) 195.1 miles
(C) 200 miles

(D) 204.3 miles
(E) 220 miles

15. Feathers cost $500 a ton for the first 12 tons and $(500 − x) a ton for any tons over 12. What is x, if it costs $10,000 for 30 tons of feathers?

(A) 270.00
(B) 277.00
(C) 277.70
(D) 277.78
(E) 280.00

16. The angles of a triangle are in the ratio 2:3:4. The largest angle in the triangle is

(A) 30°
(B) 40°
(C) 70°
(D) 75°
(E) 80°

17. Find the area of the trapezoid ABCD. AB = CD = 5, BC = 10, AD = 16, and BE is an altitude of the trapezoid.

(A) 50
(B) 52
(C) 64
(D) 80
(E) 160

18. If x is less than 2, which of the following statements are always true?

  I. x is negative.
  II. x is positive.
  III. 2x is greater than or equal to x.
  IV. x^2 is greater than or equal to x.

(A) III only
(B) IV only
(C) I and III only
(D) I, III, and IV only
(E) none of the statements

19. A worker is digging a ditch. He gets 2 assistants who work ⅔ as fast as he does. If all 3 work on a ditch they should finish it in what fraction of the time that the worker takes working alone?

(A) 3/7
(B) ½
(C) ¾
(D) 4/3
(E) 7/3

20. In a survey of political preferences, 78% of those asked were in favor of at least one of the proposals: I, II, and III. 50% of those asked favored proposal I, 30% favored proposal II, and 20% favored proposal III. If 5% of those asked favored all three of the proposals, what percentage of those asked favored more than one of the three proposals?

(A) 5
(B) 10
(C) 12
(D) 17
(E) 22

If there is still time remaining, you may review the questions in this section only.
You may not turn to any other section of the test.

Answers

Section I   Reading Comprehension

1.	(E)	8.	(D)	15.	(D)	22.	(C)
2.	(C)	9.	(C)	16.	(C)	23.	(D)
3.	(B)	10.	(C)	17.	(E)	24.	(B)
4.	(B)	11.	(C)	18.	(B)	25.	(C)
5.	(A)	12.	(C)	19.	(E)		
6.	(A)	13.	(C)	20.	(B)		
7.	(C)	14.	(C)	21.	(B)		

Section II   Problem Solving

(Numbers in parentheses indicate the section in the Mathematics Review where material concerning the question is discussed.)

1.	(D) (II-6)	6.	(E) (III-7, I-4)	11.	(E) (II-3)	16.	(B) (I-8)
2.	(E) (III-1, II-2)	7.	(D) (II-3)	12.	(B) (IV-4)	17.	(B) (I-2)
3.	(C) (I-4)	8.	(A) (I-4)	13.	(C) (IV-4)	18.	(B) (I-6)
4.	(E) (I-1)	9.	(C) (II-3, 5)	14.	(C) (IV-4)	19.	(A) (III-7, I-4)
5.	(C) (II-4)	10.	(D) (II-3)	15.	(D) (II-7)	20.	(B) (III-7)

Section III   Analysis of Situations

1.	(B)	11.	(E)	21.	(E)	31.	(B)
2.	(D)	12.	(E)	22.	(B)	32.	(C)
3.	(A)	13.	(C)	23.	(B)	33.	(E)
4.	(B)	14.	(C)	24.	(B)	34.	(B)
5.	(D)	15.	(B)	25.	(E)	35.	(C)
6.	(E)	16.	(A)	26.	(E)		
7.	(B)	17.	(B)	27.	(C)		
8.	(D)	18.	(E)	28.	(B)		
9.	(D)	19.	(B)	29.	(D)		
10.	(A)	20.	(A)	30.	(B)		

Section IV   Data Sufficiency

1.	(A)	8.	(C)	15.	(E)	22.	(D)
2.	(A)	9.	(C)	16.	(E)	23.	(C)
3.	(E)	10.	(E)	17.	(A)	24.	(B)
4.	(E)	11.	(A)	18.	(D)	25.	(A)
5.	(B)	12.	(D)	19.	(C)		
6.	(D)	13.	(B)	20.	(A)		
7.	(D)	14.	(A)	21.	(E)		

Section V   Writing Ability

1. (C)	8. (A)	15. (B)	22. (E)
2. (B)	9. (B)	16. (A)	23. (C)
3. (C)	10. (D)	17. (E)	24. (D)
4. (E)	11. (C)	18. (C)	25. (D)
5. (B)	12. (B)	19. (E)	
6. (D)	13. (A)	20. (A)	
7. (B)	14. (C)	21. (E)	

Section VI   Critical Reasoning

1. (B)	8. (C)	15. (C)	22. (D)
2. (C)	9. (B)	16. (C)	23. (B)
3. (D)	10. (E)	17. (E)	24. (D)
4. (D)	11. (A)	18. (D)	25. (D)
5. (E)	12. (B)	19. (D)	
6. (B)	13. (A)	20. (C)	
7. (C)	14. (A)	21. (A)	

Section VII   Writing Ability

1. (C)	8. (D)	15. (C)	22. (A)
2. (E)	9. (E)	16. (E)	23. (C)
3. (B)	10. (A)	17. (E)	24. (D)
4. (A)	11. (D)	18. (C)	25. (A)
5. (C)	12. (A)	19. (C)	
6. (A)	13. (B)	20. (A)	
7. (B)	14. (A)	21. (C)	

Section VIII   Problem Solving

(Numbers in parentheses indicate the section in the Mathematics Review where material concerning the question is discussed.)

1. (D) (II-3)	6. (B) (II-7)	11. (B) (I-4)	16. (E) (II-5, III-4)
2. (D) (I-4)	7. (C) (I-2, II-5)	12. (A) (II-2)	17. (B) (III-7)
3. (C) (III-7)	8. (C) (I-1)	13. (D) (II-3)	18. (E) (II-7)
4. (D) (I-7)	9. (D) (II-3)	14. (A) (I-4, II-3)	19. (A) (II-3)
5. (C) (II-1)	10. (D) (I-7)	15. (D) (II-3)	20. (D) (II-4)

Analysis

Section I   Reading Comprehension

1. **(E)** The report (on which the passage is based) is certainly not optimistic (B), but rather pessimistic in its assessment, although not specifically about the trade gap (D). Nor can the report be characterized as harshly condemnatory (A) or critical of labor unions (C). After all, as pointed out in the passage, it is labor that will suffer. The answer is (E). This is specifically supported by the first and second paragraphs.

2. **(C)** Free trade is the reduction or elimination of tariffs and duties on exports. See lines 3 and 16–18.

3. **(B)** Manufacturers that cannot increase productivity in order to lower prices will not be able to compete with duty-free imports, and will not receive adjustment assistance, i.e., subsidies or some other financial payments to buttress them in the face of foreign competition.

4. **(B)** The author's recommendation is that redundant labor should be removed. See lines 36–37.

5. **(A)** Even though the subject of trade with the Common Market (C) is discussed, the major thrust of the passage is on the consequences of free trade—in this case, with the Common Market.

6. **(A)** Only alternative I was mentioned in paragraph 1. II is incorrect because the workers will be *displaced*, not unemployed.

7. **(C)** The author blames the government for not making its position clear with regard to trade policy. See line 17.

8. **(D)** The passage specifically mentions industrial goods on line 18.

9. **(C)** The manufacturing sector is mentioned in paragraphs 3, 4, and 5; services are mentioned in paragraphs 5 and 6.

10. **(C)** This is stated in paragraph 3 of the passage.

11. **(C)** The major objective is to explain the objectives of sociology, which are the same as those of science. See line 1.

12. **(C)** A discussion of this point is given in paragraph 3. The other answers are either factually incorrect or incomplete.

13. **(C)** The final step or objective of science—according to the passage—is explanation (line 3), best stated as a causal proposition. See lines 38–39.

14. **(C)** I and II are mentioned in the first and second paragraphs. III is mentioned in lines 32–33 as one of the activities in which the scientist is *not* interested.

15. **(D)** Answers (B) and (E) are mentioned in the passage, but are secondary in importance to (D). Answer (C) is not correct, and answer (A) is not mentioned in the passage.

16. **(C)** The scientist would not accept I since angels are not considered empirical (see the last paragraph). He would not accept II; since the term *weak character* is not defined, it cannot be observed. The scientist would accept III since all the terms involved in the explanation are observable.

17. **(E)** All the other answers are mentioned in the paragraph but they are not the main topic.

18. **(B)** This is mentioned in the first and the final paragraphs. In any case, the prefix *poly* means many and the suffix *theist* means one who believes in a god or gods.

19. **(E)** Answers (A), (B) and (D) cannot be inferred from the passage. Answer (C) is roughly consonant with what the author has to say, but (E) is a stronger example of the question statement.

20. **(B)** I is incorrect since they worshipped gods in both human and other forms. See lines 24ff.

21. **(B)** Although the author states that certain cultures are more inclined to anthropocentric worship (A), he mentions it while making the point that there are those who attribute it to others, even though practicing it themselves.

22. **(C)** The paragraph indicates that if the universe is partly controlled by the "wet-god" (it rains), then the "dry-god" lacks control. This is an example of incoherence. If you pray for rain, you must also pray to prevent the "dry-god" from exercising his powers, an example of potential conflict. Hence there is hardly a commonality of interests or order in a polytheistic system.

23. **(D)** See lines 26–27.

24. **(B)** See paragraph 2.

25. **(C)** Alternative I is found in line 1; alternative II, in lines 36–37. Alternative III is incorrect; the passage also mentions Romans.

Section II   Problem Solving

1. **(D)** Since $\frac{12}{4} = 3 = \frac{36}{12}$ the ratio of one term to the previous term is 3. So if x is the next term, $\frac{x}{36} = 3$ and $x = 3(36) = 108$.

2. **(E)** The complement of x is an angle of $90 - x$ degrees, and the supplement of x is an angle of $180 - x$ degrees. Thus, we have $90 - x = \frac{1}{6}(180 - x) = 30 - \frac{1}{6}x$, so $60 = \frac{5}{6}x$ or $x = 72$.

3. **(C)** The profit was $250 on sales of $1,900, so the ratio of profit to sales is $\frac{250}{1,900} = \frac{25}{190}$ which is approximately .132 or about 13%.

4. **(E)** Since 4 is a multiple of 2, the least common multiple of 3, 4, and 5 will be the least common multiple of 2, 3, 4, and 5. 3, 4, and 5 have no common factors so the least common multiple is $3 \cdot 4 \cdot 5 = 60$.

5. **(C)** Since 10% have both brown eyes and brown hair, and 25% have brown eyes, 15% of the people have brown eyes but do not have brown hair. Thus, 40% + 15% or 55% of the people have brown eyes or brown hair or both. Therefore, 100% − 55% or 45% of the people have neither brown eyes nor brown hair.

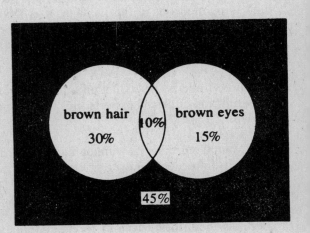

6. **(E)** Area = ½ (altitude)(base). The increased altitude is (1.05) altitude and the increased base is (1.07) base. Therefore, the increased area is ½(1.05)(1.07)(altitude)(base). So the increased area is (1.1235) area. Thus, the area has increased by 12.35%.

7. **(D)** The first 20 pounds cost 20 · 2¢ = 40¢. The package weighs 3½ pounds more than 20 pounds, so there are 3 pounds and one fraction of a pound over 20 pounds. The weight over 20 pounds will cost 4 · (1.5)¢ = 6¢. Therefore, the total cost will be 46¢.

8. **(A)** Since 5,000 − 1,000 = 4,000, there are 4,000 sheets which will be discounted. The 4,000 sheets cost 4,000¢ or $40.00 before the discount, so they will cost (.98)($40.00) or $39.20 after the 2% discount. The first 1,000 sheets cost 1¢ each so they cost 1,000¢ or $10.00. Therefore, the total cost of the 5,000 sheets will be $49.20.

9. **(C)** Let T be Tom's salary, J be John's salary, and S be Steve's salary. Then the given information is $T = (1.5)J$ and $J = (.8)S$. Changing to fractions we get $T = \frac{3}{2}J$ and $J = \frac{4}{5}S$ so $S = \frac{5}{4}J$. Therefore, $\frac{S}{T} = \frac{5}{4}J / \frac{3}{2}J = \frac{5}{4} / \frac{3}{.2} = \frac{5}{4} \cdot \frac{2}{3} = \frac{5}{6}$. The ratio is 5 to 6.

10. **(D)** If the average speed is 50 mph, then in 5 hours the driver will travel $5 \cdot 50$ miles or 250 miles. He traveled 135 miles in the first 3 hours, so he needs to travel $250 - 135 = 115$ miles in the final 2 hours.

11. **(E)** 30 workers are $\frac{3}{5}$ of 50 workers, so it should take the 30 workers $\frac{5}{3}$ as long as the 50 workers. Therefore, the 30 workers should take $\frac{5}{3} \cdot 4 = \frac{20}{3} = 6\frac{2}{3}$ hours = 6 hours and 40 minutes.

12. **(B)** The profit is indicated by the arrow.

13. **(C)** 1968 and 1971.

14. **(C)** Statement I is false since there was a loss in 1967. II is false since the profits decreased from 1968 to 1969.

15. **(D)** If $x - 2 < y$, then $x < y + 2$.

16. **(B)** The price of wheat (in dollars) will be $2(1.1)^n$ after n months. This will be greater than 2.62 when $(1.1)^n$ is greater than $2.62/2 = 1.31$. Since $1.1 \times 1.1 = 1.21$ and $1.1 \times 1.1 \times 1.1 = 1.331$, after three months the price of a bushel of corn will be less than the price of a bushel of wheat.

17. **(B)** If $\frac{1}{2} + \frac{1}{4} = \frac{x}{15}$, then since $\frac{1}{2} + \frac{1}{4} = \frac{3}{4}$, we have that $\frac{3}{4} = \frac{x}{15}$. So $x = \frac{45}{4} = 11\frac{1}{4} = 11.25$.

18. **(B)** If three of the numbers were negative, then as long as the fourth is greater than the absolute value of the sum of the other three, the sum of all four will be positive. For example, $(-50) + (-35) + (-55) + 155 = 15$.

19. **(A)** Area $= LW$. The increased length is $1.11L$ and W is unchanged; so the increased area is $(1.11L)W = (1.11)(LW) = (1.11)A$. Therefore, the increase in area is $1.11A - A = .11A$; and the area is increased by 11%.

20. **(B)** The area of the circle is $\pi \times \sqrt{2} \times \sqrt{2} = 2\pi$. Since $3^2 + 4^2 = 5^2$, the triangle in III is a right triangle. So it has an altitude and base equal to 3 and 4. Therefore, its area is $(1/2) \times 3 \times 4 = 6$, which is less than 2π because π is greater than 3.

Let ABC be the equilateral triangle of II. Then if AD is an altitude of ABC, the right triangles ABD and ACD are congruent. So BD must equal CD, which means $BD = 4/2 = 2$. Now we can compute the length of the altitude AD by the Pythagorean relation. AD is the square root of AC squared minus CD squared. So AD is the square root of $(4^2 - 2^2 = 16 - 4 = 12)$. Hence, the area of ABC is $(1/2) \times 4 \times \sqrt{12} = 2 \times 2 \times \sqrt{3} = 4\sqrt{3}$. Thus II has the largest area since $4\sqrt{3}$ is larger than 2π. ($4\sqrt{3}$ is about 6.93 and 2π is only about 6.28.)

Section III   Analysis of Situations

1. **(B)** The workers had no loyalty to the company from the "distant north." This was a *Major Factor* as far as their will to work was concerned.

2. **(D)** This was an assumption initially made by Cappa upon which he developed his managerial style. It was erroneous, of course.

3. **(A)** Motivating the workers is Cappa's *Major Objective*.

4. **(B)** Low productivity, caused mainly by lack of motivation, is a *Major Factor*.

5. **(D)** Cappa's desire to institute a bonus system (that failed) was not supported by any evidence that it could succeed.

6. **(E)** The fact that Cappa was a U.S. citizen had no apparent impact on the major problem of motivating workers or on his deciding whether to return to the U.S.

7. **(B)** Worker loyalty—or lack of it—was a *Major Factor* in determining what sort of plan

would motivate workers to increase productivity.

8. **(D)** Cappa *believed* that people everywhere are alike and will respond to cash incentives. This was an unsupported assumption on his part.

9. **(D)** Cappa *believed* that productivity would increase if workers received more authority. This assumption was not based on any facts given in the passage.

10. **(A)** Relating pay to output was a *Major Objective* desired by Cappa. Its purpose was to increase productivity, another major objective.

11. **(E)** The quality of the machinery was not a factor in any alternative course of action.

12. **(E)** Nothing in the passage mentions the location of the orange groves as an element in the decision process.

13. **(C)** Cappa tried to establish co-determination in order to increase worker motivation—an objective. Meeting with the committees was a less important consideration than implementing co-determination itself.

14. **(C)** Cappa's ambitions were a *Minor Factor* in Cappa's decision to leave for Italy. Note the three reasons for his accepting his uncle's proposition, as given in the passage: (1) the chance to be his own boss, (2) his wish to bring U.S. know-how to the firm, and (3) his desire to return to his father's homeland with some personal authority. Ambition is probably connected with these three factors, but it is of lesser importance.

15. **(B)** Cappa's plans had been stymied on more than one occasion by the recalcitrance of the union. Therefore, the power of the union was a *Major Factor* which Cappa had to take into consideration in making his final decision.

16. **(A)** Managing the Palermo printing plant was a *Major Objective* of Cappa.

17. **(B)** The chance to be his own boss was a *Major Factor* in Cappa's decision to accept his uncle's offer to run the printing plant.

18. **(E)** The sort of products produced by the Palermo plant was an *Unimportant Issue* not considered in any decision alternative.

19. **(B)** The availability of rubber in India was a *Major Factor* in Allied's consideration to invest there.

20. **(A)** The *Major Objective* of Allied was to determine whether to recruit local people or American expatriates for managerial positions in India.

21. **(E)** The fact that European countries favor centralized management was not a consideration in any alternative course of action.

22. **(B)** The selection of management for overseas operations must consider labor force traditions. If not, conflict between management and labor may occur.

23. **(B)** The cost of transferring Americans abroad is a major consideration in the alternative of hiring expatriate managers.

24. **(B)** The high divorce rates among expatriate managers is a major consideration of Allied management in deciding whether to hire local versus American managers for positions abroad.

25. **(E)** Control methods in American firms is not a consideration by Allied management in the decision to recruit personnel for the operation in India.

26. **(E)** Since no restrictions on the hiring of expatriates were formulated by the Indian government, the issue is not a consideration.

27. **(C)** The cost of transporting expatriates overseas is one part of the overall cost of relocation and is thus a *Minor Factor*.

28. **(B)** The cultural problems facing expatriate managers is a major consideration in the assignment of Americans to positions abroad.

29. **(D)** The possibility that hiring an equal number of American expatriates and Indian nationals would cause internal conflict was a *Major Assumption* of management.

30. **(B)** Allied's experience with recruitment in both their African and their Brazilian operations was a *Major Factor* or consideration in the decision to formulate a recruitment policy for India.

31. **(B)** It is stated that the successful operation of Allied was owing to a number of factors, one of which was removal of the language barrier between the subsidiary and the parent organization. A consideration in the hiring of Americans or local nationals, therefore, was the language barrier, a *Major Factor*.

32. **(C)** The cost of housing expatriates overseas was one part of the overall cost of relocating and is therefore a *Minor Factor*.

33. **(E)** The number of years that the Brazilian plant had been operating was not a consideration and is an *Unimportant Issue*.

34. **(B)** The lower national salary levels in Brazil were a *Major Factor* in the decision alternative of hiring Brazilian nationals.

35. **(C)** Overall training was a *Major Factor* in the decision to hire local nationals in Brazil. Since cross-cultural training is only one part of overall training—which includes product and technical training as well—it is a *Minor Factor*.

Section IV   Data Sufficiency

1. **(A)** STATEMENT (1) alone is sufficient. If angle ABC is a right angle, then AOC is a semicircle. Therefore, AC is a diameter.

   STATEMENT (2) alone is insufficient. There are many (an infinite number) triangles we can inscribe in the circle such that $AB = \frac{3}{4}BC$. Not all of these will have AC as a diameter.

   Therefore, STATEMENT (1) alone is sufficient, but STATEMENT (2) alone is not sufficient.

2. **(A)** To find how many gallons the tank will hold, we need to calculate the volume of the tank and then divide this by the volume of one gallon of the liquid. Therefore, STATEMENT (1) alone is sufficient.

   STATEMENT (2) alone is not sufficient (note that it gives no further information about the tank). We need to know how much space a gallon of the liquid occupies.

   Therefore, STATEMENT (1) alone is sufficient, but STATEMENT (2) alone is not.

3. **(E)** STATEMENT (1) alone is not sufficient. We still need the total weight of the books; then we can divide by the average weight to obtain the number of books.

   STATEMENT (2) tells us how much the books and the bookshelf together weigh, but we don't know how much the books weigh.

   So STATEMENTS (1) and (2) together are not sufficient.

4. **(E)** STATEMENT (1) alone is not sufficient, since many noncongruent triangles can have a side and an angle which are equal.

   By the same reasoning, STATEMENT (2) alone is not sufficient.

   STATEMENTS (1) and (2) together are not sufficient. For two triangles to be congruent, they must have two pairs of corresponding sides and the *included* angles equal. For example, the following two triangles satisfy STATEMENTS (1) and (2) and x = y but they are not congruent.

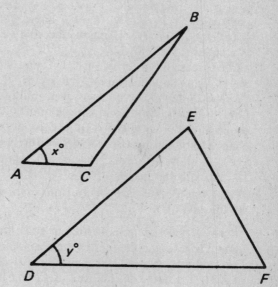

   Therefore, STATEMENTS (1) and (2) together are not sufficient.

5. **(B)** STATEMENT (2) alone is sufficient, since we can multiply $\frac{1}{9}$ by (60 × 60) to obtain the speed in mph.

   STATEMENT (1) alone is not sufficient, because the plane's flying in a circle gives us no information about the exact speed of the plane. So STATEMENT (2) alone is sufficient, but STATEMENT (1) alone is not.

6. **(D)** STATEMENT (1) alone is sufficient. If $L =$ the length of the floor, then STATEMENT (1) says the width is $\frac{1}{2}L$. The area of the floor is length times width or $(L)(\frac{1}{2}L)$ or $\frac{1}{2}L^2$. Since the area is equal to 32 square feet, we have $\frac{1}{2}L^2 = 32$ so $L^2 = 64$ and $L = 8$ feet.

STATEMENT (2) alone is sufficient. Let $W =$ the width of the floor. Then STATEMENT (2) says $W = L - 4$. So the area is $L(L - 4)$ or $L^2 - 4L$ which equals 32. Therefore, L satisfies $L^2 - 4L - 32 = 0$, and since $L^2 - 4L - 32 = (L - 8)(L + 4)$, $L^2 - 4L - 32 = 0$ if and only if $L = 8$ or $L = -4$. Since $L = -4$ has no meaning for the problem, $L = 8$.

So STATEMENT (1) alone is sufficient, and STATEMENT (2) alone is sufficient.

7. **(D)** We have to determine whether $(AB)(BC)$ which is the area of the rectangle $ABCD$ is equal to $(EH)^2$ which is the area of the square $EFGH$.

STATEMENT (1) alone is sufficient. Since ABC is a right triangle, $BC = \sqrt{(AC)^2 - (AB)^2}$, and using STATEMENT (1) we have $BC = \sqrt{(EG)^2 - \frac{1}{4}(EH)^2}$. Using the fact that $EFGH$ is a square, we know $(EG)^2 = 2(EH)^2$, so we can express BC in terms of EH. Using STATEMENT (1) we can express AB as $\frac{1}{2}EH$, so $(AB)(BC)$ can be expressed as a multiple of $(EH)^2$. Notice that to answer the question you don't have to actually set up the equation. If you work it out you will find that the area of $ABCD$ is $\frac{\sqrt{7}}{4}(EH)^2$, so the areas are not equal.

Don't waste time carrying out the extra work on the test.

STATEMENT (2) alone is sufficient since the diagonal of a rectangle divides the rectangle into two congruent triangles. Therefore, the area of $ABCD$ is equal to the area of $EFGH$ if and only if the area of ABC is equal to the area of EFG.

8. **(C)** STATEMENT (2) says $J = 2S$, where $J =$ Joan's weight and $S =$ Susan's weight. But since we don't know Joan's weight, STATEMENT (2) alone is not sufficient.

STATEMENT (1) says $J + S = 250$; so if we use STATEMENT (2) we have $2S + S = 250$ or $S = \frac{250}{3} = 83\frac{1}{3}$. But STATEMENT (1) alone is not sufficient. If we use only STATEMENT (1), we don't know how much Joan weighs. Therefore, STATEMENTS (1) and (2) together are sufficient, but neither statement alone is sufficient.

9. **(C)** In each minute, hole A drains $\frac{1}{24}$ of the tank according to STATEMENT (1). Since we have no information about B, STATEMENT (1) alone is not sufficient.

In each minute, hole B drains $\frac{1}{42}$ of the tank according to STATEMENT (2), but STATEMENT (2) gives no information about hole A. So STATEMENT (2) alone is not sufficient.

If we use STATEMENTS (1) and (2), then both holes together will drain $\frac{1}{24} + \frac{1}{42}$ or $\frac{7 + 4}{6 \times 28}$ or $\frac{11}{168}$ of the tank each minute. Therefore, it will take $\frac{168}{11}$ or $15\frac{3}{11}$ minutes for the tank to be empty. So STATEMENTS (1) and (2) together are sufficient, but neither statement alone is sufficient.

10. **(E)** STATEMENTS (1) and (2) are equivalent, since $x - y = 6$ if and only if $-2x + 2y = -2(x - y) = (-2)(6) = -12$. Each statement tells us only what $x - y$ is, and we have no other information. Therefore, each statement alone is insufficient. But since the two statements are the same, even together they are not sufficient.

11. **(A)** STATEMENT (2) alone is not sufficient, since we must know how close the circles are and we know only the radius of each circle.

STATEMENT (1) alone is sufficient. The centers of the two circles are closer than the sum of the radii. (So we can form a triangle with DF as one side and the two other sides with length 2 and R respectively; but this means that the third vertex of the triangle will be on both circle E and circle C.)

So STATEMENT (1) alone is sufficient, but STATEMENT (2) alone is not sufficient.

12. **(D)** It is sufficient to be able to find his total income for the years 1967 through 1969 since we divide the total income by 3 to obtain the average income.

STATEMENT (1) alone is sufficient. Since we know his income for 1967, we can find his income in 1968 and 1969 by using STATEMENT (1). Therefore, we can find the total income. STATEMENT (2) alone is sufficient. Add the combined income from 1968 and 1969 to the income from 1967 (which is given), and we have the total income.

Therefore, STATEMENTS (1) and (2) are each sufficient.

13. **(B)** STATEMENT (1) alone is not sufficient. $y = z$ does not imply $x = 90$. For example, in an equilateral triangle, $x = y = z$ and $x = 60$.

STATEMENT (2) alone is sufficient. Pythagoras' theorem says ACB is a right angle if and only if $(AC)^2 + (BC)^2 = (AB)^2$.

14. **(A)** STATEMENT (1) alone is sufficient. If $P =$ Paul's height, then we can write a proportion $\dfrac{P}{6} = \dfrac{9}{10}$ since their shadows are proportional to their heights. $\left[\text{Thus, } P = \dfrac{54}{10} = 5.4 \text{ feet.}\right]$

STATEMENT (2) alone is not sufficient. The distance they are apart does not give us any information about their heights.

Therefore, STATEMENT (1) alone is sufficient, but STATEMENT (2) alone is not sufficient.

15. **(E)** STATEMENT (1) alone is not sufficient. Note that $4 = (-2)^2 > 1 = (-1)^2$ but $-2 < -1$.

STATEMENT (2) alone is not sufficient. If $x + 3$ is greater than $y + 2$, then x can be less than y or greater than y. For example, $\frac{1}{2}$ is greater than 0, and $\frac{1}{2} + 3$ is greater than $0 + 2$. However, $\frac{1}{2}$ is less than 1, while $\frac{1}{2} + 3$ is greater than $1 + 2$.

STATEMENTS (1) and (2) together are not sufficient. For example, $x = -\frac{1}{2}$ is less than $y = \frac{1}{4}$, $-\frac{1}{2} + 3$ is greater than $2 + \frac{1}{4}$, and $(-\frac{1}{2})^2 = \frac{1}{4}$ is greater than $\frac{1}{16} = (\frac{1}{4})^2$. Also, $y = \frac{1}{4}$ is less than $x = 2$, $(\frac{1}{4})^2$ is less than 2^2, and $2 + 3$ is greater than $\frac{1}{4} + 2$. So STATEMENTS (1) and (2) together are not sufficient.

16. **(E)** STATEMENTS (1) and (2) together are insufficient. You need to know whether the wages of the average worker changed. 4 minutes of work in January 1981 could be worth more or less than 90¢.

17. **(A)** STATEMENT (1) alone is sufficient. STATEMENT (2) alone is not sufficient, since you do not know how many tickets are in a book.

18. **(D)** STATEMENT (1) alone is sufficient. Since $x > 0$, (1) implies $y > 0$. Hence, we can divide

the equations $x = \frac{1}{4}y$ by y to get the value of x/y.

STATEMENT (2) alone is sufficient since $y = 4x$ is equivalent to STATEMENT (1).

19. **(C)** STATEMENT (1) alone is not sufficient. Using (1) you can deduce that the area of the sector is 72/360 of the area of the circle, but you can't find the area of the circle.

STATEMENT (2) alone is not sufficient. OB is a radius of the circle, so (2) gives you the area of the circle but you can't deduce what fraction of the circle the sector is. However, STATEMENT (1) gives that information, so STATEMENTS (1) and (2) together are sufficient.

20. **(A)** STATEMENT (1) alone is sufficient. Since all the numbers are less than 30, all three must be positive for their sum to be larger than 60.

STATEMENT (2) alone is insufficient. (2) implies that x and y are positive, but gives no information about z.

21. **(E)** STATEMENTS (1) and (2) together are not sufficient. You need to know what direction it is from town B to town C, besides the distance between the towns.

22. **(D)** STATEMENT (1) is sufficient. The fact that the ratio is 4 to 1 means that the number of imported cars sold was $\frac{1}{4}$ the number of American cars sold.

STATEMENT (2) alone is sufficient, since the ratio of 4 to 1 means that 20% of all cars sold were imported cars.

23. **(C)** STATEMENTS (1) and (2) are sufficient. 40% of the 28% are families who both have income over \$25,000 and own a sailboat. Note that STATEMENT (2) alone is not sufficient. The percentage of families who own a sailboat and have an income over \$25,000 is a percentage of families in the state. In statement (2), the percentage given is a percentage of families with income over \$25,000.

24. **(B)** STATEMENT (2) alone is sufficient. Solving the equation in (2) gives $x = y$, which implies that $x - y = 0$. STATEMENT (1) alone is obviously not sufficient, since no information about y is supplied.

25. **(A)** Since the area of a circle is equal to πr^2

and the radius is positive, STATEMENT (1) alone is sufficient.

STATEMENT (2) is true for all circles, so it gives no information about the radius of this particular circle.

Section V   Writing Ability

1. **(C)** Choices (A), (B), and (E) lack parallel structure; parallel nouns should be used: *years, desire,* and *debut.* Choice (D) unnecessarily changes the infinitive *to become.*

2. **(B)** Choices (A), (C), and (E) imply that driving a car at any speed is speeding. Choice (D) is wrong, because the subjunctive mood is required in the *if* clause.

3. **(C)** Choices (A) and (B) contain a faulty comparison. The word processor *is* a modern machine, and so the word *other* must be included. In choices (D) and (E), the word *has* is unnecessary and awkward.

4. **(E)** Choices (A) and (B) suffer from dangling participles. In addition, choice (A) has an error in agreement between the singular subject (*daydreaming*) and the plural verb (*enable*). Choices (C) and (D) change the meaning of the sentence.

5. **(B)** *Due to* should not be used in place of the compound preposition *because of.* Choice (C) has an error in agreement between the singular verb (*was*) and the compound subject (*technology* and *capital*). Choice (D) is wordy and awkward.

6. **(D)** Choice (D) corrects the misplaced modifiers in choices (A), (B), and (C). Choice (E) seems to say that the owner told police as he was about to make a night deposit.

7. **(B)** The compound subject requires a plural verb. Choice (C) uses incorrect language: *both of which are each,* and choice (E) changes the meaning by using *or* instead of *and.*

8. **(A)** *Affected* (*influenced by* or *acted upon*) is the correct word. Choice (C) uses the wrong tense.

9. **(B)** The pronoun *who* is the object of the verb *regard*; therefore, it should be in the objective case, *whom.* Choice (C) misplaces the modifier *both.*

10. **(D)** To maintain parallel construction, the noun *superstition* should replace the gerund phrase *thinking in superstitious ways.* The reference of *it* or *they* in choices (B), (C), and (E) is not completely clear.

11. **(C)** All the choices but (C) include a dangling modifier, since Jung's *writings* had not broken with Freud.

12. **(B)** *Cannot scarcely, cannot hardly,* and *isn't hardly* are considered double negatives.

13. **(A)** The past perfect tense *had been described* is needed to make clear the order in which the events occurred.

14. **(C)** The correct expression is *the reason is that.* Choice (B) has an error in agreement: *background . . . have.* The idiom is *qualified for,* not *qualified to* (D).

15. **(B)** The plural subject *numbers* requires a plural verb. Choice (C) misplaces *not only*: "to warrant *not only* continuing . . . *but also* maintaining." Choice (E) lacks parallel construction: *not only continuing . . . but also to maintain.*

16. **(A)** With a compound subject (*feelings* and *conviction*), the plural verb *are* is called for. In choice (C), *irregardless* is nonstandard English.

17. **(E)** Choices (D) and (E) correct the misplaced modifier, but choice (D) has an error in parallel structure. The noun clause *what his serial number was* is not parallel with *name* and *rank.*

18. **(C)** *Finishing* is parallel to *writing.*

19. **(E)** Choices (A) and (B) suffer from the change of persons (from *anyone* to *you*). In choice (C) *would learn* is the wrong tense. Choice (D) is wordy.

20. **(A)** The word *number* is used when the quantity can be counted. Choices (C) and (D) incorrectly use *less* and *fewer*; *fewer accidents* and *lesser amount* would be correct. In choice (E) *they* has no reference.

1. **(E)** *Being that* in choices (A) and (C) is incorrect. The placement of *only* in choice (B) is wrong. Choice (D), *Seeing as how . . . .* is nonstandard.

2. **(E)** Parallel structure is violated in choices (A), (B), and (D). The placement of *also* in choice (C) is poor, for it ends the sentence on an anticlimactic note.

3. **(C)** In choices (A) and (D) *which* refers to the entire sentence rather than to a specific antecedent. (B) is not as strong a sentence as (C). Choice (E) has a dangling modifier.

4. **(D)** *The majority* calls for a singular verb (*has*). In choice (C) *lacks* should be used to agree with its subject, *one*.

5. **(D)** Choices (A), (B), and (E) omit important parts of the verb. *Hopefully* in choices (C) and (E) is wrong; although many people use it this way, most grammarians do not accept it as a substitute for *we hope*. (Strictly speaking, *hopefully* should only be used to mean *in a hopeful way*, as in *The farmer searched the skies hopefully looking for signs of rain*.)

Section VI   Critical Reasoning

1. **(B)** C, D, and E are too specific, B is more comprehensive and A is the opposite, causal relationship.

2. **(C)** An import substitution policy is designed to develop local industry and is frequently promoted by a protectionist policy, i.e. tariffs, quotas, and other constraints that either prohibit imports or tax them highly. By restricting imports or increasing their cost, locally produced products may be priced more highly than if import competition were allowed. Therefore, consumers ultimately pay the cost of higher priced (and often inferior) locally produced goods. Alternative (E) is partially correct. A protectionist policy (limiting imports) may benefit developing countries by allowing local industry to develop and may be an anathema to trading partners, but this hardly weakens the argument for a policy of economic independence as given in the statement.

3. **(D)** A and E are two extremes; B is not accurate; C is wrong and D expresses the transitory position of this period and the spreading of books.

4. **(D)** The marital status of females E affects their participation in the labor force; A and B are obvious; C also affects participation in the labor force. D has no effect on the labor supply; employment agencies direct the supply of labor, they do not affect it.

5. **(E)** A to D refer to community and land use. E relates to housing design.

6. **(B)** Two factors are noted. First, the per capita production rate has not been as high as the production increase without regard to population size. Second, the rate of increase over the last ten years has been slower. Therefore, B is correct.

7. **(C)** A, D, and E are from the statement; B is a fact not contained in the statement. C implies a westward migration instead of eastward (as stated above).

8. **(C)** Since Dyner's country produces only 2 percent of world petroleum supply, its output can hardly affect world prices.

9. **(B)** The statement is an admonition for people to be aware of "contaminents," a reference to physical and chemical hazards.

10. **(E)** Variables A, B, C, and D all affect occupational mobility. The rate of turnover (E) is another way of measuring mobility, so it cannot be an explanatory variable.

11. **(A)** Textiles are mentioned as the major export; woolens and worsteds are components of textiles. Apart from textiles, corn is mentioned as the only other significant export.

12. **(B)** 31 percent of men who operate unincorporated businesses (self-employed), completed four or more years of college, against only 19 percent of the women in the same category.

13. **(A)** The statement implies a correlation between a decline in gasoline consumption (less pollution) and a decrease in the incidence of lung cancer among white males. If lung cancer among blacks did not decrease over the same time period, one could assume that another causal or intermediate variable—other than gasoline consumption—may explain the decrease in lung cancer among white males.

14. **(A)** Production per worker is a measure of productivity. If production per worker increases, it may be a result of [in the context of (A)] either

increasing output with the same number of workers, or with fewer workers, or if the number of workers increases, increasing output proportionately. However, (A) alone is an insufficient explanation for the increased trend in food production.

15. **(C)** C reflects the intention behind the above, which stresses the facts of usage. A implies a metaphysical theory about the use of the word tall (platonic). B is an opinion opposed to that of the writer. D is a judgment on the behavior described in the abstract.

16. **(C)** While personal satisfaction is a motivating factor, the statement shows that business starts increased — since 1980 — along with a set of tax changes, promoting financial gains.

17. **(E)** A to D reflect developments in the Industrial Revolution (progress, wage improvement, etc.). Therefore, E is wrong because wages *increased.*

18. **(D)** There is no evidence for A or B, C cannot be inferred; the inference is that social class affects behavior, not that social class is more of an influence in Europe than in America. There is no assumption about the science of consumer behavior (E). All the factors in (D) are assumed to have influence upon consumer behavior, both in Europe and in America.

19. **(D)** The passage states that university expansion — north of Italy outside France and England — took place between the mid-14th century and the end of the 15th century.

20. **(C)** Even if it were true that there are more self-employed women than men, it does not explain why this number increased five times faster than men.

21. **(A)** This problem relates to "investigator paradigm" effect as stated in the passage.

22. **(D)** Land values were higher in Europe, attracting U.S. capital (A); higher duties on U.S. exports to Europe (B) brought a substitution of foreign U.S. production for exports; lower labor costs in Europe (C) meant it was cheaper to produce there. Higher liquidity (E) in the U.S. provided the capital for foreign investment. Only D is irrelevant as an explanation of direct investment.

23. **(B)** The key phrase in the passage is "tries as far as possible." Social security legislation generally adapts itself to the changing needs of society.

24. **(D)** A possibility exists that the hiring of temporary replacements and the continuation of health insurance for those on leave (zero productivity)

may be an unbearable cost for the business enterprise.

25. **(D)** The passage states that construction workers had to wear steel helmets beginning in 1955; some workers in the construction industry or in other industries may have worn them before 1955.

Section VII   Writing Ability

1. **(C)** The pronoun *each* is singular, and requires the singular verb *was required.*

2. **(E)** When only two things are being compared (in this case, stationary sites and mobile units), the word *more* rather than *most* should be used.

3. **(B)** To maintain parallel structure, a phrase beginning with a noun (*ability*) is needed.

4. **(A)** The original wording is the clearest and simplest.

5. **(C)** As originally written, the sentence is a fragment, since it lacks an independent subject and verb. Choice (C) supplies them (*He had chosen*).

6. **(A)** No error.

7. **(B)** The pronoun *she* is needed, since it is part of the compound subject of the verb *was willing*; the verb must be singular to agree with the nearest subject (*Dean*).

8. **(D)** Use *among* when three or more people or things are involved.

9. **(E)** The underlined phrase must begin with *the Governor*; otherwise, the phrase which precedes it has no clear reference. Choice (C) is verbose and rather vague.

10. **(A)** No error.

11. **(D)** The pronoun *no one* is singular, and requires the singular verb *was.* Choice (C) is awkward in comparison to choice (D).

12. **(A)** The sentence is correct as originally written. Note that the compound subject ("X, Y and Z") requires a plural verb—in this case *have replaced.*

13. **(B)** The comparative phrases *equal . . . to* and *less . . . than* must be complete in order for the sentence to make sense.

14. **(A)** Correct as originally written. The pronoun *whom* is correct, since it is the object of the verb *should blame*.

15. **(C)** Use *fewer* for countable items (such as amendments); use *less* for noncountable substances (for example, sand, water, or time).

16. **(E)** The phrase beginning *One of the costliest* must be adjacent to the phrase *the space shuttle program*, in order to make the reference clear.

17. **(E)** The past perfect tense *had appointed* is needed to clarify the order in which the events occurred.

18. **(C)** The other choices are verbose, vague, or both.

19. **(C)** Use the pronoun *whom* only for people, never for things. Choice (E) introduces *they*, a pronoun without a reference. *Best* is needed here.

20. **(A)** No error. In most *if* clauses, the past subjunctive form of the verb—with *had*—must be used.

21. **(C)** The singular verb *illustrates* is needed, since the subject is the singular *imposition*.

22. **(A)** Correct as originally written. Parallelism calls for repetition of the pronoun *by* (*less by . . . than by . . .*).

23. **(C)** The pronoun should be *he*, since it is part of the compound subject of the verb *would be*.

24. **(D)** The pronoun *it* is unnecessary, since the subject of the verb—*the Civilian Review Board*—has already appeared.

25. **(A)** No error.

Section VIII   Problem Solving

1. **(D)** Each box of dictionaries weighs $6 \times 20 = 120$ pounds. Each box of encyclopedias weighs $2 \times 75 = 150$ pounds. So the load weighs $98 \times 120 + 50 \times 150 = 19{,}260$ pounds.

2. **(D)** Mary makes $600 a month on her regular job. Therefore, she receives $600 \cdot 12 = \$7{,}200$ a year from her regular job. Her only other income is $400. So her total yearly income is $7,600. She makes $600 + $400 = $1,000 during July, so she makes $1{,}000/7{,}600 = 5/38$ which is about .13 of her annual income during July. Therefore, Mary makes about 13% of her annual income in July.

3. **(C)** The area of the triangle is ½(altitude)(base) = ½ (altitude)S. The area of the square is S^2. Therefore, ½S(altitude) = S^2, so the altitude must be $2S$.

4. **(D)** The train will average 50 mph for 3½ hours, 75 mph for 3 hours and 20 mph for half an hour. So the distance of the trip is $(3\frac{1}{2})(50) + (3)(75) + (\frac{1}{2})(20) = 175 + 225 + 10 = 410$ miles. The trip takes 7 hours. Therefore, the average speed is $410/7 = 58\frac{4}{7}$ mph.

5. **(C)**
$$(x - y)(y + 3) = x(y + 3) - y(y + 3)$$
$$= xy + 3x - y^2 - 3y$$
$$= xy - y^2 - 3y + 3x$$

6. **(B)** If $x < y$ and $y < z$, then $x < z$. All the other statements may be true but are not always true.

7. **(C)** The ratio is $\dfrac{2}{3} \Big/ \dfrac{5}{4}$ which is equal to $\dfrac{2}{3} \cdot \dfrac{4}{5}$ $= \dfrac{8}{15}$

8. **(C)** 3 divides 9 evenly and 3 divides 33 evenly, so 9 and 33 are not primes. 7, 11, 13, and 29 have no divisors except 1 and themselves, so they are all primes. Thus, the set of numbers contains 4 prime numbers.

9. **(D)** Each share is worth $13.21 - $9.50 or $3.71 more in 1970 than it was in 1960. So 100,000 shares are worth ($3.71)(100,000) or $371,000.00 more in 1970 than they were in 1960.

10. **(D)** Add up all the daily wages for the week: $40.62 + 41.35 + 42.00 + 42.50 + 39.53 = $206.00. Divide $206.00 by 5 to get the average daily wage, $41.20.

11. **(B)** If the price of a pound of apples rises 2%, then the price of ten pounds of apples rises 2%. This is because the percentage change is the same for any amount sold. Since a dozen

eggs and ten pounds of apples currently cost the same, each costs one half of the total price. Therefore, one half of the total is increased by 10% and the other half is increased by 2%, so the total price is increased by ½(10%) + ½(2%) = 6%.

12. (A) $2y = 6$, so $y = 3$. Therefore, $x + 3 = 4$; so $x = 1$.

13. (D) Each man does $\frac{1}{25}$ of the job in $1\frac{1}{2}$ hours. Thus, 15 men will do $\frac{15}{25}$ or $\frac{3}{5}$ of the job in $1\frac{1}{2}$ hours. So 15 men will complete the job in $\frac{5}{3} \cdot \frac{3}{2} = \frac{5}{2} = 2\frac{1}{2}$ hours. Another method gives $\frac{15}{25} = \frac{3/2}{x}$ where x is the time 15 men will take to complete the job. Therefore, $15x = \frac{3}{2} \cdot 25 = \frac{75}{2}$ so $x = \frac{5}{2} = 2\frac{1}{2}$.

14. (A) The car gets 100% − 12% or 88% of 20 miles to the gallon at 60 miles per hour. Thus, the car gets (.88)(20) or 17.6 miles to the gallon at 60 mph. Therefore, it can travel (11)(17.6) or 193.6 miles.

15. (D) The first 12 tons cost (12)($500) or $6,000. When you purchase 30 tons, you are buying 18 tons in addition to the first 12 tons so the additional 18 tons will cost $\$(500 - x)(18)$. Since $10,000 − $6,000 = $4,000, we get $\$9{,}000 - 18x = \$4{,}000$, and $18x = \$5{,}000$. So $x = 277.78$.

16. (E) The sum of the angles of a triangle is 180°. Let x be the number of degrees in the largest angle; then the other angles are $\frac{1}{2}x$ and $\frac{3}{4}x$ degrees. Therefore, $\frac{1}{2}x + \frac{3}{4}x + x = \frac{9}{4}x = 180°$, so $x = 80°$.

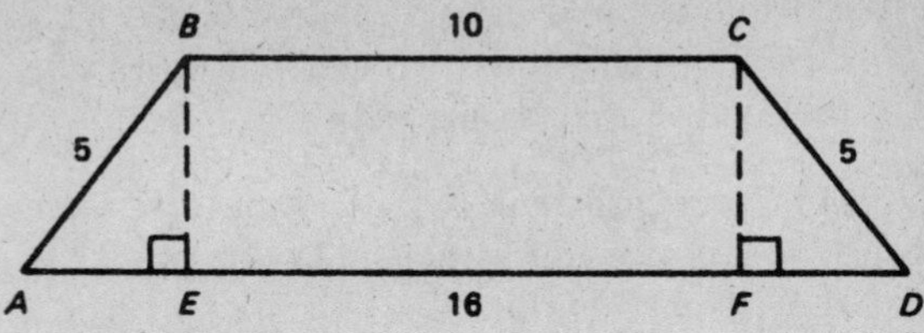

17. (B) If we draw $CF \perp AD$, then $\triangle ABE \cong \triangle DC$. and $AE = FD = 3$. Then $BE = 4$. Thus th area of the trapezoid, which equals the produc of the altitude and the average of the bases equals (4) (½) (10 + 16) = 52.

18. (E) Since −1 (a negative number) is less tha 2, and 1 (a positive number) is less than 2 neither I or II is always true.

Since −1 is less than 2 and 2 × −1 = −2 which is less than −1, III is not true.

Finally, since ½ is less than 2 but ½ × ½ = ¼, which is less than ½, IV is also no always true. Therefore, none of the statement is always true.

19. (A) Since each assistant does ⅔ as much a the worker, all 3 will accomplish 1 + 2(⅔) o 7/3 as much as the worker by himself. So the will finish the job in 1 ÷ 7/3 or 3/7 as much tim as it would take the worker by himself.

20. (D) The percent favoring at least one of th proposals is NOT the sum of 50, 30, and 2 because someone favoring 2 of the proposal will be counted twice and someone favorin all three will be counted 3 times. The correc relation is 78 = 50 + 30 + 20 − (percen favoring 2 of the proposals) − 2(percent fa voring all 3). Thus 78 = 100 − (percent fa voring 2) − 2(5), which can be solved to giv the percentage favoring 2 of the proposals c 100 − 10 − 78 = 12. Therefore the percentag favoring more than one proposal is 12 + = 17.

Evaluating Your Score

Tabulate your score for each section of Sample Test 5 according to the directions on pages 4–5 and record the results in the Self-scoring Table below. Then find your rating for each score on the Self-scoring Scale and record it in the appropriate blank.

Self-scoring Table

SECTION	SCORE	RATING
1		
2		
3		
4		
5		
6		
7		
8		

Self-scoring Scale

RATING

SECTION	POOR	FAIR	GOOD	EXCELLENT
1	0–12+	13–17+	18–21+	22–25
2	0–9+	10–13+	14–17+	18–20
3	0–17+	18–24+	25–31+	32–35
4	0–12+	13–17+	18–21+	22–25
5	0–12+	13–17+	18–21+	22–25
6	0–12+	13–17+	18–21+	22–25
7	0–12+	13–17+	18–21+	22–25
8	0–9+	10–13+	14–17+	18–20

Study again the Review sections covering material in Sample Test 5 for which you had a rating of FAIR or POOR.

To obtain an approximation of your actual GMAT score see page 5.

SIX
A LIST OF SCHOOLS REQUIRING THE GMAT

Listed below are graduate schools of business that *require* the GMAT as part of their admissions procedure.

United States

Alabama

Alabama Agricultural and Mechanical University
School of Business
Normal, AL 35762

Auburn University
Auburn School of Business
Graduate School
Auburn, AL 36830

Samford University
School of Business
Birmingham, AL 35229

Troy State University
School of Business and Commerce
Troy, AL 36081

Troy State University at Dothan
Fort Rucker School of Business and Commerce
Dothan, AL 36301

University of Alabama / Birmingham
Graduate School of Management
Birmingham, AL 35294

University of Alabama / Huntsville
School of Administrative Science
Huntsville, AL 35899

University of Alabama / University
Graduate School of Business
University , AL 35486

University of North Alabama
School of Business
Florence, AL 35630

University of South Alabama Graduate School
College of Business and Management Studies
Mobile, AL 36688

Alaska

University of Alaska / Anchorage
School of Business and Public Affairs
Anchorage, AK 99508

University of Alaska / Fairbanks
School of Management
MBA Program
Fairbanks, AK 99701

University of Alaska / Juneau
Division of Business
Juneau, AK 99801

Arizona

American Graduate School of International Management
Graduate Business Program
Glendale, AZ 85306

Arizona State University
College of Business Administration
Tempe, AZ 85287

Northern Arizona University
College of Business Administration
Flagstaff, AZ 86011

University of Arizona
College of Business and Public Administration
Graduate Programs
Tucson, AZ 85721

Arkansas

Arkansas State University
College of Business
Graduate Programs
State University, AR 72467

Harding University
Graduate School of Business
Searcy, AR 72143

University of Arkansas / Fayetteville
College of Business Administration
Fayetteville, AR 72701

University of Arkansas / Little Rock
The Graduate School
Little Rock, AR 72204

University of Central Arkansas
Graduate Business Programs
Conway, AR 72032

California

Azusa Pacific University
Division of Business Administration
Azusa, CA 91702

California Lutheran College
Graduate Program in Business Administration
Thousand Oaks, CA 91360

California State College / Bakersfield
School of Business and Public
 Administration
Graduate Programs
Bakersfield, CA 93309

California State College / San Bernadino
School of Administration
Graduate Programs
San Bernadino, CA 92346

California State College / Stanislaus
Division of Business Administration
MBA Program
Turlock, CA 95380

California State Polytechnic University / Pomona
School of Business Administration
Graduate Programs
Pomona, CA 91768

California State University / Chico
School of Business
MBA Program
Chico, CA 95929

California State University / Dominguez
Hills School of Management
Carson, CA 90747

California State University / Fresno
School of Business
Graduate Program
Fresno, CA 93740

California State University / Fullerton
School of Business Administration and
 Economics
Fullerton, CA 92634

California State University / Hayward
School of Business and Economics
Graduate Programs
Hayward, CA 94542

California State University / Long Beach
School of Business Administration
Graduate Programs
Long Beach, CA 90801

California State University / Los Angeles
School of Business and Economics
Graduate Programs
Los Angeles, CA 90032

California State University / Northridge
School of Business Administration and
 Economics
Northridge, CA 91330

California State University / Sacramento
School of Business and Public
 Administration
Sacramento, CA 95819

Chapman College
School of Business and Management
MBA Programs
Orange, CA 92666

Claremont Graduate School
Business Administration Department
Claremont, CA 91711

Golden Gate University
Graduate College and School of Accounting
San Francisco, CA 94105

Holy Names College
The MBA in Weekend College
Oakland, CA 94619

Loma Linda University
Graduate School
MBA Program
Loma Linda, CA 92350

Loyola Marymount University
College of Business Administration
MBA Program
Los Angeles, CA 90045

Monterey Institute of International Studies
Division of International Management
Graduate Programs
Monterey, CA 93940

Northrop University
College of Business and Management
Graduate Programs
Inglewood, CA 90306

Pacific Christian College
Graduate School of Business
San Diego, CA 92111

Pacific States University
College of Business Administration
Los Angeles, CA 90006

Pepperdine University
School of Business and Management
Graduate Programs
Los Angeles, CA 90044

Saint Mary's College of California
Graduate Business Programs
Moraga, CA 94575

San Diego State University
College of Business Administration
San Diego, CA 92182

San Francisco State University
School of Business
San Francisco, CA 94132

San Jose State University
School of Business
MBA Program
San Jose, CA 95192

Sonoma State University
Department of Management Studies
Graduate Program
Rohnert Park, CA 94928

Stanford University
Graduate School of Business
Stanford, CA 94305

United States International University
School of Business and Management
Graduate Programs
San Diego, CA 92131

University of California / Berkeley
Graduate School of Business
   Administration
Berkeley, CA 94720

University of California / Davis
Graduate School of Administration
Davis, CA 95616

University of California / Irvine
Graduate School of Management
Irvine, CA 92717

University of California / Los Angeles
Graduate School of Management
Los Angeles, CA 90024

University of California / Riverside
Graduate School of Administration
Riverside, CA 92521

University of Judaism
Graduate School of Management
Public Management and Administration
Los Angeles, CA 90077

University of San Diego
Graduate School of Business Administration
San Diego, CA 92110

University of San Francisco
McLaren College of Business
MBA Program
San Francisco, CA 94117

University of Santa Clara
Graduate School of Business and Administration
Santa Clara, CA 95053

University of Southern California
Graduate School of Business Administration
Los Angeles, CA 90007

Whittier College
Department of Business Administration and
  Economics
MBA Program
Whittier, CA 90608

Colorado

Colorado State University
College of Business
MBA Program
Fort Collins, CO 80523

Regis College
Special Programs
MBA Program
Denver, CO 80221

University of Colorado
Graduate School of Business Administration
Boulder, CO 80309

University of Colorado at Denver
Graduate School of Business
Denver, CO 80202

University of Denver
Graduate School of Business and Public
  Management
Denver, CO 80208

University of Southern Colorado
Graduate School of Business
Pueblo, CO 81001

Connecticut

Fairfield University
School of Business
Graduate Program
Fairfield, CT 06430

Quinnipiac College
Graduate Studies
School of Business
Hamden, CT 06518

Sacred Heart University
Division of Graduate Studies
Bridgeport, CT 06606

University of Bridgeport
Graduate School of Management
Bridgeport, CT 06601

University of Connecticut
School of Business Administration
Storrs, CT 06268

University of Hartford
Austin Dunham Barney School of Business and
  Public Administration
West Hartford, CT 06117

Western Connecticut State University
Ancell School of Business
Danbury, CT 06810

Yale University
School of Organization and Management
New Haven, CT 06520

Delaware

Delaware State College
Graduate School of Business
Dover, DE 19901

University of Delaware
College of Business and Economics
Newark, DE 19711

Wilmington College
MBA Program
New Castle, DE 19720

District of Columbia

American University
The Kogod College of Business Administration
Washington, DC 20016

George Washington University
School of Government and Business Administration
Washington, DC 20052

Georgetown University
School of Business Administration
Washington, DC 20057

Howard University
School of Business and Public Administration
Washington, DC 20001

Southeastern University
School of Business and Public Administration
Washington, DC 20024

Florida

Barry University
School of Business
Graduate Division
Miami Shores, FL 33161

Florida Agricultural and Mechanical University
Graduate Business Program
Tallahassee, FL 32307

Florida Atlantic University
College of Business and Public Administration
Boca Raton, FL 33431

Florida International University
Graduate Business Program
Miami, FL 33199

Florida State University
College of Business
Tallahassee, FL 32306

Jacksonville University
College of Business Administration
Jacksonville, FL 32211

Nova University
Center for the Study of Administration
Fort Lauderdale, FL 33314

Rollins College
Roy E. Crummer Graduate School of Business
Winter Park, FL 32789

Saint Thomas University
Division of Human Resources
Program in Advanced Accounting
Miami, FL 33054

Stetson University
School of Business Administration
DeLand, FL 32720

University of Central Florida
College of Business Administration
Orlando, FL 32816

University of Florida
Graduate School of Business Administration
Gainesville, FL 32611

University of Miami
School of Business Administration
Graduate Studies
Coral Gables, FL 33124

University of South Florida
College of Business Administration
Tampa, FL 33620

Webber College
Program in Business Administration
Babson Park, FL 33827

Georgia

Atlanta University
School of Business Administration
Atlanta, GA 30314

Augusta College
School of Business Administration
Augusta, GA 30910

Berry College
Graduate Studies
Mount Berry, GA 30149

Columbus College
School of Business
Columbus, GA 31993

Emory University
Graduate School of Business Administration
Atlanta, GA 30322

Georgia College
School of Business
Milledgeville, GA 31061

Georgia Institute of Technology
College of Management
Atlanta, GA 30332

Georgia Southern College
Graduate School of Business
Statesboro, GA 30460

Georgia State University
Graduate Division
College of Business Administration
Atlanta, GA 30303

Kennesaw College
Graduate School of Business
Marietta, GA 30061

LaGrange College
MBA Program
LaGrange, GA 30240

Mercer University / Atlanta
Division of Business and Economics
MBA Program
Atlanta, GA 30341

Mercer University / Macon
School of Business and Economics
MBA Program
Macon, GA 31207

Savannah State College
School of Business
MBA Program
Savannah, GA 31404

University of Georgia
Graduate School of Business Administration
Athens, GA 30602

Valdosta State College
School of Business Administration
Valdosta, GA 31698

West Georgia College
School of Business
Carrollton, GA 30118

Hawaii

Chaminade University of Honolulu
Business Administration Division
MBA Program
Honolulu, HI 96816

University of Hawaii at Hilo
Graduate School of Business
Hilo, HI 96720

Idaho

Boise State University
College of Business
Graduate Programs
Boise, ID 83725

Idaho State University
College of Business
MBA Program
Pocatello, ID 83209

University of Idaho
College of Business and Economics
Graduate Programs
Moscow, ID 83843

Illinois

Bradley University
College of Business Administration
MBA Program
Peoria, IL 61625

DePaul University
Graduate School of Business
Chicago, IL 60604

Eastern Illinois University
School of Business
Graduate Business Studies
Charleston, IL 61920

George Williams College
Administration and Organizational Behavior
    Graduate Business Programs
Downers Grove, IL 60515

Governors State University
College of Business and Public Administration
Graduate Programs
Park Forest South, IL 60466

Illinois Benedictine College
MBA Program
Lisle, IL 60532

Illinois Institute of Technology
Stuart School of Management and Finance
Chicago, IL 60616

Illinois State University
College of Business
Graduate Programs
Normal, IL 61761

Keller Graduate School of Management
Graduate Business Program
Chicago, IL 60606

Lake Forest School of Management
Graduate Business Program
Lake Forest, IL 60045

Lewis University
College of Business
Romeoville, IL 60441

Loyola University of Chicago
Graduate School of Business
Chicago, IL 60611

Northern Illinois University
The Graduate School
College of Business
DeKalb, IL 60115

Northwestern University
J. L. Kellogg Graduate School of Management
Evanston, IL 60201

Quincy College
Graduate School of Business
Quincy, IL 62301

Roosevelt University
Walter E. Heller College of Business Administration
Graduate Programs
Chicago, IL 60605

Rosary College
Graduate Business Programs
River Forest, IL 60305

Saint Xavier College
Graham School of Management
Chicago, IL 60655

Sangamon State University
Graduate Programs
Springfield, IL 62708

Southern Illinois University / Carbondale
Graduate School and College of
   Business Administration
Carbondale, IL 62901

Southern Illinois University / Edwardsville
School of Business
Graduate Programs
Edwardsville, IL 62026

University of Chicago
Graduate School of Business
Chicago, IL 60637

University of Illinois at Chicago
Graduate School of Business
Chicago, IL 60680

University of Illinois at Urbana-Champaign
Graduate School of Business
Urbana, IL 61801

Western Illinois University
College of Business
Graduate Programs
Macomb, IL 61455

Indiana

Ball State University
College of Business
Graduate Programs
Muncie, IN 47306

Butler University
College of Business Administration
Graduate Programs
Indianapolis, IN 46208

Indiana Central University
Graduate Division
Indianapolis, IN 46227

Indiana State University / Terre Haute
School of Business
Graduate Programs
Terre Haute, IN 47809

Indiana University / Bloomington
Graduate School of Business
Bloomington, IN 47401

Indiana University / Northwest
Division of Business and Economics
Gary, IN 46408

Indiana University / Purdue University
Division of Business and Economics
Graduate Program
Fort Wayne, IN 46805

Indiana University / Purdue University
School of Business
Indianapolis, IN 46202

Indiana University / South Bend
Division of Business and Economics
Graduate Program
South Bend, IN 46615

Purdue University
Graduate School
Department of Management
Hammond, IN 46323

Purdue University
Krannert Graduate School of Management
West Lafayette, IN 47907

Saint Francis College
Department of Business Administration
Fort Wayne, IN 46808

University of Evansville
Graduate School of Business Administration
Evansville, IN 47702

University of Notre Dame
College of Business Administration
Graduate Division
Notre Dame, IN 46556

Iowa

Drake University
College of Business Administration
Graduate Programs
Des Moines, IA 50311

Maharishi International University
Department of Business Administration
Fairfield, IA 52556

Saint Ambrose College
MBA Program
Davenport, IA 52803

University of Iowa
College of Business Administration
Graduate Programs
Iowa City, IA 52242

University of Northern Iowa
School of Business
Graduate Programs
Cedar Falls, IA 50614

Kansas

Emporia State University
Division of Business
Graduate Programs
Emporia, KS 66801

Fort Hays State University
School of Business
MBA Program
Hays, KS 67601

Kansas State University
College of Business Administration
Graduate Programs
Manhattan, KS 66506

Pittsburg State University
Kelce School of Business and Economics
MBA Program
Pittsburg, KS 66762

University of Kansas
School of Business
Graduate Programs
Lawrence, KS 66045

Washburn University
School of Business
MBA Program
Topeka, KS 66621

Wichita State University
College of Business Administration
Graduate Studies in Business
Wichita, KS 67208

Kentucky

Ballarmine College
Graduate Business Program
Louisville, KY 40205

Eastern Kentucky University
Graduate School
College of Business
Richmond, KY 40475

Morehead State University
School of Business and Economics
Morehead, KY 40351

Murray State University
College of Business and Public Affairs
Murray, KY 42071

Northern Kentucky University
Master of Business Administration
Highland Heights, KY 41076

University of Kentucky
College of Business and Economics
Lexington, KY 40506

University of Louisville
School of Business
Louisville, KY 40292

Western Kentucky University
College of Business Administration
Bowling Green, KY 42101

Louisiana

Centenary College of Louisiana
School of Business
MBA Program
Shreveport, LA 71104

Grambling State University
Graduate School of Business
Grambling, LA 71245

Louisiana State University / Baton Rouge
College of Business Administration
Graduate Division
Baton Rouge, LA 70803

Louisiana State University / Shreveport
College of Business Administration
MBA Program
Shreveport, LA 71115

Louisiana Tech University
College of Administration and Business
Graduate Programs
Ruston, LA 71272

Loyola University
College of Business Administration
Graduate Programs
New Orleans, LA 70118

McNeese State University
The Graduate School
MBA Program
Lake Charles, LA 70609

Nicholls State University
College of Business Administration
MBA Program
Thibodaux, LA 70310

Northeast Louisiana University
College of Business Administration
MBA Program
Monroe, LA 71209

Northwestern State University
College of Business and Applied Sciences
Natchitoches, LA 71457

Southeastern Louisiana University
School of Graduate Studies
MBA Program
Hammond, LA 70402

Tulane University
School of Business
MBA Program
New Orleans, LA 70118

University of New Orleans
College of Business Administration
Graduate Programs
New Orlenas, LA 70122

University of Southwestern Louisiana
College of Business Administration
MBA Program
Lafayette, LA 70504

Maine

Husson College
Graduate Studies Division
Bangor, ME 04401

Thomas College
Graduate School of Management
Waterville, ME 04901

University of Maine / Orono
College of Business Administration
The Graduate School
Orono, ME 04469

Maryland

Hood College
Graduate School
Frederick, MD 21701

Loyola College
School of Business and Management
Baltimore, MD 21210

Morgan State University
School of Graduate Studies
Baltimore, MD 21239

Mount Saint Mary's College
Graduate School of Business
Emmitsburg, MD 21727

Salisbury State College
School of Business
Salisbury, MD 21801

University of Baltimore
School of Business
Baltimore, MD 21201

University of Maryland / College Park
College of Business and Management
College Park, MD 20742

Massachusetts

American International College
School of Business Administration
Graduate Program
Springfield, MA 01109

Anna Maria College
Graduate Division, Department of Business
  Administration
Paxton, MA 01612

Assumption College
Graduate School
MBA Program
Worcester, MA 01609

Babson College
Graduate School of Business
Wellesley, MA 02157

Bentley College
Graduate School
Waltham, MA 02254

Boston College
Graduate School of Management
Chestnut Hill, MA 02167

Boston University
School of Management
Graduate Programs
Boston, MA 02215

Boston University
MBA Program
Boston, MA 02215

Clark University
Graduate School of Management
Worcester, MA 01610

Fitchburg State College
Program in Management
Fitchburg, MA 01420

Harvard University
Graduate School of Business Administration
Boston, MA 02163

Massachusetts Institute of Technology
Alfred P. Sloan School of Management
Cambridge, MA 02139

Nichols College
MBA Program
Dudley, MA 01570

Northeastern University
Graduate School of Business Administration
Boston, MA 02115

Salem State College
Program in Business Administration
Salem, MA 01970

Simmons College
Graduate School of Management
Boston, MA 02115

Southeastern Massachusetts University
MBA Program
North Dartmouth, MA 02747

Suffolk University
Graduate School of Management
Boston, MA 02108

University of Lowell
College of Management Science
Lowell, MA 01854

University of Massachusetts at Amherst
School of Business Administration
Graduate School
Amherst, MA 01003

University of Massachusetts at Boston
Graduate Business School
Boston, MA 02108

Western New England College
School of Business
Springfield, MA 01119

Worcester Polytechnic Institute
Evening School
MBA and MSM Programs
Worcester, MA 01609

Michigan

Andrews University
School of Business
Berrien Springs, MI 49104

Aquinas College
Graduate Management Program
Grand Rapids, MI 49506

Central Michigan University
School of Business Administration
Graduate Programs
Mt. Pleasant, MI 48859

Eastern Michigan University
College of Business
Graduate Programs
Ypsilanti, MI 48197

Grand Valley State Colleges
F.E. Seidman Graduate School of Business and
   Administration
Allendale, MI 49401

Lake Superior State College
Department of Business and Economics
MBA Program
Sault Ste. Marie, MI 49783

Madonna College
Graduate Studies Program
Livonia, MI 48150

Michigan State University
Graduate School of Business Administration
East Lansing, MI 48824

Michigan Technological University
School of Business and Engineering Administration
Graduate Program
Houghton, MI 49931

Northern Michigan University
School of Business and Management
MBA Program
Marquette, MI 49855

Oakland University
School of Economics and Management
Rochester, MI 48063

Saginaw Valley State College
School of Business and Management
University Center, MI 48710

University of Detroit
College of Business and Administration
Graduate Programs
Detroit, MI 48207

University of Michigan / Ann Arbor
Graduate School of Business
   Administration
Ann Arbor, MI 48109

University of Michigan / Dearborn
School of Management
MBA Program
Dearborn, MI 48128

University of Michigan / Flint
School of Management
MBA Program
Flint, MI 48503

Wayne State University
School of Business Administration
MBA Program
Detroit, MI 48202

Western Michigan University
College of Business
Kalamazoo, MI 49008

Minnesota

College of St. Thomas
Graduate Programs in Management
St. Paul, MN 55105

Mankato State University
College of Business Administration
Graduate Programs
Mankato, MN 56001

Metropolitan State University
Program in Management and Administration
St. Paul, MN 55101

Moorhead State University
MBA Program
Moorhead, MN 56560

Saint Cloud State University
College of Business
Graduate Programs
St. Cloud, MN 56301

University of Minnesota / Duluth
School of Business and Economics
MBA Program
Duluth, MN 55812

Univesity of Minnesota / Twin Cities
Graduate School of Management
Minneapolis, MN 55455

Winona State University
Department of Business Administration and
   Economics
MBA Program
Winona, MN 55987

Mississippi

Delta State University
School of Business
Graduate School
Cleveland, MS 38732

Jackson State University
School of Business and Economics
The Graduate School
Jackson, MS 39217

Millsaps College
School of Management
Jackson, MS 39210

Mississippi College
School of Business and Public Administration
Clinton, MS 39058

Mississippi State University
College of Business and Industry
Division of Graduate Studies
Mississippi State, MS 39762

University of Mississippi
School of Business Administration
University, MS 38677

University of Southern Mississippi / Gulf Coast
Coordinator of Graduate Business Studies
Long Beach, MS 39560

University of Southern Mississippi / Hattiesburg
College of Business Administration
Graduate Studies
Hattiesburg, MS 39401

William Carey College
Graduate Center for Management Development
Hattiesburg, MS 39401

Missouri

Avila College
Department of Business and Economics
MBA Program
Kansas City, MO 64145

Central Missouri State University
College of Business and Economics
Warrensburg, MO 64093

Drury College
Breech School of Business Administration
MBA Program
Springfield, MO 65802

Fontbonne College
Graduate School of Business
St. Louis, MO 63105

Lincoln University
School of Graduate Studies
MBA Program
Jefferson City, MO 65101

Maryville College
Division of Management
St. Louis, MO 63141

Northeast Missouri State University
Division of Business
Graduate Programs
Kirksville, MO 63501

Northwest Missouri State University
School of Business Administration
Graduate Programs
Maryville, MO 64468

Rockhurst College
Graduate Business Program
Kansas City, MO 64110

Saint Louis University
MBA Program
St. Louis, MO 63108

Southeast Missouri State University
College of Business
MBA Program
Cape Girardeau, MO 63701

Southwest Missouri State University
School of Business
Graduate Programs
Springfield, MO 65802

University of Missouri / Columbia
College of Business and Public
  Administration
Graduate Programs
Columbia, MO 65211

University of Missouri / Kansas City
School of Administration
Kansas City, MO 64110

University of Missouri / St. Louis
School of Business Administration
Graduate Programs
St. Louis, MO 63121

Washington University
Graduate School of Business Administration
St. Louis, MO 63130

Montana

University of Montana
School of Business Administration
Graduate Programs
Missoula, MT 59812

Nebraska

Creighton University
College of Business Administration
Graduate Programs
Omaha, NE 68178

University of Nebraska / Lincoln
College of Business Administration
Lincoln, NE 68588

University of Nebraska / Omaha
College of Business Administration
Graduate Programs
Omaha, NE 68182

Nevada

University of Nevada / Las Vegas
College of Business and Economics
Las Vegas, NV 89154

University of Nevada / Las Vegas
Las Vegas College of Hotel Administration
Las Vegas, NV 89154

University of Nevada / Reno
College of Business Administration
Reno, NV 89557

New Hampshire

Dartmouth College
Amos Tuck School of Business Administration
Hanover, NH 03755

New Hampshire College
Graduate School of Business
Manchester, NH 03104

Plymouth State College
Master of Business Administration Program
Plymouth, NH 03264

Rivier College
Graduate Department of Business Administration
Nashua, NH 03060

University of New Hampshire
Whittemore School of Business and Economics
Durham, NH 03824

New Jersey

Fairleigh Dickinson University
Samuel J. Silberman College of Business
  Administration
Madison, NJ 07940

Fairleigh Dickinson University
Graduate School of Business
Rutherford, NJ 07070

Monmouth College
MBA Program
West Long Beach, NH 07764

Montclair State College
School of Business Administration
MBA Program
Upper Montclair, NJ 07043

Rider College
Division of Graduate Studies School of Business
Lawrenceville, NJ 08648

Rutgers University / Camden
Master of Business Administration Program
Camden, NJ 08102

Rutgers University / Newark
Graduate School of Business Administration
Newark, NJ 07102

Seton Hall University
W. Paul Stillman School of Business
South Orange, NJ 07079

Stevens Institute of Technology
Department of Management Science
Hoboken, NJ 07030

Trenton State College
School of Business
Trenton, NJ 08625

William Paterson College of New Jersey
School of Management
MBA Program
Wayne, NJ 07470

New Mexico

College of Santa Fe
Graduate School of Business
Santa Fe, NM 87501

Eastern New Mexico University
College of Business
Graduate Programs
Portales, NM 88130

New Mexico Highlands University
Division of Business and Economics
MBA Program
Las Vegas, NM 87701

New Mexico State University
College of Business Administration and Economics
Graduate Programs
Las Cruces, NM 88003

University of New Mexico
Robert O. Anderson Graduate School of
  Management
Albuquerque, NM 87131

Western New Mexico University
Department of Business and Public Administration
Silver City, NM 88061

New York

Adelphi University
School of Business Administration
Garden City, NY 11530

Canisius College
School of Business Administration
Buffalo, NY 14214

City University of New York / Baruch College
School of Business and Public Administration
Graduate Studies
New York, NY 10010

City University of New York /
Graduate School and University Center
Program in Business
New York, NY 10036

Clarkson College of Technology
School of Management
Potsdam, NY 13676

College of Insurance
Graduate Program
Business Division
New York, NY 10038

College of Saint Rose
Graduate School
Social Science Division
Albany, NY 12203

Columbia University
Graduate School of Business
New York, NY 10027

Cornell University
Graduate School of Management
Ithaca, NY 14853

Cornell University
Graduate School, Hotel Administration
Ithaca, NY 14853

Dowling College
Master of Business Administration Program
Oakdale, NY 11769

Fordham University
Martino Graduate School of Business
  Administration
New York, NY 10023

Hofstra University
School of Business
Hempstead, NY 11550

Iona College
Hagan Graduate School of Business
New Rochelle, NY 10801

Long Island University / Brooklyn Center
Graduate School of Business and Public
  Administration
Brooklyn, NY 11201

Long Island University / C.W. Post Center
Graduate Programs
Greenvale, NY 11548

Long Island University / Westchester Branch
School of Business and Public Administration
Graduate Studies
Dobbs Ferry, NY 10522

Manhattan College
Graduate Division
School of Business
Riverdale, NY 10471

Marist College
Graduate Programs
Poughkeepsie, NY 12601

New York Institute of Technology
Center for Business and Economics
Old Westbury, NY 11568

New York University
Graduate School of Business Administration
New York, NY 10006

Niagara University
College of Business Administration
MBA Program
Niagara University, NY 14109

Pace University
Lubin Graduate School of Business
New York, NY 10038

Pace University / University College
Graduate School of Business
Pleasantville, NY 10570

Pace University at White Plains
Graduate School of Business
White Plains, NY 10603

Polytechnic Institute of New York / Farmingdale
Division of Management
Farmingdale, NY 11735

Polytechnic Institute of New York
Division of Management
Brooklyn, NY 11201

Polytechnic Institute of New York / Westchester
Division of Management
White Plains, NY 10605

Rensselaer Polytechnic Institute
School of Management
Troy, NY 12181

Rochester Institute of Technology
College of Business, Graduate Business Programs
Rochester, NY 14623

Russell Sage College
Department of Economics and Business
Troy, NY 12180

Russell Sage College
MBA Program
Albany, NY 12208

Saint Bonaventure University
School of Business Administration
School of Graduate Studies
St. Bonaventure, NY 14778

St. John Fisher College
Graduate School of Business
Rochester, NY 14618

Saint John's University
Graduate Division, College of Business
Administration
Jamaica, NY 11439

State University of New York at Albany
School of Business
Albany, NY 12222

State University of New York at Binghamton
School of Management
Binghamton, NY 13905

State University of New York at Buffalo
School of Management
Buffalo, NY 14214

State University of New York / Maritime College
Department of Marine Transportation
Bronx, NY 10465

Syracuse University
School of Management
Syracuse, NY 13210

Union College and University
Institute of Administration and Management
Schenectady, NY 12308

University of Rochester
Graduate School of Management
Rochester, NY 14627

North Carolina

Appalachian State University
John A. Walker College of Business
Boone, NC 28608

Campbell University
Department of Business
Buies Creek, NC 27506

Duke University
Fuqua School of Business
Durham, NC 27706

East Carolina University
School of Business
Greenville, NC 27834

Elon College
Graduate Program in Business
Elon College, NC 27244

Fayetteville State University
Graduate School of Business
Fayetteville, NC 28301

Meredith College
Department of Business and Economics
Raleigh, NC 27607

North Carolina Central University
School of Business
Durham, NC 27707

Queens College
The Graduate School
MBA Program
Charlotte, NC 28274

University of North Carolina / Chapel Hill
Graduate School of Business
Administration
Chapel Hill, NC 27514

University of North Carolina / Charlotte
College of Business Administration
Charlotte, NC 28223

University of North Carolina / Greensboro
School of Business and Economics
Greensboro, NC 27412

University of North Carolina / Wilmington
MBA Program
Wilmington, NC 28406

Wake Forest University
Babcock Graduate School of Management
Winston-Salem, NC 27109

Western Carolina University
School of Business
Graduate School
Cullowhee, NC 28723

North Dakota

North Dakota State University
MBA Program
Fargo, ND 58105

University of North Dakota
Graduate Business Programs
Grand Forks, ND 58202

Ohio

Baldwin-Wallace College
Master of Business Administration Program
Berea, OH 44017

Bowling Green State University
College of Business Administration
Bowling Green, OH 43403

Capital University
Graduate School of Administration
Columbus, OH 43209

Case Western Reserve University
Weatherhead School of Management
Cleveland, OH 44106

Cleveland State University
James J. Nance College of Business Administration
Cleveland, OH 44115

John Carroll University
School of Business
Cleveland, OH 44118

Kent State University
Graduate School of Management
Kent, OH 44242

Miami University
School of Business Administration
Oxford, OH 45056

Ohio State University
College of Administrative Science
Columbus, OH 43210

Ohio University
College of Business Administration
Athens, OH 45701

University of Akron
College of Business Administration
Akron, OH 44325

University of Cincinnati
College of Business Administration
Cincinnati, OH 45221

University of Dayton
MBA Program
School of Business Administration
Dayton, OH 45469

University of Steubenville
Department of Business
Steubenville, OH 43952

University of Toledo
College of Business Administration
Toledo, OH 43606

Wright State University
College of Business Administration
School of Graduate Studies
Dayton, OH 45435

Xavier University
Graduate Programs
Cincinnati, OH 45206

Youngstown State University
Graduate School of Business
Youngstown, OH 44555

Oklahoma

Bethany Nazarene College
College of Graduate Studies
Division of Business
Bethany, OK 73008

Central State University
School of Business
MBA Program
Edmond, OK 73034

Oklahoma City University
School of Management and Business Sciences
Graduate Programs
Oklahoma City, OK 73106

Oklahoma State University
College of Business Administration
Graduate Programs
Stillwater, OK 74078

Oral Roberts University
School of Business
Tulsa, OK 74171

Phillips University
Center of Business and Communication
MBA Program
Enid, OK 73702

University of Oklahoma
College of Business Administration
Graduate Programs
Norman, OK 73019

University of Tulsa
College of Business Administration
Graduate Programs
Tulsa, OK 74104

Oregon

Oregon State University
School of Business
Graduate Programs
Corvallis, OR 97331

Portland State University
School of Business Administration
Graduate Programs
Portland, OR 97207

Southern Oregon State College
School of Business
Graduate Programs
Ashland, OR 97520

University of Oregon
Graduate School of Management
Eugene, OR 97403

University of Portland
School of Business Administration
MBA Program
Portland, OR 97203

Willamette University
Geo. H. Atkinson Graduate School of Management
Salem, OR 97301

Pennsylvania

Bloomsburg University of Pennsylvania
School of Graduate Studies
Bloomsburg, PA 17815

Bucknell University
Department of Management
Graduate Program
Lewisburg, PA 17837

California University of Pennsylvania
Department of Business and Economics
California, PA 15419

Carnegie-Mellon University
Graduate School of Industrial Administration
Pittsburgh, PA 15213

Clarion University of Pennsylvania
School of Business Administration Graduate School
Clarion, PA 16214

Drexel University
College of Business and Administration
Philadelphia, PA 19104

Duquesne University
Graduate School of Business and Administration
Pittsburgh, PA 15282

Eastern College
Graduate Program in Business Administration
St. Davids, PA 19087

Gannon University
Master of Business Administration Program
Erie, PA 16541

Indiana University of Pennsylvania
School of Business
Graduate School
Indiana, PA 15705

Kutztown University
College of Graduate Studies
Kutztown, PA 19530

La Roche College
Graduate Studies
Pittsburgh, PA 15237

La Salle University
School of Business Administration
Philadelphia, PA 19141

Lehigh University
College of Business and Economics
Bethlehem, PA 18015

Marywood College
Graduate Program in Business and Managerial
   Science
Scranton, PA 18509

Pennsylvania State University / The Capitol Campus
Master of Administration
   Program
Middletown, PA 17057

Pennsylvania State University / University Park
Graduate Studies
College of Business Administration
University Park, PA 16802

Philadelphia College of Textiles and Science
MBA Program
Philadelphia, PA 19144

Robert Morris College
Graduate School
Coraopolis, PA 15108

Saint Joseph's University
MBA Program
Philadelphia, PA 19131

Shippensburg University of Pennsylvania
School of Business
Shippensburg, PA 17257

Temple University
School of Business Administration Graduate School
Philadelphia, PA 19122

University of Pennsylvania
The Wharton School, Graduate Division
Philadelphia, PA 19104

University of Pittsburgh
Graduate School of Business
Pittsburgh, PA 15260

University of Scranton
School of Management, Graduate School
Pittsburgh, PA 18510

Villanova University
College of Commerce and Finance
MBA Program
Villanova, PA 19085

Waynesburg College
Graduate Program in Business
Waynesburg, PA 15370

West Chester University
School of Administration and Public Affairs
West Chester, PA 19380

Widener University
Graduate Program in Business Administration
Chester, PA 19013

York College of Pennsylvania
Department of Business Administration
York, PA 17405

Rhode Island

Bryant College
Graduate School
Smithfield, RI 02917

Providence College
Graduate School
Department of Business Administration
Providence, RI 02918

University of Rhode Island
College of Business Administration
Kingston, RI 02881

South Carolina

Citadel, The
MBA Program
Department of Business Administration
Charleston, SC 29409

Clemson University
Clemson-at-Furman MBA Program
Greenville, SC 29613

Clemson University
College of Industrial Management and Textile
    Science
Clemson, SC 29631

University of South Carolina
College of Business Administration
Columbia, SC 29208

Winthrop College
School of Business Administration
Rock Hill, SC 29733

South Dakota

University of South Dakota
School of Business
Graduate Programs
Vermillion, SD 57069

Tennessee

East Tennessee State University
College of Business
The School of Graduate Studies
Johnson City, TN 37601

Memphis State University
Fogelman College of Business and Economics
Graduate School
Memphis, TN 38152

Middle Tennessee State University
Graduate Studies
School of Business
Murfreesboro, TN 37132

Tennessee State University
School of Business
Nashville, TN 37203

Tennessee Technological University
The Graduate School, Division of MBA Studies
Cookeville, TN 38501

University of Tennessee at Martin
Graduate School of Business
Martin, TN 38238

University of Tennessee / Chattanooga
School of Business Administration
Chattanooga, TN 37402

University of Tennessee / Knoxville
College of Business Administration
Knoxville, TN 37916

Vanderbilt University
Owen Graduate School of Management
Nashville, TN 37203

Texas

Baylor University
Hankamer School of Business
Graduate Programs
Waco, TX 76798

East Texas State University / Commerce
College of Business and Technology
Commerce, TX 75428

East Texas State University / Texarkana
College of Business Administration
Master's Programs
Texarkana, TX 75501

Houston Baptist University
College of Business and Economics
Graduate Programs
Houston, TX 77074

Lamar University
College of Business
MBA Program
Beaumont, TX 77710

North Texas State University
College of Business Administration
Graduate Programs
Denton, TX 76203

Pan American University
School of Business Administration
MBA Program
Edinburg, TX 78539

Prairie View A&M University
College of Business
Graduate Program
Prairie View, TX 77445

Rice University
Jesse H. Jones Graduate School of Administration
Houston, TX 77001

Saint Mary's University
School of Business and Administration
Graduate Programs
San Antonio, TX 78284

Sam Houston State University
College of Business Administration
Graduate Programs
Huntsville, TX 77341

Southern Methodist University
Edwin L. Cox School of Business
Graduate Programs
Dallas, TX 75275

Southwest Texas State University
School of Business, Graduate Division
San Marcos, TX 78666

Stephen F. Austin State University
Graduate School of Business
Nacogdoches, TX 75962

Sul Ross State University
Division of Business Administration
MBA Program
Alpine, TX 79830

Texas A&M University
College of Business Administration
Graduate Programs
College Station, TX 77843

Texas Christian University
M.J. Neeley School of Business
Fort Worth, TX 76129

Texas Southern University
School of Business
Graduate Programs
Houston, TX 77004

Texas Tech University
College of Business Administration
Graduate Programs
Lubbock, TX 79409

Texas Woman's University
Department of Business and Economics
Graduate School
Denton, TX 76204

Trinity University
Department of Business Administration
MBA Program
San Antonio, TX 78284

University of Dallas
Braniff Graduate School of Management
Irving, TX 75061

University of Houston / Clear Lake
School of Business and Public
    Administration
Graduate Programs
Houston, TX 77058

University of Houston / University Park
College of Business Administration
Graduate Programs
Houston, TX 77004

University of St. Thomas
Cameron School of Business
MBA Program
Houston, TX 77006

University of Texas / Arlington
College of Business Administration
Graduate Programs
Arlington, TX 76019

University of Texas / Austin
Graduate School of Business
Austin, TX 78712

University of Texas / Dallas
School of Management and Administration
Graduate Programs
Richardson, TX 75080

University of Texas / San Antonio
College of Business
Graduate Program
San Antonio, TX 78285

University of Texas / Tyler
School of Business Administration
MBA Program
Tyler, TX 75701

West Texas State University
School of Business
Graduate Programs
Canyon, TX 79016

Utah

Brigham Young University
Graduate School of Management
Provo, UT 84602

Southern Utah State College
Graduate School of Business
Cedar City, UT 84720

University of Utah
Graduate School of Business
Salt Lake City, UT 84112

Utah State University
College of Business
Graduate Programs
Logan, UT 84322

Weber State College
Graduate School of Business
Ogden, UT 84408

Vermont

University of Vermont
Division of Engineering
Mathematics and Business Administration
Burlington, VT 05405

Virginia

Averett College
Graduate School of Business
Danville, VA 24541

CBN University
School of Business Administration
Virginia Beach, VA 23463

College of William and Mary
School of Business Administration
Williamsburg, VA 23185

George Mason University
Graduate School
School of Business Administration
Fairfax, VA 22030

Hampton University
Graduate Studies in Business
Hampton, VA 23668

James Madison University
School of Business
Harrisonburg, VA 22807

Lynchburg College
Department of Business Administration
Lynchburg, VA 24501

Mary Washington College
Graduate Business Programs
Fredericksburg, VA 22401

Marymount College of Virginia
MBA Program
Arlington, VA 22207

Norfolk State University
School of Business
Graduate Business Program
Norfolk, VA 23504

Old Dominion University
School of Business Administration
Norfolk, VA 23508

Shenandoah College and Conservatory
MBA Program
Winchester, VA 22601

University of Richmond
Graduate Division
Richmond, VA 23173

University of Virginia
Colgate Darden Graduate School of Business
Charlottesville, VA 22906

Virginia Commonwealth University
School of Business
Richmond, VA 23284

Virginia Polytechnic Institute and State University
College of Business
Blacksburg, VA 24061

Washington

Eastern Washington University
MBA Program Office, School of Business
Cheney, WA 99004

Gonzaga University
School of Business Administration
Graduate Programs
Spokane, WA 99258

Pacific Lutheran University
School of Business Administration
MBA Program
Tacoma, WA 98447

Saint Martin's College
Graduate Studies in Management
Lacey, WA 98503

Seattle Pacific University
Master of Business Administration Program
Seattle, WA 98119

Seattle University
Albers School of Business
MBA Program
Seattle, WA 98122

University of Washington
Graduate School of Business Administration
Seattle, WA 98195

Washington State University
College of Business and Economics
Graduate Programs
Pullman, WA 99163

Western Washington University
College of Business and Economics
Graduate Programs
Bellingham, WA 98225

West Virginia

Marshall University
Graduate School
College of Business
Huntington, WV 25701

University of Charleston
Graduate School of Business
Charleston, WV 25304

West Virginia University
College of Business and Economics
Morgantown, WV 26506

Wheeling College
Graduate Business Program
Wheeling, WV 26003

Wisconsin

Marquette University
Robert A. Johnston College of Business
  Administration
Graduate Programs
Milwaukee, WI 53233

University of Wisconsin / Eau Claire
School of Business
MBA Program
Eau Claire, WI 54701

University of Wisconsin / La Crosse
College of Business Administration
MBA Program
La Crosse, WI 54601

University of Wisconsin / Madison
Graduate School of Business
Madison, WI 53706

University of Wisconsin / Milwaukee
Milwaukee School of Business Administration
Milwaukee, WI 53201

University of Wisconsin / Oshkosh
College of Business Administration
Oshkosh, WI 54901

University of Wisconsin / Parkside
Division of Business and Administrative
  Science
MBA Program
Kenosha, WI 53141

University of Wisconsin / Whitewater
College of Business and Economics
Whitewater, WI 53190

Wyoming

University of Wyoming
College of Commerce and Industry
Graduate Business Programs
Laramie, WY 82071

Guam

University of Guam
College of Business and Public Administration
Mangilao, GU 96913

Puerto Rico

Universidad del Turabo
Program in Accounting
Caguas, PR 00626

University of Puerto Rico, Mayaguez
College of Business Administration
Mayaguez, PR 00708

University of Puerto Rico / Rio Piedras
Graduate School of Business
  Administration
Rio Piedras, PR 00931

Virgin Islands

College of the Virgin Islands
Division of Business Administration
St. Thomas, VI 00801

Canada

Carleton University
Graduate School of Business
Ottawa, ON K1S5B

Concordia University
Faculty of Commerce and Administration
Montreal, PQ H3G1M

Dalhousie University
Faculty of Graduate Studies
International Business
Halifax, NS B3H3J

Lakehead University
School of Business Administration
Thunder Bay, ON P7B5E

McGill University
Faculty of Management
Montreal, PQ H3A2T

McMaster University
Faculty of Business Program in Management Science
Hamilton, ON L8S4M

Memorial University of Newfoundland
Faculty of Business Administration
St. John's, NF A1B3X

Queen's University at Kingston
School of Business
Kingston, ON K7L3N

Saint Mary's University
Faculty of Commerce
Halifax, NS B3H3C

Simon Fraser University
Faculty of Business Administration/Finance
Burnaby, BC V5A1S

Université de Sherbrooke
School of Business
Sherbrooke, PQ J1K2R

University of Alberta
Faculty of Business
Edmonton, AB T6G2R

University of British Columbia
Faculty of Commerce and Business Administration
Vancouver, BC V6T1Z

University of Calgary
Faculty of Management
Calgary, AB T2N1N

University of Manitoba
Faculty of Administrative Studies
Winnipeg, ON R3T2N

University of New Brunswick
Graduate School of Business
Fredericton, NB E3B5A

University of Saskatchewan
College of Commerce
Saskatoon, SK S7N0W

University of Toronto
School of Graduate Studies, Department of
  Management
Toronto, ON M5SMB

University of Western Ontario
School of Business Administration
London, ON N6A3K

University of Windsor
Faculty of Business Administration
Windsor, ON N9B3P

University of Ottawa
Faculty of Administration
Ottawa, ON K1N6N

Wilfrid Laurier University
School of Business and Economics
Waterloo, ON N2L3C

York University
Faculty of Administrative Studies
Downsview, ON M3J2R

BARRON'S GUIDE TO GRADUATE BUSINESS SCHOOLS

AN INDISPENSABLE DATA SOURCE FOR EVERYONE WHO PLANS TO EARN AN MBA OR ANY OTHER GRADUATE BUSINESS DEGREE

LATEST FACTS ON MORE THAN 575 SCHOOLS FROM COAST TO COAST
PLUS SELECTED SCHOOLS IN CANADA AND OTHER COUNTRIES
Enrollment • Costs • Financial Aid • Admissions Data • Average GMAT Scores • Programs • Course Requirements • Student D
Faculty Data • Computer Facilities • Library and Research Facilities • Entrance Requirements • Application Procedures •

VALUABLE INFORMATION FOR BUSINESS SCHOOL APPLICANTS
How to Choose a Business School • Recent Rankings of Top Schools • Facts About the GMAT •
Advice for Women, Minorities, and Foreign Students • Financing Your Education • What Employers Look Fo
How to Apply • Career Outlook • Typical Starting Salaries for MBAs • What Employers Look Fo

NEW: In-depth information on placement
PLUS: School locator maps, chart guide to all schools
FIFTH EDITION Eugene Miller

$12.95

At your bookseller, or order direct adding 10% postage
(minimum charge $1.50) plus applicable sales tax.

BARRON'S
Barron's Educational Series, I

More selected BARRON'S titles:

DICTIONARY OF ACCOUNTING TERMS
Joel Siegel and Jae Shim
Approximately 2500 terms are defined for accountants, business
managers, students, and small business persons.
Paperback, $8.95, Canada $13.50/ISBN 3766-9

DICTIONARY OF ADVERTISING AND DIRECT MAIL TERMS
Jane Imber and Betsy-Ann Toffler
Approximately 3000 terms are defined as reference for ad industry
professionals, students, and consumers.
Paperback, $8.95, Canada $13.50/ISBN 3765-0

DICTIONARY OF BUSINESS TERMS
Jack P. Friedman, general editor
Over 6000 entries define a wide range of terms used throughout
business, real estate, taxes, banking, investment, more.
Paperback, $8.95, Canada $13.50/ISBN 3775-8

DICTIONARY OF COMPUTER TERMS
Douglas Downing and Michael Covington
Over 600 key computer terms are clearly explained, and sample
programs included. Paperback, $8.95, Canada $13.50/ISBN 2905-4

DICTIONARY OF INSURANCE TERMS
Harvey W. Rubin
Approximately 2500 insurance terms are defined as they relate to
property, casualty, life, health, and other types of insurance.
Paperback, $8.95, Canada $13.50/ISBN 3722-3, 448 pages

BARRON'S BUSINESS REVIEW SERIES
Self-instruction guides cover topics taught in a college-level business
course, presenting essential concepts in an easy-to-follow format.
Each book paperback $8.95, Canada $13.50, approx. 288 pages
ACCOUNTING, *by Peter J. Eisen*/ISBN 3574-7
BUSINESS LAW, *by Hardwicke and Emerson*/ISBN 3495-3
BUSINESS STATISTICS, *by Downing and Clark*/ISBN 3576-3
ECONOMICS, *by Walter J. Wessels*/ISBN 3560-7
FINANCE, *by A. A. Groppelli and Ehsan Nikhbakht*/ISBN 3561-5
MANAGEMENT, *by Montana and Charnov*/ISBN 3559-3
MARKETING, *by Richard L. Sandhusen*/ISBN 3494-5

BARRON'S TALKING BUSINESS SERIES:
BILINGUAL DICTIONARIES
Five bilingual dictionaries translate about 3000 terms not found in
most foreign phrasebooks. Includes words related to accounting,
sales, banking, computers, export/import and finance.

Each book paperback, $6.95, Canada $9.95, approx. 256 pages

TALKING BUSINESS IN FRENCH, *by Beppie LeGal*/ISBN 3745-6
TALKING BUSINESS IN GERMAN, *by Henry Strutz*/ISBN 3747-2
TALKING BUSINESS IN ITALIAN, *by Frank Rakus*/ISBN 3754-5
TALKING BUSINESS IN JAPANESE, *by C. & N. Akiyama*/
  ISBN 3848-7
TALKING BUSINESS IN SPANISH, *by T. Bruce Fryer and*
  Hugo J. Faria/ISBN 3769-3

All prices are in U.S. and Canadian dollars and subject to change without notice.
At your bookseller, or order direct adding 10% postage (minimum charge
$1.50), N.Y. residents add sales tax.

Barron's Educational Series, Inc.
250 Wireless Boulevard, Hauppauge, NY 11788
Call toll-free: 1-800-645-3476, in NY 1-800-257-5729
In Canada: 195 Allstate Parkway, Markham, Ontario L3R4T8